T0214854

Lecture Notes in Computer Science   11824

More information about this series at http://www.springer.com/series/7412

Lecture Notes in Computer Science 11824

More information about this series at http://www.springer.com/series/7412

Gernot A. Fink · Simone Frintrop ·
Xiaoyi Jiang (Eds.)

Pattern Recognition

41st DAGM German Conference, DAGM GCPR 2019
Dortmund, Germany, September 10–13, 2019
Proceedings

 Springer

Editors
Gernot A. Fink (iD)
TU Dortmund University
Dortmund, Germany

Simone Frintrop (iD)
University of Hamburg
Hamburg, Germany

Xiaoyi Jiang (iD)
University of Münster
Münster, Germany

ISSN 0302-9743　　　　　　ISSN 1611-3349　(electronic)
Lecture Notes in Computer Science
ISBN 978-3-030-33675-2　　　ISBN 978-3-030-33676-9　(eBook)
https://doi.org/10.1007/978-3-030-33676-9

LNCS Sublibrary: SL6 – Image Processing, Computer Vision, Pattern Recognition, and Graphics

This Springer imprint is published by the registered company Springer Nature Switzerland AG
The registered company address is: Gewerbestrasse 11, 6330 Cham, Switzerland

Preface

It was an honor and pleasure to organize the 41st German Conference on Pattern Recognition (GCPR 2019) in Dortmund during September 10–13, 2019. In the long tradition of the DAGM conference series, GCPR returns to the Ruhr Area (after the DAGM Symposium 1980 held in Essen) and was organized in Dortmund for the first time.

The city of Dortmund is associated with a long tradition of beer brewing, which to some extent is still visible today, and, more importantly, with the steel and mining industry that dominated the Ruhr Area for almost a century. Today, all that remains of this period are museums and impressive monuments of industrial heritage. Finding new avenues for industry in the region has been a challenge for many years. Dortmund as a city mastered this challenge by transforming into what today can be considered an IT and science location. Among the several scientific institutions, TU Dortmund University is the most prominent one. Its spacious green campus in the south-west of the city offered the venue for GCPR 2019.

The call for papers for GCPR 2019 resulted in 91 submissions from institutions from 23 countries. Given the positive experiences made in the last year, where special tracks were introduced to increase the emphasis on applied research, GCPR 2019 continued to offer special tracks with dedicated track chairs. Each paper underwent a strict double-blind reviewing process, resulting in three reviews, in almost all cases from Program Committee members, sometimes with support from additional experts. In total, 43 papers were accepted for publication (an acceptance rate of 47%). From those submissions, 16 papers were selected for oral presentation and 27 contributions were chosen as posters. In accordance with the conference tradition, we organized a Young Researchers Forum to promote scientific interaction between outstanding young researchers and our community. The work of five selected students was presented at the conference and included in these proceedings. The resulting high-quality single-track program covers the entire spectrum of pattern recognition, machine learning, image processing, and computer vision. We thank all authors for their submissions to GCPR 2019 and all reviewers for their valuable assessment.

Moreover, we are glad that three internationally renowned researchers accepted our invitation to give keynote lectures, Marc Pollefeys (ETH Zurich, Switzerland), Laurens van der Maaten (Facebook AI Research, New York, USA), and Bram van Ginneken (Radboud University Medical Center Nijmegen, the Netherlands).

The technical program was complemented by two tutorials: Automated Machine Learning (Matthias Feurer and Thomas Elsken, University of Freiburg, Germany) and Vision for Robotics (Tim Patten, TU Vienna, Austria; Cesar Cadena, ETH Zurich, Switzerland). Finally, we also offered a half-day seminar on Founding a Start-up (René Grzeszick, MotionMiners, Dortmund, Germany) at the end of the conference. With this overall program we hope to continue the tradition of GCPR in providing a forum for scientific exchange at a high quality level.

The success of GCPR 2019 would not have been possible without the support of many institutions and people. We would like to thank our sponsors ZEISS (Gold Sponsor), MVTec Software GmbH (Silver Sponsor) and Amazon and Informatik Centrum Dortmund e.V. (Bronze Sponsors) as well as our donors *Gesellschaft der Freunde der TU Dortmund and Alumni der Informatik Dortmund*. We are also grateful for the kind support of TU Dortmund University and *Deutsche Arbeitsgemeinschaft für Mustererkennung e.V.* (DAGM). Special thanks go to the members of the technical support and the Local Organizing Committee. Additionally, we are grateful to Springer for giving us the opportunity of continuing to publish the GCPR proceedings in the LNCS series.

To the readers of this proceedings book: enjoy it! We look forward to having a great GCPR next year in Tübingen.

September 2019

Gernot A. Fink
Simone Frintrop
Xiaoyi Jiang

Organization

General Chair

Gernot A. Fink   TU Dortmund, Germany

Program Committee Chairs

Simone Frintrop   University of Hamburg, Germany
Xiaoyi Jiang   University of Münster, Germany

Local Chair

Stefan Dissmann   TU Dortmund, Germany

Program Committee

Christian Bauckhage   Fraunhofer IAIS, Germany
Horst Bischof   TU Graz, Austria
Thomas Brox   University of Freiburg, Germany
Andrés Bruhn   University of Stuttgart, Germany
Joachim Buhmann   ETH Zurich, Switzerland
Daniel Cremers   TU Munich, Germany
Andreas Dengel   TU Kaiserslautern, Germany
Joachim Denzler   Schiller University Jena, Germany
Paolo Favaro   University of Bern, Switzerland
Wolfgang Förstner   University of Bonn, Germany
Uwe Franke   Daimler AG, Germany
Mario Fritz   CISPA Helmholtz Center i.G., Germany
Jürgen Gall   University of Bonn, Germany
Peter Gehler   University of Tübingen, Germany
Andreas Geiger   University of Tübingen, Germany
Bastian Goldlücke   University of Konstanz, Germany
Olaf Hellwich   TU Berlin, Germany
Margret Keuper   University of Mannheim, Germany
Reinhard Koch   University of Kiel, Germany
Ullrich Köthe   Heidelberg University, Germany
Walter Kropatsch   TU Wien, Austria
Hilde Kuehne   University of Bonn, Germany
Arjan Kuijper   TU Darmstadt, Fraunhofer IGD, Germany
Christoph Lampert   IST Austria, Austria
Laura Leal-Taixe   TU Munich, Germany
Bastian Leibe   RWTH Aachen University, Germany

Track Chairs

Additional Reviewers

Technical Support, Web, and Proceedings

Kai Brandenbusch	TU Dortmund, Germany
Dominik Koßmann	TU Dortmund, Germany
Philipp Oberdieck	TU Dortmund, Germany
Fernando Moya Rueda	TU Dortmund, Germany
Fabian Wolf	TU Dortmund, Germany
Jiaqi Zhang	University of Münster, Germany

Local Organization/Conference Office

Claudia Graute	TU Dortmund, Germany
Luise Henkel	TU Dortmund, Germany

Awards

GPCR Paper Awards

GCPR 2019 Best Paper Award

Learned Collaborative Stereo Refinement

Patrick Knöbelreiter	Graz University of Technology, Austria
Thomas Pock	Graz University of Technology, Austria

GCPR 2019 Honorable Mentions

Deep Archetypal Analysis

Sebastian Mathias Keller	University of Basel, Switzerland
Maxim Samarin	University of Basel, Switzerland
Mario Wieser	University of Basel, Switzerland
Volker Roth	University of Basel, Switzerland

Non-causal Tracking by Deblatting

Denys Rozumnyi	Czech Technical University & Czech Academy of Sciences, Prague, Czech Republic
Jan Kotera	Czech Technical University & Czech Academy of Sciences, Prague, Czech Republic
Filip Šroubek	Czech Technical University & Czech Academy of Sciences, Prague, Czech Republic
Jiří Matas	Czech Technical University & Czech Academy of Sciences, Prague, Czech Republic

DAGM Awards

DAGM German Pattern Recognition Award 2019

Gerhard Pons-Moll, Max Planck Institute for Informatics, Saarbrücken, for his scientific contributions in the area of capturing and modeling people from images and 3D scans

DAGM MVTec Dissertation Award 2019

Articulated Human Pose Estimation in Unconstrained Images and Videos

Umar Iqbal	University of Bonn
Jürgen Gall (Supervisor)	University of Bonn

DAGM Best Master Thesis Award 2019

3D Instance Semantic Segmentation on Point Clouds
Cathrin Elich   RWTH Aachen
Bastian Leibe (Supervisor)   RWTH Aachen

Contents

Oral Session I: Image Processing and Analysis

Learned Collaborative Stereo Refinement.......................... 3
  Patrick Knöbelreiter and Thomas Pock

Plane Completion and Filtering for Multi-View Stereo Reconstruction...... 18
  Andreas Kuhn, Shan Lin, and Oliver Erdler

Simultaneous Semantic Segmentation and Outlier Detection in Presence
of Domain Shift 33
  Petra Bevandić, Ivan Krešo, Marin Oršić, and Siniša Šegvić

3D Bird's-Eye-View Instance Segmentation 48
  *Cathrin Elich, Francis Engelmann, Theodora Kontogianni,
  and Bastian Leibe*

Classification-Specific Parts for Improving Fine-Grained
Visual Categorization.. 62
  Dimitri Korsch, Paul Bodesheim, and Joachim Denzler

Oral Session II: Imaging Techniques, Image Analysis

Adjustment and Calibration of Dome Port Camera Systems
for Underwater Vision.. 79
  Mengkun She, Yifan Song, Jochen Mohrmann, and Kevin Köser

Training Auto-Encoder-Based Optimizers for Terahertz
Image Reconstruction 93
  *Tak Ming Wong, Matthias Kahl, Peter Haring-Bolívar,
  Andreas Kolb, and Michael Möller*

Joint Viewpoint and Keypoint Estimation with Real and Synthetic Data 107
  Pau Panareda Busto and Juergen Gall

Non-causal Tracking by Deblatting 122
  Denys Rozumnyi, Jan Kotera, Filip Šroubek, and Jiří Matas

Oral Session III: Learning

Group Pruning Using a Bounded-ℓ_p Norm for Group Gating
and Regularization 139
  *Chaithanya Kumar Mummadi, Tim Genewein, Dan Zhang,
  Thomas Brox, and Volker Fischer*

On the Estimation of the Wasserstein Distance in Generative Models   156
Thomas Pinetz, Daniel Soukup, and Thomas Pock

Deep Archetypal Analysis   171
*Sebastian Mathias Keller, Maxim Samarin, Mario Wieser,
and Volker Roth*

Oral Session IV: Image Analysis, Applications

Single Level Feature-to-Feature Forecasting
with Deformable Convolutions   189
*Josip Šarić, Marin Oršić, Tonći Antunović, Sacha Vražić,
and Siniša Šegvić*

Predicting Landscapes from Environmental Conditions Using
Generative Networks   203
*Christian Requena-Mesa, Markus Reichstein, Miguel Mahecha,
Basil Kraft, and Joachim Denzler*

Semi-supervised Segmentation of Salt Bodies in Seismic Images Using
an Ensemble of Convolutional Neural Networks   218
Yauhen Babakhin, Artsiom Sanakoyeu, and Hirotoshi Kitamura

Entrack: A Data-Driven Maximum-Entropy Approach
to Fiber Tractography   232
Viktor Wegmayr, Giacomo Giuliari, and Joachim M. Buhmann

Posters

Generative Aging of Brain MR-Images and Prediction
of Alzheimer Progression   247
Viktor Wegmayr, Maurice Hörold, and Joachim M. Buhmann

Nonlinear Causal Link Estimation Under Hidden Confounding
with an Application to Time Series Anomaly Detection   261
*Violeta Teodora Trifunov, Maha Shadaydeh, Jakob Runge,
Veronika Eyring, Markus Reichstein, and Joachim Denzler*

Iris Verification with Convolutional Neural Network
and Unit-Circle Layer   274
Radim Špetlík and Ivan Razumenić

SDNet: Semantically Guided Depth Estimation Network   288
Matthias Ochs, Adrian Kretz, and Rudolf Mester

Object Segmentation Using Pixel-Wise Adversarial Loss   303
Ricard Durall, Franz-Josef Pfreundt, Ullrich Köthe, and Janis Keuper

Visual Coin-Tracking: Tracking of Planar Double-Sided Objects 317
Jonáš Šerých and Jiří Matas

Exploiting Attention for Visual Relationship Detection 331
Tongxin Hu, Wentong Liao, Michael Ying Yang, and Bodo Rosenhahn

Learning Task-Specific Generalized Convolutions
in the Permutohedral Lattice 345
Anne S. Wannenwetsch, Martin Kiefel, Peter V. Gehler, and Stefan Roth

Achieving Generalizable Robustness of Deep Neural Networks
by Stability Training 360
Jan Laermann, Wojciech Samek, and Nils Strodthoff

2D and 3D Segmentation of Uncertain Local Collagen Fiber Orientations
in SHG Microscopy 374
Lars Schmarje, Claudius Zelenka, Ulf Geisen, Claus-C. Glüer,
and Reinhard Koch

Points2Pix: 3D Point-Cloud to Image Translation Using
Conditional GANs 387
Stefan Milz, Martin Simon, Kai Fischer, Maximillian Pöpperl,
and Horst-Michael Gross

MLAttack: Fooling Semantic Segmentation Networks
by Multi-layer Attacks 401
Puneet Gupta and Esa Rahtu

Not Just a Matter of Semantics: The Relationship Between Visual
and Semantic Similarity 414
Clemens-Alexander Brust and Joachim Denzler

DynGraph: Visual Question Answering via Dynamic Scene Graphs 428
Monica Haurilet, Ziad Al-Halah, and Rainer Stiefelhagen

Training Invertible Neural Networks as Autoencoders 442
The-Gia Leo Nguyen, Lynton Ardizzone, and Ullrich Köthe

Weakly Supervised Learning of Dense Semantic Correspondences
and Segmentation 456
Nikolai Ufer, Kam To Lui, Katja Schwarz, Paul Warkentin,
and Björn Ommer

A Neural-Symbolic Architecture for Inverse Graphics Improved
by Lifelong Meta-learning 471
Michael Kissner and Helmut Mayer

Unsupervised Multi-source Domain Adaptation Driven by Deep
Adversarial Ensemble Learning.   485
   Sayan Rakshit, Biplab Banerjee, Gemma Roig, and Subhasis Chaudhuri

Time-Frequency Causal Inference Uncovers Anomalous Events
in Environmental Systems   499
   *Maha Shadaydeh, Joachim Denzler, Yanira Guanche García,
and Miguel Mahecha*

Tongue Contour Tracking in Ultrasound Images with Spatiotemporal
LSTM Networks.   513
   Enes Aslan and Yusuf Sinan Akgul

Localized Interactive Instance Segmentation.   522
   Soumajit Majumder and Angela Yao

Iterative Greedy Matching for 3D Human Pose Tracking
from Multiple Views.   537
   Julian Tanke and Juergen Gall

Visual Person Understanding Through Multi-task
and Multi-dataset Learning.   551
   *Kilian Pfeiffer, Alexander Hermans, István Sárándi,
Mark Weber, and Bastian Leibe*

Dynamic Classifier Chains for Multi-label Learning   567
   Pawel Trajdos and Marek Kurzynski

Learning 3D Semantic Reconstruction on Octrees.   581
   Xiaojuan Wang, Martin R. Oswald, Ian Cherabier, and Marc Pollefeys

Learning to Disentangle Latent Physical Factors for Video Prediction   595
   Deyao Zhu, Marco Munderloh, Bodo Rosenhahn, and Jörg Stückler

Learning to Train with Synthetic Humans   609
   David T. Hoffmann, Dimitrios Tzionas, Michael J. Black, and Siyu Tang

Author Index   625

Oral Session I: Image Processing and Analysis

Learned Collaborative Stereo Refinement

Patrick Knöbelreiter[(✉)][iD] and Thomas Pock[iD]

Institute for Computer Graphics and Vision, Graz University of Technology,
Graz, Austria
{knoebelreiter,pock}@icg.tugraz.at

Abstract. In this work, we propose a learning-based method to denoise
and refine disparity maps of a given stereo method. The proposed variational network arises naturally from unrolling the iterates of a proximal
gradient method applied to a variational energy defined in a joint disparity, color, and confidence image space. Our method allows to learn a
robust collaborative regularizer leveraging the joint statistics of the color
image, the confidence map and the disparity map. Due to the variational
structure of our method, the individual steps can be easily visualized,
thus enabling interpretability of the method. We can therefore provide
interesting insights into how our method refines and denoises disparity maps. The efficiency of our method is demonstrated by the publicly
available stereo benchmarks Middlebury 2014 and Kitti 2015.

1 Introduction

Computing 3D information from a stereo pair is one of the most important problems in computer vision. One reason for this is that depth information is a very
strong cue to understanding visual scenes, and depth information is therefore an
integral part of many vision based systems. For example, in autonomous driving,
it is not sufficient to know the objects visible in the scene, but it is also important
to estimate the distance to these objects. A lidar scanner is often too expensive
and provides only sparse depth estimates. Therefore, it is an interesting alternative to compute depth information exclusively from stereo images. However,
the calculation of depth information from images is still a very challenging task.
Reflections, occlusions, challenging illuminations *etc.* make the task even harder.
To tackle these difficulties the computation of dense depth maps is usually split
up into the four steps (i) matching cost computation, (ii) cost aggregation, (iii)
disparity computation and (iv) disparity refinement [27]. In deep learning based
approaches (i) and (ii) are usually implemented in a matching convolutional
neural network (CNN), (iii) is done using graphical models or 3D regularization
CNNs and (iv) is done with a refinement module [29].

Electronic supplementary material The online version of this chapter (https://
doi.org/10.1007/978-3-030-33676-9_1) contains supplementary material, which is available to authorized users.

© Springer Nature Switzerland AG 2019
G. A. Fink et al. (Eds.): DAGM GCPR 2019, LNCS 11824, pp. 3–17, 2019.
https://doi.org/10.1007/978-3-030-33676-9_1

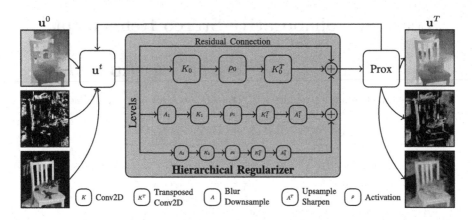

Fig. 1. Model Overview. Our model takes three inputs, an initial disparity map, confidence map and the color image. The collaborative hierarchical regularizer iteratively computes a refined disparity map and yields refined confidences and an abstracted color image as a byproduct. The subscripts indicate the level.

There are many approaches to tackle (i)–(iii). However, there are only a few learning-based works for disparity refinement (iv) (see Sect. 2). Existing work to refine the disparity map is often based on another CNN using residual connections. In this work we want to overcome these black-box refinement networks with a simple, effective and most important easily interpretable refinement approach for disparity maps. We tackle the refinement problem with a learnable hierarchical variational network. This allows us to exploit both the power of deep learning and the interpretability of variational methods. In order to show the effectiveness of the proposed refinement module, we conduct experiments on directly refining/denoising winner-takes-all (WTA) solutions of feature matching and as a pure post-processing module on top of an existing stereo method. Figure 1 shows an overview of our method. Starting from an initial disparity map the final result is iteratively reconstructed.

Contributions. We propose a learnable variational refinement network which takes advantage of the joint information of the color image, the disparity map and a confidence map to compute a regularized disparity map. We therefore show how our proposed method can be derived from the iterates of a proximal gradient method and how it can be specifically designed for stereo refinement. Additionally, we evaluate a broad range of possible architectural choices in an ablation study. Furthermore, we give insights into how our model constructs the final disparity map by visualizing and interpreting the intermediate iterates. We show the effectiveness of our method by participating on the two complementary public available benchmarks Middlebury 2014 and Kitti 2015.

2   Related Work

We propose a learnable variational model, where we use the modeling power of variational calculus to explicitly guide the refinement process for stereo. Thus, we focus on disparity refinement in the following sections.

Variational Methods. Variational methods formulate the correspondence problem as minimization of an energy functional comprising a data fidelity term and a smoothness term. We also briefly review variational optical flow methods, because stereo is a special case of optical flow, *i.e.* it can be considered as optical flow in horizontal direction only. The data-term measures usually the raw intensity difference [3,4,32] between the reference view and the warped other view. The regularizer imposes prior knowledge on the resulting disparity map. This is, the disparity map is assumed to be piecewise smooth. Prominent regularizers are the robust Total Variation (TV) [32] and the higher order generalization of TV as e.g. used by Ranftl *et al.* [20,21] or by Kuschk and Cremers [13]. Variational approaches have two important advantages in the context of stereo. They naturally produce sub-pixel accurate disparities and they are easily interpretable. However, in order to also capture large displacements a coarse-to-fine warping scheme [3] is necessary. To overcome the warping scheme without losing fine details, variational methods can also be used to refine an initial disparity map. This has *e.g.* be done by Shekhovtsov *et al.* [28] who refined the initial disparity estimates coming from a Conditional Random Field (CRF). Similarly, [22] and [16] used a variational method for refining optical flow.

Disparity Refinement. Here we want to focus on the refinement of an initial disparity map. The initial disparity map can be *e.g.* the WTA solution of a matching volume or any other output of a stereo algorithm. One important approach of refinement algorithms is the fast bilateral solver (FBS) [1]. This algorithm refines the initial disparity estimate by solving an optimization problem containing an ℓ_2 smoothness - and an ℓ_2 data-fidelity term. The fast bilateral solver is the most related work to ours. However, in this work we replace the ℓ_2 norm with the robust ℓ_1 norm. More importantly, we additionally replace the hand-crafted smoothness term by a learnable multi-scale regularizer. Another refinement method was proposed by Gidaris and Komodakis [7]. They also start with an initial disparity map, detect erroneous regions and then replace and refine these regions to get a high-quality output. Pang *et al.* [18] proposed to apply one and the same network twice. They compute the initial disparity map in a first pass, warp the second view with the initial disparity map and then compute only the residual to obtain a high quality disparity map. Liang *et al.* [14] also improved the results by adding a refinement sub-network on top of the regularization network. We want to stress that the CNN based refinement networks [14,18] do not have a specialized architecture for refinement as opposed to the proposed model.

Learnable Optimization Schemes. Learnable optimization schemes are based on unrolling the iterates of optimization algorithms. We divide the approaches into two categories. In the first category the optimization iterates are mainly used to utilize the structure during learning. For example in [23] 10 iterations of a TGV regularized variational method are unrolled and used for depth super-resolution. However, they kept the algorithm fixed, *i.e.* the only learnable parameters in the inference part are the step-sizes. Similarly, in [30] unrolling 10k iterations of the FISTA [2] algorithm is proposed. The second category includes methods where the optimization scheme is not only used to provide the structure, but it is also generalized by adding additional learnable parameters directly to the optimization iterates. For example [31] proposed a primal-dual-network for low-level vision problems, where the authors learned the inference part of a Markov Random Field (MRF) model generalizing a primal-dual algorithm. Chen *et al.* [6] generalized a reaction-diffusion model and successfully learned a model for image denoising. Based on [6] a generalized incremental proximal gradient method was proposed in [12], where the authors showed connections to residual units [8]. We built on the work of Chen *et al.*, but specially designed the energy terms for the stereo task. Additionally, we allow to regularize on multiple spatial resolutions jointly and make use of the robust ℓ_1 function in our data-terms.

3   Method

We consider images to be functions $f : \Omega \to \mathbb{R}^C$, with $\Omega \subset \mathbb{N}_+^2$ and C is the number of channels which is 3 for RGB color images. Given two images f^0 and f^1 from a rectified stereo pair, we want to compute dense disparities d such that $f^0(x) = f^1(x - \tilde{d})$, *i.e.* we want to compute the horizontal shift $\tilde{d} = (d, 0)$ for each pixel $x = (x_1, x_2)$ between the reference image f^0 and the second image f^1. Here, we propose a novel variational refinement network for stereo which operates solely in 2D image space and is thus very efficient. The input to our method is an initial disparity map $\check{u} : \Omega \to [0, D]$, where D is the maximal disparity, a reference image f^0 and a pixel-wise confidence map $c : \Omega \to [0, 1]$. The proposed variational network is a method to regularize, denoise and refine a noisy disparity map with learnable filters and learnable potential functions. Hence, the task we want to solve is the following: Given a noisy disparity map $\check{u}$, we want to recover the clean disparity with T learnable variational network steps. We do not make any assumptions on the quality of the initial disparity map, i.e. the initial disparity map may contain many strong outliers.

3.1   Collaborative Disparity Denoising

As the main contribution of this paper, we propose a method that performs a collaborative denoising in the joint color image, disparity and confidence space (see Fig. 2). Our model is based on the following three observations: (i) Depth discontinuities co-inside with object boundaries, (ii) discontinuities in the confidence image are expected to be close to left-sided object boundaries and (iii) the confidence image can be used as a pixel-wise weighting factor in the data fidelity

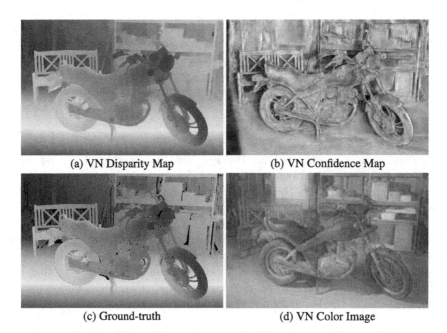

(a) VN Disparity Map   (b) VN Confidence Map

(c) Ground-truth   (d) VN Color Image

Fig. 2. Collaborative Disparity Denoising. Our method produces three outputs: (a) the refined disparity map, (b) the refined confidence map and (d) the refined color image. (c) shows the ground-truth image for comparison (black pixels = invalid). Note how our method is able to preserve fine details such as the spokes of the motorcycle.

term. Based on these three observations, we propose the following collaborative variational denoising model

$$\min_{\mathbf{u}} \mathcal{R}(\mathbf{u}) + \mathcal{D}(\mathbf{u}), \tag{1}$$

where $\mathbf{u} = (\mathbf{u}^{rgb}, u^d, u^c) : \Omega \to \mathbb{R}^5$, $i.e.$ $\mathbf{u}$ contains for every pixel an RGB color information, a disparity value and a confidence value. $\mathcal{R}(\mathbf{u})$ denotes the collaborative regularizer and it is given by a multi-scale and multi-channel version of the Fields of Experts (FoE) model [25] with L scales and K channels.

$$\mathcal{R}(\mathbf{u}; \theta) = \sum_{l=1}^{L} \sum_{k=1}^{K} \sum_{x \in \Omega} \phi_k^l \left(\left(K_k^l A^l \mathbf{u} \right) (x) \right), \tag{2}$$

where A^l are combined blur and downsampling operators, K_k^l are linear convolution operators and $\phi_k^l : \mathbb{R} \mapsto \mathbb{R}$ are non-linear activation functions. The vector θ holds the parameters of the regularizer which will be detailed later. Note that multiple levels allow the model to operate on different spatial resolutions and therefore enables the denoising of large corrupted areas. Intuitively, the collaborative regularizer captures the statistics of the joint color, confidence and disparity space. Hence, it will be necessary to learn the linear operators and the non-linear potential functions from data. It will turn out that the combination of filtering in the joint color-disparity-confidence space at multiple hierarchical pyramid levels and specifically learned channel-wise potential functions make our model very powerful.

$\mathcal{D}(\mathbf{u})$ denotes the collaborative data fidelity term and it is defined by

$$\mathcal{D}(\mathbf{u}; \theta) = \frac{\lambda}{2}\|\mathbf{u}^{rgb} - \mathbf{f}^0\|^2 + \mu\|u^c - c\|_1 + \nu\|u^d - \check{d}\|_{u^c, 1}, \tag{3}$$

where θ is again a placeholder for the learnable parameters. The first term ensures that the smoothed color image $\mathbf{u}^{rgb}$ does not deviate too much from the original color image $\mathbf{f}^0$, the second term ensures that the smoothed confidence map stays close to the original confidence map. Here we use an ℓ_1 norm in order to deal with outliers in the initial confidence map. The last term is the data fidelity term of the disparity map. It is given by an ℓ_1 norm which is pixelwise weighted by the confidence measure u^c. Hence, data fidelity is enforced in high-confidence regions and suppressed in low-confidence regions. Note that the weighted ℓ_1 norm additionally ties the disparity map with the confidence map during the steps of the variational network.

Proximal Gradient Method (PGM). We consider a PGM [19] whose iterates are given by

$$\mathbf{u}_{t+1} = \text{prox}_{\alpha_t \mathcal{D}}(\mathbf{u}_t - \alpha_t \nabla \mathcal{R}(\mathbf{u}_t)), \tag{4}$$

where α_t is the step-size, $\nabla \mathcal{R}(\mathbf{u}_t)$ is the gradient of the regularizer which is given by

$$\nabla \mathcal{R}(\mathbf{u}) = \sum_{l=1}^{L} \sum_{k=1}^{K} (K_k^l A^l)^T \rho_k^l \left(K_k^l A^l \mathbf{u}\right), \tag{5}$$

where $\rho_k^l = \text{diag}((\phi_k^l)')$. $\text{prox}_{\alpha_t \mathcal{D}}$ denotes the proximal operator with respect to the data fidelity term, which is defined by

$$\text{prox}_{\alpha_t \mathcal{D}}(\tilde{\mathbf{u}}) = \arg\min_{\mathbf{u}} \mathcal{D}(\mathbf{u}) + \frac{1}{2\alpha_t}\|\mathbf{u} - \tilde{\mathbf{u}}\|_2^2. \tag{6}$$

Note that the proximal map allows to handle the non-smooth data fidelity terms such as the ℓ_1 norm. Additionally, there is a strong link between proximal gradient methods and residual units which allows to incrementally reconstruct a solution (see Fig. 1). We provide the computation of the prox-terms in the supplementary material.

Variational Network. Our collaborative denoising algorithm consists of performing a fixed number of T iterations of the proximal gradient method Eq. (4). In order to increase the flexibility we allow the model parameters to change in each iteration.

$$\mathbf{u}_{t+1} = \text{prox}_{\alpha_t \mathcal{D}(\cdot, \theta_t)}(\mathbf{u}_t - \alpha_t \nabla \mathcal{R}(\mathbf{u}_t, \theta_t)), \ 0 \le t \le T - 1 \tag{7}$$

Following [6,12] we parametrize the derivatives of the potential functions using Gaussian radial basis functions (RBF)

$$\rho_k^{l,t}(s) = \beta_k^{l,t} \sum_{b=1}^{B} w_{k,b}^{l,t} \exp\left(-\frac{(s-\gamma_b)^2}{2\sigma^2}\right), \tag{8}$$

where γ_b are the means regularly sampled on the interval $[-3,3]$, σ is the standard deviation of the Gaussian kernel and $\beta_k^{l,t}$ is a scaling factor. The linear operators $K_k^{l,t}$ are implemented as multi-channel 2D convolutions with convolution kernels $\kappa_k^{l,t}$. In summary, the parameters in each step are given by $\theta_t = \{\kappa_k^{l,t}, \beta_k^{l,t}, w_{k,b}^{l,t}, \mu^t, \nu^t, \lambda^t, \alpha_t,\}$.

4 Computing Inputs

Our proposed refinement method can be applied to an arbitrary stereo method, provided it comes along with a cost-volume, which is the case for the majority of existing stereo methods.

Probability Volume. Assume we have given a cost-volume $v : \Omega \times \{0, \ldots, D-1\} \to \mathbb{R}$, where smaller costs mean a higher likelihood of the respective disparity values. In order to map the values onto probabilities $p : \Omega \times \{0, \ldots, D-1\}$, we make use of the "softmax" function, that is

$$p(x,d) = \frac{\exp(\frac{-v(x,d)}{\eta})}{\sum_{d'=0}^{D-1} \exp(\frac{-v(x,d')}{\eta})}, \tag{9}$$

where η influences the smoothness of the probability distribution.

Initial Disparity Map. From Eq. (9) we can compute the WTA solution by a pixel-wise arg max over the disparity dimension, i.e.,

$$\bar{d}(x) \in \arg\max_d \, p(x,d). \tag{10}$$

Moreover, we compute a sub-pixel accurate disparity map $\check{d}(x)$ by fitting a quadratic function to the probability volume. This is equivalent to perform one step of Newton's algorithm:

$$\check{d}(x) = \bar{d}(x) - \frac{\delta^+(p(x,\cdot))(\bar{d}(x))}{\delta^-(\delta^+(p(x,\cdot)))(\bar{d}(x))}, \tag{11}$$

where $\delta^{\{+,-\}}$ denote standard forward and backward differences in the disparity dimension. Furthermore, we compute the refined value of the probabilities, denoted as $\check{p}(x)$, via linear interpolation in the probability volume.

Init	Step 1	Step 2	Step 3	Step 4	Step 5	Step 6	Step 7

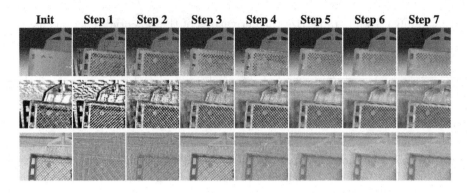

Fig. 3. Visualization of steps in the VN. Top to bottom: disparity map, confidence map, image. Left to right: Initialization, VN Steps 1–7. Note how the color image and the confidence map help to restore very fine details in the disparity map.

Initial Confidence Measure. The computation of a confidence measure of the stereo results is important for many applications and a research topic on its own [9]. Here we take advantage of the probabilistic nature of our matching costs $\check{p}(x)$. Moreover, we make use of geometric constraints by using a left-right (LR) consistency check, where the left and right images are interchanged. This allows us to identify occluded regions. We compute the probability of a pixel being not occluded as

$$p_o(x) = \frac{\max(\varepsilon - \mathrm{dist}_{lr}(x), 0)}{\varepsilon} \in [0, 1], \tag{12}$$

where

$$\mathrm{dist}_{lr}(x) = |\check{d}_l(x) + \check{d}_r(x + \check{d}_l(x))| \tag{13}$$

is the disparity difference between the left prediction $\check{d}_l$ and the right prediction $\check{d}_r$ and the parameter ε acts as a threshold and is set to $\varepsilon = 3$ in all experiments. The final confidence measure is given by

$$c(x) = \check{p}(x)p_o(x) \in [0, 1]. \tag{14}$$

Thus, we define our total confidence as the product of the matching confidence and the LR confidence. Most of the pixels not surviving the LR check are pixels in occluded regions. To get a good initialization for these pixels as well, we inpaint the disparities of these pixels from the left side. The experiments show that this significantly increases the performance of the model (see Table 1).

5   Learning

In this section we describe our learning procedure for the collaborative denoising model. To remove scaling ambiguities we require the filter kernels $\kappa_k^{l,t}$ to be zero-mean and to have an ℓ_2 norm ≤ 1. Moreover, we constraint the weights of the RBF kernels to have an ℓ_2 norm ≤ 1, too. This is defined with the following convex set:

$$\Theta = \{\theta_t : \|\kappa_k^{l,t}\| \leq 1, \ \sum \kappa_k^{l,t} = 0, \ \|w_k^{l,t}\| \leq 1\} \tag{15}$$

Fig. 4. Qualitative results on the Kitti 2015 test set. Top-to-bottom: Reference image, disparity map which is color coded with blue = far away to yellow = near, error map, where blue = correct disparity, orange = incorrect disparity. (Color figure online)

For learning, we define a loss function that measures the error between the last iterate of the disparity map u_T^d and the ground-truth disparity d^*. Note that we do not have a loss function for the confidence and the color image. Their aim is rather to support the disparity map to achieve the lowest loss. We use a truncated Huber function of the form

$$\min_{\theta \in \Theta} \sum_{s=1}^{S} \sum_{i=1}^{MN} \min \left(|u_{s,T}^d(x, \theta) - d_s^*(x)|_{\delta}, \ \tau \right) \qquad (16)$$

where τ is a truncation value, s denotes the index of the training sample and

$$|r|_{\delta} = \begin{cases} \frac{r^2}{2\delta} & \text{if } |r| \leq \delta \\ |r| - \frac{\delta}{2} & \text{else} \end{cases} \qquad (17)$$

is the Huber function.

Implementation Details. We implemented our model in the PyTorch machine learning framework[1]. We train the refinement module for 3000 epochs with a learning rate of 10^{-3} with a modified projected Adam optimizer [10]. We dynamically adjusted the stepsize computation to be constant within each parameter block in our constraint set Θ to ensure that we perform an orthogonal projectio onto the constraint set. After 1500 epochs we reduce the truncation value τ from ∞ to 3.

6   Experiments

We split the experiments into two parts. In the first part we evaluate architectural choices based on the WTA result of a matching network and compare with the

---

[1] https://pytorch.org.

Table 1. Ablation study on the Kitti 2015 dataset. Conf = Confidences, Img = Image, OccIp = Occlusion inpainting, Joint = joint training. The super-script indicates the number of steps and the filter-size while the sub-script indicates the number of levels in the variational network. $VN_4^{7,5}$ is therefore a variational network with 7 steps and 4 levels.

Model	WTA	FBF [1]	$VN_4^{7,5}$	$VN_4^{7,5}$	$VN_4^{7,5}$	$VN_4^{7,5}$	$VN_4^{7,5}$	$VN_4^{7,5}$	$VN_3^{5,7}$	$VN_2^{8,7}$	$VN_4^{14,3}$	$VN_5^{11,3}$
Conf	✓		✓	✓			✓	✓	✓	✓	✓	✓
Img	✓			✓		✓	✓	✓	✓	✓	✓	✓
OccIp	✓		✓		✓	✓	✓	✓	✓	✓	✓	✓
Joint								✓	✓	✓	✓	✓
[bad3] occ	8.24	7.48	5.42	5.12	4.43	3.77	3.46	**3.37**	3.43	3.62	4.37	4.25
[bad3] noc	6.78	6.08	4.68	3.98	3.90	3.07	2.72	**2.55**	2.58	2.97	3.71	3.49

FBS [1]. In the second part, we use the best architecture and train a variational network for refining the disparity maps computed by the CNN-CRF method [11]. We use this method to participate in the public available stereo benchmarks Middlebury 2014 and Kitti 2015. To ensure a fair comparison we choose methods with similar numbers of parameters and runtimes. Figure 3 shows how our method constructs the final result. The method recovers step-by-step fine details with the guidance of the confidences and the color image.

Kitti 2015. The Kitti 2015 dataset [17] is an outdoor dataset specifically designed for autonomous driving. It contains 200 images with available ground-truth to train a model and 200 images with withheld ground-truth which is used for testing the models on previously unseen data. The ground-truth is captured using a laser scanner and is therefore sparse in general. The cars are densified by fitting CAD models into the laser point-cloud. We report the *badX* error metric for occluded (occ) and non-occluded (noc) pixels with $X = 3$. In the badX measure the predicted disparity $\hat{d}$ is treated incorrect, if the distance to the ground-truth disparity d^* is larger than X.

Middlebury 2014. The Middlebury 2014 stereo dataset [26] is orthogonal to the Kitti 2015 dataset. It consists of 153 high resolution indoor images with highly precise dense ground-truth. The challenges in the Middlebury dataset are large, almost untextured regions, huge occluded regions, reflections and difficult lighting conditions. The generalization capability of the method is evaluated on a 15 images test-set with withheld ground-truth data. We report all available metrics, i.e., bad$\{0.5, 1, 2, 4\}$ errors, the average error (avg) and the root-mean-squared error (rms).

6.1 Ablation Study

To find the most appropriate hyper parameters for the proposed method, we generate our initial disparity map with a simple feature network. The learned features are then compared using a fixed matching function for a pre-defined number of discrete disparities.

Table 2. Performance on public benchmarks. Top = Official training set, Bottom = Official test set. Bold font: Overall best. Italic font = improvement of base-line. ∅R denotes the average rank over all metrics on the benchmarks.

| Method | Kitti 2015 | | | Middlebury 2014 | | | | | | | |
	noc	all	∅R	bad0.5	bad1	bad2	bad4	avg	rms	time	∅R
PSMNet [5]	-	**1.83**	-	90.0	78.1	58.5	32.2	9.60	21.7	2.62	44
PDS [29]	-	-	-	54.2	26.1	11.4	5.10	1.98	9.10	10	8
MC-CNN [33]	-	-	-	42.1	20.5	11.7	7.94	3.87	16.5	1.26	9
CNN-CRF [11]	-	4.04	-	56.1	25.1	10.8	6.12	2.30	9.89	3.53	10
[11] + VN (ours)	*1.90*	*2.04*	-	*41.8*	*17.1*	*7.05*	*2.96*	*1.21*	*5.80*	4.06	*2*
PSMNet [5]	**2.14**	**2.32**	17	81.1	63.9	42.1	23.5	6.68	19.4	2.62	33
PDS [29]	2.36	2.58	19	58.9	21.1	14.2	6.98	3.27	15.7	10.3	9
MC-CNN [33]	3.33	3.89	32	**41.3**	**18.0**	**9.47**	6.7	4.37	22.4	1.26	6
CNN-CRF [11]	4.84	5.50	36	60.9	31.9	12.5	**6.61**	3.02	14.4	3.53	8
[11] + VN (ours)	*4.45*	*4.85*	*33*	56.2	30.0	14.2	7.71	*2.49*	*10.8*	4.06	*6*

Feature Network. Our feature network is a modified version of the U-Net [15,24] which we use to extract features suitable for stereo matching. We kept the number of parameters low by only using 64 channels at every layer. The output of our feature network is thus a 64-dimensional feature vector for every pixel. The exact architecture is shown in the supplementary material.

Feature Matching. Next, we use the extracted features ψ^0 from the left image and ψ^1 from the right image to compute a matching score volume $\tilde{p} : \Omega \times \{0, \ldots, D-1\} \to \mathbb{R}$ with

$$\tilde{p}(x, d) = \langle \psi^0(x), \ \psi^1(x - \tilde{d}) \rangle. \tag{18}$$

We follow Sect. 4 to compute the inputs for the variational network.

Ablation Study. We systematically remove parts of our method in order to show how the final performance is influenced by the individual parts. Table 1 shows an overview of all experiments. First we investigate the influence of our data-terms, the disparity data-term, the confidence data-term and the RGB image data-term. The study shows that each of the data-terms positively influence the final performance. Especially, adding the original input image significantly increases the performance. This can be *e.g.* seen in Fig. 3, where the information of how the basket needs to be reconstructed, is derived from the input image. In the second part of the study, we evaluate different variational network architectures. To make the comparison as fair as possible, we chose the variants such that the total number of parameters is approximately the same for all architectures. The experiments show, that a compromise between number of steps, pyramid levels and filter-size yields the best results. The best performing model is the model $VN_4^{7,5}$, where the filter-size is set to 5×5 for 4 pyramid levels and 7 steps. The

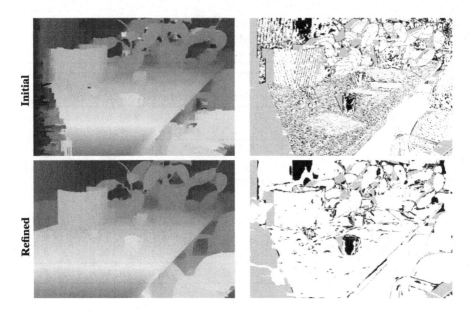

Fig. 5. Qualitative results on the Middlebury test set. Left: Color-coded disparity maps ranging from blue = far away to red = near. Right: Error maps, where white = correct and black = incorrect. The top row shows the initial disparity map (=input to the VN) and the bottom row shows our refined result. (Color figure online)

average runtime of this VN is as low as 0.09 s on an NVidia 2080Ti graphics card.

Additionally, we compare with the FBS. We therefore use exactly the same inputs as we did in our method, i.e., the refined WTA solution $\check{d}$, our confidence measure c and the RGB input image. To ensure the best performance for the FBS, we performed a grid-search over its hyper-parameters on the Kitti dataset. As shown in Table 1 the FBS clearly improves the performance upon the initial solution, but the FBS cannot compete with the proposed method.

6.2   Benchmark Performance

We use our method on top of the CNN-CRF [11] stereo method for the official test set evaluation (see Table 2). We set the temperature parameter $\eta = 0.075$ in all experiments. The average rank is computed with all published methods in the respective benchmarks with a runtime ≤ 20 s. This yields in total 71 methods on the Kitti benchmark and 50 methods on the Middlebury benchmark.

We used the model $VN_4^{7,5}$ on the Kitti dataset. As shown in Table 2 we reduce the bad3 error in both, occluded and in non-occluded regions. Figure 4 shows qualitative results with the corresponding error maps on the Kitti test set.

On the Middlebury benchmark we use the model $VN_4^{7,11}$ for all evaluations. We compare the errors on the training set with the errors on the test set (Table 2) and observe that: (i) Our method achieves the best scores in all metrics among the compared methods on the training set. (ii) This positive trend is transferred to the test set for the average error and the RMS error. (iii) The bad$\{0.5, 1\}$ errors on the test set are reduced and (iv) the bad$\{2, 4\}$ errors slightly increase on the test set compared to [11]. One reason for this is the limited amount of training data for these very high-resolution images. Figure 5 shows a qualitative example of the Middlebury test set. Note that the tabletop is nice and smooth while the sharp edges of the objects are very well preserved.

7   Conclusion and Future Work

We have proposed a learnable variational network for efficient refinement of disparity maps. The learned collaborative and hierarchical refinement method allows the use of information from the joint color, confidence and disparity space from multiple spatial resolutions. In an ablation study, we evaluated a broad range of architectural choices and demonstrated the impact of our design decisions. Our method can be applied on top of any other stereo method, with full use of additional information of a full cost volume. We demonstrated this by adding the variational refinement network on top of the CNN-CRF method and have shown improved results. Furthermore, we have proven the effectiveness of our method by participating in the publicly available stereo benchmarks of Middlebury and Kitti. In future work, we would like to include a matching score during the refinement process and perform data augmentation to increase the training set for learning.

Acknowledgements. This work was partly supported from the ERC starting grant HOMOVIS (No. 640156).

References

1. Barron, J.T., Poole, B.: The fast bilateral solver. In: Leibe, B., Matas, J., Sebe, N., Welling, M. (eds.) ECCV 2016. LNCS, vol. 9907, pp. 617–632. Springer, Cham (2016). https://doi.org/10.1007/978-3-319-46487-9_38
2. Beck, A., Teboulle, M.: A fast iterative shrinkage-thresholding algorithm for linear inverse problems. SIAM J. Imaging Sci. **2**, 183–202 (2009)
3. Brox, T., Bruhn, A., Papenberg, N., Weickert, J.: High accuracy optical flow estimation based on a theory for warping. In: Pajdla, T., Matas, J. (eds.) ECCV 2004. LNCS, vol. 3024, pp. 25–36. Springer, Heidelberg (2004). https://doi.org/10.1007/978-3-540-24673-2_3
4. Chambolle, A., Pock, T.: A first-order primal-dual algorithm for convex problems with applications to imaging. J. Math. Imaging Vis. **40**, 120–145 (2011)
5. Chang, J.R., Chen, Y.S.: Pyramid stereo matching network. In: IEEE Conference on Computer Vision and Pattern Recognition (CVPR), pp. 5410–5418 (2018)
6. Chen, Y., Yu, W., Pock, T.: On learning optimized reaction diffusion processes for effective image restoration. In: IEEE Conference on Computer Vision and Pattern Recognition (CVPR), pp. 5261–5269 (2015)
7. Gidaris, S., Komodakis, N.: Detect, replace, refine: deep structured prediction for pixel wise labeling. In: IEEE Conference on Computer Vision and Pattern Recognition (CVPR), pp. 5248–5257 (2017)

8. He, K., Zhang, X., Ren, S., Sun, J.: Deep residual learning for image recognition. In: IEEE Conference on Computer Vision and Pattern Recognition (CVPR), pp. 770–778 (2016)
9. Hu, X., Mordohai, P.: A quantitative evaluation of confidence measures for stereo vision. IEEE Trans. Pattern Anal. Mach. Intell. **34**, 2121–2133 (2012)
10. Kingma, D.P., Ba, J.: Adam: a method for stochastic optimization. arXiv preprint arXiv:1412.6980 (2014)
11. Knöbelreiter, P., Reinbacher, C., Shekhovtsov, A., Pock, T.: End-to-end training of hybrid CNN-CRF models for stereo. In: IEEE Conference on Computer Vision and Pattern Recognition (CVPR), pp. 2339–2348 (2017)
12. Kobler, E., Klatzer, T., Hammernik, K., Pock, T.: Variational networks: connecting variational methods and deep learning. In: Roth, V., Vetter, T. (eds.) GCPR 2017. LNCS, vol. 10496, pp. 281–293. Springer, Cham (2017). https://doi.org/10.1007/978-3-319-66709-6_23
13. Kuschk, G., Cremers, D.: Fast and accurate large-scale stereo reconstruction using variational methods. In: IEEE International Conference on Computer Vision Workshop, pp. 700–707 (2013)
14. Liang, Z., et al.: Learning for disparity estimation through feature constancy. In: IEEE Conference on Computer Vision and Pattern Recognition (CVPR), pp. 2811–2820 (2018)
15. Long, J., Shelhamer, E., Darrell, T.: Fully convolutional networks for semantic segmentation. In: IEEE Conference on Computer Vision and Pattern Recognition (CVPR), pp. 3431–3440 (2015)
16. Maurer, D., Stoll, M., Bruhn, A.: Order-adaptive and illumination-aware variational optical flow refinement. In: British Machine Vision Conference (2017)
17. Menze, M., Geiger, A.: Object scene flow for autonomous vehicles. In: IEEE Conference on Computer Vision and Pattern Recognition (CVPR), pp. 3061–3070 (2015)
18. Pang, J., Sun, W., Ren, J.S., Yang, C., Yan, Q.: Cascade residual learning: a two-stage convolutional neural network for stereo matching. In: IEEE International Conference on Computer Vision Workshop, pp. 887–895 (2017)
19. Parikh, N., Boyd, S., et al.: Proximal algorithms. Found. Trends Optim. **1**, 127–239 (2014)
20. Ranftl, R., Gehrig, S., Pock, T., Bischof, H.: Pushing the limits of stereo using variational stereo estimation. In: IEEE Intelligent Vehicles Symposium, pp. 401–407 (2012)
21. Ranftl, R., Bredies, K., Pock, T.: Non-local total generalized variation for optical flow estimation. In: Fleet, D., Pajdla, T., Schiele, B., Tuytelaars, T. (eds.) ECCV 2014. LNCS, vol. 8689, pp. 439–454. Springer, Cham (2014). https://doi.org/10.1007/978-3-319-10590-1_29
22. Revaud, J., Weinzaepfel, P., Harchaoui, Z., Schmid, C.: Epicflow: edge-preserving interpolation of correspondences for optical flow. In: IEEE Conference on Computer Vision and Pattern Recognition (CVPR), pp. 1164–1172 (2015)
23. Riegler, G., Rüther, M., Bischof, H.: ATGV-Net: accurate depth super-resolution. In: Leibe, B., Matas, J., Sebe, N., Welling, M. (eds.) ECCV 2016. LNCS, vol. 9907, pp. 268–284. Springer, Cham (2016). https://doi.org/10.1007/978-3-319-46487-9_17
24. Ronneberger, O., Fischer, P., Brox, T.: U-Net: convolutional networks for biomedical image segmentation. In: Navab, N., Hornegger, J., Wells, W.M., Frangi, A.F. (eds.) MICCAI 2015. LNCS, vol. 9351, pp. 234–241. Springer, Cham (2015). https://doi.org/10.1007/978-3-319-24574-4_28

25. Roth, S., Black, M.J.: Fields of experts. Int. J. Comput. Vis. **82**, 205 (2009)
26. Scharstein, D., et al.: High-resolution stereo datasets with subpixel-accurate ground truth. In: Jiang, X., Hornegger, J., Koch, R. (eds.) GCPR 2014. LNCS, vol. 8753, pp. 31–42. Springer, Cham (2014). https://doi.org/10.1007/978-3-319-11752-2_3
27. Scharstein, D., Szeliski, R.: A taxonomy and evaluation of dense two-frame stereo correspondence algorithms. Int. J. Comput. Vis. **47**, 7–42 (2002)
28. Shekhovtsov, A., Reinbacher, C., Graber, G., Pock, T.: Solving dense image matching in real-time using discrete-continuous optimization. In: Computer Vision Winter Workshop (2016)
29. Tulyakov, S., Ivanov, A., Fleuret, F.: Practical deep stereo (pds): toward applications-friendly deep stereo matching. In: Proceedings of Advances in Neural Information Processing Systems, pp. 5871–5881 (2018)
30. Vogel, C., Knöbelreiter, P., Pock, T.: Learning energy based inpainting for optical flow. In: Jawahar, C.V., Li, H., Mori, G., Schindler, K. (eds.) ACCV 2018. LNCS, vol. 11366, pp. 340–356. Springer, Cham (2019). https://doi.org/10.1007/978-3-030-20876-9_22
31. Vogel, C., Pock, T.: A primal dual network for low-level vision problems. In: German Conference on Pattern Recognition (GCPR) (2017)
32. Zach, C., Pock, T., Bischof, H.: A duality based approach for realtime TV-L1 optical flow. In: German Conference on Pattern Recognition (GCPR) (2007)
33. Žbontar, J., LeCun, Y.: Stereo matching by training a convolutional neural network to compare image patches. J. Mach. Learn. Res. **17**, 1–32 (2016)

Plane Completion and Filtering for Multi-View Stereo Reconstruction

Andreas Kuhn[1($\boxtimes$)], Shan Lin[1,2], and Oliver Erdler[1]

[1] Sony Europe B.V. – Stuttgart Technology Center, Stuttgart, Germany
andreas.kuhn@sony.com
[2] Technical University of Munich, Munich, Germany

Abstract. Multi-View Stereo (MVS)-based 3D reconstruction is a major topic in computer vision for which a vast number of methods have been proposed over the last decades showing impressive visual results. Long-since, benchmarks like Middlebury [32] numerically rank the individual methods considering accuracy and completeness as quality attributes. While the *Middlebury* benchmark provides low-resolution images only, the recently published *ETH3D* [31] and *Tanks and Temples* [19] benchmarks allow for an evaluation of high-resolution and large-scale MVS from natural camera configurations. This benchmarking reveals that still only few methods can be used for the reconstruction of large-scale models. We present an effective pipeline for large-scale 3D reconstruction which extends existing methods in several ways: (i) We introduce an outlier filtering considering the MVS geometry. (ii) To avoid incomplete models from local matching methods we propose a plane completion method based on growing superpixels allowing a generic generation of high-quality 3D models. (iii) Finally, we use deep learning for a subsequent filtering of outliers in segmented sky areas. We give experimental evidence on benchmarks that our contributions improve the quality of the 3D model and our method is state-of-the-art in high-quality 3D reconstruction from high-resolution images or large image sets.

1 Introduction

Benchmarking 3D reconstruction from real-world high-resolution images has been absent to the community since the unavailability of Strecha et al.'s [33] online service. Even though ground truth models are available for a subset of the datasets, their images basically show well-textured scenes from specific and simple camera configurations. For example, the objects are captured from a constant distance. Similar limited configurations are provided by the *DTU Robot Image* [1] and *Middlebury* [32] datasets, both consisting of images captured in a laboratory environment with relatively low resolutions.

The importance of employing a large variety of scenes and viewpoints in different kind of environments is demonstrated by the recently published benchmark datasets *ETH3D* [31] and *Tanks and Temples* [19]. Both datasets comprise ground truth models generated from high-precision laser scanners. For specific

G. A. Fink et al. (Eds.): DAGM GCPR 2019, LNCS 11824, pp. 18–32, 2019.
https://doi.org/10.1007/978-3-030-33676-9_2

training data the ground truth is publicly available. The *ETH3D* [31] dataset provides images that have been registered and aligned with the laser scans while the *Tanks and Temples* dataset [19] provides the image data only. Since data alignment is a non-trivial task, we use the *ETH3D* training dataset for the evaluation of the proposed contributions in our experiments. Finally, we show our evaluation results on the *ETH3D* Test and *Tanks and Temples* Test and Training datasets from our proposed 3D reconstruction pipeline.

1.1   Related Work

In this paper, we focus on methods allowing a high completeness of 3D models while still preserving details. **CMPMVS** [17] reconstructs surfaces (meshes) in a tetrahedral space [27] derived from noisy point clouds using visibility constraints. CMPMVS is especially strong in the reconstruction of surface parts that have not been directly derived in the Multi-View Stereo (MVS) step. For MVS an efficient plane-sweep approach is used [16]. The underlying optimization scheme has already been shown to be suitable for large-scale 3D reconstruction [26, 35]. Instead of tetrahedralization, we reconstruct point clouds with pointwise quality criterion allowing a higher level of detail without a complex optimization. **COLMAP** [29, 30] is considered widely as state of the art in effective point cloud reconstruction from images with unrestricted configurations. Impressive results were shown with diverse datasets like Photo Community Collections [29], laboratory data [32] and high-resolution imagery [30]. One of COLMAPs major contributions is the depth map generation based on PatchMatch (PM) [3, 38] including statistics for correspondence search in multiple images resulting in a higher efficiency [30]. Finally, it uses a geometric fusion of noisy depth maps into clean point clouds. The resulting point cloud can be transformed into surface meshes, e.g., by means of Poisson reconstruction [18]. **Gipuma** [11] also provides a GPU implementation of PM stereo matching including a pixelwise normal estimation. For an independent parallelization a checkerboard propagation scheme is proposed leading to a higher efficiency of the method. Depth maps are fused into a single point cloud by averaging over consistent depth and normal estimates. The Gipuma method is ranked lower in the *ETH3D* benchmark compared to alternative PM methods. **ACMH** [36] demonstrates that the checkerboard sampling allows high-quality reconstruction when using a multi-hypothesis joint view selection. When further employing a multi-scale geometric consistency guidance (**ACMM** [36]) state-of-the art quality is achieved. To this end, the completeness is improved by multi-scale geometric consistency guidance for propagating depth measurements from lower resolution levels. **LTVRE** [23] uses Semi-Global Matching (SGM) [14] to generate disparity maps and derives a pixelwise quality estimate using a Total Variation (TV) criterion [22]. The TV criterion has also been successfully applied to PM for stereo images [24]. One key contribution of LTVRE is a 3D error estimation and probabilistic fusion and filtering [21] which which improves standard local volumetric fusion while still allowing a high scalability [20]. Semi-globally optimized depth maps provide a higher completeness but are limited by their fronto-parallel assumptions.

MVE [9] is also based on a volumetric fusion of implicit functions from 3D point clouds including pointwise quality values [8]. In contrast to linear one dimensional functions, MVE considers a 3D error assigning values to voxels in a spatial neighborhood. Depth maps are estimated with a region-growing approach [12] which is less effective since it lacks completeness as it can be demonstrated with the *ETH3D* benchmark. **PMVS** [10] also employs sparse features expanded by means of a region-growing approach. The semi-dense point clouds are filtered for obtaining a higher accuracy. PMVS does show a similar relatively low quality as other methods based on region growing MVS on the *ETH3D* benchmarks. **TAPA-MVS** [28] recently demonstrated that the completeness of PM depth maps can be significantly improved by applying depth completion with plane-fitting on superpixel level as additional hypothesis.

Our method also uses COLMAP PM depth maps as input for a plane-based completion on superpixels. We extend TAPA-MVS by introducing hierarchical superpixel clustering and adaption of the plane estimation to generic MVS where no scale of the scene is available. To this end, we make use of LTVREs error propagation. In addition, we apply the plane fitting as a post-processing to PM depth maps and demonstrate a significant improvement for the completeness of 3D models with ETH3D benchmark while still preserving high resolution details.

2   Review of Suitable 3D Reconstruction Methods

As said, our method is based on ideas from MVS, error propagation and depth completion. In this section we give a summary and analysis of employed methods.

2.1   Multi-View Stereo

There are promising deep-learning-based stereo matching methods [15, 37] for accurate depth map generation. However, they are limited with large-scale scenes because they generate very large 3D cost volumes as input strongly limiting the applicability for large disparity ranges. A direct comparison on the high-resolution *ETH3D* benchmark is given by [28] demonstrating their shortcomings. We focus on methods which are feasible for high-resolution image processing.

Benchmarking shows better results for MVS estimation with PM and stereo estimation with SGM than for region-growing methods. SGM performs well on scalability, as only two images (stereo) have to be processed at a time. The final (MVS) disparity map is derived by means of pixel-wise fusion from multiple stereo disparity maps. In general, PM is feasible for processing high-resolution images as the runtime complexity increases only linearly with the image resolution (in overall pixels N), while SGM has an polynomial complexity ($\mathcal{O}(N^{1.5})$) considering the additional disparity dimension. On the other hand, SGM does not need a pixel-wise propagation of each pixel assigned to a patch neighborhood for all iterations as it only needs a scalar representation of pixel neighborhoods using Census matching costs [13]. Hence, PM needs efficient implementations, e.g., on a GPU where memory resources are limited. However, its unrestricted patch-based nature results in a higher quality reconstruction as it does not imply strong geometric priors like the fronto-parallel assumption in SGM. Therefore, we selected PM for depth-map estimation as we found that a standard GPU is sufficient to process the *ETH3D* datasets in full resolution of 25 MP.

We extend the COLMAP PM process [30] by calculating the average baseline b for multi-view configurations which is used for the subsequent completion and fusion. COLMAP PM employs a final consistency checking by projecting pixelwise estimated depths into source images. If the re-projection error and a NCC-based photometric consistency is below a threshold the pixel passes the consistency checks and is marked valid. For each pixel p in each source image i we use the finally matched pairs to estimate an average baseline:

$$b_i^p = \frac{1}{|J_i^p|} \sum_{j \in J_i^p} b_{i,j}, \ J_i^p \subset N \ , \tag{1}$$

with baseline $b_{i,j}$ between images i and j and set J image pairs out of all source images N which have been marked valid. The average baseline is important for our filtering and quality propagation to model 3D uncertainties.

2.2   Error Propagation

In the subsequent filtering, completion and fusion steps, we use the uncertainty of a 3D point as error metric [25]. We derive this uncertainty in the three space dimension from 3D Point $P = (P_x, P_y, P_z)$, focal length f, camera baseline b and expected disparity error with standard deviation Δp for a pair of registered images:

$$\Delta P_x = \Delta p \frac{P_z}{fb} \sqrt{(b - P_x)^2 + P_x^2} \ ,$$
$$\Delta P_y = \Delta p \frac{P_z}{fb} \sqrt{2P_y^2 + \frac{b^2}{2}} \ , \ \Delta P_z = \Delta p \frac{P_z^2}{fb} \sqrt{2} \ . \tag{2}$$

Kuhn et al. [23] already successfully applied this concept for MVS and showed that using $\Delta P = \Delta P_z$ as scalar error is valid because it is the dominant error when depth values are larger then two times the camera baseline. To extend the propagation to MVS instead of single stereo only, they are estimating for the average baseline over all images. In this paper we make use of the pixel-wise estimated baseline $b = b_i^p$ (Eq. (1)) from the PM process (see Sect. 2.1).

2.3   Depth Completion

The recently published depth completion method TAPA-MVS [28] has demonstrated that completion on superpixels improves the quality of 3D reconstruction significantly [31]. TAPA-MVS employs SEED superpixels [34] in two varying sizes on the input images. After the first PM iteration they filter out small peaks in the depth images and fit planes in superpixels by applying RANSAC on remaining depth measurements. In the second PM run, the completed maps are taken into account as hypothesis for pixelwise depth estimation. To handle untextured areas, a texture confidence from the local variance of an image is used [28]. We take this method as a reference and also make use of RANSAC-based plane fitting on superpixels. In contrast to TAPA-MVS, we propose a hierarchical clustering of extracted superpixels, integrate the MVS geometric error (Sect. 2.1) in the RANSAC optimization and apply the depth completion as a post-processing step for PM instead of adding an additional hypothesis. This improves the PM runtime, allows better handling of large untextured areas and the processing of generic MVS datasets. In addition, fine structured details are preserved as we keep the original PM depth values when available. We will demonstrate the qualitative improvement on the *ETH3D* benchmark. The quantitative improvement is demonstrated by processing the *Tanks and Temples* dataset, which do not provide an absolute scale, e.g., in meters like the *ETH3D* datasets.

3   Algorithm

We propose a 3D reconstruction pipeline with three major steps: 1. Depth maps generation and filtering, 2. Completion of depth maps and 3. Final filtering of outliers. In this section, we describe the individual steps.

3.1   Depth Maps Generation and Filtering

For the reconstruction of areas which have been captured by only two cameras, one cannot rely on a filtering with robust statistics because the resulting models would lack in completeness. To decimate the number of outliers, e.g., TAPA-MVS filters peaks in depth maps considering the depth difference of neighboring pixels. This is not possible for general MVS configurations because a constant depth range has to be defined. Hence, we make use of a filtering in the disparity domain as proposed by Hirschmüller [14] and used in SGM: Small peaks are clustered in the disparity map and filtered if they do not exceed a minimum cluster size. The disparity map is segmented by allowing neighboring disparities to vary by only less than one pixel. At this point SGM operates on disparity maps estimated from two images. Such clustering is suitable for SGM with its fronto parallel assumption. However, such depth maps show problems on strongly slanted surface parts. Our employed PM in contrast, allows their reconstruction and neighboring pixels could be connected even though the disparity difference is high. Hence, we do not cluster the disparity maps directly but use its derivative. We transfer depth values d from the depth maps into disparity space considering the pixel-wise average baseline b_i^p from Eq. (1) and derive the first order deviation for pixel i as follows:

$$\nabla \mathcal{D}_i^p = \nabla \frac{f\ b_i^p}{d_i^p} \qquad (3)$$

From the derivative disparity map $\nabla \mathcal{D}$ small clusters of connected components are filtered out. Because the derivative does not penalize depth values on parallel planes we additionally employ the 3D error term (Eq. 2) in the clustering, which means that neighboring values should be in a tolerantly-set noise area ΔP. The top row of Fig. 1 shows an example of filtered clusters. Neighboring depth values on the wall have varying differences in depth (≈ 0.5 m in near and ≈ 5 m in far areas). Clustering in the disparity space can handle such scale differences. Our experience shows that the filtering is working well when employing the average baseline, even though Eq. (3) considers standard stereo configurations and we use MVS-derived depth maps in varying configurations.

3.2   Depth Completion

The locally derived depth maps lack in completeness as PM disregards texture-less areas. Inspired by recently published depth filling on superpixels TAPA-MVS [28] we propose an important extension of the filling of depth maps. TAPA-MVS extracts superpixel on two levels and considers the filled depths as additional hypothesis in PM. We, in contrast, estimate the superpixels on the finer resolution and cluster them subsequently. To this end, we set a minimum number of valid depth measurements per superpixel. If the number is below a threshold the superpixel is merged with the most similar neighboring superpixel (see Fig. 1). As proposed by TAPA-MVS, the Bhattacharya distance of RGB histogramms is used as similarity metric. TAPA-MVS considers this metric for selecting mea-surements of neighboring superpixels for the RANSAC fitting depending on a similarity norm. In their method only one neighboring superpixel can be taken into account, hence, our method is more adaptive for larger untextured areas.

Having a sufficient number of depth measurements, we run the plane fitting employing a RANSAC optimization. More precisely we use RANSAC employing an M-estimator (MSAC). In TAPA-MVS the RANSAC considers inliers to be in a fixed range of 10 cm. At this point, we make use of the pixel-wise 3D error estimate. The inlier range is set relatively to the expected error defined in Eq. (2)

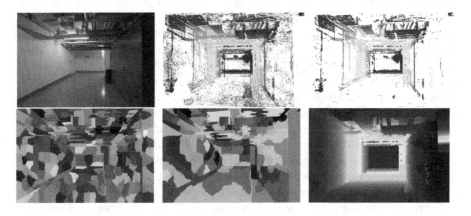

Fig. 1. Filtered (top right) and unfiltered (top centre) PM depth maps. The bottom left images shows the initial and the bottom centre the clustered superpixels. On the bottom right the depth map is filled from the RANSAC-derived planes.

and the summed cost of the relative distance is minimized:

$$\underset{K}{\operatorname{argmin}} \sum_{k \in K} \frac{||<P_k, \mathcal{P}>||}{\Delta P_k} , \qquad (4)$$

with set K as selected inlier points which minimize the sum of relative distances considering the distance $||<P_k, \mathcal{P}>||$ from point P to plane $\mathcal{P}$ and uncertainty ΔP (Eq. (2)) as normalization. If the distance from 3D point P and plane $\mathcal{P}$ is above a threshold its influence is fixed as proposed by MSAC. The normalization concerning the 3D uncertainty allows the processing of generic data where no scale is know, e.g., on the *Tanks and Temples* datasets. In addition, considering the 3D error is beneficial when having varying baseline and distances to the scene (see Fig. 1). Having a plane estimate for each superpixel, we fill the initial PM depth map with depth values by intersecting the line of sight with the estimated 3D plane. Next to runtime optimization the post-processing allows the preservation on fine-structured details from the original depth maps. PM also extracts normal vectors, which are required for our fusion method. Because our depth filtering method is implemented as postprocessing, we fill the PM normal maps by the individual normals of the superpixel-wise estimated plane.

3.3   Consistency Check and Sky Filtering

Completed depth maps still lack in quality as they include outliers from erroneously estimated planes and non-planar surfaces with low degree of texturedness. As done by PM we subsequently filter measurements by means of consistency checks. For an efficient processing we consider for each reference depth map a limited number of source depth maps that have sufficient overlap. Each depth is propagated from the reference to the source maps and backwards. If the reprojection error exceed a threshold the depth is filtered. In addition, the normal vectors are assumed to be similar. We do not employ a photometric consistency check to preserve untextured areas. Unfortunately, sky areas for outdoor scenes lead to strong artifacts that cannot be filtered geometrically. To solve for this problem, we introduce a sky area detection by means of semantic segmentation (see Fig. 2) based on DeepLabV3+ [4] which demonstrated a stable semantic segmentation on images. In order to retrain the network for binary segmentation, an enhanced dataset for sky is used comprising the following datasets: Cityscapes [7], ADE20K [39] and SkyFinder [6]. They all provide the class sky in a various of outdoor scene which we use for a binary labeling. The datasets Cityscape and ADE20 maintain a large variety of outdoor configurations while SkyFinder strengthens the stability of the retrained network for different illuminance and weather conditions. This helps to improve the ability of the network to distinguish sky and non-sky parts of each image. In order to avoid overfitting we augmented the data by cropping, rotating and flipping images. Furthermore, DeepLabV3+ is modified for binary segmentation by adjusting the loss function. We penalize wrong labeling of sky areas by a factor of 10 because sky areas appear less frequently in the training dataset.

Fig. 2. The upper row shows an input image with the binary sky map where black marked pixels represent detected sky areas. The mask is used to filter the depth map (bottom left). The bottom right image shows final depth map.

4   Experiments

We run experiments using the *ETH3D* and *Tanks and Temples* training datasets to evaluate the proposed steps of the pipeline and validated the full pipeline on the test datasets. The 13 *ETH3D* training datasets contain from 14 to 76 registered images with 24 MP resolution while the low-res training datasets contain 660 to 1200 registered images with 0.36 MP resolution. We processed the data on a 28-core 2.6 GHz machine with four Geforce GTX 1080 Ti GPUs and 11 GB memory. The initial depth maps are generated by COLMAP with the standard parameter set, except the minimum of reference images for valid depths which we set to 1 for the DSLR and to 3 for the video sequences. The PM depth maps are derived from half resolution images for the high-resolution and in full resolution for the low-resolution images. The number of source images to match the reference image against is set automatically dependent on the GPU memory.

4.1   Depth Completion

We filter the depths in each map, by setting a minimum cluster size of connected pixels which neighboring disparity gradients (see Eq. (3)) do not exceed the threshold of 1.0 pixel. We empirically found that a minimum cluster size of 100 pixels is a good trade off preserving completeness and accuracy.

A major contribution of our paper is the depth completion on growing superpixels: We generate superpixels from the input images and combine neighboring superpixels when having an insufficient number of depth values. The minimum number of depth values per superpixel is set to 4000. Similar to TAPA-MVS we use SEED superpixels [34] with a parameter of 200 superpixel per image for the initialization. Note that in contrast to TAPA-MVS we make use of the superpixel-based completion as post-processing which avoids computational complex hypothesis propagation within the MVS process and allows higher quality in high resolution areas because the original PM depth map is preserved. Note that both methods are based on COLMAP PM. For each clustered superpixel we run the RANSAC-based plane estimation allowing a maximum error of two times the standard deviation (see Eq. (2)). We set the minimum inlier rate to 30%, the maximum number of trials to 10000 and the confidence to 99.99%.

To allow a direct comparison of the depth completion part, we use the depth map fusion method provided by COLMAP which was also used by TAPA-MVS. Similar to TAPA-MVS, we changed the standard fusion parameters to maximum re-projection error of 0.5 pixels for the high-res and 0.25 pixels for the low res images and the maximum difference of the normal angle of 20°. Furthermore, we disabled the sky filtering procedure at this point to allow a direct comparison of the depth completion part. Table 1 shows the results over all *ETH3D* training datasets and a direct comparison to TAPA-MVS and COLMAP which are based on the same PM method. The latter employs the PM depthmaps without completion. As evaluation metric the standard F-Score is used combining completeness and accuracy. We evaluated the metrics on two resolutions: 1 cm and 10 cm to cover fine and coarse resolution scores. Our approach has the best F-Score values for the fine and competitive values for the coarse resolution evaluation. Note that for the final evaluation (Sect. 4.3) we do not use the COLMAP fusion parameters suggested by TAPA-MVS.

Table 1. F-Score [%] combining completeness and accuracy at a distance of 1 cm and 10 cm for all *ETH3D* high-res training datasets and their average mean (AVG). The first row show the result of our completion method with COLMAP fusion with same parameters as TAPA-MVS. The second and third row show the results of TAPA-MVS and COLMAP which are based on the same depthmaps. Best results are marked bold. Our method outperforms the baseline methods especially in fine-structured areas.

Method	AVG	Courty.	Delivery	Electro	Facade	Kicker	Meadow
Ours	**68.16** 93.34	**67.70 96.56**	**74.03 97.70**	**75.73** 95.82	**52.31 94.55**	69.00 88.33	**57.96 89.38**
TAPA	60.85 **93.69**	47.38 **96.89**	65.33 97.62	65.35 **96.15**	36.51 91.67	**75.16 94.94**	48.82 85.97
COLMAP	51.99 87.61	49.13 95.54	61.73 94.48	60.53 91.77	36.57 90.14	53.14 87.16	32.95 75.50
Method	Office	Pipes	Playgr.	Relief	Relief2	Terrace	Terrain
Ours	**61.09 86.18**	**73.73 94.33**	**55.57** 93.70	**71.09** 91.51	**67.76** 91.54	**78.92** 97.63	**81.16 96.22**
TAPA	54.70 **87.72**	63.51 91.96	53.31 **94.40**	68.36 **93.76**	64.97 **93.06**	73.37 **98.30**	74.27 95.58
COLMAP	37.10 73.41	38.68 76.86	40.49 87.33	65.72 90.05	63.08 89.87	72.11 96.48	64.60 90.46

Table 2. F-Score [%] combining completeness and accuracy at a distance of 1 cm and 10 cm for all *ETH3D* low-res training datasets as in Table 1.

Method	AVG	Delivery	Electro	Forest	Playground	Terrains
Ours	**42.66 82.11**	**32.50 79.81**	**40.83** 80.72	**46.11 88.57**	**28.69 76.43**	65.17 85.02
TAPA	38.87 81.65	22.75 77.80	34.37 **82.80**	45.53 87.23	24.02 73.54	**67.70 86.89**
COLMAP	32.32 76.00	16.26 74.84	28.69 78.71	39.99 85.35	17.68 59.56	58.96 81.54

Table 2 shows the evaluation table for the *ETH3D* video datasets containing large sets of low resolution images. Again, our method has best scores concerning the F-score when evaluating fine-structured details (1 cm distance).

4.2   Depth Filtering

Sky areas do not have a strong influence on the *ETH3D* benchmarking as they are mostly assigned to undefined areas. We found that for the *Tanks and Temples* benchmark, in contrast, artifacts appear around surfaces which have an influence on the final quality. This can be traced back to the large amount of images showing the same scene leading to a higher rate of outliers. As described in Sect. 3.3, we retrained the segmentation network DeepLabV3+ for a binary labeling of sky areas. After testing with two backbones and training steps the best performance was obtained by retraining 30000 steps with Xception [5] as backbone. The mean intersection over union (mIOU) of our sky segmentation network scores 91% accuracy for the validation dataset. In general, the sky segmentation network has the robustness against complex weather and illuminance conditions and generates stable and precise segmentation result.

We generate binary maps for each image and filter sky-labeled depth values in the final depth maps before the fusion. Even though, for some areas false positive appear, the overall improvement is obvious. Figure 3 visually shows the resulting point cloud with and without sky-labeled filtering. For a numerical evaluation we run the *Tanks and Temples* training datasets on both point clouds and show the results in Table 3. For a fair comparison we use the sky filtering in all datasets

Table 3. F-Score [%] combining completeness and accuracy at for all *Tanks and Temples* datasets. For the evaluation of Ours $\setminus \{SF\}$ the sky filtering was disabled.

Method	AVG	Barn	Caterp.	Church	Courth.	Ignatius	Meetingr.	Truck
Ours	**59.96**	**68.66**	**57.23**	**61.39**	**40.20**	**80.15**	45.36	**66.73**
Ours $\setminus\{SF\}$	59.05	66.69	56.86	61.15	37.04	79.80	**45.44**	66.43
COLMAP	53,03	47.26	54.71	52.37	38.37	78.06	34.45	64.98

Fig. 3. The images show the rendered 3D point cloud from the Barn dataset with and without filtering of sky elements. The outliers are obviously decimated.

for the final evaluation, even for the *ETH3D* and *Tanks and Temples* indoor data which slightly lowers the accuracy.

4.3   Final Evaluation

We run our pipeline also on the *ETH3D* and *Tanks and Temples* test datasets. The 12 *ETH3D* test datasets contain from 7 to 110 registered images captured with a 24 MP camera while the *Tanks and Temples* datasets contain larger sequences containing from 251 to 1105 images of 12 MP. We use the same parameters for all datasets for the final evaluation. In comparison to the standard COLMAP fusion parameters, we set the maximum difference of the surface normal angle to 20° and employ our 3D consistency. The latter allows a fusion of 3D point considering the uncertainty in 3D (see Eq. (2)). The original COLMAP fusion considers the inverse depth as a filtering criteria. We found that the improvement does not have a significant influence on the numerical benchmarking, but reduces the final point cloud size because a larger set of redundant low quality points is fused resulting in a clean point cloud.

Concerning the *ETH3D* high-res dataset (Table 4) our method outperforms TAPA-MVS also for 2 cm which is the standard evaluation on the *ETH3D* homepage. In comparison to ACMM, we obtain similar scores for the F-Score but a distinct improvement in completeness. Table 5 shows similar results for the *ETH3D* video datasets. ACMM does not participate in this benchmark.

Table 4. F-Score [%] at a distance of 2 cm which is the standard setting for the *ETH3D* high-res benchmarking. For the AVG also the completeness is listed (right) The individual rows show the results of the currently leading methods. Our method has a similar quality concerning F-Score and a higher quality concerning completeness.

Method	AVG (train)	AVG (test)	Courty.	Delivery	Electro	Facade	Kicker	Meadow	Office
Ours	**79.42 75.73**	80.38 **79.29**	84.88	**88.17**	**86.08**	69.85	75.23	68.43	**68.03**
ACMM	78.86 70.42	**80.78** 74.34	**86.89**	83.40	86.02	**70.50**	**75.28**	**71.49**	63.01
TAPA-MVS	77.69 71.45	79.15 74.49	80.68	84.52	81.36	63.14	84.77	64.82	68.72
LTVRE	61.82 49.41	76.25 66.27	72.83	77.19	64.37	58.97	33.56	28.00	52.59
COLMAP	67.66 55.13	73.01 62.98	80.49	77.98	75.29	62.95	63.62	49.96	47.32

Method	Pipes	Playgr.	Relief	Relief2	Terrace	Terrain	Botani	Boulde.	Bridge
Ours	**78.38**	71.76	81.26	80.65	88.56	**91.18**	87.71	**68.99**	83.65
ACMM	69.26	**73.57**	**84.11**	**83.98**	89.76	87.84	89.31	68.37	**89.99**
TAPA-MVS	75.91	71.86	81.62	79.55	87.80	85.24	**89.59**	62.99	88.16
LTVRE	42.21	63.93	74.52	76.28	77.15	82.13	88.60	64.38	79.24
COLMAP	50.72	58.57	76.87	75.50	84.94	75.33	87.13	65.63	88.30

Method	Door	Exhibi.	Lectur	Living.	Lounge	Observ.	Old co.	Statue.	Terrace.
Ours	91.46	63.00	**77.77**	**90.28**	**66.10**	**95.09**	61.40	**88.22**	90.94
ACMM	**91.60**	**70.28**	77.25	89.66	53.37	93.53	**74.24**	82.85	88.85
TAPA-MVS	91.51	65.77	77.14	91.09	60.91	93.21	50.26	87.05	92.17
LTVRE	89.12	70.76	69.79	87.86	49.09	93.20	56.21	80.16	86.65
COLMAP	84.19	62.96	63.80	87.69	38.04	92.56	46.66	74.91	84.24

Table 5. F-Score (left) and completenes (right) [%] at a distance of 2 cm which is the standard setting for the *ETH3D* low-res (video) benchmarking.

Method	AVG (train)	Indoor	Outdoor	AVG (test)	Indoor	Outdoor
Ours	**57.32 58.17**	**59.66** 57.60	**55.76 58.56**	57.06 58.42	48.10 **54.11**	**63.03** 61.29
TAPA-MVS	55.13 55.77	58.21 **61.18**	53.07 52.17	**58.67 58.89**	**52.34** 51.21	62.89 **64.01**
ACMH	51.50 53.77	53.46 49.88	50.20 56.37	47.97 52.68	38.24 35.79	54.45 63.93
LTVRE	53.52 41.68	58.21 44.05	51.36 40.11	53.52 43.60	45.46 37.31	58.89 47.80
COLMAP	49.91 40.86	51.76 40.09	48.68 41.37	52.32 45.89	42.45 37.03	58.89 51.79

The *Tanks and Temples* benchmark shows slightly worse results with our method in comparison to ACMM for the intermediate sequences and slightly better results for the advanced sequences. Note that the datasets do not have many flat walls which reduces the influence of our plane prior. In addition, the evaluation strongly depends on the SfM results as no ground truth camera poses is given. To demonstrate the influence, we registered the datasets with COLMAP SfM and Altizure SfM [2]. Table 6 shows that our method generates state-of-the-art results for the *Tanks and Temples* dataset.

Table 6. F-Score [%] at a employing varying distances as defined by the evaluation software and the average mean (AVG) for the intermediate and advanced *Tanks and Temples* datasets. For a comparison the currently best methods are shown. Our method generates state-of-the-art results especially when using Altizure SfM.

Method	AVG (int.)	AVG (ad.)	Family	Francis	Horse	Lighth.	M60	Panther
Altizure+Ours	55.88	**35.69**	**70.99**	49.60	40.34	**63.44**	**57.79**	58.91
COLMAP+Ours	53.39	34.59	67.32	43.28	34.45	61.17	50.59	**61.20**
ACMM	**57.27**	34.02	69.24	**51.45**	**46.97**	63.20	55.07	57.64
ACMH	54.82	33.73	69.99	49.45	45.12	59.04	52.64	52.37
COLMAP	42.14	27.24	50.41	22.25	25.63	56.43	44.83	46.97
Method	Playgr.	Train	Auditor.	Ballr.	Courtr.	Museum	Palace	Temple
Altizure+Ours	56.59	49.40	**28.33**	**38.64**	35.95	**48.36**	**26.17**	**36.69**
COLMAP+Ours	55.93	53.14	26.87	31.53	**44.70**	47.39	24.05	32.97
ACMM	**60.08**	**54.48**	23.41	32.91	41.17	48.13	23.87	34.60
ACMH	58.34	51.61	21.69	32.56	40.62	47.27	24.04	36.17
COLMAP	48.53	42.04	16.02	25.23	34.70	41.51	18.05	27.94

5   Conclusion and Outlook

In this paper we have presented a pipeline for dense reconstruction of 3D point clouds from large sets of high-resolution images. The extension of depth completion methods resulted in an improvement over the state of the art in 3D reconstruction concerning completeness and the preservation of fine details. Three major contributions are made: (1) outlier filtering, (2) depth completion on growing superpixel, (3) filtering of sky areas. The individual steps are extended by considering MVS geometry. We have shown the improvement visually and numerically on datasets from standard benchmarks in large-scale reconstruction.

In future work we will focus on the filtering part. While the completeness has been improved significantly multiple planes appear for some datasets (see Fig. 4) deteriorating the accuracy. Confidence prediction beyond geometry, e.g., by means of deep learning has potential to solve such problems.

Fig. 4. Results for two ETH3D datasets from left to right: TAPA-MVS, ACMM and Ours. Concerning the scores our method performs well on the terrains dataset (top). For the old-computer dataset (bottom) our method has a significant lower F1-Score even though we reconstruct the ground which is not available in the ground truth. Future work will focus on filtering as curved surfaces cause multiple conflicting planes

References

1. Aanæs, H., Jensen, R.R., Vogiatzis, G., Tola, E., Dahl, A.B.: Large-scale data for multiple-view stereopsis. Int. J. Comput. Vis. (IJCV) **120**(2), 153–168 (2016)
2. Altizure: Altizure the portal for realistic 3D modeling (2019). https://www.altizure.com/
3. Bleyer, M., Rhemann, C., Rother, C.: PatchMatch stereo - stereo matching with slanted support windows. In: British Machine Vision Conference (BMVC) (2011)
4. Chen, L., Zhu, Y., Papandreou, G., Schroff, F., Adam, H.: Encoder-decoder with atrous separable convolution for semantic image segmentation. CoRR abs/1802.02611 (2018). http://arxiv.org/abs/1802.02611
5. Chollet, F.: Xception: Deep learning with depthwise separable convolutions. CoRR abs/1610.02357 (2016). http://arxiv.org/abs/1610.02357
6. Chu, W.T., Zheng, X.Y., Ding, D.S.: Camera as weather sensor: estimating weather information from single images. J. Vis. Commun. Image Represent. **46**, 233–249 (2017)
7. Cordts, M., et al.: The Cityscapes dataset for semantic urban scene understanding. In: CVPR (2016)
8. Fuhrmann, S., Goesele, M.: Floating scale surface reconstruction. ACM Trans. Graph. **33**(4), 46:1–46:11 (2014)

9. Fuhrmann, S., Langguth, F., Goesele, M.: MVE: a multi-view reconstruction environment. In: Eurographics Workshop on Graphics and Cultural Heritage (2014)
10. Furukawa, Y., Ponce, J.: Accurate, dense, and robust multi-view stereopsis. IEEE Trans. Pattern Anal. Mach. Intell. (TPAMI) **32**(8), 1362–1376 (2010)
11. Galliani, S., Lasinger, K., Schindler, K.: Massively parallel multiview stereopsis by surface normal diffusion. In: ICCV (2015)
12. Goesele, M., Snavely, N., Curless, B., Hoppe, H., Seitz, S.M.: Multi-view stereo for community photo collections. In: ICCV (2017)
13. Hirschmüller, H., Scharstein, D.: Evaluation of stereo matching costs on images with radiometric differences. IEEE Trans. Pattern Anal. Mach. Intell. (TPAMI) **31**, 1582–1599 (2008)
14. Hirschmüller, H.: Stereo processing by semiglobal matching and mutual information. IEEE Trans. Pattern Anal. Mach. Intell. (TPAMI) **30**(2), 328–341 (2008)
15. Huang, P.H., Maten, K., Knop, J., Ahuja, N., Huang, J.B.: DeepMVS: learning multi-view stereopis. In: CVPR (2018)
16. Jancosek, M., Pajdla, T.: Hallucination-free multi-view stereo. In: Kutulakos, K.N. (ed.) ECCV 2010. LNCS, vol. 6554, pp. 184–196. Springer, Heidelberg (2012). https://doi.org/10.1007/978-3-642-35740-4_15
17. Jancosek, M., Pajdla, T.: Multi-view reconstruction preserving weakly-supported surfaces. In: CVPR (2011)
18. Kazhdan, M., Hoppe, H.: Screened Poisson surface reconstruction. ACM Trans. Graph. (ToG) **32**, 29:1–29:13 (2013)
19. Knapitsch, A., Park, J., Zhou, Q.Y., Koltun, V.: Tanks and temples: benchmarking large-scale scene reconstruction. ACM Trans. Graph. **36**(4), 78 (2017)
20. Kuhn, A., Mayer, H.: Incremental division of very large point clouds for scalable 3D surface reconstruction. In: International Conference on Computer Vision Workshop (ICCVW) (2015)
21. Kuhn, A., Hirschmüller, H., Mayer, H.: Multi-resolution range data fusion for multi-view stereo reconstruction. In: Weickert, J., Hein, M., Schiele, B. (eds.) GCPR 2013. LNCS, vol. 8142, pp. 41–50. Springer, Heidelberg (2013). https://doi.org/10.1007/978-3-642-40602-7_5
22. Kuhn, A., Hirschmüller, H., Scharstein, D., Mayer, H.: A TV prior for high-quality local multi-view stereo reconstruction. In: International Conference on 3D Vision (3DV) (2014)
23. Kuhn, A., Hirschmüller, H., Scharstein, D., Mayer, H.: A TV prior for high-quality scalable multi-view stereo reconstruction. Int. J. Comput. Vis. (IJCV) **124**(1), 2–17 (2017)
24. Kuhn, A., Roth, L., Frahm, J.M., Mayer, H.: Improvement of extrinsic parameters from a single stereo pair. In: IEEE Winter Conference on Application of Computer Vision (WACV) (2018)
25. Molton, N., Brady, M.: Practical structure and motion from stereo when motion is unconstrained. Int. J. Comput. Vis. (IJCV) **39**(1), 5–23 (2000)
26. Mostegel, C., Prettenthaler, R., Fraundorfer, F., Bischof, H.: Scalable surface reconstruction from point clouds with extreme scale and density diversity. In: CVPR (2017)
27. P. Labatut, J.P., Keriven, R.: Robust and efficient surface reconstruction from range data. In: Computer Graphics Forum (2009)
28. Romanoni, A., Matteucci, M.: TAPA-MVS: textureless-aware PatchMatch multi-view stereo. CoRR abs/1903.10929 (2019). https://arxiv.org/abs/1903.10929
29. Schönberger, J.L., Frahm, J.M.: Structure-from-motion revisited. In: CVPR (2016)

30. Schönberger, J.L., Zheng, E., Frahm, J.-M., Pollefeys, M.: Pixelwise view selection for unstructured multi-view stereo. In: Leibe, B., Matas, J., Sebe, N., Welling, M. (eds.) ECCV 2016. LNCS, vol. 9907, pp. 501–518. Springer, Cham (2016). https://doi.org/10.1007/978-3-319-46487-9_31

31. Schöps, T., et al.: A multi-view stereo benchmark with high-resolution images and multi-camera videos. In: CVPR (2017)

32. Seitz, S., Curless, B., Diebel, J., Scharstein, D., Szeliski, R.: A comparison and evaluation of multi-view stereo reconstruction algorithms. In: CVPR (2006)

33. Strecha, C., von Hansen, W., Gool, L.J.V., Fua, P., Thoennessen, U.: On benchmarking camera calibration and multi-view stereo for high resolution imagery. In: CVPR (2008)

34. Van den Bergh, M., Boix, X., Roig, G., Van Gool, L.: SEEDS: superpixels extracted via energy-driven sampling. Int. J. Comput. Vis. (IJCV) $111(3)$, 298–314 (2015)

35. Vu, H.H., Labatut, P., Pons, J.P., Keriven, R.: High accuracy and visibility-consistent dense multiview stereo. IEEE Trans. Pattern Anal. Mach. Intell. $34(5)$, 889–901 (2012)

36. Xu, Q., Taoi, W.: Multi-scale geometric consistency guided multi-view stereo. CoRR abs/1904.08103 (2019). https://arxiv.org/abs/1904.08103

37. Yao, Y., Luo, Z., Li, S., Fang, T., Quan, L.: MVSNet: depth inference for unstructured multi-view stereo. In: Ferrari, V., Hebert, M., Sminchisescu, C., Weiss, Y. (eds.) ECCV 2018. LNCS, vol. 11212, pp. 785–801. Springer, Cham (2018). https://doi.org/10.1007/978-3-030-01237-3_47

38. Zheng, E., Dunn, E., Jojic, V., Frahm, J.: PatchMatch based joint view selection and depthmap estimation. In: CVPR (2014)

39. Zhou, B., Zhao, H., Puig, X., Fidler, S., Barriuso, A., Torralba, A.: Scene parsing through ADE20K dataset. In: CVPR (2017)

Simultaneous Semantic Segmentation and Outlier Detection in Presence of Domain Shift

Petra Bevandić[(✉)], Ivan Krešo, Marin Oršić, and Siniša Šegvić

Faculty of Electrical Engineering and Computing, University of Zagreb,
Zagreb, Croatia
petra.bevandic@fer.hr

Abstract. Recent success on realistic road driving datasets has increased interest in exploring robust performance in real-world applications. One of the major unsolved problems is to identify image content which can not be reliably recognized with a given inference engine. We therefore study approaches to recover a dense outlier map alongside the primary task with a single forward pass, by relying on shared convolutional features. We consider semantic segmentation as the primary task and perform extensive validation on WildDash val (inliers), LSUN val (outliers), and pasted objects from Pascal VOC 2007 (outliers). We achieve the best validation performance by training to discriminate inliers from pasted ImageNet-1k content, even though ImageNet-1k contains many road-driving pixels, and, at least nominally, fails to account for the full diversity of the visual world. The proposed two-head model performs comparably to the C-way multi-class model trained to predict uniform distribution in outliers, while outperforming several other validated approaches. We evaluate our best two models on the WildDash test dataset and set a new state of the art on the WildDash benchmark.

1 Introduction

Early computer vision approaches focused on producing decent performance on small datasets. This often posed overwhelming difficulties, so researchers seldom quantified the prediction confidence. An important milestone was reached when generalization was achieved on realistic datasets such as Pascal VOC [13], CamVid [5], KITTI [14], and Cityscapes [9]. These datasets assume closed-world evaluation [38] in which the training and test subsets are sampled from the same distribution. Such setup has been able to provide a fast feedback on novel

P. Bevandić—This work has been partially supported by Croatian Science Foundation.

Electronic supplementary material The online version of this chapter (https:// doi.org/10.1007/978-3-030-33676-9_3) contains supplementary material, which is available to authorized users.

approaches due to good alignment with the machine learning paradigm. This further accelerated development and led us to the current state of research where all these datasets are mostly solved, at least in the strongly supervised setup.

Recent datasets further raise the bar by increasing the number of classes and image diversity. However, despite this increased complexity, the Vistas [35] dataset is still an insufficient proxy for real-life operation even in a very restricted scenario such as road driving. New classes like bike racks and ground animals were added, however many important classes from non-typical or worst-case images are still absent. These classes include persons in non-standard poses, crashed vehicles, rubble, fallen trees etc. Additionally, real-life images may be affected by particular image acquisition faults including hardware defects, covered lens etc. This suggests that foreseeing every possible situation may be an elusive goal, and that our algorithms should be designed to recognize image regions which are foreign to the training distribution.

The described deficiencies emphasize the need for a more robust approach to dataset design. First, an ideal dataset should identify and target a set of explicit hazards for the particular domain [46]. Second (and more important), an ideal dataset should endorse open-set recognition paradigm [38] in order to promote detection of unforeseen hazards. Consequently, the validation (val) and test subsets should contain various degrees of domain shift with respect to the training distribution. This should include moderate domain shift factors (e.g. adverse weather, exotic locations), exceptional situations (e.g. accidents, poor visibility, defects) and outright outliers (objects and entire images from other domains). We argue that the WildDash dataset [46] represents a step in the right direction, although further development would be welcome, especially in the direction of enlarging the negative part of the test dataset [3]. Models trained for open-set evaluation can not be required to predict an exact visual class in outlier pixels. Instead, it should suffice that the outliers are recognized, as illustrated in Fig. 1 on an image from the WildDash dataset.

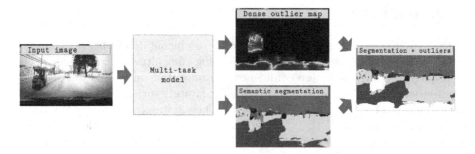

Fig. 1. The proposed approach for simultaneous semantic segmentation and outlier detection. Our multi-task model predicts (i) a dense outlier map, and (ii) a semantic map with respect to the 19 Cityscapes classes. The two maps are merged to obtain the final outlier-aware semantic predictions. Our model recognizes outlier pixels (white) on two objects which are foreign to Cityscapes: the ego-vehicle and the yellow forklift. (Color figure online)

This paper addresses simultaneous semantic segmentation and open-set outlier detection. We train our models on inlier images from two road-driving datasets: Cityscapes [9] and Vistas [35]. We consider several outlier detection approaches from the literature [2,20,21] and validate their performance on WildDash val (inliers), LSUN val [44] (outliers), and pasted objects from Pascal VOC 2007 (outliers). Our main hypotheses are (i) that training with noisy negatives from a very large and diverse dataset such as ImageNet-1k [10] can improve outlier detection, and (ii) that discriminative outlier detection and semantic segmentation can share features without significant deterioration of either task. We confirm both hypotheses by re-training our best models on WildDash val, Vistas and ImageNet-1k, and evaluating performance on the WildDash benchmark.

2   Related Work

Previous approaches to outlier detection in image data are very diverse. These approaches are based on analyzing prediction uncertainty, evaluating generative models, or exploiting a broad secondary dataset which contains both outliers and inliers. Our approach is also related to multi-task models and previous work which explores the dataset quality and dataset bias.

2.1   Estimating Uncertainty (or Confidence) of the Predictions

Prediction confidence can be expressed as the probability of the winning class or max-softmax for short [20]. This is useful in image-wide prediction of outliers, although max-softmax must be calibrated [16] before being interpreted as $P(\text{inlier}|\mathbf{x})$. The ODIN approach [31] improves on [20] by pre-processing input images with a well-tempered perturbation aimed at increasing the max-softmax activation. These approaches are handy since they require no additional training.

Some approaches model the uncertainty with a separate head which learns either prediction uncertainty [23,28] or confidence [11]. Such training is able to recognize examples which are hard to classify due to insufficient or inconsistent labels, but is unable to deal with real outliers.

A principled information-theoretic approach expresses the prediction uncertainty as mutual information between the posterior parameter distribution and the particular prediction [40]. In practice, the required expectations are estimated with Monte Carlo (MC) dropout [23]. Better results have been achieved with explicit ensembles of independently trained models [28]. However, both approaches require many forward passes and thus preclude real-time operation.

Prediction uncertainty can also be expressed by evaluating per-class generative models of latent features [30]. However, this idea is not easily adaptable for dense prediction in which latent features typically correspond to many classes due to subsampling and dense labelling. Another approach would be to fit a generative model to the training dataset and to evaluate the likelihood of a given sample. Unfortunately, this is very hard to achieve with image data [34].

2.2 Training with Negative Data

Our approach is most related to three recent approaches which train outlier detection by exploiting a diverse negative dataset [41]. The approach called outlier exposure (OE) [21] processes the negative data by optimizing cross entropy between the predictions and the uniform distribution. Outlier detection has also been formulated as binary classification [2] trained to differentiate inliers from the negative dataset. A related approach [42] partitions the training data into K folds and trains an ensemble of K leave-one-fold-out classifiers. However, this requires K forward passes. while data partitioning may not be straight-forward.

Negative training samples can also be produced by a GAN generator [15]. Unfortunately, existing works [29,37] have been designed for image-wide prediction in small images. Their adaptation to dense prediction on Cityscapes resolution would not be straight-forward [4].

Soundness of training with negative data has been challenged by [39] who report under-average results for this approach. However, their experiments average results over all negative datasets (including MNIST), while we advocate for a very diverse negative dataset such as ImageNet.

2.3 Multi-task Training and Dataset Design

Multi-task models attach several prediction heads to shared features [7]. Each prediction head has a distinct loss. The total loss is usually expressed as a weighted sum [36] and optimized in an end-to-end fashion. Feature sharing brings important advantages such as cross-task enrichment of training data [1] and faster evaluation. Examples of successful multi-task models include combining depth, surface normals and semantic segmentation [12], as well as combining classification, bounding box prediction and per-class instance-level segmentation [17]. A map of task compatibility with respect to knowledge transfer [45] suggests that many tasks are suitable for multi-task training.

Dataset quality is as a very important issue in computer vision research. Diverse negative datasets have been used to reduce false positives in several computer vision tasks for a very long time [41]. A methodology for analyzing the quality of road-driving datasets has been proposed in [47]. The WildDash dataset [46] proposes a very diverse validation dataset and the first semantic segmentation benchmark with open-set evaluation [38].

3 Simultaneous Segmentation and Outlier Detection

Our method combines two distinct tasks: outlier detection and semantic segmentation, as shown in Fig. 1. We prefer to rely on shared features in order to promote fast inference and synergy between tasks [1]. We assume that a large, diverse and noisy negative dataset is available for training purposes [2,21].

3.1   Dense Feature Extractor

Our models are based on a dense feature extractor with lateral connections [25]. The processing starts with a DenseNet [22] or ResNet [19] backbone, proceeds with spatial pyramid pooling (SPP) [18,48] and concludes with ladder-style upsampling [25,32]. The upsampling path consists of three upsampling blocks (U1-U3) which blend low resolution features from the previous upsampling stage with high resolution features from the backbone. We speed-up and regularize the learning with three auxiliary classification losses (cf. Fig. 2). These losses have soft targets corresponding to ground truth distribution across the corresponding window at full resolution [26].

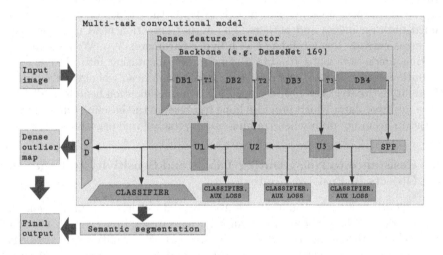

Fig. 2. The proposed two-head model: the classification head recovers semantic segmentation while the outlier detection head identifies pixels where semantic segmentation may be wrong. The output is produced by combining these two dense prediction maps.

3.2   Dense Outlier Detection

There are four distinct approaches to formulate simultaneous semantic segmentation and dense outlier detection over shared features. The C-way multi-class approach attaches the standard classification head to the dense feature extractor (C denotes the number of inlier classes). The inlier probability is formulated as max-softmax. If a negative set is available, this approach can be trained to emit low max-softmax in outliers by supplying a modulated cross entropy loss term towards uniform distribution [21,29]. The modulation factor λ_{KL} is a hyperparameter. Unfortunately, training on outliers may compromise classification accuracy and generate false positive outliers at semantic borders.

The C-way multi-label approach has C sigmoid heads. The final prediction is the class with maximum probability max-σ, whereas the inlier probability is formulated as max-σ. Unfortunately, this formulation fails to address the competition between classes, which again compromises classification accuracy.

The C+1-way multi-class approach includes outliers as the C+1-th class, whereas the inlier probability is a 2-way softmax between the max-logit over inlier classes and the outlier logit. To account for class disbalance we modulate the loss due to outliers with λ_{C+1}. Nevertheless, this loss affects inlier classification weights, which may be harmful when the negatives are noisy (as in our case).

Finally, the two-head approach complements the C-way classification head with a head which directly predicts the outlier probability as illustrated in Fig. 2. The classification head is trained on inliers while the outlier detection head is trained both on inliers and outliers. The outlier detection head uses the standard cross entropy loss modulated with hyper-parameter λ_{TH}. We combine the resulting prediction maps to obtain semantic segmentation into C+1 classes. The outlier detection head overrides the classification head whenever the outlier probability is greater than a threshold. Thus, the classification head is unaffected by the negative data, which provides hope to preserve the baseline semantic segmentation accuracy even when training on extremely large negative datasets.

3.3 Resistance to Noisy Outlier Labels and Sensitivity to Negative Objects in Positive Context

Training outlier detection on a diverse negative dataset has to confront noise in negative training data. For example, our negative dataset, ImageNet-1k, contains several classes (e.g. cab, streetcar) which are part of the Cityscapes ontology. Additionally, several stuff classes from Cityscapes (e.g. building, terrain) occur in ImageNet-1k backgrounds. Nevertheless, these pixels are vastly outnumbered by true inliers. This is especially the case when the training only considers the bounding box of the object which defines the ImageNet-1k class.

We address this issue by training our models on mixed batches with approximately equal share of inlier and negative images. Thus, we perform many inlier epochs during one negative epoch, since our negative training dataset is much larger than the inlier ones. The proposed batch formation procedure prevents occasional inliers from negative images to significantly affect the training. Additionally, it also favours stable development of batchnorm statistics. Hence, the proposed training approach stands a fair chance to succeed.

We promote detection of outlier objects in inlier context by pasting negative content into inlier training images. We first resize the negative image to 5% of the inlier image, and then paste it at random. We perform this before the cropping, so some crops may contain only inlier pixels. Unlike [3], we do not use the Cityscapes ignore class since it contains many inliers.

4 Experiments

We train most models on Vistas inliers [35] by mapping original labels to Cityscapes [9] classes. In some experiments we also use Cityscapes inliers to improve results and explore influence of the domain shift. We train all applicable models on outliers from two variants of ImageNet-1k: the full dataset (ImageNet-1k-full) and the subset in which bounding box annotations are available (ImageNet-1k-bb). In the latter case we use only the bounding box for training on negative images (the remaining pixels are ignored) and pasting into positive images.

We validate semantic segmentation by measuring mIoU on WildDash val separately from outlier detection. We validate outlier detection by measuring pixel level average precision (AP) in two different setups: (i) entire images are either negative or positive, and (ii) appearance of negative objects in positive context. The former setup consists of many assays across WildDash val and random subsets of LSUN images. The LSUN subsets are dimensioned so that the numbers of pixels in LSUN and WildDash val are approximately equal. Our experiments report mean and standard deviation of the detection AP across 50 assays. The latter setup involves WildDash val images with pasted Pascal animals. We select animals which take up at least 1% of the WildDash resolution, and paste them at random in each WildDash image.

We normalize all images with ImageNet mean and variance, and resize them so that the shorter side is 512 pixels. We form training batches with random 512×512 crops which we jitter with horizontal flipping. We set the auxiliary loss weight to 0.4 and the classifier loss weight to 0.6. We set $\lambda_{\mathrm{KL}} = 0.2$, $\lambda_{\mathrm{C}+1} = 0.05$, and $\lambda_{\mathrm{TH}} = 0.2$. We use the standard Adam optimizer and divide the learning rate of pretrained parameters by 4. All our models are trained throughout 75 Vistas epochs, which corresponds to 2 epochs of ImageNet-1k-full, or 5 epochs of ImageNet-1k-bb. We detect outliers by thresholding inlier probability at $p_{\mathrm{IP}} = 0.5$. Our models produce a dense index map for C Cityscapes classes and 1 void class. We obtain predictions at the benchmark resolution by bilinear upsampling.

We perform ODIN inference as follows. First, we perform the forward pass and the backward pass with respect to the max-softmax activation (we use temperature $\mathrm{T} = 10$). Then we determine the max-softmax gradient with respect to pixels. We determine the perturbation by multiplying the sign of the gradient with $\varepsilon = 0.001$. Finally, we perturb the normalized input image, perform another forward pass and detect outliers according to the max-softmax criterion.

4.1 Evaluation on the WildDash Benchmark

Table 1 presents our results on the WildDash semantic segmentation benchmark, and compares them to other submissions with accompanying publications.

Our two models use the same backbone (DenseNet-169 [22]) and different outlier detectors. The LDN_OE model has a single C-way multi-class head. The LDN_BIN model has two heads as shown in Fig. 2. Both models have been trained on Vistas train, Cityscapes train, and WildDash val (inliers), as well as on ImageNet-1k-bb with pasting (outliers). Our models significantly outperform

Table 1. Evaluation of the semantic segmentation models on WildDash bench

Model	Meta Avg	Classic					Negative
	mIoU	mIoU	iIoU	mIoU	iIoU		mIoU
	cla	cla	cla	cat	cat		cla
APMoE_seg_ROB [24]	22.2	22.5	12.6	48.1	35.2		22.8
DRN_MPC [43]	28.3	29.1	13.9	49.2	29.2		15.9
DeepLabv3+_CS [8]	30.6	34.2	24.6	49.0	38.6		15.7
LDN2_ROB [27]	32.1	34.4	30.7	56.6	47.6		29.9
MapillaryAI_ROB [6]	38.9	41.3	**38.0**	60.5	**57.6**		25.0
AHiSS_ROB [33]	39.0	41.0	32.2	53.9	39.3		43.6
LDN_BIN (ours, two-head)	41.8	**43.8**	37.3	58.6	53.3		**54.3**
LDN_OE (ours, C× multi-class)	**42.7**	43.3	31.9	**60.7**	50.3		52.8

all previous submissions on negative images, while also achieving the highest meta average mIoU (the principal benchmark metric) and the highest mIoU for classic images. We achieve the second-best iIoU score for classic images, which indicates underperformance on small objects. This is likely due to the fact that we train and evaluate our models on half resolution images.

4.2 Validation of Dense Outlier Detection Approaches

Table 2 compares various approaches for dense outlier detection. All models are based on DenseNet-169, and trained on Vistas (inliers). The first section shows the results of a C-way multi-class model trained without outliers, where outliers are detected with max-softmax [20] and ODIN + max-softmax [31]. We note that ODIN slightly improves the results across all experiments.

Table 2. Validation of dense outlier detection approaches. WD denotes WildDash val.

Model	ImageNet	AP WD-LSUN	AP WD-Pascal	mIoU WD
C× multi-class	✗	55.65 ± 0.80	6.01	49.07
C× multi-class, ODIN	✗	55.98 ± 0.77	6.92	**49.77**
C+1× multi-class	✓	98.92 ± 0.06	33.59	45.60
C× multi-label	✓	98.75 ± 0.07	**57.31**	42.72
C× multi-class	✓	$\mathbf{99.49 \pm 0.04}$	41.72	46.69
Two heads	✓	99.25 ± 0.04	46.83	47.37

The second section of the table shows the four dense outlier detection approaches (cf. Sect. 3) which we also train on ImageNet-1k-bb with pasting (outliers). Columns 3 and 4 clearly show that training with noisy and diverse negatives significantly improves outlier detection. However, we also note a reduction of the segmentation score as shown in the column 5. This reduction is lowest for the C-way multi-class model and the two-head model, which we analyze next.

The two-head model is slightly worse in discriminating WildDash val from LSUN, which indicates that it is more sensitive to domain shift between Vistas train and WildDash val. On the other hand, the two-head model achieves better inlier segmentation (0.7 pp, column 5), and much better outlier detection on Pascal animals (5 pp, column 4). A closer inspection shows that these advantages occur since the single-head C-way approach generates many false positive outlier detections at semantic borders due to lower max-softmax.

The C+1-way multi-class model performs the worst out of all models trained with noisy outliers. The sigmoid model performs well on outlier detection but underperforms on inlier segmentation.

4.3   Validation of Dense Feature Extractor Backbones

Table 3 explores influence of different backbones to the performance of our two-head model. We experiment with ResNets and DenseNets of varying depths. The upsampling blocks are connected with the first three DenseNet blocks, as shown in Fig. 2. In the ResNet case, the upsampling blocks are connected with the last addition at the corresponding subsampling level. We train on Vistas (inliers) and ImageNet-1k-bb with pasting (outliers).

Table 3. Validation of backbones for the two-head model. WD denotes WildDash val.

Backbone	AP WD-LSUN	AP WD-Pascal	mIoU WD
DenseNet-121	99.05 ± 0.03	55.84	44.75
DenseNet-169	**99.25 ± 0.04**	46.83	47.37
DenseNet-201	98.34 ± 0.07	36.88	**47.59**
ResNet-34	97.19 ± 0.07	47.24	45.17
ResNet-50	99.10 ± 0.04	**56.18**	41.65
ResNet-101	98.96 ± 0.06	52.02	43.67

All models achieve very good outlier detection in negative images. There appears to be a trade-off between detection of outliers at negative objects and semantic segmentation accuracy. We opt for better semantic segmentation results since WildDash test does not have negative objects in positive context. We therefore use the DenseNet-169 backbone in most other experiments due to a very good overall performance.

4.4   Influence of the Training Data

Table 4 explores the influence of inlier training data to the model performance. All experiments involve the two-head model based on DenseNet-169, which was trained on outliers from ImageNet-1k-bb with pasting.

Table 4. Influence of the inlier training dataset to the performance of the two-head model with the DenseNet-169 backbone. WD denotes WildDash val.

Inlier training dataset	AP WD-LSUN	AP WD-Pascal	mIoU WD
Cityscapes	66.57 ± 0.86	13.85	11.12
Vistas	99.25 ± 0.04	46.83	47.17
Cityscapes, Vistas	$\mathbf{99.29 \pm 0.03}$	**53.68**	**47.78**

The results suggest that there is a very large domain shift between Cityscapes and WildDash val. Training on inliers from Cityscapes leads to very low AP scores, which indicates that many WildDash val pixels are predicted as outliers with respect to Cityscapes. This suggests that Cityscapes is not an appropriate training dataset for real-world applications. Training on inliers from Vistas leads to much better results which is likely due to greater variety with respect to camera, time of day, weather, resolution etc. The best results across the board have been achieved when both inlier datasets are used for training.

Table 5 explores the impact of negative training data. All experiments feature the two-head model with DenseNet-169 trained on inliers from Vistas.

Table 5. Influence of the outlier training dataset to the performance of our two-head model with the DenseNet-169 backbone. WD denotes WildDash val.

Outlier training dataset	Outlier pasting	AP WD-Pascal	mIoU WD
ImageNet-1k-full	No	2.94	43.13
ImageNet-1k-full	Yes	45.96	43.68
ImageNet-1k-bb	Yes	**46.83**	**47.17**

The table shows that training with pasted negatives greatly improves outlier detection on negative objects. It is intuitively clear that a model which never sees a border between inliers and outliers during training does not stand a chance to accurately locate such borders during inference.

The table also shows that ImageNet-1k-bb significantly boosts inlier segmentation, while also improving outlier detection on negative objects. We believe that this occurs because ImageNet-1k-bb has a smaller overlap with respect to the inlier training data, due to high incidence of Cityscapes classes (e.g. vegetation, sky, road) in ImageNet backgrounds. This simplifies outlier detection due to decreased noise in the training set, and allows more capacity of the shared feature extractor to be used for the segmentation task. The table omits outlier detection in negative images, since all models achieve over 99 % AP on that task.

4.5   Comparing the Two-Head and C-way Multi-class Models

We now compare our two models from Table 1 in more detail. We remind that the two models have the same feature extractor and are trained on the same data. The two-head model performs better in most classic evaluation categories as well as in the negative category, however it has a lower meta average score.

Table 6 explores influence of WildDash hazards [46] on the performance of the two models. The C-way multi-class model has a lower performance drop in most hazard categories. The difference is especially large in images with distortion and overexposure. Qualitative experiments show that this occurs since the two-head model tends to recognize pixels in images with hazards as outliers (cf. Fig. 3).

Table 6. Impact of hazards to performance of our WildDash submissions. The hazards are image blur, uncommon road coverage, lens distortion, large ego-hood, occlusion, overexposure, particles, dirty windscreen, underexposure, and uncommon variations. LDN_BIN denotes the two-head model. LDN_OE denotes the C-way multi-class model.

Model	Class mIoU drop across WildDash hazards [46]									
	blur	cov.	dist.	hood	occ.	over.	part.	screen	under.	var.
LDN_BIN	−14%	−14%	−22%	−14%	**−3%**	−35%	**−3%**	−9%	**−25%**	−8%
LDN_OE	**−11%**	**−13%**	**−7%**	**−10%**	−5%	**−24%**	**0%**	**−6%**	−30%	**−7%**

Figure 3 presents a qualitative comparison of our two submissions to the WildDash benchmark. Experiments in rows 1 and 2 show that the two-head model performs better in classic images due to better performance on semantic borders. Furthermore, the two-head model is also better in detecting negative objects in positive context (ego-vehicle, the forklift, and the horse). Experiments in row 3 show that the two-head model tends to recognize all pixels in images with overexposure and distortion hazards as outliers. Experiments in rows 4 and 5 show that the two-head model recognizes entire negative images as outliers, while the C-way single-head model is able to recognize positive objects (the four persons) in negative images. These experiments suggest that both models are able to detect outliers at visual classes which are (at least nominally) not present in ImageNet-1k: ego-vehicle, toy-brick construction, digital noise, and text. Figure 4 illustrates space for further improvement by presenting a few failure cases on WildDash test.

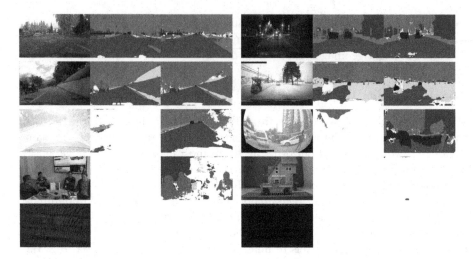

Fig. 3. Qualitative performance of our two submissions to the WildDash benchmark. Each triplet contains a test image (left), the output of the two-head model (center), and the output of the model trained to predict uniform distribution in outliers (right). Rows represent inlier images (1), outlier objects in inlier context (2), inlier images with hazards (3), out-of-scope negatives (4), and abstract negatives (5). The two-head model produces more outlier detections while performing better in classic images (cf. Table 1).

Fig. 4. Failure cases on WD test arranged as in Fig. 3. Top: the two-head model predicts outliers at trucks. Bottom left: both models fail to accurately detect birds on the road. Bottom right: both models exchange road and sky due to position bias (late experiments show this can be improved with training on smaller crops and scale jittering).

4.6   Discussion

Validation on LSUN and WildDash val suggests that detecting entire outlier images is an easy problem. A useful practical application of this result would be a module to detect whether the camera is out of order due to being covered, dirty or faulty. Validation on pasted Pascal animals suggests that detecting outliers in inlier context is somewhat harder but still within reach of modern techniques.

Evaluation on WildDash test shows that our models outperform previous published approaches. We note significant improvement with respect to state of the art in classic and negative images, as well as in average mIoU score.

Our models successfully detect all abstract and out-of-scope negatives [46], even though much of this content is not represented by ImageNet-1k classes.

Future work should address further development of open-set evaluation datasets such as [3,46]. In particular, the community would benefit from substantially larger negative test sets which should include diverse non-ImageNet-1k content, as well as outlier objects in inlier context and inlier objects in outlier context.

5 Conclusion

We have presented an approach to combine semantic segmentation and dense outlier detection without significantly deteriorating either of the two tasks. We cast outlier detection as binary classification on top of a shared convolutional representation. This allows for solving both tasks with a single forward pass through a convolutional backbone. We train on inliers from standard road driving datasets (Vista, Cityscapes), and noisy outliers from a very diverse negative dataset (ImageNet-1k). The proposed training procedure tolerates inliers in negative training images and generalizes to images with mixed content (inlier background, outlier objects). We perform extensive open-set validation on Wild-Dash val (inliers), LSUN val (outliers), and pasted Pascal objects (outliers). The results confirm suitability of the proposed training procedure. The proposed multi-head model outperforms the C-way multi-label model and the C+1-way multi-class model, while performing comparably to the C-way multi-class model trained to predict uniform distribution in outliers. We apply our two best models to WildDash test and set a new state of the art on the WildDash benchmark.

References

1. Bengio, Y., Courville, A.C., Vincent, P.: Representation learning: a review and new perspectives. IEEE Trans. Pattern Anal. Mach. Intell. **35**(8), 1798–1828 (2013)
2. Bevandic, P., Kreso, I., Orsic, M., Segvic, S.: Discriminative out-of-distribution detection for semantic segmentation. CoRR abs/1808.07703 (2018)
3. Blum, H., Sarlin, P., Nieto, J.I., Siegwart, R., Cadena, C.: The Fishyscapes benchmark: measuring blind spots in semantic segmentation. CoRR abs/1904.03215
4. Brock, A., Donahue, J., Simonyan, K.: Large scale GAN training for high fidelity natural image synthesis. In: ICLR (2019)
5. Brostow, G.J., Shotton, J., Fauqueur, J., Cipolla, R.: Segmentation and recognition using structure from motion point clouds. In: Forsyth, D., Torr, P., Zisserman, A. (eds.) ECCV 2008. LNCS, vol. 5302, pp. 44–57. Springer, Heidelberg (2008). https://doi.org/10.1007/978-3-540-88682-2_5
6. Bulò, S.R., Porzi, L., Kontschieder, P.: In-place activated BatchNorm for memory-optimized training of DNNs. CoRR, abs/1712.02616, December 5 2017
7. Caruana, R.: Multitask learning. Mach. Learn. **28**(1), 41–75 (1997). https://doi.org/10.1023/A:1007379606734

8. Chen, L.-C., Zhu, Y., Papandreou, G., Schroff, F., Adam, H.: Encoder-decoder with atrous separable convolution for semantic image segmentation. In: Ferrari, V., Hebert, M., Sminchisescu, C., Weiss, Y. (eds.) ECCV 2018. LNCS, vol. 11211, pp. 833–851. Springer, Cham (2018). https://doi.org/10.1007/978-3-030-01234-2_49

9. Cordts, M., et al.: The cityscapes dataset. In: CVPRW (2015)

10. Deng, J., Dong, W., Socher, R., Li, L., Li, K., Li, F.: ImageNet: a large-scale hierarchical image database. In: CVPR, pp. 248–255 (2009)

11. DeVries, T., Taylor, G.W.: Learning confidence for out-of-distribution detection in neural networks. CoRR abs/1802.04865 (2018)

12. Eigen, D., Fergus, R.: Predicting depth, surface normals and semantic labels with a common multi-scale convolutional architecture. In: ICCV, pp. 2650–2658 (2015)

13. Everingham, M., Gool, L., Williams, C.K., Winn, J., Zisserman, A.: The pascal visual object classes (VOC) challenge. Int. J. Comput, Vision (2010)

14. Geiger, A., Lenz, P., Stiller, C., Urtasun, R.: Vision meets robotics: the KITTI dataset. Int. J. Robot. Res. (IJRR) **32**, 1231–1237 (2013)

15. Goodfellow, I.J., et al.: Generative adversarial nets. In: NIPS (2014)

16. Guo, C., Pleiss, G., Sun, Y., Weinberger, K.Q.: On calibration of modern neural networks. In: ICML, pp. 1321–1330 (2017)

17. He, K., Gkioxari, G., Dollár, P., Girshick, R.: Mask R-CNN. In: ICCV (2017)

18. He, K., Zhang, X., Ren, S., Sun, J.: Spatial pyramid pooling in deep convolutional networks for visual recognition. In: Fleet, D., Pajdla, T., Schiele, B., Tuytelaars, T. (eds.) ECCV 2014. LNCS, vol. 8691, pp. 346–361. Springer, Cham (2014). https://doi.org/10.1007/978-3-319-10578-9_23

19. He, K., Zhang, X., Ren, S., Sun, J.: Deep residual learning for image recognition. In: CVPR, pp. 770–778 (2016)

20. Hendrycks, D., Gimpel, K.: A baseline for detecting misclassified and out-of-distribution examples in neural networks. In: ICLR (2017)

21. Hendrycks, D., Mazeika, M., Dietterich, T.: Deep anomaly detection with outlier exposure. In: ICLR (2019)

22. Huang, G., Liu, Z., Weinberger, K.Q.: Densely connected convolutional networks. In: CVPR (2017)

23. Kendall, A., Gal, Y.: What uncertainties do we need in Bayesian deep learning for computer vision? In: NIPS, pp. 5574–5584 (2017)

24. Kong, S., Fowlkes, C.: Pixel-wise attentional gating for parsimonious pixel labeling. arxiv 1805.01556 (2018)

25. Kreso, I., Krapac, J., Segvic, S.: Ladder-style DenseNets for semantic segmentation of large natural images. In: ICCV CVRSUAD 2017, pp. 238–245 (2017)

26. Kreso, I., Krapac, J., Segvic, S.: Efficient ladder-style DenseNets for semantic segmentation of large images. CoRR abs/1905.05661 (2019)

27. Kreso, I., Orsic, M., Bevandic, P., Segvic, S.: Robust semantic segmentation with ladder-DenseNet models. CoRR abs/1806.03465 (2018)

28. Lakshminarayanan, B., Pritzel, A., Blundell, C.: Simple and scalable predictive uncertainty estimation using deep ensembles. In: NIPS, pp. 6402–6413 (2017)

29. Lee, K., Lee, H., Lee, K., Shin, J.: Training confidence-calibrated classifiers for detecting out-of-distribution samples. In: ICLR (2018)

30. Lee, K., Lee, K., Lee, H., Shin, J.: A simple unified framework for detecting out-of-distribution samples and adversarial attacks. In: NeurIPS (2018)

31. Liang, S., Li, Y., Srikant, R.: Enhancing the reliability of out-of-distribution image detection in neural networks. In: ICLR (2018)

32. Lin, T., Dollár, P., Girshick, R.B., He, K., Hariharan, B., Belongie, S.J.: Feature pyramid networks for object detection. In: CVPR, pp. 936–944 (2017)

33. Meletis, P., Dubbelman, G.: Training of convolutional networks on multiple heterogeneous datasets for street scene semantic segmentation. In: IV (2018)
34. Nalisnick, E.T., Matsukawa, A., Teh, Y.W., Görür, D., Lakshminarayanan, B.: Do deep generative models know what they don't know? In: ICLR (2019)
35. Neuhold, G., Ollmann, T., Bulò, S.R., Kontschieder, P.: The mapillary vistas dataset for semantic understanding of street scenes. In: ICCV (2017)
36. Ngiam, J., Khosla, A., Kim, M., Nam, J., Lee, H., Y. Ng, A.: Multimodal deep learning. In: ICML, pp. 689–696 (2011)
37. Sabokrou, M., Khalooei, M., Fathy, M., Adeli, E.: Adversarially learned one-class classifier for novelty detection. In: CVPR, pp. 3379–3388 (2018)
38. Scheirer, W.J., de Rezende Rocha, A., Sapkota, A., Boult, T.E.: Toward open set recognition. IEEE Trans. Pattern Anal. Mach. Intell. **35**(7), 1757–1772 (2013)
39. Shafaei, A., Schmidt, M., Little, J.J.: Does your model know the digit 6 is not a cat? a less biased evaluation of "outlier" detectors. CoRR abs/1809.04729 (2018)
40. Smith, L., Gal, Y.: Understanding measures of uncertainty for adversarial example detection. In: UAI, abs/1803.08533 (2018)
41. Torralba, A., Efros, A.A.: Unbiased look at dataset bias. In: CVPR, June 2011. https://doi.org/10.1109/CVPR.2011.5995347
42. Vyas, A., Jammalamadaka, N., Zhu, X., Das, D., Kaul, B., Willke, T.L.: Out-of-distribution detection using an ensemble of self supervised leave-out classifiers. In: Ferrari, V., Hebert, M., Sminchisescu, C., Weiss, Y. (eds.) ECCV 2018. LNCS, vol. 11212, pp. 560–574. Springer, Cham (2018). https://doi.org/10.1007/978-3-030-01237-3_34
43. Yu, F., Koltun, V., Funkhouser, T.: Dilated residual networks. In: CVPR (2017)
44. Yu, F., Zhang, Y., Song, S., Seff, A., Xiao, J.: LSUN: construction of a large-scale image dataset using deep learning with humans in the loop. CoRR abs/1506.03365 (2015)
45. Zamir, A.R., Sax, A., Shen, W.B., Guibas, L.J., Malik, J., Savarese, S.: Taskonomy: disentangling task transfer learning. In: CVPR (2018)
46. Zendel, O., Honauer, K., Murschitz, M., Steininger, D., Domínguez, G.F.: Wild-Dash - creating hazard-aware benchmarks. In: Ferrari, V., Hebert, M., Sminchisescu, C., Weiss, Y. (eds.) ECCV 2018. LNCS, vol. 11210, pp. 407–421. Springer, Cham (2018). https://doi.org/10.1007/978-3-030-01231-1_25
47. Zendel, O., Murschitz, M., Humenberger, M., Herzner, W.: How good is my test data? introducing safety analysis for computer vision. Int. J. Comput. Vis. **125**(1–3), 95–109 (2017)
48. Zhao, H., Shi, J., Qi, X., Wang, X., Jia, J.: Pyramid scene parsing network. In: CVPR (2017)

3D Bird's-Eye-View Instance Segmentation

Cathrin Elich[1,2]([✉]) [ID], Francis Engelmann[1] [ID], Theodora Kontogianni[1] [ID], and Bastian Leibe[1] [ID]

[1] RWTH Technical University Aachen, Aachen, Germany
cathrin.elich@rwth-aachen.de
[2] Max Planck Institute for Intelligent Systems, Tuebingen, Germany

Abstract. Recent deep learning models achieve impressive results on 3D scene analysis tasks by operating directly on unstructured point clouds. A lot of progress was made in the field of object classification and semantic segmentation. However, the task of instance segmentation is currently less explored. In this work, we present 3D-BEVIS (*3D bird's-eye-view instance segmentation*), a deep learning framework for joint semantic- and instance-segmentation on 3D point clouds. Following the idea of previous proposal-free instance segmentation approaches, our model learns a feature embedding and groups the obtained feature space into semantic instances. Current point-based methods process local sub-parts of a full scene independently, followed by a heuristic merging step. However, to perform instance segmentation by clustering on a full scene, globally consistent features are required. Therefore, we propose to combine local point geometry with global context information using an intermediate bird's-eye view representation.

1 Introduction

The recent progress in deep learning techniques along with the rapid availability of commodity 3D sensors [1,2,15] has allowed the community to leverage classical tasks such as semantic segmentation and object detection from the 2D image space into the 3D world. In this work, we tackle the joint task of semantic segmentation and instance segmentation of 3D point clouds. Specifically, given a 3D reconstruction of a scene in the form of a point cloud, our goal is not only to estimate a semantic label for each point but also to identify each object's instance. Progress in this area is interesting to a number of computer vision applications such as automatic scene parsing, robot navigation and virtual or augmented reality.

The main differences between semantic and instance segmentation can be described as follows. While the semantic segmentation task can be interpreted as a classification task for a fixed number of known labels, the object indices for instance segmentation are invariant to permutation and the total number of objects is unknown a priori. Currently, there are two main directions to tackle instance segmentation: *Proposal-based* methods first look for interesting regions and then segment them into foreground and background [14,19,25]. Alternatively, *proposal-free* approaches learn a feature embedding space for the pixels

G. A. Fink et al. (Eds.): DAGM GCPR 2019, LNCS 11824, pp. 48–61, 2019.
https://doi.org/10.1007/978-3-030-33676-9_4

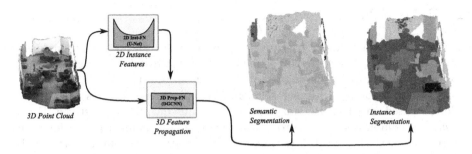

Fig. 1. We present a 2D-3D deep model for semantic instance segmentation on 3D point clouds. From left to right: The input 3D point cloud, our network architecture combining a 2D U-shaped convolutional network and a 3D graph convolutional network, actual predictions from our method.

within the image. The pixels are subsequently grouped according to their feature vector [21,23,24]. In this work, we follow the latter direction since it is straightforward to jointly perform semantic and instance segmentation for every point in the scene. Moreover, proposal-based approaches generally rely on multi-stage architectures which can be challenging to train.

Two fundamental issues need to be addressed for proposal-free instance segmentation: First, we need to learn point representations that can be grouped to object instances. Although some attempts have been made for 2D instance segmentation [6,23,24], it remains unclear what is the best way to learn instance features on 3D point clouds. This strongly relates to the second issue which deals with the scale of point clouds. A typical point cloud can have multiple millions of points along with high dimensional features, including position, color or normals. The usual approach to deal with large scenes consists in splitting the point cloud into chunks and processing them separately [27,28,34]. This is problematic for instance segmentation as large instances can extend over multiple chunks. An alternative is to downsample the original point cloud to a manageable size [33] which leads to obvious draw-backs (e.g. loss of detail) and can still fail with very large point clouds, such as in dense outdoor scenes.

In this work, we introduce a hybrid network architecture (see Fig. 1) that learns global instance features on a 2D representation of the full scene and then propagates the learned features onto subsets of the full 3D point cloud. In order to achieve this effect, we need a network architecture that supports propagation over unstructured data. The recently presented graph neural network by Wang *et al.* [35] for learning a semantic segmentation on point clouds is an adequate choice for this purpose. We present results for our model on the Stanford Indoor 3D scenes dataset [3] and the more recent ScanNet v2 dataset [11].

The key contributions of this work are as follows: (1) We present a hybrid 2D-3D network architecture for performing joint semantic and instance segmentation on large scale point clouds. (2) We show how to combine features learned from a regular 2D representation and unstructured 3D point clouds.

2   Related Work

2D Feature Learning for Instance Segmentation. Fully convolutional networks (FCN) [31] have been used as part of many successful semantic segmentation methods to provide dense semantic predictions and features [4,7,30]. Similarly, for proposal-free instance segmentation, pixel-wise features need to be inferred based on which the image pixels can subsequently be clustered. Fathi *et al.* [18] compute a cross-entropy loss on randomly sampled points for each object instance. Hsu *et al.* [21] treat the FCN-features as multinomial distributions. and rely on the KL-divergence to measure similarities between pixel distributions. Kong *et al.* [23] map pixel embeddings to a hypersphere. These embeddings are then clustered using a recurrent implementation of the mean-shift algorithm. Similar to our approach, Brabandere *et al.* [6] use a discriminative loss function to penalize large distances between pixels of the same instance and small distances between the mean embeddings of different instances.

While the above approaches are only used for 2D images, we examine instance segmentation on 3D point clouds. However, our model utilizes an additional 2D representation which has proven to be useful in previous 3D scene understanding tasks [5,8,13,32]. Building on top of these ideas for 2D feature learning, our model includes a U-shaped [30] FCN to process a 2D bird's-eye view learning globally consistent instance features for an entire scene.

Deep Learning on 3D Point Clouds. Most approaches in 2D vision tasks are taking advantage of powerful features, learned through 2D convolutions. Extending the use of convolutions to unstructured 3D point cloud data is non-trivial and has become a very active field of research [27,28,33,35]. The seminal work of Qi *et al.* [27] introduced feature learning directly on raw point clouds through a series of multi-layer perceptrons (*MLPs*) and max-pooling. Hierarchical features are added in the follow-up work [28]. In both works, the max-pooling is only able to extract global shape information. In *dynamic graph CNN* (DGCNN) [35], PointNets are further generalized by *EdgeConvs* adding local neighborhood information over a k-nearest neighbor graph. In this work, we rely on DGCNN to learn strong geometric features and simultaneously utilize it as a message passing graph network to propagate learned instance features.

3D Instance Segmentation. While recently several approaches were presented for 3D semantic segmentation [5,16,17,27–29,35] and object detection [8,26,32,37], the combined problem of these was mainly disregarded so far. The only published work that conducts instance segmentation directly on raw 3D point clouds is SGPN [34]. A pair-wise similarity matrix is computed and subsequently thresholded to generate proposals which are merged according to a confidence score. As point clouds are split into smaller blocks that are processed separately, a heuristic *GroupMerging* algorithm is required to merge identical instances. In contrast, the instance features in this work are globally coherent across a scene such that the instances can directly be extracted without the need of a merging algorithm or thresholding.

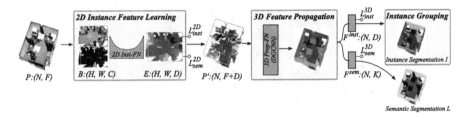

Fig. 2. 3D BEVIS framework. Given a point cloud $\mathcal{P}$, our model predicts instance labels $\mathcal{I}$ and semantic labels $\mathcal{L}$. The entire pipeline consists of three stages: First, the 2D instance feature network learns instance features $\mathcal{E}$ from a bird's-eye-view $\mathcal{B}$ of the scene. After concatenating the instance features to the original point cloud features, a 3D feature propagation network propagates and predicts instance features for all points in the scene. Our model finally predicts semantic labels $\mathcal{L}$ and instance features $\mathcal{F}^{\text{inst}}$ which are clustered to instance labels $\mathcal{I}$.

3   Model

In the following, we will present the architecture of our model 3D-BEVIS for semantic instance segmentation on 3D point clouds as visualized in Fig. 2. The input for our model is a point cloud $\mathcal{P} = \{x_i\}_{i=1}^{N}$, $i.e.$ a set of points $x_i \in \mathbb{R}^F$ where F is the dimension of the input point features. In our model, we use $F = 9$ for XYZ-position, RGB-color and normalized position with respect to the room size as in [27]. The model predicts semantic labels $\mathcal{L} = \{l_i\}_{i=1}^{N}$ and instance features $\mathcal{F}^{\text{inst}} = \{f_i\}_{i=1}^{N}$ with $f_i \in \mathbb{R}^D$ which are grouped to extract the semantic instance labels $\mathcal{I} = \{\mathcal{I}_i\}_{i=1}^{N}$. The entire framework consists of the combination of a 2D and a 3D feature network to learn point-wise instance features, followed by a clustering procedure to obtain the final instance segmentation. First, an intermediate 2D representation of the scene is utilized to learn globally consistent instant features for a scattered subset of points. These features are subsequently propagated towards the remaining points of the point cloud by applying a 3D feature propagation network. A clustering with respect to these learned features yields the final objects instances. Next, the single stages are explained in detail.

3.1   2D Instance Feature Network

To efficiently process the entire scene at once, we consider an intermediate representation $\mathcal{B} \in \mathbb{R}^{H \times W \times C}$ in the form of a bird's-eye view projection of the point cloud $\mathcal{P}$ (see Fig. 3). In contrast to previous methods [34] that independently process small chunks of the full point cloud, we are thereby able to learn instance features which are globally consistent across the point cloud. For generating this view, the points are projected onto a grid on the ground plane. If several points fall into the same cell, only the highest point above the ground plane is taken into account. We use color and height-above-ground as input channels, thus $C = 4$. The projections $\mathcal{B}$ are precomputed offline. The resulting 2D representation is the input to a fully convolutional network (FCN) [31] which predicts the instance

Input: $\mathcal{B}$ GT instance seg.   Output: $\mathcal{E}$

Fig. 3. Left to right: Input bird's-eye view $\mathcal{B}$, ground truth instance labels, predicted instance features $\mathcal{E}$ colored according to the GT instance labels. For visualization, we project the D-dimensional instance features $\mathcal{E}$ to 2D with PCA.

feature map $\mathcal{E} \in \mathbb{R}^{H \times W \times D}$. The FCN can process rooms of changing size during testing. We utilize a simple encoder-decoder architecture inspired by U-Net [30] and the FCN applied in [21]. Convolutions use a 3×3 kernel size with batch normalization, ReLU non-linearities, and skip-connections. The full architecture is shown in Fig. 4.

There are two output branches, one for semantic segmentation and one for instance segmentation. The corresponding losses are $\mathcal{L}_{\text{inst}}^{2D}$ and $\mathcal{L}_{\text{sem}}^{2D}$. $\mathcal{L}_{\text{sem}}^{2D}$ is the cross-entropy loss for semantic segmentation. The instance segmentation loss $\mathcal{L}_{\text{inst}}^{2D}$ is based on a similarity measure for pairs of pixels: $s_{i,j} = \|x_i - x_j\|_2$. From this, we define the entire loss as

$$\mathcal{L}_{\text{inst}}^{2D} = \mathcal{L}_{var} + \mathcal{L}_{dist} \tag{1}$$

with

$$\begin{aligned}
\mathcal{L}_{var} &= \sum_{c=1}^{C} \sum_{x_i, x_j \in S_c} [s_{i,j} - \delta_{var}]_+, \\
\mathcal{L}_{dist} &= \sum_{\substack{c,c'=1 \\ c \neq c'}}^{C} \sum_{\substack{x_i \in S_c \\ x_j \in S_{c'}}} [\delta_{dist} - s_{i,j}]_+
\end{aligned} \tag{2}$$

This ensures feature vectors of points belonging to the same object to be similar while encouraging a large distance in the feature space between features corresponding to different instances. Whereas the margin δ_{var} allows instance features to be spread within a certain range, δ_{dist} enforces a minimum distance between to feature vectors. $[\cdot]_+$ denotes the hinge function $\max(0, \cdot)$.

To compute the instance loss, we use the same sampling strategy as applied in [18,24]. Instead of comparing all pairs of feature vectors, we sample a subset S_c containing M pixels for each instance c.

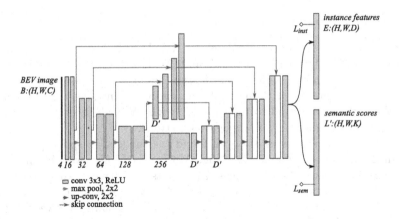

Fig. 4. 2D Instance Feature Network. U-shaped fully convolution network to learn instances features $\mathcal{E}$ from the input bird's-eye view $\mathcal{B}$. During training the network predicts semantic labels and instance features. At test time, we only forward the instance features $\mathcal{E}$.

3.2   3D Feature Propagation Network

At this stage, we have instance features $\mathcal{E}$ for all the points $\mathcal{P}_\mathcal{B} \subset \mathcal{P}$ visible in $\mathcal{B}$. These features are globally consistent and can thus be used as a basis for later grouping. Due to occlusion in the bird's-eye view projection, a fraction of the points was unregarded so far. Therefore, in this part, we use a graph neural network to propagate existing features and predict instance features for all points in $\mathcal{P}$. Specifically, we concatenate the initial point cloud features x_i with the learned instance features from $\mathcal{B}$ to obtain $\mathcal{P}'$. When generating $\mathcal{B}$, we keep track of point indices to map the learned instance features back to the point cloud $\mathcal{P}$. The instance features of unseen points in $\mathcal{P} \setminus \mathcal{P}_\mathcal{B}$ are set to zero. As graph neural network, we use the architecture from DGCNN [35] which was originally presented for learning a semantic segmentation on point clouds. Similar to the 2D instance feature network, the graph neural network has two output branches, each with an assigned loss function. The semantic segmentation loss $\mathcal{L}_{sem}^{3D}$ is again the cross-entropy loss. The instance segmentation loss $\mathcal{L}_{inst}^{3D}$ is defined as:

$$\mathcal{L}_{inst}^{3D} = \left\| \mathcal{F}^{\text{inst}} - \mathcal{F}^{\text{target}} \right\| \tag{3}$$

where $\mathcal{F}^{\text{target}} \in \mathbb{R}^{N \times D}$ are *target instance features*. The target instance feature for a point x_i is the mean over all instance features in $\mathcal{E}$ which lie in the same ground truth instance $\mathcal{I}_j$. If an instance is not visible in $\mathcal{B}$, there will be no target instance feature. Such instances are not part of the loss during training.

3.3 Instance Grouping

The last component obtains the final instance labels $\mathcal{I}$ by clustering the predicted instance features $\mathcal{F}^{\mathrm{inst}}$ using the MeanShift [9] algorithm. MeanShift does not require a pre-determined number of clusters and is thus suited for the task of instance segmentation with an arbitrary number of instances. The semantic labels $\mathcal{L}$ directly correspond to the category with the highest prediction in the semantic output branch of the propagation network.

As a final post-processing step, we found it beneficial to split up instances with an inconsistent semantic labeling. More specifically, we obtain a new instance $\mathcal{I}_c$ for every class c if at least th_c points in $\mathcal{I}$ have predicted semantic label c. th_c is chosen to be proportional to the average number of points per instance of the respective category. This helps to distinguish between objects from different classes that are hardly identified from the bird's-eye view like windows and walls.

3.4 Training Details

We train the 2D instance feature network on bird's-eye-view projections at a resolution of 3 cm (*S3DIS*) or 5 cm (*ScanNet*) per pixel. Depending on the room size, images are either cropped or padded. We deal with ceiling points by heuristically removing the highest points in each point cloud up to a threshold. As the network is fully convolutional, we can process the full image at test time. We perform data augmentation on the bird's-eye views $\mathcal{B}$ by random rotation at angles of $90°$, scaling and horizontal/vertical flipping.

To optimize the loss of the 3D feature propagation network, we pick a random position and extract 1024 points from a cylindric block with diameter $1\,\mathrm{m}^2$ or $1.5\,\mathrm{m}^2$ on the ground plane. This is comparable to the proceeding in [27,35]. The semantic losses are weighted with the negative logarithm of the class frequency. The networks are trained with the Adam optimizer [22] using exponential learning rate decay with an initial rate of 10^{-3}.

4 Experiments

We evaluate our method using two benchmark datasets on which we conduct experiments on the task of semantic and instance segmentation. We show qualitative and quantitative results on both tasks.

4.1 Settings

To evaluate our method, we need point cloud datasets with point-wise instance labels and semantic labels for each instance.

Table 1. Instance and semantic segmentation results on the S3DIS[3]
dataset. In this table, we compare methods that jointly predict semantic labels and
instance labels. Our presented method yields the best results for instance segmentation compared to both versions of SGPN. The semantic scores mainly depend on the
3D feature network and are thus comparable for SGPN$_{(DGCNN)}$ and 3D-BEVIS. Using
DGCNN as a feature network gives an important improvement.

	Instance seg.			Semantic seg.	
	$AP_{0.25}$	$AP_{0.5}$	$AP_{0.75}$	mIoU	mAcc
SGPN [34]	62.47	42.91	23.89	48.27	71.07
SGPN$_{(DGCNN)}$	70.73	58.56	39.73	**59.29**	80.71
Ours (3D-BEVIS)	**78,45**	**65,66**	**46,72**	58.37	**83.69**

Stanford Large-Scale 3D Indoor Spaces (S3DIS). [3] contains dense 3D
point clouds from 6 large-scale indoor areas consisting of 271 rooms from 3 different buildings. The points are annotated with 13 semantic classes and grouped
into instances. We follow the usual 6-fold cross validation strategy for training
and testing as used in [27].

ScanNet v2. [11] contains 3D meshes of a wide variety of indoor scenes including apartments, hotels, conference rooms and offices. The dataset contains 20
semantic classes. We use the public training, validation and test split of 1201,
312 and 100 scans, respectively.

Metrics. For semantic segmentation, we adopt the predominant metrics from
the field: intersection over union and overall accuracy. The overall accuracy is an
inadequate measure as it favors classes with many points, as it is also noted in
[33]. To report scores on instance segmentation we follow the evaluation scheme
applied in [34] to which we compare. We report the average precision (AP) of
the predicted instances with an overlap of 50 % with the ground truth instances
for the single categories as well as the AP with 25 % and 75 % overlap. We also
report results on the official ScanNet benchmark challenge [12] which uses a
stricter metric that is adapted from the CityScapes [10] evaluation. Specifically,
this metric penalizes wrong semantic labels even if the instance labels are predicted correctly. Moreover, false negatives are taken into account for the precision
score.

Table 2. Category-wise AP$_{0.5}$ on S3DIS. We receive the best results in nearly all
categories.

	Mean	Ceiling	Floor	Wall	Beam	Column	Window	Door	Table	Chair	Sofa	Bookcase	Board
SGPN	42.90	78.15	80.27	48.90	33.65	16.97	49.63	44.48	30.33	52.22	23.12	28.50	28.62
SGPN$_{DGCNN}$	58.56	**85.85**	83.15	61.65	**52.82**	47.60	55.12	62.22	34.97	66.02	42.50	55.93	54.85
3D-BEVIS	**65.66**	71.00	**96.70**	**79.37**	45.10	**64.38**	64.63	**70.15**	**57.22**	**74.22**	**47.92**	**57.97**	**59.27**

Table 3. Category-wise AP$_{0.5}$ on ScanNet. The presented scores for SGPN are extracted from [34]. As they did not provide scores for *other furniture*, this category does not contribute to the mean score.

	Mean	wall	floor	cabinet	bed	chair	sofa	table	door	window	book	picture	counter	desk	curtain	fridge	shower curtain	toilet	sink	bathtub	other furniture
SGPN* [34]	35.09	46.90	79.00	**34.10**	43.80	63.60	36.80	40.70	0.00	0.00	22.40	0.00	**26.90**	22.80	**61.10**	24.50	21.70	60.50	35.80	46.20	-
3D-BEVIS	**57.73**	**70.30**	**97.00**	29.70	**78.30**	**75.60**	**65.00**	**68.50**	**36.80**	**37.40**	**65.00**	**21.30**	14.50	**37.50**	57.80	**71.40**	**56.40**	**68.10**	**57.40**	**88.90**	38.80

Table 4. ScanNet v2 Benchmark Challenge. We report the mean average precision AP at overlap 25% (AP$_{0.25}$), overlap 50% (AP$_{0.5}$) and for overlaps in the range [0.5, 0.95] with step size 0.05 (AP). We report additional submitted scores from concurrent work that was recently accepted for publication (*). Scores from [12].

	AP	AP$_{0.5}$	AP$_{0.25}$
PMRCCN [12]	2.1	5.3	22.7
SGPN [34]	4.9	14.3	39.0
Our method	11.0	22.5	35.0
3D-SIS* [20]	16.1	38.2	55.8
GSPN* [36]	15.8	30.6	54.4

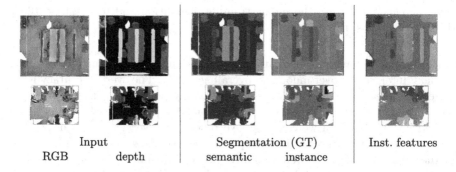

Input		Segmentation (GT)		Inst. features
RGB	depth	semantic	instance	

Fig. 5. Predicted instance features for 2D BEV. Left to right: Input RGB and depth images, ground truth semantic and instance segmentation, instance features. Instance features are mapped into RGB space by applying PCA.

Baselines. We compare our method to SGPN [34], the only published work so far in the field of semantic instance segmentation operating directly on point clouds. SGPN uses PointNet [27] as the initial feature extraction network. We conducted an additional baseline experiment SGPN$_{DGCNN}$ which replaces Point-Net by DGCNN [35]. We used the source code provided by the authors of [34], although it required some modifications to run. Due to a lack of information regarding the test split of the dataset used for the provided model, we re-trained the model. On the ScanNet dataset, we also include the PMRCNN (*Projected*

MaskRCNN) baseline experiment provided by the authors of the ScanNet benchmark challenge [12]. Their method projects predictions on 2D color images into 3D space.

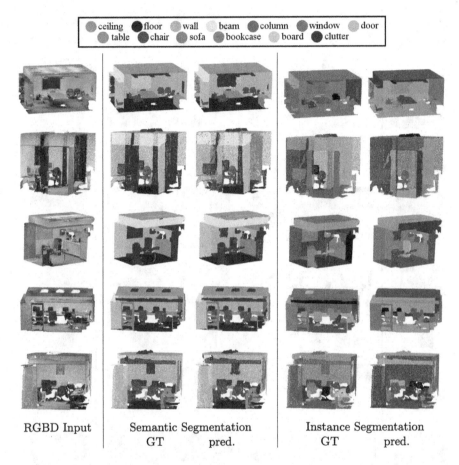

RGBD Input	Semantic Segmentation	Instance Segmentation
	GT pred.	GT pred.

Fig. 6. Qualitative results on S3DIS [3]. Left to right: Input RGB point cloud, semantic segmentation (ground truth, prediction), instance segmentation (ground truth, prediction). While we have a fixed color for each class, the color mapping for the single instances is arbitrary.

4.2 Main Results

We present quantitative and qualitative results for semantic instance segmentation. Table 1 summarizes our results on S3DIS. Category-wise scores for AP 50% are presented in Table 2. Our model outperforms both versions of SGPN over all overlap thresholds and most categories. The relatively low result for the category

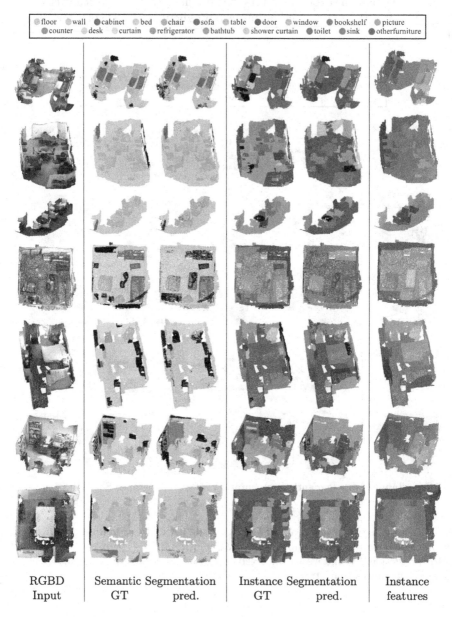

Fig. 7. Qualitative results on ScanNet [11]. Left to right: Input RGB point cloud, semantic segmentation (ground truth, prediction), instance segmentation (ground truth, prediction). While we have a fixed color for each class, the color mapping for the single instances is arbitrary.

ceiling is due to omitting the ceiling in the bird's eye view. Therefore, the distinction of several such elements is never learned. We see that DGCNN is a powerful method, it can help to significantly improve the existing approach regarding both the instance and semantic segmentation. Please note that our scores differ from the ones reported in SGPN [34]. The difficulty of reproducibility might be due to the considerable number of heuristic thresholds.

We present detailed results on ScanNet for AP 50% in Table 3. In Table 4, we report our scores on the ScanNet v2 benchmark 3D instance segmentation challenge. We get decent results compared to our baseline SGPN. Other recently submitted scores are included as well. Hou *et al.* [20] use multi-view RGB-D images as additional input. Yi *et al.* [36] predict object proposals on point clouds.

We show qualitative results of our method for instance and semantic segmentation on S3DIS [3] in Fig. 6 and ScanNet [11] in Fig. 7 at the end this paper. Our model can successfully distinguish between several objects of the same category as can be seen *e.g.* regarding multiple chairs within a scene. Visualized inferred features for the 2D bird's eye views are depicted in Fig. 5.

5   Discussion and Conclusion

The bird's-eye view used in this work has proven to be very powerful to compute globally consistent features. However, there are intrinsic limitations, *e.g.* vertically oriented objects are not well visible in this 2D representation. The same is true for scenes including numerous occluded objects. An obvious extension could be to include multiple 2D views of the scene. Compared to previous work [34], our model is able to learn global instance features which are consistent over a full scene. Thus, the presented method overcomes the necessity for a heuristic post-processing step to merge instances.

In this work, we explored the relatively new field of instance segmentation on 3D point clouds. We have proposed a 2D-3D deep learning framework combining a U-shaped fully convolution network to learn globally consistent instance features from a bird's-eye view in combination with a graph neural network to propagate and predict point features in the 3D point cloud. Future work could look at alternative 2D representations to overcome the limitations of the bird's-eye view.

References

1. Intel RealSense Stereoscopic Depth Cameras. Computing Research Repository CoRR abs/1705.05548
2. Matterport: 3D models of interior spaces. http://matterport.com. Accessed 1 Aug 2019
3. Armeni, I., et al.: 3D semantic parsing of large-scale indoor spaces. In: IEEE Conference on Computer Vision and Pattern Recognition (CVPR) (2016)
4. Badrinarayanan, V., Kendall, A., Cipolla, R.: SegNet: a deep convolutional encoder-decoder architecture for image segmentation. IEEE Trans. Pattern Anal. Mach. Intell. (PAMI) (2015)

5. Boulch, A., Guerry, J., Le Saux, B., Audebert, N.: SnapNet: 3D point cloud semantic labeling with 2D deep segmentation networks. Comput. Graph. (2017)
6. Brabandere, B.D., Neven, D., Gool, L.V.: Semantic instance segmentation with a discriminative loss function. In: IEEE Conference on Computer Vision and Pattern Recognition Workshops (CVPRW) (2017)
7. Chen, L.-C., Zhu, Y., Papandreou, G., Schroff, F., Adam, H.: Encoder-decoder with atrous separable convolution for semantic image segmentation. In: Ferrari, V., Hebert, M., Sminchisescu, C., Weiss, Y. (eds.) ECCV 2018. LNCS, vol. 11211, pp. 833–851. Springer, Cham (2018). https://doi.org/10.1007/978-3-030-01234-2_49
8. Chen, X., Ma, H., Wan, J., Li, B., Xia, T.: Multi-view 3D object detection network for autonomous driving. In: IEEE Conference on Computer Vision and Pattern Recognition (CVPR) (2017)
9. Comaniciu, D., Meer, P.: Mean shift: a robust approach toward feature space analysis. IEEE Trans. Pattern Anal. Mach. Intell. (PAMI) (2002)
10. Cordts, M., et al.: The cityscapes dataset for semantic urban scene understanding. In: IEEE Conference on Computer Vision and Pattern Recognition (CVPR) (2016)
11. Dai, A., Chang, A.X., Savva, M., Halber, M., Funkhouser, T., Nießner, M.: ScanNet: richly-annotated 3D reconstructions of indoor scenes. In: IEEE Conference on Computer Vision and Pattern Recognition (CVPR) (2017)
12. Dai, A., Chang, A.X., Savva, M., Halber, M., Funkhouser, T., Nießner, M.: ScanNet benchmark challenge. http://kaldir.vc.in.tum.de/scannet_benchmark/ (2018). Accessed 19 May 2019
13. Dai, A., Nießner, M.: 3DMV: joint 3D-multi-view prediction for 3D semantic scene segmentation. In: Ferrari, V., Hebert, M., Sminchisescu, C., Weiss, Y. (eds.) ECCV 2018. LNCS, vol. 11214, pp. 458–474. Springer, Cham (2018). https://doi.org/10.1007/978-3-030-01249-6_28
14. Dai, J., He, K., Sun, J.: Instance-aware semantic segmentation via multi-task network cascades. In: IEEE Conference on Computer Vision and Pattern Recognition (CVPR) (2016)
15. Engelmann, F.: FabScan-Affordable 3D Laser Scanning of Physical Objects (2011)
16. Engelmann, F., Kontogianni, T., Leibe, B.: Dilated point convolutions: on the receptive field of point convolutions. computing research repository, CoRR abs/1907.12046 (2019)
17. Engelmann, F., Kontogianni, T., Schult, J., Leibe, B.: Know what your neighbors do: 3D semantic segmentation of point clouds. In: Leal-Taixé, L., Roth, S. (eds.) ECCV 2018. LNCS, vol. 11131, pp. 395–409. Springer, Cham (2019). https://doi.org/10.1007/978-3-030-11015-4_29
18. Fathi, A., et al.: Semantic instance segmentation via deep metric learning. Computing research repository CoRR abs/1703.10277 (2017)
19. He, K., Gkioxari, G., Dollar, P., Girshick, R.B.: Mask R-CNN. In: International Conference on Computer Vision (ICCV) (2017)
20. Hou, J., Dai, A., Nießner, M.: 3D-SIS: 3D semantic instance segmentation of RGB-D scans. In: IEEE Conference on Computer Vision and Pattern Recognition (CVPR) (2019)
21. Hsu, Y.C., Xu, Z., Kira, Z., Huang, J.: Learning to cluster for proposal-free instance segmentation. In: International Conference on Neural Networks (IJCNN) (2018)
22. Kingma, D.P., Ba, J.: Adam: a method for stochastic optimization. In: International Conference on Learning Representations (ICLR) (2015)
23. Kong, S., Fowlkes, C.: Recurrent pixel embedding for instance grouping. In: IEEE Conference on Computer Vision and Pattern Recognition (CVPR) (2018)

24. Newell, A., Huang, Z., Deng, J.: Pixels to graphs by associative embedding. In: Neural Information Processing Systems (NIPS) (2017)
25. Pinheiro, P.O., Collobert, R., Dollar, P.: Learning to segment object candidates. In: Neural Information Processing Systems (NIPS) (2015)
26. Qi, C.R., Liu, W., Wu, C., Su, H., Guibas, L.J.: Frustum PointNets for 3D Object Detection from RGB-D Data. In: IEEE Conference on Computer Vision and Pattern Recognition (CVPR) (2018)
27. Qi, C.R., Su, H., Mo, K., Guibas, L.J.: PointNet: deep learning on point sets for 3D classification and segmentation. In: IEEE Conference on Computer Vision and Pattern Recognition (CVPR) (2017)
28. Qi, C.R., Yi, L., Su, H., Guibas, L.J.: PointNet++: deep hierarchical feature learning on point sets in a metric space. In: Neural Information Processing Systems (NIPS) (2017)
29. Rethage, D., Wald, J., Sturm, J., Navab, N., Tombari, F.: Fully-convolutional point networks for large-scale point clouds. In: Ferrari, V., Hebert, M., Sminchisescu, C., Weiss, Y. (eds.) ECCV 2018. LNCS, vol. 11208, pp. 625–640. Springer, Cham (2018). https://doi.org/10.1007/978-3-030-01225-0_37
30. Ronneberger, O., Fischer, P., Brox, T.: U-Net: convolutional networks for biomedical image segmentation. In: Navab, N., Hornegger, J., Wells, W.M., Frangi, A.F. (eds.) MICCAI 2015. LNCS, vol. 9351, pp. 234–241. Springer, Cham (2015). https://doi.org/10.1007/978-3-319-24574-4_28
31. Shelhamer, E., Long, J., Darrell, T.: Fully Convolutional Networks for Semantic Segmentation. IEEE Trans. Pattern Anal. Mach. Intell. (PAMI) (2017)
32. Simon, M., Milz, S., Amende, K., Gross, H.: Complex-YOLO: real-time 3D object detection on point clouds. Computing research repository CoRR abs/1803.06199 (2018)
33. Tatarchenko, M., Park, J., Koltun, V., Zhou, Q.Y.: Tangent convolutions for dense prediction in 3D. In: IEEE Conference on Computer Vision and Pattern Recognition (CVPR) (2018)
34. Wang, W., Yu, R., Huang, Q., Neumann, U.: SGPN: similarity group proposal network for 3D point cloud instance segmentation. In: IEEE Conference on Computer Vision and Pattern Recognition (CVPR) (2018)
35. Wang, Y., Sun, Y., Liu, Z., Sarma, S.E., Bronstein, M.M., Solomon, J.M.: Dynamic graph CNN for learning on point clouds. Computing research repository CoRR abs/1801.07829 (2018)
36. Yi, L., Zhao, W., Wang, H., Sung, M., Guibas, L.J.: GSPN: generative shape proposal network for 3D instance segmentation in point cloud. In: IEEE Conference on Computer Vision and Pattern Recognition (CVPR) (2019)
37. Zhou, Y., Tuzel, O.: VoxelNet: end-to-end learning for point cloud based 3D object detection. In: IEEE Conference on Computer Vision and Pattern Recognition (CVPR) (2018)

Classification-Specific Parts for Improving Fine-Grained Visual Categorization

Dimitri Korsch[1(✉)], Paul Bodesheim[1], and Joachim Denzler[1,2]

[1] Computer Vision Group, Friedrich-Schiller-University Jena, Jena, Germany
dimitri.korsch@uni-jena.de
[2] Michael Stifel Center Jena, Jena, Germany

Abstract. Fine-grained visual categorization is a classification task for distinguishing categories with high intra-class and small inter-class variance. While global approaches aim at using the whole image for performing the classification, part-based solutions gather additional local information in terms of attentions or parts. We propose a novel classification-specific part estimation that uses an initial prediction as well as back-propagation of feature importance via gradient computations in order to estimate relevant image regions. The subsequently detected parts are then not only selected by a-posteriori classification knowledge, but also have an intrinsic spatial extent that is determined automatically. This is in contrast to most part-based approaches and even to available ground-truth part annotations, which only provide point coordinates and no additional scale information. We show in our experiments on various widely-used fine-grained datasets the effectiveness of the mentioned part selection method in conjunction with the extracted part features.

1 Introduction

Fine-grained visual categorization (FGVC) is a challenging subdiscipline of computer vision and aims at distinguishing similar classes of objects that belong to a common major class like birds [19,21], cars [11] or flowers [13]. The latest FGVC challenges (like [20]) highlight both importance and difficulties of fine-grained categorization. As shown by others before, a careful selection of data [1] or gathering additional data from the Internet [10] for the pretraining of a convolutional neural network (CNN) can yield impressive state-of-the-art results.

In general, the proposed solutions found in the literature can be divided into algorithms working with global image features [12,16] and part-based or attention-based methods [3,4,7,22,23]. From the empirical results reported in these works, it is difficult to conclude which basic approach (global or part-based) works best, since both are competitive in terms of recognition performance. Due to the fact that categories of fine-grained recognition tasks often differ only in

Electronic supplementary material The online version of this chapter (https://doi.org/10.1007/978-3-030-33676-9_5) contains supplementary material, which is available to authorized users.

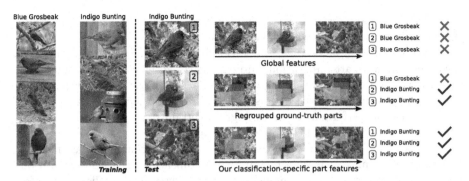

Fig. 1. An example from our experiments as a motivation for our approach: two visually similar classes are confused by a baseline classifier with global features. A part-based classifier using ground-truth annotations for anatomical parts is able to correct some of the predictions due to additional local information. However, our parts are estimated using a-posteriori classification knowledge and therefore focus on distinguishing highly similar classes. This allows for resolving misclassifications with the additional benefits of automatically determining the spatial extent of each part and being independent from manual annotations.

small details, part-based features that consider local image regions seem to be promising because they are able to explicitly focus on such distinct patterns. For example, if two bird species can only be distinguished by a characteristic spot on the head, a part feature representing the image region covered by the head of the bird would be beneficial for separating these two classes. Furthermore, parts can support the classification in case of only few training samples or highly imbalanced class distributions in the training set, e.g., by applying transfer learning techniques [5]. For analyzing classification results and failure cases, the attribution of classifier decisions to features and relevant image regions is an important step and parts are helpful for detailed investigations in order to gain a better understanding of the specific recognition task and the problem domain.

If ground-truth (GT) annotations for part locations are provided, they are usually referring to an underlying concept, e.g., the anatomical parts of a bird such as head, beak, belly, wings, and legs. Although being plausible from a human perspective, these parts may not be the best choice for achieving the highest classification accuracy with a machine learning model. In addition, not all annotated parts are equally relevant for every test image and it can be shown that an optimal part selection would lead to superior performance compared to state-of-the-art methods using all available parts [8]. Especially in case of noise, few characteristic parts can be outweighed by the remaining larger set of irrelevant parts that confuse the classifier and lead to misclassifications. In our experiments, we have observed that quality of parts is more important for an improved classification accuracy than quantity. For example, if we regroup the provided ground-truth parts for the CUB-200-2011 birds dataset [21] in more coarse but also more distinct parts, namely "head", "body", "legs", and "tail", the recognition performance can be enhanced.

However, since ground-truth annotations are not available for all applications and manual part annotations are expensive, an efficient and robust part detector is required. Such a detector has to deal with the following two main questions. First, what are the interesting and important locations that enhance the classification performance? Second, given certain part location, how and to which extent should the part features be extracted?

In this work, we tackle those questions and show that our classification-specific part estimation is able to improve classification accuracies on various fine-grained datasets. By studying failure cases of a baseline classifier that makes use of either global image features or part-based features extracted from available ground-truth annotations of the CUB-200-2011 birds dataset [21], we have observed that many class confusions occur between visually very similar classes (more details in Sect. 3 and Fig. 2). Hence, the idea of our approach is to identify relevant parts based on an initial classification with global features. By considering only the most important features for this initial decision, we estimate parts that are likely to be relevant for visually similar classes as well. With these new parts that are specifically estimated for a given test image based on additional knowledge from an initial classification, we aim at resolving misclassifications between very similar classes. This scenario is also visualized in Fig. 1.

Our proposed approach consists of the following steps. First, we perform a feature selection in order to estimate the most important features for the current classification task using a baseline classifier with global image features. The idea is then to estimate the most important regions in the image with respect to the actual classification task by only taking the most important features for the part localization into account. From these regions, we estimate parts as bounding boxes with automatically determining the spatial extent (scale) of each part. This is an advantage over most part-based approaches and ground-truth annotations. These provide only x and y coordinates of the part locations such that the size of each part has to be selected appropriately (and is usually fixed for all parts and all images). Given the newly estimated parts, we extract features for these parts as a rich representation that can then be used to improve the classification. More details are given in Sect. 3.

As it is common practice for many computer vision applications nowadays, our classification scheme relies on features computed with a CNN (called CNN features). Such features can easily be computed by applying either a pretrained CNN model as it is or a pretrained model that has been fine-tuned on the training set of the desired application. In our experiments (Sect. 4) we show that our approach: (i) improves the performance of the baseline methods, (ii) is competitive with other part-based classification approaches, and (iii) achieves state-of-the-art accuracies in some applications.

2   Related Work

Fine-grained visual categorization is a challenging and non-trivial classification task. Hence, there are diverse ways to tackle the problem. On the one hand, there are approaches that only use the global information of the image. The idea is either to use a clever way of pretraining the classifier or to use different feature pooling strategies. On the other hand, part-based approaches are applied which differ in the various part detection and extraction techniques.

2.1   Global Feature Representations

First, we consider approaches using only the global information of the image. Cui et al. [1] use a smart strategy in order to pretrain a CNN by taking large-scale datasets like ImageNet or iNaturalist into account, which offer a lot of data. Unfortunately, the difference between these datasets and the desired fine-grained datasets is too big. Hence, they suggest to preselect certain classes from the large-scale datasets which match best to the fine-grained training images and show that this preselection improves the performance drastically.

Krause et al. [10] enrich the training data with images from the Internet. They use Google Image Search in order to gather additional images for every training class. Though, the retrieved samples may not belong to the queried class, they show that even this noisy data improves the recognition performance by a large amount. Nevertheless, they cannot ensure that the collected data does not contain some images from the validation or the test set, since all these images are also publicly available. Hence, although an impressive effectiveness of noisy data is shown, one should look at the reported results with caution.

Other approaches focus on advanced ways of feature pooling. Here, bilinear pooling by Lin et al. [12] or more general the alpha-pooling by Simon et al. [16] are the most common techniques. Their aim is to highlight features that may have a greater impact on the classification task.

2.2   Part-Based Recognition Approaches

The second main direction for tackling fine-grained recognition tasks consists of methods that rely on part-based representations. A straightforward way of implementing a part-based recognition system is to employ the ground-truth part annotations if they exist (e.g., for the CUB-200-2011 birds dataset [21]). Since these annotations are expensive and most fine-grained datasets do not provide them, weakly supervised part detectors are a common choice [3,7,15,23]. The only supervision that these detectors use are class label annotations.

Fu et al. [3] and Zheng et al. [23] present similar approaches to extend CNNs with attention networks. The first work considers adjusting the attention recurrently and extracting additional information defined by the attention on different scales. On the other hand, the later work extracts multiple attentions in a single step. The extraction is done by localizing interesting areas from feature maps, regrouping them, and using these grouped areas as parts. In both cases, the whole system is trained end-to-end.

He *et al.* [7] propose a sophisticated reinforcement learning method in order to estimate how many and which image regions are helpful to distinguish the categories. They use multi-scale image representations in order to localize the object and then estimate discriminative part regions.

Simon *et al.* [15] identify part proposals with the aid of back-propagation. Afterwards, these proposals are used to fit a constellation model that determines which of the proposals are more likely to identify real parts. The part proposals with the highest match are then used to extract part features on different scales.

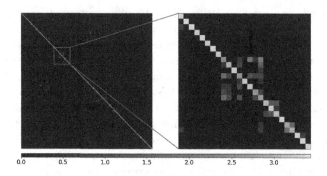

Fig. 2. Confusion matrix created from CUB-200-2011 predictions using global features only. The values are absolute number of correct predictions in log-scale. Similar classes have consecutive class indexes and are confused more often. Here you can see the classes 59–66, which are different gull species, e.g. California Gull, Herring Gull, Ivory Gull or Western Gull

3   Classification-Specific Part Estimation

In this section we describe our classification-specific part estimation approach that makes use of an initial classification based on global image features. The goal is to estimate parts depending on this first (and probably wrong) decision, such that these parts can help to spot the tiny details. These details are important for distinguishing visually similar classes in order to either confirm an initially correct classification based on the specific part features or to correct an initially wrong classification due to an enhanced representation of the important parts only. Here, we assume that many confusions of a classifier based on the global image features occur between visually very similar classes and that in those cases, the small details that are characteristic for distinguishing them are not well represented by the global features (which in general have to work for distinguishing all classes). Figure 2 visualizes this confusion and confirms our assumption. Hence, we look for the important image regions that have led to the initial classification. Then we derive new parts from these regions under the assumption that the resulting parts are also more relevant for disentangling

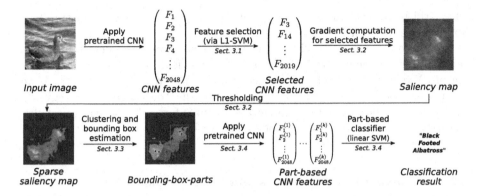

Fig. 3. The pipeline for our classification-specific part estimation.

visually similar classes. Our estimated parts are therefore classification-specific rather than based on human knowledge, e.g., from an anatomical point of view in case of the birds.

The pipeline we propose in this paper is visualized in Fig. 3 and will be outlined in the following. First, we describe the feature selection method (Sect. 3.1). Next, based on these selected features, we illustrate how relevant pixels and image regions are identified as candidates for the part locations (Sect. 3.2). Third, we explain our algorithm for estimating bounding-box-parts with the advantage of automatically determining the scale of each part (Sect. 3.3). Finally, an overview about the part feature extraction from the classification-specific bounding-box-parts and about the part-based classification is given in Sect. 3.4.

3.1 Feature Selection

Nowadays, a common approach in computer vision tasks is to use a pretrained neural network like a CNN, fine-tune its parameters on a dataset for the desired application, and extract features by concatenating the outputs of its penultimate layer in order to obtain a high-level descriptions of the image content. Our approach relies on those CNN features, which typically results in high-dimensional feature vectors ($D = 2048$ in our case). In case of a fine-grained recognition task, the recognition system often has to focus on some specific information within the features in order to spot tiny details that distinguish two similar classes.

Therefore, we first perform a feature selection in order to estimate the most important features for the current classification task. This is done by utilizing a sparsity-inducing classifier equipped with L1-regularization, which could be either a corresponding classification layer in a CNN that allows for end-to-end learning or an L1-regularized linear SVM classifier for the CNN features. Optimization with L1-regularization forces the classifier decisions to be performed on only a small subset of the CNN features. In our experiments, we tried both and found empirically that an SVM performs better in terms of recognition accuracy while still being fast during learning due to efficient SVM solvers in standard libraries like liblinear [2].

In the end, our feature selection is classification-based and determines relevant features for the underlying task by optimizing feature weights during learning of SVM classifiers. Since we consider multi-class recognition scenarios, we train a separate classifier for each class using the "one-vs-rest" strategy. As the result, we obtain a subset of relevant features for each class that best distinguishes this class from all the other classes by only selecting features with nonzero weights.

3.2   Identifying Relevant Pixels and Image Regions

The main idea within our part detection approach is to estimate the most important regions in the image with respect to the actual classification task. Hence, the part localization should only take those important features into account, which have been computed with the classification-based feature selection from the previous section. To this end, we use gradient maps [17] to identify the most relevant pixels in the image (indicated by large gradients), which have the largest influence on the feature extraction from the CNN model. By restricting the gradient map computations to only the previously selected subset of features, regions with large gradients are more adjusted to the classification task compared to propagating back the gradients of all features to the input image. Since our feature selection is based on a multi-class one-vs-rest SVM classifier, only selected features of the class assigned by this classifier are used for the gradient map computations. Thus, we incorporate knowledge of a baseline classifier with global features in our part detection algorithm.

The gradient maps are treated as saliency maps in our approach in order to guide the part detection and they depend on the used CNN features. In case of many currently used CNN architectures (Inception [18], ResNet [6], etc.), features are computed by averaging the values within each of the D output channel of the last convolutional layer. Typically, these output channels are called feature maps and the aforementioned average pooling results in a single number for each feature map. Given D feature maps $\boldsymbol{F}^{(1)}(\boldsymbol{I})$, ..., $\boldsymbol{F}^{(D)}(\boldsymbol{I})$ of size $s \times u$ for an image $\boldsymbol{I}$, this pooling step for computing the elements $f^{(d)}(\boldsymbol{I})$ of the D-dimensional feature vector $\boldsymbol{f}(\boldsymbol{I})$ can be written as follows:

$$f^{(d)}(\boldsymbol{I}) = \frac{1}{s \cdot u} \sum_{j=1}^{s} \sum_{j'=1}^{u} F_{j,j'}^{(d)}(\boldsymbol{I}) \quad \forall \, d \in \{1, \ldots, D\} \, . \tag{1}$$

Consequently, each value in a feature vector corresponds to a single feature map and since the feature selection method mentioned in Sect. 3.1 is applied to the feature vectors, it can also be viewed as applying the feature selection to the feature maps, i.e., the output channels of the last convolutional layer.

Like Simonyan *et al.* [17] and Simon *et al.* [15], we use back-propagation through the CNN to identify the regions of interest for each selected feature map. Based on the feature map subset $\mathfrak{D} \subset \{1, \ldots, D\}$ chosen by the feature selection from Sect. 3.1, we compute a saliency map $M(I)$ for an image I as follows:

$$M_{x,y}(I) = \frac{1}{|\mathfrak{D}|} \sum_{d \in \mathfrak{D}} \left| \frac{\partial}{\partial I_{x,y}} f^{(d)}(I) \right| = \frac{1}{|\mathfrak{D}|} \sum_{d \in \mathfrak{D}} \left| \frac{\partial}{\partial I_{x,y}} \frac{1}{s \cdot u} \sum_{j=1}^{s} \sum_{j'=1}^{u} F_{j,j'}^{(d)}(I) \right| . \quad (2)$$

After estimating the saliency maps, we normalize the resulting values to the range $[0 \dots 1]$ and determine a threshold to discard pixels and regions of low saliency at an early stage. We use the mean saliency value as a threshold. We have also tested Otsu's thresholding method [14] and it achieved similar performance. The resulting sparse saliency map, which now contains only pixels with large saliency values, is used in the next step for estimating location and spatial extent of parts.

3.3   Estimating Bounding-Box-Parts

Given an image and a sparse saliency map that discards pixels with low saliency, a set of k peaks $P = \{p_1, \dots, p_k\}$ with largest saliency can be computed using non-maximum suppression. Each peak serves as the initialization for a new part location. We then determine a region of high saliency around each peak, which directly defines the spatial extent of the estimated part. Like Zhang et al. [22], we achieve this by k-means clustering of pixel coordinates (x, y) and the saliencies $M_{x,y}$ (Eq. 2). Additionally, we also consider the RGB values at the corresponding positions in the input image. The clusters are initialized with the previously determined peaks $p_1, \dots, p_k$.

This has the effect that the number of selected peaks determines the number of clusters and hence the number of parts to detect. Second, since the peaks are sorted by their saliency values, the most important part is identified by the first cluster. Afterwards, it is easy to translate the clusters into bounding boxes for the parts. For each cluster we estimate the upper left and lower right corners in order to maximize the recall of the cluster pixels surrounded by the corners. The motivation behind the recall maximization is to get bounding boxes that contain as few false negatives as possible.

The resulting bounding boxes serve as parts for the following part-based classification with the advantage that we automatically determine the spatial extent (scale) of the parts by inferring the size of the bounding boxes based on the clustering and the regression. In contrast to this, most approaches estimate only x and y coordinates of the part locations such that the size of each part has to be selected appropriately. The same holds for the ground-truth annotations of many fine-grained datasets [19,21]. In most cases, the size for all parts of an image is fixed, which is obviously not very suitable since parts often have different extents in the image, e.g., consider bird parts that correspond to an eye and a wing.

With our part estimation strategy, we are able to automatically determine different sizes for different parts depending on the content of the image. Hence,

we want to emphasize again that we treat parts as bounding boxes with estimated position *and* estimated spatial extent in our framework rather than only
considering point locations with fixed extent.

3.4 Part Feature Extraction and Part-Based Classification

After we have estimated the bounding boxes around the maximum peaks of
the sparse saliency map for each image, we extract CNN features from these
bounding boxes. This is achieved by treating each bounding box as a single
image that is then processed by a pretrained CNN to extract meaningful features
from the penultimate layer. Note that this could even be the same CNN that was
initially used to extract global image features for the part localization and we use
the same CNN architecture for both steps. The resulting part features and the
global features are then concatenated prior to applying a linear SVM classifier.
This classifier has been trained using part features of the training images that
have been computed with our part estimation approach described before.

To summarize, our part descriptors are classification-specific in the sense that
we estimate location and spatial extent of parts via bounding boxes based on
an initial classifier decision with its involved feature selection, i.e., our estimated
parts focus on the important aspects that are relevant for the classification.

4   Experiments

4.1   Datasets and Implementation

Datasets. All of the experiments are performed on widely used fine-grained
datasets. These datasets belong to a single common domain (birds, cars, flowers,
etc.). Though, some of these datasets provide additional part or bounding box
annotations besides the class annotations, we use only the class labels in our
experiments. A short description of these datasets can be found in the following.

CUB-200-2011 [21] consists of 5994 training and 5794 test images from 200
different bird species. Besides the class labels, this dataset provides bounding
box and part annotations.

NA-Birds [19] is similar to the CUB-200-2011 dataset. It provides besides
class annotations also ground-truth part annotations. This dataset is more challenging, since it has 555 classes spread over 23 929 training and 24 633 test
images. Although there are more training samples, the training set is not as
balanced as the training set of the CUB-200-2011 dataset. Additionally, this
dataset provides a hierarchy information about the classes.

Stanford-Cars [11] contains 8144 training and 8041 test images for 196 car
models. This dataset provides only bounding box annotations.

Flowers-102 [13] has 102 different flower species spread over 2040 training
and 6149 test images. Class labels are the only provided annotations.

Table 1. Comparison of our part extraction algorithm with and without our proposed feature selection method (**bold** = best per dataset).

	CUB-200-2011	NA-Birds	Flowers-102	Stanford-Cars
Global features (baseline)	88.5	87.5	**97.8**	91.5
Our parts				
No feature selection	89.1	88.4	97.0	92.2
With feature selection (Sect. 3.1)	**89.5**	**88.5**	96.9	**92.5**

Implementation. As backbone for our method, we use the ResNet-50 [6] CNN architecture for Stanford-Cars and Inception-V3 CNN architecture [18] for the other datasets. For different datasets we use CNN weights proposed by Cui et al. [1]. These weights are pretrained on either the ImageNet or the iNaturalist 2017 dataset. To allow for fair comparisons with the recognition performances mentioned in [1], we use ImageNet weights for Stanford-Cars and iNaturalist weights for all other datasets. This separation makes sense, since iNaturalist consists of living things only, which matches the datasets of flowers and birds best. On the other hand, ImageNet classes are more variable and contain also objects and vehicles, which is more suitable for a dataset of car images. For every fine-grained dataset, we fine-tune a CNN on the corresponding training set, perform the feature selection, part localization and part extraction. Finally, the extracted part features and the global feature are concatenated and a linear SVM classifier is trained. In order to match the number of regrouped ground-truth parts for the CUB-200-2011 dataset mentioned in the introduction, we use $k = 4$ in the part localization step, which results in four parts.

4.2   Results

Feature Selection Evaluation. First, we show that the usage of a classification-specific feature selection improves the quality of the extracted parts. For this experiment, we first compute the gradients from the entire feature vector with respect to the input image. Based on this gradient, we detect parts and extract features as mentioned before in Sects. 3.2, 3.3, and 3.4. The results obtained with these features can then be compared to the results of our approach. Although the features derived from gradients of the entire feature vector improve the recognition performance compared to the linear classification baseline, using feature selection as presented in Sect. 3.1 yields a larger improvement, as shown in Table 1. We observe that the feature selection is an important ingredient in our approach. The additional information, in form of the part features determined from the gradients of the entire feature vector, improves the classification performance. Nevertheless, the benefits of the feature selection indicate that this additional information should be picked with care.

The saliency maps that determine the parts are computed by the sum of the gradients of every single CNN feature with respect to the input image (Eq. 2). Hence, the feature selection reduces the summation to selected gradients only.

This means that in the experiment with feature selection, we use less information but this information is more precise which results in better classification performance. These findings hold for all presented datasets except for the flowers dataset. In case of flowers we see that the baseline linear classifier performs best. One possible explanation is overfitting to the training data. Compared to other datasets, there are on average only 20 training samples per class. The other datasets contain an average of 30 to 40 samples per class.

Furthermore, as Fig. 4 shows, the number of selected features by a L1-regularized linear classifier is beneath 3% for used datasets. As a consequence, the number of aggregated gradients (Eq. 2) is also beneath 3%. This fact and the results from Table 1 confirm the assumption, that quality of selected information is more important than the quantity.

Part Feature Evaluation. Second, we compare the recognition performance of our extracted parts with the one obtained with ground-truth parts. We have chosen the CUB-200-2011 dataset for this experiment, since it is one of the few

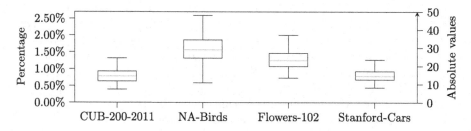

Fig. 4. Since we perform multi-class classification with the "one-vs-rest" strategy, we obtain for each class a vector of sparse weights for the linear SVM due to the L1 regularization. The distribution of the number of nonzero weights over the different classes (different "one-vs-rest" models) is shown for each dataset that is used in our experiments. Note that both relative and absolute quantities are shown (for 2048 features in total), which correspond to the number of selected features.

Table 2. Evaluation of the extracted parts on the CUB-200-2011 dataset. Note that we have used the same CNN to extract features from the different part locations: ground-truth (GT), regrouped GT, NAC parts [15], and our classification-specific parts (**bold** = best, *italic* = best without GT annotations).

	Global features	Parts only	Parts + global	# of parts
Global features (baseline)	88.5	–	–	–
GT parts	–	87.9	89.8	15
Regrouped GT parts	–	86.9	**90.2**	4
NAC part locations of [15]	–	87.9	89.0	20
Our parts	–	87.4	*89.5*	4

datasets that provides these annotations. As indicated in the introduction, we also regrouped the provided ground-truth parts in more coarse but also more distinct parts, namely "head", "body", "legs", and "tail". Compared to original ground-truth part annotations, our experiments show that these parts yield a better recognition performance (Table 2). This indicates again that the quality of parts is more important than the quantity. In the same table, we compare our classification-specific part detection with the part-based approach of Simon *et al.* [15], who have provided their extracted part locations. Additionally, we report in the table the recognition based on the global feature only. Best results are achieved when combining part features and the global image feature. While using ground-truth part annotations is slightly better, we are able to achieve better recognition results than the NAC parts proposed by Simon *et al.* [15]. Thus, our approach yields competitive recognition accuracies without relying on ground-truth part annotations, which makes it applicable in a wider range of applications where part annotations are not available.

Comparison to State-of-the-Art. Finally, we compare our proposed method with current state-of-the-art approaches on commonly used fine-grained datasets. The results are shown in Table 3 and the mentioned baseline uses only global image features extracted from the whole image. Furthermore, we differentiate between methods that use only the global information and part-based methods. Besides the method of Cui *et al.*, which utilizes clever pretraining of the CNN weights, we compare to other methods that use sophisticated pooling methods: bilinear pooling [12] and alpha-pooling [16]. We also report recognition results and the number of used parts for other part-based approaches. Note that none

Table 3. Comparison of our part-based approach for fine-grained recognition with various state-of-the-art methods (**bold** = best, *italic* = best part-based).

		CUB-200-2011	NA-Birds	Flowers-102	Stanford-Cars	Maximum # of parts
Global features	Linear SVM (baseline)	88.5	87.5	**97.8**	91.5	–
	Lin *et al.* [12]	84.1	–	–	91.3	–
	Simon *et al.* [16]	86.5	–	96.7	91.6	–
	Cui *et al.* [1]	89.6	87.9	97.7	**93.5**	–
Part-based features	Simon *et al.* [15]	81.0	–	95.3	–	20
	Krause *et al.* [9]	82.0	–	–	92.6	30
	Fu *et al.* [3]	85.3	–	–	92.5	2
	Zhang *et al.* [22]	85.4	–	–	92.3	4
	Zheng *et al.* [23]	86.5	–	–	92.8	5
	He *et al.* [7]	87.2	–	–	*93.3*	15
	Ge *et al.* [4]	*90.4*	–	–	–	10
	Our parts	89.5	**88.5**	*96.9*	92.5	4

of the approaches used ground-truth part annotations, neither during training nor in the test phase.

Table 3 shows that our approach is competitive in various fine-grained applications and achieves state-of-the-art performance on the NA-Birds dataset. For the CUB-200-2011 dataset, we outperform a lot of part-based methods even if they are using much more parts. This highlights once again that the quality of the parts is important and that our estimated parts contain meaningful information in only four locations.

5   Conclusion

In this paper, we proposed a weakly supervised classification-specific part estimation approach for fine-grained visual categorization. Unlike other part-based approaches, we estimate the part extents based on an initial classification of the whole image. We have shown that part features extracted in a classification-specific manner result in improved categorization performance. Furthermore, each estimated bounding box part has an implicit spatial extent that automatically determines an appropriate scale of the part.

References

1. Cui, Y., Song, Y., Sun, C., Howard, A., Belongie, S.: Large scale fine-grained categorization and domain-specific transfer learning. In: The IEEE Conference on Computer Vision and Pattern Recognition (CVPR), June 2018. https://doi.org/10.1109/cvpr.2018.00432
2. Fan, R.E., Chang, K.W., Hsieh, C.J., Wang, X.R., Lin, C.J.: LIBLINEAR: a library for large linear classification. J. Mach. Learn. Res. **9**(Aug), 1871–1874 (2008)
3. Fu, J., Zheng, H., Mei, T.: Look closer to see better: recurrent attention convolutional neural network for fine-grained image recognition. In: The IEEE Conference on Computer Vision and Pattern Recognition (CVPR), July 2017. https://doi.org/10.1109/cvpr.2017.476
4. Ge, W., Lin, X., Yu, Y.: Weakly supervised complementary parts models for fine-grained image classification from the bottom up (2019)
5. Göring, C., Rodner, E., Freytag, A., Denzler, J.: Nonparametric part transfer for fine-grained recognition. In: 2014 IEEE Conference on Computer Vision and Pattern Recognition (CVPR), pp. 2489–2496 (2014)
6. He, K., Zhang, X., Ren, S., Sun, J.: Deep residual learning for image recognition. In: Proceedings of the IEEE Conference on Computer Vision and Pattern Recognition, pp. 770–778 (2016)
7. He, X., Peng, Y., Zhao, J.: Which and how many regions to gaze: focus discriminative regions for fine-grained visual categorization. Int. J. Comput. Vis. 1–21 (2019). https://doi.org/10.1007/s11263-019-01176-2
8. Korsch, D., Denzler, J.: In defense of active part selection for fine-grained classification. Pattern Recogn. Image Anal. 658–663 (2018). https://doi.org/10.1134/S105466181804020X

9. Krause, J., Jin, H., Yang, J., Fei-Fei, L.: Fine-grained recognition without part annotations. In: Proceedings of the IEEE Conference on Computer Vision and Pattern Recognition, pp. 5546–5555 (2015). https://doi.org/10.1109/cvpr.2015.7299194

10. Krause, J., et al.: The unreasonable effectiveness of noisy data for fine-grained recognition. In: Leibe, B., Matas, J., Sebe, N., Welling, M. (eds.) ECCV 2016. LNCS, vol. 9907, pp. 301–320. Springer, Cham (2016). https://doi.org/10.1007/978-3-319-46487-9_19

11. Krause, J., Stark, M., Deng, J., Fei-Fei, L.: 3D object representations for fine-grained categorization. In: 4th International IEEE Workshop on 3D Representation and Recognition (3dRR-13) (2013). https://doi.org/10.1109/iccvw.2013.77

12. Lin, T.Y., RoyChowdhury, A., Maji, S.: Bilinear CNN models for fine-grained visual recognition. In: The IEEE International Conference on Computer Vision (ICCV), pp. 1449–1457 (2015). https://doi.org/10.1109/iccv.2015.170

13. Nilsback, M.E., Zisserman, A.: Automated flower classification over a large number of classes. In: Proceedings of the Indian Conference on Computer Vision, Graphics and Image Processing, December 2008

14. Otsu, N.: A threshold selection method from gray-level histograms. IEEE Trans. Syst. Man Cybern. 9(1), 62–66 (1979)

15. Simon, M., Rodner, E.: Neural activation constellations: unsupervised part model discovery with convolutional networks. In: The IEEE International Conference on Computer Vision (ICCV), December 2015

16. Simon, M., Rodner, E., Darell, T., Denzler, J.: The whole is more than its parts? from explicit to implicit pose normalization. IEEE Trans. Pattern Anal. Mach. Intell. 1–13 (2018). https://doi.org/10.1109/TPAMI.2018.2885764

17. Simonyan, K., Vedaldi, A., Zisserman, A.: Deep inside convolutional networks: visualising image classification models and saliency maps. arXiv preprint arXiv:1312.6034 (2013)

18. Szegedy, C., Vanhoucke, V., Ioffe, S., Shlens, J., Wojna, Z.: Rethinking the inception architecture for computer vision. In: The IEEE Conference on Computer Vision and Pattern Recognition (CVPR), June 2016

19. Van Horn, G., et al.: Building a bird recognition app and large scale dataset with citizen scientists: the fine print in fine-grained dataset collection. In: 2015 IEEE Conference on Computer Vision and Pattern Recognition (CVPR), pp. 595–604, June 2015. https://doi.org/10.1109/cvpr.2015.7298658

20. Van Horn, G., et al.: The inaturalist species classification and detection dataset. In: Proceedings of the IEEE Conference on Computer Vision and Pattern Recognition, pp. 8769–8778 (2018). https://doi.org/10.1109/cvpr.2018.00914

21. Wah, C., Branson, S., Welinder, P., Perona, P., Belongie, S.: The caltech-ucsd birds-200-2011 dataset. Technical Report CNS-TR-2011-001, California Institute of Technology (2011)

22. Zhang, J., Zhang, R., Huang, Y., Zou, Q.: Unsupervised part mining for fine-grained image classification. arXiv preprint arXiv:1902.09941 (2019)

23. Zheng, H., Fu, J., Mei, T., Luo, J.: Learning multi-attention convolutional neural network for fine-grained image recognition. In: The IEEE International Conference on Computer Vision (ICCV) (2017). https://doi.org/10.1109/iccv.2017.557

Oral Session II: Imaging Techniques, Image Analysis

Adjustment and Calibration of Dome Port Camera Systems for Underwater Vision

Mengkun She[1,2], Yifan Song[1(✉)], Jochen Mohrmann[1], and Kevin Köser[1]

[1] GEOMAR Helmholtz Centre for Ocean Research Kiel, Kiel, Germany
{mshe,ysong,jmohrmann,kkoeser}@geomar.de
[2] School of Civil Engineering, Chongqing University, Chongqing, China

Abstract. Dome ports act as spherical windows in underwater housings through which a camera can observe objects in the water. As compared to flat glass interfaces, they do not limit the field of view, and they do not cause refraction of light observed by a pinhole camera positioned exactly in the center of the dome. Mechanically adjusting a real lens to this position is a challenging task, in particular for those integrated in deep sea housings. In this contribution a mechanical adjustment procedure based on straight line observations above and below water is proposed that allows for accurate alignments. Additionally, we show a chessboard-based method employing an underwater/above-water image pair to estimate potentially remaining offsets from the dome center to allow refraction correction in photogrammetric applications. Besides providing intuition about the severity of refraction in certain settings, we demonstrate the methods on real data for acrylic and glass domes in the water.

1 Introduction

More than half of Earth's surface is located in the deep ocean. Despite of several decades of underwater photogrammetry (see e.g. [3, 4, 7, 16, 20]), visual mapping of the oceans is by far less developed than from land, air or space, partially because of limited visibility, attenuation and scattering of light as well as the need for more complex observation models due to refraction at the interfaces of camera housings. These housings are required to protect cameras from the surrounding water, and also from the pressure that increases approximately by one bar per ten meter ocean depth. Light rays from objects in the water typically travel through some transparent window into the interior of a housing filled with air surrounding a camera. Because of the different optical densities of water, glass and air, these rays change direction when they pass the interfaces in a non-orthogonal direction (see Fig. 1, left). It has been shown that when using a pinhole camera behind a *flat port*, the overall system becomes a non-single viewpoint camera [23] which makes applications like SLAM and dense reconstruction much more complicated [8, 21]. For instance, the projection of a 3D point into the image requires solution of a twelfth degree polynomial [1]. Additionally, because of strong refraction of

ⓒ Springer Nature Switzerland AG 2019
G. A. Fink et al. (Eds.): DAGM GCPR 2019, LNCS 11824, pp. 79–92, 2019.
https://doi.org/10.1007/978-3-030-33676-9_6

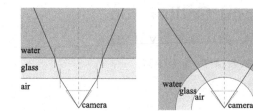 

Fig. 1. Left: Incoming light rays are refracted at the flat glass port. Center: If a pinhole camera is positioned at the center of a spheric glass window, a dome port, no refraction occurs because all rays pass the interfaces orthogonal to the surface. Right: Pressure housing with dome port of 5 cm radius and 7 mm glass thickness for 6000 m ocean depth.

outer rays flat ports limit the field of view of the overall system to below 100°. To avoid these limitations spherical glass domes can be used as windows (so-called *dome ports*). In case a camera is exactly positioned at the center of the dome, all principal rays will pass the air-glass-water interfaces at 90°, avoiding refraction (see Fig. 1, center). However, when the system is not exactly centered (see Fig. 5), non-linear, depth-dependent distortion will occur [10]. Consequently, it is very important to adjust the lens to the dome center and to know the remaining offset in order to allow proper correction of the undesired refraction effects. Finding a lens' nodal point and centering it in the dome is not always an easy task because the dome port might actually only be a fraction of a sphere, rather than a half-sphere, or the center point might be hard to gauge because of the flange construction, in particular for deep sea housings. In this contribution we propose both a mechanical adjustment procedure with visual feedback to align a camera with a dome port as well as a method to estimate a possibly remaining offset. In the next section, our novel contributions will be discussed together with the state of the art in the literature. In Sect. 3 the mechanical procedure to adjust the lens with the dome is described before Sect. 4 derives the calibration procedure. In Sect. 5, we provide detailed evaluation on synthetic ground truth data as well as offset experiments on acrylic domes and a stereo camera system with thick glass domes of a deep sea instrument, before we conclude in Sect. 6.

2   State of the Art and Contributions

The most common systems for capturing underwater imagery use cameras in underwater pressure housings with either a flat or a dome port. Flat ports are easier to make and therefore typically cheaper. The downside is that cameras behind a flat port will suffer from refraction because of the different media [9], making the overall system a non-single viewpoint camera [23]. This invalidates concepts like the pinhole camera model, including epipolar geometry and common multi-view relations, and complicates robust estimation, outlier detection and bundle adjustment, as for instance projection of a 3D point into the camera requires solution of a high degree polynomial [1]. Besides limited field of view, for deep ocean applications mechanical stability becomes an issue: Here, larger flat windows need to be either of very strong material such as sapphire or have to be several centimeters thick. The spherical structure of dome ports on the other hand is better suited for higher pressures. The field of view is not limited and pinhole cameras centered in the dome will not suffer from refraction, i.e. photogrammetry and computer vision theory for pinholes in air is applicable. A detailed discussion, also about sharpness and focus issues can be found in [14].

In presence of refraction, camera parameters differ in air and in water [4,11]. Besides generic ray-based [5] or specialized lookup-table-based representations [12] there are two main mathematical ways of formalizing underwater cameras, either to model and to obtain physical refraction parameters that refer to camera, housing and water [8,23] or to approximate the underwater camera system, including the housing, by a pinhole camera [20]. In the second concept, when used for flat-port systems, some refraction effects are absorbed into camera parameters such as focal length and radial distortion. Since refraction effects are distance-dependent this concept works best for a predefined, fixed working distance [20] and is problematic in SLAM scenarios where robots see 3D scenes from significantly different distances. Also dome port cameras have been calibrated using pinhole camera calibration techniques [15,17] assuming a dome-center aligned pinhole. In contrast, in this contribution, we explicitly investigate remaining misalignments and their effects, and follow the concept of modeling and calibrating the physical parameters of the system.

In general, very little work has been published for refraction and calibration with dome ports. The dome port scenario can be split into two subproblems, the mechanical adjustment procedure, to bring a pinhole into the center of a dome port, and the calibration of a potentially remaining offset. The first sub-problem is a similar task as is required in panorama photography, where photographers rotate a camera ideally around its nodal point (the "pinhole") to produce a series of images taken from the same position. Several techniques exist to identify the nodal point of a lens [18], e.g. using a second camera to photograph the iris of the first camera [15], by bringing calibration objects in line [22] and there are even databases for common lenses [19]. The nodal point of the lens and the rotation center of the tripod are typically measured by separate processes, and the camera is mounted in the ad-hoc calculated offset, without a feedback loop for adjustment. Here, it is not obvious how accurately one has to measure the position. For panorama photography of far away landscapes, small errors in the point of rotation are usually neglectable compared to the distance to the scene. In contrast, in photogrammetric underwater applications a millimeter offset can mean substantial refraction errors as will be shown in Fig. 6. Consequently, in this contribution, an adjustment procedure with feedback loop is proposed.

The second subproblem requires identification of the remaining miscalibration. To our knowledge, the only work in the literature that is concerned about this issue is by Kunz and Singh [10], which is the starting point for our work. Unfortunately, the authors motivate the problem only using synthetic data and sketch some ideas about offset computation without reporting results. In contrast, in the remainder of this contribution we will show a new calibration procedure that we evaluate for acrylic and glass domes.

  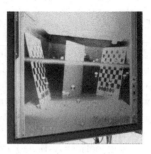

Fig. 2. Left: Technical drawing of deep sea housing with mechanics for camera adjustments towards the dome port. Center: dome port (half underwater) attached to tank. Right: View through dome (after adjustment), with straight lines crossing the surface.

3   Mechanical Adjustment of Cameras

Using the pinhole camera model with underwater dome port cameras requires centering the lens with the dome port as good as possible. The key assumption here is that the lens does not exhibit a caustic in air (see [5]), i.e. it can be considered a pinhole. Within the three possible degrees of freedom (3D offset of the pinhole from dome center), the positioning in camera forward/backward direction poses the largest challenge, as both the lens and the dome port pressure housing are typically rotationally symmetric and their axes can be aligned (already by construction) with high precision. This section proposes a method for mechanically aligning the camera in the difficult forward/backward direction, using the concept of optical feedback control. In principle, this through-the-lens approach allows to adjust the lens, until refraction in this particular camera-lens-dome system becomes neglectable or cannot be observed. Measuring the error in pixels enables also to easily transfer the concept to other lenses that require different spatial alignment accuracy in millimeters without actually having to know that accuracy requirement.

For the mechanical alignment we propose to mount the camera at the flange of the dome port as depicted in Fig. 2 (left). In our design the distance between the camera and the dome can be varied using a screw mechanism (moving 1 mm backward/forward per screw rotation). Besides this option, many other constructions are possible where the lens is moved in forward/backward direction while staying centered in the other directions.

Then the dome port should be positioned at a water tank (see Fig. 2, center), such that the dome is half-way underwater and looks parallel to the water surface. In case the camera is centered perfectly, no refraction will occur and the underwater part and the above water part of the image will be consistent. Straight lines that cross the water surface will simply continue. Figure 3 shows the corresponding images of a chessboard. The task of finding the correct camera position now translates to finding the position at which straight lines in 3D

Fig. 3. Simulated Chessboard images with parts above and below the water line. The lens is misaligned forward (left), aligned (center), misaligned backwards (right).

remain straight across the water boundary. By manually adjusting the mechanics and viewing the live images, one can determine the correct position easily.

As is well-known in underwater photography (compare also [15]), dome ports change the focus of the camera, because only the principal rays will not be refracted (see Fig. 4). Consequently, different focus or small apertures (large F-numbers) are required to produce an image that is sharp in the underwater part and in the in-air part at the same time. Since the scene is static, small apertures can be compensated by long exposure times. Additionally, if the proposed calibration is performed over larger distances, then the attenuation of light in the water could cause the underwater image part to be much darker than the image part that is in air, which can be alleviated by using underwater lights. Finally, once the straight 3D lines look straight in the camera, we can continue with subpixel offset estimation as outlined in the next section.

4   Calibration of Dome Port Systems

This section describes how to calculate the remaining offsets using an image of a chessboard in air and in water at the same extrinsic settings. It is assumed that the radius, thickness and material of the dome as well as the optical properties of the water are known. The overall approach consists of five steps: (1) Standard "in-air" perspective camera calibration is performed. (2) The camera

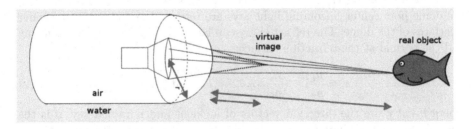

Fig. 4. Focus change induced by dome ports underwater. As can be seen, the principal ray observing the fish is not refracted, but the other rays collected by the lens intersect the dome in a non-orthogonal fashion. This requires setting a much closer focus underwater than in air and poses a challenge for a common lens setting for both.

is positioned in the dome port and mechanically adjusted to its sphere center by using the method described in Sect. 3. (3) A chessboard is photographed by the system in air, e.g. in a tank without water. The relative orientation between chessboard and camera is computed by pose estimation. (4) The chessboard (staying at the same relative orientation to the camera) is photographed by the system in water, e.g. the tank is filled. Potential displacements of chessboard corners between the in-air and in-water images are due to refraction induced by the remaining decentering errors. (5) The dome center offset that minimizes the 2D coordinate difference between real measured underwater points and re-projected underwater points (considering refraction) is sought.

4.1 In-Air Perspective Calibration

The in-air perspective calibration is a standard camera calibration procedure using calibration targets (e.g. [24]). In the following we will use homogeneous coordinates to formalize the camera model as commonly used (compare [6]): A 3D point is denoted by $\widetilde{\mathbf{P}} = [X, Y, Z, 1]^T$ and its corresponding 2D image position is $\widetilde{\mathbf{p}} = [u, v, 1]^T$. The camera model is formulated as:

$$\widetilde{\mathbf{p}} \simeq \mathbf{K}[\mathbf{R} \mid -\mathbf{RC}]\widetilde{\mathbf{P}} \qquad \text{with} \qquad \mathbf{K} = \begin{bmatrix} f_x & 0 & c_x \\ 0 & f_y & c_y \\ 0 & 0 & 1 \end{bmatrix} \qquad (1)$$

where $\mathbf{R}$ and $\mathbf{C}$ are the rotation matrix and camera center that transform from world coordinates to camera coordinates. $\mathbf{K}$ denotes the intrinsic parameters ((f_x, f_y) the focal lengths and (c_x, c_y) the principal point). Additionally, lens distortion parameters can be considered in the perspective camera model as widely used in many calibration tools [2]. However, for the sake of readability, and without loss of generality, in the following derivations we will simply use the matrix $\mathbf{K}$ to account for intrinsic parameters.

4.2 Refractive Back Projection Through Dome Ports

In the underwater case, when the camera center is not exactly positioned at the dome port center, incoming light rays are refracted at the outer and inner interfaces of the dome. The refracted ray can be computed from the incident ray and the normal at the refraction surface:

$$\mathbf{r} = \frac{n_i}{n_r}\mathbf{i} + (\frac{n_i}{n_r}\cos\theta_i - \sqrt{1 - \sin^2\theta_r})\mathbf{n} \qquad (2)$$

where $\mathbf{i}$ and $\mathbf{r}$ are the direction vectors of incident and refracted ray, $\mathbf{n}$ is the normal vector at the intersection point, all those vectors are normalized. n_i and n_r are the indices of refraction for different media. θ_i is the incident angle and can be calculated by $\theta_i = \arccos(-\mathbf{i} \cdot \mathbf{n})$. θ_r is the refraction angle, which can be derived from the incident angle according to Snell's law $n_i \sin\theta_i = n_r \sin\theta_r$.

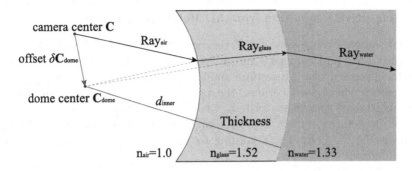

Fig. 5. Refraction of viewing ray in misaligned dome port.

In the local camera coordinate system, for a homogeneous 2D point $\tilde{p}$ in the underwater image, the viewing ray from the point is determined by

$$\overrightarrow{\mathbf{Ray}}_{air} = \frac{\mathbf{K}^{-1}\tilde{p}}{\|\mathbf{K}^{-1}\tilde{p}\|_2} \tag{3}$$

If the camera center is set off from the dome center by $\delta\mathbf{C}_{\mathrm{dome}} = (\delta X_{\mathrm{dome}}, \delta Y_{\mathrm{dome}}, \delta Z_{\mathrm{dome}})$, the viewing ray from the image is refracted twice on the air-glass and glass-water interfaces, as shown in Fig. 5. For each refraction, the intersection on the interface is determined by intersecting a ray with a sphere, where spheres can be represented as implicit quadric surfaces [6], e.g. all points $\tilde{\mathbf{P}}_u$ on the unit sphere fulfill $\tilde{\mathbf{P}}_u^T\mathbf{Q}\tilde{\mathbf{P}}_u = 0$ with the unit sphere in diagonal matrix notation $\mathbf{Q} = \mathrm{diag}\{1,1,1,-1\}$. The inner and outer spheres of the dome then can be transformed from the unit dome sphere as follows:

$$\mathbf{H}(d, \delta\mathbf{C}_{\mathrm{dome}}) = \begin{bmatrix} d & 0 & 0 & \delta X_{\mathrm{dome}} \\ 0 & d & 0 & \delta Y_{\mathrm{dome}} \\ 0 & 0 & d & \delta Z_{\mathrm{dome}} \\ 0 & 0 & 0 & -1 \end{bmatrix}$$

$$\mathbf{D}(d, \delta\mathbf{C}_{\mathrm{dome}}) = (\mathbf{H}^{-1})^T\mathbf{Q}\mathbf{H}^{-1}, \tag{4}$$

where d indicates the radius of inner and outer sphere of the dome.

The ray-sphere intersection point $\tilde{\mathbf{P}}_{a/g}$ on the air-glass interface is satisfying

$$\tilde{\mathbf{P}}_{a/g}^T\mathbf{D}_{air}\tilde{\mathbf{P}}_{a/g} = 0 \quad \text{with} \quad \tilde{\mathbf{P}}_{a/g} = \lambda_{air}\overrightarrow{\mathbf{Ray}}_{air} \tag{5}$$

which boils down to a single quadratic equation in λ_{air}. Once the intersection is determined, the normal vector can be derived and the refracted ray $\overrightarrow{\mathbf{Ray}}_{glass}$ can be calculated by Eq. 2. For the glass-water interface, the intersection point $\tilde{\mathbf{P}}_{g/w}$ can be calculated in the same way by

$$\tilde{\mathbf{P}}_{g/w}^T\mathbf{D}_{glass}\tilde{\mathbf{P}}_{g/w} = 0 \quad \text{with} \quad \tilde{\mathbf{P}}_{g/w} = \tilde{\mathbf{P}}_{a/g} + \lambda_{glass}\overrightarrow{\mathbf{Ray}}_{glass} \tag{6}$$

allowing to compute the outer interface point and ray direction in the water.

4.3   Refractive Projection from 3D Points on a Plane

Since no compact representation of the projection from a 3D point $\mathbf{P}_i$ into a misaligned dome port camera is known, we use an iterative back-projection approach to implement the projection, similar in spirit to [10]. As we will use it for projecting chessboard corners, the problem can be simplified by working in the chessboard coordinate system, where all 3D points have $Z = 0$. Essentially, to implement *refractive projection* the euclidean distance between the back-projected 3D point $\hat{\mathbf{P}}_i$ (according to Sect. 4.2) and the real model point $\mathbf{P}_i$ is minimized.

$$\mathbf{p}_{i,proj} = \underset{\mathbf{p}_{i,proj}}{\mathrm{argmin}} \| \mathbf{P}_i - \hat{\mathbf{P}}_i(\mathbf{K}, \mathbf{R}, \mathbf{C}, \delta\mathbf{C}_{dome}) \|^2 \tag{7}$$

In order to solve this equation, one can project a real model point $\mathbf{P}_i$ into image space at $\mathbf{p}_i$ as an initial guess by applying a standard perspective projection. Then a ray from $\mathbf{p}_i$ is shot back to 3D space according to Sect. 4.2. Afterwards, the intersection of the double refracted ray and the chessboard plane is computed by finding the point on the ray with Z-component equal to 0, which we consider the back-projected point. The residual is the euclidean distance of these two points, which we minimize using the Gauss-Newton algorithm to obtain the originally sought 2D projection $\mathbf{p}_{i,proj}$.

4.4   Calibration of Remaining Offsets

To compute the actual 3D offset of a camera from the dome center, an air-water image pair of a chessboard at the same position and orientation is acquired. In case the camera is perfectly centered, the corners in the two images will be exactly at the same location. Displacements indicate that there is refraction due to a centering offset (as the pose stayed the same). Assuming Gaussian noise on the detected chessboard corners, the estimation of the 3D offset $\delta\mathbf{C}_{dome}$ can be formulated in the Gauss-Markov model [13], essentially minimizing the energy:

$$E(\delta\mathbf{C}_{dome}) = \sum_{i \in \Omega} \| \mathbf{p}_{i,water} - \mathbf{p}_{i,proj}(\mathbf{p}_{i,air}, \delta\mathbf{C}_{dome}, \mathbf{K}, \mathbf{R}, \mathbf{C}) \|^2 \tag{8}$$

where $\mathbf{p}_{i,water}$ and $\mathbf{p}_{i,air}$ are obtained from the chessboard detection in water and in air separately. $\mathbf{R}$ and $\mathbf{C}$ encode the pose information of the camera relative to the chessboard which can be extracted from the set of in-air 3D-2D correspondences (standard pose estimation). $\mathbf{p}_{i,proj}$ is the projection of the chessboard point $\mathbf{P}_i$ through the dome port in the underwater case.

As an initial hypothesis for optimization, zero offset can be assumed, for which the projection yields to the in-air corner positions. We obtain the parameters according to Gauss-Newton optimization in the Gauss-Markov model as outlined in [13, Section 2]. The derivatives can be computed by finite differences approximation.

| (a) 0.1cm offset and 20cm depth | (b) 0.2cm offset and 20cm depth | (c) 0.1cm offset and 500cm depth | (d) 0.2cm offset and 500cm depth |

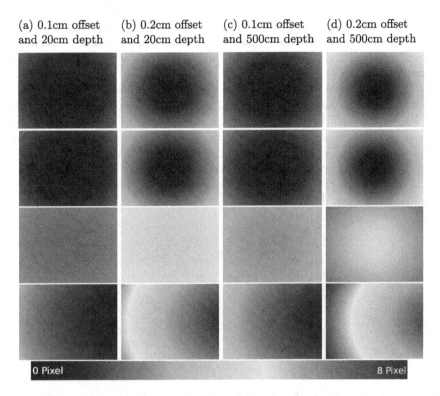

Fig. 6. Magnitude of simulated pixel distortions for different offsets between camera and dome port center. The Pixel are projected from a sphere around the dome port with different depths. From top to bottom: Offset directions forward along the principal axis, backwards along principal axis, orthogonal to principal axis and along a combined direction forward and orthogonal to principal axis (displacement enlarged by $\sqrt{2}$).

5   Evaluation

In order to obtain better insights into the observable magnitudes of refraction, first synthetic ground truth experiments are performed that resemble the parameters of our real 50 mm dome port for close range photogrammetry (20 cm) or mapping from a distance (5 m). The virtual camera was placed at positions with different offsets to the dome center. 3D points on the plane were projected to the image space by using standard perspective projection and dome port refractive projection. The magnitude of pixel displacement between different projections are visualized in Fig. 6.

Simulated Data. To validate the offset estimation algorithm, 3D chessboard coordinates with square size 20 cm × 20 cm were simulated, taken by a camera with image resolution of 1280 × 1024, focal length $f_x = f_y = 1700$ and principal point $c_x = 640.5$, $c_y = 512.5$. The dome port was simulated with radius of 50 mm and thickness of 7 mm. The chessboard corners were projected onto the image plane using standard perspective projection and refractive dome port projection, in order to generate in-air and in-water "image pairs". Afterwards, Gaussian noise with different noise level was added to the simulated points in the images.

In this experiment, the camera was simulated at different positions with respect to the dome port: $\delta_1 = (0.01, 0.01, 0.01)$, $\delta_2 = (0.002, 0.003, 0.004)$. The noise level σ varies from 0.1 pixels to 0.5 pixels, we performed 50 trials on each position and each noise level. The average absolute value of the relative error is measured between estimated parameters and ground truth. As it is shown in Fig. 7, δ_x and δ_y always give better estimates than δ_z. The main reason is that the offset along the principal axis has less effect on the image displacement compared to the side directions.

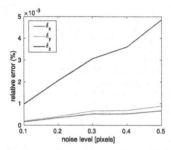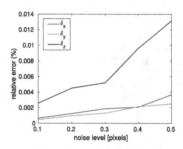

Fig. 7. Error of estimated offset parameters for different Gaussian noise levels. Left: simulated camera at offset $\delta_1 = (0.01, 0.01, 0.01)$ with respect to dome port. Right: simulated camera at offset $\delta_2 = (0.002, 0.003, 0.004)$.

Calibration Validation Using an Acrylic Dome. The proposed method was then examined on real data. This experiment aims to verify the calculation of offsets between camera and dome center. The setup consists of a low cost webcam within an acrylic dome, which has a radius of 77.45 mm and thickness of 2.4 mm.

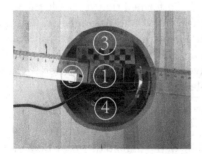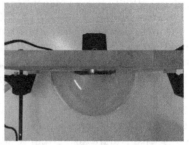

Fig. 8. Experimental settings of the webcam with an acrylic dome. Left: Top view with test positions, Right: Side view.

The in-air calibration of the webcam was performed using a standard toolbox [2]. During the experiments, the webcam was placed at different positions in the dome port (see Fig. 8), which are described in terms of the initial position close to ① the center of the dome port: ② offset 15 mm along Z-axis, ③ offset 15 mm along Y-axis, ④ offset −15 mm along Y-axis, ⑤ offset 20 mm along X-axis. The calibration results are shown in Table 1.

Table 1. Calibration results of the low cost webcam with acrylic dome ports

	Offsets			Residual [pixel]	
	δ_x [mm]	δ_y [mm]	δ_z [mm]	Before calibration	After calibration
Test ①	0.8071	3.3953	1.8441	5.6855	0.8051
Test ②	1.5459	4.5547	15.7268	7.8347	0.6356
Test ③	−0.6054	17.6406	−0.7525	30.1930	1.6123
Test ④	1.1253	−11.7163	5.2843	19.2762	0.8741
Test ⑤	−14.3336	0.3173	0.1010	23.8291	0.5925

The experiment shows that the proposed calibration algorithm provides reasonable offset values. When using the computed offsets, the residuals of the re-projection error are significantly improved and the computed offsets agree very well with the physically measured offsets. Remaining differences can be explained by the inaccurate experiment setup and the imperfection of the cheap acrylic dome which is not an optical instrument.

Deep Sea Glass Dome Stereo System. The proposed technique has also been applied to a stereo camera system (two Basler cameras with 1280×1024 resolution) with high quality glass domes (radius 50.10 mm and thickness 7 mm). The cameras were first mechanically adjusted according to the proposed approach of Sect. 3. The result of the mechanical adjustment procedure can be seen in Fig. 2 (right), the calibration and evaluation results are shown in the Table 2.

Table 2. Calibration results of the stereo cameras with glass dome ports.

	Offsets			Residual [pixel]	
	δ_x [mm]	δ_y [mm]	δ_z [mm]	Before calibration	After calibration
Master camera	0.0490	0.5033	−0.2967	2.9552	0.2847
Slave camera	−0.2431	0.0012	0.0324	6.5177	0.4120

As it can be seen, the mechanical adjustment is able to align the camera center to the dome center in sub-millimeter accuracy.

As a second evaluation the stereo system is calibrated in air, and submerged into water. Then we plot the epipolar lines of some chessboard corners from left image to right image (see Fig. 9 left). Using the in-air calibration there are significant errors in the epipolar lines. Using the calibration of the offset of the dome port, the epipolar lines cross the corresponding chessboard corners in the right image almost perfectly (see Fig. 9 right), which demonstrates that the offset calibration is useful.

Fig. 9. Epipolar lines of chessboard corners from right camera plotted in left camera image. Left: before offset calibration, Right: after offset calibration.

6   Conclusion

To avoid refraction and to allow for using the pinhole camera model and well-known multiple view relations, dome ports can be used for underwater vision. However, it is important to position the camera exactly at the center of the dome, which is not an easy task because the dome port might actually only be a fraction of a sphere, rather than a half-sphere, or the center point might be hard to gauge because of the flange of the pressure housing, in particular for deep sea housings. At the same time, the nodal point of the camera cannot be seen easily and has to be measured in any case.

In this contribution we have shown a method with visual feedback to mechanically align the camera with the center of an optical dome port and have proven that we can achieve sub-millimeter accuracy using the method. Additionally, we have presented a new calibration algorithm based on an air-water image pair of a chessboard in order to estimate the remaining refraction effects. Using the calibration information, residual errors can be improved and epipolar geometry can be made much more consistent. The result can therefore be used as a correction term in photogrammetric measurements or could also be used to further improve the mechanical adjustment. On top of these new methods, we have also presented sensitivity analyses to provide intuition about expectable refraction given inaccurate alignments. Future work should integrate these findings into an underwater camera calibration toolbox.

Acknowledgements. The authors would like to thank Matthias Wieck for designing and manufacturing the mechanical alignment mount for the dome port camera system and Dr. Anne Jordt for sharing refraction source code. This publication has been cofunded by the German Research Foundation (Deutsche Forschungsgemeinschaft, DFG) – Projektnummer 396311425, through the Emmy Noether Programme. This publication also been cofunded by the European Union's Horizon 2020 research and innovation programme under grant agreement No. 690416-H2020-SC5-2015-onestage (ROBUST). The authors of this paper are also grateful for support from the Chinese Scholarship Council (CSC) for Yifan Song.

References

1. Agrawal, A., Ramalingam, S., Taguchi, Y., Chari, V.: A theory of multi-layer flat refractive geometry. In: CVPR (2012)
2. Bouguet, J.: Camera calibration toolbox for matlab. http://www.vision.caltech.edu/bouguetj/calib_doc/index.html. Accessed 19 May 2019
3. Drap, P.: Underwater photogrammetry for archaeology. In: da Silva, D.C. (ed.) Special Applications of Photogrammetry, Chap. 6. IntechOpen, Rijeka (2012). https://doi.org/10.5772/33999
4. Fryer, J.G., Fraser, C.S.: On the calibration of underwater cameras. Photogram. Rec. **12**, 73–85 (1986)
5. Grossberg, M.D., Nayar, S.K.: The raxel imaging model and ray-based calibration. Int. J. Comput. Vis. **61**(2), 119–137 (2005)
6. Hartley, R., Zisserman, A.: Multiple View Geometry in Computer Vision, 2nd edn. Cambridge University Press, New York (2004)
7. Harvey, E.S., Shortis, M.R.: Calibration stability of an underwater stereo-video system: implications for measurement accuracy and precision. Mar. Technol. Soc. J. **32**, 3–17 (1998)
8. Jordt, A., Köser, K., Koch, R.: Refractive 3D reconstruction on underwater images. Methods Oceanogr. **15–16**, 90–113 (2016). https://doi.org/10.1016/j.mio.2016.03.001. http://www.sciencedirect.com/science/article/pii/S2211122015300086
9. Kotowski, R.: Phototriangulation in multi-media photogrammetry. In: International Archives of Photogrammetry and Remote Sensing XXVII (1988)
10. Kunz, C., Singh, H.: Hemispherical refraction and camera calibration in underwater vision. In: OCEANS 2008, pp. 1–7, 15–18 September 2008. https://doi.org/10.1109/OCEANS.2008.5151967
11. Lavest, J.M., Rives, G., Lapresté, J.T.: Underwater camera calibration. In: Vernon, D. (ed.) ECCV 2000. LNCS, vol. 1843, pp. 654–668. Springer, Heidelberg (2000). https://doi.org/10.1007/3-540-45053-X_42
12. Luczynski, T., Pfingsthorn, M., Birk, A.: The pinax-model for accurate and efficient refraction correction of underwater cameras in flat-pane housings. Ocean Eng. **133**, 9–22 (2017). https://doi.org/10.1016/j.oceaneng.2017.01.029. http://www.sciencedirect.com/science/article/pii/S0029801817300434
13. McGlone, J.C. (ed.): Manual of Photogrammetry, 5th edn. ASPRS, Maryland (2004)
14. Menna, F., Nocerino, E., Remondino, F.: Optical Aberrations in Underwater Photogrammetry with Flat and Hemispherical Dome Ports, vol. 10332 (2017). https://doi.org/10.1117/12.2270765

15. Menna, F., Nocerino, E., Fassi, F., Remondino, F.: Geometric and optic characterization of a hemispherical dome port for underwater photogrammetry. Sensors **16**(1), 48 (2016). https://doi.org/10.3390/s16010048. http://www.mdpi.com/1424-8220/16/1/48

16. Moore, E.J.: Underwater photogrammetry. Photogram. Rec. **8**(48), 748–763 (1976). https://onlinelibrary.wiley.com/doi/abs/10.1111/j.1477-9730.1976.tb00852.x

17. Nocerino, E., Menna, F., Fassi, F., Remondino, F.: Underwater calibration of dome port pressure housings. In: ISPRS - International Archives of the Photogrammetry, Remote Sensing and Spatial Information Sciences, pp. 127–134, March 2016. https://doi.org/10.5194/isprs-archives-XL-3-W4-127-2016

18. PanoramicPhotoGuide: Finding the nodal point. https://panoramic-photo-guide.com/finding-the-nodal-point.html. Accessed 19 May 2019

19. PanoTools.org: Entrance pupil database. https://wiki.panotools.org/Entrance_Pupil_Database. Accessed 19 May 2019

20. Shortis, M.: Calibration techniques for accurate measurements by underwater camera systems. Sensors **15**(12), 30810–30826 (2015). https://doi.org/10.3390/s151229831. http://www.mdpi.com/1424-8220/15/12/29831

21. Song, Y., Köser, K., Kwasnitschka, T., Koch, R.: Iterative refinement for underwater 3D reconstruction: application to disposed underwater munitions in the baltic sea. In: ISPRS - International Archives of the Photogrammetry, Remote Sensing and Spatial Information Sciences XLII-2/W10, pp. 181–187 (2019). https://doi.org/10.5194/isprs-archives-XLII-2-W10-181-2019. https://www.int-arch-photogramm-remote-sens-spatial-inf-sci.net/XLII-2-W10/181/2019/

22. TheDigitalPicture: How to find the nodal point for your lens. https://the-digital-picture.com/News/News-Post.aspx?News=27452. Accessed 19 May 2019

23. Treibitz, T., Schechner, Y., Kunz, C., Singh, H.: Flat refractive geometry. IEEE Trans. Pattern Anal. Mach. Intell. **34**(1), 51–65 (2012). https://doi.org/10.1109/TPAMI.2011.105

24. Zhang, Z.: Flexible camera calibration by viewing a plane from unknown orientations. In: Proceedings of the International Conference on Computer Vision, pp. 666–673. Corfu, Greece (1999). http://www.citeulike.org/user/snsinha/article/238276

Training Auto-Encoder-Based Optimizers for Terahertz Image Reconstruction

Tak Ming Wong[1,2(✉)] ⓘ, Matthias Kahl[1,3] ⓘ, Peter Haring-Bolívar[1,3] ⓘ,
Andreas Kolb[1,2] ⓘ, and Michael Möller[1,4] ⓘ

[1] Center for Sensor Systems (ZESS), University of Siegen, 57076 Siegen, Germany
tak.wong@uni-siegen.de
[2] Computer Graphics and Multimedia Systems Group,
University of Siegen, 57076 Siegen, Germany
[3] Institute for High Frequency and Quantum Electronics (HQE),
University of Siegen, 57068 Siegen, Germany
[4] Computer Vision Group, University of Siegen, 57076 Siegen, Germany

Abstract. Terahertz (THz) sensing is a promising imaging technology
for a wide variety of different applications. Extracting the interpretable
and physically meaningful parameters for such applications, however,
requires solving an inverse problem in which a model function determined by these parameters needs to be fitted to the measured data.
Since the underlying optimization problem is nonconvex and very costly
to solve, we propose learning the prediction of suitable parameters from
the measured data directly. More precisely, we develop a model-based
autoencoder in which the encoder network predicts suitable parameters and the decoder is fixed to a physically meaningful model function,
such that we can train the encoding network in an unsupervised way.
We illustrate numerically that the resulting network is more than 140
times faster than classical optimization techniques while making predictions with only slightly higher objective values. Using such predictions
as starting points of local optimization techniques allows us to converge
to better local minima about twice as fast as optimizing without the
network-based initialization.

1 Introduction

Terahertz (THz) imaging is an emerging sensing technology with a great potential for hidden object imaging, contact-free analysis, non-destructive testing and
stand-off detection in various application fields, including semi-conductor industry, biological and medical analysis, material and quality control, safety and
security [4,14,27]. The physically interpretable quantities relevant to the aforementioned applications, however, cannot always be measured directly. Instead,
in THz imaging systems, each pixel contains implicit information about such
quantities, making the *inverse problem* of inferring these physical quantities a
challenging problem with high practical relevance.

© Springer Nature Switzerland AG 2019
G. A. Fink et al. (Eds.): DAGM GCPR 2019, LNCS 11824, pp. 93–106, 2019.
https://doi.org/10.1007/978-3-030-33676-9_7

As we will discuss in Sect. 2, at each pixel location $\boldsymbol{x}$ the relation between the desired (unknown) parameters $\overline{\boldsymbol{p}}(\boldsymbol{x}) = (\hat{e}(\boldsymbol{x}), \sigma(\boldsymbol{x}), \mu(\boldsymbol{x}), \phi(\boldsymbol{x})) \in \mathbb{R}^4$, i.e., the electric field amplitude $\hat{e}$, the position of the surface μ, the width of the reflected pulse σ, and the phase ϕ, and the actual measurements $g(\boldsymbol{x}) \in \mathbb{R}^{n_z}$ can be modelled via the equation $g(\boldsymbol{x}, z) = (f_{\hat{e}, \sigma, \mu, \phi}(z_i))_{i \in \{1, \ldots, n_z\}} + \text{noise}$, where

$$f_{\hat{e}, \sigma, \mu, \phi}(z) = \hat{e}\,\text{sinc}\,(\sigma(z - \mu)) \exp\left(-i(\omega z - \phi)\right), \tag{1}$$

$$\text{sinc}(t) = \begin{cases} \dfrac{\sin(\pi t)}{\pi t} & t \neq 0, \\ 1 & t = 0, \end{cases} \tag{2}$$

and $(z_i)_{i \in \{1, \ldots, n_z\}}$ is a device-dependent sampling grid z_{grid}. More details of the THz model are described in [32]. Thus, the crucial step in THz imaging is the solution of optimization problem of the form

$$\min_{\hat{e}, \sigma, \mu, \phi} \quad \text{Loss}(f_{\hat{e}, \sigma, \mu, \phi}(z_{grid}), g(\boldsymbol{x})), \tag{3}$$

at each pixel $\boldsymbol{x}$, possibly along with additional regularizers on the unknown parameters. Even with simple choices of the loss function such as an ℓ^2-squared loss, the resulting fitting problem is highly nonconvex and global solutions become rather expensive. Considering that the number $(n_x \cdot n_y)$ of pixels, i.e., of optimization problem (3) to be solved, typically is in the order of hundred thousands to millions, even local first order or quasi-Newton methods become quite costly: For example, running the build-in Trust-Region solver of MATLAB® to reconstruct a 446×446 THz image takes over 170 min.

In this paper, we propose to train a neural network to solve the per-pixel optimization problem (3) directly. We formulate the training of the network as a model-based autoencoder (AE), which allows us to train the corresponding network with real data in an unsupervised way, i.e., without ground truth. We demonstrate that the resulting optimization network yields parameters $(\hat{e}, \sigma, \mu, \phi)$ that result in only slightly higher losses than actually running an optimization algorithm, despite the advantage of being more than 140 times faster. Moreover, we demonstrate that our network can serve as an excellent initialization scheme for classical optimizers. By using the network's prediction as a starting point for a gradient-based optimizer, we obtain lower losses and converge more than 2x faster than classical optimization approaches, while benefiting from all theoretical guarantees of the respective minimization algorithm.

This paper is organized as follows: Section 2 gives more details on how THz imaging systems work. Section 3 summarizes the related work on learning optimizers, machine learning for THz imaging techniques, and model-based autoencoders. Section 4 describes model-based AEs in contrast to classical supervised learning approaches in detail, before Sect. 5 summarizes our implementation. Section 6 compares the proposed approaches to classical (optimization-based) reconstruction techniques in terms of speed and accuracy before Sect. 7 draws conclusions.

2   THz Imaging Systems

There are several approaches to realizing THz imaging, e.g. femtosecond laser based scanning system [7,12], synthetic aperture systems [8,20], and hybrid systems [15]. A typical approach to THz imaging is based on the Frequency Modulated Continuous Wave (FMCW) concept [8], which uses active frequency modulated THz signals to sense reflected signals from the object. The reflected energy and phase shifts due to the signal path length make 3D THz imaging possible.

In Fig. 1, the setup of our electronic FMCW-THz 3D imaging system is shown. More details on the THz imaging system are described in [8].

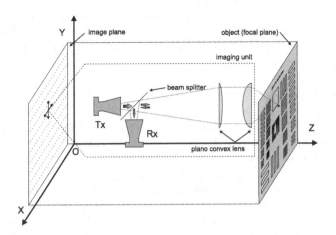

Fig. 1. THz 3D imaging geometry. Both transmitter (Tx) and receiver (Rx) are mounted on the same platform. The imaging unit, consisting of Tx, Rx and optical components, are moved along the x and y direction using stepper motors and linear stages. This imaging unit takes a depth profile of the object at each lateral position, in order to acquire a full THz 3D image.

In this paper, we denote by $g_t(\boldsymbol{x}, t)$ the measured demodulated time domain signal of the reflected electric field amplitude of the FMCW system at lateral position $\boldsymbol{x} \in \mathbb{R}^2$. In FMCW radar signal processing, this continuous wave temporal signal is converted into frequency domain by a Fourier transform [23,28]. Since the linear frequency sweep has a unique frequency at each spatial position in z-direction, the converted frequency domain signal directly relates to the spatial azimuth (z-direction) domain signal

$$g_c(\boldsymbol{x}, z) = \mathcal{F}\{g_t(\boldsymbol{x}, t)\}. \tag{4}$$

The resulting 3D image $g_c \in \mathbb{C}^{n_x \times n_y \times n_z}$ is complex data in the spatial domain, representing per-pixel complex reflectivity of THz energy. The quantities n_x, n_y, n_z resemble the discretization in vertical, horizontal and depth-direction, respectively. Equivalently, we may represent g_c by considering the real and imaginary parts as two separate channels, resulting a 4D real data tensor $g \in \mathbb{R}^{n_x \times n_y \times n_z \times 2}$.

Since the system is calibrated by amplitude normalization with respect to an ideal metallic reflector, a rectangular frequency signal response is ensured for the FMCW frequency dependance [8]. After the FFT in (4), the z-direction signal envelope is an ideal sinc function as continuous spatial signal amplitude, giving rise to the physical model given in (1) in the introduction.

In (1), the electric field amplitude $\hat{e}$ is the reflection coefficient for the material, which is dependent on the complex dielectric constant of the material and helps to identify and classify materials. The depth position μ is the position at which maximum reflection occurs, i.e., the position of the surface reflecting the THz energy. σ is the width of the reflected pulse, which includes information on the dispersion characteristics of the material. The phase ϕ of the reflected wave depends on the ratio of real to imaginary parts of the dielectric properties of the material. Thus, the parameters $\overline{p} = (\hat{e}, \sigma, \mu, \phi)$ contain important information about the geometry as well as the material of the imaged object, which is of interest in a wide variety of applications.

3 Related Work

Due to the revolutionary success (convolutional) neural networks have had on computer vision problems over the last decade, researchers have extended the fields of applications of neural networks significantly. A particularly interesting concept is to learn the solution of complex, possibly nonconvex, optimization problems. Different lines of research have considered directly learning the optimizer itself, e.g. modelled as a recurrent neural network [2], or rolling out optimization algorithms and learning the incremental steps, e.g. in the form of parameterized proximal operators in [18]. Further hybrid approaches include optimization problems in the networks' architecture, e.g. [1], or combining optimizers with networks that have been trained individually [5,21]. The recent work of Moeller et al. [22] trains a network to predict descent directions to a given energy in order to give provable convergence results on the learned optimizer.

Objectives similar to the one arising in the training of our model-based AEs are considered, for instance, for solving inverse problems with deep image priors [31] or deep decoders [11]. These works, however, consider the input to the networks being fixed random noise and have to solve an optimization problem for the networks weights for each inverse problems, such that they are regularization-by-parametrization approaches rather than learned optimizers.

The most related prior work is the 3D face reconstruction network from Tewari et al. [30]. They aimed at finding a semantic code vector from a given facial image such that feeding this code vector into a rending engine yields an image similar to the input image itself. While this problem had been addressed using optimization algorithms a long time ago [3] (also known under the name of analysis-by-synthesis approaches), the approach by Tewari et al. [30] replaced the optimizer with a neural network and kept the original cost function to train the network in an unsupervised way. The resulting structure resembles an AE in which the decoder fixed to the forward model and was therefore coined model-based AE. As we will discuss in the next section, the idea of model-based AEs generalizes far beyond 3D face reconstruction and can be used to boost the THz parameter identification problem significantly.

Finally, a recent work has exploited deep learning techniques in Terahertz imaging in [19], but the considered application of super-resolving the THz amplitude image by training a convolutional neural network on synthetically blurred images is not directly related to our proposed approach.

4   A Model-Based Autoencoder for THz Image Reconstruction

Let us denote the THz input data by $g \in \mathbb{R}^{n_x \times n_y \times n_z \times 2}$, and consider our four unknown parameters $(\hat{e}, \sigma, \mu, \phi)$ to be $\mathbb{R}^{n_x \times n_y}$ matrices, allowing each parameter to change at each pixel. Under slight abuse of notation we can interpret all operations in (1) to be pointwise and again identify complex values with two real values in order to have $f_{\hat{e},\sigma,\mu,\omega,\phi}(z_{grid}) \in \mathbb{R}^{n_x \times n_y \times n_z \times 2}$, where $z_{grid} = (z_i)_{i \in \{1,...,n_z\}}$ denotes the depth sampling grid. Concatenating all four matrix valued parameters into a single parameter tensor $\boldsymbol{P} \in \mathbb{R}^{n_y \times n_x \times 4}$, our goal can be formalized as finding $\boldsymbol{P}$ such that $f_{\boldsymbol{P}}(z_{grid}) \approx g$.

A classical supervised machine learning approach to problems with known forward operator is illustrated in Fig. 2 for the example of THz image reconstruction: The explicit forward model f is used to simulate a large set of images g from known parameters P which can subsequently be used as training data for predicting P via a neural network $\mathcal{G}(g; \theta)$ depending on weights θ. Such supervised approaches with simulated training data are frequently used in other image reconstruction areas, e.g. super resolution [9,16], or image deblurring [24,26]. The accuracy of networks trained on simulated data, however, crucially relies on precise knowledge of the forward model and the simulated noise. Slight deviations thereof can significantly degrade a network performance as demonstrated in [25], where deep denoising networks trained on Gaussian noise were outperformed by BM3D when applied to realistic sensor noise.

Instead of pursuing the supervised learning approach described above, we replace $\bar{p} = (\hat{e}, \sigma, \mu, \phi)$ in the optimization approach (3) by a suitable network $\mathcal{G}(g; \theta)$ that depends on the raw input data g and learnable parameters θ, that can be trained in an *unsupervised* way *on real data*. Assuming we have multiple examples g^k of THz data, and choosing the loss function in (3) as an ℓ^2-squared loss, gives rise to the unsupervised training problem

$$\min_{\theta} \sum_{\text{training examples } k} \|f_{\mathcal{G}(g^k;\theta)}(z_{grid}) - g^k\|_F^2. \tag{5}$$

As we have illustrated in Fig. 3, this training resembles an AE architecture: The input to the network is data g^k which gets mapped to parameters P that – when fed into the model function f – ought to reproduce g^k again.

Opposed to the straight forward supervised learning approach, the proposed approach (5) has two significant advantages

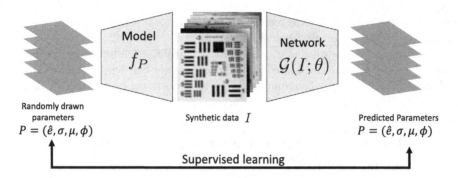

Fig. 2. Classical supervised learning strategy with simulated data: The forward model f_P (e.g. from (1)) is used to simulate data g, which can subsequently be fed into a network to be trained to reproduce the simulation parameters in a supervised way.

- It allows us to train the network in an *unsupervised* way, i.e., on real data, and therefore learn to deal with measurement-specific distortions.
- The cost function in (5) implicitly handles the scaling of different parameters, and therefore circumvents the problem of defining meaningful cost functions on the parameter space: Simple parameter discrepancies such as $\|P_1 - P_2\|_2^2$ for two different parameters sets P_1 and P_2 largely depend on the scaling of the individual parameters and might even be meaningless, e.g. for cyclic parameters such as the phase offset ϕ.

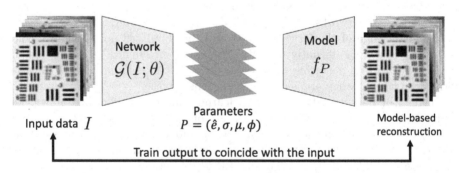

Fig. 3. A model-based AE for THz image reconstruction: The input data g is fed into a network $\mathcal{G}$ whose parameters θ are trained in such a way that feeding the network's prediction $\mathcal{G}(g; \theta)$ into a model function f again reproduces the input data g. Such an architecture resembles an AE with a learnable encoder and a model-based decoder and allows an unsupervised training on real data.

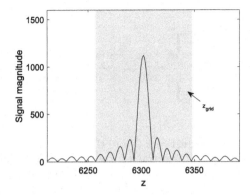

Fig. 4. Magnitude of a sample point of measured THz signal. The main lobe and major side-lobes are included in the grid window, which is colored in gray.

5 Encoder Network Architecture and Training

5.1 Data Preprocessing

As illustrated in the plot of the magnitude of an exemplary measured THz signal shown in Fig. 4, the THz energy is mainly focused in the main lobe and first side-lobes of the sinc function. Because the physical model remains valid in close proximity of the main lobe only, we preprocess the data to reduce the impressively large range of 12600 measurements per pixel. We, therefore, crop out 91 measurements per pixel centered around the main lobe, whose position is related to the object distance and to the parameter μ. Details of the cropping window are described in [32]. We represent the THz data in a 4D real tensor $g \in \mathbb{R}^{n_x \times n_y \times n_z \times 2}$, where $n_x = n_y = 446$, and n_z is the size of the cropping window, i.e. 91 in our case.

5.2 Encoder Architecture and Training

For the encoder network $\mathcal{G}(g; \theta)$ we pick a spatially decoupled architecture using 1×1 convolutions on g only, leading to a signal-by-signal reconstruction mechanism that allows a high level of parallelism and therefore maximizes the reconstruction speed on a GPU. The specific architecture (illustrated in Fig. 5) applies a first set of convolutional filters on the real and imaginary part separately, before concatenating the activations, and applying three further convolutional filters on the concatenated structure. We apply batch-normalization (BN) [13] after each convolution and use leaky rectified linear units (LeReLU) [10] as activations. Finally, a fully connected layer reduces the dimension to the desired size of four output parameters per pixel. To ensure that the amplitude is physically meaningful, i.e., non-negative, we apply an absolute value function on the first component. Interestingly, this choice compared favorably to a plain rectified linear unit when the network is trained.

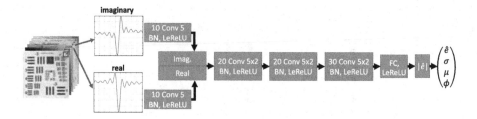

Fig. 5. Architecture of encoding network $\mathcal{G}(g; \theta)$ that predicts the parameters: At each pixel the real and imaginary part is extracted, convolved, concatenated and processed via three convolutional and 1 fully connected layer. To obtain physically meaningful (non-negative) amplitudes, we apply an absolute value function to the first component.

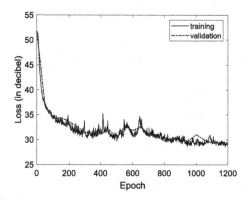

Fig. 6. The average losses of the training and validation sets over 1200 epochs on a decibel scale illustrate that there is almost no generalization gap between training and validation.

We train our model optimizing (5) using the Adam optimizer [17] on 80% of the 446×446 pixels from a real (measured) THz image for 1200 epochs. The remaining 20% of the pixels serve as a validation set. The batch size is set to 4096. The initial learning rate is set to 0.005, and is reduced by a factor of 0.99 every 20 epochs. Figure 6 illustrates the decay of the training and validation losses over 1200 epochs. As we can see, the validation loss nicely resembles the training loss with almost no generalization gap.

6   Numerical Experiments

We evaluate the proposed model-based AE on two datasets, which are acquired using the setup described in Sect. 2, namely the *MetalPCB* dataset and the *StepChart* dataset. The MetalPCB dataset is measured by a nearly planar copper target etched on a circuit board (Fig. 7a), which includes *metal* and *PCB* material regions, in the standard size scale of USAF target *MIL-STD-150A* [29]. After the preprocessing described in Sect. 5.1, the MetalPCB dataset

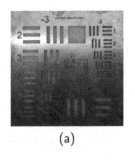

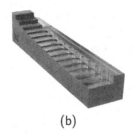

(a)   (b)

Fig. 7. Objects of evaluated datasets (a) MetalPCB dataset (b) StepChart dataset

has $446 \times 446 \times 91$ sample points. The StepChart dataset is based on an aluminum object (Fig. 7b) with sharp edges to evaluate the distance measurement accuracy using a 3D object. The StepChart dataset has $113 \times 575 \times 91$ sample points after preprocessing.

In order to evaluate the optimization quality on different materials and structures, MetalPCB dataset is evaluated in regions: *PCB region* is a local region that contains PCB material only, *Metal region* is a local region that contains copper material only, and *All region* is the entire image area. Similarly, the StepChart dataset is evaluated by 3 regions: *Edge region* is the region that contains physical edges, *Steps region* is the center planar region of each steps, and *All region* is the entire image area. This segmentation is done, because the THz measurements of the highly specular aluminum target results in strong multi-path interference artifacts at the edges that should be investigated separately.

The proposed model-based AE is trained on the MetalPCB dataset only, while the parameter inference is made for both the MetalPCB and StepChart datasets. This cross-referencing between two datasets can verify whether the proposed AE method is modelling the physical behavior of the system without overfitting to a specific dataset or recorded material.

To compare with the classical optimization methods, the parameters are estimated using the Trust-Region Algorithm (TRA) [6], which is implemented in MATLAB® . The TRA optimization requires a proper definition of the parameter ranges. Furthermore, it is very sensitive with respect to the initial parameter set. We, therefore, carefully select the initial parameters by sequentially estimating them from the source data (see [32] for more details). Still, the optimization may result in a parameter set with significant loss values; see Sect. 6.2.

The trained encoder network is independent of any initialization scheme as it tries to directly predict optimal parameters from the input data. While the network alone gives remarkably good results with significantly lower runtimes than the optimization method, there is no guarantee that the network's predictions are critical points of the energy to be minimized. This motivates the use of the encoder network as an initialization scheme to the TRA, specifically because the TRA guarantees the monotonic decrease of objective function such that using the TRA on top of the network can only improve the results. We abbreviate this approach to *AE+TRA* for the rest of this paper.

To fairly compare all three approaches, the optimization time of TRA and the inference time of the AE are both recorded by an Intel® i7-8700K CPU computation, while the AE is trained on a NVIDIA® GTX 1080 GPU. The PyTorch source code is available at https://github.com/tak-wong/THz-AutoEncoder.

6.1   Loss and Timing

Table 1. Loss and timing enhancement based on the proposed model-based AE

Dataset (Region)	Measurement	TRA	AE	AE+TRA
MetalPCB (All)	Average loss	693.9	886.3	**442.2**
MetalPCB (PCB)	Average loss	**589.0**	872.6	**589.0**
MetalPCB (Metal)	Average loss	519.6	446.1	**115.7**
StepChart (All)	Average loss	3815.1	5148.3	**3675.3**
StepChart (Edges)	Average loss	4860.4	6309.1	**2015.7**
StepChart (Steps)	Average loss	1152.5	2015.7	**1150.3**
MetalPCB	Training time (sec.)	**none**	9312.8	9312.8
MetalPCB	Run time (sec.)	10391.2	[a]**73.5**	[b]4854.7
StepChart	Run time (sec.)	3463.9	[a]**22.8**	[b]1712.4

[a] Inference time
[b] Run time is the sum of AE inference and TRA optimization time

In Table 1, the average loss in (5) and the timing are shown for the Trust-Region Algorithm (TRA), the Autoencoder (AE) and the joint AE+TRA approaches, respectively. We can see that the proposed encoder network achieves a lower average loss than the TRA method in the metal region of the MetalPCB dataset, it yields higher average losses than the TRA on both datasets. It is encouraging to see that although the AE was trained on the MetalPCB dataset, the relative performance in comparison to the TRA does not decay too significantly when changing to an entirely unseen data set with a different material, with the AE loss being 21.7% and 25.9% higher than the TRA loss on the MetalPCB and StepChart data sets, respectively. If such a sacrifice in accuracy is acceptable, the speed-up in runtime is tremendous with the AE being over 140 times faster than the TRA (for both methods being evaluated on a CPU). Note that even the sum of training and inference time are smaller for the proposed AE than the runtime of the TRA on the MetalPCB dataset.

Interestingly, the combined AE+TRA approach of initializing the TRA with the encoder network's prediction leads to better losses than the TRA alone in all regions. Additionally, the AE-initialized TRA converged more than 2 times faster due to the stopping criterion being reached earlier.

We note that the losses of all approaches are significantly higher for the StepCart data set than they are for the MetalPCB. This is because the aluminum StepChart object (Fig. 7b) has a more complex physical structure than the MetalPCB object, which results in a mixture of scattered THz pulses by multipath interference effects in all object regions. Incorporating such effects in the reflection model of (1) could therefore be an interesting aspect of future research for improving the explainability of the measured data with the physical model.

6.2   Quality Assessment of THz Images

In THz imaging, the *intensity* image I that is equal to the squared amplitude, i.e. $I = \hat{e}^2$ is the most important criteria for quality assessment. Note that the intensity could be inferred directly from the data by considering that (1) yields

$$f_{\hat{e},\sigma,\mu,\phi}(\mu) \cdot f^*_{\hat{e},\sigma,\mu,\phi}(\mu) = \hat{e}^2 \cdot \text{sinc}^2(0) = \hat{e}^2 = I \qquad (6)$$

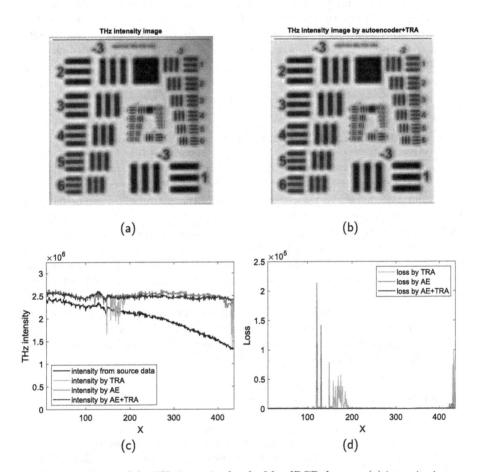

(a)   (b)

(c)   (d)

Fig. 8. Comparison of the THz intensity for the MetalPCB dataset: (a) intensity image extracted from the source data without any model-based processing (in red: the pixel line for plots (c) and (d)); (b) image extracted by the proposed AE+TRA approach (in red: the pixel line for plots (c) and (d)); (c) plot of the intensity extracted along the horizontal line in the copper region; (d) plot of the per-pixel loss by TRA, AE, and AE+TRA approaches along the horizontal line in the copper region. (Color figure online)

where f^* is the complex conjugate of f. As we illustrate in Fig. 8, the model-based approach is not only capable of extracting all relevant parameters, i.e., $\hat{e}$, μ, σ and ϕ, but, compared to values directly extracted from the source data, the resulting intensity I is more homogeneous in homogeneous material regions. The homogeneity of the directly extracted intensity results from the very low depth of field of THz imaging systems in general, combined with the slight non-planarity of the MetalPCB target. As depicted in Fig. 8c, the intensity variations along the selected line in the homogeneous copper region are reduced using the three model-based methods, i.e. TRA, AE, and AE+TRA. However, due to the crucial selection of the initial parameters (see discussion at the beginning of Sect. 6), the TRA optimization results exhibit significant amplitude fluctuations and loss values (Fig. 8d) in the two horizontal sub-regions $x \in [150, 200]$ and $x > 430$. The proposed AE and AE+TRA methods, however, deliver superior results with respect to the main quality measure applied in THz imaging, i.e. to the intensity homogeneity and the loss in model fitting. Still, the AE approach shows very few extreme loss values, while the AE+TRA method's loss values are consistently low along the selected line in the homogeneous copper region.

7   Conclusions and Future Work

In this paper, we propose a model-based autoencoder for THz image reconstruction. Comparing to a classical Trust-Region optimizer, the proposed autoencoder gets within 25% margin to the objective value of the optimizer, while being more than 140 times faster. Using the network's prediction as an initialization to a gradient-based optimization scheme improves the result over a plain optimization scheme in terms of objective values while still being two times faster. We believe that these are very promising results for training optimizers/initialization schemes for parameter identification problems in general by exploiting the idea of model-based autoencoders for unsupervised learning.

Future research will include exploiting spatial information during the reconstruction as well as considering joint parameter identification and reconstruction problems such as denoising, sharpening, and super-resolving parameter images such as the amplitude images shown in Fig. 8b.

References

1. Amos, B., Kolter, J.Z.: OptNet: differentiable optimization as a layer in neural networks. In: Proceedings of International Conference on Machine Learning (2017)
2. Andrychowicz, M., et al.: Learning to learn by gradient descent by gradient descent. In: Proceedings of International Conference on Neural Information Processing Systems (NIPS) (2016)
3. Blanz, V., Vetter, T.: A morphable model for the synthesis of 3d faces. In: Proceedings of SIGGRAPH, pp. 187–194. ACM Press/Addison-Wesley Publishing Co., New York, NY, USA (1999). https://doi.org/10.1145/311535.311556
4. Chan, W.L., Deibel, J., Mittleman, D.M.: Imaging with terahertz radiation. Rep. Prog. Phys. **70**(8), 1325 (2007)

5. Chang, J.H., Li, C.L., Poczos, B., Kumar, B.V., Sankaranarayanan, A.: One network to solve them all – solving linear inverse problems using deep projection models. In: Proceedings of IEEE International Conference on Computer Vision (2017)
6. Coleman, T.F., Li, Y.: An interior trust region approach for nonlinear minimization subject to bounds. SIAM J. Optim. **6**(2), 418–445 (1996)
7. Cooper, K.B., Dengler, R.J., Llombart, N., Thomas, B., Chattopadhyay, G., Siegel, P.H.: THz imaging radar for standoff personnel screening. IEEE Trans. Terahertz Sci. Technol. **1**(1), 169–182 (2011)
8. Ding, J., Kahl, M., Loffeld, O., Haring Bolívar, P.: THz 3-D image formation using sar techniques: simulation, processing and experimental results. IEEE Trans. Terahertz Sci.Technol. **3**(5), 606–616 (2013)
9. Dong, C., Loy, C.C., He, K., Tang, X.: Learning a deep convolutional network for image super-resolution. In: Fleet, D., Pajdla, T., Schiele, B., Tuytelaars, T. (eds.) ECCV 2014. LNCS, vol. 8692, pp. 184–199. Springer, Cham (2014). https://doi.org/10.1007/978-3-319-10593-2_13
10. Glorot, X., Bordes, A., Bengio, Y.: Deep sparse rectifier neural networks. In: Proceedings of the Fourteenth International Conference on Artificial Intelligence and Statistics, pp. 315–323 (2011)
11. Heckel, R., Hand, P.: Deep decoder: Concise image representations from untrained non-convolutional networks. In: International Conference on Learning Representations (2019)
12. Hu, B.B., Nuss, M.C.: Imaging with terahertz waves. Opt. Lett. **20**(16), 1716–1718 (1995)
13. Ioffe, S., Szegedy, C.: Batch normalization: Accelerating deep network training by reducing internal covariate shift. In: Proceedings of International Conference on Machine Learning (2015)
14. Jansen, C., Wietzke, S., Peters, O., Scheller, M., Vieweg, N., Salhi, M., Krumbholz, N., Jördens, C., Hochrein, T., Koch, M.: Terahertz imaging: applications and perspectives. Appl. Opt. **49**(19), E48–E57 (2010)
15. Kahl, M., et al.: Stand-off real-time synthetic imaging at mm-wave frequencies. In: Passive and Active Millimeter-Wave Imaging XV. vol. 8362, p. 836208 (2012)
16. Kim, J., Kwon Lee, J., Mu Lee, K.: Accurate image super-resolution using very deep convolutional networks. In: Proceedings IEEE Conference on Computer Vision and Pattern Recognition, pp. 1646–1654 (2016)
17. Kingma, D.P., Ba, J.: Adam: A method for stochastic optimization. arXiv preprint arXiv:1412.6980 (2014)
18. Kobler, E., Klatzer, T., Hammernik, K., Pock, T.: Variational networks: connecting variational methods and deep learning. In: Roth, V., Vetter, T. (eds.) GCPR 2017. LNCS, vol. 10496, pp. 281–293. Springer, Cham (2017). https://doi.org/10.1007/978-3-319-66709-6_23
19. Long, Z., Wang, T., You, C., Yang, Z., Wang, K., Liu, J.: Terahertz image super-resolution based on a deep convolutional neural network. Appl. Opt. **58**(10), 2731–2735 (2019)
20. McClatchey, K., Reiten, M., Cheville, R.: Time resolved synthetic aperture terahertz impulse imaging. Appl. Phys. Lett. **79**(27), 4485–4487 (2001)
21. Meinhardt, T., Moeller, M., Hazirbas, C., Cremers, D.: Learning proximal operators: using denoising networks for regularizing inverse imaging problems. In: Proceedings of IEEE International Conference on Computer Vision (2017)
22. Moeller, M., Möllenhoff, T., Cremers, D.: Controlling neural networks via energy dissipation (2019). https://arxiv.org/abs/1904.03081

23. Munson, D.C., Visentin, R.L.: A signal processing view of strip-mapping synthetic aperture radar. IEEE Trans. Acoust. Speech Signal Process. **37**(12), 2131–2147 (1989)
24. Nah, S., Hyun Kim, T., Mu Lee, K.: Deep multi-scale convolutional neural network for dynamic scene deblurring. In: Proceedings of IEEE Conference on Computer Vision and Pattern Recognition, pp. 3883–3891 (2017)
25. Plötz, T., Roth, S.: Benchmarking denoising algorithms with real photographs. In: Proceedings of IEEE Conference on Computer Vision and Pattern Recognition (2017)
26. Schuler, C.J., Hirsch, M., Harmeling, S., Schölkopf, B.: Learning to deblur. IEEE Trans. Pattern Anal. Mach. Intell. (PAMI) **38**(7), 1439–1451 (2016)
27. Siegel, P.H.: Terahertz technology. IEEE Trans. Microw. Theory Tech. **50**(3), 910–928 (2002)
28. Skolnik, M.I.: Radar Handbook. McGraw-Hill Book Co., New York (1970)
29. Standard, M.: Photographic lenses (1959). http://www.dtic.mil/dtic/tr/fulltext/u2/a345623.pdf
30. Tewari, A., et al.: MoFA: model-based deep convolutional face autoencoder for unsupervised monocular reconstruction. In: Proceedings of IEEE International Conference on Computer Vision (2017)
31. Ulyanov, D., Vedaldi, A., Lempitsky, V.: Deep image prior. In: Proceedings of IEEE Conference on Computer Vision and Pattern Recognition (2018)
32. Wong, T.M., Kahl, M., Haring Bolívar, P., Kolb, A.: Computational image enhancement for frequency modulated continuous wave (FMCW) THz image. J. Infrared Millimeter Terahertz Waves **40**(7), 775–800 (2019)

Joint Viewpoint and Keypoint Estimation with Real and Synthetic Data

Pau Panareda Busto$^{(\boxtimes)}$ (ID) and Juergen Gall (ID)

Computer Vision Group, University of Bonn, Bonn, Germany
s6papana@uni-bonn.de

Abstract. The estimation of viewpoints and keypoints effectively enhance object detection methods by extracting valuable traits of the object instances. While the output of both processes differ, i.e., angles vs. list of characteristic points, they indeed share the same focus on how the object is placed in the scene, inducing that there is a certain level of correlation between them. Therefore, we propose a convolutional neural network that jointly computes the viewpoint and keypoints for different object categories. By training both tasks together, each task improves the accuracy of the other. Since the labelling of object keypoints is very time consuming for human annotators, we also introduce a new synthetic dataset with automatically generated viewpoint and keypoints annotations. Our proposed network can also be trained on datasets that contain viewpoint and keypoints annotations or only one of them. The experiments show that the proposed approach successfully exploits this implicit correlation between the tasks and outperforms previous techniques that are trained independently.

1 Introduction

Many camera-based applications need to identify and analyse certain object classes for a better understanding of their surroundings. While 2D object detection is often a starting point, it is usually required to extract more detailed information from the detected objects. For instance, 2D keypoints provide additional details regarding the shape of an object and the 3D viewpoint provides the information about the orientation of an object. Both tasks, however, are correlated since the locations of the 2D keypoints depend on the orientation of the object and the 2D keypoints are a cue for the 3D orientation. In this work, we exploit this implicit correlation and introduce a joint model for 3D viewpoint and 2D keypoint estimation. The proposed network generalises the human pose estimator by Wei et al. [31] to multiple objects and it is trained jointly for the two tasks. For the 3D viewpoint estimation, we propose a simple yet effective multi-granular viewpoint classification approach.

The labelling process for training our network requires nonetheless large amounts of accurate labelled data. While human annotations excel in annotating object instances by bounding boxes, they fail to accurately estimate fine 3D viewpoints [18]. The same applies for annotating keypoints, which require

© Springer Nature Switzerland AG 2019
G. A. Fink et al. (Eds.): DAGM GCPR 2019, LNCS 11824, pp. 107–121, 2019.
https://doi.org/10.1007/978-3-030-33676-9_8

pixel precision and a correct handling of occlusions. In order to alleviate the collection of training data, we propose two solutions. Firstly, we design our network such that it can be trained with images from different datasets. The datasets can provide annotations for only viewpoints, keypoints or both. Secondly, we make use of synthetic data to increase the amount of training samples since computer generated images are a quick way to collect many training samples, as well as precise ground truth. Specifically, we introduce a novel synthetic dataset that includes not only viewpoints, but also accurate keypoints.

We evaluate our method on 12 popular classes of the *ObjectNet3D* [34] dataset, which contains both viewpoint and keypoint annotations. We demonstrate that our method outperforms current well established methods for multi-class viewpoint and keypoint estimation.

2 Related Work

2.1 Viewpoint Estimation

We divide viewpoint estimation techniques in two categories: regression methods that compute the pose by optimising in a continuous space [6,10,22] and classification-based methods that simplify the span of viewpoints into a limited set of discrete bins. From the latter, focus of our work, Liebelt and Schmid [13] optimise a multi-view linear SVM and classify local features to select the winning viewpoint based on a voting approach. Busto et al. [17,18] also use linear SVMs in a one-vs-all multi-class approach to refine coarse annotated viewpoints. Su et al. [25] propose a classification-based CNN model with one bin per degree, i.e. 360 bins for the azimuth angle, and a Gaussian function that spreads the optimisation to neighbouring bins. The training phase uses millions of synthetic samples to compensate the fine viewpoint representation. A coarser discretisations was proposed by Tulsiani and Malik [29], which showed better accuracies when trained on real data. Massa et al. [15] concluded that classification-based approaches obtain better viewpoint accuracies than regression techniques when jointly trained with an object detector in different popular CNN architectures. It has also been shown by Ghodrati et al. [8] that these methods using global features extracted from the 2D bounding boxes outperform more complex methods trained on 3D data. More recently, Divon and Tal [4] introduced a triplet loss to increase the dissimilarity of viewpoints that are far apart. Viewpoint estimation can also benefit from 3D object detections, as shown by Kehl et al. [11], who extended a popular real-time object detector with 3D viewpoint predictions.

Close in spirit to our work, other approaches already used the spatial information of keypoints to estimate accurate viewpoints. Torki and Elgammal [27] learn a regression function to compute the azimuth angle of vehicles based on pre-computed local features and their spatial arrangements. Pepik et al. [21] extend the deformable part model [5] to 3D objects, optimising at the same time the location and the viewpoint of the object for a fixed number of bins. Concretely for hand pose estimation, Zimmermann and Brox [37] compute the camera parameters by using keypoint confidence maps as input of the network.

A deep regression technique is presented by Wu et al. [32], where 2D keypoints are used to estimate the camera parameters after concatenating several fully connected layers. Lately, Grabner et al. [9] use the Perspective-n-Point algorithm to extract the viewpoint from a detected 3D bounding box.

2.2 Keypoint Estimation

Research in keypoint estimation has mostly been centred on human articulated poses [1,3,26,28]. In this paper, we expand the CNN model for human pose estimation proposed by Wei et al. [31], who optimised confidence maps for each keypoint. This model appends the later portion of the network several times, i.e., the input of the new stage comes from the output of the previous one, creating larger receptive fields. The deeper the stacked network the more it suppresses ambiguities and better captures the spatial layout of the keypoints. Newell et al. [16] refined this architecture by adding transposed convolutions at the end of each stage for finer confidence maps.

Previous to our work, keypoint estimation in rigid objects has already been in focus. Long et al. [14] initially addressed the capabilities of CNNs for keypoint estimation by dividing the last convolutional layer in smaller cells and training each keypoint as an independent class in a multi-class SVM. Moving towards a purely neural network approach, Tulsiani and Malik [29] concatenate the spatial information in a fully connected layer and only activate through the network those receptive fields that include the corresponding keypoints. The prediction is further refined with independently computed viewpoints. The human pose estimation by [16] has been modified by [19,36] to detected 3D keypoints of multiple rigid classes to consequently estimate the translation and rotation of the object by fitting the keypoints into a shape model.

2.3 Synthetic Data

Synthetic dataset has been used for many years to easily increase the amount of training samples in object detection tasks [20,23]. In recent years, new datasets based on computer generated models with accurate 3D pose information have been proposed. For instance, ShapeNet [2] provides a large dataset of 3D graphics models for hundreds of object classes. Its drawback comes from the low quality of most of their 3D models. From another perspetive, other approaches [30,33] compensate the lack of photo-realism in synthetic images by aligning 3D models with real samples for accurate 3D pose annotations.

3   Joint Viewpoint and Keypoint Estimation

In this work, we propose a multi-task network that leverages 3D viewpoint and 2D keypoint estimation. We assume that an object has been already detected and our goal is to estimate the keypoints as well as the viewpoint. Our network is trained for all object classes $C = \{c_1, \ldots, c_{|C|}\}$ where the number of keypoints

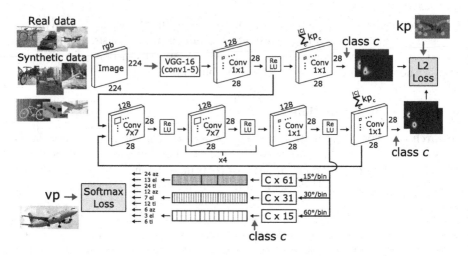

Fig. 1. Overview of the proposed multi-class CNN for joint viewpoint and keypoint estimation. The network uses a multi-stage architecture. The first row shows the first stage, which predicts for each keypoint per class a heatmap. For the later stages (second row), the features of the first and the previous stage after the last ReLU are used as input. At each stage, an L2-loss is used, which compares the predicted heatmaps for the class of the training sample to the ground truth heatmaps. After the last stage, additional layers for viewpoint estimation are added (third row). We use a multi-resolution loss where fully connected layers map the $128 \times 28 \times 28$ features to nine vectors corresponding to three different discretisations ($15°$, $30°$, $60°$) of azimuth (az), elevation (el) and tilt (ti).

per object class K_c varies. A second important aspect of the network is that it can be trained on various types of data including real and synthetic data at the same time. Since the data might be annotated for only one of the two tasks, $\mathcal{M}$ denotes the set of training samples with viewpoint and 2D keypoint annotations, $\mathcal{N}$ denotes the set with only viewpoint annotations and $\mathcal{O}$ the set with only keypoint annotations. An overview of the proposed CNN architecture is presented in Fig. 1. We first discuss the parts that are relevant for keypoint estimation.

3.1   Keypoint Estimation

The proposed network is a multi-stage architecture with intermediate loss functions after each stage and the first part is similar to the convolutional pose machines [31], which is a multi-stage network for 2D human pose estimation. The cropped image of an detected object is fed to a VGG-16 model [24] and additional convolutional layers are used to generate heatmaps for each keypoint and each object class. In total, we have $\sum_{c \in C} K_c$ heatmaps, where K_c denotes the number of keypoints of the c-th class. Since the object class c is known for an image during training, the L_2-loss is computed only for the heatmaps of the corresponding class. At the first stage $s = 1$, the loss is therefore given by

$$\mathcal{L}_{kp_s} = \sum_{x_i \in \{\mathcal{M}, \mathcal{O}\}} \frac{1}{K_{c_i}} \sum_{k=1}^{K_{c_i}} \left\| y_{i,k} - f_s(x_i)_{c,k} \right\|_2^2, \tag{1}$$

where x_i denotes a training sample from the set $\mathcal{M}$ or $\mathcal{O}$ and $f_s(x_i)$ denotes all heatmaps that are predicted for the stage s. The estimated heatmap for the k-th keypoint of class c is then denoted by $f_s(x_i)_{c,k}$ and $y_{i,k}$ is the corresponding ground-truth heatmap for the training sample x_i. The L2-loss is computed over all pixels in the heatmap, but we write $\|a - b\|_2^2$ instead of $\sum_{\omega \in \Omega} \|a(\omega) - b(\omega)\|_2^2$.

As in [31], we do not use one stage but 6 stages. For each stage except of the first one, we use the heatmaps of the previous stage and the feature maps of the first stage after the last ReLU layer as input. Since heatmaps are computed at each stage s, we sum the loss functions (1) over all stages, i.e., $\sum_s \mathcal{L}_{kp_s}$.

3.2   Viewpoint Estimation

As shown in Fig. 1, the proposed network not only predicts the 2D keypoints but also the 3D viewpoint encoded by the three angles $\{\phi, \psi, \theta\}$, which denote azimuth ($\phi \in [0°, 360°]$), elevation ($\psi \in [-90°, 90°]$) and in-plane rotation ($\theta \in [-180°, 180°]$), respectively. We opt for a classification-based approach to estimate the viewpoints and discretise each angle using a bin size of 15°. We obtain the probabilities for each bin by a fully connected layer and a softmax layer for each angle. The cross-entropy loss for bin size $b = 15°$ is then given by

$$\mathcal{L}_{vp_b} = \sum_{x_i \in \{\mathcal{M}, \mathcal{N}\}} \sum_{v \in \{\phi, \psi, \theta\}} - \log \left(f_b(x_i)_{c,v,v_i} \right), \tag{2}$$

where x_i denotes a training sample from the set $\mathcal{M}$ or $\mathcal{N}$, v_i denotes the ground-truth bin for angle v and $f_b(x_i)$ denotes the vector with the bin probabilities for all classes and angles. The estimated probability for the v_i-th bin of class c and angle v is then denoted by $f_b(x_i)_{c,v,v_i}$.

In addition, the network predicts during training the viewpoint for each class for two coarser discretisations of the angles, namely for 60° and 30°. In this way, the coarse discretisations guide the network to the correct bin of the finer discretisation and improve the accuracy as we will show as part of the experimental evaluation. The multi-task loss for the network is then expressed as

$$\mathcal{L} = \sum_s \mathcal{L}_{kp_s} + \sum_b \mathcal{L}_{vp_b}. \tag{3}$$

Since we aim at a finer viewpoint prediction than 15°, we upsample the estimated viewpoint probabilities to an angular resolution of 1° during inference. To this end, we interpolate the probabilities by applying a cubic filter [12] as illustrated in Fig. 2. For the azimuth and the in-plane rotation, we convolve the discrete bins as a circular array.

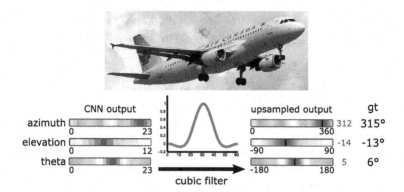

Fig. 2. Using a cubic filter, the probabilities of the viewpoint quantised at 15° are upsampled to an angle resolution of 1°. Note that we have 24 bins for azimuth and θ since they are circular, but only 13 bins for elevation where the 7th bin is centred at zero elevation and the outer bins have only 7.5°.

4 Experiments

In this section we evaluate the performance of our method, denoted as JVK (*Joint Viewpoint and Keypoints*), and compare its results with several popular viewpoint and keypoint estimation algorithms. We train our network for 12 popular object categories, i.e., $|C| = 12$, namely: *airplane, bicycle, boat, bottle, bus, car, chair, diningtable, motorbike, sofa, train* and *tvmonitor*. We then evaluate our method on the test images of the *ObjectNet3D* [34] dataset. The source code is available at https://github.com/Heliot7/viewpoint-cnn-syn.

4.1 Datasets

ObjectNet3D [34] is a large dataset that contains real images of 100 object categories. From all of them, the 12 classes that we selected include not just viewpoints from aligned 3D shapes, but also manually annotated keypoints. The selected subset is evenly separated between training and test data with 11421 and 11327 images, respectively. Most of the classes contain between 500 and 1000 samples in every set. The classes *bottle* and *diningtable* are above 1000 samples and *car* above 2000 samples.

ShapeNet [2] is a large-scale dataset of 3D shapes whose most relevant subset contains the 12 object categories, providing a considerable amount of models for each class. Although this setting allows for an extensive image dataset with a great variety of object orientations, the low quality of the renderings produce training samples that greatly differ from real images. This dataset only provides 3D viewpoints, automatically generated from the camera parameters in the image rendering. For our experiments, we make use of all models and generate 100000 images per class with random camera viewpoints, i.e., 1200000 images in total.

New Synthetic Data: In this work, we introduce a new synthetic dataset from 3D graphics models for the 12 object categories. For each class, we collect 10 graphics models with higher levels of realism and more detailed meshes compared to ShapeNet. In addition to the 3D viewpoint annotations that are directly extracted from the camera rotation, we go one step further and introduce automatically generated 2D keypoints. In order to easily obtain keypoints from synthetic data, we firstly set deformable spheres in the 3D rendered model locations that we consider to be valid using the keypoints from ObjectNet3D as reference. Figure 3a shows some 3D graphics models with spheres placed as keypoints. Then, we project the centre of each sphere to pixel coordinates for a given camera orientation to create the 2D keypoints. For the projection, we take occlusions into account. We generate synthetic data with 10000 samples per class with random orientations. Examples of rendered images are illustrated in Fig. 3b with the 2D bounding boxes and the visible 2D keypoints. The resulting images also include a background image from the KITTI dataset [7].

4.2   Network Configuration

We train the proposed CNN model for a total of 150000 iterations when using only real images for training, 250000 iterations when including one of the two synthetic datasets and 350000 iteration for all 3 datasets. The weight decay is set to 0.0005 and the learning rate to 0.00005, which is multiplied by 0.1 every 100000 iterations. The input image will be cropped in all experiments to 224×224 pixels while preserving the aspect ratio. The batch contains 20 samples per iteration where we sample uniformly across the datasets if we use more than one for training. In addition, standard data augmentation techniques are employed during the training of the network: flipping, in-plane rotation $[-45°, 45°]$, image scaling (0.4,1.0) and translation. However, we only add the transformed image if the intersection over union of the transformed bounding box compared to the original one is above 0.8.

For the test phase, we will extract the samples of each object class using their annotated 2D bounding boxes, i.e., without any prior object detector. We run 5 passes with different scaling factors and average all of them to obtain the final confidence map of keypoints and 3D viewpoints.

From our model, we analyse two modifications. In JVK-KP, we only train the keypoint estimation, ignoring the viewpoint extension. Then, JVK denotes the standard network for both keypoint and viewpoint sections. We also modify the training datasets that we utilise, combining the real samples from ObjectNet3D [34] with manually labelled viewpoints and keypoints (Re), ShapeNet [2] images with only viewpoints (Sh) and our novel synthetic dataset with generated viewpoints and keypoints (Sy).

(a) Rendered models with spheres as keypoints   (b) Generated 2D images

Fig. 3. In (a) we show renderings of our graphics models with spheres that represent each keypoint for *cars*, *chairs* and *motorbikes*. In (b) we provide some examples of automatically generated images with their 2D bounding boxes and the projected keypoints that are visible.

Table 1. Keypoint estimation on the ObjetNet3D dataset [34] for 12 object classes. We report the keypoint localisation metric (PCK) introduced by [35].

ObjectNet3D [34] (12 classes)		aero	bike	boat	bottle	bus	car	chair	dtable	mbike	sofa	train	tv	Avg.
PCK $\alpha = 0.1$	VpKp [29] (192)	74.4	80.6	60.7	81.9	80.7	89.6	71.1	52.4	78.0	76.2	57.4	47.1	70.8
	VpKp [29] (384)	80.1	88.6	70.7	90.0	93.7	96.5	76.7	65.4	85.2	89.1	68.7	78.7	82.0
	VpKp [29] (192-384)	84.1	90.0	74.4	91.3	94.4	97.5	84.9	73.3	87.4	91.0	71.3	80.1	85.0
	VpKp [29] (pLike)	82.7	90.7	69.2	92.6	95.8	95.6	89.5	76.3	85.9	92.5	72.0	80.3	85.3
	JVK-KP (Re)	85.7	92.7	74.8	**94.5**	98.1	98.4	89.4	83.9	89.7	93.8	73.4	75.7	87.5
	JVK (Re-Sh)	87.9	94.7	75.3	94.3	**98.6**	**98.5**	89.6	**84.5**	90.6	**94.0**	75.0	77.0	88.3
	JVK-KP (Re-Sy)	87.7	95.2	73.6	93.9	97.8	**98.5**	90.1	81.5	91.3	93.5	**75.2**	83.4	88.5
	JVK (Re-Sy)	88.8	95.2	75.1	93.6	98.0	**98.5**	90.9	83.6	91.2	93.8	73.3	82.3	88.7
	JVK (Re-Sy-Sh)	**89.5**	**95.9**	**77.1**	93.9	98.2	**98.5**	**91.5**	83.3	**93.0**	93.9	74.2	**84.0**	**89.4**

4.3 Keypoint Estimation

To measure the quality of our keypoint localisation, we use the PCK$[\alpha = 0.1]$ evaluation introduced by Yang and Ramanan [35]. An estimated keypoint is valid if the Euclidean distance with respect to the corresponding ground truth is below $\alpha \times max(h, w)$, where h and w are the height and width of the object's bounding box, respectively.

As a baseline, we compare our method with the popular keypoint estimation for rigid objects [29] (VpKp). We report the results of VpKp with 192×192 input resolution (192), 384×384 input resolution (384), both resolutions trained one after the other (192-384) and in a setting where the viewpoint is first estimated for the low resolution and used as input to refine the keypoints for the higher resolution (pLike).

We report the results in Table 1. Firstly, we observe that JVK-KP (Re), which uses the same real data as in VpKp, already outperforms all variations of VpKp. For instance, our method has $+2.2\%$ accuracy compared to VpKp (pLike). In contrast to VpKp that requires several sequential steps and higher resolutions, we only require a small amount of forward passes of our network with rescaled images. If we compare our modifications, we see a comparable improvement when including synthetic images with only keypoints, JVK-KP (Re-Sy), or only viewpoints, JVK (Re-Sh). This shows the benefits of estimating 3D viewpoint and 2D keypoints jointly. The network trained with all three training datasets (Re-Sy-Sh) obtains the best overall PCK accuracy, which is $+0.7\%$ higher compared to the result without Shapenet (Re-Sy).

4.4 Viewpoint Estimation

We evaluate our viewpoint estimation using two widely used metrics. The first metric [29] is the geodesic distance between the ground truth and predicted rotation matrices from ϕ, ψ and θ, which is given by

$$\Delta(R_{gt}, R_{pred}) = \frac{||log(R_{gt}^T R_{pred})||_F}{\sqrt{2}}. \tag{4}$$

The viewpoint is considered to be correct if the distance is below $\frac{\pi}{6}$ rad ($Acc\frac{\pi}{6}$). The second measure is the median error (MedError).

For this evaluation against other CNN-based approaches, we take as baseline a standard regression approach by [15], where continous angles are seen as a circular array and represented in $\mathbb{R}^2$. VpKp [29] proposes a classification-based viewpoint with also several discretisation levels. Then, Render4CNN [25] presents a very fine discretisation with Gaussian filters to leverage the neighbouring bins by using millions of synthetic images. Finally, we re-train a VGG-16 [24] model for testing different classification-based configurations (Class): with only one level of discretisation (15°), our proposed approach with 3 quantisations with 15°, 30° and 60°, and including the upsampling with cubic filtering (upsamp.).

The evaluation results for all the presented baselines and our configurations are shown in Table 2. Generally, we observe that the regression technique obtains similar results compared to other classification-based techniques. However, the cubic interpolation provides a significant reduction in median error and accuracy that favors classification approaches. Compared to the same configuration without upsampling, the error is reduced by $-1.6°$ and the accuracy increases by $+0.8\%$. The fine discretisaton of Render4CNN fails to compute robust viewpoints and ends up being the worst performing method by a large margin. Using real images from ObjectNet3D would not solve the problem, since the amount of training samples is too scarce for the large number of bins per angle. Class-15-30-60 outperforms Class-15, showing that learning several angle quantisations at the same time provides better results. When we compare JVK with Class, we observe that including a specific network for keypoint estimation allows for better viewpoint accuracies and reduced angle errors. JVK (Re) demonstrates to be superior compared Class upsampling (Re) by $+2\%$ in accuracy and $-1.7°$ in the median error. Although the gap is significantly smaller when training the networks with synthetic data, JVK trained with additional synthetic data achieves the best overall results. Specifically, the results of JVK trained on our new synthetic data are comparable to the ones using ShapeNet, but employing 10 times less samples. The better quality and additional labelled data of our dataset play an important role in improving the overall results.

4.5   Qualitative Results

For completeness, we also show some qualitative results in Fig. 4. For each class, we show the results for the first three test images of ObjectNet3D [34]. We observe that the predicted 2D keypoints and 3D viewpoints are in alignment. The majority of the few wrongly estimated keypoints and viewpoints are due to lateral symmetries of objects.

Table 2. Viewpoint estimation on the ObjectNet3D dataset [34] from ground truth bounding boxes. We report the percentage of estimated viewpoints with a geodesic error below $\pi/6$ rad ($Acc\frac{\pi}{6}$) and the median error (MedError).

ObjectNet3D [34] (12 classes)		aero	bike	boat	bottle	bus	car	chair	dtable	mbike	sofa	train	tv	Avg.
$Acc\frac{\pi}{6}$	Regression (Re) [15]	79.9	81.0	66.7	93.3	92.8	96.7	90.8	79.3	83.0	96.1	94.9	89.7	87.0
	VpKp (Re) [29]	88.7	79.4	74.3	91.7	96.7	96.3	92.2	82.3	80.8	95.4	95.7	83.1	88.0
	Render4CNN (Sh) [25]	71.0	76.1	45.1	83.7	86.3	89.9	88.5	63.0	68.4	90.4	82.3	92.3	78.1
	Class-15 (Re)	83.6	77.0	71.9	89.6	95.4	95.0	90.4	84.8	76.6	95.4	93.5	79.1	86.0
	Class-15-30-60 (Re)	85.8	81.5	71.9	92.4	96.1	95.9	92.7	85.5	81.1	95.1	94.6	83.7	87.9
	Class-15-30-60 upsamp. (Re)	86.7	82.5	73.5	92.8	95.9	96.6	93.1	85.7	81.6	96.0	94.5	85.2	88.7
	Class (Re-Sy)	88.4	85.8	76.5	94.5	96.9	96.8	95.6	86.5	88.5	96.5	94.3	87.5	90.7
	Class (Re-Sh)	91.5	85.4	80.3	94.5	97.6	97.3	97.5	86.8	86.6	97.8	95.5	89.9	91.7
	Class (Re-Sy-Sh)	90.7	85.7	81.0	93.8	98.0	97.1	97.9	88.3	88.5	97.9	94.6	90.3	92.0
	JVK (Re)	86.3	85.1	79.0	94.5	98.5	97.8	92.2	87.7	87.5	97.1	95.1	87.5	90.7
	JVK (Re-Sy)	89.8	88.9	78.6	95.5	98.3	97.4	93.5	87.3	90.5	97.2	94.0	88.9	91.7
	JVK (Re-Sh)	87.7	86.8	80.6	95.1	97.8	98.3	96.2	89.2	91.3	98.1	94.5	92.0	92.3
	JVK (Re-Sy-Sh)	87.8	87.0	79.8	95.0	98.7	97.5	96.0	86.6	90.7	98.3	95.8	92.7	92.2
MedError	Regression (Re)	13.4	16.7	18.6	8.2	4.3	4.8	9.9	11.5	16.4	9.1	6.4	13.0	11.0
	VpKp (Re) [29]	12.2	16.0	15.4	12.7	6.8	8.9	11.6	11.1	16.8	12.3	8.0	14.0	12.2
	Render4CNN (Sh) [25]	14.9	18.6	35.5	11.4	8.2	7.5	9.5	17.4	20.1	12.9	13.0	14.6	15.3
	Class-15 (Re)	13.0	17.0	15.8	10.0	5.9	8.1	10.3	9.3	18.1	11.7	8.1	15.0	11.9
	Class-15-30-60 (Re)	11.7	15.2	15.2	9.3	5.8	8.0	9.7	9.5	17.3	11.3	8.0	14.1	11.3
	Class-15-30-60 upsamp. (Re)	9.8	13.8	13.6	8.6	4.5	5.5	7.6	7.3	15.6	9.4	6.9	13.2	9.7
	Class (Re-Sy)	9.0	12.5	12.5	8.0	4.2	5.1	7.2	6.8	13.0	8.6	6.1	11.4	8.7
	Class (Re-Sh)	8.0	11.5	11.2	8.4	4.2	4.9	6.9	6.7	13.0	8.3	6.0	10.5	8.3
	Class (Re-Sy-Sh)	8.3	10.9	10.8	7.4	4.2	4.4	6.9	6.5	12.3	7.9	6.0	10.2	8.0
	JVK (Re)	8.5	11.2	12.3	7.5	4.1	3.7	7.3	6.1	12.4	8.1	5.5	9.7	8.0
	JVK (Re-Sy)	8.3	10.0	12.0	7.4	3.6	3.7	6.5	6.0	11.5	7.7	5.6	8.9	7.6
	JVK (Re-Sh)	8.4	10.4	11.2	7.4	4.0	3.9	6.5	5.6	12.1	7.5	5.7	9.6	7.7
	JVK (Re-Sy-Sh)	8.1	10.7	11.4	7.6	4.0	3.8	7.2	6.0	11.7	7.7	5.9	9.5	7.8

Fig. 4. Qualitative results for the proposed approach JVK (Re-Sy-Sh). The directional arrow represents the projected 3D viewpoint. Blue (dots) and red (crosses) denote correct and wrong estimations based on the PCK$[\alpha = 0.1]$ or Acc$(\pi/6)$ measure, respectively. (Color figure online)

5 Conclusion

In this paper we have presented an approach for joint viewpoint and keypoint estimation for multiple rigid object classes. The approach includes a simple yet effective branch for viewpoint estimation with different discretisation levels and cubic upsampling that produce more accurate results. In contrast to previous methods that train a separate approach for each task, we have shown that viewpoint and keypoint estimation benefit from each other. Our approach also handles different kinds of training datasets containing real or synthesized images, as well as datasets where only one of the tasks is annotated. We evaluated our approach on ObjectNet3D where it outperforms previous approaches.

Acknowledgement. The work has been supported by the ERC Starting Grant ARCA (677650).

References

1. Belagiannis, V., Zisserman, A.: Recurrent human pose estimation. In: IEEE International Conference on Automatic Face & Gesture Recognition, pp. 468–475 (2017)
2. Chang, A.X., et al.: Shapenet: An information-rich 3D model repository. CoRR abs/1512.3012 (2015)
3. Chu, X., Yang, W., Ouyang, W., Ma, C., Yuille, A.L., Wang, X.: Multi-context attention for human pose estimation. In: IEEE Conference on Computer Vision and Pattern Recognition, pp. 5669–5678 (2017)
4. Divon, G., Tal, A.: Viewpoint estimation–insights & model. In: IEEE European Conference on Computer Vision, pp. 252–268 (2018)
5. Felzenszwalb, P., Girshick, R., McAllester, D., Ramanan, D.: Object detection with discriminatively trained part-based models. IEEE Trans. Pattern Anal. Mach. Intell. **32**(9), 1627–1645 (2010)
6. Fenzi, M., Leal-Taixe, L., Rosenhahn, B., Ostermann, J.: Class generative models based on feature regression for pose estimation of object categories. In: IEEE Conference on Computer Vision and Pattern Recognition, pp. 755–762 (2013)
7. Geiger, A., Lenz, P., Urtasun, R.: Are we ready for autonomous driving? The KITTI vision benchmark suite. In: IEEE Conference on Computer Vision and Pattern Recognition, pp. 3354–3361 (2012)
8. Ghodrati, A., Pedersoli, M., Tuytelaars, T.: Is 2D information enough for viewpoint estimation? In: British Machine Vision Conference, pp. 1–12 (2014)
9. Grabner, A., Roth, P.M., Lepetit, V.: 3D pose estimation and 3D model retrieval for objects in the wild. In: IEEE Conference on Computer Vision and Pattern Recognition, pp. 3022–3031 (2018)
10. He, K., Sigal, L., Sclaroff, S.: Parameterizing object detectors in the continuous pose space. In: IEEE European Conference on Computer Vision, pp. 450–465 (2014)
11. Kehl, W., Manhardt, F., Tombari, F., Ilic, S., Navab, N.: SSD-6D: making RGB-based 3D detection and 6D pose estimation great again. In: IEEE International Conference on Computer Vision, pp. 1521–1529 (2017)
12. Keys, R.G.: Cubic convolution interpolation for digital image processing. IEEE Trans. Acoust. Speech Signal Process. **29**(6), 1153–1160 (1981)

13. Liebelt, J., Schmid, C.: Multi-view object class detection with a 3D geometric model. In: IEEE Conference on Computer Vision and Pattern Recognition, pp. 1688–1695 (2010)
14. Long, J.L., Zhang, N., Darrell, T.: Do convnets learn correspondence? In: Advances in Neural Information Processing Systems, pp. 1601–1609 (2014)
15. Massa, F., Marlet, R., Aubry, M.: Crafting a multi-task CNN for viewpoint estimation. In: British Machine Vision Conference (2016)
16. Newell, A., Yang, K., Deng, J.: Stacked hourglass networks for human pose estimation. In: IEEE European Conference on Computer Vision, pp. 483–499 (2016)
17. Panareda Busto, P., Gall, J.: Viewpoint refinement and estimation with adapted synthetic data. Comput. Vis. Image Underst. **169**, 75–89 (2018)
18. Panareda Busto, P., Liebelt, J., Gall, J.: Adaptation of synthetic data for coarse-to-fine viewpoint refinement. In: British Machine Vision Conference (2015)
19. Pavlakos, G., Zhou, X., Chan, A., Derpanis, K.G., Daniilidis, K.: 6-DoF object pose from semantic keypoints. In: IEEE International Conference on Robotics and Automation, pp. 2011–2018 (2017)
20. Peng, X., Sun, B., Ali, K., Saenko, K.: Learning deep object detectors from 3D models. In: IEEE International Conference on Computer Vision, pp. 1278–1286 (2015)
21. Pepik, B., Stark, M., Gehler, P., Schiele, B.: Teaching 3D geometry to deformable part models. In: IEEE Conference on Computer Vision and Pattern Recognition, pp. 3362–3369 (2012)
22. Pepik, B., Stark, M., Gehler, P., Ritschel, T., Schiele, B.: 3D object class detection in the wild. In: IEEE Conference on Computer Vision and Pattern Recognition: Workshops, pp. 1–10 (2015)
23. Pishchulin, L., Jain, A., Wojek, C., Andriluka, M., Thormählen, T., Schiele, B.: Learning people detection models from few training samples. In: IEEE Conference on Computer Vision and Pattern Recognition, pp. 1473–1480 (2011)
24. Simonyan, K., Zisserman, A.: Very deep convolutional networks for large-scale image recognition. CoRR abs/1409.1556 (2014)
25. Su, H., Qi, C.R., Li, Y., Guibas, L.J.: Render for CNN: viewpoint estimation in images using CNNs trained with rendered 3D model views. In: IEEE International Conference on Computer Vision, pp. 2686–2694 (2015)
26. Tompson, J., Goroshin, R., Jain, A., LeCun, Y., Bregler, C.: Efficient object localization using convolutional networks. In: IEEE Conference on Computer Vision and Pattern Recognition, pp. 648–656 (2015)
27. Torki, M., Elgammal, A.: Regression from local features for viewpoint and pose estimation. In: IEEE International Conference on Computer Vision, pp. 2603–2610 (2011)
28. Toshev, A., Szegedy, C.: Deeppose: Human pose estimation via deep neural networks. In: IEEE Conference on Computer Vision and Pattern Recognition, pp. 1653–1660 (2014)
29. Tulsiani, S., Malik, J.: Viewpoints and keypoints. In: IEEE Conference on Computer Vision and Pattern Recognition, pp. 1510–1519 (2015)
30. Wang, Y., et al.: 3D pose estimation for fine-grained object categories. In: IEEE European Conference on Computer Vision: Workshops (2018)
31. Wei, S.E., Ramakrishna, V., Kanade, T., Sheikh, Y.: Convolutional pose machines. In: IEEE Conference on Computer Vision and Pattern Recognition, pp. 4724–4732 (2016)
32. Wu, J., et al.: Single image 3d interpreter network. In: IEEE European Conference on Computer Vision, pp. 365–382 (2016)

33. Xiang, Y., Mottaghi, R., Savarese, S.: Beyond pascal: a benchmark for 3D object detection in the wild. In: IEEE Winter Conference on Applications of Computer Vision, pp. 75–82 (2014)
34. Xiang, Y., et al.: Objectnet3D: a large scale database for 3D object recognition. In: IEEE European Conference on Computer Vision, pp. 160–176 (2016)
35. Yang, Y., Ramanan, D.: Articulated pose estimation with flexible mixtures-of-parts. In: IEEE Conference on Computer Vision and Pattern Recognition, pp. 1385–1392 (2011)
36. Zhou, X., Karpur, A., Luo, L., Huang, Q.: Starmap for category-agnostic keypoint and viewpoint estimation. In: IEEE European Conference on Computer Vision, pp. 318–334 (2018)
37. Zimmermann, C., Brox, T.: Learning to estimate 3D hand pose from single RGB images. In: IEEE International Conference on Computer Vision, pp. 4903–4911 (2017)

Non-causal Tracking by Deblatting

Denys Rozumnyi[1][(✉)] [ID], Jan Kotera[2] [ID], Filip Šroubek[2] [ID], and Jiří Matas[1] [ID]

[1] Centre for Machine Perception, Department of Cybernetics, Faculty of Electrical Engineering, Czech Technical University in Prague, Prague, Czech Republic
rozumden@cmp.felk.cvut.cz
[2] Institute of Information Theory and Automation, Czech Academy of Sciences, Prague, Czech Republic

Abstract. Tracking by Deblatting (Deblatting = *debl*urring and m*atting*) stands for solving an inverse problem of deblurring and image matting for tracking motion-blurred objects. We propose non-causal Tracking by Deblatting which estimates continuous, complete and accurate object trajectories. Energy minimization by dynamic programming is used to detect abrupt changes of motion, called bounces. High-order polynomials are fitted to segments, which are parts of the trajectory separated by bounces. The output is a continuous trajectory function which assigns location for every real-valued time stamp from zero to the number of frames. Additionally, we show that from the trajectory function precise physical calculations are possible, such as radius, gravity or sub-frame object velocity. Velocity estimation is compared to the high-speed camera measurements and radars. Results show high performance of the proposed method in terms of Trajectory-IoU, recall and velocity estimation.

1 Introduction

The field of visual object tracking has received huge attention in recent years [6,7,20]. The developed techniques cover many problems and various methods were proposed, such as single object tracking [1,9,17,19], long-term tracking [10], methods with re-detection and learning [3,12,13,18], or multi-view [8] and multi-camera [14] methods.

Detection and tracking of fast moving objects is an underexplored area of tracking. In a paper focusing on tracking objects that move very fast with respect to the camera, Rozumnyi et al. [15] presented the first algorithm that tracks such objects, i.e. objects that satisfy the Fast Moving Object (FMO) assumption – the object travels a distance larger than its size during exposure time. The method [15] operates under restrictive conditions – the motion-blurred object should be visible in the difference image and trajectories in each frame should be approximately linear.

Recently, a method called Tracking by Deblatting[1] (TbD) has been introduced by Kotera et al. [5] to alleviate some of these restrictions. TbD performs significantly better than [15] and for a larger range of scenarios. The method solves two inverse problems of

---

[1] Deblatting = *debl*urring and m*atting*.

Electronic supplementary material The online version of this chapter (https://doi.org/10.1007/978-3-030-33676-9_9) contains supplementary material, which is available to authorized users.

G. A. Fink et al. (Eds.): DAGM GCPR 2019, LNCS 11824, pp. 122–135, 2019.
https://doi.org/10.1007/978-3-030-33676-9_9

  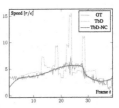

Tracking by Deblatting [5]   Non-causal trajectory estimation   Speed estimation

Fig. 1. Trajectory reconstruction using the proposed non-causal Tracking by Deblatting (middle) compared to the causal TbD [5] (left). Color denotes the trajectory accuracy, from red (complete failure) to green (high accuracy). Ground truth trajectory (yellow) from high-speed camera is shown under the estimated trajectory. Speed estimation is shown on the right. Ground truth speeds (olive) are noisy due to discretization and TbD speed estimation (lightgray) is inaccurate, which is fixed by the proposed TbD-NC (purple). (Color figure online)

deblurring and image matting, and estimates object trajectories as piece-wise parabolic curves in each frame individually.

In its core, TbD assumes causal processing of video frames, i.e. the trajectory reported in the current frame is estimated using only information from previous frames. Applications of detection and tracking of fast moving objects do not usually require online and causal processing. Moreover, non-causal trajectory estimation brings many advantages, such as complete and accurate trajectories, which were among TbD limitations, e.g. failures at contact with a player or missing detection.

We study non-causal Tracking by Deblatting and show that global analysis of FMOs leads to accurate estimation of FMO properties, such as nearly uninterrupted trajectory, velocity and shape. The paper makes the following contributions:

– We introduce global non-causal method, referred here as TbD-NC, for estimating *continuous* object trajectories by optimizing a global criterion on the whole sequence. Segments without bounces are found by an algorithm based on dynamic programming, followed by fitting of polynomials using a least squares linear program. Recovered trajectories give object location in every real-valued time stamp.
– Compared to the causal tracker, TbD-NC reduces by a factor of 10 the number of frames where the trajectory estimation completely fails.
– We show that TbD-NC increases the precision of the recovered trajectory to a level that allows good estimates of object velocity and size. Figure 1 shows an example.

2 Related Work

Tracking methods that consider motion blur have been proposed in [11, 16, 21], yet there is an important distinction between models therein and the problem considered here. Unlike in case of object motion, the blur is assumed to be caused by camera motion, which results in blur affecting the whole image and in the absence of alpha blending of the tracked object with the background.

To our knowledge, there are only a few published methods that tackle the problem of detection and tracking of motion-blurred objects. The first publication was the work by Rozumnyi et al. [15]. The method assumes linear motion and trajectories are calculated by morphological thinning of the difference image between the given frame and the estimated background. In this paper, the first dataset with FMOs was introduced, however it contains only ground truth masks without trajectories and it cannot be used to evaluate trajectory accuracy. Deblurring of FMOs also appeared in the paper by Kotera et al. [4], focusing only on deblurring without taking into account tracking or detection.

TbD [5] is the only method that uses motion blur and deblurring to improve tracking results and performs parametric fit to estimate intra-frame trajectories. The TbD dataset presented therein is another dataset with FMOs which contains ground truth trajectories and can be used for evaluating trajectory accuracy. A brief overview of TbD follows. The acquisition model with fast moving objects proposed in [5, 15] is defined as

$$I = H * F + (1 - H * M)B, \tag{1}$$

where $I: D \rightarrow \mathbb{R}^3$ is the current image frame defined in image domain $D \subset \mathbb{R}^2$, which is modelled by two terms. The first term is the motion-blurred object model F along the trajectory given by the blur kernel $H: D \rightarrow \mathbb{R}$. The second term represents the influence of the background B and it depends on the indicator function M of object model F. The blur is then modelled by convolution and the background is estimated as a median of previous 3 to 5 frames. The camera is assumed to be static. We consider color images in this work and the median operator as well as convolutions are performed on each color channel separately. TbD introduces a prior on the blur kernel H and it is represented in each frame t by a continuous trajectory function $C_t: [0, 1] \rightarrow \mathbb{R}^2$. The TbD outputs are individual trajectories C_t and blur kernels H_t in every frame. The outputs serve as inputs to the proposed TbD-NC method.

3   Non-causal Tracking by Deblatting

TbD-NC is based on post-processing of individual trajectories from TbD. The final output of TbD-NC consists of a single trajectory $C_f(t): [0, N] \subset \mathbb{R} \rightarrow \mathbb{R}^2$, where N is a number of frames in the given sequence. The function $C_f(t)$ outputs precise object location for any real number between zero and N. Each frame has unit duration and the object in each frame is visible only for duration of exposure fraction $\epsilon \leq 1$. Function $C_f(t)$ is continuous and piecewise polynomial

$$C_f(t) = \sum_{k=0}^{d_s} \bar{c}_{s,k} t^k \quad t \in [t_{s-1}, t_s], s = 1..S, \tag{2}$$

with S polynomials, where polynomial with index s has degree d_s and it is represented by its coefficient matrix $\bar{c}_s \in \mathbb{R}^{2,d_s}$. Columns of the matrix, denoted as $\bar{c}_{s,k} \in \mathbb{R}^2$, correspond to coefficients of two polynomials for x and y axis. The degree depends on the size of time-frame in which the polynomial is fitted to. Variables t_s form a splitting of the whole interval between 0 and N, i.e. that $0 = t_0 < t_1 < ... < t_{S-1} < t_S = N$.

Polynomials of degree 2 (parabolic functions) can model only free falling objects under the gravitational force. In many cases forces, such as air resistance or wind, also influence the object. They are difficult to model mathematically by additional terms. Furthermore, we would like to keep the function linear with respect to the weights. Taylor expansion will lead to a polynomial of higher degree, which means that these forces can be approximated by adding degrees to the fitted polynomials. We validated experimentally that 3rd and 4th degrees are essential to explain object motion in standard scenarios. Degrees 5 and 6 provide just a small improvement, whereas degrees higher than 6 tend to overfit. Circular motion can also be approximated by (2).

A rough overview of the structure of the proposed method follows. The whole approach to estimate the piecewise polynomial function (2) is based on three main steps. In the first step, the sequence is decomposed into non-intersecting parts. Each part is converted into a discrete trajectory by minimizing using dynamic programming an energy function which combines information from partial trajectories estimated by the causal TbD, curvature penalizer to force smooth trajectories and constraints on start and end points. In the second step, the discrete trajectory is further decomposed into segments by detecting bounces. Then, segments define frames which are used for fitting each polynomial. In the third step, polynomials of orders up to six are fitted into segments without bounces, which define the final trajectory function $C_f(t)$.

Splitting into Segments. When tracking fast moving objects in long-term scenarios, objects commonly move back and forth, especially in rallies. During their motion, FMOs abruptly change direction due to contact with players or when they bounce off static rigid bodies. We start with splitting the sequence into differentiable parts, i.e. detecting *bounces* – abrupt changes of object motion due to contact with other stationary or moving objects. Parts of the sequence between bounces are called *segments*. Segments do not contain abrupt changes of motion and can be approximated by polynomial functions. Theoretically, causal TbD could detect bounces by fitting piecewise linear functions in one frame, but usually blur kernels are noisy and detecting bounces in just one frame is unstable. This inherent TbD instability can be fixed by non-causal processing.

To find segments and bounces, we split the sequence into *non-intersecting parts* where the object does not intersect its own trajectory, i.e. either horizontal or vertical component of motion direction has the same polarity. Between non-intersecting parts we always report bounces. Energy minimization by dynamic programming is used to convert blur kernels H_t from all frames in the given non-intersecting part into a single discrete trajectory. The proposed dynamic programming approach finds the global minimum of the following energy function

$$E(P) = - \sum_{x=x_b}^{x_e} \sum_{t=t_s-1}^{t_s} H_t(x, P_x) + \kappa_1 \sum_{x=x_b+2}^{x_e} \left| (P_x - P_{x-1}) - (P_{x-1} - P_{x-2}) \right|$$
$$+ \kappa_2(C^x_{t_s-1}(0) - x_b) + \kappa_3(x_e - C^x_{t_s}(1)), \quad (3)$$

where variable P is a discrete version of trajectory C and it is a mapping which assigns y coordinate to each corresponding x coordinate. P is restricted to the image domain. The first term is a data term of estimated blur kernels in all frames with the negative sign in front of the sum which accumulates more values from blur kernels while our energy function is being minimized. The second term penalizes direction changes

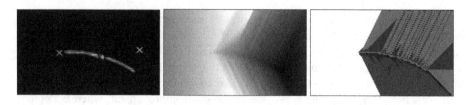

Fig. 2. Example of dynamic programming. Estimated discrete trajectory P is marked in red, starting point $C_{t_{s-1}}(0)$ by green cross, and ending point $C_{t_s}(1)$ by yellow cross. These points were deliberately moved further away to show robustness of the approach. Left image: accumulated blur kernels from two consecutive frames $H_{t_{s-1}}$ and H_{t_s} in joint coordinate system. Middle image: value of the energy function at each pixel from black (lowest) to white (highest). Right image: pixels where moving down by 1 is optimal are marked in dark green, down by 2 in bright green, up by 1 in dark red, up by 2 in bright red and moving straight in grey. Pixels, where reporting a starting point x_b is optimal, are white. The minimal value of the energy function is at the most right red pixel x_e in the left image. The whole trajectory is then estimated from right to left by backtracking until the next minimizing pixel is reported as a starting point (white space). (Color figure online)

and it is defined as the difference between directions of two following points and it is an approximation of the second order derivative of P. This term makes trajectories smoother and κ_1 serves as a smoothing parameter. The last two terms enforce that the starting point and the ending point are not far from the ones in the non-intersecting part. $C_{t_{s-1}}^x(0)$ and $C_{t_s}^x(1)$ denote x coordinate of the starting point at frame t_{s-1} and the ending point at frame t_s of causal TbD output. Note that in the last two terms there is no absolute value function and the sign is different, because they try to make trajectories shorter and they compete with the first term which prefers longer trajectories, e.g. either making trajectory longer is worth it in terms of values in blur kernels. Without the first term, the optimal trajectory would be of zero length, i.e. just a point. Discrete trajectory P is defined from x_b until x_e and these two variables are also being estimated. The ending point $C_{t_s}(1)$ is assumed to be on the right side from the starting point $C_{t_{s-1}}(0)$, and the image is flipped otherwise. All κ_i parameters were set to 0.1.

The energy E (3) is minimized by a dynamic programming (DP) approach. Accumulated blur kernels H_t are sorted column-wise (H_t) or row-wise (H_t transpose) to account for camera rotation or objects travelling from top to bottom. For both options we find the global minimum of E and the one with lower energy is chosen. Let us illustrate the approach for the column-wise sorting. The row-wise case is analogous. DP starts with the second column and processes columns from left to right. We compute energy E for each pixel by comparing six options and choosing the one with the lowest E: either adding to the trajectory one pixel out of five nearest pixels in the previous column with y coordinate difference between $+2$ and -2, or choosing the current pixel as the starting point. Both the minimum energy (Fig. 2 middle) and the decision option (Fig. 2 right) in every pixel is stored. When all columns are checked, the minimum in (Fig. 2 middle) is selected as the end point and the trajectory is estimated by backtracking following decisions in (Fig. 2 right). Backtracking finishes when a pixel is reached with the starting-point decision (white in Fig. 2 right).

Fig. 3. TbD-NC processing steps. From left to right, top to bottom: causal TbD [5] output, splitting into segments, fitting polynomials to segments, final TbD-NC output. Top row: trajectories for all frames overlaid on the first frame, Trajectory-IoU accuracy measure color coded from red (failure) to green (success) by scale (top left corner). Bottom row: bounces between segments (magenta, red), fitted polynomials (green), extrapolation to the first and second frame (yellow). Arrows indicate motion direction. Best viewed when zoomed in a reader. (Color figure online)

When each non-intersecting part is converted into 1D signal, it becomes easier to find bounces. We are looking for points with abrupt changes of direction. When w pixels to the left and w pixels to the right of the given point have a change of direction higher than some threshold, then this point is considered a bounce. In case of circular motion with no hard bounces, the approach finds a most suitable point to split the circle. After this step, the sequence is split into segments which are separated by bounces.

Fitting Polynomials. The output discrete trajectory P has a two-fold purpose. First, it is used to estimate bounces and define segments, and second to estimate which frames belong to the segment and should be considered for fitting polynomials. To this end, we assign starting and ending points of each frame, i.e. $C_t(0)$ and $C_t(1)$, to the closest segment. For fitting we use only frames that completely belong to the segment, i.e. $C_t(0)$ and $C_t(1)$ are closer to this segment than to any other. The degree of a polynomial is a function of the number of frames ($N_s = t_s - t_{s-1} + 1$) belonging to the segment

$$d_s = \min(6, \lceil N_s/3 \rceil). \tag{4}$$

Fig. 4. Trajectory recovery for selected sequences from the TbD dataset. Top row: trajectories estimated by the causal TbD [5] overlaid on the first frame. TIoU (7) with ground truth trajectories from a high-speed camera is color coded by scale in Fig. 3. Bottom row: trajectory estimates by the proposed TbD-NC which outputs continuous trajectory for the whole sequence. The yellow curves underneath denote ground truth. Arrows indicate the direction of motion. (Color figure online)

The polynomial coefficients are found by solving a linear least-squares problem

$$\min_{\bar{c}_s} \sum_{t=t_{s-1}}^{t_s} \|\mathcal{C}_f(t) - \mathcal{C}_t(0)\|^2 + \|\mathcal{C}_f(t + \epsilon) - \mathcal{C}_t(1)\|^2 \\ \text{s. t.} \quad \mathcal{C}_f(t_{s-1}) = \mathcal{C}_{t_{s-1}}(0) \quad \text{and} \quad \mathcal{C}_f(t_s + \epsilon) = \mathcal{C}_{t_s}(1),$$

(5)

where s denotes the segment index. Equality constraints force continuity of the curve throughout the whole sequence, i.e. we get curves of differentiability class C^0. The least-squares objective enforces similarity to the trajectories estimated during the causal TbD pipeline. The final trajectory $\mathcal{C}_f$ is defined over the whole sequence and the last visible point in the frame t which is $\mathcal{C}_t(1)$ corresponds to $\mathcal{C}_f(t + \epsilon)$ in the sequence time-frame, where the exposure fraction ϵ is assumed to be constant in the sequence. The exposure fraction is estimated as an average ratio of the length of trajectories $\mathcal{C}_t$ in each frame and the distance between adjacent starting points

$$\epsilon = \frac{1}{N-1} \sum_{t=1}^{N-1} \frac{\|\mathcal{C}_t(1) - \mathcal{C}_t(0)\|}{\|\mathcal{C}_{t+1}(0) - \mathcal{C}_t(0)\|}.$$

(6)

Frames which are only partially in segments contain bounces. We replace them with a piecewise linear polynomial which connects the last point from the previous segment, bounce point found by dynamic programming and the first point from the following segment. Frames between non-intersecting parts are also interpolated by piecewise linear polynomial which connects the last point of the previous segment, point of intersection of these two segments and the first point of the following segment. Frames which are before the first detection or after the last non-empty $\mathcal{C}_t$ are extrapolated by the closest segment. Figure 3 shows an example of splitting a sequence into segments which are used for fitting polynomials. More examples of full trajectory estimation are in Fig. 4.

4   Experiments

Experiments are done on the TbD dataset [5] with the ground truth trajectories from a high-speed camera. We use Trajectory Intersection over Union (TIoU) proposed by Kotera et al. [5] to measure the accuracy of estimated trajectories, which is defined as

$$\text{TIoU}(\mathcal{C}, \mathcal{C}^*) = \int_t \text{IoU}\left(M^*_{\mathcal{C}(t)}, M^*_{\mathcal{C}^*(t)}\right) dt, \tag{7}$$

where the estimated trajectory $\mathcal{C}$ is compared to the ground-truth trajectory $\mathcal{C}^*$. The ground truth object appearance mask M^* is used to measure IoU at different points x on the trajectory, denoted by M^*_x. Time t is discretized into 10 evenly spaced time-stamps to approximate integral.

Table 1. TIoU (7) and recall (Rcl) on the TbD dataset – comparison of TbD, FuCoLoT, FMO methods and the proposed TbD-NC. FuCoLoT is a standard, well-performing [7], near real-time tracker. For each sequence, the highest TIoU is highlighted in italics and recall in bold.

Sequence	Frames	FuCoLoT [10]		FMO [15]		TbD [5]		TbD-NC	
		TIoU	Rcl	TIoU	Rcl	TIoU	Rcl	TIoU	Rcl
badminton_white	40	.286	0.39	.242	0.34	.694	0.97	*.783*	**1.00**
badminton_yellow	57	.123	0.22	.236	0.31	.677	0.91	*.780*	**1.00**
pingpong	58	.065	0.14	.064	0.12	.523	0.91	*.643*	**1.00**
tennis	38	.294	0.89	.596	0.78	.673	0.97	*.750*	**1.00**
volleyball	41	.496	0.79	.537	0.72	.795	0.97	*.857*	**1.00**
throw_floor	40	.275	0.63	.272	0.37	.810	**1.00**	*.855*	**1.00**
throw_soft	60	.463	0.95	.377	0.57	.652	0.97	*.761*	**1.00**
throw_tennis	45	.239	0.98	.507	0.65	.850	**1.00**	*.878*	**1.00**
roll_golf	16	.360	**1.00**	.187	0.71	.873	**1.00**	*.894*	**1.00**
fall_cube	20	.324	0.67	.408	0.78	.721	**1.00**	*.757*	**1.00**
hit_tennis	30	.330	0.93	.381	0.68	.667	0.93	*.714*	**1.00**
hit_tennis2	26	.226	0.79	.414	0.71	.616	0.83	*.682*	**0.92**
Average	39	.290	0.70	.352	0.56	.713	0.96	*.779*	**0.99**

Table 2. Comparison of TbD-NC with TbD [5]. TbD failure is defined as frames where TIoU (7) equals to zero. TbD-NC decreases the number of frames with failure by a factor of 10.

	TbD [TIoU]	TbD-NC [TIoU]	TbD [%]	TbD-NC [%]
TbD Fails	0.000	0.382	4.7	0.4
TbD TIoU> 0	0.744	0.800	95.3	99.6

Comparison to baselines on the TbD dataset is presented in Table 1. We use the recently introduced long-term tracker FuCoLoT [10] as a baseline standard tracker, the FMO method [15] as a baseline for a tracker specialized on fast moving objects and Tracking by Deblatting [5] (causal TbD with a template) as a well-performing method for establishing trajectories in each frame. The proposed TbD-NC outperforms all baselines in both recall and TIoU. Recall is 100% in all cases except one, where the first detection appeared only on the seventh frame and extrapolation to the first six frames was not successful. Table 2 shows that TbD-NC corrects complete failures of causal TbD when TIoU is zero, e.g. due to wrong predictions or other moving objects. TbD-NC also improves TIoU of successful detection by fixing small local errors, e.g. when the blur is misleading or fitting in one frame is not precise.

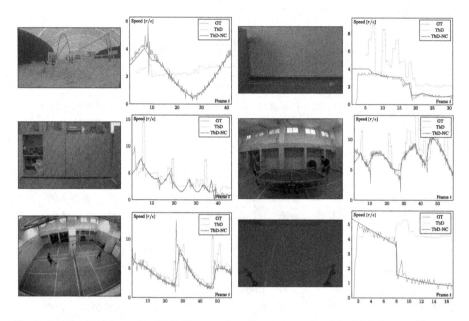

Fig. 5. Speed estimation using TbD-NC on selected sequences from the TbD dataset. Trajectories estimated by TbD-NC are overlaid on the first frame of each sequence. Graphs contain the speed estimation by TbD [5] (lightgray) and TbD-NC (purple) in radii per exposure compared to "ground truth" speeds (olive) calculated from high speed camera. The noise and oscillations in GT are caused by discretization. Mean differences to GT for all sequences are shown in Table 4. (Color figure online)

Speed Estimation. Tbd-NC provides the trajectory function $C_f(t)$, which is defined for each real-valued time stamp t between 0 and the number of frames. Taking the norm of the derivative of $C_f(t)$ gives a real-valued function of object velocity, measured in pixels per exposure. To normalize it with respect to the object, we divide it by the radius and report speed in radii per exposure. The results are visualized in Fig. 5 where sequences are shown together with their speed functions. The ground-truth speed was estimated from a high-speed camera footage having 8 times higher frame rate. The object center was detected in every frame and the GT speed was then calculated from the distance between the object centers in adjacent frames. Deliberately, we used no prior information (regularization) to smooth the GT speed and therefore it is noisy as can be seen in Fig. 5. We also report average absolute differences between GT and the estimated speed in Table 4. The error is mostly due to the noise in GT.

Speed Estimation Compared to Radar Guns. In sports, such as tennis, radar guns are commonly used to estimate the speed of serves. In this case, only the maximum speed is measured and the strongest signal usually happens immediately after the racquet hits the ball. Hrabalík [2] gathered the last 10 serves of the final match of 2010 ATP World Tour. The serves were found on YouTube from a spectator's viewpoint. Ground truth was available from another footage which showed the measured speeds from radar guns (example in Fig. 6). A real-time version of FMO detector in [2] achieved precise estimates of the speeds with the average error of 4.7%, where the error is computed as an absolute difference to the ground truth velocity divided by the ground truth velocity.

Unfortunately, the ATP footage from spectator's viewpoint is of a very poor quality and the tennis ball is visible only as several pixels. Deblurring does not perform well when a video has low resolution or the object of interest is poorly visible. To test only the performance of full trajectory estimation (TbD-NC), we manually simulated FMO detector by annotating only start and end points of the ball trajectory in several frames after the hit for every serve. Then the time-stamp t_{hit} is found, such that the final trajectory $C_f(t_{hit})$ at this point is the closest to the hit point. Then $\|C_f'(t_{hit})\|$ is the speed measured by TbD-NC. The pixel-to-miles transformation was computed by measuring the court size in the video (1519 pixels) and dividing it by the tennis standards (78 feet). The camera frame rate was set to the standard 29.97 fps. Additionally, due to severe camera motion, the video was stabilized by computing an affine

Table 3. Speed estimation compared to the radar gun (GT). We used the last 10 serves of the final match of 2010 ATP World Tour. The lowest error for each serve is marked in italics.

Serve	Duration [frames]	GT [mph]	Hrabalík [2] Speed [mph]	Error [%]	TbD-NC Speed [mph]	Error [%]
1	23	108	105.6	2.2	108.0	*0.0*
2	32	101	103.8	2.8	101.6	*0.6*
3	62	104	106.5	*2.4*	110.4	6.1
4	75	113	101.7	10.0	115.8	*2.5*
5	82	104	91.9	11.6	106.9	*2.8*
6	30	127	127.4	*0.3*	126.3	0.6
7	34	112	116.1	*3.7*	107.5	4.0
8	78	125	123.2	*1.4*	130.3	4.2
9	67	99	88.3	10.8	89.7	*9.4*
10	90	108	110.2	2.0	106.2	*1.6*
Mean	57	110.1	107.5	4.7	110.3	*3.2*

Spectator's view   Front view (speed in top left)   Cropped

Fig. 6. Radar gun measurements. Speed was automatically estimated by TbD-NC method from the video on the left. Ground truth acquisition from YouTube video is shown in the middle and the right images. Table 3 compares estimates to the ground truth.

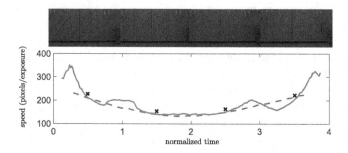

Fig. 7. Estimating the object velocity from blur kernels. In four consecutive frames (top row), object trajectories were estimated with TbD. The bottom plot shows the velocity calculated from the blur kernels (solid red) and the ground-truth (dashed blue line) obtained by a high-speed camera. Black crosses show the average velocity per frame calculated from the trajectory length. (Color figure online)

transformation between consecutive frames using feature matching as in [15]. Table 3 compares the speed estimated by TBD-NC and FMO methods to the ground truth from the radar. The proposed TbD-NC method is more precise than the FMO method and in several cases the speed is estimated with GT error close to zero.

Speed from the Blur Kernel. Apart from estimating speed by taking the norm of the derivative of $C_f(t)$, we can also directly estimate speed from the blur kernel H. The values in the blur kernel are directly proportional to time the object spent in that location. For example, if half of the exposure time the object was moving with a constant velocity and than it stopped and stayed still, the blur kernel will have constant intensity values terminated with a bright spot that will be equal to the sum of intensities of all other pixels. Estimating speed from blur intensity values is however not very reliable due to noise in H. Figure 7 illustrates a case where this approach works. All pixels in the blur kernel H which lay on the trajectory C are used for calculating the object velocity.

Shape and Gravity Estimation. In many situations, gravity is the only force that has non-negligible influence. Then, fitting polynomials of second order is sufficient. If parameters of the polynomial are estimated correctly, and the real gravity is given, then

Table 4. Estimation of radius, speed and gravity by TbD-NC on the TbD dataset [5]. The speed estimation is compared to GT from a high-speed camera. Radius is calculated when assuming Earth gravity, or vice versa. Standard object sizes are taken as GT for radius.

Sequence	Speed	Radius			Gravity	
	Mean Diff. $[r/\epsilon]$	GT [cm]	Est. [cm]	Err. [%]	Est. $[ms^{-2}]$	Err. [%]
badminton_white	0.57	–	–	–	–	–
badminton_yellow	0.65	–	–	–	–	–
pingpong	0.66	2.00	1.99	0.3	9.53	2.8
tennis	0.56	–	–	–	–	–
volleyball	0.45	10.65	10.47	1.7	10.50	7.2
throw_floor	0.61	3.60	3.47	3.7	10.21	4.2
throw_soft	0.42	3.60	3.72	3.3	9.52	2.9
throw_tennis	1.31	3.43	3.69	7.6	9.19	6.2
roll_golf	2.54	–	–	–	–	–
fall_cube	2.24	2.86	2.63	8.0	10.66	8.8
hit_tennis	0.43	–	–	–	–	–
hit_tennis2	1.28	–	–	–	–	–
Average	0.98	–	–	4.1	9.93	5.3

transforming pixels to meters in the region of motion is feasible. Gravity is represented by a parameter a, which has units $[px(\frac{1}{f}s)^{-2}]$, where the frame rate is denoted by f. If we assume the gravity of Earth $g \approx 9.8[ms^{-2}]$, f is known and a is estimated by curve fitting, the formula to convert pixels to meters becomes $p = g/(2af^2)$, where p are meters in one pixel on the object in motion. The radius estimation by this approach is shown in Table 4. Only half of the TbD dataset is used, i.e. sequences where the object was undergoing only motion given by the gravity (throw, fall, ping pong, volleyball). In other cases such as roll and hit, the gravity has almost no influence and this approach cannot be used. The badminton sequences have large air resistance and the tennis sequence was recorded outside during strong wind. When gravity was indeed the only strong force, the estimation has average error 4.1%. The variation of gravity on Earth is mostly neglectable, but knowing exact location where videos have been recorded might even improve results. Alternatively, when the real object size is known, we can estimate gravity, e.g. when throwing objects on another planet and trying to guess which planet it is. In this case, the formula can be rewritten to estimate g. Results are also shown in Table 4 and the average error is 5.3% when compared to the gravity on Earth. This shows robustness of the approach in both estimating radius and gravity.

Temporal Super-Resolution. Among other applications of TbD-NC are fast moving object removal and temporal super-resolution. The task of temporal super-resolution stands for creating a high-speed camera footage out of a standard video and consists of three steps. First, a video free of fast moving objects is produced which is called fast moving object removal. For all FMOs which are found in every frame, we replace them with the estimated background. Second, intermediate frames between adjacent frames are calculated as their linear interpolation. Objects which are not FMOs will look natural after linear interpolation. Then, trajectory $C_f(t)$ is split into the required number of pieces, optionally with shortening to account for the desired exposure fraction. Third, the object model (F, M) is estimated and used to synthesize the formation model with FMOs (1). Examples of these applications are provided in the supplementary material.

5   Conclusion

We proposed a non-causal Tracking by Deblatting (TbD-NC) which estimates accurate and complete trajectories of fast moving objects in videos. TbD-NC is based on globally minimizing an optimality condition which is done by dynamic programming. High-order polynomials are then fitted to trajectory segments without bounces. The method performs well on the recently proposed TbD dataset and complete failures appear 10 times less often. From the estimated trajectories, we are able to calculate precise object properties such as velocity or shape. The speed estimation is compared to the data obtained from a high-speed camera and radar guns. Novel applications such as fast moving objects removal and temporal super-resolution are shown.

Acknowledgements. This work was supported by the Czech Science Foundation grant GA18-05360S and the Czech Technical University student grant SGS17/185/OHK3/3T/13.

References

1. Danelljan, M., Hager, G., Shahbaz Khan, F., Felsberg, M.: Accurate scale estimation for robust visual tracking. In: Proceedings of the British Machine Vision Conference. BMVA Press (2014). https://doi.org/10.5244/C.28.65
2. Hrabalík, A.: Implementing and applying fast moving object detection on mobile devices, master's thesis. Czech Technical University in Prague, Faculty of Electrical Engineering (2017)
3. Kalal, Z., Mikolajczyk, K., Matas, J.: Tracking-learning-detection. IEEE Trans. Pattern Anal. Mach. Intell. **34**(7), 1409–1422 (2012). https://doi.org/10.1109/TPAMI.2011.239
4. Kotera, J., Šroubek, F.: Motion estimation and deblurring of fast moving objects. In: 2018 25th IEEE International Conference on Image Processing (ICIP), pp. 2860–2864, October 2018. https://doi.org/10.1109/ICIP.2018.8451661
5. Kotera, J., Rozumnyi, D., Šroubek, F., Matas, J.: Intra-frame Object Tracking by Deblatting. arXiv e-prints arXiv:1905.03633, May 2019
6. Kristan, M., et al.: The visual object tracking VOT2016 challenge results. In: Hua, G., Jégou, H. (eds.) ECCV 2016. LNCS, vol. 9914, pp. 777–823. Springer, Cham (2016). https://doi.org/10.1007/978-3-319-48881-3_54
7. Kristan, M., et al.: The sixth visual object tracking VOT2018 challenge results. In: Leal-Taixé, L., Roth, S. (eds.) ECCV 2018. LNCS, vol. 11129, pp. 3–53. Springer, Cham (2019). https://doi.org/10.1007/978-3-030-11009-3_1
8. Kroeger, T., Dragon, R., Van Gool, L.: Multi-view tracking of multiple targets with dynamic cameras. In: Jiang, X., Hornegger, J., Koch, R. (eds.) GCPR 2014. LNCS, vol. 8753, pp. 653–665. Springer, Cham (2014). https://doi.org/10.1007/978-3-319-11752-2_54
9. Lukežič, A., Vojíř, T., Zajc, L.C., Matas, J., Kristan, M.: Discriminative correlation filter with channel and spatial reliability. In: 2017 IEEE Conference on Computer Vision and Pattern Recognition (CVPR), pp. 4847–4856, July 2017. https://doi.org/10.1109/CVPR.2017.515

10. Lukežič, A., Zajc, L.Č., Vojíř, T., Matas, J., Kristan, M.: FuCoLoT – a fully-correlational long-term tracker. In: Jawahar, C.V., Li, H., Mori, G., Schindler, K. (eds.) ACCV 2018. LNCS, vol. 11362, pp. 595–611. Springer, Cham (2019). https://doi.org/10.1007/978-3-030-20890-5_38

11. Ma, B., Huang, L., Shen, J., Shao, L., Yang, M., Porikli, F.: Visual tracking under motion blur. IEEE Trans. Image Process. **25**(12), 5867–5876 (2016). https://doi.org/10.1109/TIP.2016.2615812

12. Moudgil, A., Gandhi, V.: Long-term visual object tracking benchmark. arXiv preprint arXiv:1712.01358 (2017)

13. Mueller, M., Smith, N., Ghanem, B.: A benchmark and simulator for UAV tracking. In: Leibe, B., Matas, J., Sebe, N., Welling, M. (eds.) ECCV 2016. LNCS, vol. 9905, pp. 445–461. Springer, Cham (2016). https://doi.org/10.1007/978-3-319-46448-0_27

14. Ristani, E., Tomasi, C.: Features for multi-target multi-camera tracking and re-identification. In: 2018 IEEE/CVF Conference on Computer Vision and Pattern Recognition, pp. 6036–6046, June 2018. https://doi.org/10.1109/CVPR.2018.00632

15. Rozumnyi, D., Kotera, J., Šroubek, F., Novotný, L., Matas, J.: The world of fast moving objects. In: 2017 IEEE Conference on Computer Vision and Pattern Recognition (CVPR), pp. 4838–4846, July 2017. https://doi.org/10.1109/CVPR.2017.514

16. Seibold, C., Hilsmann, A., Eisert, P.: Model-based motion blur estimation for the improvement of motion tracking. Comput. Vis. Image Underst. **160**, 45–56 (2017). https://doi.org/10.1016/j.cviu.2017.03.005

17. Tang, M., Yu, B., Zhang, F., Wang, J.: High-speed tracking with multi-kernel correlation filters. In: 2018 IEEE/CVF Conference on Computer Vision and Pattern Recognition, pp. 4874–4883, June 2018. https://doi.org/10.1109/CVPR.2018.00512

18. Tao, R., Gavves, E., Smeulders, A.W.: Tracking for half an hour. arXiv preprint arXiv:1711.10217 (2017)

19. Vojir, T., Noskova, J., Matas, J.: Robust scale-adaptive mean-shift for tracking. In: Kämäräinen, J.-K., Koskela, M. (eds.) SCIA 2013. LNCS, vol. 7944, pp. 652–663. Springer, Heidelberg (2013). https://doi.org/10.1007/978-3-642-38886-6_61

20. Wu, Y., Lim, J., Yang, M.: Online object tracking: A benchmark. In: 2013 IEEE Conference on Computer Vision and Pattern Recognition, pp. 2411–2418, June 2013. https://doi.org/10.1109/CVPR.2013.312

21. Wu, Y., Ling, H., Yu, J., Li, F., Mei, X., Cheng, E.: Blurred target tracking by blur-driven tracker. In: 2011 International Conference on Computer Vision, pp. 1100–1107, November 2011. https://doi.org/10.1109/ICCV.2011.6126357

Oral Session III: Learning

Group Pruning Using a Bounded-ℓ_p Norm for Group Gating and Regularization

Chaithanya Kumar Mummadi[1,2]($\boxtimes$) (ID), Tim Genewein[1] (ID), Dan Zhang[1] (ID),
Thomas Brox[2] (ID), and Volker Fischer[1] (ID)

[1] Bosch Center for Artificial Intelligence, Robert Bosch GmbH, Renningen, Germany
ChaithanyaKumar.Mummadi@de.bosch.com
[2] University of Freiburg, Freiburg im Breisgau, Germany

Abstract. Deep neural networks achieve state-of-the-art results on several tasks while increasing in complexity. It has been shown that neural networks can be pruned during training by imposing sparsity inducing regularizers. In this paper, we investigate two techniques for group-wise pruning during training in order to improve network efficiency. We propose a gating factor after every convolutional layer to induce channel level sparsity, encouraging insignificant channels to become exactly zero. Further, we introduce and analyse a bounded variant of the ℓ_1 regularizer, which interpolates between ℓ_1 and ℓ_0-norms to retain performance of the network at higher pruning rates. To underline effectiveness of the proposed methods, we show that the number of parameters of ResNet-164, DenseNet-40 and MobileNetV2 can be reduced down by 30%, 69%, and 75% on CIFAR100 respectively without a significant drop in accuracy. We achieve state-of-the-art pruning results for ResNet-50 with higher accuracy on ImageNet. Furthermore, we show that the light weight MobileNetV2 can further be compressed on ImageNet without a significant drop in performance.

1 Introduction

Modern deep neural networks are notoriously known for requiring large computational resources, which becomes particularly problematic in resource-constrained domains, such as in automotive, mobile or embedded applications. Neural network *compression* methods aim at reducing the computational footprint of a neural network while preserving task performance (e.g. classification accuracy) [4,34]. One family of such methods, *Network pruning*, operates by removing unnecessary weights or even whole neurons or convolutional featuremaps ("channels") during or after training, thus reducing computational resources needed at test time or deployment. A simple relevance-criterion for pruning weights is weight-magnitude: "small" weights contribute relatively little to the overall computation (dot-products and convolutions) and can thus be removed.

However, weight-pruning leads to unstructured sparsity in weight matrices and filters. While alleviating storage demands, it is non-trivial to exploit

---

T. Genewein—Currently at DeepMind.

© Springer Nature Switzerland AG 2019
G. A. Fink et al. (Eds.): DAGM GCPR 2019, LNCS 11824, pp. 139–155, 2019.
https://doi.org/10.1007/978-3-030-33676-9_10

unstructured sparsity for reducing computational burden during forward-pass operation. This effect becomes even more pronounced on today's standard hardware for neural network computation (GPUs), which is typically designed for massively parallel operation. In contrast to individual-weight pruning, neuron- and featuremap-pruning allows dropping whole slices of weight matrices or tensors, which straightforwardly leads to a reduction of forward-pass FLOPS, energy consumption as well as on- and off-line memory requirements. However, it is more intricate to determine the relevance of whole neurons/featuremaps than that of weights.

In this paper, we propose and evaluate a method for *group-wise* pruning. A group typically refers to all weights that correspond to a neuron or convolutional filter, but could in principle also be chosen to correspond to different sub-structures such as larger parts of a layer or even whole blocks/layers in architectures with skip-connections. The central idea of our method is the addition of a "trainable gate", that is a *parameterized, multiplicative factor*, per group. During training, the gate-parameter is learned for each gate individually, allowing the network to learn the relevance of each neuron/featuremap. After training, groups of low relevance can be straightforwardly identified and pruned without significant loss in accuracy. The resulting highly structured sparsity patterns can be readily used to reduce the size of weight-matrices or -tensors. An important aspect of our method is that we use a sparsity-inducing regularizer during training to force a maximally large number of gates towards zero. We empirically compare different choices for this sparsity-inducing regularizer and in addition to previously proposed ℓ_1 or ℓ_2 norms, we propose and evaluate a smoothened version of the ℓ_0 norm (which can also be viewed as a saturating version of an ℓ_p norm). The latter allows for a certain decoupling of parameter-importance and parameter-magnitude, which is in contrast to standard regularizers that penalize parameters of large magnitude regardless of their importance.

- We investigate the effect of group pruning using bounded ℓ_p norms for group gating and regularization on different network architectures (LeNet5, DenseNet, ResNet and MobileNetV2) and data-sets (MNIST, CIFAR100, ImageNet) achieving comparable or superior compression and accuracy.
- We show that our gating function drives the gating factors to become exactly zero for the insignificant channels during training.
- Applying ℓ_2 regularizer on our gating parameters, rather than on weights, leads to significant pruning for ResNet and DenseNet without a drop in accuracy and further improves the accuracy of MobileNetV2 on both CIFAR100 and ImageNet.
- We also propose a bounded variant of the common ℓ_1 regularizer to achieve higher pruning rates and retain generalization performance.

2   Related Work

Neural Network Compression. Most approaches in the literature resort to *quantization* and/or *pruning*. In this context, quantization refers to the reduction of required bit-precision of computation—either of weights only [3,9,12,40] or both weights and activations [5,11,20,33,38]. Network pruning attempts to reduce the number of model parameters and is often performed in a single step after training, but some variants also perform gradual pruning during training [7,12,14] or even prune and re-introduce weights in a dynamic process throughout training [10,13]. In contrast to individual weight pruning [12], group-pruning methods (pruning entire neurons or feature-maps that involve groups of weights) lead to highly structured sparsity patterns which easily translate into on-chip benefits during a forward-pass [2,36,41].

Pruning and quantization can also be combined [1,6,12,35]. Additionally, the number of weights can be reduced *before* training by architectural choices as in SqueezeNet [21] or MobileNets [17]. As we show in our experiments, even parameter-optimized architectures such as MobileNets can still benefit from post-training pruning.

Relevance Determination and Sparsity-Inducing Regularization. Many pruning methods evaluate the relevance of each unit (weight, neuron or featuremap) and remove units that do not pass a certain relevance-threshold [10,12,13,24]. Importantly, optimizing the relevance-criterion that is later used for pruning thus becomes a secondary objective of the training process—in this case via weight-magnitude regularization. An undesirable side-effect of ℓ_1- or ℓ_2-weight-decay [15] when used for inducing sparsity is that important, non-pruned weights still get penalized depending on their magnitude, leading to an entanglement of parameter-importance and magnitude. An ideal sparsity-inducing regularizer would act in an (approximately) binary fashion, similar to how the ℓ_0 norm simply counts number of non-zero parameters, but is not affected by the magnitude of the non-zero parameters. The problem of determining the relevance of model parameters has also been phrased in a Bayesian fashion via *automatic relevance determination* (ARD) and sparse Bayesian learning [22,28,31], which has recently been successfully applied to weight-pruning [29], weight ternarization [1] and neuron-/featuremap-pruning by enforcing group-sparsity constraints [6,8,25,32]. These methods require (variational) inference over the parameter posterior instead of standard training.

Neuron-/Featuremap-Pruning. Determining the importance of neurons or feature maps is non-trivial [2,36,41]. Approaches are based on thresholding the norm of convolutional kernels or evaluating activation-statistics. However, both approaches come with certain caveats and shortcomings [30,39]. Some methods try to explicitly remove neurons that do not have much impact on the final network prediction [18,23,30]. Other methods propose a more complex optimization procedure with intermediate pruning steps and fine-tuning [16,27], such that the non-pruned network can gradually adjust to the missing units.

Our approach is closely related to [26], who also use trainable, multiplicative gates for neuron-/featuremap-pruning. However, in their formulation gates Bernoulli random variables. Accordingly, learning of their gate parameters is done via (variational) Bayesian inference. In contrast, our method allows network training in a standard-fashion (with an additional regularizer term) without requiring sampling of gate parameters, or computing expected gradients across such samples. Other closely related works are [24,39], who induce sparsity on the multiplicative scaling factor γ of Batch Normalization layers and later use the magnitude of these factors for pruning channels/featuremaps. Similarly, [19] use a trainable, linear scaling factor on neurons/featuremaps with an ℓ_1-norm sparsity-inducing regularizer. We perform experiments to directly compare our method against all the above closely related works. Additionally, we reimplement the technique proposed by [24] and treat it as a baseline to compare our results against it in all experiments.

3 Bounded-$\ell_{p,0}$ Norm

The p-norm (a.k.a. ℓ_p-norm) and 0-norm of a vector $x \in \mathbb{R}^n$ of dimension n are respectively defined as:

$$\|x\|_p := \left(\sum_{i=1}^{n} |x_i|^p \right)^{1/p} \qquad \|x\|_0 := \sum_{i=1}^{n} (1 - \mathbf{1}_0(x_i)). \qquad (1)$$

Here, $\mathbf{1}_a(b)$ being the function which is one iff $a = b$ and zero otherwise. While the p-norms constitute norms in the mathematical sense, the 0-norm (a.k.a. *discrete metric*), does not due to the violation of the triangle inequality. It is constant everywhere and hence gradient based optimization techniques are unusable. We use a differentiable function adapted from [37], which around 0 interpolates, controlled by a parameter $\sigma > 0$, between the p- and 0-norm:

Definition 1. *For $\sigma > 0$, we call the mapping $\|.\|_{bound\text{-}p,\sigma} : \mathbb{R}^n \to \mathbb{R}_+$ with*

$$\|x\|_{bound\text{-}p,\sigma} := \sum_{i=1}^{n} 1 - exp\left(-\frac{|x_i|^p}{\sigma^p} \right) \qquad (2)$$

*the **bounded-$\ell_{p,0}$ norm** or **bounded-ℓ_p norm**. Figure 1 illustrates the bounded-$\ell_{p,0}$ norm with $p = 1, 2$ and different σ. One sees that $\|x\|_{bound\text{-}p,\sigma}$ is bounded to $[0, n)$ and differentiable everywhere except $x_i = 0$ for one or more coefficients of x. Further, in contrast to the 0-norm, it has a non-zero gradient almost everywhere.*

Lemma 1. *The bounded-$\ell_{p,0}$ norm has the following properties:*

- *For $\sigma \to 0^+$ the bounded-norm converges towards the 0-norm:*

$$\lim_{\sigma \to 0^+} \|x\|_{bound\text{-}p,\sigma} = \|x\|_0. \qquad (3)$$

- *In case $|x_i| \approx 0$ for all coefficients of x, the bounded-norm of x is approximately equal to the p-norm of x weighted by $1/\sigma$:*

$$\|x\|_{bound\text{-}p,\sigma} \approx \left\| \frac{x}{\sigma} \right\|_p^p \qquad (4)$$

Proof. See Sect. A1 for proof.

4   Methodology

With the use of the bounded-ℓ_p norm introduced in the previous section, we subsequently present a simple and straightforward technique to perform *group wise pruning* in deep CNNs. Here, *group* is referred to as a set of weights, e.g., a filter in a convolutional layer associated to a feature map or, in case of a fully connected layer, a single target neuron.

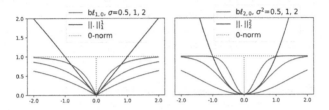

Fig. 1. Illustration of bounded-$\ell_{p,0}$ (b$\ell_{p,0}$) norms with $p \in \{1, 2\}$: Interpolation from ℓ_1-norm to 0-norm (left) and from ℓ_2-norm to 0-norm (right) with different σ.

Bounded-ℓ_1 Regularizer: It is a common practice to use sparsity inducing ℓ_1 penalty to shrink parameters during training. [24] has performed channel-wise pruning by imposing ℓ_1 penalty on the scaling factor γ of Batch Normalization (BN) layers that correspond to featuremaps in convolutional layers. We denote these scaling factors as *linear gates* in this work. Thus, the total loss L consists of the standard empirical loss l and an additional ℓ_1 penalty on the linear gates:

$$\mathcal{L} = \sum_{(x,y)} l\left(f\left(x, W\right), y\right) + \lambda \sum_{\gamma \in G} |\gamma| \qquad (5)$$

where f denotes the deep neural network, x, y denote training input and target, W denotes the network weights, γ denotes a single scaling factor from the aggregated set of all linear gates G. The ℓ_1 regularizer acts upon all linear gates and pushes them towards zero. The channels with linear gates whose magnitude is less than the relevance threshold are then pruned to obtain a narrow network. Here, the linear gates should accomplish two different tasks (i) get optimized along the other network parameters to improve the network performance and (ii) shrink down towards zero to induce channel level sparsity in the network. The hyperparameter λ defines the strength of the regularizer and controls the trade-off between primary objective and ℓ_1 penalty. Increasing λ would yield higher pruning rates at the cost of reduced network performance. The ℓ_1 regularizer penalizes each parameter at a same rate irrespective of its role and importance in accomplishing the primary objective. In general, not all parameters should receive equal penalty. We address this issue by employing a norm as defined in Eq. (2) as a sparsity inducing regularizer with $p = 1$ and denote it as bounded-ℓ_1 regularizer as it is bounded to $[0, 1]$.

Figure 1(left) shows that the bounded-ℓ_1 norm is a variant of the normal ℓ_1 norm and both penalize larger parameters. Importantly for the bounded variant, the penalty on larger weights does not increase as strong as for the normal norm, and only smaller weights are penalized comparably. Larger parameters, for which the bounded variant saturates, become primarily subject to the task loss. In other words, for the bounded variant, the penalty for large parameters becomes decoupled from the size of the parameters and converges to a constant value whereas for small parameters the penalty is relative large and forces them to even smaller values. Similar to the ℓ_1 penalty, the bounded ℓ_1 norm can be added as a regularization term in the objective function.

$$\mathcal{L}^* = \sum_{(x,y)} l\left(f\left(x, W\right), y\right) + \lambda \sum_{\gamma \in G} \left[1 - e^{-\frac{|\gamma|}{\sigma}}\right] \tag{6}$$

The gradient of the parameter γ w.r.t. ℓ_1 and bounded-ℓ_1 regularization equals:

$$\frac{\partial \mathcal{L}_{\text{reg}}}{\partial \gamma} = \lambda \cdot \text{sign}\left(\gamma\right), \qquad \frac{\partial \mathcal{L}_{\text{reg}}^*}{\partial \gamma} = \lambda \cdot \text{sign}\left(\gamma\right) \frac{e^{-\frac{|\gamma|}{\sigma}}}{\sigma} \tag{7}$$

The above equations indicate that the ℓ_1 norm updates gradients at a scale of λ irrespective of their magnitude. On the other hand, bounded-ℓ_1 norm provides no or small gradients for parameters with higher magnitude and large gradients for smaller parameters. In this manner, parameters with larger values receive gradients mainly from the first part of $\mathcal{L}^*$, being informative to accomplish the primary classification task.

Another interesting property of such norm is: The hyperparameter σ scales the regularization strength by controlling the interpolation between the ℓ_1- and 0-norm. As σ gets smaller, the bounded-ℓ_1 norm converges to the 0-norm according to Lemma 1. Larger σ allows regularization of all parameters whereas smaller σ guides the regularizer to penalize only parameters of smaller magnitude while liberating the larger ones. Larger values of σ enforce weaker regularization and smaller values enforce stronger regularization (also compare Fig. 1).

Given the behavior of σ, we can schedule it by gradually reducing its value during training. In doing so, the norm initially regularizes a larger number of parameters and then gradually shrinks down the insignificant ones towards zero while simultaneously filtering out the important ones. We can imagine the scheduling of σ as opening the gates of the 0-norm to make it differentiable which allows the insignificant parameters to fall into the valley of the norm and gradually close the gates to leave out the important parameters. It is fairly straightforward to include the hyperparameter σ also in the case of the ℓ_1 norm by replacing $|\gamma|$ with $\frac{|\gamma|}{\sigma}$ in Eq. (5) but it is similar to scaling the hyperparameter λ to $\frac{\lambda}{\sigma}$ in this case. The scheduling of σ in ℓ_1-norm increases its regularization strength and pushes down all the parameters towards zero which affects task performance of the network.

Bounded-ℓ_2 for Group Gating: Both the ℓ_1 and bounded-ℓ_1 regularizers bring down the scalar parameters towards zero but never make them exactly zeros (refer Fig. 3). This limitation always demands the setting of a relevance threshold to prune the parameters and then later requires fine-tuning for a number of iterations to stabilize the task performance of the pruned network. To this end, we propose to use the same bounded-ℓ_p norm that is defined in Eq. (2) as an additional layer in the network with $p = 2$ and $\sigma = 1$. To this, we refer to as a gating layer of *exponential gates* (with gating parameters g) which is placed after every convolutional or fully connected layer or before a BN layer in the network. This layer serves as a multiplicative gating factor for every channel in the preceding convolutional layer. The gating layer has the same number of gates as the number of channels where each gate gets multiplied to an output channel of a convolutional layer.

$$x = \text{conv}\,(input)\,; \quad y_k = x_k \cdot \left(1 - e^{-g_k^2}\right) \tag{8}$$

where x and y are the output of the convolutional and gating layer respectively and k indexes the channel of the convolutional layer. Since the gates are added as a layer in the network, we train the gating parameters g together with the network weights W. In contrast to the *linear gates* γ of BN, we impose the penalty only on the parameters g of *exponential gates*, yielding the loss function:

$$\mathcal{L} = \sum_{(x,y)} l\left(f\left(x, g, W\right), y\right) + \lambda \sum_{g \in G} R\left(g\right) \tag{9}$$

The first part of the loss function corresponds to the standard empirical loss of the neural network and $R(.)$ is the penalty term on the gating parameters g which could be either ℓ_2, ℓ_1, or the bounded-ℓ_1 regularizer. Two interesting properties of the *exponential gates* which makes them distinctive from the *linear gates* are (i) its values are bounded to the range $[0, 1)$, (ii) the quadratic exponential nature of the gates fused with the regularizer shrink down the outcome of the gates towards zero rapidly. The regularized *exponential gates* which are jointly optimized with the network weights act as a channel selection layer in the network. These gates actively differentiate the insignificant channels from significant ones during the training phase and gradually turn them off without affecting the network's performance. In Sect. 5, we empirically show that these exponential gating layers assist the regularizers to drive the insignificant channels to become exactly zero and later compress the network after removing such channels.

The *exponential gating layer* can be added to the network with or without BN. In case the gating layer is followed by BN, the statistics from the nulled-out channels remains constant across all the mini-batches since the gate is deterministic and gets multiplied to every input sample. Thus, both the running estimates of its computed mean and variance of the BN is zero for the nulled-out channels. The multiplicative scaling factor γ of BN does not show any effect on those channels but its additive bias β might change the zero channels to non-zero. This can be seen as adding a constant to the zero channels which can be easily alleviated by few iterations of fine-tuning the pruned network. In case the gating layers are added to a CNN without BN, we can prune channels in the network without any need of explicit fine-tuning since the insignificant channels become exactly zero after getting multiplied with the gates during the training phase. As a final note, the additional *exponential gating layer* increases the number of trainable parameters in the network but these gates can be merged into the weights of the associated convolutional filter after pruning.

In next section, we empirically evaluate the above-proposed techniques to achieve channel level sparsity, namely, (i) bounded-ℓ_1 norm to prune a larger number of parameters and preserve the task accuracy, and (ii) additional gating layer in CNNs to support the regularizers to achieve exactly zero channels.

5   Experimental Results

We demonstrate the significance of both, the *exponential gating layer* and the *bounded-ℓ_1* regularizer, on different network architectures and datasets, i.e., LeNet5-Caffe on MNIST, DenseNet-40, ResNet-164, MobileNetV2 on CIFAR100 and ResNet-50, MobileNetV2 on ImageNet dataset. We refer to Sect. A2 for the experiment details such as data preprocessing, architecture configuration, and hyperparameter selection. We use the threshold point 10^{-4} on the linear gates and threshold zero on the exponential gates to prune the channels.

CIFAR100. The results are summarized in Fig. 2. We compare the trade-off between classification accuracy on test data against the pruning rates obtained from different regularizers and gates. We report the average results over 3 different runs. Here, $\sigma_{constant}$ refers to the hyperparameter σ that is set to a constant value throughout the training process. We also investigated the influence of scheduling σ in case of bounded-ℓ_1 regularizer and compared the results against scheduling σ in ℓ_1 regularizer.

From Fig. 2, it can be seen that the bounded-ℓ_1 regularizer on the linear gates results in a higher pruning rate with an accuracy comparable to the ℓ_1 regularizer in ResNet-164 and provides a higher accuracy than the ℓ_1 regularizer in MobileNetV2. On the other hand, the addition of exponential gating layers in ResNet-164 and MobileNetV2 greatly increases the pruning rates and accuracy upon the linear gate. The bounded-ℓ_1 regularizer further improves the accuracy of ResNet-164 with exponential gating layer to 77.28% and 76.58% at different regularization strengths with pruning rates 30.73% and 47% respectively. In case of MobileNetV2, ℓ_1 on exponential gating layer results pruning rate of 75.83% with an accuracy 75.33%.

In contrast to the other networks, the pruning results of bounded-ℓ_1 regularizer and exponential gating layer in DenseNet-40 are identical to the results of the ℓ_1 regularizer on linear gate. However, the addition of exponential gating layer when combined with the ℓ_2 regularizer encourages channel pruning with a marginal drop in performance in both ResNet-164 and DenseNet-40 architectures, whereas the gate improves the classification performance in case

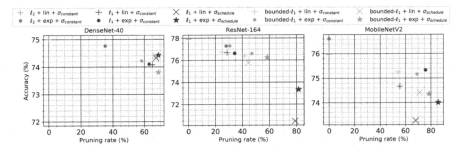

Fig. 2. Comparing trade-off between pruning rates and accuracies of different regularizers ℓ_2, ℓ_1 and bounded-ℓ_1 with different gates (linear, exponential) at constant and scheduled σ on DenseNet-40, ResNet-164 and MobileNetV2 on CIFAR100. In DenseNet-40, the scheduled ℓ_1 regularizer on exponential gate achieves slightly higher pruning and accuracy rate than the other methods. In ResNet-164, two identical markers represent settings with different regularization strengths. Here, bounded-ℓ_1 on exponential gate achieves higher pruning rates with approximately same line of accuracy with other methods. In MobileNetV2, bounded-ℓ_1 on linear gate outperforms ℓ_1 on linear gate in terms of accuracy with approximately similar pruning rate for both the cases of σ (constant and scheduled). However, ℓ_1 on exponential gate with constant σ preserves the accuracy with higher pruning rate. Thus, the networks with exponential gating layers has higher pruning rates than the linear gates with the accuracy close to baseline. On the other hand, bounded-ℓ_1 improves accuracy on linear gates in MobileNetV2 and on both gates in ResNet-164 when compared with ℓ_1 regularizer.

of MobileNetV2. We can also observe that scheduling σ for the ℓ_1 regularizer significantly drops the accuracy and increases the pruning rate in both MobileNetV2 and ResNet-164. Scheduling in the bounded-ℓ_1 regularizer also increases the pruning rate while retaining the accuracy close to the baseline margin. In MobilenetV2, scheduling the regularizer in bounded-ℓ_1 yields higher accuracy and pruning rate on linear gate when compared to the scheduled ℓ_1 regularizer. In ResNet-164, the pruning rate raises from 47% to 58.5% with an accuracy drop from 76.58% to 76.23% in case of exponential gate with scheduled bounded-ℓ_1 regularizer. On the other hand, the impact of the scheduler remains comparable, for both the regularizers in DenseNet-40 and scheduling ℓ_1 regularizer on exponential gate increases the pruning rate to 69% with 74.42% accuracy.

We compare pruning rates between linear and exponential gates and their accuracy trade-off at different threshold points in Fig. 3. We prune channels with gate values less or equal to the threshold and further fine-tune the network for a maximum of three epochs. Across the three different architectures both gates maintain the same accuracy until a critical threshold. The pruning rate of the exponential gates are significantly larger than the linear gates in ResNet-164, MobileNetV2 and comparable in DenseNet-40. In particular, the magnitude of non-zero exponential gates lies in $[10^{-3}, 0.1]$ and pruning at the threshold larger than 10^{-3} removes all channels in the network. Below 10^{-3} the exponential gates

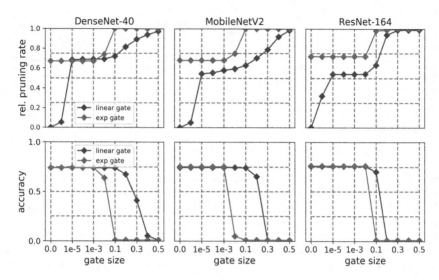

Fig. 3. Comparison of pruning rates (top row) and accuracies (bottom row) on CIFAR100 over different threshold points between linear gate (blue) and the exponential gate (red), both of which are applied in combination with ℓ_1 regularization. Units that do not pass the threshold on the gate values $|g|$ for the linear gates and $(1 - e^{-g^2})$ for exponential gates are pruned. Here, pruning rate of networks with exponential gates is superior or comparable to the linear gate at different threshold values. With the exponential gates, the achieved best pruning rates are insensitive to the selection of the threshold within the range $[0, 10^{-3}]$. In particular, the threshold zero being (nearly) optimum indicates that the exponential gates can exactly zeroing out removable channels. This observation also holds when combining with the ℓ_2 and bounded-ℓ_1 regularizers. (Color figure online)

achieve the optimum performance, i.e., largest pruning rate without loss of the classification accuracy. It is noted that the threshold zero is attainable, indicating that exponential gates can exactly null out removable channels. On contrary, the linear ones gate them with a sufficiently small value (about 10^{-5} in the case of Fig. 3), thereby necessitating the search of a precise pruning threshold.

MNIST. We also test our method on the MNIST dataset using the *LeNet5-Caffe* model. We compare our results with ℓ_0 regularization from [26]. We present different models that are obtained from different regularizers and the weight decay is set to be zero when using the ℓ_1 or bounded-ℓ_1 regularization. From the results shown in Table 1, it can be observed that network with *exponential gating layer* on different regularizers yield more narrow models than the previous method with lower test errors.

ImageNet. We also present pruning results of ResNet-50 and MobileNetV2 for the ImageNet dataset. On ResNet-50, we primarily investigate the significance of the *exponential gating layer* with ℓ_1 and ℓ_2 regularization. From Fig. 4, it can be seen that the *exponential gating layer* combined with the ℓ_2 regularizer

Table 1. Comparing pruning results of architecture *LeNet-5-Caffe 20-50-800-500* on MNIST dataset from different regularizers like ℓ_0 from [26] and ℓ_1, ℓ_2, Bounded-ℓ_1 on the network with *exponential gating layers*. We show the resulting architectures obtained from different pruning methods and their test error rate. It can be seen that our architectures are narrower than the one from previous method with comparable or smaller test error rates.

Method	Pruned architecture	Error(%)
ℓ_0, [26]	20-25-45-462	0.9
ℓ_0, [26]	9-18-65-25	1.0
ℓ_2, $\lambda_2 = $ 5e-4	8-19-117-24	0.79
ℓ_1, $\lambda_1 = $ 1e-3	8-13-37-25	0.98
bounded-ℓ_1, $\lambda_1 = $ 4e-3	9-17-43-25	0.92
bounded-ℓ_1, $\lambda_1 = $ 3e-3	9-20-54-27	0.67

outperforms ResNet-101(v1) from [39] in terms of pruning rate and accuracy. ℓ_1 regularization further penalizes the gating parameters and achieves 39% and 73% sparsity in the network with a drop of 1.3% and 5.4% Top-1 accuracy respectively at different regularization strengths. We compare these results and show that our method prunes more parameters than the previous pruning methods with the same line of accuracy.

Table 2. Results on MobileNetV2 trained for 100 epochs on ImageNet. *Bounded-ℓ_1 on linear gate* achieves higher accuracy than ℓ_1 *on linear gate* and closer to the standard training with reduced number of parameters. On the other hand, exponential gate with ℓ_1 regularizer reduces number of parameters without a significant drop in accuracy and improves accuracy when combined with ℓ_2 regularizer. Here M stands for Millions.

Network- MobileNetV2	Top-1 %	Top-5 %	#Params	#FLOPS
Standard training $\lambda_2 = $ 1e-5	70.1	89.25	3.56 M	320.2 M
$\ell_1 + lin$, $\lambda_1 = $ 5e-5, $\lambda_2 = $ 1e-5	69.54	89.14	3.37 M	275.0 M
bounded-$\ell_1 + lin$, $\lambda_1 = $ 5e-5, $\lambda_2 = $ 1e-5	69.9	89.17	3.40 M	280.0 M
$\ell_2 + exp$, $\lambda_2 = $ 4e-5	**70.7**	90.0	3.56 M	312.8 M
$\ell_1 + exp$, $\lambda_1 = $ 5e-5, $\lambda_2 = $ 4e-5	69.9	89.438	**3.00 M**	280.0 M

On MobileNetV2, we compare ℓ_1 against bounded-ℓ_1 on linear gate and ℓ_1 against ℓ_2 on exponential gate. From Table 2, it can be observed that the *bounded-ℓ_1 on linear gate* achieves higher accuracy than its counterpart ℓ_1 *on linear gate* with a slightly higher number of parameters. On the other hand, ℓ_1 penalty on exponential gate prunes a larger number of parameters and approximately keeps the accuracy of standard training whereas ℓ_2 on exponential gate improves the Top-1 accuracy by 0.6%.

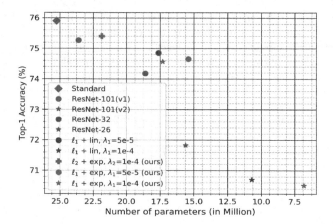

Fig. 4. Comparing our pruning results of ResNet-50 (ℓ_2 & ℓ_1 on *exponential gating layer*, $\ell_2 + exp$ and $\ell_1 + exp$) on ImageNet dataset against the previous methods like ResNet-101(v1) and ResNet-101(v2) from [39], ResNet-32 and ResNet-26 which are obtained from block pruning on ResNet-50 [19]. We also compared our results against the method ℓ_1 *on linear gate* ($\ell_1 + lin$) from [24] by implementing it on ResNet-50. Here, 'Standard' refers to the baseline model without pruning. We show the trade-off between top1-accuracy and number of remaining parameters of the network from different methods. It can be seen that the network from $\ell_2 + exp$ has about similar accuracy as ResNet-101(v1) but prunes 1.75M more parameters than the latter. Similarly, network from $\ell_1 + exp$ with $\lambda_1 = $ 5e-5 and 1e-4 prunes 2M and 3.5M more parameters respectively and has comparable accuracy with the other methods.

6   Conclusion

In this work, we propose a straightforward and easy to implement novel approach for group-wise pruning of DNNs. We introduce *exponential gating layers*, which learn importance of the channels during training and drive the insignificant channels to become exactly zero. Additionally, we propose *bounded-ℓ_1* regularization to penalize the gate parameters based on their magnitude. Different combinations of these techniques (gating functions and regularizers) are evaluated for a set of common DNN architectures for image classification. We found that the combination of exponential gating function with an ℓ_1 or its bounded variant is superior than the other approaches (cf. Fig. 2). Finally, these techniques result in higher compression rates with accuracy comparable to existing pruning approaches on ImageNet (cf. Fig. 4).

Supplementary material

A1   Proof of Lemma 1 (Lemma 1):

To improve readability, we will restate Lemma 1 from the main text:
    The mapping $\|.\|_{\text{bound-}p,\sigma}$ has the following properties:

- For $\sigma \rightarrow 0^+$ the bounded-norm converges towards the 0-norm:

$$\lim_{\sigma \to 0^+} \|x\|_{\text{bound-}p,\sigma} = \|x\|_0. \tag{1}$$

- In case $|x_i| \approx 0$ for all coefficients of x, the bounded-norm of x is approximately equal to the p-norm of x weighted by $1/\sigma$:

$$\|x\|_{\text{bound-}p,\sigma} \approx \left\| \frac{x}{\sigma} \right\|_p^p \tag{2}$$

Proof. The first statement Eq. (1) can easily be seen using:

$$\lim_{\sigma \to 0} \exp\left(-\frac{|x_i|^p}{\sigma^p}\right) = \mathbf{1}_0(x_i)$$

For the second statement Eq. (2) we use the taylor expansion of exp around zero to get:

$$
\begin{aligned}
\|x\|_{\text{bound-}p,\sigma} &= \sum_{i=1}^{n} 1 - \exp\left(-\frac{|x_i|^p}{\sigma^p}\right) \\
&= \sum_{i=1}^{n} 1 - \sum_{j=0}^{\infty} \left(-\frac{|x_i|^p}{\sigma^p}\right)^j \frac{1}{j!}
\end{aligned}
\tag{3}
$$

For $|x_i| \approx 0$ we keep only the leading coefficient $j = 1$ yielding:

$$\|x\|_{\text{bound-}p,\sigma} \approx \sum_{i=1}^{n} \frac{|x_i|^p}{\sigma^p} = \left\| \frac{x}{\sigma} \right\|_p^p.$$

A2   Experiment Details

Both CIFAR100 and ImageNet datasets are augmented with standard techniques like random horizontal flip and random crop of the zero-padded input image and further processed with mean-std normalization. The architecture MobileNetV2 is originally designed for the task of classification on ImageNet dataset. We adapt the network[1] to fit the input resolution 32×32 of CIFAR100. ResNet-164 is a pre-activation ResNet architecture containing 164 layers with bottleneck structure while DenseNet with 40 layer network and growth rate 12 has been used. All the networks are trained from scratch (weights with random initialization and bias is disabled for all the convolutional and fully connected layers) with a hypeparameter search on regularization strengths λ_1 for ℓ_1 or bounded-ℓ_1 regularizers and weight decay λ_2 on each dataset. The scaling factor γ of BN is initialized with 1.0 in case of *exponential gate* while it is initialized with 0.5 for *linear gate* as described in [24] and bias β to be zero. The hyperparameter σ in

---

[1] We changed the average pooling kernel size from 7×7 to 4×4 and the stride from 2 to 1 in the first convolutional layer and also in the second block of bottleneck structure of the network.

bounded-ℓ_1 regularizer is set to be 1.0 when the scheduling of this parameter is disabled. All the gating parameters g are initialized with 1.0.

We use the standard categorical cross-entropy loss and an additional penalty is added to the loss objective in the form of weight decay and sparsity induced ℓ_1 or bounded-ℓ_1 regularizers. Note that ℓ_1 and bounded-ℓ_1 regularization acts only on the gating parameters g whereas weight decay regularizes all the network parameters including the gating parameters g. We reimplemented the technique proposed in [24] which impose ℓ_1 regularization on scaling factor γ of Batch Normalization layers to induce channel level sparsity. We refer this method as ℓ_1 *on linear gate* and compare it against our methods *bounded-ℓ_1 on linear gate*, ℓ_1 *on exponential gate* and *bounded-ℓ_1 on exponential gate*. We train ResNet-164, DenseNet-40 and ResNet-50 for 240, 130 and 100 epochs respectively. Furthermore, learning rate of ResNet-164, DenseNet-40 and ResNet-50 is dropped by a factor of 10 after $(30, 60, 90)$, $(120, 200, 220)$, $(100, 110, 120)$ epochs. The networks are trained with batch size 128 using the SGD optimizer with initial learning rate 0.1 and momentum 0.9 unless specified. Below, we present the training details of each architecture individually.

LeNet5-Caffe: Since this architecture does not contain Batch Normalization layers, we do not compare our results with the method ℓ_1 *on linear gate*. We train the network with *exponential gating layers* that are added after every convolution/fully connected layer except the output layer and apply different regularizers like ℓ_1, bounded-ℓ_1 and weight decay separately to evaluate their pruning results. We set the weight decay to zero when training with ℓ_1 or bounded-ℓ_1 regularizers. The network is trained for 200 epochs with the weight decay and 60 epochs in case of other regularizers.

ResNet-50: We train the network with *exponential gating layers* that are added after every convolutional layer on ImageNet dataset. We evaluate performance of the network on different values of regularization strength λ_1 like 10^{-5}, 5×10^{-5} and 10^{-4}. The weight decay λ_2 is enabled for all the settings of λ_1 and set to be 10^{-4}. We analyzed the influence of *exponential gate* and compared against the existing methods.

ResNet-164: We use a dropout rate of 0.1 after the first Batch Normalization layer in every Bottleneck structure. Here, every convolutional layer in the network is followed by an *exponential gating layer*.

DenseNet-40: We use a dropout of 0.05 after every convolutional layer in the Dense block. Here, the *exponential gating layer* is added after every convolutional layer in the network except the first convolutional layer.

MobileNetV2: On CIFAR100, we train the network for 240 epochs where learning rate drops by 0.1 at 200 and 220 epochs. A dropout of 0.3 is applied after the global average pooling layer. On ImageNet, we train this network for 100 epochs which is in contrast to the standard training of 400 epochs. We start with learning rate 0.045 and reduced it by 0.1 at 30, 60 and 90 epochs. We evaluate performance of the network on *exponential gate* over the *linear gate* with ℓ_1 regularizer and also tested the significance of bounded-ℓ_1 on *linear gate*. *Exponential gating layer* is added after every standard convolutional/depthwise separable convolutional layer in the network.

On CIFAR100, we investigate the influence of weight decay, ℓ_1 and bounded-ℓ_1 regularizers, the role of *linear* and *exponential gates* on every architecture. We also study the influence of scheduling σ in both ℓ_1 and bounded-ℓ_1 regularizers on this dataset. For MobileNetV2, we initialize σ with 2.0 and decay it at a rate of 0.99 after every epoch. In case of ResNet-164 and DenseNet-40, we initialize the hyperparameters λ_1 and λ_2 with 10^{-4} and 5×10^{-4} respectively and σ with 2.0. We increase the λ_1 to 5×10^{-4} after 120 epochs and σ drops by 0.02 after every epoch until the value of σ reaches to 0.2 and later decays at a rate of 0.99.

References

1. Achterhold, J., Koehler, J.M., Schmeink, A., Genewein, T.: Variational network quantization. In: ICLR2018 (2018)
2. Alvarez, J.M., Salzmann, M.: Learning the number of neurons in deep networks. In: Advances in Neural Information Processing Systems (NIPS), pp. 2270–2278 (2016)
3. Chen, W., Wilson, J., Tyree, S., Weinberger, K., Chen, Y.: Compressing neural networks with the hashing trick. In: International Conference on Machine Learning (ICML), pp. 2285–2294 (2015)
4. Cheng, Y., Wang, D., Zhou, P., Zhang, T.: A survey of model compression and acceleration for deep neural networks. arXiv:1710.09282 (2017)
5. Courbariaux, M., Hubara, I., Soudry, D., El-Yaniv, R., Bengio, Y.: Binarized neural networks: Training deep neural networks with weights and activations constrained to $+1$ or -1. arXiv:1602.02830 (2016)
6. Federici, M., Ullrich, K., Welling, M.: Improved Bayesian compression. arXiv:1711.06494 (2017)
7. Frankle, J., Carbin, M.: The lottery ticket hypothesis: Finding small, trainable neural networks. arXiv:1803.03635 (2018)
8. Ghosh, S., Yao, J., Doshi-Velez, F.: Structured variational learning of Bayesian neural networks with horseshoe priors. arXiv:1806.05975 (2018)
9. Gong, Y., Liu, L., Yang, M., Bourdev, L.: Compressing deep convolutional networks using vector quantization. arXiv:1412.6115 (2014)
10. Guo, Y., Yao, A., Chen, Y.: Dynamic network surgery for efficient DNNs. In: Advances In Neural Information Processing Systems (NIPS), pp. 1379–1387 (2016)
11. Gysel, P., Pimentel, J., Motamedi, M., Ghiasi, S.: Ristretto: a framework for empirical study of resource-efficient inference in convolutional neural networks. IEEE Trans. Neural Netw. Learn. Syst. **29**(11), 5784–5789 (2018)
12. Han, S., Mao, H., Dally, W.J.: Deep compression: compressing deep neural networks with pruning, trained quantization and Huffman coding. In: International Conference on Learning Representations (ICLR) (2016)
13. Han, S., et al.: DSD: regularizing deep neural networks with dense-sparse-dense training flow. In: International Conference on Learning Representations (ICLR) (2017)
14. Han, S., Pool, J., Tran, J., Dally, W.: Learning both weights and connections for efficient neural network. In: Advances in Neural Information Processing Systems (NIPS), pp. 1135–1143 (2015)

15. Hanson, S.J., Pratt, L.Y.: Comparing biases for minimal network construction with back-propagation. In: Advances in Neural Information Processing Systems (NIPS), pp. 177–185 (1989)
16. He, Y., Zhang, X., Sun, J.: Channel pruning for accelerating very deep neural networks. In: International Conference on Computer Vision (ICCV), vol. 2 (2017)
17. Howard, A.G., et al.: Mobilenets: Efficient convolutional neural networks for mobile vision applications. arXiv:1704.04861 (2017)
18. Hu, H., Peng, R., Tai, Y.W., Tang, C.K.: Network trimming: a data-driven neuron pruning approach towards efficient deep architectures. arXiv:1607.03250 (2016)
19. Huang, Z., Wang, N.: Data-driven sparse structure selection for deep neural networks. arXiv:1707.01213 (2017)
20. Hubara, I., Courbariaux, M., Soudry, D., El-Yaniv, R., Bengio, Y.: Quantized neural networks: training neural networks with low precision weights and activations. J. Mach. Learn. Res. (JMLR) 18(1), 6869–6898 (2017)
21. Iandola, F.N., Han, S., Moskewicz, M.W., Ashraf, K., Dally, W.J., Keutzer, K.: Squeezenet: Alexnet-level accuracy with 50x fewer parameters and <0.5 mb model size. arXiv:1602.07360 (2016)
22. Karaletsos, T., Rätsch, G.: Automatic relevance determination for deep generative models. arXiv:1505.07765 (2015)
23. Li, H., Kadav, A., Durdanovic, I., Samet, H., Graf, H.P.: Pruning filters for efficient convnets. In: International Conference on Learning Representations (ICLR) (2017)
24. Liu, Z., Li, J., Shen, Z., Huang, G., Yan, S., Zhang, C.: Learning efficient convolutional networks through network slimming. In: 2017 IEEE International Conference on Computer Vision (ICCV), pp. 2755–2763. IEEE (2017)
25. Louizos, C., Ullrich, K., Welling, M.: Bayesian compression for deep learning. In: Advances in Neural Information Processing Systems (2017)
26. Louizos, C., Welling, M., Kingma, D.P.: Learning sparse neural networks through L_0 regularization. In: ICLR 2018 (2018)
27. Luo, J.H., Wu, J., Lin, W.: Thinet: a filter level pruning method for deep neural network compression. In: ICCV 2017 (2017)
28. MacKay, D.J.: Probable networks and plausible predictions - a review of practical Bayesian methods for supervised neural networks. Netw. Comput. Neural Syst. 6(3), 469–505 (1995)
29. Molchanov, D., Ashukha, A., Vetrov, D.: Variational dropout sparsifies deepneural networks. In: ICML 2017 (2017)
30. Molchanov, P., Tyree, S., Karras, T., Aila, T., Kautz, J.: Pruning convolutional neural networks for resource efficient inference. In: ICLR2017 (2017)
31. Neal, R.M.: Bayesian Learning for Neural Networks. Ph.D. thesis, University of Toronto (1995)
32. Neklyudov, K., Molchanov, D., Ashukha, A., Vetrov, D.: Structured Bayesian pruning via log-normal multiplicative noise. arXiv:1705.07283 (2017)
33. Rastegari, M., Ordonez, V., Redmon, J., Farhadi, A.: XNOR-net: imagenet classification using binary convolutional neural networks. In: Leibe, B., Matas, J., Sebe, N., Welling, M. (eds.) ECCV 2016. LNCS, vol. 9908, pp. 525–542. Springer, Cham (2016). https://doi.org/10.1007/978-3-319-46493-0_32
34. Sze, V., Chen, Y.H., Yang, T.J., Emer, J.: Efficient processing of deep neural networks: A tutorial and survey. arXiv:1703.09039 (2017)
35. Ullrich, K., Meeds, E., Welling, M.: Soft weight-sharing for neural network compression. In: ICLR 2017 (2017)

36. Wen, W., Wu, C., Wang, Y., Chen, Y., Li, H.: Learning structured sparsity in deep neural networks. In: Advances in Neural Information Processing Systems, pp. 2074–2082 (2016)
37. Weston, J., Elisseeff, A., Schölkopf, B., Tipping, M.: Use of the zero-norm with linear models and kernel methods. J. Mach. Learn. Res. (JMLR) **3**, 1439–1461 (2003)
38. Wu, S., Li, G., Chen, F., Shi, L.: Training and inference with integers in deep neural networks. arXiv:1802.04680 (2018)
39. Ye, J., Lu, X., Lin, Z., Wang, J.Z.: Rethinking the smaller-norm-less-informative assumption in channel pruning of convolution layers. arXiv:1802.00124 (2018)
40. Zhou, A., Yao, A., Guo, Y., Xu, L., Chen, Y.: Incremental network quantization: Towards lossless CNNs with low-precision weights. arXiv:1702.03044 (2017)
41. Zhou, H., Alvarez, J.M., Porikli, F.: Less is more: towards compact CNNs. In: Leibe, B., Matas, J., Sebe, N., Welling, M. (eds.) ECCV 2016. LNCS, vol. 9908, pp. 662–677. Springer, Cham (2016). https://doi.org/10.1007/978-3-319-46493-0_40

On the Estimation of the Wasserstein Distance in Generative Models

Thomas Pinetz[1(✉)], Daniel Soukup[1], and Thomas Pock[1,2]

[1] Center for Vision, Automation and Control, Austrian Institute of Technology,
Vienna, Austria
Thomas.Pinetz@ait.ac.at
[2] Institute of Computer Graphics and Vision,
Graz University of Technology, Graz, Austria

Abstract. Generative Adversarial Networks (GANs) have been used to model the underlying probability distribution of sample based datasets. GANs are notoriuos for training difficulties and their dependence on arbitrary hyperparameters. One recent improvement in GAN literature is to use the Wasserstein distance as loss function leading to Wasserstein Generative Adversarial Networks (WGANs). Using this as a basis, we show various ways in which the Wasserstein distance is estimated for the task of generative modelling. Additionally, the secrets in training such models are shown and summarized at the end of this work. Where applicable, we extend current works to different algorithms, different cost functions, and different regularization schemes to improve generative models.

1 Introduction

GANs [10] have been successfully applied to tasks ranging from superresolution [15], denoising [7], data generation [2], data refinement [26], style transfer [32], and to many more [14]. The core principle of GANs is to pit two models, most commonly Neural Networks (NNs), against each other in a game theoretic way [10]. The first NN, denoted generator, tries to fit the data distribution of a dataset $\mathcal{X}$, and the second network, denoted discriminator, learns to distinguish between generated data and real data. Both networks learn during a so called GAN game and the final output is a generator network, which fits the real data distribution. Still, the optimization dynamics of those networks are notoriously difficult and not well understood [18], leading to survey works concluding that no work has yet consistently outperformed the original non-saturating GAN formulation [16]. One key theoretical advancement is, that the previously used Jensen-Shannon divergence is ill defined in case of limited overlap [1]. One common way to circumvent this problem is to use different loss functions like the non-saturating loss [10] or the Wasserstein distance [2]. Minimizing the Wasserstein distance yields clear convergence guarantees, given that the generator network is powerful enough [2]. Still current formulations of the Wasserstein GAN

Electronic supplementary material The online version of this chapter (https:// doi.org/10.1007/978-3-030-33676-9_11) contains supplementary material, which is available to authorized users.

G. A. Fink et al. (Eds.): DAGM GCPR 2019, LNCS 11824, pp. 156–170, 2019.
https://doi.org/10.1007/978-3-030-33676-9_11

(WGAN) heavily dependent on the hyperparameter setting [16]. Our aim with this work is to explain why this is the case and what can be done to train WGANs successfully.

We review the usage of the Wasserstein distance as it is utilized in generative modelling, showcase the pitfalls of various algorithms and we propose possible alternatives.

As summary, our contributions are as follows:

- A review and overview of common WGAN algorithms and their respective limitations.
- A practical guide on how to apply WGANs to new datasets.
- An extension to the squared entropy regularization for Optimal Transport [5], by using the Bregman distance and moving the center of the regularization.
- An extension on the currently available approaches to ensure Lipschitz continuous discriminator networks.

The remainder of this paper is organized as follows. In Sect. 2, a recap of the Wasserstein distance in the context of GANs is given. Sections 3 and 4 describe all the algorithms in detail. Section 5, shows our experimental results. Our findings are summarized in Sect. 6 and conclusions given in Sect. 7.

2   Preliminaries: Wasserstein Distance

The p-th Wasserstein distance is defined between two probability distributions μ, ν on a metric space (M, c) as follows:

$$W_c^p(\mu, \nu) = \inf_{\pi \in \Pi(\mu,\nu)} \left\{ \int_{M \times M} c^p(x, y) d\pi(x, y) \right\}^{\frac{1}{p}}, \tag{1}$$

where $c(x, y)$ defines the ground cost. In this work, only the W_c^1 distance is considered in a discrete setting. This simplifies the whole problem to the following linear program:

$$W_c(\mu, \nu) = \min_{T \in U(\mu,\nu)} \langle T, C \rangle_F, \tag{2}$$

where $U(\mu, \nu) = \{T \in \mathbb{R}^{n \times m} | T\mathbb{1}_n = \mu, T^T\mathbb{1}_m = \nu\}$, $C_{ij} = c(x_i, y_j)$ and $\langle T, C \rangle_F = \sum_i \sum_j T_{ij} C_{ij}$ for any function (not necessarily a distance) c. This optimization problem has the following dual formulation:

$$W_c(\mu, \nu) = \max_{\alpha, \beta} \alpha^T \mu + \beta^T \nu \quad s.t. \quad \alpha_i + \beta_j \le C_{ij} \quad \forall i, j \tag{3}$$

Based on the optimality condition of linear programing an analytical solution for β is given by $\beta_j = \max_i C_{ij} - \alpha_i \quad \forall j$. By replacing the dual variables α,

β with functions, namely $f(x_i) = \alpha_i$ and $f^c(y_j) = \max_i C_{ij} - \alpha_i$, the following formulation is obtained:

$$W_c(\mu, \nu) = \max_{f, f^c} \mathbb{E}_{x \sim \mu}[f(x_i)] + \mathbb{E}_{y \sim \nu}[f^c(y_j)],$$
$$\text{s.t.} \quad f(x_i) + f^c(y_j) \leq C_{ij} \quad \forall i, j. \tag{4}$$

In case c is a distance d, it has been proven in [28] that $f^c(x) = -f(x)$. Using that result and rearranging the constraints yields $f(x_i) - f(y_j) \leq 1 \cdot d(x_i, y_j)$, which is satisfied for all functions, which have Lipschitz constant $Lip(f) \leq 1$. This establishes the Kantorovich-Rubinstein duality, which is used in WGANs:

$$W(\mu, \nu) = \max_{Lip(f) \leq 1} \mathbb{E}_{x \sim \mu}[f(x)] - \mathbb{E}_{w \sim \nu}[f(w)] \tag{5}$$

The objective in WGANs is to leverage the Wasserstein distance to train a NN to model the underlying distribution ν, given an empirical distribution $\hat{\nu}$. In the GAN framework the generated distribution is constructed by using a known base distribution e.g. $z \sim N(\mathbf{0}, \mathbf{I})$, and transforming z using a NN with parameters θ as follows: $\mu_\theta \sim g(z; \theta)$. The parameters θ are then learned by minimizing the distance between the parametric distribution and the empiric one ($\hat{\nu}$) using the following loss function:

$$L(\nu, \theta) = \min_\theta W_c(\hat{\nu}, \mu_\theta) \tag{6}$$

Due to changes in the generator parameters θ during the optimization process, the Wasserstein distance problem changes and is reevaluated in each iteration. Therefore, the speed of computation is essential. In the OT literature an additional regularization term $h(x)$ is added to improve the speed of convergence, while yielding sub-optimal results [8]. This results in the following formulation:

$$W_{c,\epsilon}(\mu, \nu) = \min_{T \in U(\mu, \nu)} \langle T, C \rangle_F + \epsilon h(T) \tag{7}$$

We discriminate between two different methodologies of algorithms, namely sub-optimal fullbatch methods and stochastic methods. The following algorithms for solving the Wasserstein distance problem to learn generative models are incorporated in our work:

1. Fullbatch Methods
   (a) Unregularized Wasserstein Distance (Eq. (2))
       i. Primal Dual Hybrid Gradient solver (PDHG)
   (b) Regularized Wasserstein Distance (Eq. (7)
       i. Negative Entropy Regularization
           A. Sinkhorn [8] (Sinkhorn)
           B. Sinkhorn-Center [30] (Sinkhorn-Center)
       ii. Quadratic Regularization
           A. FISTA (FISTA)
           B. FISTA-Center (FISTA-Center)

2. Stochastic Methods (Eq. (5))
   (a) Regularized NNs:
       i. WGAN with Gradient Penalty [12] (WGAN-GP)
   (b) Constrained NNs:
       i. WGAN with Spectral Normalization [19] (WGAN-SN)
       ii. WGAN with convolutional Spectral Normalization (WGAN-SNC)

The main iterations for all algorithms are detailed in the supplementary material.

3   Fullbatch Methods

Fullbatch estimation means taking a data-batch of size n of both probability densities and solving the Wasserstein distance for this subset $(\mathcal{X}_i, \mathcal{Y}_i^\theta)$. The idea is that the estimated Wasserstein distance is representative for the entire dataset. This is done by setting the probability for each image in the batch $x_{\{1,\dots,n\}} \in \mathcal{X}$ to $\mu(x) = \frac{1}{n}$. By the optimality conditions of convex problems, the so-called transport map T is recovered. T is a mapping between elements in $\hat{\nu}$ and μ_θ and is plugged into the following equation to learn the generative model:

$$L(\theta) = \min_\theta \langle T, c(\mathcal{X}_i, \mathcal{Y}_i^\theta) \rangle_F \qquad (8)$$

Note, that it is not necessary to differentiate through the computation of T, due to the envelope theorem as has been noted in [24, 30].

There are two main advantages of doing the fullbatch estimation. First, the convex solvers have convergence guarantees, which are easily checked in practice [5]. Second, the convergence speed is faster than with stochastic estimates [25].

3.1   Unregularized Solver

As a baseline, a solver for the unregularized Wasserstein distance is proposed. Therefore, the Primal-Dual Hybrid Gradient (**PDHG**) method [6] is used. To apply the PDHG, the problem is transformed into a saddle point problem as follows:

$$W_c(\mu, \nu) = \max_{\lambda_1, \lambda_2} \min_{t \geq 0} \langle \begin{bmatrix} \lambda_1 \\ \lambda_2 \end{bmatrix}, Kt \rangle_F + c^T t - \lambda_1^T \mu - \lambda_2^T \nu, \qquad (9)$$

where T, C are reshaped to one dimensional vectors t, c and the constraints $T\mathbb{1}_n$, $T^T\mathbb{1}_m$ are combined to Kt. The full computation of the saddle point formulation and the steps of the algorithms are shown in the supplementary material.

3.2   Regularized Optimal Transport

Generative modelling solving the unregularized Wasserstein distance problem
is computationally infeasible [9]. However, the solution to this problem in the
OT literature is to solve for the regularized Wasserstein distance instead [17]. In
this work, either negative entropy regularization or quadratic regularization are
utilized, which are defined as:

$$h_e(x) = -\sum_i x_i \log(x_i), \qquad h_q(x) = \frac{1}{2}||x||^2 \qquad (10)$$

Negative entropy regularization leads to the **Sinkhorn** algorithm [8]. While
the Sinkhorn algorithm converges rapidly, it also tends to be numerically unstable and only a small range of values for ϵ lead to satisfactory results. One approach to reduce instabilities is to adopt a Bregman distance[1] based proximal
regularization term:

$$W_c^\epsilon(\mu,\nu) = \min_{T \in U(\mu,\nu)} \langle T, C \rangle_F + \epsilon D_h(T, T^k) \qquad (11)$$

Xie et al. [30] proposed to use a modified Sinkhorn-Knopp algorithm
(**Sinkhorn-Center**) with the steps given in the supplementary material.

Another way to combat the numerical stability problems and blurry transport
maps is to use quadratic regularization [5]. By plugging the quadratic regularization into the regularized Wasserstein distance, the following dual function is
obtained:

$$W_{c,\epsilon} = \max_{\alpha,\beta} \alpha^T \mu + \beta^T \nu - \frac{1}{2\epsilon} \sum_{ij} [\alpha_i + \beta_j - C_{ij}]_+^2. \qquad (12)$$

The dual problem can be directly solved by the FISTA algorithm [3]. FISTA
was chosen due to its optimal convergence guarantees for problems like this and
due to its simple iterates as is shown in the supplementary material. The trans-
port map T is given by: $T = \frac{1}{\epsilon} \sum_{ij} [\alpha_i + \beta_j - C_{ij}]_+$. To improve the convergence
speed and allow higher values for ϵ, we also consider a proximal regularized
version. The cost function, whose derivation is contained in the supplementary
material is:

$$W_c^\epsilon = \max_{\alpha,\beta} \alpha^T \mu + \beta^T \nu - \sum_j \sup_{t_j \geq 0} \langle t_j, \alpha + \beta_j \mathbb{1} - C_j \rangle - \frac{\epsilon}{2}||t_j - t_j^k||_2^2 \qquad (13)$$

This is again solved using the FISTA algorithm as further described in the
supplementary material, with $T = T^n$.

---

[1] The Bregman distance is defined as follows: $D_h(x,z) = h(x) - (h(z) + \langle \nabla h(z), x - z \rangle)$.

4   Stochastic Estimation Methods

Full batch methods rely on the option to use batches, which are indicative for the entire problem. The required batch size is enormous for large scaled tasks [20]. In practice, the fact that close points in the data space have similar values for their Lagrangian multipliers suggest the usage of functions, which have this property intrinsically. Therefore, the Wasserstein distance is commonly approximated with a NN. The Kantorovich-Rubinstein duality leads to a natural formulation using a NN, named f:

$$W_c(\mu, \nu_\theta) = \max_{Lip(f) \leq 1} \min_\theta \mathbb{E}_{x \sim \mu}[f(x)] - \mathbb{E}_{z \sim N(\mathbf{0}, \mathbf{I})}[f(g_\theta(z))] \tag{14}$$

The key part of this formulation is the Lipschitz constraint [21]. In practice, one of two ways is used to ensure the Lipschitzness of a NN, which is either by adding a constraint penalization to the loss function or constraining the NN to only allow 1-Lipschitz functions.

4.1   Lipschitz Regularization

Here the following observation is used. If $||g|| \leq 1$ holds for $g \in \partial f$, then $Lip(f) \leq 1$. By observing this fact, a simple regularization scheme, named gradient penalty, has been proposed and is widely used in practice [12]:

$$GP(x) = \lambda(||\nabla f(x)||_2 - 1)^2$$
$$\forall x \in \mathbb{R}^n \quad \exists y \in \mathcal{X}, z \in \mathbb{R}^d, \alpha \in [0,1] \subset \mathbb{R} \quad \text{s.t.} \quad x = \alpha y + (1-\alpha)g_\theta(z) \tag{15}$$

One thing to note in this formulation the number of constraints is proportional to the product of the number of samples, generated images and the granularity of α, which makes the algorithm only slowly converging.

4.2   Lipschitz Constrained NN

One can interpret NNs as hierarchical functions, which are composed of matrix multiplications, convolutions (also denoted as matrix multiplications) and non-linear activation functions σ_i:

$$f(x) = \sigma_0(W_0(\sigma_1(W_1(...\sigma_n(W_n x))))) \tag{16}$$

The Lipschitz constants of such a function can be bounded from above by the product of the Lipschitz constant of its layers:

$$Lip(f) \leq \Pi_i^l Lip(f_i), \tag{17}$$

where $f_i(x) = \sigma_i(W_i x)$. Therefore, if each layer is 1-Lipschitz the entire NN is 1-Lipschitz. Common activation functions like ReLU, leaky ReLU, sigmoid, tanh, and softmax are 1-Lipschitz. Therefore, if the linear maps W_i are 1-Lipschitz so

---

Algorithm 1: Power method: Requires the matrix W and number of iterations n with default value 1.

Result: The spectral normalized weight matrix W_s

$u^0 = N(\mathbf{0}, \mathbf{I})$

for $k = 1, ..., n$ **do**

$\quad\quad u^{k+\frac{1}{2}} = W^T W k$

$\quad\quad u^{k+1} = \dfrac{u^{k+\frac{1}{2}}}{||u^{k+\frac{1}{2}}||_2}$

end

$W_s = \dfrac{W}{||W u^n||_2}$

---

is the entire network as well [11]. The Lipschitz constant of the linear maps are given by their spectral norm $||W||_2$. In the WGAN-SN algorithm, the spectral norm is computed using the power method [19]. The power method (Alg. 1) converges linearly depending on the ratio of the two largest eigenvectors λ_1, λ_2: $O((\frac{|\lambda_1|}{|\lambda_2|})^k)$ [11]. For matrices this is done by using simple matrix multiplications. For convolutions, in the **WGAN-SN** algorithm the filter kernels are reshaped to 2D, the power method is applied and then the result is reshaped back [19]. It is trivial to construct cases, where this is arbitrarily wrong [11] and in Fig. 4 the deviation from 1-Lipschitzness is demonstrated. A more detailed example is shown in the supplementary material. Therefore, a mathematically correct algorithm, namely the **WGAN-SNC** is proposed, where we apply a forward and a backward convolution onto a vector x in each iteration, which actually mimics the matrix multiplication of the induced matrix by the convolution. Gouk et al. [11] proposed a similar power method for classification and projected the weights back onto the feasible set after each update step for a classification network. In the supplementary material it is shown empirically on simple examples that this is too prohibitive to estimate the Wasserstein distance reliably. Therefore, the WGAN-SNC algorithm applies power method as a projection layer, similar to the WGAN-SN algorithm. In that layer, the u variable persists across update steps, an additional iteration is run during training, and the projection is used for backpropagation.

5   Experiments

The base architecture for all the NNs in this work is a standard convolutional NN as is used by the WGAN-SN [19], which is based on the DCGAN [22]. Details are described in the supplementary material. The default optimizer is the Adam optimizer with the parameter setting from the WGAN-GP [12] setting ($lr = 0.0001$, $betas = (0.0, 0.9)$). We use 1 discriminator iteration for WGAN-SN(C) algorithms and 5 for WGAN-GP.

5.1 MNIST Manifold Comparison

Here, the impact of the cost function on the generated manifold is investigated. The L2-norm is compared to the L1-norm, cosine-distance [24] and SSIM distance [29]. For this example a generator NN was trained with 1 hidden layer with 500 neurons taking $z \sim U^2(0,1)$ as input and producing an image as output. This network is then trained using the Sinkhorn-Knopp algorithm on a batch of 1000 samples, the manifold of which is shown in Fig. 1. In accordance to the image processing literature, the L1 norm produces crisper images and transitions between the images then the other cost functions. However, not all the images in the manifold show digits. On the other hand the L2 norm produces digit images everywhere, similar to the output of the WGAN-GP algorithm on large datasets, but the transitions are blurry. The cosine-distance is just a normalized and squared L2-distance. Still, the resulting manifold is quite different, as it fails to capture all the digits. Also the images are blurrier than using the actual L2-norm. This leads to the conclusion that by normalizing the images, information is lost and it is harder to separate different images. While the SSIM does generate realistic digit images, it fails at capturing the entire distribution of images, e.g. digits 4 or 6 do not occur in the manifold.

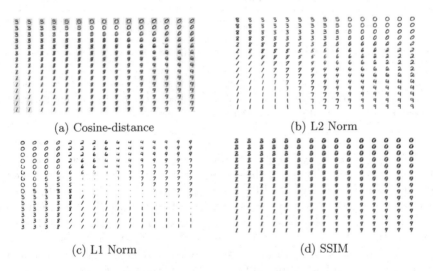

(a) Cosine-distance

(b) L2 Norm

(c) L1 Norm

(d) SSIM

Fig. 1. Impact of different cost functions on the MNIST manifold, trained using a Sinkhorn-GAN. Notice, the different interpolations between the digits (L1 sharper, L2 blurrier) and image quality (L1 some images show no digit) and the occurrence of each digit in the manifold (SSIM is missing 2,4,5,6).

5.2 Hyperparameter Dependence

In this section the hyperparameter dependence of the stochastic algorithms is tested on simple image based examples. For this reason, two batches with size

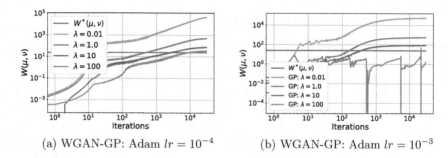

(a) WGAN-GP: Adam $lr = 10^{-4}$ (b) WGAN-GP: Adam $lr = 10^{-3}$

Fig. 2. Optimizer impact on using Gradient Penalty. Notice that the stability changes as the learning rate is changed and the hyperparamter λ is changed. Additionally, the slow rate of convergence and the deviation from 1-Lipschitzness are shown here.

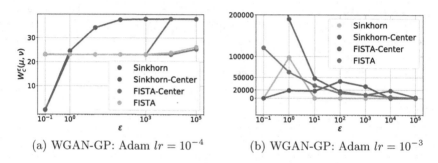

(a) WGAN-GP: Adam $lr = 10^{-4}$ (b) WGAN-GP: Adam $lr = 10^{-3}$

Fig. 3. Impact of the regularization term on the estimated Wasserstein distance and the number of iterations until convergence. The stability issues of the Sinkhorn(-Center) algorithms for $0.1 \geq \epsilon$ and $\epsilon \geq 10$ are demonstrated here.

$n = 500$ are sampled randomly from the CIFAR dataset and the Wasserstein distance is estimated based on those samples. $n = 500$ is used, due to memory restrictions of our GPU and therefore being able to use full batch gradient descent, even for the NN approaches. The results are shown in Fig. 2. One can see the stability of the gradient penalty depends on the learning rate of the optimizer and the setting for the lagrangian multiplier λ. That parameter sensitivity explains the common observation that the Wasserstein estimate heavily oscillates in the initial $10k$ iterations of the generator. Additionally, the estimate has still not converged even after $30k$ full batch iterations.

As a comparison we show the dependence of the fullbatch estimates on their hyperparameter ϵ in Fig. 3. For the entropy regularized versions ϵ defines a trade-off between numerical stability and getting good results, where moving the center drastically increases the range of good ϵ values. On the other hand, for the quadratically regularized versions, ϵ is a tradeoff between the runtime and the quality of the estimation.

5.3   Limitations of Fullbatch Methods

In the following two experiments, we show that cost functions without adversarial training do not work well without enormous batch sizes. To showcase, the ability of current generative models, we learn a mapping from a set of noise vectors to a set of images using the Wasserstein distance for a batch of size 4000. The resulting images are shown in the supplementary material for all algorithms. To show that this is not easy to scale to larger datasets, another experiment is designed: the transport map is learned for two different batches taken from CIFAR. The results for an ever increasing number of samples in a batch is shown in Fig. 5. This shows an empirical evaluation of the statistical properties of the Wasserstein distance. The estimate decreases with sample size n in the order $O(\sqrt{n})$ [4,27]. Even though, those images are sampled from the same distribution, the cost is still higher than using blurred images. Samples produced by the sinkhorn solver (Fig in supplementary material) produce an average estimate of 16 of the Wasserstein distance, which is smaller than samples taken from the dataset itself using the L2-norm. Therefore, it is better for the generator to produce samples like this.

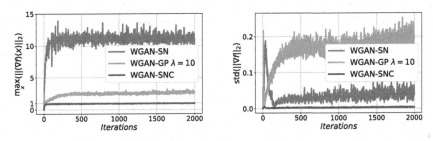

Fig. 4. Empirical Gradnorm of the stochastic algorithms. WGAN-SNC produces stable gradients close to 1 during training, while the other methods fail to do so.

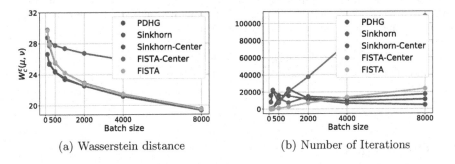

(a) Wasserstein distance   (b) Number of Iterations

Fig. 5. Wasserstein distance and number of iterations until convergence for a specific batch size using L2-norm between random samples on CIFAR.

5.4   Comparison of Algorithms

Salimans et al. [24] demonstrated, that with enough computational power it is possible to get state-of-the-art performance using fullbatch methods. However, we do not posses that kind of computational power and therefore the setting proposed by Genevay et al. [9] was used. We used a standard DCGAN, with a batchsize of 200, which reproduces their results for the Sinkhorn GAN. For the full batch methods, instead of minimizing the Wasserstein distance, the Sinkhorn divergence[2] is minimized instead [9]. The cost function is the mean squared error on an adversarial learned feature space. If the adversarial feature space is only learned on the Wasserstein distance, then features are just pushed away from each other. The Sinkhorn divergence on the other hand also has attractor terms, which forces the network to encode images from the same distribution similarly.

Related GAN algorithms, which also use full batch solvers have been evaluated using the Inception Score [23] (IS) and a comparison to them is shown in Table 1. For the other methods, we also evaluated using the Fréchet Inception Distance (FID) [13] in Table 2. In the constrained setting, the fullbatch WGANs in their current form are competitive or better to similar fullbatch algorithms like the MMD GAN. However, the stochastic methods work better for larger scaled tasks. The WGAN-SN performs better than the one using Gradient Penalty, and performs similarly to the WGAN-SNC. One thing to note is that the WGAN-SN actually works better using a hinge loss, even though no theoretical justification is given for that [19].

Table 1. Inception Score comparison of full batch methods for CIFAR.

MMD [9]	Sinkhorn [9] $\epsilon = 10^3$	Sinkhorn-Center $\epsilon = 10^3$	FISTA $\epsilon = 500$	FISTA-Center $\epsilon = 10^4$
4.04 ± 0.07	4.10 ± 0.12	4.69 ± 0.03	4.25 ± 0.051	4.61 ± 0.023

Table 2. Visual Quality comparison of Inception Score (IS, higher is better) and FID (lower is better). Note, that the WGAN SN results are our own, as the authors [19] did not evaluate the model using the Wasserstein loss.

-	FISTA-Center	Sinkhorn [9]	WGAN-GP [19]	WGAN SN	WGAN SN conv
IS	4.61 ± 0.023	4.14 ± 0.06	6.68 ± 0.06	6.80 ± 0.07	6.93 ± 0.08
FID	-	-	40.1	40.94 ± 0.55	38.26 ± 0.68

6   Discussions

Based on our experimental results, we want to share the following empirical insights to successfully train WGANs for various tasks.

---

[2] Sinkhorn divergence $\bar{W}_{c,\epsilon}(\mu, \nu) = 2W_{c,\epsilon}(\mu, \nu) - W_{c,\epsilon}(\mu, \mu) - W_{c,\epsilon}(\nu, \nu)$

- **Stochastic vs full batch Estimation**: If it is possible to compute the Wasserstein distance for a given problem accurately enough with a full batch approach, then there are a lot of advantages using this approach, like convergence guarantees, better Wasserstein estimates and a clear interpretation of hyperparameters. Depending on the batch size the optimization algorithm might be quite slow though. On the other hand full batch estimation is not possible with simple cost functions for real world image datasets as we show for the CIFAR dataset (see samples in supplementary material).
- **Cost function:** The cost function controls the geometry of the resulting generated distribution (see Fig. 1). For example the L1-norm results in sharper images and sharper interpolations than the L2-norm [31] (see Fig. 1).
- **Useful Baseline:** The batch wise estimation gives an indication of the Wasserstein distance given two batches of the dataset. This in turn is used to give an estimate on how well the NN architecture and training algorithm are able to fit the data. (see Fig. 2)
- **Full batch estimation**
  - **Squared vs Entropy regularization** (see Fig. 5): entropy regularization converges extremely fast for large values of ϵ, however, the performance quickly deteriorates even for small changes in ϵ. Quadratic regularization on the other hand works numerically very stable for any value of ϵ we tested (see Fig. 3). Proximal regularization allows for more stability in the algorithm by only minorly changing the algorithm.
  - **Batch size:** As a rule of thumb a larger batchsize is better than a smaller one to accurately estimate the Wasserstein distance. Estimating the necessary batchsize is done using indicative batches (e.g. starting batch and batches from the data distribution).
  - **Convergence guarantees**: Full batch methods provably converge to the global optimal solution and therefore accurately estimate the Wasserstein distance with a clear meaning of each hyperparameter (see Fig. 3).
- **Stochastic estimation**
  - **Convergence**: In principle, methods based on NNs, take longer to converge, have no convergence guarantees and it is hard to tell, if they really approximate a Wasserstein distance. Additionally, it is unclear how gradients of intermediate approximations relate to a converged approximation, resulting in the mystifying nature of WGAN training.
  - **Projection**: Projecting onto the feasible set is too restrictive. Therefore, the projection is done as part of the loss function (see Fig. in supplementary material).
  - **Hyperparameter dependence**: Current methods are extremely dependent on hyperparameters (GP on λ [16], and on the optimizer [19] and SN on the network architecture) (see Fig. 2 and 4).
  - **Gradient norm of NNs**: Current methods to ensure Lipschitzness in NNs have in common, that while the actual Lipschitz constant is different from 1, it is empirically stable. (see Fig. 4)

7   Conclusions and Practical Guide

We have reviewed and extended various algorithms for computing and minimizing the Wasserstein distance between distributions as part of a large generative systems. To make use of those insights in ones problems is to look at the Wasserstein distance between indicative batches, e.g. the initial batches produced by the generator and batches from the data distribution. This also gives a way to gauge how long a NN will take to converge and which hyperparameters have an impact on the estimation. Estimating the Wasserstein distance on indicative batches can safely be done with a regularized solver, due to the small differences in the Wasserstein estimates. For entropy regularization, we encourage to use proximal regularization. If the full batch estimation of the gradient is sufficient, then using a full batch GANs provides reliable results. However, for most GAN benchmarks this is not the case and then Gradient Penalty tends to work well, but is really slow. WGAN-SN is a lot faster, but mathematically incorrect. We propose a theoretically sound version of this, while showing similar performance on CIFAR. The cost function used in the Wasserstein distance controls the geometry of the generated manifold and therefore determines the interpolations between the images. The high cost between different samples taken from the same dataset shows problems with current non-adversarial cost functions on generative tasks and is a first step towards modelling better cost functions.

References

1. Arjovsky, M., Bottou, L.: Towards principled methods for training generative adversarial networks. arXiv preprint arXiv:1701.04862 (2017)
2. Arjovsky, M., Chintala, S., Bottou, L.: Wasserstein gan. arXiv preprint arXiv: 1701.07875(2017)
3. Beck, A., Teboulle, M.: A fast iterative shrinkage-thresholding algorithm for linear inverse problems. SIAM J. Imaging Sci. **2**(1), 183–202 (2009)
4. Bigot, J., Cazelles, E., Papadakis, N.: Central limit theorems for sinkhorn divergence between probability distributions on finite spaces and statistical applications. arXiv preprint arXiv:1711.08947 (2017)
5. Blondel, M., Seguy, V., Rolet, A.: Smooth and sparse optimal transport. arXiv preprint arXiv:1710.06276 (2017)
6. Chambolle, A., Pock, T.: A first-order primal-dual algorithm for convex problems with applications to imaging. J. Math. Imaging Vis. **40**(1), 120–145 (2011)
7. Chen, J., Chen, J., Chao, H., Yang, M.: Image blind denoising with generative adversarial network based noise modeling. In: Proceedings of the IEEE Conference on Computer Vision and Pattern Recognition, pp. 3155–3164 (2018)
8. Cuturi, M.: Sinkhorn distances: lightspeed computation of optimal transport. In: Advances in Neural Information Processing Systems, pp. 2292–2300 (2013)
9. Genevay, A., Peyré, G., Cuturi, M.: Learning generative models with sinkhorn divergences. In: International Conference on Artificial Intelligence and Statistics, pp. 1608–1617 (2018)
10. Goodfellow, I., et al.: Generative adversarial nets. In: Advances in Neural Information Processing Systems, pp. 2672–2680 (2014)

11. Gouk, H., Frank, E., Pfahringer, B., Cree, M.: Regularisation of neural networks by enforcing lipschitz continuity. arXiv preprint arXiv:1804.04368 (2018)
12. Gulrajani, I., Ahmed, F., Arjovsky, M., Dumoulin, V., Courville, A.C.: Improved training of wasserstein gans. In: Advances in Neural Information Processing Systems, pp. 5769–5779 (2017)
13. Heusel, M., Ramsauer, H., Unterthiner, T., Nessler, B., Hochreiter, S.: Gans trained by a two time-scale update rule converge to a local nash equilibrium. In: Advances in Neural Information Processing Systems, pp. 6626–6637 (2017)
14. Karras, T., Laine, S., Aila, T.: A style-based generator architecture for generative adversarial networks. arXiv preprint arXiv:1812.04948 (2018)
15. Ledig, C., et al.: Photo-realistic single image super-resolution using a generative adversarial network. arXiv preprint (2017)
16. Lucic, M., Kurach, K., Michalski, M., Gelly, S., Bousquet, O.: Are gans created equal? a large-scale study. In: Advances in Neural Information Processing Systems, pp. 700–709 (2018)
17. Luise, G., Rudi, A., Pontil, M., Ciliberto, C.: Differential properties of sinkhorn approximation for learning with wasserstein distance. In: Advances in Neural Information Processing Systems, pp. 5859–5870 (2018)
18. Mescheder, L., Nowozin, S., Geiger, A.: The numerics of gans. In: Advances in Neural Information Processing Systems, pp. 1823–1833 (2017)
19. Miyato, T., Kataoka, T., Koyama, M., Yoshida, Y.: Spectral normalization for generative adversarial networks. arXiv preprint arXiv:1802.05957 (2018)
20. Peyré, G., Cuturi, M., et al.: Computational optimal transport. Found. Trends® Mach. Learn. 11(5–6), 355–607 (2019)
21. Qin, Y., Mitra, N., Wonka, P.: Do gan loss functions really matter? arXiv preprint arXiv:1811.09567 (2018)
22. Radford, A., Metz, L., Chintala, S.: Unsupervised representation learning with deep convolutional generative adversarial networks. arXiv preprint arXiv:1511.06434 (2015)
23. Salimans, T., Goodfellow, I., Zaremba, W., Cheung, V., Radford, A., Chen, X.: Improved techniques for training gans. In: Advances in Neural Information Processing Systems, pp. 2234–2242 (2016)
24. Salimans, T., Zhang, H., Radford, A., Metaxas, D.: Improving gans using optimal transport. arXiv preprint arXiv:1803.05573 (2018)
25. Sanjabi, M., Ba, J., Razaviyayn, M., Lee, J.D.: On the convergence and robustness of training gans with regularized optimal transport. In: Advances in Neural Information Processing Systems, pp. 7091–7101 (2018)
26. Shrivastava, A., Pfister, T., Tuzel, O., Susskind, J., Wang, W., Webb, R.: Learning from simulated and unsupervised images through adversarial training. In: Proceedings of the IEEE Conference on Computer Vision and Pattern Recognition, pp. 2107–2116 (2017)
27. Singh, S., Póczos, B.: Minimax distribution estimation in wasserstein distance. arXiv preprint arXiv:1802.08855 (2018)
28. Villani, C.: Optimal Transport: Old and New. Grundlehren der mathematischen Wissenschaften, vol. 338. Springer Science & Business Media, Berlin (2008). https://doi.org/10.1007/978-3-540-71050-9
29. Wang, Z., Bovik, A.C., Sheikh, H.R., Simoncelli, E.P.: Image quality assessment: from error visibility to structural similarity. IEEE Trans. Image Process. 13(4), 600–612 (2004)
30. Xie, Y., Wang, X., Wang, R., Zha, H.: A fast proximal point method for wasserstein distance. arXiv preprint arXiv:1802.04307 (2018)

31. Zhao, H., Gallo, O., Frosio, I., Kautz, J.: Loss functions for image restoration with neural networks. IEEE Trans. Comput. Imaging **3**(1), 47–57 (2017)
32. Zhu, J.Y., Park, T., Isola, P., Efros, A.A.: Unpaired image-to-image translation using cycle-consistent adversarial networks. arXiv preprint (2017)

Deep Archetypal Analysis

Sebastian Mathias Keller$^{(\boxtimes)}$ ⓘ, Maxim Samarin ⓘ, Mario Wieser ⓘ,
and Volker Roth ⓘ

University of Basel, Basel, Switzerland
`sebastianmathias.keller@unibas.ch`

Abstract. Deep Archetypal Analysis (DeepAA) generates latent representations of high-dimensional datasets in terms of intuitively understandable basic entities called *archetypes*. The proposed method extends linear Archetypal Analysis (AA), an unsupervised method to represent multivariate data points as convex combinations of extremal data points. Unlike the original formulation, Deep AA is generative and capable of handling side information. In addition, our model provides the ability for data-driven representation learning which reduces the dependence on expert knowledge. We empirically demonstrate the applicability of our approach by exploring the chemical space of small organic molecules. In doing so, we employ the archetype constraint to learn two different latent archetype representations for the *same* dataset, with respect to two chemical properties. This type of supervised exploration marks a distinct starting point and let us steer de novo molecular design.

1 Introduction

Archetypal analysis (AA) is of particular interest when a given data set is assumed to be a superposition of various populations or mechanisms. For a given number of k archetypes, linear AA finds an optimal approximation of the data convex hull, i.e. a polytope, with respect to a given loss function. All data points can then be described as convex mixtures of these k extreme points. In evolutionary biology this has led to the interpretation of archetypes as the representatives most adapted to a given task while non-archetypal representatives are described as mixtures of these extreme or pure types – able to perform a variety of tasks but non of them optimally [28]. We identified several limitations of the linear AA model which we would like to address. (I) For data points on a linear submanifold, e.g. a plane in $\mathbb{R}^2$, a strictly monotone transformation should in general have no influence on which points are identified as archetypes. But such a transformation would in fact introduce a non-zero curvature to that submanifold. As a consequence it would become impossible for *linear* AA to approximate equally well the data convex hull, given the same number k of archetypes

---

Electronic supplementary material The online version of this chapter (https://doi.org/10.1007/978-3-030-33676-9_12) contains supplementary material, which is available to authorized users.

G. A. Fink et al. (Eds.): DAGM GCPR 2019, LNCS 11824, pp. 171–185, 2019.
https://doi.org/10.1007/978-3-030-33676-9_12

as before. (II) Using linear AA to explore a dataset and uncover meaningful archetypes usually requires some form of prior knowledge. Either by knowing how many archetypes k are necessary to have an acceptable trade-off between interpretability and error *or* by having domain knowledge about which dimensions of the dataset can/should be omitted, scaled or combined. This procedure of injecting *side information* to the exploration of a given dataset is unpractical at best, impossible even if no intuition about a given problem can be formed. Often side information is available in form of scalar labels, but of course side information could be any kind of richly structured data. When learning a representation of the data, linear AA offers no possibility to incorporate such side information by which to guide the selection of an optimal number of archetypes as well as the relevant dimensions. (III) Linear AA is non-generative. But especially the prospect of incorporating differentiated side information makes the ability to generate new samples – conditioned on that side information – more attractive. Closely related to that is the ability to interpolate which, in the sense of AA, would be expressed as a *geometric* interpolation within a coordinate system spanned by the k archetypes.

In the following we will propose solutions to these limitations in order to extend the area of applicability of AA. In short this entails recasting linear AA as a latent space model within the framework of the Deep Variational Information Bottleneck. Of course this means that our extension constitutes a non-linear version of AA. Extensions into non-linearity have been proposed in the past based on kernelization but such frameworks remain less flexible still in comparison to a learned deep network architecture. But with this increase in flexibility comes a certain trade-off: without side information to guide the learning of a meaningful latent representation the result might be without significance as increased flexibility implies a multitude of possible latent representations dependent only on the side information on which any learning process should therefore be conditioned.

Literature. Linear "Archetypal Analysis" (AA) was first proposed by Cutler and Breiman [8]. Since its conception AA has known several advancements on the algorithmic as well as the application side. An extension to (non-linear) Kernel AA is proposed by [3,20], algorithmic improvements by adapting a Frank–Wolfe type algorithm to calculate the archetypes are made by [4] and the extension by [27] introduces a probabilistic version of AA. Archetypal style analysis [33] applies AA to the learned image representations in deep neural networks for artistic style manipulation. In [22] the authors are concerned with model selection by asking for the optimal number of archetypes for a given dataset while [15] addresses in part the shortcoming of AA we describe in the introduction under (ii). Although AA did not prevail as a commodity tool for pattern analysis it has for example been used by [5] to find archetypal images in large image collections or by [7] to perform the analogous task for large document collections. For the human genotype data studied by [13], inferred archetypes are interpreted as representative populations for the measured genotypes. And in [10] AA is used to analyse galaxy spectra which are viewed as weighted superpositions of the emissions from stellar populations, nebular emissions and nuclear activity. Our work builds upon Variational Autoencoders (VAEs), arguably the most prevalent representatives of the class of "Deep Latent Variable Models". VAEs were introduced by [18,25] and use an inference network to perform a variational approximation of the posterior distribution of the latent variable. Important work in this direction include [14,17,24]. More recently, [1] has discovered a close connection between VAE and the Information Bottleneck principle [31]. Here, the Deep Variational Information Bottleneck (DVIB) is a VAE where X is replaced by Y in the decoder. Subsequently, the DVIB has been extended in multiple directions such as sparsity [32] or causality [21].

At the same time as our work, *AAnet* was published by [9]. There the authors introduce a neural network based extension of linear archetypal analysis on the basis of standard non-variational autoencoders. In their work two regularization terms, applied to an intermediate representation provide the latent archetypal convex representation of a non-linear transformation of the input. In contrast to our work which is based on probabilistic generative models (VAE, DVIB), *AAnet* attempts to emulate the generative process by adding noise to the latent representation during training. Further, no side information is incorporated which can – and in our opinion should – be used to constrain potentially *over-flexible* neural networks and guide the optimisation process towards learning a meaningful representation.

Contribution. We propose *Deep Archetypal Analysis* (DeepAA) which is a novel, non-linear extension of the original model proposed by [8]. By introducing *DeepAA* within a DVIB framework we address several issues of the original model. Unlike the original model, *DeepAA* (i) is able to identify meaningful archetypes even on non-linear data manifolds, (ii) does not rely on expert knowledge when combining relevant dimensions or learning appropriate transformations (e.g. scaling) and (iii) is able to incorporate side information into the learning process in order to regularize and guide the learning process towards meaningful latent representations. On a large scale experiment we demonstrate the usefulness of *DeepAA* in a setting with side information on the QM9 dataset which contains the chemical structures and properties of 134 kilo molecules [23,26]. As modern chemistry and material science are increasingly concerned with material property prediction, we show that *DeepAA* can be used to *systematically* explore vast chemical spaces in order to identify starting points for further chemical optimisation.

2 Method

2.1 Linear Archetypal Analysis

Linear AA [8] is a form of non-negative matrix factorization where a matrix $X \in \mathbb{R}^{n \times p}$ of n data vectors is approximated as $X \approx ABX = AZ$ with $A \in \mathbb{R}^{n \times k}$,

$B \in \mathbb{R}^{k \times n}$, and usually $k < \min\{n, p\}$. In AA parlance, the *archetype* matrix $Z \in \mathbb{R}^{k \times p}$ contains the k archetypes $\mathbf{z}_1, .., \mathbf{z}_j, .., \mathbf{z}_k$ and the model is subject to the following constraints:

$$a_{ij} \geq 0 \ \wedge \ \sum_{j=1}^{k} a_{ij} = 1, \quad b_{ji} \geq 0 \ \wedge \ \sum_{i=1}^{n} b_{ji} = 1 \tag{1}$$

Constraining the entries of A and B to be non-negative and demanding that both weight matrices are row stochastic, implies a representation of the data vectors $\mathbf{x}_{i=1..n}$ as a weighted sum of the rows of Z while simultaneously representing the archetypes $\mathbf{z}_{j=1..k}$ themselves as a weighted sum of the n data vectors in X:

$$\mathbf{x}_i \approx \sum_{j=1}^{k} a_{ij} \mathbf{z}_j = \mathbf{a}_i Z, \quad \mathbf{z}_j = \sum_{i=1}^{n} b_{ji} \mathbf{x}_i = \mathbf{b}_j X \tag{2}$$

Due to the constraints on A and B in Eq. 1 both the representation of $\mathbf{x}_i$ and $\mathbf{z}_j$ in Eq. 2 are *convex* combinations. Therefore the archetypes approximate the data convex hull and increasing the number k of archetypes improves this approximation. The central problem of AA is finding the weight matrices A and B for a given data matrix X.

A probabilistic formulation of linear AA is provided in [27] where it is observed that AA follows a simplex latent variable model and normal observation model. The generative process for the observations $\mathbf{x}_i$ in the presence of k archetypes with archetype weights $\mathbf{a}_i$ is given by

$$\mathbf{a}_i \sim \text{Dir}_k(\boldsymbol{\alpha}) \quad \wedge \quad \mathbf{x}_i \sim \mathcal{N}(\mathbf{a}_i Z, \epsilon^2 \mathbf{I}), \tag{3}$$

with uniform concentration parameters $\alpha_j = \alpha$ for all j summing up to $\mathbf{1}^\top \boldsymbol{\alpha} = 1$. That is the observations $\mathbf{x}_i$ are distributed according to an isotropic Gaussian with means $\boldsymbol{\mu}_i = \mathbf{a}_i Z$ and variance ϵ^2.

2.2 Deep Variational Information Bottleneck

We propose a model to generalise linear AA to the non-linear case based on the Deep Variational Information Bottleneck framework since it allows to incorporate side information Y by design and is known to be equivalent to the VAE in the case of $Y = X$, as shown in [1]. In contrast to the data matrix X in linear AA, a non-linear transformation $f(X)$ giving rise to a latent representation T of the data suitable for (non-linear) archetypal analysis is considered. I.e. the latent representation T takes the role of the data X in the previous treatment.

The DVIB combines the information bottleneck (IB) with the VAE approach [18,31]. The objective of the IB method is to find a random variable T which, while compressing a given random vector X, preserves as much information about a second given random vector Y. The objective function of the IB is as follows

$$\min_{p(\mathbf{t}|\mathbf{x})} I(X; T) - \lambda I(T; Y), \tag{4}$$

where λ is a Lagrange multiplier and I denotes the mutual information. Assuming the IB Markov chain $T - X - Y$ and a parametric form of Eq. 4 with parametric conditionals $p_\phi(\mathbf{t}|\mathbf{x})$ and $p_\theta(\mathbf{y}|\mathbf{t})$, Eq. 4 is written as

$$\max_{\phi,\theta} -I_\phi(\mathbf{t};\mathbf{x}) + \lambda I_{\phi,\theta}(\mathbf{t};\mathbf{y}). \tag{5}$$

As derived in [32], the two terms in Eq. 5 have the following forms:

$$I_\phi(T;X) = D_{KL}\left(p_\phi(\mathbf{t}|\mathbf{x})p(\mathbf{x})\|p(\mathbf{t})p(\mathbf{x})\right) = \mathbb{E}_{p(\mathbf{x})}D_{KL}\left(p_\phi(\mathbf{t}|\mathbf{x})\|p(\mathbf{t})\right) \tag{6}$$

and

$$\begin{aligned} I_{\phi,\theta}(T;Y) &= D_{KL}\left(\left[\int p(\mathbf{t}|\mathbf{y},\mathbf{x})p(\mathbf{y},\mathbf{x})\,d\mathbf{x}\right]\|p(\mathbf{t})p(\mathbf{y})\right) \\ &= \mathbb{E}_{p(\mathbf{x},\mathbf{y})}\mathbb{E}_{p_\phi(\mathbf{t}|\mathbf{x})}\log p_\theta(\mathbf{y}|\mathbf{t}) + h(Y). \end{aligned} \tag{7}$$

Here $h(Y) = -\mathbb{E}_{p(\mathbf{y})}\log p(\mathbf{y})$ denotes the entropy of Y in the discrete case or the differential entropy in the continuous case. The models in Eq. 6 and 7 can be viewed as the encoder and decoder, respectively. Assuming a standard prior of the form $p(\mathbf{t}) = \mathcal{N}(\mathbf{t};0,I)$ and a Gaussian distribution for the posterior $p_\phi(\mathbf{t}|\mathbf{x})$, the KL divergence in Eq. 6 becomes a KL divergence between two Gaussian distributions which can be expressed in analytical form as in [18]. $I_\phi(T;X)$ can then be estimated on mini-batches of size m as

$$I_\phi(\mathbf{t};\mathbf{x}) \approx \frac{1}{m}\sum_i D_{KL}\left(p_\phi(\mathbf{t}|\mathbf{x}_i)\|p(\mathbf{t})\right). \tag{8}$$

As for the decoder, $\mathbb{E}_{p(\mathbf{x},\mathbf{y})}\mathbb{E}_{p_\phi(\mathbf{t}|\mathbf{x})}\log p_\theta(\mathbf{y}|\mathbf{t})$ in Eq. 7 is estimated using the reparametrisation trick proposed by [18,25]:

$$I_{\phi,\theta}(\mathbf{t};\mathbf{y}) = \mathbb{E}_{p(\mathbf{x},\mathbf{y})}\mathbb{E}_{\varepsilon\sim\mathcal{N}(0,I)}\sum_i \log p_\theta\left(\mathbf{y}_i|\mathbf{t}_i = \boldsymbol{\mu}_i(\mathbf{x}) + diag\left(\boldsymbol{\sigma}_i(\mathbf{x})\right)\varepsilon\right) + \text{const.} \tag{9}$$

Note that without loss of generality we can assume $Y = (Y',X)$ in Eq. 5 and with $Y = X$ the original VAE is retrieved. The former will be used in the Sect. 3.3 experiment where side information Y' is available.

2.3 Deep Archetypal Analysis

Deep Archetypal Analysis can then be formulated in the following way. For the sampling of $\mathbf{t}_i$ in Eq. (9) the probabilistic AA approach as in Eq. (3) can be used which leads to

$$\mathbf{t}_i \sim \mathcal{N}\left(\boldsymbol{\mu}_i(\mathbf{x}) = \mathbf{a}_i Z,\ \sigma_i^2(\mathbf{x})\mathbf{I}\right), \tag{10}$$

where the mean $\boldsymbol{\mu}_i$ given through $\mathbf{a}_i$ and variance σ_i^2 are non-linear transformations of the data point $\mathbf{x}_i$ learned by the encoder. We note that the means $\boldsymbol{\mu}_i$ are convex combinations of weight vectors $\mathbf{a}_i$ and the archetypes $\mathbf{z}_{j=1..k}$ which in return are considered to be convex combinations of the means $\boldsymbol{\mu}_{i=1..m}$ and

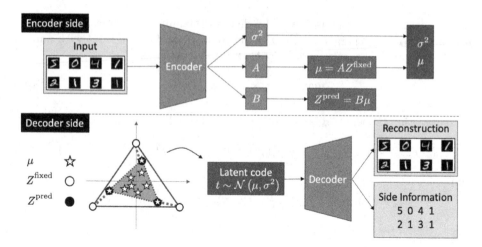

Fig. 1. Illustration of the *DeepAA* model. **Encoder side**: Learning weight matrices A and B allows to compute the archetype loss ℓ_{AT} in Eq. (11) and sample latent variables $\mathbf{t}$ as described in Eq. (10). The constraints on A and B in Eq. (1) are enforced by using softmax layers. **Decoder side**: Z^{fixed} represent the fixed archetype positions in latent space while Z^{pred} are given by the convex hull of the transformed data point means μ during training. Minimizing ℓ_{AT} corresponds to minimizing the red dashed (pairwise) distances. The input is reconstructed from the latent variable $\mathbf{t}$. In the presence of side information, the latent representation allows to reproduce the side information Y' as well as the input X. (Color figure online)

weight vectors $\mathbf{b}_j$.[1] By learning weight matrices $A \in \mathbb{R}^{m \times k}$ and $B \in \mathbb{R}^{k \times m}$ which are subject to the constraints formulated in Eq. (1) and parameterised by ϕ, a non-linear transformation of data X is learned which drives the structure of the latent space to form archetypes whose convex combination yield the transformed data points. A major difference to linear AA is that for *DeepAA* we cannot identify the positions of the archetypes $\mathbf{z}_j$ as there is no absolute frame of reference in latent space. We thus position k archetypes at the vertex points of a $(k-1)$-simplex and collect these *fixed* coordinates in the matrix Z^{fixed}. These requirements lead to an additional archetypal loss of

$$\ell_{\text{AT}} = ||Z^{\text{fixed}} - BAZ^{\text{fixed}}||_2^2 = ||Z^{\text{fixed}} - Z^{\text{pred}}||_2^2, \tag{11}$$

where $Z^{\text{pred}} = BAZ^{\text{fixed}}$ are the *predicted* archetype positions given the learned weight matrices A and B. For $Z^{\text{pred}} \approx Z^{\text{fixed}}$ the loss function ℓ_{AT} is minimized and the desired archetypal structure is achieved. The objective function of *DeepAA* is then given by

$$\max_{\phi, \theta} -I_\phi(\mathbf{t}; \mathbf{x}) + \lambda I_{\phi, \theta}(\mathbf{t}; \mathbf{y}) - \ell_{\text{AT}}. \tag{12}$$

---

[1] Note that $i = 1..m$ (and not up to n), which reflects that deep neural networks usually require batch-wise training with batch size m.

A visual illustration of *DeepAA* is given in Fig. 1. The constraints on A and B can be guaranteed by using softmax layers and *DeepAA* can be trained with a standard stochastic gradient descent technique such as Adam [16].

3 Experiments

3.1 Artificial Experiments

Data Generation. For our experiments we generate data $\mathbf{X} \in \mathbb{R}^{n \times 8}$ that are a convex mixture of k archetypes $\mathbf{Z} \in \mathbb{R}^{k \times 8}$ with $k \ll n$. The generative process for the data $\mathbf{x_i}$ follows Eq. (3) where $\mathbf{a}_i$ are stochastic weight vectors denoting the fraction of each of the k archetypes $\mathbf{z}_j$ needed to represent the data point $\mathbf{x}_i$. Here, we generate $n = 10000$ data points of which $k = 3$ are true archetypes. We set the variance to $\sigma^2 = 0.05$. We embed our linear 3-dim data manifold in a $n = 8$ dimensional space. Note that although classical and deep archetypal analysis is always performed on the full data set we only use a fraction of the data when visualizing our results.

Linear Archetypal Analysis – Linear Data. Linear archetypal analysis is performed using the efficient Frank-Wolfe procedure proposed in [4]. The input data is 8-dimensional and consequently the dimensionality of the archetypes is $\mathbf{Z} \in \mathbb{R}^{3 \times 8}$. For visualization we then use PCA to recover the original 3-dimensional manifold. The first three principal components of the ground truth data are shown in Fig. 2 as well as the computed archetypes (green triangles). The positions of the computed archetypes are in very good agreement with the ground truth. In these experiments, the data generating process is known and the number of archetypes $k = 3$ can be considered as an available *side information*.

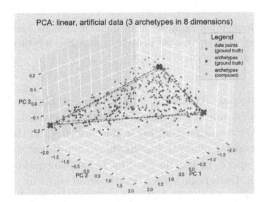

Fig. 2. PCA projection of 8-dim data after performing linear archetypal analysis. The original linear data submanifold is a convex combination of 3 archetypes. (Color figure online)

Linear Archetypal Analysis – Non-linear Data. Introducing a non-linearity to the data, e.g. by applying the exponential to a dimension of $\mathbf{X}$, results in a curved data submanifold as shown in Fig. 3a. For example ratios of power or field quantities are usually measured in decibels which is the logarithm of the these ratios. An exponentiation, i.e. introducing a strictly monotone transform, should in general not change which data points are identified as archetypes nor the number of archetypes necessary to obtain a given loss value. Figure 3a demonstrates that linear archetypal analysis is unable to recover the true archetypes on the same dataset used in the previous experiment but *after* a strictly monotone transform had been applied. Moreover to obtain a similar reconstruction loss as for the *linear* submanifold at least 5 archetypes are necessary as can be seen in Fig. 3b. Although the additional two archetypes are necessary to better approximate the data convex hull it would be counter-intuitive to interpret them as *extremes* of the dataset.

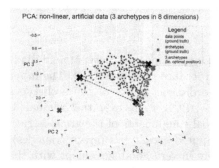 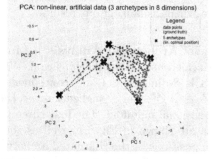

(a) A curved 2-dim manifold. None of the three archetypes identified by linear archetypal analysis can be interpreted as extremes.

(b) Linear archetypal analysis requires at least five archetypes to describe the data convex hull reasonably well.

Fig. 3. While linear archetypal analysis is in general able to approximate the data convex hull given a large enough number of archetypes, their interpretation as extremal elements is in general not ensured.

Non-linear Archetypal Analysis – Non-linear Data. Deep archetypal analysis *without explicit* side information is used to learn a latent linear archetypal representation. We consider as implicit side information the knowledge that 3 archetypes were used to generate our artificial non-linear data and therefore chose a 2-dim latent space. In Fig. 4a the first three principal components of the 8-dim data are shown. Data points have been colored according to the third principal component. In Fig. 4b the learned latent space shows that the archetypes A, B and C have been mapped to the appropriate vertices of the latent simplex. Moreover the sequence of color stripes shown in Fig. 4a has correctly been mapped into latent space. Within the latent space data points are again described as convex linear combinations of the latent archetypes. Latent data points can also be reconstructed in the original data space through the learned decoder

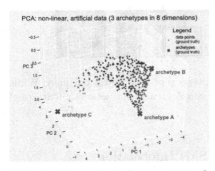

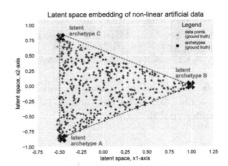

(a) The first three principal components of a non-linear 8-dim manifold. Despite the curvature only three *true* archetypes exist.

(b) 2-dim latent space learned by deep archetypal analysis. Side information used was the known number of archetypes.

Fig. 4. Deep archetypal analysis maps the archetypes from data space onto the vertices of the simplex and conserves the stripe pattern visible in the data space.

network. The network architecture used for this experiment was a simple feed-forward network (2 layered encoder and decoder), training for 20 epochs with a batch size of 100 and a learning rate of 0.001.

3.2 Generative Aspects and Model Selection

DeepAA allows to generate samples by specifying the mixture coefficients or proportions each archetype shall have in the make-up of a new sample. As a proof of concept, archetypal faces in the large-scale CelebFaces Attributes (CelebA) dataset [19] are learned and new faces generated.

In our experiment we adopt the "Deep Feature Consistent Variational Autoencoder" proposed by [12] which makes use of a (feature) perceptual loss as the reconstruction loss. In our implementation, we use the VAE-123 model of the original paper with the modification as depicted in Fig. 1. We train our model with the Adam optimizer [16] at a learning rate of 0.0005 and we set the first moment decay rate to $\beta_1 = 0.5$. Training is performed with a batch size of 64 for 10 epochs and 90%/10% split of the dataset for training/testing. In the experiment, no side information was used. In order to identify the appropriate number of archetypes we propose a model selection technique similar to the "elbow" method by [11]: The (minimal) reconstruction loss for different numbers of archetypes, evaluated on the test set, is recorded as shown in Fig. 6a. The optimal number of archetypes is considered to be the point where the curve starts converging, which in our case is at 35 archetypes (archetypal faces can be found in the supplement). Figure 5 displays an exemplary interpolation of generated faces: Starting at the latent coordinates which represent the face of a young man we move along a straight line in direction of a vertex point of the latent space simplex. While moving along this line we decode, at regular intervals, a total of six latent samples.

Fig. 5. Interpolation sequence towards an archetype representing an old man: While approaching the archetype (archetype B3 in the supplement), characteristic features of the archetypal face are reinforced.

3.3   Exploring Chemical Spaces with Side Information

Dataset: As mentioned in the introduction, archetypal analysis lends itself to a distinctly evolutionary interpretation. Although this is certainly a more biological perspective, the basic principle can be transferred to other fields such as chemistry. In this experiment we explore the chemical space which is the space of all molecules that already exist or can be produced. As side information we use the *heat capacity* C_v which quantifies the amount of energy (in Joule) needed to increase 1 Mol of molecules by $1\,K$ at constant volume. Here, a high C_v is especially important for a huge number of applications such as thermal energy storage [6]. In our experiments, we use the QM9 dataset [23,26] which was calculated on ab initio DFT method based structures and properties of 134k organic molecules with up to nine atoms (C, O, N, or F), without counting hydrogen.

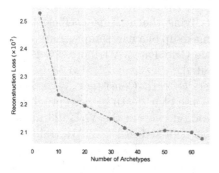
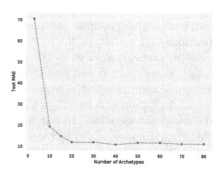

(a) CelebA: Reconstruction loss with varying number of archetypes.

(b) QM9: Test MAE with a varying number of archetypes.

Fig. 6. Model selection curves: reconstruction loss vs the number of archetypes.

Set-Up: We extracted 204 features for every molecule by using the Chemistry Development Kit [29]. The neural architectures used have 3 hidden layers with 1024, 512 and 256 neurons, respectively and ReLU activation functions.

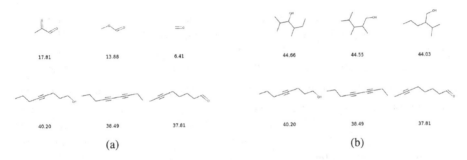

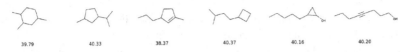

Fig. 7. The panels illustrate a comparison between two archetypes where the labels represent the corresponding heat capacity. Here, the columns denote the molecules that are closest to the specific archetype and the rows are the archetypes. Panel (a) compares a long chain versus a short chain archetype. Panel (b) compares archetypal molecules with the same mass but different shapes.

Fig. 8. Interpolation between two archetypes produced by our model. The label denote the molecules' heat capacity. While we show only one example, the same results can also be observed for other archetype combinations.

We train our model in a *supervised* fashion, by reconstructing the molecule and the side information simultaneously. In Experiment 1, we continuously increase the number of latent dimensions to perform model selection. In Experiment 2 and 3, we fix the number of latent dimensions to 19 which corresponds to 20 archetypes. During training, we steadily increase the Lagrange multiplier λ by 1.01 every 500 iterations. Our model is trained with the Adam optimizer [16] with an initial learning rate of 0.01. We decay the learning rate with an exponential decay by 0.95 every 10k iterations. In addition, we use a batch size of 2048 and train the model for 350k iterations. The dataset is divided in a training and test split of 90/10%.

In **Experiment 1**, we asses the MAE error when varying the number of archetypes in Fig. 6b. In our case, we perform model selection by observing where the MAE converges (starting from 20 archetypes) to select the optimal number of archetypes. Obviously, if the number of archetypes is smaller, it becomes more difficult to reconstruct the data. This stems from the fact there exist a large number of molecules with almost the same heat capacity but with a different shape. Thus, molecules with different shapes are mapped to archetypes with the same heat capacity which makes it hard to resolve the many-to-one mapping in the latent space.

In **Experiment 2**, we identify archetypal molecules that are associated with a particular heat capacity. In this setting, we focus on 20 archetypes (Fig. 6b) to obtain the optimal exploration-exploitation trade-off. While focusing only on a small selection of archetypes, we provide the full list in the supplement. In chemistry, the heat capacity is defined as $C_v = \frac{d\epsilon}{dT}\big|_{v=const}$ where ϵ denotes the energy of a molecule and T is the temperature. The energy can be further decomposed into $\epsilon = \epsilon^{Tr} + \epsilon^R + \epsilon^V + \epsilon^E$ where Tr depicts translation, R rotation, V vibration and E the electric contribution, respectively [2,30]. Building upon this knowledge, we compare different archetypal molecules associated with a particular heat capacity (Fig. 7). Here, the rows correspond to archetypes and the columns depict the three closest test molecules to the archetype. In Fig. 7a we illustrate two archetypes with a high and low heat capacity. The first row archetype has a lower heat capacity because of its shorter chain and more double bonds. Due to these properties, the archetype is more stable which results in a lower vibrational energy V and subsequently in a lower heat capacity. Figure 7b plots both a non-linear and a linear archetypal molecule with the same atomic mass. Here, the linear molecule loses one of its rotational modes due to its geometry. Therefore, the second row archetype has a lower rotational energy R compared to the first row archetype, leading to a lower heat capacity.

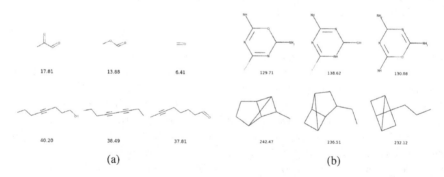

(a)   (b)

Fig. 9. The panels illustrate a comparison between archetypes with side information with the highest and lowest property values. Here, the labels correspond to the heat capacity (a) and the band gap energy (b). The columns denote the molecules that are closest to a specific certain and the rows denote the archetypes. Panel (a) depicts archetypal heat capacity molecules and Panel (b) shows archetypal band gap energy molecules.

In **Experiment 3**, we focus on the interpolation between two archetypes. We do so by plotting the test samples which are closest to the linear connection between the two archetypes. Here, we observe a smooth transition from a ring molecule to a linear molecule with the same heat capacity. Along these archetypes, which both are similar in heat capacities but differ in shape, a molecule can only change its shape but it cannot go beyond a particular heat capacity. Results are shown in Fig. 8.

Finally, in **Experiment 4**, we demonstrate that our model structures latent spaces according to the side information provided. Consequently, a molecule being a mixture of archetypes with respect to heat capacity might become archetypal with respect to another property. Here, we compare the discovered archetypes for two specific chemical properties, heat capacity and band gap energy. In Fig. 9, we plot the archetypes with the highest and lowest heat capacity (Fig. 9a) and the highest and lowest band gap energy (Fig. 9b), respectively. The extreme archetypes significantly differ in their structure as well as their atomic composition based on their property. For example, the archetype with low heat capacity are rather small with only a few C and O atoms. In contrast, the archetype with a low band gap energy are composed as rings with N and H atoms. A more detailed comparison between all archetypes can be found in the supplement.

4 Conclusion

In this paper, we introduced a novel neural network based approach to learn a structured latent representation of a given dataset. The structure we impose onto the latent space allows to characterize this space through its most extremal or *archetypal* representatives. In doing so, we build upon the linear AA approach and combine this concept with the deep IB principle to obtain a non-linear archetype model. In contrast to the classical approach our method offers three advantages: First, our model introduces a data-driven representation learning which reduces the dependence on expert knowledge. Second, we learn appropriate transformations to obtain meaningful archetypes even on non-linear data manifolds. Third, we are able to incorporate side information into the learning process. This counteracts overly flexible deep neural networks in order to identify meaningful archetypes with specific properties and facilitate an interpretable exploration of the latent space representations. Our experiment on the QM9 molecular dataset demonstrate the applicability of our method in an important real world setting.

Acknowledgements. S. Keller is partially supported by the Swiss National Science Foundation project CR32I2 159682. M. Samarin is supported by the Swiss National Science Foundation grant 407540 167333 as part of the Swiss National Research Programme NRP 75 "Big Data". M. Wieser is partially supported by the NCCR MARVEL, funded by the Swiss National Science Foundation and SNSF grant 51MRP0158328 (SystemsX.ch).

References

1. Alemi, A.A., Fischer, I., Dillon, J.V., Murphy, K.: Deep variational information bottleneck. CoRR abs/1612.00410 (2016). http://arxiv.org/abs/1612.00410
2. Atkins, P., de Paula, J.: Atkins' Physical Chemistry. OUP, Oxford (2010)

3. Bauckhage, C., Manshaei, K.: Kernel archetypal analysis for clustering web search frequency time series. In: 22nd International Conference on Pattern Recognition, pp. 1544–1549, August 2014. https://doi.org/10.1109/ICPR.2014.274

4. Bauckhage, C., Kersting, K., Hoppe, F., Thurau, C.: Archetypal analysis as an autoencoder. In: Workshop New Challenges in Neural Computation 2015, pp. 8–16, October 2015. https://www.techfak.uni-bielefeld.de/~fschleif/mlr/mlr_03_2015.pdf

5. Bauckhage, C., Thurau, C.: Making archetypal analysis practical. In: Denzler, J., Notni, G., Süße, H. (eds.) DAGM 2009. LNCS, vol. 5748, pp. 272–281. Springer, Heidelberg (2009). https://doi.org/10.1007/978-3-642-03798-6_28

6. Cabeza, L.F., et al.: Lithium in thermal energy storage: a state-of-the-art review. Renew. Sustain. Energy Rev. **42**, 1106–1112 (2015)

7. Canhasi, E., Kononenko, I.: Weighted hierarchical archetypal analysis for multi-document summarization. Comput. Speech Lang. **37** (2015). https://doi.org/10.1016/j.csl.2015.11.004

8. Cutler, A., Breiman, L.: Archetypal analysis. Technometrics **36**(4), 338–347 (1994). https://doi.org/10.1080/00401706.1994.10485840. http://digitalassets.lib.berkeley.edu/sdtr/ucb/text/379.pdf

9. van Dijk, D., Burkhardt, D., Amodio, M., Tong, A., Wolf, G., Krishnaswamy, S.: Finding archetypal spaces for data using neural networks. arXiv preprint arXiv:1901.09078 (2019)

10. Chan, B.H.P., Mitchell, D., Cram, L.: Archetypal analysis of galaxy spectra. Mon. Not. Roy. Astron. Soc. **338** (2003). https://doi.org/10.1046/j.1365-8711.2003.06099.x

11. Hart, Y., et al.: Inferring biological tasks using pareto analysis of high-dimensional data. Nat. Methods **12**(3), 233 (2015)

12. Hou, X., Shen, L., Sun, K., Qiu, G.: Deep feature consistent variational autoencoder. In: IEEE Winter Conference on Applications of Computer Vision (WACV), pp. 1133–1141. IEEE (2017)

13. Huggins, P., Pachter, L., Sturmfels, B.: Toward the human genotope. Bull. Math. Biol. **69**(8), 2723–2735 (2007). https://doi.org/10.1007/s11538-007-9244-7

14. Jang, E., Gu, S., Poole, B.: Categorical reparameterization with Gumbel-Softmax. In: International Conference on Learning Representations (ICLR) (2017)

15. Kaufmann, D., Keller, S., Roth, V.: Copula archetypal analysis. In: Gall, J., Gehler, P., Leibe, B. (eds.) GCPR 2015. LNCS, vol. 9358, pp. 117–128. Springer, Cham (2015). https://doi.org/10.1007/978-3-319-24947-6_10

16. Kingma, D.P., Ba, J.: Adam: a method for stochastic optimization. abs/1412.6980 (2014)

17. Kingma, D.P., Mohamed, S., Rezende, D.J., Welling, M.: Semi-supervised learning with deep generative models. In: Advances in Neural Information Processing Systems 27: Annual Conference on Neural Information Processing Systems 2014, 8–13 December 2014, Montreal, pp. 3581–3589 (2014)

18. Kingma, D.P., Welling, M.: Auto-encoding variational Bayes. CoRR abs/1312.6114 (2013)

19. Liu, Z., Luo, P., Wang, X., Tang, X.: Deep learning face attributes in the wild. In: Proceedings of International Conference on Computer Vision (ICCV), December 2015

20. Mørup, M., Hansen, L.K.: Archetypal analysis for machine learning and data mining. Neurocomputing **80**, 54–63 (2012)

21. Parbhoo, S., Wieser, M., Roth, V.: Causal deep information bottleneck. arXiv e-prints arXiv:1807.02326, July 2018

22. Prabhakaran, S., Raman, S., Vogt, J.E., Roth, V.: Automatic model selection in archetype analysis. In: Pinz, A., Pock, T., Bischof, H., Leberl, F. (eds.) DAGM/OAGM 2012. LNCS, vol. 7476, pp. 458–467. Springer, Heidelberg (2012). https://doi.org/10.1007/978-3-642-32717-9_46

23. Ramakrishnan, R., Dral, P.O., Rupp, M., von Lilienfeld, O.A.: Quantum chemistry structures and properties of 134 kilo molecules. Sci. Data 1 (2014)

24. Rezende, D., Mohamed, S.: Variational inference with normalizing flows. In: Bach, F., Blei, D. (eds.) Proceedings of the 32nd International Conference on Machine Learning. Proceedings of Machine Learning Research, vol. 37, pp. 1530–1538. PMLR, Lille, 07–09 July 2015

25. Rezende, D.J., Mohamed, S., Wierstra, D.: Stochastic backpropagation and approximate inference in deep generative models 32(2), 1278–1286 (2014)

26. Ruddigkeit, L., van Deursen, R., Blum, L.C., Reymond, J.L.: Enumeration of 166 billion organic small molecules in the chemical universe database GDB-17. J. Chem. Inf. Model. 52(11), 2864–2875 (2012). https://doi.org/10.1021/ci300415d. pMID: 23088335

27. Seth, S., Eugster, M.J.A.: Probabilistic archetypal analysis. Mach. Learn. 102(1), 85–113 (2016). https://doi.org/10.1007/s10994-015-5498-8

28. Shoval, O., et al.: Evolutionary trade-offs, pareto optimality, and thegeometry of phenotype space. Science 336(6085), 1157–1160 (2012). https://doi.org/10.1126/science.1217405. http://science.sciencemag.org/content/336/6085/1157

29. Steinbeck, C., Han, Y.Q., Kuhn, S., Horlacher, O., Luttmann, E., Willighagen, E.: The Chemistry Development Kit (CDK): an open-source Java library for chemo- and bioinformatics. J. Chem. Inf. Comput. Sci. 43(2), 493–500 (2003)

30. Tinoco, I.: Physical Chemistry: Principles and Applications in Biological Sciences. No. S. 229-313 in Physical Chemistry: Principles and Applications in Biological Sciences. Prentice Hall, Englewood Cliffs (2002)

31. Tishby, N., Pereira, F.C., Bialek, W.: The information bottleneck method. arXiv preprint arXiv:physics/0004057 (2000)

32. Wieczorek, A., Wieser, M., Murezzan, D., Roth, V.: Learning sparse latent representations with the deep copula information bottleneck. In: International Conference on Learning Representations (ICLR) (2018)

33. Wynen, D., Schmid, C., Mairal, J.: Unsupervised learning of artistic styles with archetypal style analysis. In: Advances in Neural Information Processing Systems, pp. 6584–6593 (2018)

Oral Session IV: Image Analysis, Applications

Single Level Feature-to-Feature Forecasting with Deformable Convolutions

Josip Šarić[1]([✉]), Marin Oršić[1], Tonći Antunović[2], Sacha Vražić[2], and Siniša Šegvić[1]

[1] University of Zagreb, Faculty of Electrical Engineering and Computing, Zagreb, Croatia
josip.saric@fer.hr
[2] Rimac Automobili, Sveta Nedelja, Croatia

Abstract. Future anticipation is of vital importance in autonomous driving and other decision-making systems. We present a method to anticipate semantic segmentation of future frames in driving scenarios based on feature-to-feature forecasting. Our method is based on a semantic segmentation model without lateral connections within the upsampling path. Such design ensures that the forecasting addresses only the most abstract features on a very coarse resolution. We further propose to express feature-to-feature forecasting with deformable convolutions. This increases the modelling power due to being able to represent different motion patterns within a single feature map. Experiments show that our models with deformable convolutions outperform their regular and dilated counterparts while minimally increasing the number of parameters. Our method achieves state of the art performance on the Cityscapes validation set when forecasting nine timesteps into the future.

1 Introduction

Ability to anticipate the future is an important attribute of intelligent behavior, especially in decision-making systems such as robot navigation and autonomous driving. It allows to plan actions not only by looking at the past, but also by considering the future. Accurate anticipation is critical for reliable decision-making of autonomous vehicles. The farther the forecast, the longer the time to avoid undesired outcomes of motion. We believe that semantic forecasting will be one of critical concepts for avoiding accidents in future autonomous driving systems.

There are three meaningful levels at which forecasting could be made: raw images, feature tensors, and semantic predictions. Forecasting raw images [20, 26] is known to be a hard problem. Better results have been obtained with direct forecasting of semantic segmentation predictions [18]. The third approach is to forecast feature tensors instead of predictions [25]. Recent work [17] proposes a

---

Electronic supplementary material The online version of this chapter (https:// doi.org/10.1007/978-3-030-33676-9_13) contains supplementary material, which is available to authorized users.

G. A. Fink et al. (Eds.): DAGM GCPR 2019, LNCS 11824, pp. 189–202, 2019.
https://doi.org/10.1007/978-3-030-33676-9_13

bank of feature-to-feature (F2F) models which target different resolutions along the upsampling path of a feature pyramid network [16]. Each F2F model receives corresponding features from the four previous frames (t, t−3, t−6, t−9) and forecasts the future features (t+3 or t+9). The forecasted features are used to predict instance-level segmentations [8] at the corresponding resolution level.

This paper addresses forecasting of future semantic segmentation maps in road driving scenarios. We propose three improvements with respect to the original F2F approach [17]. Firstly, we base our work on a single-frame model without lateral connections. This requires only one F2F model which targets the final features of the convolutional backbone. These features are very well suited for the forecasting task due to high semantic content and coarse resolution. Secondly, we express our F2F model with deformable convolutions [31]. This greatly increases the modelling power due to capability to account for different kinds of motion patterns within a single feature map. Thirdly, we provide an opportunity for the two independently trained submodels (F2F, upsampling path) to adapt to each other by joint fine-tuning. This would be very difficult to achieve with multiple F2F models [17] since the required set of cached activations would not fit into GPU memory. Thorough forecasting experiments on Cityscapes val [4] demonstrate state-of-the-art mid-term (t+9) performance and runner-up short-term (t+3) performance where we come second only to [24] who require a large computational effort to extract optical flow prior the forecast. Two experiments on Cityscapes test suggest that our performance estimates on the validation subset contain very little bias (if any).

2   Related Work

Semantic Segmentation. State of the art methods for semantic segmentation [3,14,28,30] have overcome the 80% mIoU barrier on Cityscapes test. However, these methods are not well suited for F2F forecasting due to huge computational cost and large GPU memory footprint. We therefore base our research on a recent semantic segmentation model [22] which achieves a great ratio between accuracy (75.5 mIoU Cityscapes test) and speed (39 Hz on GTX1080Ti with 2 MP input). This model is a great candidate for F2F [17] forecasting due to a backbone with low-dimensional features (ResNet-18, 512D) and a lean upsampling path similar to FPN [16]. In particular, we rely on a slightly impaired version of that model (72.5 mIoU Cityscapes val) with no lateral connections in the upsampling path.

Raw Image Forecasting. Predicting future images is interesting because it opens opportunities for unsupervised representation learning on practically unlimited data. It has been studied in many directions: exploiting adversarial training [20] anticipating arbitrary future frames [26], or leveraging past forecasts to autoregressively anticipate further into the future [11].

Feature Forecasting. Feature-level forecasting has been first used to anticipate appearance and actions in video [25]. The approach uses past features to forecast the last AlexNet layer of a future frame. Later work [17] forecasts convolutional features and interprets them with the Mask-RCNN [8] head of the single-frame model. F2F approaches are applicable to dense prediction tasks such as panoptic segmentation [13], semantic segmentation [30], optical flow [23] etc.

Semantic Segmentation Forecasting. Luc et al. [18] set a baseline for direct semantic segmentation forecasting by processing softmax preactivations from past frames. Nabavi et al. [21] train an end-to-end model which forecasts intermediate features by convolutional LSTM [27]. Bhattacharyya et al. [1] use Bayesian learning to model the multi-modal nature of the future and directly predict future semantic segmentation of road driving scenes. None of the previously mentioned approaches utilize optical flow despite its usefulness for video recognition [7]. Jin et al. [10] jointly forecast semantic segmentation predictions and optical flow. They use features from the optical flow subnet to provide better future semantic maps. Terwilliger et al. [24] predict future optical flow and obtain future prediction by warping the semantic segmentation map from the current frame.

Convolutions with a Wide Field of View. Convolutional models [15] proved helpful in most visual recognition tasks. However, stacking vanilla convolutional layers often results in undersized receptive field. Consequently, the receptive field has been enlarged with dilated convolutions [29] and spatial pyramid pooling [30]. However, these techniques are unable to efficiently model geometric warps required by F2F forecasting. Early work on warping convolutional representations involved a global affine transformation at the tensor level [9]. Deformable convolutions [5] extend this idea by introducing per-activation convolutional warps which makes them especially well-suited for F2F forecasting.

3   Single-Level F2F Model with Deformable Convolutions

We propose a method for semantic segmentation forecasting composed of (i) feature extractor (ResNet-18), (ii) F2F forecasting model, and (iii) upsampling path, as illustrated in Fig. 1 (b). Yellow trapezoids represent ResNet processing blocks RB1–RB4 which form the feature extractor. The red rectangle represents the F2F model. The green rhombus designates spatial pyramid pooling (SPP) while the blue trapezoids designate modules which form the upsampling path.

Figure 1(a) shows the single-frame model which we use to train the feature extractor and the upsampling path. We also use this model as an oracle which predicts future segmentation by observing a future frame. Experiments with the oracle estimate upper performance bound of semantic segmentation forecasting.

3.1   Training Procedure

The training starts from a public parameterization of the feature extractor pretrained on ImageNet [6]. We jointly train the feature extractor and the upsampling path for single-frame semantic segmentation [22]. We use that model to extract features at times $t-9$, $t-6$, $t-3$, and t (sources), as well as at time $t+dt$ (target). We then train the F2F model with L2 loss in an unsupervised manner. However, the forecasting induces a covariate shift due to imperfect F2F prediction. Therefore, we adapt the upsampling path to noisy forecasted features by fine-tuning the F2F model and the upsampling path using cross-entropy loss with respect to ground truth labels. We update the F2F parameters by averaging gradients from F2F L2 loss and the backpropagated cross-entropy loss.

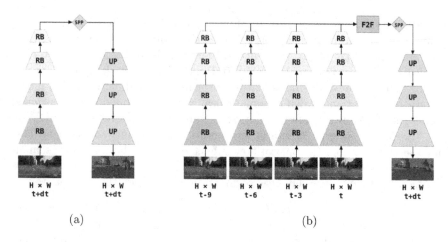

(a)   (b)

Fig. 1. Structural diagram of the employed single-frame model (a) and the proposed compound model for forecasting semantic segmentation (b). The two models share the ResNet-18 feature extractor (yellow) and the upsampling path (green, blue). (Color figure online)

3.2 Proposed Feature-to-Feature Model

We propose a single-level F2F model operating on features from the last convolutional layer of ResNet-18. We formulate our model as a sequence of N deformable convolutions and denote it as DeformF2F-N. The first convolution of the sequence has the largest number of input feature maps since it blends features from all previous frames. Therefore we set its kernel size to 1×1. All other convolutions have 3×3 kernels and 128 feature maps, except the last one which recovers the number of feature maps to match the backbone output.

The proposed formulation differs from the original F2F architecture [17] in three important details. Firstly, we forecast backbone features instead of features from the upsampling path. Backbone features have a larger dimensionality, and are closer to ImageNet pre-trained parameters due to reduced learning rate during joint training. Hence, these features are more distinctive than features trained for recognition of only 19 classes. Forecasting SPP features decreased the validation performance for 1 % point (pp) mIoU in early experiments.

Secondly, we use a single-level F2F model which performs the forecasting at a very coarse resolution (1/32 of the original image). This is beneficial since small feature displacements simplify motion prediction (as in optical flow). Early multi-level forecasting experiments decreased performance for 2pp mIoU.

Thirdly, we use thin deformable convolutions [5] instead of thick dilated ones. This decreases the number of parameters and improves the performance as presented in ablation experiments. Feature-to-feature forecasting is rather geometrically than semantically heavy, since the inputs and the outputs are at the same semantic level. Regular convolutions lack the potential to learn geometrical transformations due to fixed grid sampling locations. In deformable convolutions, the grid sampling locations are displaced with learned per-pixel offsets which are inferred from the preceding feature maps. We believe that learnable displacements are a good match for F2F transformation since they are able to model semantically aware per-object dynamics across observed frames.

3.3   Inference

The proposed method requires features from four past frames. These features are concatenated and fed to the F2F module which forecasts the future features. The future features are fed to the upsampling path which predicts the future semantic segmentation. A perfect F2F forecast would attain performance of the single-frame model applied to the future frame, which we refer to as oracle.

The proposed method is suitable for real-time semantic forecast since the feature extractor needs to be applied only once per frame. Consider the computational complexity of the single-frame model as baseline. Then the only overhead for a single forecast corresponds to caching of four feature tensors evaluating the F2F model. If we require both the current prediction and a single forecast, then the overhead would additionally include one evaluation of the upsampling path.

4   Experiments

We perform experiments on the Cityscapes dataset [4] which contains 2975 training, 500 validation and 1525 test images with dense labels from 19 classes. The dataset includes 19 preceding and 10 succeeding unlabeled frames for each image. Each such mini-clip is 1.8 s long. Let $\mathbf{X}$ denote features from the last convolutional layer of ResNet-18. The shape of these features is $512 \times H/32 \times W/32$, where 512 is the number of feature maps, while H and W are image dimensions. Then, the model input is a tuple of features $(\mathbf{X}_{t-9}, \mathbf{X}_{t-6}, \mathbf{X}_{t-3}, \mathbf{X}_t)$. The model output are future features $\mathbf{X}_{t+3}$ (short-term prediction, 0.18 s) or $\mathbf{X}_{t+9}$ (mid-term prediction, 0.54 s) [17] which in most experiments correspond to the labeled frame in a mini-clip.

4.1   Implementation Details

We use the deformable convolution implementation from [2]. The features are pre-computed from full-size Cityscapes images and stored on SSD drive. We optimize the L2 regression loss with Adam [12]. We set the learning rate to 5e-4 and train our F2F models for 160 epochs with batch size 12 in all experiments. We fine-tune our model with SGD with learning rate set to 1e-4 and batch size 8 for 5 epochs. The training takes around 6 h on a single GTX1080Ti.

We measure semantic segmentation performance on the Cityscapes val dataset. We report the standard mean intersection over union metric over all 19 classes. We also measure mIoU for 8 classes representing moving objects (person, rider, car, truck, bus, train, motorcycle, and bicycle).

4.2 Comparison with the State of the Art on Cityscapes Val

Table 1 evaluates several models for semantic segmentation forecasting. The first section shows the performance of the oracle, and the copy-last-segmentation baseline which applies the single-frame model to the last observed frame. The second section shows results from the literature. The third section shows our results. The last section shows our result when F2F model is trained on two feature tuples per mini-clip. The row Luc F2F applies the model proposed in [17] as a component of our method. The methods DeformF2F-5 and DeformF2F-8 correspond to our models with 5 and 8 deformable convolutions respectively. The suffix FT denotes that our F2F model is fine-tuned with cross entropy loss.

Table 1. Semantic forecasting on the Cityscapes validation set.

	Short-term		Mid-term	
	mIoU	mIoU-MO	mIoU	mIoU-MO
Oracle	72.5	71.5	72.5	71.5
Copy last segmentation	52.2	48.3	38.6	29.6
Luc Dil10-S2S [18]	59.4	55.3	47.8	40.8
Luc Mask-S2S [17]	/	55.3	/	42.4
Luc Mask-F2F [17]	/	61.2	/	41.2
Nabavi [21]	60.0	/	/	/
Terwilliger [24]	**67.1**	**65.1**	51.5	46.3
Bhattacharyya [1]	65.1	/	51.2	/
Luc F2F (our implementation)	59.8	56.7	45.6	39.0
DeformF2F-5	63.4	61.5	50.9	46.4
DeformF2F-8	64.4	62.2	52.0	48.0
DeformF2F-8-FT	64.8	62.5	**52.4**	**48.3**
DeformF2F-8-FT (2 samples per seq.)	65.5	63.8	**53.6**	**49.9**

Poor results of copy-last-segmentation reflect the difficulty of the forecasting task. Our method DeformF2F-8 outperforms Luc F2F for 4.6pp mIoU. In comparison with the state-of-the-art, we achieve the best mid-term performance, while coming close to [24] in short-term, despite a weaker oracle (72.5 vs 74.3 mIoU) and not using optical flow. Cross entropy fine-tuning improves results by 0.4pp mIoU both for the short-term and the mid-term model. We applied DeformF2F-8-FT to Cityscapes test and achieved results similar to those on the validation set: 64.3 mIoU (short-term) and 52.6 mIoU (mid-term).

The last result in the table shows benefits of training on more data. Here we train our F2F model on two farthest tuples (instead of one) in each mini-clip. Cross entropy fine-tuning is done in the regular way, since groundtruth is available only in the 19th frame in each mini-clip. We notice significant improvement of 0.7 and 1.2pp mIoU for short-term and mid-term forecast respectively.

4.3 Single-Step vs. Autoregressive Mid-Term Forecast

There are two possible options for predicting further than one step into the future: (i) train a separate single-step model for each desired forecast interval, (ii) train only one model and apply it autoregressively. Autoregressive forecast applies the same model in the recurrent manner, by using the current prediction as input to each new iteration. Once the model is trained, the autoregression can be used to forecast arbitrary number of periods into the future. Unfortunately, autoregression accumulates prediction errors from intermediate forecasts. Hence, the compound forecast tends to be worse than in the single-step case.

Table 2. Validation of auto-regressive mid-term forecast on Cityscapes val.

DeformF2F-8 variant	Mid-term	
	mIoU	mIoU-MO
single-step	**52.4**	**48.3**
autoregressive 3×	48.7	43.5
autoregressive 3× fine-tuned	51.2	46.5

Table 2 validates autoregressive models. The first row shows our single-step model (cf. Table 1) for mid-term forecast. The middle row shows the baseline autoregressive forecast with our corresponding short-term model. The last row shows improvement due to recurrent fine-tuning for mid-term prediction, while initializing with the same short-term model as in the middle row. Fine-tuning brings 2.5pp mIoU improvement with respect to the autoregressive baseline. Nevertheless, the single-step model outperforms the best autoregressive model.

Table 3 shows per-class auto-regressive performance for different forecasting offsets. The three sections correspond to the oracle, two single-step models,

Table 3. Single-step and autoregressive per-class results on Cityscapes val. Rows denoted with [†] are evaluated only on Frankfurt sequences where long clips are available.

	road	sidewalk	building	wall	fence	pole	traffic light	traffic sign	vegetation	terrain	sky	person	rider	car	truck	bus	train	motorcycle	bicycle	mean
Oracle	97.5	81.6	90.7	50.1	53.4	56.1	60.3	70.8	90.9	60.9	92.9	75.9	53.0	93.2	67.4	84.4	72.0	54.5	71.7	72.5
Short-term	96.1	73.9	87.0	47.9	50.8	35.8	51.4	57.2	86.7	56.0	88.7	58.8	41.4	86.3	64.8	75.2	63.7	48.5	60.6	64.8
Mid-term	93.2	61.2	79.6	41.6	45.1	15.1	31.9	33.2	78.3	49.1	80.1	39.1	24.6	72.9	60.0	63.5	46.5	37.5	41.9	52.4
AR-3[†]	95.8	71.1	84.9	42.0	52.2	35.0	46.2	53.5	85.0	50.0	88.0	59.0	36.6	86.2	68.5	71.7	60.6	51.8	58.0	63.0
AR-6[†]	94.3	64.2	80.9	37.6	48.6	23.5	35.4	40.6	80.1	46.8	82.8	48.4	26.3	78.8	64.9	66.0	50.0	44.5	49.4	56.0
AR-9[†]	93.4	61.1	78.0	37.7	46.2	17.5	28.4	30.9	77.0	44.5	79.3	41.8	23.2	74.4	63.7	60.7	34.0	42.1	43.5	51.5
AR-12[†]	92.6	57.7	75.3	36.5	44.1	13.5	21.5	25.4	74.2	42.2	75.7	35.5	18.3	69.8	57.1	53.8	29.6	37.7	37.3	47.3
AR-15[†]	91.6	53.8	72.9	35.7	42.0	10.8	17.9	20.1	71.1	36.4	71.6	31.6	13.2	64.5	40.6	48.0	34.7	24.4	32.9	42.9
AR-18[†]	90.7	51.4	71.0	33.9	40.9	09.1	14.7	15.6	68.9	34.5	69.0	29.2	12.4	60.4	38.2	46.6	16.8	25.1	28.2	39.9

and autoregressive application of the last model from Table 2. Autoregressive experiments have been performed on 267 sequences from the Frankfurt subset of Cityscapes val. Long clips are not available for other cities.

The performance drop due to forecasting is largest for class person among all of moving object classes. We believe that this is because persons are articulated: it is not enough for the model to determine the new position of the object center, the model also needs to determine positions and poses of the parts (legs and arms). Poles seem to be the hardest static class because of their thin shape. Qualitative results (e.g. last two rows of Fig. 4) show that pole often gets dominated by large surrounding classes (building, sidewalk, road etc.).

Figure 2 plots mIoU results from the third section of Table 3 for various temporal offsets of the future frame, and explores contribution of autoregressive fine-tuning. We show mIoU and mIoU-MO (solid and dashed lines resp.) for a straight autoregressive model (red), and a model that was autoregressively fine-tuned for mid-term forecast (blue).

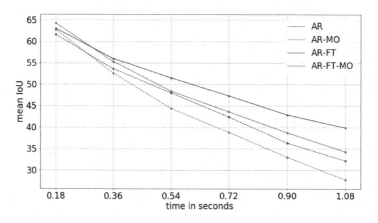

Fig. 2. Autoregressive mIoU performance at different forecasting offsets for the straight short-term model (red) and the model fine-tuned for mid-term prediction (blue). (Color figure online)

4.4   Validation of Deformable Convolutions

Table 4 compares the mIoU performance and the number of parameters for various design choices. Our DeformF2F-5 model achieves a 4-fold decrease in the number of parameters with respect to Luc F2F. Dilated and deformable convolutions achieve the largest impact in mid-term forecasting where the feature displacements are comparatively large. Dilation achieves a slight improvement on mid-term prediction. Deformable convolutions improve both the short-term and mid-term results while significantly outperforming the dilation models. This clearly validates the choice of deformable convolutions for F2F forecasting.

Table 4. Validation of plain, 2× dilated and deformable convolutions on Cityscapes.

	Short-term		Mid-term		#params
	mIoU	mIoU-MO	mIoU	mIoU-MO	
Luc F2F	59.8	56.7	45.6	39.0	5.50M
ConvF2F-5	60.4	56.6	43.8	36.3	1.30M
DilatedF2F-5	60.0	56.9	45.6	38.8	1.30M
DeformF2F-5	**63.4**	**61.5**	**50.9**	**46.4**	1.43M

4.5 Ablation of the Number of Input Frames

Table 5 investigates the impact of the number of input frames to short-term and mid-term performance. We always sample frames three steps apart. For instance, the second row in the table observes frames at $t-6$, $t-3$, and t. The model operating on a single frame performs significantly worse than the models which observe multiple frames. Such model can only predict the movement direction from object posture and/or orientation, while it is often very hard to forecast the magnitude of motion without looking at least one frame in the past. Models operating on two and three frames produce comparable short-term forecast with respect to the four frame model. Adding more frames from the past always improves the accuracy of mid-term forecasts. This suggests that the models benefit from past occurrences of the parts of the scene which are disoccluded in the forecasted frame. This effect is visible only in mid-term prediction, since such occlusion-disocclusion patterns are unlikely to occur across short time intervals.

Table 5. Ablation of the number of input frames. Two input frames are enough for short-term forecasting. More input frames improve performance of mid-term forecasts.

	#frames	Short-term		Mid-term	
		mIoU	mIoU-MO	mIoU	mIoU-MO
DeformF2F-8	4	64.4	62.2	**52.0**	**48.0**
	3	64.4	62.5	50.9	46.2
	2	**64.5**	**62.6**	50.7	46.2
	1	57.7	54.3	44.2	37.8

4.6 Could a Forecast Improve the Prediction in the Current Frame?

We consider an ensemble of a single-frame model which observes the current frame and a forecasting model which observes past frames. The predictions of the ensemble are a weighted average of softmax activations of the two models:

$$P(\mathbf{Y}_{t+3}|\mathbf{X}_{t-9}, .., \mathbf{X}_{t+3}) = \lambda \cdot P(\mathbf{Y}_{t+3}|\mathbf{X}_{t+3}) + (1-\lambda) \cdot P(\mathbf{Y}_{t+3}|\mathbf{X}_{t-9}, .., \mathbf{X}_t). \quad (1)$$

Similar results are achieved for $\lambda \in [0.7, 0.9]$. Table 6 presents experiments on Cityscapes val. The first two rows show the oracle and our best short-term model. The third row ensembles the previous two models according to (1). We observe 0.3pp improvement over the single-frame model. This may be interesting in autonomous driving applications which would need semantic segmentation for the current and the future frame in each time instant. In that case, the proposed ensemble would require no additional cost, since the forecast from the previous time instant can be cached. On the other hand, evaluating an ensemble of two single-frame models would imply double computational complexity.

Table 6. Performance of the ensemble of a single-frame model which observes the current frame with a forecasting model which observes only the four past frames.

	mIoU	mIoU-MO
Single frame model	72.5	71.5
DeformF2F-8-FT	64.8	62.5
Ensemble	**72.8**	**71.8**

4.7   Qualitative Results

Figures 3 and 4 show forecasted semantic segmentation on Cityscapes val for short-term and mid-term predictions respectively. We observe loss of spatial detail when forecasting sequences with greater dynamics and when predicting further into the future (cf. the first row in Figs. 3 and 4). The row 4 in Fig. 4 shows a red car turning left. Our model inferred the future spatial location of the car quite accurately. The last row shows a car which disoccludes the road opposite the camera. Our model correctly inferred the car motion and in-painted the disoccluded scenery in a feasible although not completely correct manner.

Fig. 3. Short-term semantic segmentation forecasts (0.18 s into the future) for 3 sequences. The columns show (i) the last observed frame, (ii) the future frame, (iii) the groundtruth segmentation, (iv) our oracle, and (v) our semantic segmentation forecast.

Fig. 4. Mid-term semantic segmentation predictions (0.5 s into the future) for 5 sequences. The columns show (i) the last observed frame, (ii) the future frame, (iii) the ground truth segmentation, (iv) our oracle, and (v) our semantic segmentation forecast.

Effective Receptive Field. We express the effective receptive field by measuring partial derivation of log-max-softmax [19] with respect to the four input images. The absolute magnitude of these gradients quantifies the importance of particular pixels for the given prediction. Figure 5 visualizes the results for our DeformF2F-8-FT mid-term model. The four leftmost columns show input images, while the two rightmost columns show the future image (unavailable to the model), and the semantic forecast. The green dot in the two rightmost columns designates the examined prediction. The red dots designate pixels in which the absolute magnitude of the gradient of the examined prediction is larger than a threshold. The threshold is dynamically set to the value of the k-th (k = 3000, top 0.15%) largest gradient within the last observed frame (t). In other words, we show pixels with top k gradients in the last observed frame, as well as a selection of pixels from the other frames according to the same threshold. We notice that most important pixels come from the last observed frame. Row 1 considers a static pixel which does not generate strong gradients in frames t−3, t−6, and t−9. Other rows consider dynamic pixels. We observe that the most important pixels for a given prediction usually correspond to object location in past frames. Distances between object locations in the last observed and the forecasted frame are often larger than 300 pixels. This emphasizes the role of deformable convolutions since the F2F model with plain convolutions is unable to compensate for such large offsets. The figure also illustrates the difficulty of forecasting in road-driving videos, and the difference of this task with respect to single-frame semantic segmentation. These visualizations allow us to explain and interpret successes and failures of our model and to gauge the range of its predictions. In particular we notice that most mid-term decisions rely only on

Fig. 5. Effective receptive field of mid-term forecast in 4 sequences. Columns show the four input frames, the future frame t+9 and the corresponding semantic segmentation forecast. We show pixels with the strongest gradient of log-max-softmax (red dots) in a hand-picked pixel (green dot) w.r.t. the each of the input frames. (Color figure online)

pixels from the last two frames. This is in accordance with mid-term experiments from Table 5 which show that frames t−6 and t−9 contribute only 1.3pp mIoU.

5   Conclusion and Future Work

We have presented a novel method for anticipating semantic segmentation of future frames in driving scenarios based on feature-to-feature (F2F) forecasting. Unlike previous methods, we forecast the most abstract backbone features with a single F2F model. This greatly improves the inference speed and favors the forecasting performance due to coarse resolution and high semantic content of the involved features. The proposed F2F model is based on deformable convolutions in order to account for geometric nature of F2F forecasting. We use a lightweight single-frame model without lateral connections, which allows to adapt the upsampling path to F2F noise by fine-tuning with respect to groundtruth labels. We perform experiments on the Cityscapes dataset. To the best of our knowledge, our mid-term semantic segmentation forecasts outperform all previous approaches. Our short-term model comes second only to a method which uses a stronger single-frame model and relies on optical flow. Evaluation on Cityscapes test suggests that our validation performance contains very little bias (if any). Suitable directions for future work include adversarial training of the upsampling path, complementing image frames with optical flow, investigating end-to-end learning, as well as evaluating performance on the instance segmentation task.

Acknowledgment. This work has been funded by Rimac Automobili. This work has been partially supported by European Regional Development Fund (DATACROSS) under grant KK.01.1.1.01.0009. We thank Pauline Luc and Jakob Verbeek for useful discussions during early stages of this work.

References

1. Bhattacharyya, A., Fritz, M., Schiele, B.: Bayesian prediction of future street scenes using synthetic likelihoods. arXiv preprint arXiv:1810.00746 (2018)
2. Chen, K., et al.: mmdetection. https://github.com/open-mmlab/mmdetection (2018)
3. Chen, L.C., Papandreou, G., Kokkinos, I., Murphy, K., Yuille, A.L.: Deeplab: semantic image segmentation with deep convolutional nets, atrous convolution, and fully connected crfs. IEEE Trans. Pattern Analysis Mach. Intell. **40**(4), 834–848 (2018)
4. Cordts, M., et al.: The cityscapes dataset for semantic urban scene understanding. In: Proceedings of the IEEE Conference on Computer Vision and Pattern Recognition, pp. 3213–3223 (2016)
5. Dai, J., et al.: Deformable convolutional networks. In: ICCV, pp. 764–773 (2017)
6. Deng, J., Dong, W., Socher, R., Li, L.J., Li, K., Fei-Fei, L.: Imagenet: a large-scale hierarchical image database. In: 2009 IEEE Conference on Computer Vision and Pattern Recognition, pp. 248–255. IEEE (2009)
7. Feichtenhofer, C., Pinz, A., Zisserman, A.: Convolutional two-stream network fusion for video action recognition. In: 2016 IEEE Conference on Computer Vision and Pattern Recognition, CVPR 2016, Las Vegas, NV, USA, 27–30 June 2016, pp. 1933–1941 (2016)
8. He, K., Gkioxari, G., Dollár, P., Girshick, R.: Mask r-cnn. In: Proceedings of the IEEE International Conference on Computer Vision, pp. 2961–2969 (2017)
9. Jaderberg, M., Simonyan, K., Zisserman, A., Kavukcuoglu, K.: Spatial transformer networks. In: NIPS, pp. 2017–2025 (2015)
10. Jin, X., et al.: Predicting scene parsing and motion dynamics in the future. In: Advances in Neural Information Processing Systems, pp. 6915–6924 (2017)
11. Kalchbrenner, N., et al.: Video pixel networks. In: Proceedings of the 34th International Conference on Machine Learning-Volume 70, pp. 1771–1779 (2017). JMLR.org
12. Kingma, D.P., Ba, J.: Adam: a method for stochastic optimization. arXiv preprint arXiv:1412.6980 (2014)
13. Kirillov, A., He, K., Girshick, R., Rother, C., Dollár, P.: Panoptic segmentation. arXiv preprint arXiv:1801.00868 (2018)
14. Krešo, I., Krapac, J., Šegvić, S.: Efficient ladder-style densenets for semantic segmentation of large images. arXiv preprint arXiv:1905.05661 (2019)
15. LeCun, Y., Bengio, Y., et al.: Convolutional networks for images, speech, and time series. Handb. Brain Theory Neural Networks **3361**(10), 1995 (1995)
16. Lin, T.Y., Dollár, P., Girshick, R., He, K., Hariharan, B., Belongie, S.: Feature pyramid networks for object detection. In: Proceedings of the IEEE Conference on Computer Vision and Pattern Recognition, pp. 2117–2125 (2017)
17. Luc, P., Couprie, C., Lecun, Y., Verbeek, J.: Predicting future instance segmentation by forecasting convolutional features. In: Proceedings of the European Conference on Computer Vision (ECCV), pp. 584–599 (2018)
18. Luc, P., Neverova, N., Couprie, C., Verbeek, J., LeCun, Y.: Predicting deeper into the future of semantic segmentation. In: Proceedings of the IEEE International Conference on Computer Vision, pp. 648–657 (2017)
19. Luo, W., Li, Y., Urtasun, R., Zemel, R.: Understanding the effective receptive field in deep convolutional neural networks. In: Advances in Neural Information Processing Systems, pp. 4898–4906 (2016)

20. Mathieu, M., Couprie, C., LeCun, Y.: Deep multi-scale video prediction beyond mean square error. arXiv preprint arXiv:1511.05440 (2015)
21. Nabavi, S.S., Rochan, M., Wang, Y.: Future semantic segmentation with convolutional LSTM. In: BMVC (2018)
22. Oršić, M., Krešo, I., Bevandić, P., Šegvić, S.: In defense of pre-trained imagenet architectures for real-time semantic segmentation of road-driving images. arXiv preprint arXiv:1903.08469 (2019)
23. Sun, D., Yang, X., Liu, M.Y., Kautz, J.: Pwc-net: CNNs for optical flow using pyramid, warping, and cost volume. In: Proceedings of the IEEE Conference on Computer Vision and Pattern Recognition, pp. 8934–8943 (2018)
24. Terwilliger, A.M., Brazil, G., Liu, X.: Recurrent flow-guided semantic forecasting. arXiv preprint arXiv:1809.08318 (2018)
25. Vondrick, C., Pirsiavash, H., Torralba, A.: Anticipating the future by watching unlabeled video. arXiv preprint arXiv:1504.08023 2 (2015)
26. Vukotić, V., Pintea, S.-L., Raymond, C., Gravier, G., van Gemert, J.C.: One-step time-dependent future video frame prediction with a convolutional encoder-decoder neural network. In: Battiato, S., Gallo, G., Schettini, R., Stanco, F. (eds.) ICIAP 2017. LNCS, vol. 10484, pp. 140–151. Springer, Cham (2017). https://doi.org/10. 1007/978-3-319-68560-1_13
27. Xingjian, S., Chen, Z., Wang, H., Yeung, D.Y., Wong, W.K., Woo, W.c.: Convolutional LSTM network: a machine learning approach for precipitation nowcasting. In: Advances in Neural Information Processing Systems, pp. 802–810 (2015)
28. Yang, M., Yu, K., Zhang, C., Li, Z., Yang, K.: Denseaspp for semantic segmentation in street scenes. In: CVPR, pp. 3684–3692 (2018)
29. Yu, F., Koltun, V.: Multi-scale context aggregation by dilated convolutions. arXiv preprint arXiv:1511.07122 (2015)
30. Zhao, H., Shi, J., Qi, X., Wang, X., Jia, J.: Pyramid scene parsing network. In: The IEEE Conference on Computer Vision and Pattern Recognition (CVPR), July 2017
31. Zhu, X., Hu, H., Lin, S., Dai, J.: Deformable convnets v2: more deformable, better results. arXiv preprint arXiv:1811.11168 (2018)

Predicting Landscapes from Environmental Conditions Using Generative Networks

Christian Requena-Mesa[1,2,3(✉)] ⓘ, Markus Reichstein[3,4] ⓘ,
Miguel Mahecha[3,4] ⓘ, Basil Kraft[3] ⓘ, and Joachim Denzler[2,4] ⓘ

[1] Climate Informatics, Institute of Data Science, German Aerospace Center,
Jena, Germany
[2] Computer Vision Group, Friedrich-Schiller-Universität, Jena, Germany
[3] Max-Planck-Institute for Biogeochemistry, Jena, Germany
crequ@bgc-jena.mpg.de
[4] Michael Stifel Center Jena for Data-Driven and Simulation Science, Jena, Germany

Abstract. Landscapes are meaningful ecological units that strongly depend on the environmental conditions. Such dependencies between landscapes and the environment have been noted since the beginning of Earth sciences and cast into conceptual models describing the interdependencies of climate, geology, vegetation and geomorphology. Here, we ask whether landscapes, as seen from space, can be statistically predicted from pertinent environmental conditions. To this end we adapted a deep learning generative model in order to establish the relationship between the environmental conditions and the view of landscapes from the Sentinel-2 satellite. We trained a conditional generative adversarial network to generate multispectral imagery given a set of climatic, terrain and anthropogenic predictors. The generated imagery of the landscapes share many characteristics with the real one. Results based on landscape patch metrics, indicative of landscape composition and structure, show that the proposed generative model creates landscapes that are more similar to the targets than the baseline models while overall reflectance and vegetation cover are predicted better. We demonstrate that for many purposes the generated landscapes behave as real with immediate application for global change studies. We envision the application of machine learning as a tool to forecast the effects of climate change on the spatial features of landscapes, while we assess its limitations and breaking points.

1 Introduction

The Earth's land surface can be considered a mosaic of landscapes [6]. Landscapes are the material-physical entities that comprise the structures of nature [12]: ecological meaningful units that have a characteristic ordering of elements [23].

Electronic supplementary material The online version of this chapter (https:// doi.org/10.1007/978-3-030-33676-9_14) contains supplementary material, which is available to authorized users.

© Springer Nature Switzerland AG 2019
G. A. Fink et al. (Eds.): DAGM GCPR 2019, LNCS 11824, pp. 203–217, 2019.
https://doi.org/10.1007/978-3-030-33676-9_14

Landscapes result from the long-term interaction of abiotic, biotic and anthropogenic processes. The relation between landscapes and the climatic, geological, and anthropogenic factors is, however, rather conceptual. The totality of interactions and processes that determine the landscapes are impossible to simulate numerically as of today. This fact holds true to such extent that, to the best of our knowledge, landscape imagery prediction is yet to be attempted. We aim to analyze whether the relation between forming factors and landscapes can be mapped with a statistical method. Our goal is to reconstruct the 2D aerial view (multispectral) of the landscapes from a set of 2D environmental conditions. Furthermore, we assess the use of predicting landscapes as a tool for climate change and landscape change studies.

The study of Earth at the landscape scale gained momentum in the last decades benefiting from the use of geographic information systems and the high availability of remotely sensed imagery [8,11,18,24,27]. Remotely sensed images are a measure of the radiation reflected by the surface. The observed reflections at certain wavelength are information rich snapshots that can be used to diagnose features such as land-cover type, ecosystem spatial structure, vegetation health, water availability or human impact [2,9,25]. Predicting the aerial image comes close to predicting the landscapes and their spatial arrangement. From the satellite image, one could derive many high level aspects of the landscapes and ecosystems with existing earth observation tools.

Landscapes are formed by a wide range of components and processes. Factors that determine a landscape can be categorized into largely independent ones (e.g. climate or geology) and dependent ones (e.g. soil or vegetation). A change on the independent factor leads to a change of the dependent ones, for example, changes on abiotic factors generally lead to changes in biotic components (such as shifting position or composition). Previous work to classify the landscapes has determined and ranked the forming factors by importance [3,19,23]

$$L = f(C, G, H, S, V, F, U, S). \tag{1}$$

Where L is the Landscape, C is climate, G the geology and geomorphology, H the hydrology, S the soil, V the vegetation, F the fauna, U the land use and S the landscape structure. Developing over the work of [23] we can further reduce the conceptual relationship into the essential independent forming factors

$$L = f(Clim, Geo, AI). \tag{2}$$

Where $Clim$ is the broadened climate, Geo is the lithology and topography and AI are the anthropogenic interventions. As the dependent factors (e.g. soil or vegetation) can be thought of as a function of the independent ones (climate and geology) direct knowledge is not strictly necessary. In addition we broad the definition of climate to encompass all of the meteorological hydrology.

Mechanistic or statistical approaches are scarce, or only address certain aspects (e.g. geomorphological models). Advances in deep learning allow for unsupervised content-based data driven modeling, i.e, neural networks capable of learning the relationship between the spatial features present in the input and output from available data [15]. Ideally, these networks can accommodate the non-linearities that best approximate the functional relation between environmental factors and landscapes generating realistic spatial representations of the landscapes. We aim to demonstrate that it is possible to predict landscapes -as seen from space- that behave as real for hypothetical environmental conditions. We attempt to map the climatic, topographic and anthropogenic factors onto sentinel-2 visible and near-IR bands using a conditional generative adversarial network (cGAN) [22]. We will assess its limitations and usability as a tool for climate change studies. One of the main applications envisioned for the proposed approach is forecasting landscape change under future climate projections.

2   Materials and Methods

Generative adversarial networks (GANs) estimate a generative model via an adversarial process in which two neural networks are trained simultaneously: a generative network G that captures the data distribution and a discriminative network D that estimates the probability of a sample coming from the training set rather than from G. Both networks are co-trained: the network G tries to maximize the probability of D making a mistake while the network D tries to discriminate data generated by G from true samples [10].

In addition, cGANs learn a mapping from input conditions and r probabilistic latent space to the output. Later developed topologies such as the U-Net GAN [15] allow for the input conditions to have two spatial dimensions. With the use of skip-connection between symmetrical convolutional and deconvolutional layers, the conditions do not only determine the features that shall be present in the output, but where those must appear. This is important since, the location of a feature on one of the conditioning variables, e.g., a mountain range in the altitude predictor, must be reflected on the same location on the generated landscape. The mapping from the probabilistic space is relevant since the conditioning variables do not deterministically determine landscapes.

2.1   Problem and Notations

To model the problem's uncertainty, we define the ground truth as a probability distribution over the imagery conditioned on the set of environmental conditions C. In training we have access to one sample of the target landscapes for each set of environmental conditions. We train a neural network G to approximate the sought function Eq. (2), returning landscapes as seen from space when fed with the environmental conditions

$$G(C, r; \theta) \approx f(Clim, Geo, AI). \tag{3}$$

where θ denotes the network parameter and r is a random variable from which to map the multiple plausible outputs. During test time multiple samples of r could be used to generate different plausible landscapes for the same set of environmental conditions.

2.2   Data

Satellite imagery sensed on April 2017 by Sentinel-2 was matched with 32 environmental predictors representing the *Clim*, *Geo*, and *AI* forming factors for 94, 289 locations. The dataset covers 10% of the emerged Earth surface on 1857 blocks of 110×110 Km randomly distributed across the planet. Each location will serve as a single sample with 256 × 256 pixels, 32 input environmental variables and 4 output multispectral variables. Climatic variables (*Clim*) were represented by a subset of WorldClim v2 [14]. Altitude and lithology (*Geo*) variables, were represented by STRM v4 [16] and GLiM [13]. In addition, we used three of the GlobeLand30's [17] classes as a proxy for anthropogenic large scale interventions (*AI*). All of the environmental variables were resampled to 256 · 256 pixeles to match the resolution of the imagery.

2.3   Experimental Design

Two experiments were designed to asses (1) the ability of the proposed approach to generate landscape imagery and (2) its generalization capability under different spatial block designs to find limitations and describe possible consequences of extrapolation.

Experiment One. We first compare five models of different architectural complexity, from a fully connected network to the complex cGAN detailed in the models subsection. For this experiment train and test samples were drawn from a completely randomized pool, 80% of which were used for training and 20% for testing. With this experiment we expect to unveil whether there is a significant performance improvement between the proposed cGAN approach and baseline machine learning methods.

Experiment Two. We trained the cGANs of different complexity and the baseline fully connected model under different spatial block designs. Landscapes that are close on the surface of the planet tend to be similar [26]. We split the train and test sets into 3 experimental treatments: a complete randomization of the test and train sets as a baseline; a block design where the test locations must be at least 100 km from the closest training sample; and a third treatment where landscapes in the Americas are predicted by a model trained solely with Asia, Africa and Europe. We expect to be able to measure the negative consequences of overfitting that might arise when extrapolating to locations far from those used for training, and thus, combinations of input conditions never seen during training.

Models. Two cGANs were trained inheriting the architecture of the original pix2pix network [15]: a low complexity one (GAN 1 Gb) with few learnable filters per layer and a high complexity one (GAN 7 Gb), named after the total size of the weights on disk. Alongside with the cGANs a fully connected model lacking spatial context was trained as a baseline. In addition, two handicapped cGAN models were trained in order to compare equally complex models that lack one of the key features. One handicapped cGAN was trained over a modified train set with no spatial features due to random permutation of pixels. It is to expect that this handicapped cGAN will not take advantage of convolutions. The second handicapped cGAN was deprived of the discriminator loss. We would expect it to fail to produce landscapes with sharp photointerpretable features. Further detail of the networks' architectures can be found in the supplementary material.

Analysis. Domain experts can visually determine whether a pair of satellite images resemble the same ecosystem, have a similar climate or have a relatable landscape structures. Experts can identify if a satellite image is realistic or faulty. However, human perception based metrics are costly, time inefficient and prone to bias; therefore, computerized metrics are needed for the objective comparison of models of results over thousands of samples. The generated landscapes must resemble the target ones, however the generated landscapes do not have to match the targets pixel to pixel. Per pixel error metrics are not adequate since the features of interest on landscapes are of supra-pixel scale, and can appear on different places in the generated imagery.

We tested the generated landscapes by comparing the high level landscape patch metrics [4] to the target landscapes. Landscape metrics are typically used for the objective description of landscape structure. These are central to the study of landscape ecology and biodiversity and habitat analysis [28]. We make use of landscape level patch metrics as a mean to compare landscape composition and structure. While our quantitative analysis is focused on the landscape metrics, it is important to note that predicting these metrics is not the objective of our work. Our objective is to generate landscape images that behave realistic, and we make use of the landscape metrics as a mean of automatizing the evaluation.

In order to compute patch metrics of a landscape, segmentating into landscape units is needed first. These landscape units typically have a semantic meaning such as *forest* or *industrial* and the segmentation process is often carried out by humans. However, in an effort to automatize the analysis, we opted for an unsupervised non-semantic segmentation. The generated and the target satellite imagery was unsupervisedly segmented via K-means clustering using the red, green, blue and near-infrared bands as input variables. The individual pixels were segmented into 20 clusters. A value of $K = 20$ was selected since this is a typical number of land cover units seen in semantically segmented land cover products [7]. For robustness, the analysis was repeated under different landscape segmentations, clustering it in an undersegmentation scenario (K = 8) and oversegmentation scenario ($K = 60$). A total of 8 K-means were trained using $3,000,000$ pixels (3% of total) extracted randomly from $1,500$ randomly selected target images (8% of total). Once trained, in a cross-validation fashion, segmentation was performed for 8 randomly selected subsets of size $1,500$ sample pairs (each pair consisting of a target and generated landscape).

As landscape metrics are often redundant [5], we selected five representative landscape level metrics of diverse nature based on expert criteria: Shannon diversity index, patch cohesion, connectance, mean fractal dimensionality and effective mesh size. Landscape metrics were computed using FRAGSTATS v4 [21]. Our final evaluation measure is the robust biweight midcorrelation [29] computed as in [20] between generated and target landscapes for patch metrics.

3 Results

3.1 Quantitative Analysis

Experiment One. Landscapes level metrics' correlation between generated and target landscapes on our first experiment can be seen in Fig. 1. The proposed model (GAN 1 Gb) is best at producing landscapes whose patch level metrics resemble the target landscapes. The handicapped models, in spite of having the same number of total weights as the proposed GAN, fail to reproduce the landscape metrics to the same degree. This indicates both, the use of a discriminative training and the capability of mapping spatial features, are key for a high performace. The pixel based 'FC' model is the least capable of generating landscapes whose landscapes composition and structure resemble the targets. Results evidence that for best performance, models that can make explicit use of spatial neighboring on the input features and can generate the landscape as a whole rather than per pixel are needed. In addition, the best performing models are those using a discriminative loss, rather than simple per pixel error metrics. Further evaluation with undersegmented and oversegmented landscapes also lead to similar results (supplementary Figs. 2 and 3). This indicates that the findings are not dependent on the segmentation process used for calculating the landscape metrics.

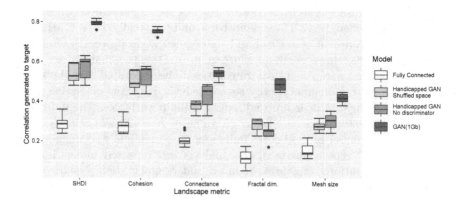

Fig. 1. Intermodel comparison (20 landcover units). Correlation between landscape metrics of generated and target landscapes. Shannon diversity index (SHDI), patch cohesion, patch connectance, average patch fractal dimensionality and effective mesh size were computed for both, real landscapes, and landscapes generated given the environmental conditions on the test locations.

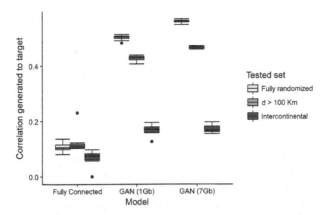

Fig. 2. Model generalizability. Correlation between target and generated landscapes' averaged patch metrics. The baseline FC and the two models representing the proposed approach (GAN 1 Gb and GAN 7 Gb) are compared over 3 different test sets. The fully randomized test set is well represented by the training data. The intercontinental set has sample locations on the Americas for models trained with locations on Asia, Europe and Africa. In the intermediate case, the locations are at least 100 Km apart from the closest location used for training.

Experiment Two. On our second experiment we compared our approach and the baseline on a test set that is vaguely represented by the test set due to distance between samples, some extrapolation occurs at prediction time. Landscapes level metrics' correlation generated to target for the proposed model and the baseline can be seen in Fig. 2. The proposed GAN models (1 Gb and 7 Gb) outperform the simple baseline method FC. We observe all models suffer some kind of performance decay as location of the testing set samples is further from the train locations. The FC model's performance decays the least with distance, this is to expect of a model that does not suffer from overfitting. The performance of the more complex GAN models decays strongly with extrapolation. While the GAN 7 Gb model slightly outperforms the GAN 1 Gb model on the fully randomized test set and the short distance test, performance becomes similar on the harder intercontinental test. This indicates some level of overfitting to train locations. While the performance decay due to extrapolation is the largest on the GAN 7 Gb, it is to note that it still outperforms the simpler method that does not use spatial context.

Normalized Difference Vegetation Index Prediction. Summary statistics for the prediction of the overall amount of vegetation for all models can be seen in Table 1. As NDVI is a simple ratio between different spectral bands, these results can also be understood as the ability of the models to predict overall reflectance.

The simpler models perform close to the GAN models. This effect might be due to the unnecessity of context and spatial features as NDVI is averaged across

Table 1. Generated to target correlation for the Normalized Difference Vegetation Index

	FC	Spatially shuffled	No discriminator	GAN (1 Gb)	GAN (7 Gb)
Fully randomized	0.934	0.989	0.995	0.991	0.965
d > 100 Km	0.903			0.980	0.978
Intercontinental	0.716			0.749	0.718

the image. While by a small margin, the more complex models (GAN 1 Gb and GAN 7 Gb) outperform the FC baseline models. The higher performance cannot be attributed to the capability of these models to learn spatial features or the discriminative loss, since both handicapped models also outperform the baseline. Therefore, the most plausible cause for the higher performance is the sheer size of the models. Similar to what has been observed for the landscape metrics, the simpler baseline method performance does not decrease as steeply as the GANs when predicting intercontinentally; however, the absolute performance of the GANs is still superior even when extrapolation is done.

3.2   Visual Analysis

Experiment One. We first present generated and target landscapes on an ideal scenario where the train dataset represents very well the cases in the test set due to spatial proximity (Fig. 3). Landscape reconstructions based on per pixel mapping (FC model) gives overly a close rendition of reflectance across all bands, i.e., colors resemble the target with few exceptions (as seen in sample 14VNK37). Nonetheless, these generated samples lack the characteristic spatial features of landscapes. This is visible on an agricultural area where the model produces an image that lacks the spatial features of agricultural fields (sample 37SGA21). These samples can hardly be understood as satellite imagery, preventing photointerpretation. Moreover the spatial heterogeneity seen in the output of the fully connected model is directly determined by the spatial heterogeneity of the input condition variables.

The spatially shuffled handicapped GAN faces similar visual problems as the FC model. Although overall colors seem accurate, it still fails to project the expected spatial features of real landscapes as it lacks content-based generation. The outputs are noisier than the fully connected model, possibly due to the spatially shuffling of pixels on the training set and the discriminative loss, i.e., noisy samples, similar to those used for training, had a smaller discriminative loss. The 'No discriminator' handicapped GAN, in contrast, can make use of convolutions but lacks the discriminative training. It generates outputs that contain spatial features loosely resembling those of real landscapes; however, these are smoother. This is an expected artifact when using solely mean squared error as training loss.

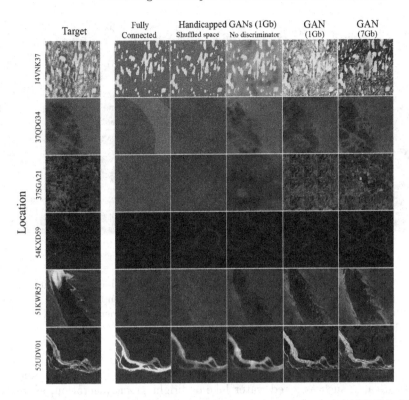

Fig. 3. Sample generated landscapes across the tested models. Visible bands on test locations belonging to the fully randomized test set. Model complexity increases from left to right. The six displayed locations were drafted at random.

GAN models (1 Gb and 7 Gb) generate crisper images. These contain spatial features that humans can recognize as part of landscapes that are not determined by the spatial features in the predictors. The lower complexity model (GAN 1 GB) seems to lack the ability to learn enough spatial features on its generator, and under some circumstances generates mosaicking patterns (as seen in sample 37SGA21) while the model with higher number of convolutional filters per layer (GAN 7 Gb) seems to be able to cope better with spatially homogenous predictors. However, it is still susceptible to generate visually faulty landscapes as seen in sample 52UDV01. Under simple visual inspection, the proposed models (GAN 1 Gb and 7 Gb) seem to be the ones generating imagery that is most readily accessible to photointerpretation.

Experiment Two. We trained the models with samples from Europe, Africa and Asia to later generate samples for environmental conditions occurring on the Americas. Samples from a good and a bad case were re-mosaicked for display on Fig. 4. While Laguna Salada landscape does not show large scale artifacts,

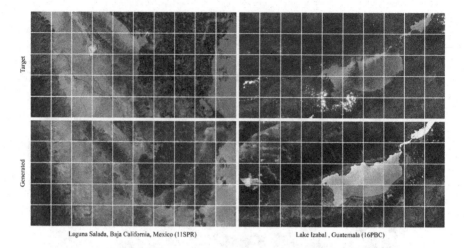

Fig. 4. Generated test samples by a GAN (7 Gb) for the intercontinental test set. The model used to generate the landscapes was trained solely with imagery of Europe, Africa and Asia, however the input conditions given to generate the images occur in the Americas. Each square image was generated independently and mosaicked to display a larger area. (Color figure online)

Lake Izabal landscape displays colors and features that are not possible on a real landscape, such as a red water lake or bright green vegetation, as well as, repetitive patterns.

4   Discussion

We tackled the prediction of landscapes as seen from space by linking reflectance and environmental conditions with a generative neural network. The proposed approach is able to generate photointerpretable satellite imagery. This is the first time it has been achieved. We unveiled that both, a discriminative loss and spatial context are key for the good performance of the model. In addition, spatial extrapolation to new areas is possible to some extent.

Nonetheless, there are artifacts of different nature in the generated imagery, especially for the test locations that are far from the train locations. We hypothesize these artifacts could be caused by a combination of the following reasons: (1) the deep dreamy appearance might be a negative consequence of the discriminative loss; (2) the model might be overfitting our training set; (3) the input environmental conditions were never seen during training; (4) the processes involved in creating landscapes are not identical in different parts of the planet. These results highlight the importance, when using this approach as a tool, of training the model with a set of samples that is as relevant as possible to the problem to be solved.

4.1   Predicting Landscapes as a Tool

Predicting landscapes could become an important tool for the study of ecological change at the landscape scale. However, further effort is needed as the proposed approach is by no means exempt of flaws and projecting future climate scenarios is only valid under rigorous assumptions.

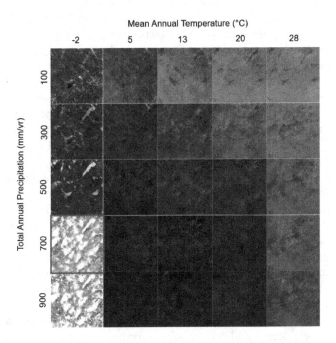

Fig. 5. Satellite imagery generated for hypothetical environmental conditions. Annual precipitation and temperature were modified over a real location in northern Canada (56°48'37"N, 106°32'36") in order to display the ability of the model to create novel landscapes for hypothetical climate scenarios. The real landscape is marked in red. (Color figure online)

One of the main applications envisioned for the proposed approach is forecasting landscape change under future climate projections. In Fig. 5 a sample test location is altered both, annual precipitation and mean annual temperature, in order to display the capability of the model to reimagine landscapes under different environments. Validating the landscapes depicted in Fig. 5 is not possible; however, the increase of vegetation cover and the desertification as temperature and precipitation varies is consistent with our expectation. While, made up predictors generate landscapes never seen and thus, difficult to validate, we have tested against predictors found in real world mid distance (more than 100 Km away) and long distance (intercontinentally) and the landscapes generated do resemble the real landscapes to a high extent.

There are, however, limitations to be taken into account before using these models for projecting future landscapes. Our approach, in its current status, does not account for the temporal processes; instead, if we were to predict future scenarios we would be assuming space for time, e.g., sometime warmer in the future must look like somewhere warmer today. However, this assumption only holds if you allow ample time for the landscape to achieve a new steady state after the intervention. When climatic conditions change rapidly, landscape change lags behind, and thus, modelling the landscapes inertia and temporal dynamics is necessary. Also with global change other factors such as CO_2 change, having an important effect on vegetation that a static model cannot predict. In addition, in order to generate landscapes for hypothetical environmental conditions, we assume that the system is currently in steady state. However, we know that current climate is trending [1]. Therefore, since our train set landscapes are not in equilibrium with the environmental conditions, our ability to predict landscapes for the future climates is further detrimented. The data driven modelling of the evolution of landscapes over time given the environmental conditions might server as a fix to most of the flaws previously mentioned.

Although landscapes are shaped by past environmental conditions, for simplicity, we have assumed that present day conditions are sufficient. As a matter of fact, present day conditions may serve as a proxy for past climatic conditions. While this is true for orbital processes, it is not for the tectonic processes or glaciations [30].

Predicting the landscape patch composition and structure is not the only use that can be made of the imagery. The generated satellite imagery can be potentially used across many disciplines. There are many available tools for different scientific purposes that make use of satellite imagery to gather information. It is unknown whether the quality of the generated imagery is sufficient for these tools to work seamlessly and will require specific testing for the different use cases.

4.2   Problems

Predicting landscapes as seen from space is an ill-posed problem. Landscapes are stochastic and chaotic systems and their evolution is conditioned on an unknown initial state. For added difficulty, landscapes have become dependent on complex societal and economical systems that are hard to predict as well. We cannot expect our method or any future method to predict landscapes without flaws and compromises.

We have experienced technical problems. We observe mode collapse. The GAN network we use [15] does not explicitly model the uncertainty since no r probabilistic space is used during the generative process. Instead, it does so in a weak manner by having an active dropout during test time as explained in [15]. When fed the same set of environmental conditions, the network outputs nearly identical landscapes. Later developed network architectures, such as those using an implicit probabilistic space and making use of Wasserstein distance during training might mitigate the observed mode collapse. Predicting the full set of landscapes that are plausible for a set of environmental conditions is key in order to have a measure of uncertainty over our prediction.

4.3 Future Work

Predicting imagery of landscapes is a valid line of research; furthermore, future improvements in deep learning must be expected making the prediction of satellite imagery more feasible.

- Modeling explicitly landscape evolution over time could greatly benefit the usability as a tool.
- Improve landscape comparison metrics: comparing generated and target landscapes is not trivial. Learned perceptual similarity based metrics [31] might be a faster and better option then landscape metrics.
- Extract knowledge from the network. Exploring the latent space might give us new insight to the importance of the forming factors, the relation between them and help clustering the surface of Earth landscape-wise.
- Build a working stochastic generator. Generate the multiple plausible landscapes that can be arise from each set of environmental factors.

5   Summary and Conclusion

We have tackled the prediction of landscapes as seen from space by approximating the conceptual model with a generative neural network. The proposed approach demonstrates that a minimum set of environmental conditions is enough to predict landscapes. Our trained model allows to generate close to realistic landscapes for hypothetical environmental scenarios that have some degree of photointerpretability. To the best of our knowledge, this is the first time that environmental predictors are used to infer the aerial view of landscapes.

The predicted images of the landscapes have spatial features that are not dictated by the predictors, but introduced by the generative model. These spatial features add for the interpretability as evidenced by our experiments (Fig. 3), making the generated landscapes behave closer to the real ones as evidenced by patch level landscape metrics Fig. 1). We contribute our dataset covering 10% of the emerged surface of Earth and matched with the pertinent 32 environmental predictors (detailed in Supplementary Material) for further development. We believe this is an important step for the data-driven modeling and forecasting of Earth surface.

The use of a discriminative loss and spatial context is crucial in order to generate landscape images susceptible to photointerpretation. We see how a minimum set of with only present day environmental conditions provide enough information to infer the aerial view of a landscape. We demonstrate for the first time that landscapes, as seen from space, can be predicted by pertinent environmental conditions, opening a new data-driven way to study the landscape evolution.

References

1. Allen, M.R., et al.: IPCC fifth assessment synthesis report-climate change 2014 synthesis report (2014)
2. Brando, V.E., Dekker, A.G.: Satellite hyperspectral remote sensing for estimating estuarine and coastal water quality. IEEE Trans. Geosci. Remote Sens. **41**(6), 1378–1387 (2003)
3. Bunce, R.G.H., Barr, C., Clarke, R., Howard, D., Lane, A.: Land classification for strategic ecological survey. J. Environ. Manage. **47**(1), 37–60 (1996)
4. Cardille, J.A., Turner, M.G.: Understanding landscape metrics. In: Gergel, S.E., Turner, M.G. (eds.) Learning Landscape Ecology, pp. 45–63. Springer, New York (2017). https://doi.org/10.1007/978-1-4939-6374-4_4
5. Cushman, S.A., McGarigal, K., Neel, M.C.: Parsimony in landscape metrics: strength, universality, and consistency. Ecol. Ind. **8**(5), 691–703 (2008)
6. Forman, R.T.: Some general principles of landscape and regional ecology. Landscape Ecol. **10**(3), 133–142 (1995)
7. Fox, J., Vogler, J.B.: Land-use and land-cover change in montane mainland southeast asia. Environ. Manag. **36**(3), 394–403 (2005)
8. Franklin, S., Dickson, E., Hansen, M., Farr, D., Moskal, L.: Quantification of landscape change from satellite remote sensing. Forestry Chronicle **76**(6), 877–886 (2000)
9. Getzin, S., Wiegand, K., Schöning, I.: Assessing biodiversity in forests using very high-resolution images and unmanned aerial vehicles. Methods Ecol. Evol. **3**(2), 397–404 (2012)
10. Goodfellow, I., et al.: Generative adversarial nets. In: Advances in neural information processing systems, pp. 2672–2680 (2014)
11. Groom, G., Mücher, C., Ihse, M., Wrbka, T.: Remote sensing in landscape ecology: experiences and perspectives in a european context. Landscape Ecol. **21**(3), 391–408 (2006)
12. Haase, G., Richter, H.: Current trends in landscape research. GeoJournal **7**(2), 107–119 (1983)
13. Hartmann, J., Moosdorf, N.: The new global lithological map database GLiM: a representation of rock properties at the Earth surface. Geochemistry, Geophysics, Geosystems, 13(12) (2012)
14. Hijmans, R.J., Cameron, S., Parra, J., Jones, P., Jarvis, A., Richardson, K.: WorldClim-Global Climate Data. Free Climate Data for Ecological Modeling and GIS (2015)
15. Isola, P., Zhu, J.Y., Zhou, T., Efros, A.A.: Image-to-image translation with conditional adversarial networks. arXiv preprint (2017)
16. Jarvis, A., Reuter, H.I., Nelson, A., Guevara, E.: Hole-filled srtm for the globe version, 4 (2008)
17. Jun, C., Ban, Y., Li, S.: China: open access to Earth land-cover map. Nature **514**(7523), 434 (2014)
18. Kerr, J.T., Ostrovsky, M.: From space to species: ecological applications for remote sensing. Trends Ecol. Evol. **18**(6), 299–305 (2003)
19. Klijn, J.: Hierarchical concepts in landscape ecology and its underlying disciplines. DLO winand staring centre report 100, (1995)
20. Langfelder, P., Horvath, S.: Fast R functions for robust correlations and hierarchical clustering. J. Stat. Softw. **46**(11), i11 (2012)

21. McGarigal, K., Cushman, S.A., Neel, M.C., Ene, E.: FRAGSTATS v4: Spatial Pattern Analysis Program for Categorical and Continuous Maps. University of Massachusettes, Amherst, MA. http://www.umass.edu/landeco/research/fragstats/fragstats.html (2007) (2012). https://doi.org/citeulike-article-id:287784

22. Mirza, M., Osindero, S.: Conditional generative adversarial nets. arXiv preprint arXiv:1411.1784 (2014)

23. Mücher, C.A., Klijn, J.A., Wascher, D.M., Schaminée, J.H.: A new european landscape classification (lanmap): a transparent, flexible and user-oriented methodology to distinguish landscapes. Ecol. Ind. **10**(1), 87–103 (2010)

24. Newton, A.C., et al.: Remote sensing and the future of landscape ecology. Prog. Phys. Geogr. **33**(4), 528–546 (2009)

25. Otterman, J.: Anthropogenic impact on the albedo of the earth. Climatic Change **1**(2), 137–155 (1977)

26. Roberts, D.R., et al.: Cross-validation strategies for data with temporal, spatial, hierarchical, or phylogenetic structure. Ecography **40**(8), 913–929 (2017)

27. Simmons, M., Cullinan, V., Thomas, J.: Satellite imagery as a tool to evaluate ecological scale. Landscape Ecol. **7**(2), 77–85 (1992)

28. Uuemaa, E., Antrop, M., Roosaare, J., Marja, R., Mander, Ü.: Landscape metrics and indices: an overview of their use in landscape research. Living Rev. Landscape Res. **3**(1), 1–28 (2009)

29. Wilcox, R.R.: Robust generalizations of classical test reliability and cronbach's alpha. Br. J. Math. Stat. Psychol. **45**(2), 239–254 (1992)

30. Zachos, J., Pagani, M., Sloan, L., Thomas, E., Billups, K.: Trends, rhythms, and aberrations in global climate 65 ma to present. Science **292**(5517), 686–693 (2001)

31. Zhang, R., Isola, P., Efros, A.A., Shechtman, E., Wang, O.: The unreasonable effectiveness of deep features as a perceptual metric. In: Proceedings of the IEEE Conference on Computer Vision and Pattern Recognition, pp. 586–595 (2018)

Semi-supervised Segmentation of Salt Bodies in Seismic Images Using an Ensemble of Convolutional Neural Networks

Yauhen Babakhin[1]([✉]), Artsiom Sanakoyeu[2], and Hirotoshi Kitamura[3]

[1] H2O.ai, Minsk, Belarus
yauhen.babakhin@h2o.ai
[2] Heidelberg Collaboratory for Image Processing, IWR, Heidelberg University, Heidelberg, Germany
[3] Ritsumeikan University, Kyoto, Japan

Abstract. Seismic image analysis plays a crucial role in a wide range of industrial applications and has been receiving significant attention. One of the essential challenges of seismic imaging is detecting subsurface salt structure which is indispensable for the identification of hydrocarbon reservoirs and drill path planning. Unfortunately, the exact identification of large salt deposits is notoriously difficult and professional seismic imaging often requires expert human interpretation of salt bodies. Convolutional neural networks (CNNs) have been successfully applied in many fields, and several attempts have been made in the field of seismic imaging. But the high cost of manual annotations by geophysics experts and scarce publicly available labeled datasets hinder the performance of the existing CNN-based methods. In this work, we propose a semi-supervised method for segmentation (delineation) of salt bodies in seismic images which utilizes unlabeled data for multi-round self-training. To reduce error amplification during self-training we propose a scheme which uses an ensemble of CNNs. We show that our approach outperforms state-of-the-art on the TGS Salt Identification Challenge dataset and is ranked the first among the 3234 competing methods. The source code is available at GitHub.

1 Introduction

One of the major challenges of seismic imaging is localization and delineation of subsurface salt bodies. The precise location of salt deposits helps to identify reservoirs of hydrocarbons, such as crude oil or natural gas, which are trapped by overlying rock-salt formations due to the exceedingly small permeability of the latter.

Modern seismic imaging techniques result in large amounts of unlabeled data which have to be interpreted. Unfortunately, the exact identification of large salt deposits is notoriously difficult [20] and often requires manual interpretation of

© Springer Nature Switzerland AG 2019
G. A. Fink et al. (Eds.): DAGM GCPR 2019, LNCS 11824, pp. 218–231, 2019.
https://doi.org/10.1007/978-3-030-33676-9_15

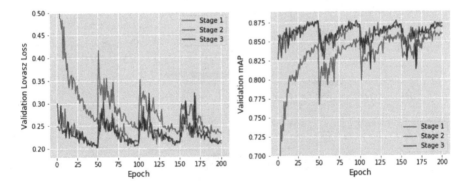

Fig. 1. Progress of the validation loss (top) and the validation mAP score (bottom) during training our U-ResNet34 model on TGS Salt Identification Challenge dataset [21] for $K = 3$ rounds. Every next round the model converges faster and achieves better local minima. Loss spikes every 50 epochs correspond to the cycles of the cosine annealing learning rate schedule.

seismic images by the domain experts. Despite being highly time-consuming and expensive, manual interpretation induces a subjective human bias, which can lead to potentially dangerous situations for oil and gas company drillers.

In recent years, a number of tools for automatic or semi-automatic seismic interpretation have been proposed [3,7,12,17,35,44,45,50] to speed-up the interpretation process and, to some extent, reduce the human bias. However, these methods do not generalize well for complex cases since they rely on handcrafted features.

The advent of convolutional neural networks (CNNs) brought significant advancements in different problems and several attempts have been made to apply CNNs in the field of seismic imaging [10,41,43,49]. CNNs overcome the need for manual feature design and show superior performance on the tasks of the salt body delineation compared to the methods based on the handcrafted features. However, a low amount of publicly available annotated seismic images hinder the performance of the existing CNN-based methods since CNNs are notoriously hungry for data.

To overcome the shortage of labeled data, we propose a semi-supervised method for segmentation of salt bodies in seismic images which can make use of abundant unlabeled data. The unlabeled images are utilized for self-training [40]. The proposed self-training procedure (see Fig. 2) is an iterative process which extends the labeled dataset by alternating between training the model and pseudo-labeling (i.e. imputing the labels on the unlabeled data). We do K rounds of retraining the model (see the straining in Fig. 1). At the first round, we train model solely on the available labeled data and then predict labels on the unlabeled data. Every next round we use for training both original labeled data and the pseudo-labels obtained at the previous round. The error amplification is a well-known problem in self-training [28] when the error is accumulated during

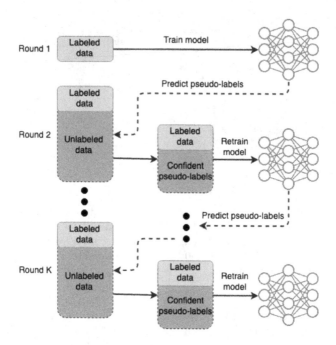

Fig. 2. The pipeline of the proposed self-training procedure. We do K rounds of retraining the model. Every round we train the model on the available labeled data and predicted confident pseudo-labels for the unlabeled data. *All* pseudo-labels are recalculated at the end of every round.

self-training rounds and the models tend to generate less reliable predictions during the time. To mitigate it we propose to train an ensemble of CNNs and predict labels on the unlabeled data using the average voting of the models in the ensemble. Average voting scheme corrects examples which could be mislabeled by one of the models, hence facilitates more reliable pseudo-labeling. Moreover, to further reduce the error amplification we retrain our models from scratch and predict labels for *all* unlabeled examples every round in similar spirit as [28].

We conduct experiments on the largest available to our knowledge dataset for salt body delineation – TGS Salt Identification Challenge dataset [21]. This dataset was collected by TGS, the world's leading geoscience data company, and was provided in the Kaggle competition. Our approach achieves state-of-the-art performance on this dataset featuring the *first place* in the global ranking among 3234 competitors.

In summary, the contribution of this work is as follows: (i) we propose an iterative self-training approach for semantic segmentation which benefits from unlabeled data; (ii) we build a sophisticated network architecture which is tailored for the task of salt body delineation (see Fig. 3); (iii) we evaluate our approach on a real-world salt body delineation dataset – TGS Salt Identification Challenge [21], where the proposed method achieves the state-of-the-art performance outperforming *all* other competing teams.

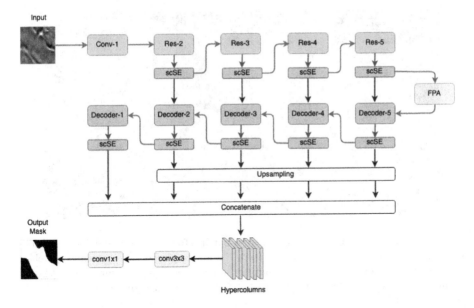

Fig. 3. The outline of the U-ResNet34/U-ResNeXt50 architecture proposed. The difference between U-ResNet34 and U-ResNeXt50 is only in the structure of the encoder blocks (green). We insert scSE modules [37] after each encoder (green) and decoder (purple) blocks. Encoder blocks are connected with the corresponding decoder blocks using skip-connections. We use a Feature Pyramid Attention module (FPA) [14] after the last encoder block. All outputs of the decoder blocks are upsampled to have the same size as the output of the last decoder bock. Obtained feature maps are concatenated together into hypercolumns [15], which are used for prediction of the segmentation mask after applying two convolutional layers. (Color figure online)

2   Related Work

A lot of research efforts have been devoted to interpretation of seismic images [3,35,39,45,50]. With the advent of CNNs, several approaches have been proposed for supervised seismic image interpretation using deep learning [8,41,49]. But the small size of the available datasets and lack of the annotations seismic image interpretation did not allow to unfold the full potential of the CNNs.

The recent trend in the Computer Vision community is unsupervised or self-supervised learning [1,2,5,9,19,24,27,33,38] which can make use of abundant unlabeled visual data available on the internet and avoid costly manual annotations. Another class of methods which lies between completely unsupervised methods and supervised methods is semi-supervised learning. It jointly utilizes a large amount of unlabeled data, together with the labeled data [51]. The semi-supervised technique most relevant to our work is self-training [29,40,47]. In the self-training, a classifier is trained with an initially small number of labeled examples, then it predicts labels for unlabeled points. After that, the classifier is retrained with its own most confident predictions, together with initially pro-

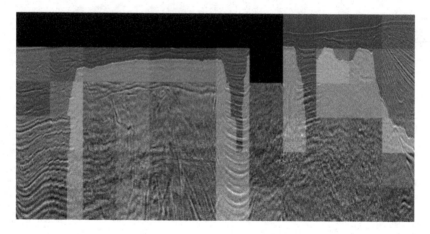

Fig. 4. Example of the 6 × 12 mosaic of train patches from the TGS Salt Identification Challenge dataset [21]. Each patch is 101 × 101 pixels. Green patches denote patches without the salt boundary; green/red patches indicate patches containing the salt body boundary; black color means missing mosaic patches. (Color figure online)

vided labeled examples. However existing self-training approaches [11,30,31,48] are based on hand-crafted features which are much more limited than the features learned by CNNs. [26,42] use CNNs in the self-training framework, but they apply it to relatively simple classification datasets like MNIST [25] and CIFAR-10 [23]. The most relevant self-training approach which is based on CNN features is [13], which is designed for image classification task and uses pretrained CNNs as the fixed feature-extractors while training SVM classifier on top. In contrast, our approach is the first to our knowledge which proposes a self-training procedure for semantic segmentation task and it learns CNN features end-to-end. Moreover, our method reduces the error amplification [28] by using an ensemble of the networks and by retraining from scratch and recalculating pseudo-labels every training round.

Another work related to ours is [34]. Authors try to mitigate the high cost of manual annotations of seismic images by introducing an approach which can utilize sparse annotations instead of the commonly used dense segmentation masks.

3   Method

The salt body delineation problem can be reduced to the task of semantic image segmentation [10], therefore we design our model to predict a binary segmentation mask [6] for the salt body. We will further use the terms segmentation and delineation interchangeably in the text.

In this section, we first present the proposed iterative self-training procedure (Sect. 3.1) which can make use of unlabeled samples for training. Then we describe the ensemble used for training and the network architectures in detail (Sect. 3.2).

3.1 Self-training Process

Since the labeled data available for the salt body delineation task is scarce, we propose to produce pseudo-labels for unlabeled data and use the pseudo-labels along with ground truth labels to train the model. We refer to this process as self-training. Our self-training procedure is a K-round iterative process where each round has 2 steps: (a) training the model using the labeled dataset extended with pseudo-labels; (b) updating pseudo-labels for unlabeled data.

During the first round, we train the model using the ground truth labels only. Then we predict pseudo-labels for all unlabeled data by assigning to each pixel in the image the most probable class. Unreliable predictions can be filtered out by removing images with the low-confidence pseudo-labels (i.e. when confidence $conf(\cdot) < thresh$). We define the confidence of the predicted segmentation mask as the negative mean entropy of the pixel labels in the mask.

Every next round, we first (a) retrain the model using jointly ground truth labels and confident pseudo-labels; and then (b) update the pseudo-labels for all unlabeled data using the new model. It is crucial to reset model weights before every round of self-training not to accumulate errors in pseudo-labels during multiple rounds [28].

To further improve the robustness of the generated pseudo-labels and prevent over-fitting to the errors of the sole model, we jointly train an ensemble of CNNs with different backbone architectures. In this case, the pseudo-labels are produced by averaging the predictions of all models in the ensemble. And every next round each model in the ensemble utilizes the confident knowledge of the entire ensemble from the previous round expressed and aggregated in the pseudo-labels. We summarize the full self-training procedure in Algorithm 1 and visualize it in Fig. 2.

3.2 Network Architecture

We start building our networks inspired by seminal U-Net architecture [36], which has an encoder, a decoder and skip connections between encoder and decoder blocks with similar spatial resolution. However, training the encoder from scratch is difficult given a limited amount of labeled data. Hence, we opt to use an Imagenet pretrained CNN as the backbone for the encoder [18]. In particular, we build an ensemble of two models: the first one uses ResNet34 [16] as the encoder backbone (we will refer to it as U-ResNet34) and the second one with ResNeXt50 [46] as the encoder backbone (we will refer to it as U-ResNeXt50).

We propose a number of modifications to the architecture to make it more effective for salt body delineation task. We use several types of attention mechanisms in the network. The encoder and decoder consist of repeating blocks separated by down-sampling and up-sampling respectively. First, we insert concurrent spatial and channel Squeeze & Excitation modules (scSE) [37] after each encoder and decoder block. scSE modules can be interpreted as some sort of attention mechanism: they rescale individual dimensions of the feature maps by increasing the importance of informative features and suppressing the less relevant ones.

Algorithm 1: The proposed self-training procedure

Input: Labeled data $\mathcal{D}_{gt} = (X, Y)$, where X is the set of images and Y is their corresponding ground truth labels; unlabeled images $\hat{X}$; number of training epochs T; number of self-training rounds K; model $\phi(\cdot, \theta)$ with learnable parameters θ.

1 $\mathcal{D} \leftarrow \mathcal{D}_{gt}$;   ▷ initialize the training set
2 **for** $k \leftarrow 1$ *to* K **do**
3 │ Initialize θ using a pretrained Imagenet model;
4 │ Train model $\phi(\cdot, \theta)$ on $\mathcal{D}$ for T epochs;
5 │ Predict pseudo-labels $\hat{Y}$ for each element in $\hat{X}$;
6 │ $\mathcal{D}_{pseudo} \leftarrow (\hat{X}, \hat{Y})$;
7 │ Remove images with low-confidence pseudo-labels from $\mathcal{D}_{pseudo}$;
8 │ $\mathcal{D} \leftarrow \mathcal{D}_{gt} \cup \mathcal{D}_{pseudo}$;
9 **end**

Result: Model parameters θ.

Additionally, in the bottleneck block between the encoder and the decoder we use Feature Pyramid Attention module [14], which increases the receptive field by fusing features from different pyramid scales.

Another powerful design decision for exploiting feature maps from different scales is Hypercolumns [15]. Instead of using only the last layer of the decoder for prediction of the segmentation mask, we stack the upsampled feature maps from all decoder blocks and use them as the input to the final layer. It allows getting more precise localization and captures the semantics at the same time. To produce the final segmentation mask, we feed Hypercolumns through a 3×3 convolution followed by the final 1×1 convolution. We present our final network architecture in Fig. 3.

4   Experiments

4.1   Dataset: TGS Salt Identification Challenge

TGS Salt Identification Challenge is a Machine Learning competition on a Kaggle platform [21]. The data for this competition represents 2D image slices of 3D view of earth's interior. It was collected using reflection seismology method (similar to X-ray, sonar, and echolocation). For this reason, input data is a set of single-channel grayscale images showing the boundaries between different rock types at various locations chosen at random in the subsurface. For the competition purposes, large-size images were transformed into 101×101 pixel crops by the organizers. Further, each pixel is classified as either salt or sediment and binary masks are provided. To visualize the data we assembled a mosaic using the several small patches from the dataset (see Fig. 4). The goal of the competition is to segment regions that contain salt. Note that if the 101×101 image contains all the salt pixels, it is treated as an empty mask in the data. Such peculiarity is explained by the organizers as they are more interested in segmenting salt deposit boundaries instead of full-body salt.

The whole dataset has been split into three parts: train, public test, and private test. The train set consists of 4000 images together with binary masks and is used for models developing. The public test set has around 6000 images and is used for evaluating the models during the competition. Lastly, private test set has around 12000 images and is used to determine the final competition standings. Overall, the test dataset contains 18000 unlabeled images (public + private test) which we can use for self-training.

To track the local quality of the models and prevent overfitting we used 5-fold cross-validation. Thus, every model is trained five times (one per fold).

Table 1. Results and ablation studies. The first section of the table shows the performance of a single U-ResNet34 without any usage of pseudo-labels. The second block shows the quality increase after several self-training rounds for a single U-ResNet34 model. The third block shows results for multiple self-training rounds using the ensemble of U-ResNet34 and U-ResNeXt50 networks which achieves state-of-the-art performance. Finally, our best model is compared with another approach presented in [22] on the same dataset.

Method	Private test mAP	Public test mAP	Private LB place
Our U-ResNet34 *Round 1 ablation studies*			
Single best snapshot	0.8682	0.8431	200
+ TTA	0.8739 (+0.6%)	0.8498	144
+ Multiple snapshots	0.8777 (+0.4%)	0.8552	99
+ Multiple folds	0.8834 (+0.6%)	0.8629	61
+ Train 200 epochs more	0.8845 (+0.1%)	0.8644	51
Our U-ResNet34			
Round 1	0.8834	0.8629	61
Round 2	0.8898 (+0.6%)	0.8719	20
Round 3	0.8915 (+0.2%)	0.8715	12
Ensemble of Rounds 2 and 3	0.8917 (+0.1%)	0.8727	10
Our U-ResNet34 + U-ResNeXt50			
Round 1	0.8853	0.8677	46
Round 2	0.8919 (+0.7%)	0.8748	10
Round 3	0.8953 (+0.4%)	0.8759	5
Ensemble of Rounds 2 and 3	**0.8964** (+0.1%)	**0.8766**	1
[22]	0.8880	0.8663	27

Evaluation Metric. The metric used in this competition is defined as the mean average precision at 10 different intersection over union (IoU) thresholds $t = (0.50, 0.55, \ldots, 0.95)$. The IoU of a predicted set of salt pixels and a set of true salt pixels is calculated as:

$$IoU(A, B) = \frac{A \cap B}{A \cup B}. \tag{1}$$

Let Y be a ground truth set of pixels and Y' be a set of pixels predicted by a model. At each threshold t, a precision value is calculated based on the following rules:

$$P(t) = \begin{cases} 0, & \text{if } |Y| = 0 \text{ and } |Y'| > 0 \\ 0, & \text{if } |Y| > 0 \text{ and } |Y'| = 0 \\ 1, & \text{if } |Y| = 0 \text{ and } |Y'| = 0 \\ IoU(Y, Y') > t, & \text{if } |Y| > 0 \text{ and } |Y'| > 0 \end{cases} \tag{2}$$

Then, the average precision of a single image is calculated as the mean of the above precision values at each IoU threshold:

$$AP = \frac{1}{10} \sum_{i=1}^{10} P(t_i). \tag{3}$$

The final evaluation score (mAP) is calculated as the mean taken over the individual average precisions of each image in the test dataset.

4.2   Implementation Details

We employ an ensemble of two U-Nets with Imagenet-pretrained encoder backbones: U-ResNet34 and U-ResNeXt50. The output of the ensemble is the average of the predictions of two models in the ensemble.

All images are resized to the size of 202×202 pixels and then padded to the size of 256×256 pixels. We do $K = 3$ rounds of self-training and $T = 200$ training epochs per round. Increasing the number of rounds did not lead to significant improvements of the results. We use cosine annealing learning rate policy [32] resetting the learning rate every 50 epochs (cf. loss spikes in Fig. 1 every 50 epochs). The learning rate starts from 0.001 and decays to 0.0001 every cycle.

Model weights are "warmed-up" using binary cross-entropy loss during the first 50 epochs. After that, we minimize Lovasz loss function [4] for 150 epochs, which allows a direct optimization of the IoU metric. The warm-up phase is necessary because we noticed that the network gets stuck in a very bad local optimum when the Lovasz loss is used from the very beginning.

Additionally, to get a more robust ensemble at the end of every round we average the predictions of 4 snapshots, which are saved every 50 epochs. When predicting pseudo-labels for all unlabeled data we do not remove the low-confidence predictions (i.e. $thresh = -\inf$) and use all 18000 pseudo-labeled images for training in the next round. We noticed that this strategy yielded better results than using only confident pseudo-labels.

During the first self-training round, we train the ensemble on the provided 4000 labeled images and generate 18000 pseudo-labels for unlabeled images. At rounds 2 and 3 we train the network for T epochs solely on the pseudo-labeled data and then fine-tune for another T epochs on the ground truth labeled training images. During initial experiments, we observed that jointly training on the ground-truth labeled images and pseudo-labeled images led to inferior results.

After each stage, we obtain 4 network snapshots for each of 5 folds giving 20 snapshots in total for a single network architecture. Since we use an ensemble of U-ResNet34 and U-ResNeXt50, it results in 40 models in total which are combined together for inference using the average voting.

For the final prediction on the test set, we use an ensemble of Round 2 and Round 3 models, which gives the best performing results on the public and private test sets (see Table 1).

To ensure the reproducibility, we will release the source code for our approach after the acceptance of the paper.

4.3   Results

We now compare our approach to the other state-of-the-art approaches. The detailed results are presented in Table 1. We evaluate using 3 metrics: private test mAP; public test mAP; place the model achieves on the private leaderboard (LB).

The table is split into three sections. The first section shows the results of the single U-ResNet34 model without the usage of pseudo-labels (i.e. Round 1 only). The second section ("Our U-ResNet34") shows results for 3 rounds of self-training using our U-ResNet34 model only (no ensemble used). And the third section ("Our U-ResNet34 + U-ResNeXt50") shows the results for 3 rounds of self-training using the ensemble of U-ResNet34 and U-ResNeXt50.

Training U-ResNet34 for 200 epochs gives 0.8834 mAP on private test. If we continue training the same model for another 200 epochs, it gives only a minor improvement by 0.1%.

However, the proposed self-training procedure allows to further improve the score using the unlabeled data while regular training does not help anymore. Round 2 of self-training significantly improves the performance: private test mAP score is increased by 0.6% bringing the model 41 positions up the leaderboard. Round 3 further improves the mAP score on the private test by 0.2% and moves us to the 12-th position on the leaderboard. This time the improvement is not so large as after Round 2, nevertheless it shows that applying multiple self-training rounds allows the model to iteratively increase the quality. Finally, a simple average of Round 2 and Round 3 models gives an extra 0.1% performance boost and brings us to the 10 place on the leaderboard (see "Ensemble of Round 2 and Round 3" in the second section of Table 1). Figure 1 shows the validation loss and mAP during different rounds of self-training. We observe that the model achieves better validation score every consequent round of self-training.

Our ensemble of U-ResNet34 and U-ResNeXt50 achieves the top-1 score on the private and public leaderboards showing the state-of-the-art performance on this dataset after two rounds of self-training. It has mAP score 0.8964 on the private LB (see "Ensemble of Round 2 and Round 3" in the third section of Table 1). For comparison, this ensemble surpasses the approach from the 27-th position described in [22] by 0.9%.

4.4   Ablation Study

In this section, we investigate improvements that can be gained using only one model architecture. The results of the ablations studies are reported in the first section of the Table 1.

We start with a single best snapshot of U-ResNet34 model which yields 0.8682 private test mAP (200-th place on the private leaderboard). The first idea is to use Test Time Augmentations (TTA): instead of predicting on a single test image, we average predictions on the original test image and its horizontal flip. Such an approach gives 0.6% performance boost almost for free.

The next idea is to utilize multiple snapshots. As was shown in the previous section, the cosine annealing learning rate schedule allows us to obtain multiple local optima in a single training loop. We can create an ensemble of all the snapshots instead of using only the latest snapshot. Such a method gives another 0.4% performance improvement.

Finally, we can further increase the diversity of the models training them on different data subsets. The most obvious choice, in this case, is to use k-fold data split and train k different models. This simple idea gives another substantial improvement of 0.6% mAP score relative to the previous one. It corresponds to the 40 positions increase on the private leaderboard.

5   Conclusion

We introduced an iterative self-training approach for semantic segmentation which can be effectively used in the limited labeled data setup by using unlabeled data to boost the model performance. Moreover, we designed a sophisticated network architecture for the task of salt body delineation and evaluated the proposed approach on a real-world salt body delineation dataset – TGS Salt Identification Challenge [21]. Our approach shows the best performance in the TGS Salt Identification Challenge [21] reaching the top-1 position on the leaderboard among the 3234 competing teams, which proves its effectiveness for the task.

References

1. Bautista, M.A., Sanakoyeu, A., Tikhoncheva, E., Ommer, B.: CliqueCNN: deep unsupervised exemplar learning. In: Advances in Neural Information Processing Systems, pp. 3846–3854 (2016)
2. Bautista, M.A., Sanakoyeu, A., Ommer, B.: Deep unsupervised similarity learning using partially ordered sets. In: Proceedings of the IEEE Conference on Computer Vision and Pattern Recognition, pp. 1923–1932 (2017)
3. Bedi, J., Toshniwal, D.: SFA-GTM: seismic facies analysis based on generative topographic map and RBF. arXiv preprint arXiv:1806.00193 (2018)
4. Berman, M., Rannen Triki, A., Blaschko, M.B.: The lovász-softmax loss: a tractable surrogate for the optimization of the intersection-over-union measure in neural networks. In: Proceedings of the IEEE Conference on Computer Vision and Pattern Recognition, pp. 4413–4421 (2018)
5. Büchler, U., Brattoli, B., Ommer, B.: Improving spatiotemporal self-supervision by deep reinforcement learning. In: Ferrari, V., Hebert, M., Sminchisescu, C., Weiss, Y. (eds.) ECCV 2018. LNCS, vol. 11219, pp. 797–814. Springer, Cham (2018). https://doi.org/10.1007/978-3-030-01267-0_47
6. Chen, L.C., Papandreou, G., Kokkinos, I., Murphy, K., Yuille, A.L.: Semantic image segmentation with deep convolutional nets and fully connected crfs. arXiv preprint arXiv:1412.7062 (2014)
7. Di, H., Shafiq, M., AlRegib, G.: Multi-attribute k-means clustering for salt-boundary delineation from three-dimensional seismic data. Geophys. J. Int. 215(3), 1999–2007 (2018)
8. Di, H., Wang, Z., AlRegib, G.: Real-time seismic-image interpretation via deconvolutional neural network. In: SEG Technical Program Expanded Abstracts 2018, pp. 2051–2055. Society of Exploration Geophysicists (2018)
9. Doersch, C., Gupta, A., Efros, A.A.: Unsupervised visual representation learning by context prediction. In: Proceedings of the IEEE International Conference on Computer Vision, pp. 1422–1430 (2015)
10. Dramsch, J.S., Lüthje, M.: Deep-learning seismic facies on state-of-the-art CNN architectures. SEG Technical Program Expanded Abstr. 2018, 2036–2040 (2018)
11. Fazakis, N., Karlos, S., Kotsiantis, S., Sgarbas, K.: Self-trained LMT for semisupervised learning. Comput. Intell. Neurosci. 2016, 10 (2016)
12. Halpert, A., Clapp, R.G.: Salt body segmentation with dip and frequency attributes. Stanford Explor. Project 113, 1–12 (2008)
13. Han, W., Feng, R., Wang, L., Cheng, Y.: A semi-supervised generative framework with deep learning features for high-resolution remote sensing image scene classification. ISPRS J. Photogrammetry Remote Sens. 145, 23–43 (2018)
14. Li, H., Xiong, P., An, J., Wang, L.: Pyramid attention network for semantic segmentation. In: Proceedings of the British Machine Vision Conference (BMVC) (2018)
15. Hariharan, B., Arbeláez, P., Girshick, R., Malik, J.: Hypercolumns for object segmentation and fine-grained localization. In: Proceedings of the IEEE Conference on Computer Vision and Pattern Recognition, pp. 447–456 (2015)
16. He, K., Zhang, X., Ren, S., Sun, J.: Deep residual learning for image recognition. In: Proceedings of the IEEE Conference on Computer Vision and Pattern Recognition, pp. 770–778 (2016)
17. Hegazy, T., AlRegib, G.: Texture attributes for detecting salt bodies in seismic data. In: SEG Technical Program Expanded Abstracts 2014, pp. 1455–1459. Society of Exploration Geophysicists (2014)

18. Iglovikov, V., Shvets, A.: TernausNet: U-Net with VGG11 encoder pre-trained on ImageNet for image segmentation. arXiv preprint arXiv:1801.05746 (2018)
19. Jiang, H., Larsson, G., Maire, M., Shakhnarovich, G., Learned-Miller, E.: Self-supervised relative depth learning for urban scene understanding. In: Ferrari, V., Hebert, M., Sminchisescu, C., Weiss, Y. (eds.) ECCV 2018. LNCS, vol. 11215, pp. 20–37. Springer, Cham (2018). https://doi.org/10.1007/978-3-030-01252-6_2
20. Jones, I.F., Davison, I.: Seismic imaging in and around salt bodies. Interpretation 2(4), SL1–SL20 (2014)
21. Kaggle: TGS salt identification challenge (2018). https://www.kaggle.com/c/tgs-salt-identification-challenge. Accessed 20 Oct 2018
22. Karchevskiy, M., Ashrapov, I., Kozinkin, L.: Automatic salt deposits segmentation: a deep learning approach. arXiv Machine Learning (2018)
23. Krizhevsky, A., Hinton, G.: Learning multiple layers of features from tiny images. Technical report. Citeseer (2009)
24. Larsson, G., Maire, M., Shakhnarovich, G.: Learning representations for automatic colorization. In: European Conference on Computer Vision, pp. 577–593 (2016)
25. LeCun, Y., et al.: Backpropagation applied to handwritten zip code recognition. Neural Comput. 1(4), 541–551 (1989)
26. Lee, D.H.: Pseudo-label: the simple and efficient semi-supervised learning method for deep neural networks. In: Workshop on Challenges in Representation Learning, ICML, vol. 3, p. 2 (2013)
27. Lee, H.Y., Huang, J.B., Singh, M., Yang, M.H.: Unsupervised representation learning by sorting sequences. In: Proceedings of the IEEE International Conference on Computer Vision, pp. 667–676 (2017)
28. Lee, H.W., Kim, N.r., Lee, J.H.: Deep neural network self-training based on unsupervised learning and dropout. Int. J. Fuzzy Log. Intell. Syst. 17(1), 1–9 (2017)
29. Li, M., Zhou, Z.-H.: SETRED: self-training with editing. In: Ho, T.B., Cheung, D., Liu, H. (eds.) PAKDD 2005. LNCS (LNAI), vol. 3518, pp. 611–621. Springer, Heidelberg (2005). https://doi.org/10.1007/11430919_71
30. Livieris, I.: A new ensemble semi-supervised self-labeled algorithm. Informatica 49, 221–234 (2019)
31. Livieris, I., Kanavos, A., Tampakas, V., Pintelas, P.: An ensemble SSL algorithm for efficient chest x-ray image classification. J. Imaging 4(7), 95 (2018)
32. Loshchilov, I., Hutter, F.: SGDR: stochastic gradient descent with warm restarts. arXiv preprint arXiv:1608.03983 (2016)
33. Noroozi, M., Favaro, P.: Unsupervised learning of visual representations by solving jigsaw puzzles. In: Leibe, B., Matas, J., Sebe, N., Welling, M. (eds.) ECCV 2016. LNCS, vol. 9910, pp. 69–84. Springer, Cham (2016). https://doi.org/10.1007/978-3-319-46466-4_5
34. Peters, B., Granek, J., Haber, E.: Multi-resolution neural networks for tracking seismic horizons from few training images. arXiv preprint arXiv:1812.11092 (2018)
35. Pitas, I., Kotropoulos, C.: A texture-based approach to the segmentation of seismic images. Pattern Recogn. 25(9), 929–945 (1992)
36. Ronneberger, O., Fischer, P., Brox, T.: U-Net: convolutional networks for biomedical image segmentation. In: Navab, N., Hornegger, J., Wells, W.M., Frangi, A.F. (eds.) MICCAI 2015. LNCS, vol. 9351, pp. 234–241. Springer, Cham (2015). https://doi.org/10.1007/978-3-319-24574-4_28
37. Roy, A.G., Navab, N., Wachinger, C.: Concurrent spatial and channel 'Squeeze & Excitation' in fully convolutional networks. In: Frangi, A., Schnabel, J., Davatzikos, C., Alberola-López, C., Fichtinger, G. (eds.) MICCAI 2018. LNCS, vol. 11070, pp. 421–429. Springer, Cham (2018). https://doi.org/10.1007/978-3-030-00928-1_48

38. Sanakoyeu, A., Bautista, M.A., Ommer, B.: Deep unsupervised learning of visual similarities. Pattern Recogn. **78**, 331–343 (2018)
39. Telford, W.M., Telford, W., Geldart, L., Sheriff, R.E., Sheriff, R.: Applied Geophysics, vol. 1. Cambridge University Press, Cambridge (1990)
40. Triguero, I., García, S., Herrera, F.: Self-labeled techniques for semi-supervised learning: taxonomy, software and empirical study. Knowl. Inf. Syst. **42**(2), 245–284 (2015)
41. Waldeland, A.U., Jensen, A.C., Gelius, L.J., Solberg, A.H.S.: Convolutional neural networks for automated seismic interpretation. Lead. Edge **37**(7), 529–537 (2018)
42. Wang, G., Xie, X., Lai, J., Zhuo, J.: Deep growing learning. In: IEEE International Conference on Computer Vision (ICCV), pp. 2831–2839. IEEE (2017)
43. Wang, W., Yang, F., Ma, J.: Automatic salt detection with machine learning. In: 80th EAGE Conference and Exhibition 2018 (2018)
44. Wrona, T., Pan, I., Gawthorpe, R.L., Fossen, H.: Seismic facies analysis using machine learning. Geophysics **83**(5), O83–O95 (2018)
45. Wu, X.: Methods to compute salt likelihoods and extract salt boundaries from 3D seismic images. Geophysics **81**(6), IM119–IM126 (2016)
46. Xie, S., Girshick, R., Dollár, P., Tu, Z., He, K.: Aggregated residual transformations for deep neural networks. In: Proceedings of the IEEE Conference on Computer Vision and Pattern Recognition, pp. 1492–1500 (2017)
47. Yarowsky, D.: Unsupervised word sense disambiguation rivaling supervised methods. In: 33rd Annual Meeting of the Association for Computational Linguistics (1995)
48. Yu, Z., et al.: Progressive semisupervised learning of multiple classifiers. IEEE Trans. Cybern. **48**(2), 689–702 (2018)
49. Zeng, Y., Jiang, K., Chen, J.: Automatic seismic salt interpretation with deep convolutional neural networks. arXiv preprint arXiv:1812.01101 (2018)
50. Zhao, T., Jayaram, V., Roy, A., Marfurt, K.J.: A comparison of classification techniques for seismic facies recognition. Interpretation **3**(4), SAE29–SAE58 (2015)
51. Zhu, X.J.: Semi-supervised learning literature survey. Technical report. University of Wisconsin-Madison Department of Computer Sciences (2005)

Entrack: A Data-Driven Maximum-Entropy Approach to Fiber Tractography

Viktor Wegmayr[(✉)], Giacomo Giuliari, and Joachim M. Buhmann

ETH Zurich, Zurich, Switzerland
vwegmayr@inf.ethz.ch

Abstract. The combined effort of brain anatomy experts and computerized methods has continuously improved the quality of available gold-standard tractograms for diffusion-weighted MRI. These prototypical tractograms contain information that can be utilized by other brain mapping applications. However, this transfer requires data-driven tractography algorithms, which learn from example tractograms, to deliver the obtained knowledge to other diffusion-weighted MRI data. The value of these data-driven methods would be greatly enhanced, if they could also estimate and control the uncertainty of their predictions. These reasons lead us to propose a generic machine learning method for probabilistic tractography. We demonstrate the general approach with a basic Fisher-von-Mises distribution to model local fiber direction. The distributional parameters are inferred from diffusion data by a neural network. For training the neural network, we derive an analytic, entropy-regularized cost function, which allows to control model uncertainty in accordance with the level of noise in the data. We highlight the ability of our method to quantify the probability of a given fiber, which makes it a useful tool for outlier detection. The tracking performance of the model is evaluated on the ISMRM 2015 Tractography Challenge.

Keywords: Diffusion weighted MRI · Probabilistic tractography · Brain · Machine learning · Neural networks

1 Introduction

While fiber tractography from diffusion-weighted magnetic resonance imaging (DWI) is a key technology in clinical neuroscience [9], it is notorious for lacking a reliable gold-standard [14]. Even though some initiatives have made attempts to provide high-quality reference tractograms [6,12,16], they remain difficult to obtain. In such a situation, it is crucial to distill as much information as possible from the few available data, and transfer it to new tractography tasks.

Machine learning (ML) [11] provides suitable tools for this kind of data-driven tractography. Several recent works have indeed attested great potential to ML-based tractography [13,15,23]. It was also found in previous work that ML

© Springer Nature Switzerland AG 2019
G. A. Fink et al. (Eds.): DAGM GCPR 2019, LNCS 11824, pp. 232–244, 2019.
https://doi.org/10.1007/978-3-030-33676-9_16

models trained on fibers produced by another algorithm (teacher) can generalize very well to new DWI data, and even improve over the teacher [24]. However, data-driven ML models for tractography would benefit from the advantages of probabilistic models, which are common in traditional (i.e. non-learning) tractography [1,3,21].

Probabilistic algorithms provide an estimate of their uncertainty, and they can consider several, similarly likely outcomes in ambiguous situations. Recent research in computer vision also demonstrates the benefit of taking into account the intrinsic uncertainty of the data, also called aleatoric noise [10]. However, while probabilistic models *may* incorporate uncertainty, they still tend to become deterministic in practice, due to overfitting to the training objective.

In this work, we introduce a probabilistic ML model for tractography, and present a principled maximum-entropy regularization to mitigate overfitting. We call our approach Entrack, and outline its three main components in the following. First, we choose a parametric directional distribution, such as the Fisher-von-Mises (FvM) distribution [18], to model the local distribution of fiber directions. Second, the parameters of this distribution are inferred from local diffusion data by an ML model trained on reference fibers. For the FvM, these parameter are mean direction and concentration. More specifically, we implement a neural network (NN) model, because of its flexible architecture, and its ability to learn appropriate feature transformations automatically. Lastly, the optimization of the NN weights is guided by an entropy-regularized likelihood, also known as the Gibbs free energy. The amount of regularization is controlled by a temperature parameter, which allows to match the uncertainty of the model to the noise in the data.

Using the ISMRM 2015 benchmark, we show that entropy regularization indeed helps to obtain better tractography scores. During prediction, fiber tracking proceeds sequentially, and at each step it considers diffusion data within the spatial neighborhood of the current position. Thus, the parameters of the directorial FvM distribution change along the predicted path, effectively taking into account the heteroscedasticity of fiber uncertainty. While being a competitive tractography model in its own right, Entrack also enables local fiber uncertainty quantification, and detection of outlier fibers. Lastly, the transparent derivation within the maximum entropy framework reveals numerous potential extensions to the Entrack method.

2 Background

2.1 Diffusion-Weighted MRI and Tractography

Diffusion-Weighted MRI measurements formally yield one k-dimensional vector for each image voxel. The vector components represent the MRI signal measured along a fixed set of k spatial *directions*. Low signals are recorded along directions where water can diffuse easily, i.e. where the local tissue structure favors random water motion. Consequently, DWI is a probe for local tissue architecture, which makes it an excellent tool to investigate anisotropic tissues such as the white matter of the brain [4]. More precisely, the white matter consists of myelinated axon bundles, which connect different brain regions. These bundles, or tracts, are the reason for anisotropic water diffusion in the white matter, so that it can be probed with DWI [2]. Typically, raw DWI measurements are converted to a more compact data representation, such as orientation distribution functions [20] illustrated in Fig. 1a.

Tractography refers to the inverse problem of reconstructing the original tissue connections from local DWI data. In simple words, Tractography tries to connect voxels to answer questions like "Is there a path from voxel A to voxel B?". It finds clinical application in preoperative planning, and research about stroke and dementia [25]. We illustrate a tractography result, also referred to as tractogram, in Fig. 1b. The major challenge in Tractography is ambiguity due to partial volume effects. While axon diameters are on the scale of μm, the DWI resolution is merely on the scale of mm. This lack of resolution makes it hard to disambiguate locations where fibers cross, touch, or fan apart.

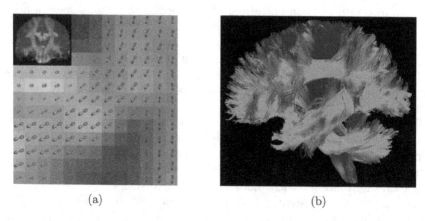

(a)   (b)

Fig. 1. Illustration of diffusion MRI, and a resulting tractogram. RGB color corresponds to the local xyz fiber orientation. (a) DWI data represented by local orientation distribution functions (b) The Tractometer reference tractogram [6] (Color figure online)

2.2 Uncertainty Quantification

In general, caution is necessary when we rely on model predictions in situations where human judgment is limited. These situations arise when it is difficult to establish a gold-standard, because the data representation is not intuitive for humans. This is certainly the case in tractography, as it is hard to interpret even the simplest useful representation of DWI data, which is a three-dimensional

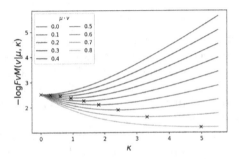

Fig. 2. Illustration of loss attenuation for the FvM distribution. Each line shows the negative log-likelihood for a fixed value of $\langle \mu, v \rangle$. For high deviation between prediction μ and observation v (*red lines*), the minimum (*black crosses*) is realized at a low certainty κ, while small deviations (*green lines*) can have their minima at higher certainties. (Color figure online)

vector field. In this situation, it is particularly desirable when model predictions come with an estimate of their uncertainty. More precisely, we are referring to the notion of aleatoric uncertainty, i.e the noise inherent to observations, which can not be reduced, even if we collect more data [10].

We illustrate this concept with the Fisher-von-Mises (FvM) distribution, which is a central component of this work. It is a unimodal, directional distribution defined on the sphere. For unit-length vectors v, the FvM density is given by $p(v) = C(\kappa) \exp\left(\kappa \langle \mu, v \rangle\right) \equiv \text{FvM}(v \mid \mu, \kappa)$, with $C(\kappa) = \kappa/(4\pi \sinh \kappa)$ and $\langle \mu, v \rangle = \sum_{i=1}^{3} \mu_i v_i$. It involves two parameters, i.e. the unit-length mean direction μ, and the scalar concentration $\kappa \in \mathbb{R}^{+}$.

In a deterministic setting, the corresponding loss L of a prediction μ, given an observation v, would simply be the negative scalar product, i.e. $L(\mu) = -\langle \mu, v \rangle$. Instead, in the probabilistic setting, we define the loss as the negative log-likelihood of the observation v under the *predicted distribution* $\text{FvM}(\mu, \kappa)$. To put it differently, instead of directly estimating the local fiber direction, we estimate the parameters μ, κ of the local directional distribution. Formally, the loss becomes $L(v) = -\log \text{FvM}(v \mid \mu, \kappa) = -\log C(\kappa) - \kappa \mu^{\top} v$.

This objective exhibits the property of loss attenuation [10], which means that a large deviation between prediction and observation can be compensated by an increased uncertainty, i.e. a lower concentration κ. We illustrate loss attenuation for the FvM distribution in Fig. 2.

Moreover, we can account for the *heteroscedasticity* of noise, if we make the estimated certainty a function of the input data x, i.e. $\kappa = \kappa(x)$. In the case of tractography, we can thus compare the certainty of predicted directions at different locations in the brain, depending on the local diffusion data, which takes the role of x.

2.3   Maximum-Entropy Regularization

In practice, the benefits of a probabilistic objective, as discussed in the previous section, may be reduced due to overfitting. Overfitting occurs, if the model complexity is large, as it is for neural networks. However, as we can see in Fig. 2, when the training loss goes to zero, the uncertainty is driven to zero, too, i.e. $\kappa \to \infty$. The predicted FvM distribution would put all the probability mass on a single direction, i.e. the mean direction.

As a consequence, the entropy of the output distributions is also minimal, which is detrimental for its robustness to noise, because is known from robust inference that the lower the entropy of a distribution, the more susceptible it is to perturbation of its constraints [19]. In our setting, this perturbation is equivalent to data fluctuations.

To maintain the benefits of a probabilistic objective, and its robustness against noise, we need regularization, which keeps the model from collapsing to zero uncertainty, i.e. minimal entropy. Indeed, this is in line with the fundamental Maximum Entropy Principle, which states that if two distributions have the same expected loss, the distribution with the higher entropy is more robust [8]. Formally, this is captured by the free energy functional $G(p)$ of a distribution p:

$$G(p) = \mathbb{E}_p[R] - T \cdot \mathbb{H}[p] = \mathbb{E}_{p(v)}[R(v) + T \cdot \log p(v)]. \tag{1}$$

The expected cost $R(v)$, over all predictions v under p, is denoted by $\mathbb{E}_p[R]$, and the entropy of p is denoted by $\mathbb{H}[p]$. The temperature parameter T should reflect the amount of noise in the data, i.e. low temperature for little, and high temperature for large noise. In practice, the temperature is determined by cross-validation with a score of interest, such as the scores of the ISMRM 2015 Tractography Challenge [6].

3   Methods

3.1   The Maximum-Entropy Objective for Tractography

In the following we describe the specifics of the Entrack model, and how it is derived from the principles described in Sect. 2.

We consider a tractogram as a set of N fiber polygons. Each fiber polygon $i = 1, \ldots, N$ is described by a tuple of $j = 1, \ldots, n_i$ fiber segment vectors $v_j^i \in \mathbb{R}^3$, i.e. the tuple $(v_1^i, \ldots, v_{n_i}^i)$. While this joint formulation is fairly general, we need to make some simplifications about the cost R of a tractogram to obtain analytical results from Eq. (1).

Making the assumption that fibers are independent, we can write the cost in the form $R = \sum_{i=1}^N R_i(v_1^i, \ldots, v_{n_i}^i)$. Moreover, we reduce the cost of a single fiber into the costs of its individual segments, i.e. $R_i(v_1^i, \ldots, v_{n_i}^i) = \sum_{j=1}^{n_i} R_j^i(v_j^i)$. As in Sect. 2, we choose the negative scalar product between segment v_j^i and its observation $\hat{v}_j^i$ as the segment cost, i.e. $R_j^i(v_j^i) = -\langle v_j^i, \hat{v}_j^i \rangle$. Combining this choice for the cost with the choice of the FvM as variational distribution, we can formulate the free energy $G(p_j^i) \equiv G(\mu_j^i, \kappa_j^i)$ for a single segment j:

$$G(\mu_j^i, \kappa_j^i) = - \int_{\|v\|_2=1} \langle v, \hat{v}_j^i \rangle \mathrm{FvM}(v \mid \mu_j^i, \kappa_j^i) dv - \mathbb{H}[\mathrm{FvM}(v \mid \mu_j^i, \kappa_j^i)]. \qquad (2)$$

Indeed, the free energy for a segment can be calculated analytically:

$$G(\mu_j^i, \kappa_j^i) = -W(\kappa_j^i) \cdot \langle \mu_j^i, \hat{v}_j^i \rangle - T \cdot H(\kappa_j^i). \qquad (3a)$$

$$W(\kappa) = \|\mathbb{E}_{\mathrm{FvM}(v \mid \mu, \kappa)}[v]\|_2 = \frac{\cosh \kappa}{\sinh \kappa} - \frac{1}{\kappa}. \qquad (3b)$$

$$H(\kappa) = \mathbb{H}\left[\mathrm{FvM}(v \mid \mu, \kappa)\right] = 1 - \frac{\kappa}{\tanh \kappa} - \log \frac{\kappa}{4\pi \sinh \kappa}. \qquad (3c)$$

The free energy in Eq. (3a) has a similar loss attenuating property as discussed before in Sect. 2.2. As shown in Fig. 3b, higher deviations $\langle \mu, \hat{v} \rangle$ cause the free energy minima to shift towards higher uncertainty, i.e. lower κ. Moreover, the minima are realized at higher certainty for lower temperature, i.e. when less entropy regularization is used.

The functions $W(\kappa)$ and $H(\kappa)$ have very intuitive meanings. They are the norm of the first moment, and the entropy of a $\mathrm{FvM}(\mu, \kappa)$ distribution, respectively. We illustrate both functions in Fig. 3a.

The total free energy objective over the set of all segment parameters $\{\mu_j^i, \kappa_j^i\}$ is obtained by summing up all segment contributions, i.e. $G(\{p_j^i\}) \equiv G(\{\mu_j^i, \kappa_j^i\}) = \sum_{i,j} G(p_j^i)$.

In principle, any appropriate directional distribution could serve as variational approximation of p_j^i. We choose the family of FvM distributions due to its analytic tractability, which enables us to demonstrate the concept of Entrack without too much technical involvement. Besides, the FvM distribution is actually a maximum entropy distribution itself. For linear costs $R(v) = -\langle v, \hat{v} \rangle$ and $\|v\|_2 = 1$, the maximum entropy solution $p^*(v)$ of Eq. (1) is $\mathrm{FvM}(\hat{v}, \frac{1}{T})$.

3.2 Learning the Conditional Segment Distribution

Given a training tractogram, i.e. a set $\{(\hat{v}_1^1, \ldots, \hat{v}_{n_1}^1), \ldots, (\hat{v}_1^N, \ldots, \hat{v}_{n_N}^N)\}$, the direct optimization of $G(\{\mu_j^i, \kappa_j^i\})$ - just as a function of $\{\mu_j^i, \kappa_j^i\}$ - would be fairly straight forward. The reason is that each contribution $G(\mu_j^i, \kappa_j^i)$ can be optimized independently. Simple calculation shows that $\mu_j^i = \hat{v}_j^i$ and $f(\kappa_j^i, T) = 0$, where f is a non-linear, implicit equation for κ_j^i, which is the same for all segments. In words, the "learned" distribution would simply have the training tractogram as mean, and a location-independent variance, which solely depends on the temperature. Clearly, this trivial copy of the training tractogram will not generalize to DWI data of an unseen brain.

Instead, the segment parameters $\{\mu_j^i, \kappa_j^i\}$ should be functions of the diffusion data, i.e. $\mu_j^i = \mu_\theta(\mathbf{B}_j^i, \mathbf{v}_j^i)$ and $\kappa_j^i = \kappa_\phi(\mathbf{B}_j^i, \mathbf{v}_j^i)$, where $\mathbf{B}_j^i$ is a $k \times k \times k$ block of diffusion data around the location of the segment, and $\mathbf{v}_j^i$ are m fiber segments preceding the segment, i.e. $\mathbf{v}_j^i = (v_{j-1}^i, \ldots, v_{j-m}^i)$. The functional forms of μ_θ and κ_ϕ are also design choices, but it is desirable to choose flexible functions that can appropriately fit the relationship between diffusion data and the local distribution of fiber direction. For this reason, we choose neural networks, which are instantiated in Sect. 4.2. Note, the optimization with respect to the neural network weights $\{\theta, \phi\}$ is now a high-dimensional, and non-convex problem. We state the loss function to make it explicit:

$$L(\{\theta, \phi\}) = \sum_{i=1}^{N} \sum_{j=1}^{n_i} G\left(\mu_\theta(\mathbf{B}_j^i, \mathbf{v}_j^i), \kappa_\phi(\mathbf{B}_j^i, \mathbf{v}_j^i)\right). \tag{4}$$

Importantly, once the weights are found, we are able to predict the distributional parameters (μ, κ) for unseen input data $(\mathbf{B}, \mathbf{v})$. This means, we have truly learned the patterns in the training tractogram, and we can generalize them on new data.

3.3   Inference for Fiber Tracking

We follow the streamlining procedure described in [24], but recap it shortly for completeness.

Having learned the functions μ_θ, κ_ϕ, they can be used to track fibers iteratively from seed points, which are typically on the boundary between white and gray matter. During one iteration, we query the diffusion data $\mathbf{B}$ around the current location, and the preceding m segments $\mathbf{v}$. If preceding vectors are not available, e.g. at the beginning of a fiber, we set them to zero. Using this data as input, we predict the distributional parameters of the direction for the next move, i.e. $\mu_\theta(\mathbf{B}, \mathbf{v})$, and $\kappa_\phi(\mathbf{B}, \mathbf{v})$. Now we can either move deterministically along the most likely direction μ_θ, or stochastically along a sampled direction $v \sim \text{FvM}(\mu_\theta, \kappa_\phi)$. After moving along the chosen direction for a fixed step size α, the iteration is repeated until the white/gray matter boundary is reached again, or a maximum length is exceeded.

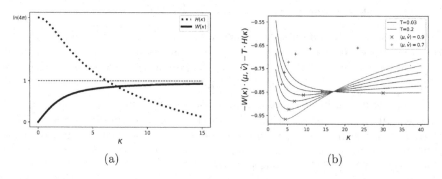

(a)   (b)

Fig. 3. (a) Illustration of the entropy $H(\kappa)$ (*dotted*) and first moment norm $W(\kappa)$ (*solid*) of a FvM(μ, κ) distribution. (b) Illustration of the free energy minima (*crosses*) for a single segment as a function of κ, i.e. Eq. (3a), for different deviations $\langle \mu, \hat{v} \rangle$ ($\times$ *and* $+$), and temperatures T. Colors indicates high T (*red*), and low T (*blue*). We omitted the lines for $\langle \mu, \hat{v} \rangle = 0.7$ to avoid clutter. (Color figure online)

4 Experiments

4.1 Data

Diffusion-weighted MRI data used in this work was obtained from the MGH-USC Human Connectome Project (HCP) database [7], and from the Tractometer (TM) project [6]. The TM data also includes 25 well-prepared fiber bundles with 200k fibers, which serves as our gold-standard. Training samples are obtained from a given tractogram by decomposing its fibers into tuples of $(\mathbf{B}, \mathbf{v}, \hat{v})$, i.e. into fiber segments $\hat{v}$ together with their local diffusion data $\mathbf{B}$, and their preceding directions $\mathbf{v}$. For models trained on HCP data, we use only training fibers with a minimum length of 30 mm, while we use all fibers when training on Tractometer data.

4.2 Implementation

Neural Network Architecture. As discussed in Sect. 3.2, we implement the functions μ_θ, κ_ϕ as neural networks, which are described here in more detail.[1] First, the inputs $(\mathbf{B}, \mathbf{v})$ are both flattened and then concatenated to form one input vector. The input vector goes through a sequence of fully-connected layers, which are shared between the output heads for μ and κ. The last shared layer is duplicated, and provides the same input to both output branches, which add their own sequence of layers on top. All layer specifications are detailed in Fig. 4. The output head for μ yields the unit-length mean-direction, whereas the second head yields the scalar, positive-valued concentration κ.

Input Representation. The neural network takes two components as input. The first is diffusion data around the current location. Diffusion measurements are represented with a spherical-harmonics expansion up to order $l = 4$, which means the diffusion signal at each voxel has 15 feature values. The spatial extent of the diffusion data taken into account is $3 \times 3 \times 3$ voxels, centered on the current position. In total, this results in $3 \times 3 \times 3 \times 15 = 405$ diffusion features. The second input component is given by $m = 4$ preceding fiber vectors, which gives a total of 12 features.

Optimization. The optimization is performed with standard stochastic gradient descent. We use a learning rate of 0.05, batch size of 512 and train for 10 epochs on a given data set. Additionally, we clip the gradient to a maximal global norm of 5. While the general free energy loss in Eq. (1) involves cumbersome expectations, the loss derived analytically in Eq. (4) enables a more stable training process, because it avoids the estimation of stochastic gradients.

---

[1] Code available at https://github.com/vwegmayr/entrack

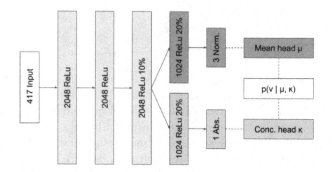

Fig. 4. Neural Network Layers. Inputs (*white box*) flow from left to right, first through shared layers (*gray boxes*), before the two output heads for the mean (*green boxes*) and concentration (*yellow boxes*) branch off. All layers are fully-connected (*arrows*). Numbers indicate number of hidden units, followed by the layer's activation function (ReLU: rectified linear unit, Norm: normalization to unit length, Abs: absolute value), and Dropout percentage, if applicable. (Color figure online)

4.3   Optimal Temperature

To show that entropy regularization, i.e. having $T > 0$, indeed improves fiber tracking performance, we train the Entrack model at different temperatures on the TM data, and report validation scores in Fig. 5.

We observe that all scores obtain their optima at a non-zero temperature ($T^* \approx 10^{-3}$), which confirms that entropy regularization is beneficial in the presence of data fluctuations. For lower temperatures, the model overfits the training data. For higher temperatures, the model is over-regularized. In both cases, the performance is reduced compared to the optimal temperature.

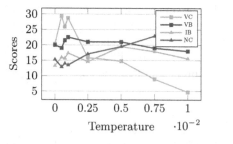
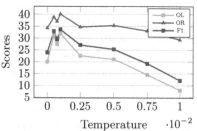

Fig. 5. Cross-validation for the optimal temperature T^*. The model is trained on the TM data set, and the following scores are reported: valid connections (*VC*, %), valid bundles (*VB*, out of 25), invalid bundles (*IB*, scaled by $\frac{1}{10}$), non-connections (*NC*, %), mean overlap (*OL*, %), mean overreach (*OR*, %) and mean F1 score (*F1*, %). The marker shapes (■/▲) indicate higher/lower is better, respectively. A detailed explanation of the scores is given in the Tractometer paper, and the corresponding challenge website [6].

4.4 Probabilistic Fiber Analysis

In addition to fiber tracking, the Entrack model also enables probabilistic evaluation of streamlines, because it provides a proper probability density over fibers. Thus, it is possible to compare tractography results, or to detect outliers. Due to our independence assumptions, it is simple to evaluate the probability of an entire fiber:

$$p(v_1, \ldots, v_n) = \prod_{i=1}^{n} p(v_i \mid \mathbf{B}_i, \mathbf{v}_i). \tag{5}$$

We note that longer fibers are *not* biased towards lower probabilities, because the segment density factors in Eq. (5) are not bound to be smaller than 1.

We show two applications of Eq. (5) in Fig. 6. First, the Entrack model enables to pinpoint fibers with low probability as shown by the red loops in Figs. 6a and b. In this experiment, we trained the model on the TM data, and used it to evaluate the probability of the same TM fibers. As the TM data is well prepared, hardly any outliers can be recognized by visual inspection. However, using the fiber probabilities produced by Entrack, we can identify some anatomically implausible loops. In contrast to e.g. curvature based filters, the Entrack model can distinguish strongly bending fibers that are supported by the diffusion data.

The second application concerns estimation of local fiber uncertainty. The concentration parameter κ of the FvM distribution corresponds to the degree of certainty the model has about the fiber direction in a given point. In Fig. 6c we can observe that the concentration/certainty is larger at the core of bundles, i.e. where the diffusion data tends to be less ambiguous. Areas that are closer to the white matter boundary, such as bundle outlines, have lower concentration, presumably because the diffusion signal is weaker in those areas. In particular, fiber end points exhibit the lowest concentrations, as they are located right at the white matter boundary, as shown in Fig. 6d.

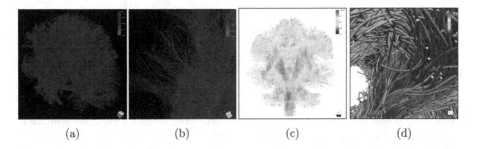

| (a) | (b) | (c) | (d) |

Fig. 6. (a) Illustration of fibers with high probability (*blue*), and low probability (*red*). (b) Enhanced view of an implausible loop (*red, center*). (c) Illustration of the spatial variation of the certainty κ. Bundle cores tend to be more certain (*red*), while the certainty of their outlines is reduced (*green*). (d) Enhanced view of increased uncertainty at fiber ends (*blue*). (Color figure online)

4.5 Generalization Ability

As mentioned in Sect. 1, data-driven tractography methods aim to enable information transfer from a given training tractogram to new applications on unseen data.

To demonstrate the generalization ability of the Entrack model, we train it on one subject of the HCP data set (ID 978578), using the iFOD2 implementation of MRtrix [21,22] to generate training fibers. After training and cross-validation of T, the model is used to predict fibers on the TM data set. For prediction, we use a step size α for streamlining, which is 75% of the voxelsize. The predicted fibers are then scored by the TM benchmark utility. For scoring, we produce 50k fibers with a minimum length of 25α, and a maximum length of 550α. Comparison to other data-driven approaches is provided in Table 1, which includes only results that were not trained on the TM test data, but rather on a separate data set. While the work of [15] reports encouraging results using recurrent neural networks, they only provide TM scores obtained by models, which were trained *and* tested on the TM data.

Table 1 indicates that no current data-driven method clearly outperforms the rest. The Entrack model achieves scores comparable to the other works, indicating its usefulness as predictive model for fiber tracking, in addition to its benefits of uncertainty quantification, and outlier detection.

Table 1. Evaluation on the Tractometer. Please refer to Fig. 5 for a description of the scores. We don't include NC in this table, because it was only available for Entrack.

Model	VB	IB	VC	OL	OR	F1
iFOD2 [21]	**23**	83	**62%**	40%	38%	39%
Wegmayr [24]	22	**75**	34%	14%	**29%**	21%
Neher [13]	**23**	94	52%	**59%**	37%	n.a.
Entrack	**23**	85	51%	23%	39%	27%

5 Discussion

Entrack represents a probabilistic framework for ML approaches to fiber tractography, which enables uncertainty quantification. The need for such an approach has been articulated in previous work [15,24].

Other works, which output probability vectors directly, e.g. by using the probabilities of a random forest classifier [13], can *not* provide uncertainty quantification. To do so, it would be necessary to predict a distribution over probabilities, such as the Dirichlet distribution as demonstrated by [17]. The Entrack model uses a neural network to predict the parameters of a Fisher-von-Mises distribution over local fiber direction. The prediction takes into account local diffusion data, and preceding fiber segments.

To increase robustness, and avoid overfitting, we derive an entropy-regularized cost function within the general Maximum-Entropy framework [8]. Entropy-regularization is necessary to reduce overfitting by maintaining a non-zero uncertainty, and we demonstrate its positive effect on generalization in Fig. 5. We note that the work of [17], which investigates uncertainty quantification in the context of classification, also introduces a similar regularization term. However, it is presented ad hoc as a Kullback-Leibler divergence with the uniform distribution, without mentioning its relationship to the concept of Maximum-Entropy.

The Entrack approach is very flexible, and can be combined with other recent works such as recurrent neural networks modeling the sequential nature of streamlines [15]. Even though we instantiate our approach with the unimodal FvM distribution and non-recurrent, fully-connected NNs, its fiber predictions generalize well to the ISMRM 2015 phantom, after being trained on real HCP brain data. We obtain Tractometer scores that are comparable to the current state-of-the-art in data-driven tractography, however none of the compared methods outperforms the rest in every score as shown in Table 1. We emphasize again that, in addition to fiber tracking, Entrack enables quantification of local fiber uncertainty, and detection of outlier fibers.

In future work, it would be interesting to explore multiple potential extensions of the presented approach. For example, the FvM distribution is its own conjugate prior, which would allow to incorporate the information of preceding fiber segments in a more principled way than just adding them as input features. Moreover, the choice of the parametric distribution is not limited to the FvM distribution. An interesting alternative could be the antipodally symmetric Bingham distribution, which also features a non-isotropic covariance matrix [5]. Mixture-models could go beyond unimodal distributions to account for several fiber directions at a single location. The Entrack framework provides room for many modeling choices in closed form, but it in principle it also applies to models, which are not analytically tractable.

References

1. Aganj, I., et al.: A hough transform global probabilistic approach to multiple-subject diffusion MRI tractography. Med. Image Anal. 15(4), 414–425 (2011). https://doi.org/10.1016/j.media.2011.01.003
2. Beaulieu, C.: The basis of anisotropic water diffusion in the nervous system - a technical review. NMR Biomed. 15(7–8), 435–455 (2002)
3. Behrens, T.E.J., et al.: Probabilistic diffusion tractography with multiple fiber orientations: what can we gain? NeuroImage 34(1), 144–155 (2007). https://doi.org/10.1016/j.neuroimage.2006.09.018
4. Bihan, D.L., Iima, M.: Diffusion magnetic resonance imaging: what water tells us about biological tissues. In: PLoS Biology (2015)
5. Bingham, C.: An antipodally symmetric distribution on the sphere. Ann. Stat. 2(6), 1201–1225 (1974). https://doi.org/10.1214/aos/1176342874

6. Côté, M.A., et al.: Tractometer: towards validation of tractography pipelines. Med. Image Anal. **17**(7), 844–857 (2013). http://www.tractometer.org/ismrm_2015_challenge/evaluation

7. Fan, Q., et al.: MGH-USC human connectome project datasets with ultra-high b-value diffusion MRI. NeuroImage **124**, 1108–1114 (2016)

8. Jaynes, E.T.: Information theory and statistical mechanics. Phys. Rev. **106**, 620–630 (1957). https://doi.org/10.1103/PhysRev.106.620

9. Johansen-Berg, H., et al.: Just pretty pictures? what diffusion tractography can add in clinical neuroscience. Curr. Opin. Neurol. **19**, 379–385 (2006)

10. Kendall, A., Gal, Y.: What uncertainties do we need in Bayesian deep learning for computer vision? In: NIPS (2017)

11. Murphy, K.P.: Machine learning - a probabilistic perspective. In: Adaptive Computation and Machine Learning Series (2012)

12. Neher, P.F., et al.: Fiberfox: facilitating the creation of realistic white matter software phantoms. Magn. Reson. Med. **72**(5), 1460–1470 (2014). https://doi.org/10.1002/mrm.25045

13. Neher, P.F., et al.: Fiber tractography using machine learning. NeuroImage **158**, 417–429 (2017)

14. Nimsky, C., Bauer, M., Carl, B.: Merits and limits of tractography techniques for the uninitiated. In: Schramm, J. (ed.) Advances and Technical Standards in Neurosurgery. ATSN, vol. 43, pp. 37–60. Springer, Cham (2016). https://doi.org/10.1007/978-3-319-21359-0_2

15. Poulin, P., et al.: Learn to track: deep learning for tractography. In: Descoteaux, M., Maier-Hein, L., Franz, A., Jannin, P., Collins, D.L., Duchesne, S. (eds.) MICCAI 2017. LNCS, vol. 10433, pp. 540–547. Springer, Cham (2017). https://doi.org/10.1007/978-3-319-66182-7_62

16. Poupon, C., et al.: A diffusion hardware phantom looking like a coronal brain slice. In: Proceedings of the International Society for Magnetic Resonance in Medicine (2010)

17. Sensoy, M., Kaplan, L., Kandemir, M.: Evidential Deep Learning to Quantify Classification Uncertainty, pp. 3179–3189 (2018)

18. Straub, J.: Bayesian inference with the von-Mises-fisher distribution in 3D (2017). http://people.csail.mit.edu/jstraub/download/straub2017vonMisesFisher Inference.pdf. Accessed 09 Feb 2018

19. Tikochinsky, Y., Tishby, N.Z., Levine, R.D.: Alternative approach to maximum-entropy inference. Phys. Rev. A **30**, 2638–2644 (1984)

20. Tournier, J.D., et al.: Robust determination of the fibre orientation distribution in diffusion MRI: non-negativity constrained super-resolved spherical deconvolution. NeuroImage **35**, 1459–1472 (2007)

21. Tournier, J.D., et al.: Improved probabilistic streamlines tractography by 2nd order integration over fibre orientation distributions. In: Proceedings of International Society for Magnetic Resonance in Medicine (ISMRM) (2010)

22. Tournier, J.D., et al.: MRtrix: diffusion tractography in crossing fiber regions. Int. J. Imaging Syst. Technol. (2012). http://www.mrtrix.org/

23. Wasserthal, J., et al.: Direct White Matter Bundle Segmentation using Stacked U-Nets. CoRR (2017)

24. Wegmayr, V.: Data-driven fiber tractography with neural networks. In: ISBI (2018)

25. Yamada, K., Sakai, K., Akazawa, K., Yuen, S., Nishimura, T.: MR tractography: a review of its clinical applications. Magn. Reson. Med. Sci. **8**(4), 165–174 (2009). MRMS : an official journal of Japan Society of Magnetic Resonance in Medicine

Posters

Generative Aging of Brain MR-Images and Prediction of Alzheimer Progression

Viktor Wegmayr$^{(\boxtimes)}$, Maurice Hörold, and Joachim M. Buhmann

ETH Zurich, Zurich, Switzerland
vwegmayr@inf.ethz.ch

Abstract. Predicting the age progression of individual brain images from longitudinal data has been a challenging problem, while its solution is considered key to improve dementia prognosis. Often, approaches are limited to group-level predictions, lack the ability to extrapolate, can not scale to many samples, or do not operate directly on image inputs. We address these issues with the first approach to artificial aging of brain images based on Wasserstein Generative Adversarial Networks. We develop a novel recursive generator model for brain image time series, and train it on large-scale longitudinal data sets (ADNI/AIBL). In addition to thorough analysis of results on healthy and demented subjects, we demonstrate the predictive value of our brain aging model in the context of conversion prognosis from mild cognitive impairment to Alzheimer's disease. Conversion prognosis for a baseline image is achieved in two steps. First, we estimate the future brain image with the Generative Adversarial Network. This follow-up image is passed to a CNN classifier, pre-trained to discriminate between mild cognitive impairment and Alzheimer's disease. It estimates the Alzheimer probability for the follow-up image, which represents an effective measure for future disease risk.

Keywords: WGAN · Deep learning · Brain aging · Alzheimer · MRI

1 Introduction

Growing collections of longitudinal brain MRI data have been a driving factor of brain aging research [27]. They have lead to a better understanding of the spatio-temporal structure of brain changes during aging [3,25], and how it interacts with pathologies, in particular Alzheimer's disease (AD). Thus, there is agreement that predictive models of brain aging hold great promise for the early prognosis of AD onset [1,21].

However, it has been difficult to predict the age progression of an individual brain, due to the high dimensionality of the respective brain imagery, and the relative scarcity of samples. Some approaches reduce the complexity of disease progression by prediction at population-level, using voxel-wise regression [16,31].

Geodesic Regression defines a popular framework to interpolate image time series [22]. Even though recent work has reduced its computational demands [10],

© Springer Nature Switzerland AG 2019
G. A. Fink et al. (Eds.): DAGM GCPR 2019, LNCS 11824, pp. 247–260, 2019.
https://doi.org/10.1007/978-3-030-33676-9_17

its ability to extrapolate, or even predict subject-specific progression, remains limited. The work of [5] has addressed extrapolation, and individual predictions in the context of large deformation diffeomorphic metric mapping (LDDMM), but their results were restricted to the progression of subcortical structures.

Recently, [24] proposed a pipeline combining LDDMM, convolutional and recurrent Neural Networks. Their model learns sequences of deformations to predict individual brain image progression. However, their model does not learn the progression end-to-end from image data, but depends on the LDDMM output.

A closely related area of research addresses face (image) aging, which attempts to solve the same basic problem as brain aging, i.e. predicting the temporal progression of face appearance in an image. In contrast to brain aging, the most recent approaches to face aging almost exclusively rely on conditional (Wasserstein) Generative Adversarial Networks (WGAN) [2,19,23,32]. More specifically, the estimation of the aged faces is conditioned on an input image of the respective young face. In general, this technique is known as image-to-image translation [15]. A major difference between brain and face data is that the latter is subject to many factors of variation, while brain image acquisition is fairly standardized. Within the brain MRI domain, WGANs have recently been used to model the effects of AD in brain images [7,8]. Their goal is to attribute the effects of AD to changes in the image, e.g. reduced volume of certain brain regions like the hippocampus.

Motivated by these recent successes, we propose the first approach to brain image aging based on conditional WGANs. We develop a novel recursive WGAN model for the estimation of image progression, which directly receives image data as input in an end-to-end fashion. It makes efficient use of longitudinal data, and its optimization with mini-batch gradient descent is computationally efficient. Our model can predict subject-specific progression, and extrapolate it beyond the last observation.

Importantly, we demonstrate that estimation of the aging process improves the accuracy of predicting whether an individual will progress from mild cognitive impairment (MCI) to Alzheimer's disease, which is a prognostic problem of high clinical relevance.

Preliminary results of this research have been reported in [29]; this work substantially extends the analysis and evaluation, including experiments on synthetic data, discussion of different diagnosis groups, and predictions for different follow-up times.

2   Methods

The proposed generative brain aging model is based on Wasserstein Generative Adversarial Networks (WGAN) [20]. The WGAN is an improvement of the original GAN model [13], which was based on the Jensen-Shannon divergence. The Wasserstein distance is a dissimilarity between probability distributions, also known as Earth Mover distance due to its relationship with optimal transport theory. Formally, we seek to generate samples from an aging distribution

$\mathbb{P}(x_0, x_1, \delta)$, where x_0 denotes the baseline image, x_1 the follow-up image, and $\delta = t_1 - t_0$ the time difference between baseline and follow-up. The WGAN model approximates the real aging distribution by iteratively updating two networks, namely the generator network g and the critic network c. This iteration minimizes the dual form of the Wasserstein distance $W(\mathbb{P}_r, \mathbb{P}_g)$ between the generator distribution $\mathbb{P}_g$, and the data distribution $\mathbb{P}_r$:

$$W(\mathbb{P}_r, \mathbb{P}_g) = \sup_{\|c\|_L \leq 1} \mathbb{E}_{\mathbb{P}_r(x_0, \delta)} \Big[\mathbb{E}_{\mathbb{P}_r(x_1|x_0, \delta)}[c(x_0, x_1, \delta)] - \mathbb{E}_{\mathbb{P}_g(x_1|x_0, \delta)}[c(x_0, x_1, \delta)] \Big]$$

We have re-written the Wasserstein distance in terms of conditional distributions to point out the relationship between our model, and the common formulation. In our setting, the generator distribution $\mathbb{P}_g(x_1|x_0, \delta)$ reduces to a deterministic generator function $x_1 = g(x_0, \delta)$. The critic is a function of all inputs $c(x_0, x_1, \delta)$, as it judges whether the changes from x_0 to x_1 correspond to realistic aging over a time δ.

Both, generator and critic functions are implemented as deep CNNs. The generator has a U-Net architecture [28], i.e. the image input first runs through an encoder sequence of convolutional layers, which decrease in spatial size, but increase in the number of feature maps. These features are consequently upsampled again through a decoder sequence of transposed convolution layers to yield the output image. The detailed generator architecture is illustrated in Fig. 1. The critic network has the same architecture as the encoder of the generator, but its output layers compute a single scalar instead of decoding a brain image. We detail the critic network in Sect. 3.1. A similar architecture was employed by [7] for visual feature attribution of Alzheimer's disease.

However, to account for the longitudinal data structure, we need a generator which is able to perform aging across different follow-up times, because it would be rather wasteful to train a separate WGAN for each δ. A simple approach would be to condition the generator on an additional δ feature to encode the requested follow-up time. Unfortunately, this approach proved unsuccessful in our experiments. Instead, we propose a recursive generator model. A single pass through the generator produces aging by an incremental time step ϵ, so we denote this generator as g_ϵ. To produce an image after some follow-up time δ, the generator is iterated for $k = \lceil \frac{\delta}{\epsilon} \rceil$ times:

$$x_1 = \underbrace{g_\epsilon \circ \cdots \circ g_\epsilon}_{k\text{-times}}(x_0) \tag{1}$$

In the actual implementation, the recursion is unrolled as in recurrent neural networks (RNNs). However, our recursive model does not have a hidden state as in RNNs, but simply reuses its output as the input for the next iteration. Evidently, the generator model assumes that aging only depends on the current observation. Moreover, it is stationary, as it assumes that aging is independent of the subject's age. This simplifying assumption is also made in other work, e.g. [24].

3   Experiments

3.1   Implementation

As mentioned in Sect. 2, the critic network has the same architecture as the encoder part of the generator shown in Fig. 1, but adds different classification layers instead of the decoder part.

More specifically, after the last 128 feature maps of the encoder, it continues with another 2×2 max-pooling layer, three more 3×3 convolutional layers with 256 channels each, finally followed by a 1×1 linear convolution to reduce the number of channels to 1. The critic output is simply the mean of the final feature map. All activation functions in generator and critic are ReLUs, except the linear output layers, and the generator output layer, which requires a tanh activation function. We use batch normalization only for the convolutional layers of the generator, but not in the critic.

In our experiments we always use a 60/20/20 train/validation/test split for hyper-parameter estimation and model selection. WGAN models are trained for 20000 steps with a batch size of 16 using the ADAM optimizer with a learning rate of 10^{-4}. As a starting point for our WGAN implementation, we used the code of [7]. The code implementing the generative brain aging model is available at https://github.com/vwegmayr/brain-aging.

Moreover, we use a CNN model analogous to the critic network for MCI/AD classification. It differs from the critic in the final layers. More specifically, the 1×1 convolution in the critic is replaced with a reduce-mean over the spatial dimensions, resulting in a vector of 256 features. A subsequent linear layer computes two logits for the classes MCI and AD. In contrast to the critic, all convolutional layers in the classifier use batch normalization.

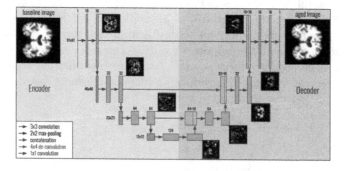

Fig. 1. Architecture of the brain aging generator. Lateral numbers indicate the spatial extent of the feature maps, top numbers indicate the number of feature maps. Inset images exemplify feature map appearance. Architecture of the brain aging generator. Lateral numbers indicate the spatial extent of the feature maps, top numbers indicate the number of feature maps. Inset images exemplify feature map appearance.

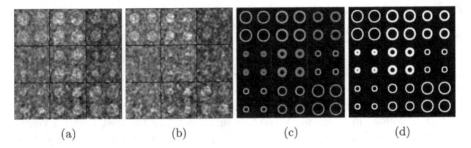

Fig. 2. Nine synthetic test examples on a 3×3 grid. (a) Generator inputs. (b) Shrinked circles produced by generator. (c) Difference maps $x_1 - x_0$ between generator inputs and outputs. (d) Real difference maps.

3.2 Synthetic Data

To validate the proposed generative brain aging model, we conduct experiments on a synthetic data distribution, which is intended to mimic atrophy in real brain tissue. The distribution is defined over tuples (x_0, x_1, δ). The first two components x_0 and x_1 are 112×112 grayscale images containing four bright disks on a background of smoothed Gaussian noise as shown in Fig. 2a. The scalar δ defines how much the disk radius in x_1 is shrinked relative to x_0. In our simulation, we use four different initial disk radii, and three different amounts of shrinkage. As documented in Fig. 2, the WGAN model can successfully generate x_1, conditioned on (x_0, δ). We also measure the normalized correlation coefficient (NCC) between the generated and the ground truth difference maps. The model achieves a mean NCC test score of 0.972 ± 0.006, which confirms its basic ability to model the temporal evolution of images.

3.3 Brain Data

Data used in preparation of this article were obtained from the Alzheimer's Disease Neuroimaging Initiative database (ADNI) [9], and from the Australian Imaging, Biomarker & Lifestyle Flagship Study of Ageing (AIBL) [17]. In total, the assembled data set contains 4115 baseline/follow-up image pairs from 2224 subjects. In terms of diagnosis, 2865 pairs are labeled as healthy control (HC), 843 as MCI, and 407 as AD. The mean age of subjects at image acquisition was 75.3 ± 7.3 years. We did not observe a substantial age difference between different diagnoses. Images are preprocessed by brain extraction, *rigid* registration to a common template, down-sampling to $91 \times 109 \times 91$, and voxel intensity scaling to $[-1, 1]$. As common practice to facilitate efficient experimentation (e.g. [8, 18, 24]), we choose to represent each sample with a single coronal slice (y = 59). The slice at y = 59 was chosen to yield a good section of the ventricles, and the hippocampus, which are known to be particularly affected by aging and dementia [25].

3.4   Generative Brain Aging

For all WGAN experiments, we choose an incremental time step $\epsilon = 1$ year, i.e. one pass through the generator corresponds to one year of aging. While the typical follow-up timestep in our data set is six months, we considered changes during such a short time as too subtle for the given image noise level. Besides, smaller time steps require more iterations, which would prolong model training. Moreover, follow-up times for WGAN training δ range between 1 and 5 years. As the empirical follow-up times are not always exact multiples of $\epsilon = 1$ year, we allow for a tolerance of ± 0.2 years between the empirical follow-up time and the number of generator iterations. For implementation purposes, pairs in a training batch have the same δ. Batches with different δ are fed in round-robin order.

Visual Validation. To observe whether the WGAN model captures group-specific aging characteristics we re-train it on three differently composed groups, i.e. one consisting only of HC samples, one with only AD samples, and one with samples from all three diagnoses HC+MCI+AD. We show detailed predictions of each model for one random healthy test subject in Fig. 3. As expected, we observe that the amount of atrophic changes (shown in blue) is the least for the WGAN trained on healthy subjects only, while it is the most for the WGAN trained only an AD subjects. Moreover, individual brain structure is preserved, while changes due to aging, such as progressive enlargement of the ventricles, are captured. However, some changes are not aligned with the ground-truth aging. This is likely due to the circumstance that rigid registration of all images to one template is insufficient to properly align successive images of the same individual. These alignment differences introduce confounding changes unrelated to aging. While Fig. 3 shows the progression of one subject for different WGANs, Fig. 5 illustrates the progression of HC, MCI, and AD subjects using the same WGAN. In the same example, we also show extrapolation of the aging prediction up to 30 years into the future. The iterated predictions are stable, but as the WGAN is trained only on follow-up times up to five years, the predicted brain composition starts to degrade after ca. ten years.

Group Comparison sMCI/pMCI. When a person is diagnosed with MCI, it is of high interest to estimate if they are at risk to progress to AD at a certain time in the future. We refer to this estimation as conversion prognosis. Moreover, we refer to those who progress to AD after *exactly* Δ years as $pMCI_\Delta$, while we refer to those who remain MCI for *at least* Δ as $sMCI_\Delta$. As a preliminary for subject-specific predictions (Sect. 3.5), we test if the generative aging model can estimate changes that are relevant to recognize differences between $s/pMCI_\Delta$ on a *group level*. To do so, we use a WGAN trained on HC+MCI+AD to predict the image progression for the two test groups $s/pMCI_\Delta$. Then we estimate the evolution of dementia risk p_{AD} based on the generated images with the pre-trained MCI/AD classifier described above. We emphasize that the $s/pMCI_\Delta$ samples are not used in the classifier training. We note, it is necessary to use the

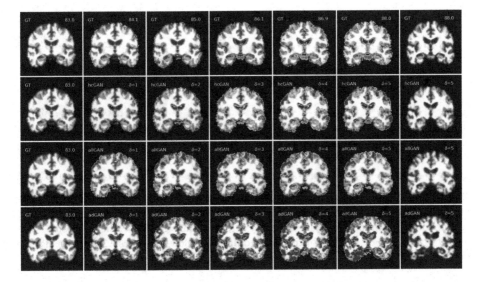

Fig. 3. First row: Ground-truth (GT) sequence of brain images acquired at 1-year intervals from the same HC subject. **Second row:** Images generated by WGAN trained only on HC. **Third row:** WGAN trained on HC+MCI+AD. **Fourth row:** WGAN trained only on AD. The last two columns show the final image after five years with, and without difference map overlay. Red color indicates positive changes, while blue indicates negative changes. The changes in each column refer to GT at 83 yrs, i.e. they should be interpreted cumulatively. (Color figure online)

classifier to estimate p_{AD}, because we have the disease labels only for training samples, but not for generated samples. In this analysis we use samples with a common follow-up time of $\Delta = 4$ years, as indicated by the colored bars in Fig. 4b, which also shows the $s/pMCI_\Delta$ class distribution for shorter follow-up times. While we have $sMCI_4 \subset sMCI_3 \subset sMCI_2 \subset sMCI_1$, the sample sets of $pMCI_\Delta$ don't share any samples. We observe that four generative aging steps (equivalent to four years) increase the median AD risk of the pMCI group by 0.59, while it does not significantly increase for the sMCI group. We illustrate the evolution of the AD risk distribution over generator iterations in Fig. 4a. While the sMCI group shows mainly small, and gradual increases of AD risk, the subjects in the pMCI group more often show larger, and sudden increases in AD risk. This result demonstrates that the generative aging model tends to produce more disease-like changes in the pMCI group than in the sMCI group, which indicates its usefulness to enhance disease-patterns for the early detection of AD.

Image Prediction Error. As for the synthetic difference maps, we measure NCC test scores between generated brain difference maps, and ground-truth. We obtain a mean NCC test score of 0.21 ± 0.08, which is relatively low compared to the result on synthetic data, but significantly higher than the mean NCC

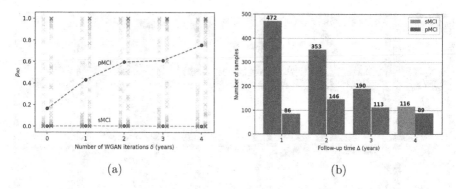

(a)   (b)

Fig. 4. (a) Distribution of AD risk p_{AD} over generator iterations δ for sMCI (orange) and pMCI (blue) cohorts. Round markers indicate the median p_{AD}. We reduce the opacity of sample markers to give a better impression of their density. (b) $sMCI_\Delta/pMCI_\Delta$ class distributions for different follow-up times Δ. (Color figure online)

score between difference maps of randomly paired subjects, which is 0.03±0.14. Moreover, these results are comparable to [7], who reports mean NCC scores of 0.25 ± 0.15 between generated and observed AD effect maps.

Besides NCC, the work [24] reports a pixel-wise mean squared error $6 \pm 1 \cdot 10^{-4}$. For $\delta = 1$ we obtain an MSE of $5 \pm 3 \cdot 10^{-3}$ between baseline image and follow-up image. This difference is considerably higher, likely because [24] uses non-linear, pair-wise image registration. We also illustrate how the MSE increases over follow-up times in Fig. 6a. As expected, the difference between prediction and ground-truth images slightly increases for longer follow-up times.

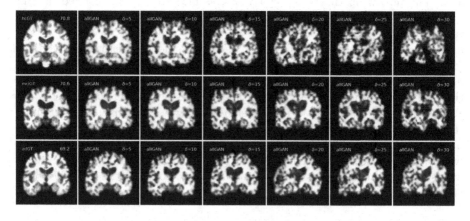

Fig. 5. Progression of three different subjects generated by a WGAN trained on HC+MCI+AD. Top row: HC subject. Middle row: MCI subject. Bottom row: AD subject.

3.5   Conversion Prognosis

After evaluation of the generative aging model, we now investigate its impact on conversion prognosis, i.e. the classification of MCI baseline images into sMCI and pMCI. For training we split the subjects into five groups, i.e. one HC group, one AD group, and three MCI groups, depending on the follow-up time Δ used for prognosis. The first, *stable MCI* (sMCI) group contains images from subjects who are diagnosed as MCI for at least Δ years after their baseline image was acquired. The second *progressive MCI* (pMCI) MCI group converts from MCI to AD after exactly Δ years. The remaining MCI subjects are assigned to the third MCI group, e.g. MCI subjects who have follow-ups only for less than Δ years. Please refer to [29] for a more formal description of the data splitting procedure. To recap the proposed procedure for conversion prognosis: Given the baseline image of an MCI subject in question, we first generate the estimated follow-up image after Δ years, iterating the generator $\left[\frac{\Delta}{\epsilon}\right]$ times. Then we estimate the AD probability p_{AD} with the pre-trained MCI/AD classifier. Finally, we classify a sample as pMCI, if p_{AD} is larger than a threshold γ, which is the only parameter that needs to be determined from the sMCI/pMCI data. We call this procedure *generative prognosis* for short. The WGAN model and the MCI/AD classifier are trained on data from HC, MCI, and AD, while the sMCI and pMCI sets are kept aside for cross-validation. Cross-validation is performed only for the threshold γ, because neither the WGAN, nor the MCI/AD classifier need to be fitted to the sMCI/pMCI data. As we have only very few sMCI/pMCI samples (116/89 subjects for $\Delta = 4$, see Fig. 4b), we perform a triple 5-fold cross-validation, i.e. three times with randomly re-shuffled samples. On each training fold, the threshold γ is optimized for accuracy, and then used on the test fold to estimate generalization performance.

Baselines for Conversion Prognosis. To investigate the advantage, and potential, of generative prognosis, we compare it to three different baselines described in the following.

- **Direct Prognosis:** This approach simply fine-tunes the binary MCI/AD classifier directly to the few examples of sMCI/pMCI. This means, the classifier previously trained on MCI/AD provides its weights as initialization for re-training the classifier on sMCI/pMCI, but now its outputs stand for p_{sMCI} and p_{pMCI}. While this approach is simple, it is likely to overfit the complex CNN model on (too) few samples.
- **Pseudo Prognosis:** Instead of estimating future p_{AD} on the generated follow-up image x_1, we estimate it on the current baseline x_0. This way we measure the status quo probability of AD instead of its future value, hence the name "pseudo" prognosis. As in generative prognosis, only the threshold γ is fitted to the sMCI/pMCI data, while p_{AD} is estimated by the pre-trained MCI/AD classifier. So the only difference between pseudo and generative prognosis is the additional estimation of the follow-up image. This enables us to separate out the contribution of the generative aging step to discriminate between sMCI and pMCI.

Table 1. Median performance metrics of sMCI/pMCI classification. **WGAN** is the proposed generative prognosis approach, while $WGAN^*$ uses ground-truth information. Competing results are selected to use only MRI data at baseline.

	$WGAN^*$	**WGAN**	Pseudo	Direct	[11]	[33]	[14]	[12]	[4]	[30]
Accuracy (%)	80 ± 6	73 ± 4	70 ± 6	56 ± 14	75	72	70	77	63	65
Recall (%)	74 ± 6	75 ± 8	53 ± 9	83 ± 22	-	-	-	-	64	77
Precision (%)	80 ± 10	68 ± 5	71 ± 11	51 ± 17	-	-	-	-	73	48

- **Ideal WGAN***: Instead of estimating the follow-up image by generative aging, we use the ground-truth follow-up image as input to the pre-trained MCI/AD classifier. The estimated probability p_{AD} is thresholded as before. This procedure is only feasible in hindsight, because in practice we do not have access to the real follow-up image. For this procedure, we can estimate how well the WGAN model approximates temporal changes that are relevant for conversion prognosis. To put it differently, using the real follow-up image corresponds to an ideal approximation of the aging distribution, which represents an upper bound on the WGAN contribution to conversion prognosis.

The results of conversion prognosis with $\Delta = 4$ are summarized in Table 1. As expected, direct prognosis achieves the lowest test accuracy of 0.56. Generative prognosis considerably improves to 0.73 test accuracy (p = 0.003), and it also has a slight advantage over pseudo prognosis, which achieves 0.70 test accuracy (p = 0.127). These results demonstrate that aging changes induced by generative aging enhance the discrimination between sMCI and pMCI, i.e. the classifier benefits from the image feature changes generated by the WGAN. Moreover, the ideal $WGAN^*$ achieves 0.80 test accuracy, which shows that the generated images are close to the real follow-up images in terms of predictive performance. We also include results of other recent works on conversion prognosis in Table 1. Even though these works are highly tuned to the classification between sMCI/pMCI, their accuracies (between 0.63 to 0.77) are not significantly higher than generative aging combined with plain classification, which in fact fits only a single threshold parameter γ to the sMCI/pMCI data. We emphasize again that conversion prognosis is different from disease diagnosis. While diagnosis attempts to classify the *current* health status of a subject, prognosis aims to predict if they will develop AD *in the future*.

Follow-Up Time. The follow-up time Δ between acquisition of the baseline image and the follow-up image is an important variable in conversion prognosis. It has been observed that conversion prognosis is more difficult for smaller Δ, but reasonable conversion prognosis can be achieved with as little as two years between first diagnosis and follow-up examination [6,26], as it takes time for AD effects to manifest clearly in MRI. In addition to the $\Delta = 4$ experiments described before, we compare generative prognosis for $\Delta \in \{2, 3, 4\}$ years.

Note, WGAN training is not affected by Δ, but only the composition of the sMCI/pMCI sets (see also Fig. 4b), and the number of generator iterations during inference. The sMCI/pMCI class distribution is not well balanced for every Δ (pMCI ratio is 0.15, 0.29, 0.43 for $\Delta = 2, 3, 4$). As a consequence, in these experiments we decide to cross-validate the threshold γ for F1-score instead of accuracy. This choice also explains why the results for $\Delta = 4$ are not congruent with those in Table 1. The results confirm the trend mentioned before, i.e. conversion prognosis is more accurate for longer follow-up times. The test accuracy is 0.51/0.68/0.70 for $\Delta = 2, 3, 4$, which is also illustrated in Fig. 6b.

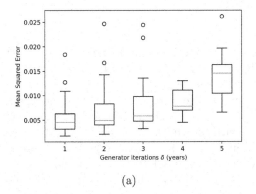

(a)

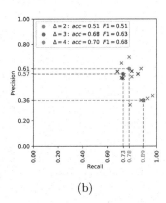

(b)

Fig. 6. (a) Pixel-wise mean squared test error between generated and real HC images. The WGAN was trained on HC+MCI+AD. (b) Comparison of generative prognosis for three different follow-up times $\Delta \in \{2, 3, 4\}$ *years*. In this experiment we performed one round of 5-fold cross-validation, i.e. each cross represents the result of one test fold.

4 Discussion

4.1 Generative Aging

In this section we discuss strengths, and limitations of our approach. The convolutional WGAN model allows us to approximate the data distribution with less bias than for example models based on diffeomorphic deformations, which interpret changes as deviations from the identity mapping. Conversely, this constraint leads to sharper images, and tends to better preserve subject identity. We also consider it an advantage that the WGAN model can be trained directly on image inputs, and does not require additional modules for feature extraction. Another aspect is that the loss currently only depends on the last output. In general, it could be advantageous to include also intermediate outputs of the recursion into the loss. While the proposed generator model is recursive, it does not use a hidden state to store information between iterations as in RNNs. We decided to avoid this additional complexity, as both RNNs, and GANs are notorious for being hard to train, let alone their combination. However, it should be considered in future work. Moreover, a fixed incremental time step in the generator is restrictive when the empirical data is sampled at irregular time intervals, or would require many iterations. It would also be desirable to include the absolute age of a subject into the generation process to account for the fact that brain aging is not independent of age. Another, conceptually obvious extension of our work would be to process full 3D brain images. However, training times of WGAN models increased in our experiments from a few hours for 2D slices to almost a week for 3D volumes on a single NVIDIA Titan-X GPU, thereby severely limiting our means to explore potential benefits from 3D data.

4.2 Conversion Prognosis

Based on brain MRI scans, we propose a simple prognosis method to predict whether a person diagnosed with MCI will convert to AD in the near future. It separates prognosis into two meaningful steps, i.e. aging and subsequent diagnosis. While training data for direct prognosis is very scarce, sufficient observations are available for the separate predictions steps. The WGAN model for aging can be trained on any pair of brain images with known time difference. The MCI/AD classifier can be learned from any brain imagery for which we know the disease label. In contrast to the sMCI/pMCI label, the MCI/AD labels do not require several scans to be determined, which makes them much more abundant. Essentially, the separation into aging and subsequent diagnosis can be considered as a means of transfer learning from data-richer tasks. This way, the essential feature of future AD probability can be extracted more robustly, because we avoid over-fitting to the scarce sMCI/pMCI data.

5 Conclusion

To the best of our knowledge, we have presented the first conditional WGAN model for brain image aging. In contrast to WGAN models for visual feature attribution, we address the longitudinal aspect of temporal brain data with a novel recursive generator model. Compared to most previous work on brain aging, the presented model can predict subject-specific progression based on a single baseline image. Prediction is fast, because it only requires a few passes through the generator. The model is trained end-to-end on image data, and optimized with mini-batch gradient descent, which scales to large sample sizes. We extensively analyse and validate the generative brain image aging model on synthetic and real data, with particular attention to the difference between healthy and demented subjects. In addition, we demonstrate that the proposed brain image aging model improves the accuracy of conversion prognosis in conjunction with a standard convolutional MCI/AD classifier. Despite its simplicity, this combination achieves results competitive with current approaches dedicated solely to the prediction of future conversion from MCI to AD based on brain MRI.

References

1. Alberdi, A., et al.: On the early diagnosis of Alzheimer's Disease from multimodal signals: a survey. Artif. Intell. Med. **71**, 1–29 (2016)
2. Antipov, G., Baccouche, M., Dugelay, J.L.: Face aging with conditional generative adversarial networks. In: 2017 IEEE International Conference on Image Processing (ICIP), pp. 2089–2093 (2017)
3. Giorgio, A., et al.: Age-related changes in grey and white matter structure throughout adulthood. In: NeuroImage (2010)
4. Cheng, B., et al.: Domain transfer learning for MCI conversion prediction. IEEE Trans. Biomed. Eng. **62**, 1805–1817 (2012)
5. Bône, A., et al.: Prediction of the progression of subcortical brain structures in Alzheimer's disease from baseline. In: GRAIL/MFCA/MICGen@MICCAI (2017)
6. Cabral, C., et al.: Predicting conversion from MCI to AD with FDG-PET brain images at different prodromal stages. Comput. Biol. Med. **58**, 101–109 (2015)
7. Baumgartner, C.F., et al.: Visual feature attribution using wasserstein GANs. In: CVPR (2018)
8. Bowles, C., et al.: Modelling the progression of Alzheimer's disease in MRI using generative adversarial networks. In: Medical Imaging: Image Processing (2018)
9. Jack, C.R., et al.: The Alzheimer's disease neuroimaging initiative (ADNI): MRI methods. J. Magn. Reson. Imaging JMRI **27**, 685–691 (2008)
10. Ding, Z., Fleishman, G., Yang, X., Thompson, P., Kwitt, R., Niethammer, M.: Fast predictive simple geodesic regression. In: Cardoso, M.J., et al. (eds.) DLMIA/ML-CDS -2017. LNCS, vol. 10553, pp. 267–275. Springer, Cham (2017). https://doi.org/10.1007/978-3-319-67558-9_31
11. Lu, D., et al.: Multimodal and multiscale deep neural networks for the early diagnosis of Alzheimer's disease using structural MR and FDG-PET images. In: Scientific Reports (2018)
12. Moradi, E., et al.: Machine learning framework for early MRI-based Alzheimer's conversion prediction in MCI subjects. NeuroImage **104**, 398–412 (2015)
13. Goodfellow, I.J., et al.: Generative adversarial nets. In: NIPS (2014)
14. Korolev, I.O., et al.: Predicting progression from mild cognitive impairment to Alzheimer's dementia using clinical, MRI, and plasma biomarkers via probabilistic pattern classification. In: PloS One (2016)
15. Isola, P., Zhu, J.Y., Zhou, T., Efros, A.A.: Image-to-image translation with conditional adversarial networks. In: 2017 IEEE Conference on Computer Vision and Pattern Recognition (CVPR), pp. 5967–5976 (2017)
16. Dukart, J., et al.: Generative FDG-PET and MRI model of aging and disease progression in Alzheimer's disease. PLoS Comput. Biol. **9**(4), e1002987 (2013)
17. Ellis, K.A., et al.: The Australian imaging, biomarkers and lifestyle (AIBL) study of aging: methodology and baseline characteristics of 1112 individuals recruited for a longitudinal study of Alzheimer's disease. Int. Psychoger. **21**, 672–687 (2009)
18. Lin, W., et al.: Convolutional neural networks-based MRI image analysis for the Alzheimer's disease prediction from mild cognitive impairment. Front. Neurosci. (2018)
19. Liu, S., Sun, Y., Zhu, D., Bao, R., Wang, W., Shu, X., Yan, S.: Face aging with contextual generative adversarial nets. In: ACM Multimedia (2017)
20. Arjovsky, M., et al.: Wasserstein generative adversarial networks. In: Proceedings of the 34th International Conference on Machine Learning, Proceedings of Machine Learning Research, vol. 70, pp. 214–223 (2017)

21. Mueller, S.G., et al.: Ways toward an early diagnosis in Alzheimer's disease: the Alzheimer's disease neuroimaging initiative (ADNI). Alzheimer's Dement. **1**, 55–66 (2005)
22. Niethammer, M., Huang, Y., Vialard, F.-X.: Geodesic regression for image time-series. In: Fichtinger, G., Martel, A., Peters, T. (eds.) MICCAI 2011. LNCS, vol. 6892, pp. 655–662. Springer, Heidelberg (2011). https://doi.org/10.1007/978-3-642-23629-7_80
23. Palsson, S.: Generative adversarial style transfer networks for face aging. In: 2018 IEEE/CVF Conference on Computer Vision and Pattern Recognition Workshops (CVPRW), pp. 2165–21658 (2018)
24. Pathan, S., Hong, Y.: Predictive image regression for longitudinal studies with missing data. In: Medical Imaging with Deep Learning (MIDL) (2018)
25. Peters, R.: Ageing and the brain. Postgrad. Med. J. **82**(964), 84–88 (2006)
26. Querbes, O., et al.: Early diagnosis of Alzheimer's disease using cortical thickness: impact of cognitive reserve. Brain J. Neurol. **132**, 2036–2047 (2009)
27. Resnick, S.M., Pham, D.L., Kraut, M.A., Zonderman, A.B., Davatzikos, C.: Longitudinal magnetic resonance imaging studies of older adults: a shrinking brain. J. Neurosci. Official J. Soc. Neurosci. **23**(8), 3295–3301 (2003)
28. Ronneberger, O., Fischer, P., Brox, T.: U-net: convolutional networks for biomedical image segmentation. In: Bildverarbeitung für die Medizin (2017)
29. Wegmayr, V., Hörold, M., Buhmann, J.M.: Generative aging of brain MRI for early prediction of MCI-AD conversion. In: 2019 IEEE 16th International Symposium on Biomedical Imaging (ISBI 2019) (2019)
30. Wolz, R., et al.: Multi-method analysis of MRI images in early diagnostics of Alzheimer's disease. In: PloS One (2011)
31. Huizinga, W., et al.: A spatio-temporal reference model of the aging brain. NeuroImage **169**, 11–22 (2018)
32. Yang, H., Huang, D., Wang, Y., Jain, A.K.: Learning face age progression: a pyramid architecture of GANs. In: 2018 IEEE/CVF Conference on Computer Vision and Pattern Recognition, pp. 31–39 (2018)
33. Sun, Z., et al.: Detection of conversion from mild cognitive impairment to Alzheimer's disease using longitudinal brain MRI. Front. Neuroinform. (2017)

Nonlinear Causal Link Estimation Under Hidden Confounding with an Application to Time Series Anomaly Detection

Violeta Teodora Trifunov[1,2](✉)[iD], Maha Shadaydeh[1][iD], Jakob Runge[2][iD],
Veronika Eyring[4,5][iD], Markus Reichstein[3,6][iD], and Joachim Denzler[1,3][iD]

[1] Computer Vision Group, Friedrich Schiller University Jena, Jena, Germany
violetateodora.trifunov@uni-jena.de
[2] Climate Informatics Group, Deutsches Zentrum für Luft- und Raumfahrt e.V.
(DLR), Institute for Data Science, Jena, Germany
[3] Michael Stifel Center Jena for Data-Driven and Simulation Science, Jena, Germany
[4] Deutsches Zentrum für Luft- und Raumfahrt e.V. (DLR), Institut für Physik der
Atmosphäre, Oberpfaffenhofen, Germany
[5] University of Bremen, Institute of Environmental Physics (IUP), Bremen, Germany
[6] Max Planck Institute for Biogeochemistry, Jena, Germany

Abstract. Causality analysis represents one of the most important tasks when examining dynamical systems such as ecological time series. We propose to mitigate the problem of inferring nonlinear cause-effect dependencies in the presence of a hidden confounder by using deep learning with domain knowledge integration. Moreover, we suggest a time series anomaly detection approach using causal link intensity increase as an indicator of the anomaly. Our proposed method is based on the Causal Effect Variational Autoencoder (CEVAE) which we extend and apply to anomaly detection in time series. We evaluate our method on synthetic data having properties of ecological time series and compare to the vector autoregressive Granger causality (VAR-GC) baseline.

1 Introduction

Causality analysis represents one of the most important tasks when examining dynamical systems such as ecological time series. Its principal difficulties are hidden causes of the observed phenomena, in addition to the often-found nonlinearities in the data. We propose to mitigate the problem of inferring nonlinear cause-effect dependencies in the presence of a hidden confounder by using deep learning together with domain knowledge. Moreover, we suggest a time series anomaly detection approach using causal link intensity increase as an indicator of the anomaly.

In ecosystems for instance, considering the problem of confounding is important when trying to determine a causal link between gross primary production (GPP) and the ecosystem respiration (R_{eco}). Since both of these variables are influenced by the global radiation (R_g), one cannot be certain that the causal

© Springer Nature Switzerland AG 2019
G. A. Fink et al. (Eds.): DAGM GCPR 2019, LNCS 11824, pp. 261–273, 2019.
https://doi.org/10.1007/978-3-030-33676-9_18

link between them is not influenced by this variable. Therefore, not considering a confounder may lead to incorrect conclusions. Two variables, W and Y, are said to be *confounded* if there exists another variable Z that causes both W and Y. In order to verify whether the confounder is influencing the link between W and Y, we need to intervene on W in the sense of do-Calculus [15] and thereby remove any influence of Z on W. If the intervention on W does not affect the outcome, it is clear that the causal link between W and Y is influenced exclusively by the hidden confounder Z itself.

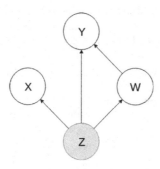

Fig. 1. Causal graphical model portraying hidden confounding with one proxy. Variable Y denotes an outcome, W an intervention variable, Z an unobserved confounder and X denotes a proxy variable providing noisy views on the hidden confounder Z.

When a confounder is observed, the usual approach for accounting for its effect is to "control" for it, for instance by covariate-adjusted regression or propensity score regression [12]. However, if a confounder is hidden or unmeasured, it is impossible to estimate the effect of the intervention on the outcome without further assumptions [15]. This is, nevertheless, a problem of utmost importance in observational studies, Simpson's paradox [23] being a good example of the type of bias that may occur in causal inference if unmeasured confounding is not properly dealt with. One way to tackle this issue is by using a proxy to the hidden confounder instead of the confounder itself. In the previously described ecosystem example, the air temperature (T) can be utilized as a proxy to the confounder R_g. Figure 1 depicts a version of this problem in the form of a causal graphical model when there is only one proxy variable, as suggested by [13]. For more general proxy models, as well as conditions under which they could be identified, see [14].

In ecological time series, variables often contain trends or periodic components such as diurnal and seasonal cycles. These act as an unobserved confounder, concealing the true causal effect between the affected variables. It was recently shown in [21] that time domain causality analysis of ecosystem variables based on vector autoregressive Granger Causality (VAR-GC) [7], may result in spurious causal links due to the diurnal or seasonal cycle. To tackle this issue, the authors in [21] proposed to use the parametric frequency domain representation of VAR-GC. It was further shown in [19,20] that anomalous events can be detected as those events where the causal intensities between the variables in certain frequency bands differ considerably from the average causal intensities. The application of our method to anomaly detection builds upon these findings. Namely, we estimate the causal link intensity between confounded variables and by observing an increase of this estimation, we are able to detect anomalies. Moreover, our work extends to a setting where seasonal cycles or trends are acting as the unobserved confounder. Additionally, we are able to perform causal inference of not only linear, but also the nonlinear inter-variable relationships, which are difficult to consider using GC methods. Our suggested method is based on the causal effect variational autoencoder (CEVAE) [13], a deep graphical model designed to estimate the unknown latent space summarizing the confounders and the causal effect by relying on a noisy proxy of the hidden confounder, as seen in Fig. 1. It is required that the causal graphical model used by the CEVAE satisfies the back-door criterion [15] in order for it to be possible to use the do-Calculus and calculate the desired causal effect. We extend CEVAE for ecological time series and use it to infer a nonlinear causal link between variables confounded by the periodic component such as the seasonal or diurnal cycle. We apply our proposed method in this setting to estimate the intensity of the previously mentioned causal link. By being able to do so, we use its increase to detect anomalies. Furthermore, we are, to the best of our knowledge, first to use this deep graphical model for anomaly detection. In summary, our method which builds upon the CEVAE is in line with the trend to apply deep learning in Earth system analysis for describing the spatio-temporal dependency of ecosystems on climate and the interacting geo-factors as recognized by [17].

In Sect. 2, we discuss methods of causality analysis and anomaly detection on time series, whereas we devote Sect. 3 to outlining the CEVAE method along with our adaptation of it to ecological data. In Sect. 4 we describe synthetic data used to evaluate our method, followed by experimental results and the comparison to the VAR-GC method. Finally, Sect. 5 concludes our paper.

2   Related Work

The analysis of causal dependencies in time series has become a focal point of study in various fields such as engineering, finance, the physical and life sciences [18]. The main assumption of this probabilistic concept of causality is that causes always come before their effects in time. This means that if one time series causes another series, knowing the former series should be helpful for predicting future values of the latter series after influences of all other variables have been considered. A standard method used for this purpose is Granger Causality (GC) applied in the setting of no hidden confounding [4] and only when causal links are linear. These limitations persist in anomaly detection methods relying on GC for time series [16]. Seeking to improve the conventional way of causality analysis, several deep learning approaches have been suggested. One such approach is introduced for inferring interactions between variables while learning the dynamics in an unsupervised manner [10]. Furthermore, Causal Effect Network (CEN) [11] has been proposed for assessing causal relationships of time series, as well as their time delays between different processes. However, these methods cannot be applied when causal inter-variable relations are nonlinear, nor when they are driven by a hidden confounder. In [24], causality between the global radiative forcing and the annual global mean surface temperature anomalies (GMTA) is measured as the time rate of information flowing from one time series to another. A different branch of research that deals with modelling the latent variable space using deep graphical models was introduced in the recent years, specifically by the introduction of a Variational Autoencoder (VAE) in [9]. It is a deep learning method combined with a directed probabilistic graphical model for efficient inference in the presence of continuous latent variables with intractable posterior distributions. Moreover, it represents a crucial building block of a CEVAE [13], which allows for estimation of the unknown latent space and inference of the causal links between the confounded variables. Our work extends the capabilities of a CEVAE to time series, as well as to its novel application to anomaly detection using an increase of the causal link intensity.

An unsupervised method for discovering anomalies considering intervals of multivariate time series is proposed by [1]. It proposes that instead of regarding one point at the time, it is beneficial to compare probability distribution of samples within an interval to that of the rest of the data. A recently developed method for anomaly detection of time series using a Variational Recurrent Autoencoder (VRAE) [5] is proposed in [2]. It applies a latent-space detection approach which considers the variability of the latent representations, as well as their expectation and computes the anomaly score using the median Wasserstein distance [25] between a test sample and other samples within the test set of latent representations.

Our method differs substantially from other anomaly detection approaches as we rely on causal link intensity changes in the presence of an unobserved confounder for detecting anomalies in ecological time series which has, to the best of our knowledge, not been done so far.

3   Methodology

3.1   Causal Effect Variational Autoencoder

Based on a VAE [9] and a TARnet [22] generative model structure, CEVAE [13] is a deep learning method dealing with hidden confounding as it estimates the latent space and summarizes the causal effect of discrete or continuous, non-sequential variables, using a noisy proxy related to the confounder, as shown in Fig. 1. One of its original applications was to medical data, so that in Fig. 1 W denotes treatment, Y an outcome of the treatment, whereas a hidden confounder Z represents the socio-economic status of each patient and its proxy X represents patient's income for the previous year and a place of residence. The main objective was, therefore, recovering the Individual Treatment Effect (ITE) and the Average Treatment Effect (ATE) defined in (1) and (2), respectively:

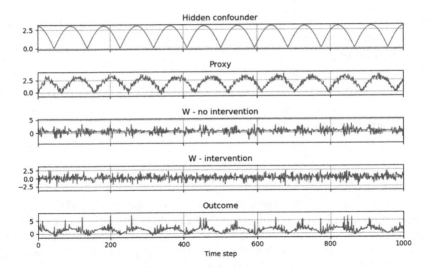

Fig. 2. Synthetic data. The first row shows the hidden confounder Z with parameters $b = 5$ and $f = 36.5$; the second row shows the noisy proxy X for $s = 500$ and $\beta = 0.3$; the third row shows variable W for $\mu_w = 0.55$ and $e = 0.4$ without intervention; the fourth row shows variable W with intervention; the fifth row shows the outcome Y for $g = 0.8$ and $\alpha = 3$.

$$ITE(x) := \mathbb{E}(Y|X = x, do(W = w^1)) - \mathbb{E}(Y|X = x, do(W = w^0)) \quad (1)$$

$$ATE := \mathbb{E}(ITE(x)) \quad (2)$$

These metrics are defined for each value x of variable X, and by w^1 we denote applied treatment, while values of W when no treatment is applied are denoted by w^0. ATE is easily calculated once we recover the ITE, and to do that we need to recover the joint probability $p(Z, X, W, Y)$, as shown by Theorem 1 in [13]. Obtaining this joint distribution is done through a model network of a CEVAE by estimating the true posterior over Z which depends on X, W and Y, whereas Z itself is modelled by the standard normal distribution. The estimate of the posterior is then inferred via TARnet [22] by splitting it for each intervention group in W. It is then possible to construct a single objective for the inference and model networks, i.e. the *variational lower bound*

$$\mathcal{L} = \sum_{i=1}^{N} \mathbb{E}_{q(z_i|x_i,w_i,y_i)}(\log p(z_i) - \log q(z_i|x_i, w_i, y_i)$$
$$+ \log p(x_i, w_i|z_i) + \log p(y_i|w_i, z_i)) \quad (3)$$

of the causal graphical model from Fig. 1. By x_i we denoted an input data point, w_i corresponds to the treatment assignment, y_i to the outcome of the specific treatment, z_i corresponds to the latent hidden confounder and by q we denote estimation of the probability distribution with the same arguments. Finally, since it is necessary to know the intervention assignment w together with its outcome

y before inferring the posterior distribution over Z, two auxiliary distributions are introduced, helping to predict w_i and y_i for new samples, so the variational lower bound becomes

$$\mathcal{F}_{CEVAE} = \mathcal{L} + \sum_{i=1}^{N} (\log q(w_i = w_i^* | x_i^*) + \log q(y_i = y_i^* | x_i^*, w_i^*)), \qquad (4)$$

where x_i^*, w_i^*, y_i^* are the observed values for the input, intervention and outcome variables in the training set.

3.2   CEVAE for Ecological Time Series

When analysing ecological time series, one often encounters variables having periodic components such as diurnal and seasonal cycles. This can make it difficult to infer inter-variable causal dependencies as the underlying cycle may be influencing them as well. Synthetic data we use for the evaluation of our method, shown in Fig. 2, is generated such that these periodic components act as the hidden confounder. Our task is to infer the causal link intensity between W and Y in the presence of this confounder and detect anomalies induced by the causal link intensity's increase. In contrast to the conventional CEVAE setting, our intervention variable W is a time series. This means we needed to find a different way of intervening on W in order to estimate the desired cause-effect relations. To further put the CEVAE into our context, we adjust several required probability distributions. Namely, we model a conditional distribution of W given Z as defined in (5).

$$p(W|Z) = \mathcal{N}(\mu_w, \sigma_w^2), \quad [\,\mu_w, \sigma_w] = f_1(Z) \qquad (5)$$

Estimation of this distribution is obtained through the use of the proxy X:

$$q(W|X) = \mathcal{N}(\mu_{\hat{w}}, \sigma_{\hat{w}}^2), \quad [\,\mu_{\hat{w}}, \sigma_{\hat{w}}] = f_2(X) \qquad (6)$$

Functions f_1 and f_2 are feedforward neural networks with three layers. To measure the intervention effect of W to Y we extend ITE to the case of a sequential intervention and define the Interval Intervention Effect (IIE) and the Average Intervention Effect (AIE):

$$IIE(x) := \mathbb{E}(Y | x_i \leq X \leq x_{i+1}, do(W = w^1))$$
$$- \mathbb{E}(Y | x_i \leq X \leq x_{i+1}, do(W = w^0)) \qquad (7)$$

$$AIE := \mathbb{E}(IIE(x)) \qquad (8)$$

In (7) and (8), x_0 and x_i are the interval limits for $i \in \{1, \ldots m\}$ and $m = 256$, as we regularly quantize variable X into an 8-bit word, whereas w^1 and w^0 denote intervention or no intervention on W, respectively.

For detecting anomalies in the intervention variable W under hidden confounding, we utilize the increase of the intensity of the causal link from W to Y regardless of its linearity and deploy a sliding window approach documenting the estimated AIE for each window.

3.3   Vector Autoregressive Granger Causality

The main assumption of Granger causality (GC) [7] is that causes precede their effects and can be used for their prediction. Let $u_i, i = 1, \cdots, N$ be the time series of N ecological variables. Each time series $u_i(t), t = 1, \cdots, k$ is a realization of length k real valued discrete stationary stochastic process $U_i, i = 1, \cdots, N$. These N time series can be represented by a pth order vector autoregressive model (VAR(p)) of the form

$$\begin{bmatrix} u_1(t) \\ \vdots \\ u_N(t) \end{bmatrix} = \sum_{r=1}^{p} A_r \begin{bmatrix} u_1(t-r) \\ \vdots \\ u_N(t-r) \end{bmatrix} + \begin{bmatrix} \epsilon_1(t) \\ \vdots \\ \epsilon_N(t) \end{bmatrix}. \tag{9}$$

The residuals $\epsilon_i, i = 1, \cdots, N$ form a white noise stationary process with covariance matrix Σ. The model parameters at time lags $r = 1, \cdots, p$ comprise the matrix $A_r = [a_{ij}(r)]_{N \times N}$. Let Σ_j be the covariance matrix of the residual ϵ_j associated to u_j using the model in (9), and let Σ_j^{i-} denote the covariance matrix of this residual after excluding the ith raw and column in A_r. The time domain VAR-GC of u_i on u_j conditioned on all other variables is defined by [6]

$$\gamma_{i \to j} = \ln \frac{|\Sigma_j^{i-}|}{|\Sigma_j|}. \tag{10}$$

4   Experiments

By experiments on synthetic data we first demonstrate that our method is sensitive to the increase of the nonlinear causal link's intensity between the confounded variables, which we then exploit to achieve the second goal of this work, i.e. to apply CEVAE for detecting anomalies. In regard of the neural network architecture, we closely followed [13]. We used feedforward neural networks, namely f_1 and f_2 having 3 hidden layers, with ELU [3] nonlinearity and 200 neurons in each layer. We note, however, that more hidden layers can be used. We modelled variable Z as normally distributed with 20 dimensions, due to its latency. We used a small weight decay term for all parameters, with $\lambda = 0.0001$. For optimization, Adamax [8] was utilized with a learning rate of 0.01. Furthermore, early stopping according to the lower bound on a validation set was performed. For obtaining the outcomes $p(y|x_i \leq X \leq x_{i+1}, do(W = w^1))$ and $p(y|x_i \leq X \leq x_{i+1}, do(W = w^0))$ we averaged over 100 samples from the approximate posterior $q(Z|X) = \sum_w \int q(Z|w, y, X) q(y|w, X) q(w|X) dy$.

4.1   Synthetic Data

The synthetic data was created according to causal relationships of the graphical model in Fig. 1, which we consider to be the ground truth. In real data, these

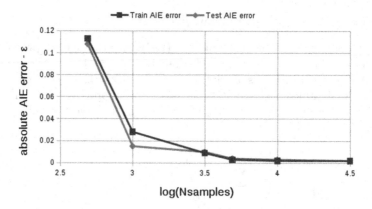

Fig. 3. Absolute error of AIE estimation on synthetic data samples for $\alpha = 1$, $\beta = 0.3$ and quantization level $m = 2^8$. We note that absolute AIE error ϵ is already quite small for the sample size $N = 1000$.

causal relationships are extracted from the prior expert knowledge. We create a hidden confounder Z as:

$$Z_t = |b \cdot \cos(\frac{\pi}{2} \cdot \frac{t}{f})|, \text{ for } b, f \in \mathbb{R} \tag{11}$$

where $t \in \{0, \ldots N\}$ and N denotes the sample size. It is defined to resemble a periodic component such as daily or seasonal cycle often encountered in ecological time series. Noisy proxy X is defined through shifting Z by a constant $s \in \mathbb{N}$ and the noise level $\beta \in (0, 1)$:

$$X_t = Z_{t-s} + \beta \cdot \epsilon_X, \text{ for } \epsilon_X \sim \mathcal{N}(0, 1). \tag{12}$$

The intervention variable W is modelled to be influenced by the unobserved confounder as follows:

$$W_t \sim \mathcal{N}(\mu_w, e \cdot Z_t), \ e \in (0, 1) \tag{13}$$

As an intervention, we consider values of the intervention variable where values of the proxy's periodic component are less than its half. This type of the intervention was chosen in order for it to satisfy the properties of *do*-calculus. Moreover, it allows for an almost straightforward application of our method to real data. Namely, after intervention, causal link between W and its parent Z should either be removed or so small, that it can be neglected.

The outcome Y is modelled to be influenced by both the hidden confounder Z and the intervention variable W with added Gaussian noise as:

$$Y_t = 0.7 \cdot Z_t + g^{-(\alpha \cdot (W_t - \mu_w) + \mu_w)} + \epsilon_Y, \text{ for } \epsilon_Y \sim \mathcal{N}(0, 0.1), \ g \in (0, 1) \tag{14}$$

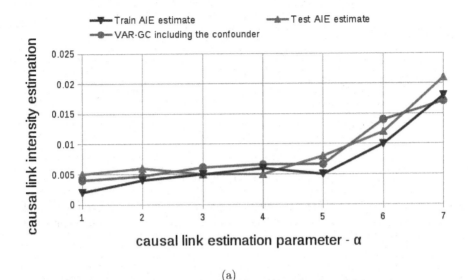

(a)

(b)

Fig. 4. (a) Causal link estimation results of our method in comparison to the vector autoregressive Granger causality. Blue and orange curves show our method's estimation of the AIE during training and test, respectively, for $\beta = 0.3$, $m = 2^8$, $s = 500$ and sample size $N = 1000$. Green curve shows results of the VAR-GC when the confounder Z is included. (b) Causal link estimation results of the VAR-GC method when the confounder is hidden. We note that our method performs better than VAR-GC baseline when the confounder is excluded and comparatively well to the VAR-GC with the included confounder. (Color figure online)

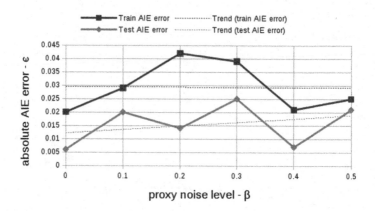

Fig. 5. Proxy noise level vs absolute AIE error ϵ for $\alpha = 2$, $m = 2^8$, $s = 500$ and sample size $N = 1000$. We observe that trend lines of the absolute AIE error for different values of the proxy noise level β are very close to constant.

4.2 Causal Link Intensity Estimation

In the case when $\alpha \in (0, 1)$, perturbations in the variance of W are very small and we consider them neither as the intervention nor as the anomaly. We rather focus on causal link intensity estimation for $\alpha \geq 1$. A relationship between α, the parameter of a function proportional to the causal link's intensity, and the AIE metric's estimation is shown in Fig. 4(a). This illustrates our method's sensitivity to the increase of the causal link strength between the confounded variables, predicting its estimation accordingly. To choose the most suitable sample size, we conducted an experiment in which we ran our method for nonlinear causal link intensity estimation with different values of N to choose the most suitable sample size. We used the absolute AIE error

$$\epsilon = |AIE^* - AIE| \tag{15}$$

for measuring our method's accuracy. This was done for each sample size $N \in \{500, 1000, 3000, 5000, 10000, 30000\}$ as seen in Fig. 3. Here AIE* denotes the predicted average intervention effect, while its ground truth value is denoted by AIE. Finally, we have chosen $N = 1000$ for our sliding window size.

As the baseline, we applied the VAR-GC method to all four variables $u_1 = W$, $u_2 = Y$, $u_3 = X$ and $u_4 = Z$ from Fig. 2 and compared it to our method during training and testing, as shown in Fig. 4(a). We note that our method behaves comparatively well to this baseline when the confounding variable Z was included. To determine if VAR-GC can detect the increase of the nonlinear causal link's strength between W and Y without the use of the confounder Z, we excluded it and observed that it is not the case, as shown in Fig. 4(b).

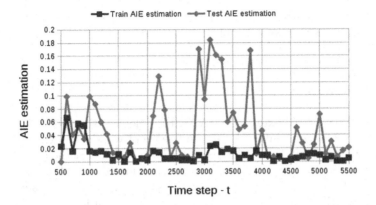

Fig. 6. Anomaly detection for $\alpha = 3$, $\beta = 0.3$, $m = 2^8$, $s = 500$, $N = 6000$ and ground truth anomaly with $\alpha = 7$ positioned at $t \in \{2500, \ldots, 4499\}$. Marked samples on the X-axis denote window centres for each sliding window.

4.3   Proxy Noise Levels

Since the confounder is unobserved, we wanted to ensure that the proxy we are using is not influencing the causal link between W and Y. To this end, we have performed a proxy noise level experiment as seen in Fig. 5. We observe that, on average, changes in the absolute AIE error, as defined in (15), for different values of the proxy noise level β are constant. Therefore, we conclude that the proxy variable X is not influencing the causal link between W and Y. This means that the hidden confounder Z is not causing the link between the confounded variables, but that W is the actual cause of the outcome Y.

4.4   Anomaly Detection in Synthetic Data

Using a sliding window approach and estimating the AIE of W on Y, we propose to detect anomalies in cause-effect relationship intensity between those two variables. We create the anomaly as an increased value of α in (14) by a certain value $a \in \mathbb{N}$ in a particular time interval. More precisely, in this interval the outcome variable becomes:

$$Y_t = 0.7 \cdot Z_t + g^{-((\alpha+a) \cdot (W_t - \mu_w) + \mu_w)} + \epsilon_Y, \text{ for } \epsilon_Y \sim \mathcal{N}(0, 0.1), \ g \in (0, 1) \quad (16)$$

Specifically, in our approach a window consisting of 1000 samples is shifted by 100 in each iteration. We train the adapted CEVAE on time series data, as described in the beginning of this section, using data with an intervention on W i.e. where values of the proxy's periodic component are less than its half, and test on data containing the anomaly. Figure 6 shows our anomaly detection results for the nonlinear coupling between W and Y defined in (14) for $g = 0.8$, $\alpha = 3$ and $\alpha = 7$ for the interval containing the anomaly. The AIE estimation in Fig. 6 is depicted after training and testing, where each value on the x-axis corresponds to each window's centre. Significantly higher AIE intensity from 2200 to about 4000 samples indicates considerable increase in the causal intensity and thus a possible anomaly.

5   Conclusion

In this paper, we have extended CEVAE to ecological time series in order to tackle the problem of nonlinear causal inference of variables in the presence of an unobserved confounder. Furthermore, we have shown that the proxy variable is not influencing the causal link between the confounded variables, meaning that the confounder itself is not the cause of the said link. After successfully establishing our method's sensitivity to increase of the causal link intensity on synthetic data, we utilized its estimates to detect anomalies induced by its increase. We used the VAR-GC method as a baseline and obtained better results when the confounder was hidden. To strengthen our method, we intend to incorporate time-delay embeddings as well as recurrent neural networks for time series anomaly detection.

References

1. Barz, B., Rodner, E., Guanche, Y., Denzler, J.: Detecting regions of maximal divergence for spatio-temporal anomaly detection. IEEE Trans. Pattern Anal. Mach. Intell. **41**, 1088–1101 (2019)
2. Cardoso Pereira, J.P.: Unsupervised anomaly detection in time series data using deep learning. Master's thesis, Instituto Superior Tecnico Lisboa (2018)
3. Clevert, D.A., Unterthiner, T., Hochreiter, S.: Fast and accurate deep network learning by exponential linear units (ELUs). arXiv:1511.07289 [cs.LG] (2016)
4. Eichler, M.: Causal Inference in Time Series Analysis. Wiley Series in Probability and Statistics, pp. 327–354. Wiley, United States (2012). https://doi.org/10.1002/9781119945710.ch22
5. Fabius, O., van Amersfoort, J.R.: Variational recurrent auto-encoders. arXiv:1412.6581v6 [stat.ML] (2014)
6. Geweke, J.: Measurement of linear dependence and feedback between multiple time series. J. Am. Stat. Assoc. **77**, 304–313 (1982)
7. Granger, C.W.J.: Investigating causal relations by econometric models and cross-spectral methods. Econometrica J. Econometric Soc. **37**(3), 424–438 (1969)
8. Kingma, D.P., Adam, J.B.: A method for stochastic optimization. In: International Conference on Learning Representations (ICLR) (2015)
9. Kingma, D.P., Welling, M.: Auto-encoding variational Bayes. In: Proceedings of the 2nd International Conference on Learning Representations (ICLR), arXiv: 1312.6114 [stat. ML] (2014)
10. Kipf, T., Fetaya, E., Wang, K.C., Welling, M., Zemel, R.: Neural relational inference for interacting systems. In: Internvational Conference on Machine Learning 2018 (ICML), arXiv:1802.04687v2 [stat.ML] (2018)
11. Kretschmer, M., Coumou, D., Donges, J.F., Runge, J.: Using causal effect networks to analyze different arctic drivers of midlatitude winter circulation. J. Climate **29**, 4069–4081 (2016)

12. Li, L., Kleinman, K., Gillman, M.W.: A comparison of confounding adjustment methods with an application to early life determinants of childhood obesity. J. Dev. Orig. Health Dis. **5**(6), 435–447 (2014)
13. Louizos, C., Shalit, U., Mooij, J., Sontag, D., Z., R., Welling, M.: Causal effect inference with deep latent-variable models. In: Advances in Neural Information Processing Systems, vol. 30, pp. 6446–6456 (2017)
14. Miao, W., Geng, Z., Tchetgen Tchetgen, E.: Identifying causal effects with proxy variables of an unmeasured confounder. In: arXiv preprint arXiv:1609.08816 (2016)
15. Pearl, J.: Causality. Cambridge University Press, New York (2009)
16. Qiu, H., Liu, Y., Subrahmanya, N.A., Li, W.: Granger causality for time-series anomaly detection. In: 2012 IEEE 12th International Conference on Data Mining, pp. 1074–1079, December 2012. https://doi.org/10.1109/ICDM.2012.73
17. Reichstein, M., Camps-Valls, G., Stevens, B., Jung, M., Denzler, J., Carvalhais, N.: Prabhat: deep learning and process understanding for data-driven earth system science. Nature **566**, 195–204 (2019)
18. Runge, J.: Causal network reconstruction from time series: from theoretical assumptions to practical estimation. Chaos Interdisc. J. Nonlinear Sci. **28**(7), 075310 (2018)
19. Shadaydeh, M., Denzler, J., Guanche, Y., Mahecha, M.: Time-frequency causal inference uncovers anomalous events in environmental systems. In: GCPR (2019)
20. Shadaydeh, M., Guanche, Y., Mahecha, M., Denzler, J.: BACI deliverable 5.4: methods for attribution scheme and near real-time BACI. Technical report (2018). http://baci-h2020.eu/index.php/Outreach/Deliverables
21. Shadaydeh, M., Guanche, Y., Mahecha, M., Reichstein, M., Denzler, J.: Causality analysis of ecological time series: a time-frequency approach. In: Climate Informatics Workshop 2018 (2018)
22. Shalit, U., Johansson, F., Sontag, D.: Estimating individual treatment effect: generalization bounds and algorithms. In: arXiv:1606.03976v5 [stat.ML] (2016)
23. Simpson, E.H.: The interpretation of interaction in contingency tables, pp. 238–241, No. 13 in B (1951)
24. Stips, A., Macias, D., Coughlan, C., Gracia-Gorriz, E., Liang, X.S.: On the causal structure between co_2 and global temperature. Sci. Rep. **6**(21691) (2016). https://doi.org/10.1038/srep21691
25. Villani, C.: The wasserstein distances. Optimal Transport. Grundlehren der mathematischen Wissenschaften (A Series of Comprehensive Studies in Mathematics), vol. 338, pp. 93–111. Springer, Heidelberg (2009). https://doi.org/10.1007/978-3-540-71050-9_6

Iris Verification with Convolutional Neural Network and Unit-Circle Layer

Radim Špetlík[1]($\boxtimes$) and Ivan Razumenić[2]

[1] Czech Technical University, 120 00 Prague, Czech Republic
spetlrad@cmp.felk.cvut.cz
[2] Microsoft Development Center Serbia, 11070 Belgrade, Serbia

Abstract. We propose a novel convolutional neural network to verify a match between two normalized images of the human iris. The network is trained end-to-end and validated on three publicly available datasets yielding state-of-the-art results against four baseline methods. The network performs better by a 10% margin to the state-of-the-art method on the CASIA.v4 dataset. In the network, we use a novel "Unit-Circle" layer which replaces the Gabor-filtering step in a common iris-verification pipeline. We show that the layer improves the performance of the model up to 15% on previously-unseen data.

1 Introduction

Iris verification is a biometric technique used for human identification. Given a pair of images of human irises, the task is to decide whether the irises match. Iris verification is applied widely, e.g., in border control, citizen authentication, or in forensics [21].

Common iris-verification pipeline has three steps – iris detection, feature extraction, and matching (see Fig. 1, interested reader is referred, e.g., to [5]). First, an iris is found and normalized. Second, the normalized iris is typically convolved with Gabor filters and converted into a "bitcode", i.e. a matrix of binary numbers. Third, two bitcodes are compared. The bitcodes match if their Hamming distance is smaller than a given threshold.

Feature extraction and matching are highly data-dependent in a common iris-verification pipeline and therefore require parameter-tuning. Since the task is not convex, an exhaustive search for parameters is performed. In this paper, we propose a method which replaces the feature extraction and matching part of the iris verification pipeline with a single fully convolutional neural network (CNN) and a single learning rule – the backward propagation of errors or backpropagation. The network is trained end-to-end with the binary cross-entropy loss. The input of the network is a pair of normalized irises, the output is a single number which is interpreted as a posterior probability of a match (see Fig. 2).

R. Špetlík—Work performed partly during an internship at Microsoft Development Center Serbia.

G. A. Fink et al. (Eds.): DAGM GCPR 2019, LNCS 11824, pp. 274–287, 2019.
https://doi.org/10.1007/978-3-030-33676-9_19

CNNs in iris verification are used for better feature encoding in the metric-learning setup. In the metric learning, images of a single iris are considered to be examples from the same class; the task is to minimize the intra-class distances, while, at the same time, maximize the inter-class distances. Two irises match if the distance of their CNN encodings is lower than a given threshold. In our method, we compare two images of irises directly, interpreting the output of the network as the "probability of a match". Furthermore, we introduce a novel "Unit-Circle layer" that replaces the feature extraction step in a common iris verification pipeline.

(a) detection (b) normalization (c) feature (d) mask   (e) matching
                          extraction extraction

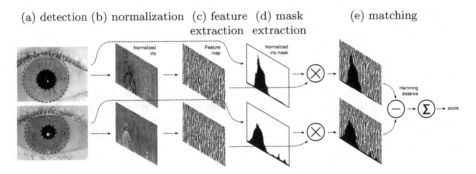

Fig. 1. Common iris-verification pipeline. An iris is (a) detected, (b) normalized and (d) its mask is found, (c) the features are extracted. Two irises match (e) if the Hamming distance of their bitcodes multiplied by their masks (score) is lower than a given threshold t.

The contributions of this paper are the following: (i) we propose a novel method of iris verification that replaces feature extraction and matching steps of a commonly used iris verification pipeline. We replace it with a single convolutional neural network (IrisMatch-CNN) trained end-to-end that is robust to changes in the iris image acquisition setup, (ii) as opposed to the metric-learning iris verification, we compare two images of irises directly and learn the network with the binary cross-entropy loss, (iii) we evaluate the method on three public datasets against four methods achieving state-of-the-art results.

2   Related Work

To the best of our knowledge, there is only one work [8] in which a convolutional neural network (CNN) extracts the features and performs the iris verification at the same time. However, the method is designed to verify a match only between a pair of heterogeneous irises, i.e. irises from different sources.

Commonly, researchers in the iris verification domain use a CNN to better encode the iris features. In the following text, we present the methods that use a CNN at some point in the iris verification pipeline.

CNN as the Feature Extractor. We start with the methods that use a CNN as the feature extraction tool.

[11] use a pre-trained CNN network to produce a feature vector used for verification. The verification is performed with a support vector machine.

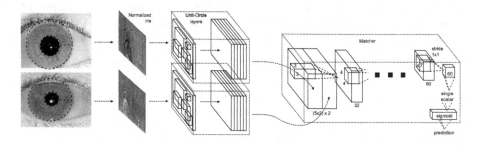

Fig. 2. Iris verification with IrisMatch-CNN. Two irises are detected and normalized. The normalized irises are fed into the Unit-Circle (U-C) layers. The responses from the U-C layers are concatenated and fed into the Matcher convolutional network. A single scalar is produced – the probability of a match. Two irises match if the probability is greater than a given threshold. Compare with a common iris verification pipeline in Fig. 1.

In [19], a deep CNN generates a compact representation of iris and periocular regions. The input of the network is a normalized iris image, the output is a 256-dimensional feature vector. Cosine similarity, ℓ^1 norm, ℓ^2 norm, and covariance measures are used to match two feature vectors.

In our experiments, we follow the methodology presented in [21]. The authors propose a deep learning framework composed of a CNN that generates iris descriptors and a sub-network that provides a mask identifying iris regions meaningful for matching. The network is trained using a specially designed *Extended Triplet Loss* that incorporates bit-shifting and non-iris masking. The input of the network is a normalized iris image. The output is a feature map that is, together with the mask, used to perform the matching. Matching is done by computing the Hamming distance of two binarized feature maps, taking into account their masks. Experiments on four publicly available databases are presented in which the introduced method outperforms four iris recognition approaches.

Another approach that uses CNN to decode features is presented in [17]. The learning of the network is formulated as a classification problem. The input is a normalized iris image and output is a C-dimensional softmax layer where each class corresponds to a set of irises of a particular person. After the training is finished, the fifth convolutional layer is used as a feature map. To improve robustness, custom ordinal measure is computed that produces a binary vector which is used to perform the matching.

[6] present a *deep* CNN that encodes the iris into a 4096-dimensional feature vector. The learning is stated as a classification problem where each class corresponds to a set of irises of a single person. After the training, the output

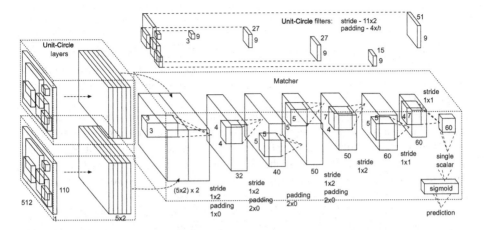

Fig. 3. Architecture of the IrisMatch-CNN. Two normalized-iris images are fed into the Unit-Circle (U-C) layers. The responses from the U-C layers are concatenated and fed into the Matcher convolutional network. A single scalar is produced – the probability of a match. The variable h stands for an integer part of half the width of the corresponding filter.

of the second last fully connected layer is used to compute a similarity score – the Euclidean distance. The input of the network is a gray-scale iris image normalized to polar coordinates.

CNN used Differently than the Feature Extractor. We follow with three works that use the CNN in another way than just an extractor of the features.

Authors of [8] design a CNN to verify the relationship between two heterogeneous iris images. A "pairwise filter" layer is introduced to extract features from a pair of normalized irises from different sources. For a single pair of irises, six input pairs are generated, explicitly encoding iris rotations and ordering of pairs. The output of the network is a similarity score – 1 if the two normalized irises belong to the same identity, 0 otherwise. Experiments only for irises from heterogeneous sources are presented. It is not clear which loss function is used.

A CNN in [14] distinguishes between corresponding/noncorresponding patches on a normalized iris image. The output of the network is a single scalar – a probability that the patches correspond. The output of the CNN serves as an input to a Markov random field used to infer a deformation model between a pair of iris images. Given the deformation parameters, the histogram of magnitudes and phase angles are computed. Classification is done with a binary classifier.

A pre-trained ResNet18 in [10] verifies if two irises match. Each (presumably normalized) iris is passed through the ResNet18, which extracts n-dimensional feature vectors. Absolute difference of the two vectors is computed and fed to a single layer of two perceptrons, one for the class "match", the other for class "non-match".

3   Method

We propose a convolutional neural network (CNN) to verify a match of two normalized iris images (see Fig. 3). The input of the network is a pair of normalized iris images. The output is a single scalar interpreted as the posterior probability of the match.

The verification has two parts. First, the features are extracted with a novel "Unit-Circle layer". Second, the features are concatenated and fed into the "Matcher" – a fully convolutional neural network which outputs a single scalar, the probability of the match. When used together, the Unit-Circle layer and Matcher CNN creates a network architecture to which we refer as to the IrisMatch-CNN.

Let $\mathcal{T} = \{(\mathbf{x}_1^j, \ldots, \mathbf{x}_{N_j}^j) \in \mathcal{X}^{N_j} \mid j = 1, \ldots, l\}$ be the training set that contains l tuples of normalized-iris images $\mathbf{x} \in \mathcal{X}$. Each tuple contains N_j images of the same iris. Symbol $\mathcal{X}$ denotes the set of all input iris images.

Unit-Circle Layer. Let $c(\mathbf{x}_k; \phi)$ be the output of a standard convolutional layer with a single input channel and two output channels for the k-th normalized iris image, where ϕ is a concatenation of the parameters of the filter. We define the output of the *Unit-Circle layer* $\mathring{c}(\mathbf{x}_k; \phi)$ on the i-th row and j-th column as

$$\mathring{c}_{(i,j)}(\mathbf{x}_k; \phi) = \frac{c_{(i,j)}(\mathbf{x}_k; \phi)}{\left\| c_{(i,j)}(\mathbf{x}_k; \phi) \right\|_2}. \tag{1}$$

In other words, the output of the Unit-Circle layer (U-C layer) is the output of a standard convolutional layer that is normalized along the output channel dimension – the convolutional layer must have one input channel and two output channels. After the normalization, each pixel in the two-dimensional output of the U-C lies on the unit circle.

When multiple U-C layers are used, we define the concatenation of their responses $\mathring{c}(\mathbf{x}_k; \Phi) = (\mathring{c}^1(\mathbf{x}_k; \phi^1), \ldots, \mathring{c}^F(\mathbf{x}_k; \phi^F))$, where F is the number of U-C layers, $\mathring{c}^F(\mathbf{x}_k; \phi^F)$ is the response of the F-th U-C filter, Φ is a concatenation of all parameters of the F filters. In IrisMatch-CNN, five U-C layers are used, i.e. we get five pairs of responses or 10 output channels for each normalized image of iris.

We follow a custom padding strategy. In the vertical direction, we pad by zeroes. Since the normalized image is stored in the polar coordinates, in the horizontal direction and left side of the image we: (i) compute h – integer part of half the width of the filter, (ii) create a copy of the normalized iris by selecting h pixels from the right side of the image, (iii) append the copy to the left side of the image. We repeat for the right side.

Matcher. The Matcher is a fully convolutional neural network that produces a single scalar – the probability that two irises match. Let $g(\overline{\mathbf{x}}_{q,r}; \Psi)$ be the output of the Matcher CNN for the pair of q-th and r-th normalized-iris images and Ψ a concatenation of all convolutional filter parameters. The input of the Matcher CNN is $\overline{\mathbf{x}}_{q,r} = (\overset{\bullet}{c}(\mathbf{x}_q; \Phi), \overset{\bullet}{c}(\mathbf{x}_r; \Phi))$, where $\overset{\bullet}{c}(\mathbf{x}_q; \Phi)$ is the output of *all* U-C layers for the normalized iris $\mathbf{x}_q$ and Φ is a concatenation of the parameters of filters of all U-C layers.

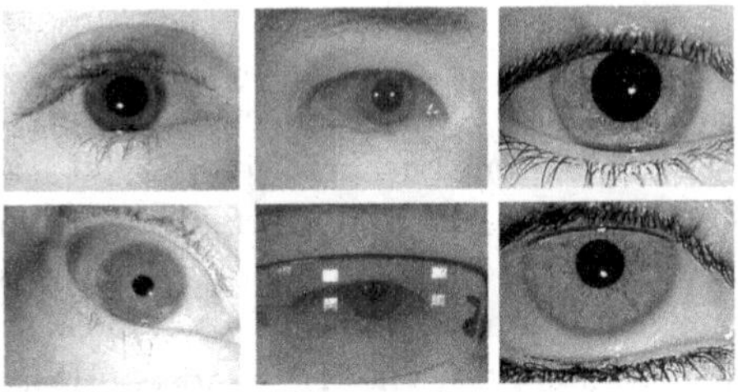

training	authentic / imposter
ND-IRIS-0405	2, 655, 213 / 563, 657, 472
CASIA v4	20, 068 / 2, 619, 167
IITD	1, 410 / 277, 221

testing	authentic / imposter
ND-IRIS-0405	14, 791 / 5, 743, 130
CASIA v4	20, 702 / 2, 969, 533
IITD	2, 240 / 624, 400

(a) Sample images from ND-IRIS-0405, CA- SIA v4, and IITD database. Top: dilated pupil, bottom: constricted pupil.

(b) Dataset statistics. The number of positive (authentic) and negative (imposter) pairs in the training and testing sets.

Fig. 4. Overview of the datasets used in the experiments.

In other words, the input of the network is created as follows. A normalized iris is fed into the U-C layers. The output of the U-C layers is concatenated. The same procedure is repeated for the second normalized iris. Finally, the two sets of responses are concatenated creating the input of the Matcher network. Note that the normalized-iris images are fed through the same set of U-C layers.

Learning. The binary cross-entropy is used as the objective function. If two irises match, the desired prediction is 1.0, 0.0 otherwise. In all experiments, the Matcher network was trained first - the weights of the U-C layers were initialized randomly and fixed. After approx. 100 epochs, we started training the weights of the whole IrisMatch-CNN. We applied this scheme to speed up the training – if the whole network was trained from the beginning, the network converged approx. 10 times slower or did not converge at all. The training data are heavily imbalanced towards the negative class (up to 216 : 1 ratio). We balanced the classes by randomly selecting the N_p negative examples, where N_p is the number of positive examples. We repeated the sub-sampling of the negative class in each epoch.

Technical Details. In the Matcher CNN, standard blocks of convolutions and Exponential Linear Unit [4] activation functions were used. Also, batch normalization and dropout was applied. We trained the network in the *PyTorch 1.0* library with the Adam optimizer and the learning rate set to 0.01. The set of all input normalized-iris images $\mathcal{X} = \mathbb{R}^{110 \times 512}$. The output of *all* U-C layers for the normalized-iris image $\overset{\bullet}{c}(\mathbf{x}; \boldsymbol{\Phi}) = (\overset{\partial}{c}^1(\mathbf{x}; \phi_1), \ldots, \overset{\partial}{c}^5(\mathbf{x}; \phi_5))$. Stride and padding are the same in all five layers.

The training set was split to the training and validation subset with the ratio of $10:1$. IrisMatch-CNN has 416.930 parameters in total (compare with approx. $12 \cdot 10^6$ of [10]).

4   Experiments

The quality of iris detection and segmentation has a severe effect on the performance of iris recognition pipeline [7]. Since different authors use different iris segmentation methods, reproducibility of the results reported in iris-verification papers is usually low. Therefore, we follow the methodology of [21] – the authors made their codes public along with the segmentations.

In the experiments, we evaluate the methods with the True Accept Rate (TAR) for a given False Accept Rate (FAR). FAR is a fraction of non-matching pairs classified as matches, TAR is a fraction of matching pairs of iris images classified as matches.

Datasets. As discussed earlier in this section, we follow the evaluation procedure introduced in [21]. However, we were not able to retrieve the "WVU Non-ideal Iris Database - Release 1" since it is currently available only to the residents of the United States. Therefore, we present the results on three datasets – ND-IRIS-0405, CASIA v4, and IITD. See Fig. 4 for the number of samples in the training and testing subsets and for sample images. In case of all datasets, the iris segmentations provided in the scripts of [21] were used to extract the iris in the testing sets. For the training sets, the irises were segmented with a method introduced in [20]. The models with the highest TAR on the validation subset were selected for the evaluation on the test set.

ND-IRIS-0405. The ND-IRIS-0405 Iris Image Dataset (ICE 2006) [3] contains $64{,}980$ iris samples from 356 subjects. The training set for this database was composed of the left eye images from all subjects and the test set from the first 10 right eye images from all subjects.

CASIA Iris Image Database V4 - Distance. The "distance" subset of the CASIA dataset [1] contains $2{,}446$ samples from 142 subjects. The "distance" subset is composed of images of the upper part of a face – each image contains both eyes. The authors of [21] provide segmentation of eyes for the subjects in the testing set. For the training set, the eyes were localized with the *IntraFace* facial landmarks detector [18] using the facial landmarks near the eyes. The training set contains only the right eye images, the test set includes only the left eye images.

IITD Iris Database. The IITD database [2] includes $2{,}240$ image samples from 224 subjects. There are only right eye images in the training set. In the test set, only the first five left eye images were used.

4.1 Comparative Study

In this experiment, a comparative study on three public datasets against four state-of-the-art methods is presented.

First, we shortly describe the methods. The most widely deployed iris feature descriptor is the Gabor-filter-based *IrisCode* [5]. It is a highly competitive method suitable for a performance benchmark [21]. A popular public implementation of *IrisCode* is an open source tool for iris recognition *OSIRIS v4.1* [12]. It uses a band of tunable 2D Gabor filters encoding the iris features at different scales. Another *IrisCode* method [9] uses 1D log-Gabor filter(s) to extract the features. *Ordinal* is an approach checking the consistency of Ordinal measures in irises [15].

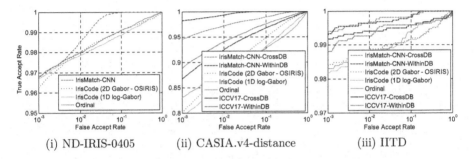

(i) ND-IRIS-0405   (ii) CASIA.v4-distance   (iii) IITD

Fig. 5. Comparative study on three public datasets against four state-of-the-art methods. The proposed IrisMatch-CNN method yields the best results in the case of all three databases. Results as reported in [21]. Note that we were not able to reproduce the results of [21] on the ND-IRIS-0405 database. We, therefore, exclude the ICCV17 method from the comparison in case of this database.

Table 1. False reject rates (FRR) at **0.1%** false accept rate (FAR) and equal error rates (EER). Results as reported in [21]. We were not able to reproduce the ICCV17-WithinDB results on the ND-IRIS-0405 database. We, therefore, exclude them from the table.

	ND-IRIS-0405		CASIA.v4-distance		IITD	
	FRR	EER	FRR	EER	FRR	EER
IrisCode (OSIRIS)	3.73%	1.70%	19.93%	6.39%	1.61%	1.11%
Ordinal	3.22%	1.74%	16.93%	7.89%	1.70%	1.25%
ICCV17-CrossDB	/	/	13.27%	4.54%	0.82%	0.64%
ICCV17-WithinDB	—		11.15%	3.85%	1.19%	0.73%
Ours-CrossDB	/	/	5.81%	2.18%	**0.65%**	**0.41%**
Ours-WithinDB	**3.20%**	**1.29%**	**1.67%**	**0.87%**	0.68%	0.43%

The *ICCV17* and IrisMatch-CNN methods are presented in two configurations. "CrossDB" means that the model was trained only on the training set of the ND-IRIS-0405 database and "WithinDB" means that the model was also fine-tuned on the training set of the target database. We present the results reported in [21] – the results were reproduced with the scripts provided by the authors. However, despite significant efforts, we were not able to reproduce the results in case of ND-IRIS-0405 database. We therefore exclude the ICCV17 method from the comparison in case of this database. Note that in all experiments presented in [21], the vertical resolution of the normalized iris image is 64 pixels. The IrisMatch-CNN was developed with the input vertical resolution of 110 pixels. Therefore, we resize to the required vertical resolution using the linear interpolation. All methods were extensively tuned on the target databases to ensure a fair comparison – the details are provided in [21].

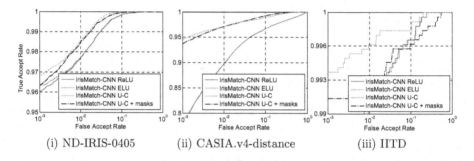

(i) ND-IRIS-0405   (ii) CASIA.v4-distance   (iii) IITD

Fig. 6. Effect of the Unit-Circle layers on the performance of IrisMatch-CNN. The ℓ_2 normalization was replaced by the ReLU and ELU non-linearities and the model was learnt for 1000 epochs. In "masks" experiment, iris masks were concatenated to outputs of the Unit-Circle layers.

Taking look at Fig. 5 and Table 1, IrisMatch-CNN yields the best results in case of all three databases. We see that, compared to the other methods, the performance of IrisMatch-CNN shows a different trend – TAR tends to be higher for a wider range of FAR, which is especially visible in case of the ND-IRIS-0405 database. We believe that this tendency is caused by the binary cross-entropy objective function.

Let us examine "CrossDB" and "WithinDB" setups in Fig. 5. The results of IrisMatch-CNN on the IITD database do not differ much between these two settings. A difference of approx. 3% in favour of "WithinDB" setup is visible in case of the CASIA database. We conclude that IrisMatch-CNN generalizes well between different databases, i.e. the method is robust to changes in the iris image acquisition setup.

4.2   Effect of Unit-Circle layers on performance

We developed the Unit-Circle (U-C) layer as a replacement of the Gabor filtering step in the iris recognition pipeline. We interpret the outputs of the U-C layer as responses lying on the unit circle in a two-dimensional plane. In the following experiment, we replaced the ℓ^2 normalization in the U-C layer by two non-linearities – by the Rectified Linear Unit, or ReLU, and the Exponential Linear Unit [4], or ELU. We trained the IrisMatch-CNN network with each non-linearity on the training set of the ND-IRIS-0405 database for $1,000$ epochs, selecting the model with the best validation performance.

As seen in Fig. 6 in case of all three databases, the TAR is higher for the network in which the U-C layers are used. From the plots (ii) and (iii), we conclude that the U-C layers improve generalization on unseen data.

4.3 Effect of Iris Masks on Performance

The input of IrisMatch-CNN is a pair of normalized irises. In this experiment, we also included the masks estimated by the ICCV17 mask sub-network so that the input of the IrisMatch-CNN network is a pair of normalized irises with their masks. The normalized-iris mask is shown in Fig. 1. In a common iris-verification pipeline, it marks the areas not suitable for matching – e.g., eyelids, sclera, or reflections.

The results are shown in Fig. 6. There is no significant improvement when also the masks are included. Therefore, we conclude that the IrisMatch-CNN network is capable of determining the "good areas to match" by itself.

4.4 Effect of Iris-Segmentation Method on IrisMatch-CNN performance

In this experiment, the task was to examine the robustness of IrisMatch-CNN against the change of the iris segmentation method. In our datasets, we segment the iris with the total variation method [20]. In this experiment, we employed a publicly available iris-verification software *OSIRIS v4.1* that uses the Viterbi method [16]. We created two modified test subsets from the ND-IRIS-0405 and CASIA.v4 databases (see Fig. 7b for statistics). We followed the left/right eye splits in the testing datasets. However, we used all images that were successfully extracted by both the methods. The presented results were retrieved by the IrisMatch-CNN network that was trained on the standard training subset of the ND-IRIS-0405 database.

There is a much better performance visible in Fig. 7a in case of ND-IRIS-0405. The test set used in other experiments contains only the first 10 right eye images from all subjects. In this experiment, we did not follow this limitation. Instead, we used all iris images that were successfully segmented by both the methods. This condition resulted in an "easy-to-verify" set of normalized irises. However, for the database on which the IrisMatch-CNN was trained the switch between the total variation method and the Viterbi method makes no difference in performance.

However, the results on the CASIA.v4-distance database give us a different view. The total variation method gives better TAR by 10% for a 10^{-3} FAR than the Viterbi method. We conclude, that the IrisMatch-CNN method is not robust to changing the capture settings (i.e. the database) and the segmentation method at the same time.

Note that we excluded the IITD database from this experiment since the number of authentic pairs in the testing set, which we got by the previously described construction, was less than $1,000$.

4.5 Heterogeneous Iris Verification

In this experiment, we inspect the performance of the IrisMatch-CNN model in the heterogeneous iris verification. In this type of verification, two images of irises are compared, but each iris is from a different source (as opposed to the previous experiments, in which the pair of irises was always from the same source).

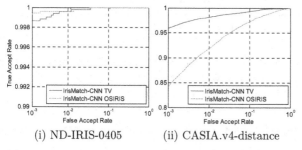

(i) ND-IRIS-0405	(ii) CASIA.v4-distance

(a) Iris-segmentation experiment results. Solid blue: irises segmented with the total variation method [20], orange dashed: irises segmented with the Viterbi method [16].

authentic	
ND-IRIS-0405	$21,886$
CASIA v4	$13,231$
imposter	
ND-IRIS-0405	$13,505,915$
CASIA v4	$1,711,922$

(b) Statistics of test dataset used in iris-segmentation experiment.

Fig. 7. Effect of iris-segmentation method on IrisMatch-CNN performance. The network was trained only on the ND-IRIS-0405 training set. The test datasets are described in Sect. 4.4 (see also Fig. 7b).

For the purpose of this experiment, we use the ND-CrossSensor2013 database[1]. In this database, each iris is captured with both the LG2200 and LG4000 iris sensors. We follow the experimental protocols introduced by the authors of the database. More specifically, we use the "SigSets2013-Small-LG4000-LG2200" protocol that specifies which irises should be compared. In this protocol, there is a total number of $99,690,130$ comparisons. However, we segmented the normalized irises with the total variation method [20] and we were not able to segment the whole dataset. Therefore, in our experiment, there is a total number of $18,000,588$ comparisons (see Fig. 8c for numbers of positive class, or authentic, and negative class, or imposter, pairs).

Figure 8b shows results of two experiments. In the first experiment, we used the model trained on the ND-IRIS-0405 database training subset (see Fig. 5 for

---

[1] Available at https://cvrl.nd.edu.

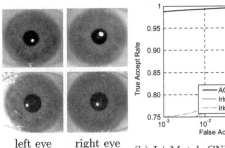

ND-CrossSensor2013	
training	
authentic	15,071
imposter	2,366,456
testing	
authentic	41,876
imposter	17,958,712

left eye   right eye

(a) ND-CrossSensor2013 database. Detail of iris, same subject. Top: LG2200, bottom: LG4000 sensor.

(b) IrisMatch-CNN evaluated on ND-CrossSensor2013 database (see Fig. 8c). Solid: ACSTL as reported in [13], dashed: IrisMatch-CNN trained on ND-IRIS-0405 database, dot dash: fine-tuned.

(c) Statistics of the testing and training subsets of ND-CrossSensor2013 database.

Fig. 8. Heterogeneous iris verification. Evaluated on the ND-CrossSensor2013 database. We used the IrisMatch-CNN model from the ND-IRIS-0405 comparative study. For the fine-tuning, the same model was trained for $1,000$ epochs and the one yielding the best validation true accept rate for 10^{-3} false accept rate was selected.

results on other datasets). In the second experiment, we fine-tuned the model on the training subset of the ND-CrossSensor2013 database. Compared to the results reported by the ACSTL Cross-Sensor Comparison Competition Team 2013 [13], our models perform more than 20% worse at the false accept rate of 10^{-3}. We believe that this is caused by the architecture of the IrisMatch-CNN – we use the same set of Unit-Circle layers for both input images of irises. In fact, our experiment verifies results of [8]. The authors design a special "pairwise bank filter" to account for differences between the heterogeneous irises, i.e. irises from different sources. In our case, the source of the difference between the irises is the capturing device. Compared to the LG4000-based sensors, the LG2200-based sensors produce blurry images commonly with a strong interlacing (see Fig. 8a). We conclude, that IrisMatch-CNN is not suitable for heterogeneous iris verification.

5   Conclusion

In this paper, we introduced a novel convolutional neural network architecture IrisMatch-CNN yielding state-of-the-art results in the iris-verification task on the ND-IRIS-0405, CASIA.v4-distance, and IITD databases. The input of the network is a normalized-iris image, the output is a single scalar interpreted as the probability of a match. A novel Unit-Circle layer was introduced that improves robustness of the model (i.e. the ability of the model to generalize on previously-unseen data), which is verified in experiments. We presented experiments in which a different iris-segmentation method: (a) does not affect the performance when evaluated on previously-seen data (b) decreases the performance otherwise. Lastly, we showed that IrisMatch-CNN is not suitable for heterogeneous iris verification, i.e. for matching two irises when each is from a different source.

Acknowledgments. Radim Špetlík was supported by the OP VVV funded project CZ.02.1.01/0.0/0.0/16_019/0000765 and by CTU student grant SGS17/185/OHK3/3T/13.

References

1. CASIA.v4 Iris Database. http://www.cbsr.ia.ac.cn/china/Iris%20Databases%20CH.asp
2. IIT Delhi Iris Database. http://www4.comp.polyu.edu.hk/~csajaykr/IITD/Database_Iris.htm
3. Bowyer, K.W., Flynn, P.J.: The ND-IRIS-0405 iris image dataset. Technical report, Notre Dame CVRL
4. Clevert, D.A., Unterthiner, T., Hochreiter, S.: Fast and accurate deep network learning by exponential linear units (ELUs). arXiv:1511.07289 (Nov 2015)
5. Daugman, J.: How iris recognition works. IEEE Trans. Circ. Syst. Video Technol. **14**(1), 21–30 (2004). https://doi.org/10.1109/TCSVT.2003.818350
6. Gangwar, A., Joshi, A.: DeepIrisNet: deep iris representation with applications in iris recognition and cross-sensor iris recognition. In: 2016 IEEE International Conference on Image Processing (ICIP), pp. 2301–2305, September 2016. https://doi.org/10.1109/ICIP.2016.7532769
7. Li, Y.H., Huang, P.J., Juan, Y.: An Efficient and Robust Iris Segmentation Algorithm Using Deep Learning (2019). https://doi.org/10.1155/2019/4568929
8. Liu, N., Zhang, M., Li, H., Sun, Z., Tan, T.: DeepIris: learning pairwise filter bank for heterogeneous iris verification. Pattern Recogn. Lett. **82**, 154–161 (2016). https://doi.org/10.1016/j.patrec.2015.09.016
9. Masek, L.: Recognition of human iris patterns for biometric identification. Technical report (2003)
10. Menon, H., Mukherjee, A.: Iris biometrics using deep convolutional networks. In: 2018 IEEE International Instrumentation and Measurement Technology Conference (I2MTC), pp. 1–5, May 2018. https://doi.org/10.1109/I2MTC.2018.8409594
11. Nguyen, K., Fookes, C., Ross, A., Sridharan, S.: Iris recognition with off-the-shelf CNN features: a deep learning perspective. IEEE Access **6**, 18848–18855 (2018). https://doi.org/10.1109/ACCESS.2017.2784352
12. Othman, N., Dorizzi, B., Garcia-Salicetti, S.: OSIRIS: an open source iris recognition software. Pattern Recogn. Lett. **82**, 124–131 (2016). https://doi.org/10.1016/j.patrec.2015.09.002
13. Popescu-Bodorin, N., et al.: Cross-sensor iris recognition: LG4000-to-LG2200 comparison. arXiv:1801.01695, January 2018
14. Proença, H., Neves, J.C.: IRINA: iris recognition (even) in inaccurately segmented data. In: 2017 IEEE Conference on Computer Vision and Pattern Recognition (CVPR), pp. 6747–6756, July 2017. https://doi.org/10.1109/CVPR.2017.714
15. Sun, Z., Tan, T.: Ordinal measures for iris recognition. IEEE Trans. Pattern Anal. Mach. Intell. **31**(12), 2211–2226 (2009). https://doi.org/10.1109/TPAMI.2008.240

16. Sutra, G., Garcia-Salicetti, S., Dorizzi, B.: The Viterbi algorithm at different resolutions for enhanced iris segmentation. In: 2012 5th IAPR International Conference on Biometrics (ICB), pp. 310–316, March 2012. https://doi.org/10.1109/ICB.2012. 6199825

17. Tang, X., Xie, J., Li, P.: Deep convolutional features for iris recognition. In: Zhou, J., et al. (eds.) CCBR 2017. LNCS, vol. 10568, pp. 391–400. Springer, Cham (2017). https://doi.org/10.1007/978-3-319-69923-3_42

18. Xiong, X., Torre, F.D.l.: Supervised descent method and its applications to face alignment. In: 2013 IEEE Conference on Computer Vision and Pattern Recognition, pp. 532–539, June 2013. https://doi.org/10.1109/CVPR.2013.75

19. Zhang, Q., Li, H., Sun, Z., Tan, T.: Deep feature fusion for iris and periocular biometrics on mobile devices. IEEE Trans. Inf. Forensics Secur. **13**(11), 2897–2912 (2018). https://doi.org/10.1109/TIFS.2018.2833033

20. Zhao, Z., Kumar, A.: An accurate iris segmentation framework under relaxed imaging constraints using total variation model. In: 2015 IEEE International Conference on Computer Vision (ICCV), pp. 3828–3836, December 2015. https://doi.org/10. 1109/ICCV.2015.436

21. Zhao, Z., Kumar, A.: Towards More Accurate Iris Recognition Using Deeply Learned Spatially Corresponding Features, pp. 3809–3818 (2017)

SDNet: Semantically Guided Depth Estimation Network

Matthias Ochs[1($\boxtimes$)], Adrian Kretz[1], and Rudolf Mester[1,2]

[1] VSI Lab, Goethe University, Frankfurt am Main, Germany
matthias.ochs@vsi.cs.uni-frankfurt.de
[2] Norwegian Open AI Lab, CS Dept. (IDI), NTNU, Trondheim, Norway

Abstract. Autonomous vehicles and robots require a full scene understanding of the environment to interact with it. Such a perception typically incorporates pixel-wise knowledge of the depths and semantic labels
for each image from a video sensor. Recent learning-based methods estimate both types of information independently using two separate CNNs.
In this paper, we propose a model that is able to predict both outputs simultaneously, which leads to improved results and even reduced
computational costs compared to independent estimation of depth and
semantics. We also empirically prove that the CNN is capable of learning more meaningful and semantically richer features. Furthermore, our
SDNet estimates the depth based on ordinal classification. On the basis
of these two enhancements, our proposed method achieves state-of-the-
art results in semantic segmentation and depth estimation from single
monocular input images on two challenging datasets.

1 Introduction

Many computer vision applications rely on or at least can increase their performance, if pixel-wise depth information is available in addition to the input image.
Based on this depth information, geometric relationships in the environment
can be explained better and can support, for instance, the scene understanding
in robotics, autonomous driving, image editing or 3D modeling/reconstruction
(Fig. 1).

Unfortunately, estimating the depth from a single monocular image is an ill-
posed problem, which cannot be solved without further knowledge. In this paper,
we propose a deep learning-based approach, where this additional information
is learned in a supervised manner from the geometric cues of many training
samples by a CNN. The network architecture of this CNN is inspired by the
DeepLabv3+ model from [2] and extended by two subnets to simultaneously
predict the depth and semantic labels. Due to this combined prediction, our
net learns semantically richer and more stable features in the Atrous Spatial
Pyramid Pooling (ASPP) module, which results in an improved estimation of
both. Following the insights of [6] and having in mind that depths follow a natural
order, we regard the depth estimation as an ordinal classification problem and
not as a regression-based one. This ensures that the neural network converges

© Springer Nature Switzerland AG 2019
G. A. Fink et al. (Eds.): DAGM GCPR 2019, LNCS 11824, pp. 288–302, 2019.
https://doi.org/10.1007/978-3-030-33676-9_20

Input	SDNet	Output
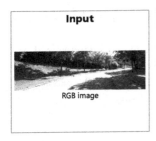	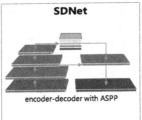	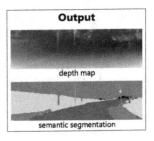

Fig. 1. Our proposed SDNet estimates pixel-wise depth and semantic labels from a single monocular input image based on a modified DeepLabv3+ architecture.

faster and that the resulting depth maps are more precise and can retrieve more details of fine structures and small objects. In the evaluation section, we show that SDNet yields state-of-the-art results on two datasets while still being able to generalize to other datasets as well.

2   Related Work

In this section, we review classical as well as deep learning based methods for solving the depth estimation problem. In most classical approaches [20, 24, 25], hand-crafted features are extracted from the monocular images, which are then used to predict the depth map by optimizing a probabilistic model like, a Markov random field (MRF) or conditional random field (CRF). Ladicky et al. [15] estimate the depth based on different canonical views and show that semantic knowledge helps to improve the prediction. This is verified for stereo-matching methods by [26, 31], too. In this paper, we empirically prove that this concept also holds for depth estimation from a single monocular image with a CNN.

Besides these classical techniques, many recent approaches make use of Convolutional Neural Networks (CNNs). These techniques can be divided into two categories: supervised and unsupervised learning methods. Supervised learning techniques include models which are trained on stereo images, but which can infer depth maps on monocular images. [12] propose an approach which follows this paradigm. They use the correlations of CNN feature maps of stereo images and derive the unary matching costs. The depth maps are then computed by using a CRF. But there are also CNNs [8, 21, 23, 28], which try to find stereo correspondences to estimate the disparity/depth.

The previously mentioned approaches are trained in a supervised manner. [14] introduce a semi-supervised approach, where the loss function includes an additional unsupervised term. This term captures the stereo alignment error of two images given an approximate depth map. The approaches of [7, 30] and [9] use modifications of this alignment error to train networks in a completely unsupervised way. Since ground truth depth maps are not necessary with these approaches, it is possible to make use of much larger training databases. These unsupervised techniques tend to produce much smoother and thus more inaccurate depth map than supervised techniques, though.

Fu et al. [6] introduced DORN, which is a CNN trained in a supervised way and achieves current state-of-the-art results. Instead of using regression to estimate the depth of each pixel, the depths are discretized and ordinal classification is used. We also use a similar idea for our depth estimation.

3   Approach

In this section, we introduce our proposed model, which classifies the depth based on ordinal depth classes while simultaneously inferring the semantic labels for each pixel, too. This has the advantage that more meaningful features are learned in the final layers of the encoder, from which both the semantic segmentation and the depth estimation can benefit. This allows the CNN to describe, detect and classify objects more accurately.

3.1   Architecture

The network architecture of our model is depicted in Fig. 2. It is similar to the DeepLabv3+ model from [2], which represents the current state of the art for semantic segmentation.

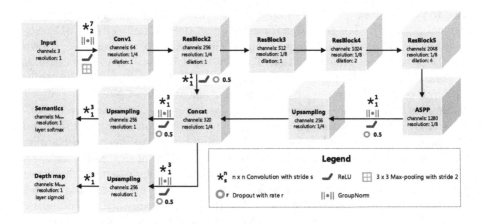

Fig. 2. Encoder-decoder architecture of SDNet with ASPP module. The decoder consists of two subnets, which predict the pixel-wise depths and semantic labels.

Theoretically, every encoder, e.g. ResNets or InceptionNets, can be used to extract feature maps which serve as input for the ASPP module. Due to limited computational capacity and real-time requirements, we use a ResNet-50 in this work. The ResNet is configured as proposed by [2] (dilation rate, multi grid, output stride of 8, atrous convolution, etc.). With the combination of this encoder and the ASPP module, SDNet is capable of extracting features on multiple scales, which improves the results significantly. The ASPP module is also adopted from DeepLabv3+, except that we use group normalization [29] instead of batch normalization, which applies to all normalization layers in the CNN. Furthermore, we add dropout layers, as shown in Fig. 2. Compared to DORN [6], our ASPP module is *fully-convolutional* and thus our CNN is not dependent on a predefined input resolution.

Unlike DeepLabv3+, our decoder consists of two subnets. First, the decoder interpolates the semantically meaningful feature maps from the ASPP module which are then concatenated with feature maps from the second ResBlock. These feature maps provide additional structural information and are able to recognize fine structures in the image. The resulting feature maps serve as input for our two subnets. In the first subnet, the semantic labels are estimated. The second subnet determines the depth. Both output layers of the two subnets compute class probabilities, which is done by a softmax function for the semantics and by a sigmoid layer for the depths.

3.2 Discretization

For ordinal regression, the continuous depth must be discretized so that a particular class c can be assigned to each depth d. Normally, the depths $d \in [d_{\min}, d_{\max}]$ are divided linearly into classes between the minimum and maximum depth. However, this partitioning has the disadvantage that an erroneous estimation of a depth class at shallow depths causes a larger relative estimation error compared to a faulty estimated large depth.

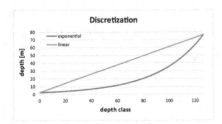 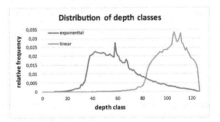

Fig. 3. The left plot shows the exponential and linear discretization of the depths with $M_{\mathrm{depth}} = 128$ in the interval [2 m, 80 m]. In the right histogram, the relative frequency of these exponential and linear discretized depth classes are shown over all existing depths of the KITTI depth prediction training dataset.

This relative error can be reduced by either defining the classes by their inverse depths $\rho = \frac{1}{d}$, or by choosing a more complex mapping function, e.g., [6] chose a logarithmic mapping function for discretization. In this work, we split the inverse depth into discrete classes c_i using an exponential function

$$c_i = \rho_{\min} \cdot \exp\left(\log\left(\frac{\rho_{\max}}{\rho_{\min}}\right) \cdot \frac{i-1}{M_{\mathrm{d}}-1}\right), \quad i \in \{1, \ldots M_{\mathrm{d}}\} \qquad (1)$$

where M_d corresponds to the number of depth classes. In the left plot of Fig. 3, both the linear and the exponential mapping functions are shown. On the basis of this graph, one can see that due to the exponential character, more discretization levels or classes are available for small and medium depths than for larger ones. Thus, the relative prediction errors of an estimator should be correspondingly smaller. In the adjacent histogram, the relative frequencies of these two depth classes are shown using the depths found in the KITTI depth prediction training data. A uniform distribution of these classes would be ideal for training a CNN. By a suitable choice of the mapping function, such as the proposed exponential, the depth distribution can be approximated to be a uniform one.

In contrast to the semantic classes, the depth classes follow an ordinal relation. This means that a larger depth class c_i is always included in the smaller ones: $\{c_1 \preccurlyeq c_2 \preccurlyeq \ldots c_i \ldots \preccurlyeq c_{M_d}\}$. By this concept, an inverse depth ρ which actually belongs to the class c_i, also belongs to the classes $c_1, \ldots, c_{i-1}$. This ordered classification was introduced for neural networks by [3] and [22]. [6] and we use this idea, and show that an ordinal classification is advantageous over a standard classification or regression based estimation of depth values.

3.3   Output and Loss

As described in Sect. 3.1, SDNet returns the result of the semantic segmentation and depth estimation in two separate subnets. The output and the loss of the semantic subnet follow the standard multi-class classification for each pixel $k \in 1, \ldots, K$, where K is the number of pixels in the image. Hence, the semantic subnet outputs logits $\boldsymbol{y}_k^s \in \mathbb{R}^{M_s}$, where M_s is equal to the number of semantic classes. The logits $\boldsymbol{y}_k$ are then converted into probabilities $\boldsymbol{p}_k^s$ by using the softmax function. As training loss, we use the multi-class cross entropy with $\boldsymbol{t}_k^s \in \{0, 1\}^{M_s}$ as the one-hot-encoded vector representing the ground truth:

$$L_{k,\text{sem}}(\boldsymbol{\theta}; \boldsymbol{p}_k^s, \boldsymbol{t}_k^s) = -\frac{1}{M_s} \cdot \sum_i t_{k,i}^s \log p_{k,i}^s, \tag{2}$$

where $\boldsymbol{\theta}$ are the trainable parameters in the CNN.

This vanilla multi-class classification cannot be used for the ordered depth classes, because a single pixel can belong to multiple labels (multi-label classification), whereas each depth class is not dependent on the others. Thus, it is regarded as a binary classification problem for each class c_i and pixel k. The depth logits $\boldsymbol{y}_k^d \in \mathbb{R}^{M_d}$ are transformed by the sigmoid function to probabilities $\boldsymbol{p}_k^d$, where $p_{i,k}^d \in [0, 1]$ indicates whether the pixel k belongs to class c_i or not. Then, SDNet calculates the following multi-hot-encoded vector for each pixel:

$$\boldsymbol{z}_k^d = \left[\sigma(p_{k,1}^d), \ldots, \sigma(p_{k,M_d}^d) \right]^T, \quad \text{with}$$

$$\sigma(x) = \begin{cases} 1, & \text{if } x \geq 0.5 \\ 0, & \text{otherwise.} \end{cases} \tag{3}$$

To preserve the ordered relation of the classes, the components of the classified vector y_i are accumulated until the first entry of the vector z_k^d is 0. This sum then corresponds to the class of the pixel:

$$c_k = \sum_i \eta(z_k^d, i), \quad \text{with}$$

$$\eta(z_k^d, i) = \begin{cases} 1, & \text{if } i = 1 \text{ and } z_{k,i}^d = 1 \\ 1, & \text{if } \eta(z_k^d, i-1) = 1 \text{ and } z_{k,i}^d = 1 \\ 0, & \text{otherwise.} \end{cases} \quad (4)$$

To train the depth part of SDNet, we choose the following binary cross entropy loss and the ground truth vector t_k^d is formulated as a multi-hot-encoded vector for class c_k:

$$L_{k,\text{depth}}(\boldsymbol{\theta}; \boldsymbol{p}_k^d, \boldsymbol{t}_k^d) = -\frac{1}{M_d} \cdot \sum_i t_{k,i}^d \log p_{k,i}^d + (1 - t_{k,i}^d) \log(1 - p_{k,i}^d). \quad (5)$$

Thus, the total loss is the mean of two individual losses over all pixels in the batch, with λ acting as a coupling constant:

$$L(\boldsymbol{\theta}; \boldsymbol{p}_k, \boldsymbol{t}_k) = \frac{1}{K} \sum_k L_{k,\text{depth}}(\boldsymbol{\theta}; \boldsymbol{p}_k^d, \boldsymbol{t}_k^d) + \lambda \cdot L_{k,\text{sem}}(\boldsymbol{\theta}; \boldsymbol{p}_k^s, \boldsymbol{t}_k^s). \quad (6)$$

To weight both loss terms similarly, $\lambda = 10$ was empirically determined. We have also analyzed additional loss terms, such as regularization of the predicted depth map by its gradient as proposed by [14] and [9], or the absolute sum of the depth values from [32]. Another possible improvement would be the use of class balancing factors or the focal loss from [18]. However, all of these improvements have not produced any additional positive effects, so we disregarded them.

4   Evaluation and Experiments

This section describes the training of SDNet in more detail. Both, the predicted depth and semantic segmentation are evaluated and achieve state-of-the-art results in the KITTI depth prediction (KD) benchmark [27] and the KITTI pixel-level semantic segmentation (KS) benchmark [1]. In addition, we demonstrate the generalization of SDNet to other data on Cityscapes (CS) [4] and compare our semantic segmentation results with a modified DeepLabv3+ model. We use the same evaluation metrics as in [5] and the official benchmarks.

Both the evaluation and ablation studies show that a joint estimation of depths and semantic labels is preferable to an independent estimation, because it yields superior results. This observation indicates that a CNN is learning semantically more meaningful features. Using these features, the CNN can detect and recognize objects better, which in turn improves both predictions. Additionally, the experiments also show that depths can be estimated more precisely using classes rather than a regression-based approach.

4.1 Training Protocol

To train the SDNet, we used the three datasets mentioned above in the following order. First, we train on the 3000 samples of fine-annotated training data from CS, which contain both semantic information and depth maps from SGBM [11]. These depth maps are relatively dense compared to LIDAR measurements from KITTI, but they are also less accurate and exhibit the typical stereo artifacts. Thus, SDNet was also trained with the 85898 samples of training data from KD, in which LIDAR measurements were accumulated over several frames to get denser depth maps. There is no semantic information available for this data, so only the depth part of SDNet could be trained with KD. However, KITTI published a training dataset (KS) with 200 images containing semantic annotations. LIDAR data also exists for this dataset, so that all necessary data is available for a complete training of SDNet.

Due to the different resolutions and the limited GPU memory, we randomly cropped the images to 768×352 pixel at each epoch. Furthermore, we used random flipping and the standard color jittering as data augmentation techniques. We initialized the encoder with pre-trained weights from ImageNet and froze the parameters of the first and the second ResNet block during training. We used Adam as optimizer and a batch size of 4. The weight-decay factor and dropout rate was set to 0.0005 and 0.5 respectively. The best results were achieved when using 128 depth classes to split the depth interval of $[2\,m, 80\,m]$.

In the first training phase, SDNet was trained on CS and KD with 50.000 iterations each and an initial learning rate of 0.0001. For training on KD, λ was set to 0 because there is no semantic data and thus only the depth subnet should be trained. In all other cases $\lambda = 10$ was chosen. The second training phase consists of fine-tuning on KS, where both subnets are optimized using learning rate of 0.00001 and 3000 iterations.

During deployment, there is no need to divide the input images, because SDNet is fully-convolutional. Thus, the output can be estimated on arbitrary sized input images. Similarly, as suggested by [9], SDNet also predicts the output of the flipped input image. The final prediction is then computed by merging these two outputs, which makes the result more robust to occlusion and outliers.

4.2 KITTI Dataset

The depth estimation and semantic segmentation were evaluated by several evaluations within KD and KS, and compared to state-of-the-art methods. Before KITTI published its benchmark for the monocular depth estimation in 2018, it was common to evaluate the results using an unofficial dataset suggested by [5].

The Eigen test dataset consists of 697 images, which are selected from 29 different sequences of the KITTI raw dataset. The evaluation in Table 1 proves that SDNet achieves very good results in all metrics and is only outperformed by DORN. Moreover, the qualitative comparison of the predicted depth maps in Fig. 4 shows that SDNet can reproduce the depths more accurately and with

Table 1. Evaluation and comparison with other approaches on the test split by Eigen et al. [5]. In the upper part of this table, the depth is evaluated in range of [0m; 80m] whereas the maximum depth was reduced to 50 m in the lower part.

Method	ARD ↓	SRD ↓	RMSE ↓	RMSE$_{Log}$ ↓	$\delta < 1.25$ ↑	$\delta < 1.25^2$ ↑	$\delta < 1.25^3$ ↑
Fu et al. [6]	0.072	0.307	2.727	0.120	0.932	0.985	0.995
SDNet	0.079	0.504	3.700	0.167	0.921	0.968	0.983
Yang et al. [32]	0.097	0.734	4.442	0.187	0.888	0.958	0.980
Kuznietsov et al. [14]	0.113	0.741	4.621	0.189	0.862	0.960	0.986
Godard et al. [9]	0.114	0.898	4.935	0.206	0.861	0.949	0.976
Eigen et al. [5]	0.190	1.515	7.156	0.270	0.692	0.899	0.967
Liu et al. [19]	0.217	1.841	6.986	0.289	0.647	0.882	0.961
Saxena et al. [25]	0.280	3.012	8.734	0.361	0.601	0.820	0.926
Fu et al. [6]	0.071	0.268	2.271	0.116	0.936	0.985	0.995
SDNet	0.075	0.430	3.199	0.163	0.926	0.970	0.984
Yang et al. [32]	0.092	0.547	3.390	0.177	0.898	0.962	0.982
Kuznietsov et al. [14]	0.108	0.595	3.518	0.179	0.875	0.964	0.988
Godard et al. [9]	0.108	0.657	3.729	0.194	0.873	0.954	0.979
Garg et al. [7]	0.169	1.080	5.104	0.273	0.740	0.904	0.962

more details compared to other methods, whose depth maps usually look more blurred. Further examples of depth estimation on KS can be found in Fig. 6.

Besides to this unofficial analysis, the estimated depths of SDNet were also evaluated on the official KD benchmark, which consists of 500 test images. The images depict different driving situations, so that the network has to generalize in order to perform well in this benchmark. The results are shown in Table 2, where only previously published methods have been listed and, again, SDNet achieves state-of-the-art results. Based on the D1 error images in Fig. 5, which shows the deviation to the ground truth for some test images, it can be recognized that the predicted depth of SDNet is erroneous especially at large depths. One reason for this could be that the maximum depth class has been set to 80 m. This also explains the relatively small gap to DORN at the Eigen evaluation, in which the maximum depth is limited to 50 m or 80 m.

Additionally, the predicted semantic segmentation of SDNet was also evaluated on the KS benchmark, which consists of 200 images. The results obtained in this benchmark can be found in Table 3. Although, the focus of SDNet is the estimation of depth and in consequence the semantic segmentation has not been purposefully optimized and has only been used to learn more meaningful features, SDNet also achieves state-of-the-art results in this benchmark.

In Fig. 6, sample results are shown on this test dataset. It can be seen that the results of semantic segmentation and depth estimation correlate directly with each other. For example, if a pixel is assigned to a wrong semantic class,

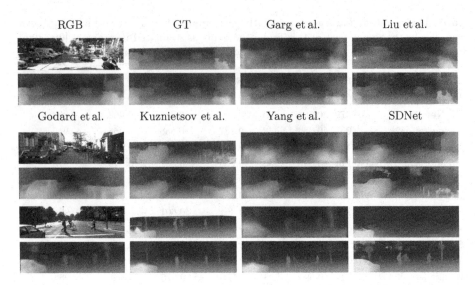

Fig. 4. Qualitative comparison with other state-of-the-art methods on KITTI Eigen test dataset. The ground truth depth maps are interpolated from the sparse LIDAR measurements for better visualization. Our approach can retrieve the depths for small objects and fine structures better than other methods.

then mostly the depth prediction is also incorrect. If, on the other hand, the depth or semantic class has been correctly classified, then in most cases the other output is correct as well.

4.3   Cityscapes Dataset

Both outputs of SDNet were also evaluated on CS to show the generalization capability of SDNet. Unfortunately, there is no benchmark for depth estimation, which is why the results could only be assessed qualitatively. In Fig. 7, the estimated depth maps of SDNet and [14] are exemplarily shown for CS. One can clearly see that the SDNet depths are more detailed compared to Kuznietsov et al.. For example, the depth for the persons in front of the Brandenburg Gate and the gate itself are retrieved well by SDNet in contrast to [14], where the depths are noticeably more blurry. Aside from the depths, the semantic segmentation of SDNet is also shown in this figure. Qualitatively, the predicted semantics yield correct and good results, with a few exceptions. This can also be shown by the quantitative results on CS.

Table 2. Official results of the KITTI depth prediction benchmark [27] (as of May 01, 2019). This table includes only already published methods. If several results of one method are ranked, then only the best is taken.

Method	SiLog [100 · log(m)]	SRD in %	ARD in %	iRMSE [1/km]
DORN [6]	11.67	2.21	9.04	12.23
VGG16-UNet [10]	13.41	2.86	10.06	15.06
DABC [17]	14.49	4.08	12.72	15.53
SDNet	14.68	3.90	12.31	15.96
APMoE [13]	14.74	3.88	11.74	15.63
CSWE [16]	14.85	3.48	11.84	16.38
DHGRL [33]	15.47	4.04	12.52	15.72

Fig. 5. D1 error of the SDNet depth estimate from the ground truth on three exemplary images from the KITTI Depth Prediction test dataset. The errors were computed by KITTI and blue represents a small deviation and red a large one. (Color figure online)

4.4 Ablation Studies

We also perform ablation studies on the KD validation data to empirically prove that our contributions/enhancements result in verifiable improvements. These experiments can be divided into three parts: i.e. loss function, discretization levels and architecture. The results are shown in Table 4. As a baseline configuration for SDNet, a ResNet-50 with group normalization layers is chosen as encoder and the proposed ordinal BCE loss is used as loss function from Eq. 5.

Table 3. Official results of the KITTI pixel-level semantic segmentation benchmark [1] (as of May 01, 2019). This list includes only already published methods.

Method	IoU class	iIoU class	IoU cat	iIoU cat
SegStereo [31]	59.10	28.00	81.31	60.26
SDNet	51.14	17.74	79.62	50.45
APMoE [13]	47.96	17.86	78.11	49.17

Thus, the CNN is trained only on the depths and the semantic loss is completely ignored. The depth interval $[2\,\text{m}; 80\,\text{m}]$ is divided into $M_d = 128$ classes.

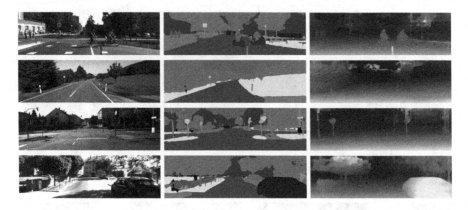

Fig. 6. Qualitative results of semantic segmentation and depth estimation using examples from KS test dataset.

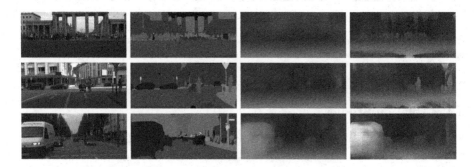

Fig. 7. Qualitative results of the semantic segmentation and the depth estimation based on exemplary examples from the CS test dataset. The first column depict the input image and the second the predicted semantics. In the last two columns, the depth maps of [14] (third column) and SDNet (last column) are shown.

The performance of the network can be increased, if the semantic loss is added to the loss. Hence, the network can learn superior features that do not solely depend on the depth, but also on the semantics. As a result, as shown here empirically, a better performance can be achieved. In addition, the ordered classification of the depths is superior to a regression approach with MAE.

The depth estimation achieves the best results, when dividing the depth interval into 128 classes. Although the accuracy is larger for less classes, the

Table 4. Ablation studies on the KD validation dataset for different configurations. As baseline, we use SDNet without semantic loss ($\lambda = 0$).

Method	SiLog [$100 \cdot \log(m)$]	ARD in %	RMSE [m]	iRMSE [1/km]	Accuracy in %
Sem. loss ($\lambda = 10$)	14.83	9.39	3.11	12.17	20.10
MAE	18.80	12.11	4.03	15.30	-
$M_{\text{depth}} = 96$	16.04	10.88	3.30	13.28	22.50
$M_{\text{depth}} = 160$	15.57	10.06	3.23	12.87	15.50
BatchNorm	15.84	10.31	3.42	12.77	18.95
ResNet-101	16.25	10.89	3.44	13.12	18.24
Baseline	15.38	9.92	3.30	12.55	20.50

prediction results get worse, because the discretization error increases with fewer number of classes. On this basis, 128 classes have proven to be the best trade-off.

Replacing the ResNet-50 by a ResNet-101 as an encoder, was supposed to increase performance, because even better features can be extracted. However, the evaluation shows that exactly the opposite was the case. The reasons for this could be that larger networks generally are harder to train. Therefore, adjustments or fine-tuning had to be made in the training protocol, which was not done (e.g. additional warm-up phase or adjustment of the learning rate). Additionally, the change of the normalization method was also evaluated. By default, batch normalization layers are used in the ResNets, but these proved disadvantageous for small batch sizes. Therefore, these layers have been replaced by group normalization layers, which had a positive effect on all metrics.

5   Summary and Conclusion

In this paper, we propose the novel SDNet for the simultaneous prediction of pixel-wise depths and semantic labels from a single monocular image. The architecture of SDNet is based on the DeepLabv3+ model, which we have extended. The depths are determined by ordered classes rather than the classic regression-based approach. In comparison to other methods, the input image is also segmented semantically. These two modifications turn out to be beneficial as the CNN learns semantically richer features, resulting in significant better results.

In a further stage, a new error or uncertainty measure could be developed on basis of the output, because prediction errors occur mostly in both predictions. This knowledge could be used for such a measure. Another improvement of SDNet would be that a better encoder than ResNet-50 is used. But this implies also that hyper-parameters must be tuned during training, which by itself could be an improvement. Nevertheless, SDNet yields state-of-the-art results for both semantic segmentation and depth estimation on various datasets.

Acknowledgement. This project (HA project no. 626/18-49) is financed with funds of LOEWE – Landes-Offensive zur Entwicklung Wissenschaftlich-öko- nomischer Exzellenz, Förderlinie 3: KMU-Verbundvorhaben (State Offensive for the Development of Scientific and Economic Excellence).

We also gratefully acknowledge the support of NVIDIA Corporation with the donation of the Titan Xp GPU used for this research.

References

1. Alhaija, H., Mustikovela, S., Mescheder, L., Geiger, A., Rother, C.: Augmented reality meets computer vision: efficient data generation for urban driving scenes. Int. J. Comput. Vis. (IJCV) **126**(9), 961–972 (2018)
2. Chen, L.-C., Zhu, Y., Papandreou, G., Schroff, F., Adam, H.: Encoder-decoder with atrous separable convolution for semantic image segmentation. In: Ferrari, V., Hebert, M., Sminchisescu, C., Weiss, Y. (eds.) ECCV 2018. LNCS, vol. 11211, pp. 833–851. Springer, Cham (2018). https://doi.org/10.1007/978-3-030-01234-2_49
3. Cheng, J., Wang, Z., Pollastri, G.: A neural network approach to ordinal regression. In: International Joint Conference on Neural Networks, pp. 1279–1284 (2008)
4. Cordts, M., et al.: The cityscapes dataset for semantic urban scene understanding. In: Conference on Computer Vision and Pattern Recognition (CVPR), pp. 3213–3223 (2016)
5. Eigen, D., Puhrsch, C., Fergus, R.: Depth map prediction from a single image using a multi-scale deep network. In: Advances in Neural Information Processing Systems (NIPS), pp. 2366–2374 (2014)
6. Fu, H., Gong, M., Wang, C., Batmanghelich, K., Tao, D.: Deep ordinal regression network for monocular depth estimation. In: Conference on Computer Vision and Pattern Recognition (CVPR), pp. 2002–2011 (2018)
7. Garg, R., B.G., V.K., Carneiro, G., Reid, I.: Unsupervised CNN for single view depth estimation: geometry to the rescue. In: Leibe, B., Matas, J., Sebe, N., Welling, M. (eds.) ECCV 2016. LNCS, vol. 9912, pp. 740–756. Springer, Cham (2016). https://doi.org/10.1007/978-3-319-46484-8_45
8. Gidaris, S., Komodakis, N.: Detect, replace, refine: deep structured prediction for pixel wise labeling. In: Conference on Computer Vision and Pattern Recognition (CVPR), pp. 7187–7196 (2017)
9. Godard, C., Mac Aodha, O., Brostow, G.J.: Unsupervised monocular depth estimation with left-right consistency. In: Conference on Computer Vision and Pattern Recognition (CVPR), pp. 6602–6611 (2017)
10. Guo, X., Li, H., Yi, S., Ren, J., Wang, X.: Learning monocular depth by distilling cross-domain stereo networks. In: Ferrari, V., Hebert, M., Sminchisescu, C., Weiss, Y. (eds.) ECCV 2018. LNCS, vol. 11215, pp. 506–523. Springer, Cham (2018). https://doi.org/10.1007/978-3-030-01252-6_30
11. Hirschmüller, H.: Stereo processing by semiglobal matching and mutual information. IEEE Trans. Pattern Anal. Mach. Intell. (TPAMI) **30**(2), 328–341 (2008)
12. Knöbelreiter, P., Reinbacher, C., Shekhovtsov, A., Pock, T.: End-to-end training of hybrid CNN-CRF models for stereo. In: Conference on Computer Vision and Pattern Recognition (CVPR), pp. 1456–1465 (2017)
13. Kong, S., Fowlkes, C.: Pixel-wise attentional gating for parsimonious pixel labeling. In: Winter Conference on Applications of Computer Vision (WACV) (2019)

14. Kuznietsov, Y., Stückler, J., Leibe, B.: Semi-supervised deep learning for monocular depth map prediction. In: Conference on Computer Vision and Pattern Recognition (CVPR), pp. 2215–2223 (2017)
15. Ladický, L., Shi, J., Pollefeys, M.: Pulling things out of perspective. In: Conference on Computer Vision and Pattern Recognition (CVPR), pp. 89–96 (2014)
16. Li, B., Dai, Y., He, M.: Monocular depth estimation with hierarchical fusion of dilated CNNs and soft-weighted-sum inference. Pattern Recogn. **83**, 328–339 (2018)
17. Li, R., Xian, K., Shen, C., Cao, Z., Lu, H., Hang, L.: Deep attention-based classification network for robust depth prediction. CoRR arXiv, 1807.03959 [cs.CV] (2018)
18. Lin, T., Goyal, P., Girshick, R., He, K., Dollar, P.: Focal loss for dense object detection. IEEE Trans. Pattern Anal. Mach. Intell. (TPAMI) (2018)
19. Liu, F., Shen, C., Lin, G., Reid, I.: Learning depth from single monocular images using deep convolutional neural fields. IEEE Trans. Pattern Anal. Mach. Intell. (TPAMI) **38**(10), 2024–2039 (2016)
20. Liu, M., Salzmann, M., He, X.: Discrete-continuous depth estimation from a single image. In: Conference on Computer Vision and Pattern Recognition (CVPR), pp. 716–723 (2014)
21. Mayer, N., et al.: A large dataset to train convolutional networks for disparity, optical flow, and scene flow estimation. In: Conference on Computer Vision and Pattern Recognition (CVPR), pp. 4040–4048 (2016)
22. Niu, Z., Zhou, M., Wang, L., Gao, X., Hua, G.: Ordinal regression with multiple output CNN for age estimation. In: Conference on Computer Vision and Pattern Recognition (CVPR), pp. 4920–4928 (2016)
23. Pang, J., Sun, W., SJ. Ren, J., Yang, C., Yan, Q.: Cascade residual learning: a two-stage convolutional neural network for stereo matching. In: International Conference on Computer Vision (ICCV) - Workshop, pp. 887–895 (2017)
24. Saxena, A., Chung, S.H., Ng, A.Y.: Learning depth from single monocular images. In: Advances in Neural Information Processing Systems (NIPS), pp. 1161–1168 (2005)
25. Saxena, A., Sun, M., Ng, A.Y.: Make3D: learning 3D scene structure from a single still image. IEEE Trans. Pattern Anal. Mach. Intell. (TPAMI) **31**(5), 824–840 (2009)
26. Schneider, L., et al.: Semantic stixels: depth is not enough. In: Intelligent Vehicles Symposium (IV), pp. 110–117 (2016)
27. Uhrig, J., Schneider, N., Schneider, L., Franke, U., Brox, T., Geiger, A.: Sparsity invariant CNNs. In: International Conference on 3D Vision (3DV) (2017)
28. Žbontar, J., LeCun, Y.: Stereo matching by training a convolutional neural network to compare image patches. J. Mach. Learn. Res. (JMLR) **17**, 2287–2318 (2016)
29. Wu, Y., He, K.: Group normalization. In: Ferrari, V., Hebert, M., Sminchisescu, C., Weiss, Y. (eds.) ECCV 2018. LNCS, vol. 11217, pp. 3–19. Springer, Cham (2018). https://doi.org/10.1007/978-3-030-01261-8_1
30. Xie, J., Girshick, R., Farhadi, A.: Deep3D: fully automatic 2D-to-3D video conversion with deep convolutional neural networks. In: Leibe, B., Matas, J., Sebe, N., Welling, M. (eds.) ECCV 2016. LNCS, vol. 9908, pp. 842–857. Springer, Cham (2016). https://doi.org/10.1007/978-3-319-46493-0_51
31. Yang, G., Zhao, H., Shi, J., Deng, Z., Jia, J.: SegStereo: exploiting semantic information for disparity estimation. In: Ferrari, V., Hebert, M., Sminchisescu, C., Weiss, Y. (eds.) ECCV 2018. LNCS, vol. 11211, pp. 660–676. Springer, Cham (2018). https://doi.org/10.1007/978-3-030-01234-2_39

32. Yang, N., Wang, R., Stückler, J., Cremers, D.: Deep virtual stereo odometry: leveraging deep depth prediction for monocular direct sparse odometry. In: Ferrari, V., Hebert, M., Sminchisescu, C., Weiss, Y. (eds.) ECCV 2018. LNCS, vol. 11212, pp. 835–852. Springer, Cham (2018). https://doi.org/10.1007/978-3-030-01237-3_50
33. Zhang, Z., Xu, C., Yang, J., Tai, Y., Chen, L.: Deep hierarchical guidance and regularization learning for end-to-end depth estimation. Pattern Recogn. **83**, 430–442 (2018)

Object Segmentation Using Pixel-Wise Adversarial Loss

Ricard Durall[1,2,3(✉)], Franz-Josef Pfreundt[1], Ullrich Köthe[4],
and Janis Keuper[1,5]

[1] Fraunhofer ITWM, Kaiserslautern, Germany
ricard.durall.lopez@itwm.fraunhofer.de
[2] IWR, University of Heidelberg, Heidelberg, Germany
[3] Fraunhofer Center Machine Learning, Kaiserslautern, Germany
[4] Visual Learning Lab Heidelberg, Heidelberg, Germany
[5] Institute for Machine Learning and Analytics,
Offenburg University, Offenburg, Germany

Abstract. Recent deep learning based approaches have shown remarkable success on object segmentation tasks. However, there is still room for further improvement. Inspired by generative adversarial networks, we present a generic end-to-end adversarial approach, which can be combined with a wide range of existing semantic segmentation networks to improve their segmentation performance. The key element of our method is to replace the commonly used binary adversarial loss with a high resolution pixel-wise loss. In addition, we train our generator employing stochastic weight averaging fashion, which further enhances the predicted output label maps leading to state-of-the-art results. We show, that this combination of pixel-wise adversarial training and weight averaging leads to significant and consistent gains in segmentation performance, compared to the baseline models.

1 Introduction

The semantic segmentation task consists of assigning a pre-defined class label to each pixel in an image. Due to its multi-domain versatility, it has become an important application in the field of computer vision. Most of current state-of-the-art methods [2,3,19,21,25,27,36] rely on convolutional neural networks (CNN) approaches as a key part of their implementation. Nevertheless, semantic segmentation remains challenging: The reduced amount of available labeled pixel-wise data (i.e., each pixel has been annotated), the lack of context information, the huge variety of scenarios in which segmentation can be applied, are just a few examples that make it still hard to solve the segmentation task.

Electronic supplementary material The online version of this chapter (https:// doi.org/10.1007/978-3-030-33676-9_21) contains supplementary material, which is available to authorized users.

© Springer Nature Switzerland AG 2019
G. A. Fink et al. (Eds.): DAGM GCPR 2019, LNCS 11824, pp. 303–316, 2019.
https://doi.org/10.1007/978-3-030-33676-9_21

In this paper, we address the task of object segmentation by proposing an adversarial learning scheme which adds a pixel-wise adversarial loss to the classical topology. Inspired by generative adversarial networks (GAN) [7], which are being employed in quite a number of different fields, we use a discriminative network to generate additional information useful for the segmentation task. In our GAN-based semantic segmentation method, we can distinguish between the generative network (generator) and the discriminative network (discriminator). On one side, the generator creates fine label maps by optimizing an objective function that combines a multi-class cross entropy loss together with the adversarial loss. On the other side, the discriminator tries to determine whether a given input segmentation map comes from the training data (real) or belongs to the generated data (fake).

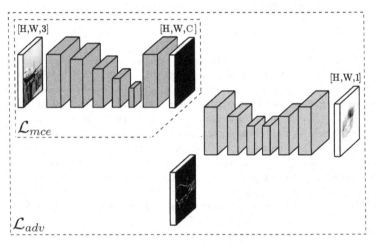

Fig. 1. The segmentation network (orange/left) is fed with RGB images as input, and produces pixel-wise predicted maps as output. The discriminator (green/right) network is fed with the predicted maps or with the ground-truth label maps and determines if they are either real or false at pixel-wise level. (Color figure online)

Summarizing, the contributions of our work are the following

- We present a generic adversarial framework that leads to more accurate segmentation results than standalone segmentator.
- We introduce a simple encoder-decoder structure together with the pixel-wise loss function which define the discriminator.
- The generator uses a weight averaging technique that allows traditional machine learning optimizers such as Stochastic Gradient Descent (SGD) to find broader minima with almost no extra computational cost.
- Our experimental results show an improvement in labeling accuracy on both Pascal VOC 2012 and SegTrack-v2 datasets.

The rest of the paper is organized as follows. In the next section, we review related methods for semantic segmentation. In Sect. 3, we introduce our approach, where we first provide a brief background of generative adversarial networks, and then we describe the design and methodology of our proposed architecture. Experimental results are shown in Sect. 4, where we report our results in Pascal VOC 2012 and SegTrack-v2 datasets. In Sects. 5 and 6 is presented an experimental ablation study and the conclusions, respectively.

2   Related Work

2.1   Generative Adversarial Networks

Goodfellow et al. proposed an adversarial framework [7] capable of learning deep generative models. It can be described as a minmax game between the generator G, which learns how to generate samples which resemble real data, and a discriminator D, which learns to discriminate between real and fake data. Throughout this process, G indirectly learns how to model the input image distribution p_{data} by taking samples z from a fixed distribution p_z (e.g. Gaussian) and forcing the generated samples $G(z)$ to match the natural images x. The objective loss function is defined as

$$\min_G \max_D \mathcal{L}(D, G) = \mathbb{E}_{\mathbf{x} \sim p_{\text{data}}}\left[\log\left(D(x)\right)\right] + \mathbb{E}_{z \sim p_z}\left[\log(1 - D(G(z)))\right]. \qquad (1)$$

GANs have drawn significant attention from the computer vision community. Numerous works such as [1,8,26,28] have further extended and improved the original vanilla GAN [7]. Moreover, it has been used in a wide variety of applications including image generation [16,26], domain adaptation [11,14,30,37], object detection [18,33], video applications [23,31,32] and semantic segmentation [12,22,29,34].

2.2   Semantic Segmentation

CNN-based approaches have become very popular within the computer vision field. Semantic segmentation has not been an exception and many promising ideas have been based on CNNs. Some of their key contributions are the introduction of fully convolutional networks [2,21], the usage of pre-trained models (mostly based on ImageNet [5]) and the implementation of long and short skip connections for improving the gradient flow [27]. As a result, much accurate semantic segmentation results have been achieved. More recent state-of-the-art results, have employed advanced typologies [3,19,25,36] along with new proposals such dilated convolution [35] to increase the receptive field size, improved pyramid techniques [36] and even new loss functions like [12,22,24].

2.3   Adversarial Training for Semantic Segmentation

Unlike aforementioned methods regarding semantic segmentation, adversarial training for semantic segmentation uses an extra network, usually called discriminator, which provides feedback to the generator based on differences between the predictions and the ground-truth. Such a feedback is often modeled as an additional loss term. The same mechanism has been successfully applied to several semantic tasks such as medical image analysis and image-to-image translation [14,37].

In this work, we propose to use this adversarial methodology to learn the target distribution in a minmax fashion game between the generator and the discriminator. This approach is flexible enough to detect mismatches between model predictions and the ground-truth, without having to explicitly define these. As a result, more accurate segmentation masks than with traditional segmentation networks can be obtained.

3 Method

3.1 Model Architecture

As shown in Fig. 1, the proposed model architecture consists of two parts: the segmentation network and the discrimination network.

Segmentation/Generation Network. Given the generic attribute of the proposed framework, any network architecture designed for semantic segmentation task is suitable for being the segmentator. Its objective is to map an input image of dimension H × W × 3, to probability maps of size H × W × C, being C the number of semantic classes.

Discrimination Network. As discriminator, we introduce an encoder-decoder structure (see Fig. 2) which resembles an Auto-Encoder (AE) but without an explicit latent layer (bottleneck). It has H × W × C as an input image size and H×W×1 as an output confidence map size.

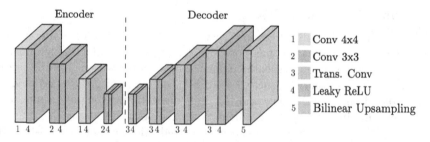

Fig. 2. The schematics of the proposed discriminator network.

3.2 Adversarial Framework

The generator and the discriminator are trained to optimize their corresponding loss function in an alternating fashion.

Training Generator. Given an input image $\mathbf{x}$ and its label y, the trainable parameters from the discriminator (θ_{disc}) are fixed and the generator parameters (θ_{gen}) are trained for one step. The objective function is defined as

$$\mathcal{L}_{\text{gen}}(\mathbf{x}, y; \theta_{\text{gen}}, \theta_{\text{disc}}) = \mathcal{L}_{\text{mce}}(G(\mathbf{x}; \theta_{\text{gen}}), y) + \lambda \mathcal{L}_{\text{adv}}(G(\mathbf{x}; \theta_{\text{gen}}); \theta_{\text{disc}}). \quad (2)$$

The loss function has two terms, the multi-class cross entropy ($\mathcal{L}_{\text{mce}}$) and the adversarial term ($\mathcal{L}_{\text{adv}}$). Furthermore, there is an extra term λ that provides control on the influence that the adversarial part has in the generator. While the $\mathcal{L}_{\text{mce}}$ uses the images $\mathbf{x}$ as an input to encourage G to predict the right class label at each pixel location, the $\mathcal{L}_{\text{adv}}$ tries to fool the discriminator by producing feature maps $\hat{y}$ close to the ground-truth distribution labels y, in order to further to recover high frequency details which have been overlooked by the generator. The $\mathcal{L}_{\text{mce}}$ can be seen as a modified version of binary cross entropy to tackle with multi-class problems. It is calculated by examining each pixel value individually and measures the distance (error) between each predicted pixel probability distribution and its real probability distribution over the classes. It can be defined as

$$\mathcal{L}_{\text{mce}} = -\sum_{h,w} \sum_{c \in C} y^{(h,w,c)} log(\hat{y}^{(h,w,c)}). \quad (3)$$

The $\mathcal{L}_{\text{adv}}$ can be seen as a binary cross entropy loss function applied to every single pixel. Such a multi-output discriminator was introduced by PatchGAN [14]. The idea is that while training the generator, the outputs from the discriminator (pixel-wise level) have to be 1, therefore classified as true, and consequently having an error equal to 0. It can be defined as

$$\mathcal{L}_{\text{adv}}(\hat{y}; \theta_{\text{disc}}) = \mathcal{L}_{\text{bce}}(\hat{y}, 1; \theta_{\text{disc}}) = -\sum_{h,w} log(D(\hat{y}; \theta_{\text{disc}})^{(h,w)}). \quad (4)$$

Training Discriminator. When the parameters from the generator (θ_{gen}) have already been updated, these are fixed and then we train on the D for one step. This time the gradients come from discriminator's objective function defined as

$$\mathcal{L}_{\text{disc}}(\hat{y}, y; \theta_{\text{disc}}) = \mathcal{L}_{\text{bce}}(\hat{y}, 0; \theta_{\text{disc}}) + \mathcal{L}_{\text{bce}}(y, 1; \theta_{\text{disc}}). \quad (5)$$

In this part of the training, given y the outputs from the discriminator have to be 1, therefore classified as true, and given $\hat{y}$ have to be 0, therefore classified as fake. Thus, on the one hand, the generator tries to minimize the adversarial loss ($\mathcal{L}_{\text{bce}}(\hat{y}, 1; \theta_{\text{disc}}) \rightarrow 0$, see Eq. (4)). On the other hand, the discriminator aims to maximize it ($\mathcal{L}_{\text{bce}}(\hat{y}, 0; \theta_{\text{disc}}) \rightarrow 0 \equiv \mathcal{L}_{\text{bce}}(\hat{y}, 1; \theta_{\text{disc}}) \rightarrow 1$, see Eq. (5)). This adversarial training described, follows the minmax game written as

$$\min_{\theta_{\text{gen}}} \max_{\theta_{\text{disc}}} \mathcal{L}(\theta_{\text{gen}}, \theta_{\text{disc}}). \quad (6)$$

Step by step, both the generator and the discriminator networks improve at their tasks. As a result, during inference the generative network produces label maps that are similar to the ground-truth.

3.3 Pixel-Wise Adversarial Loss

One key aspect in any adversarial setting is the composition of the adversarial loss. Previous publications use a loss based on traditional vanilla GAN, using a single binary decision per image. However, in this work we employ a different loss function, the pixel-wise adversarial loss. It makes a binary decision at pixel level. In other words, there are as many binary decisions as pixels in the input image (See in Fig. 3). Such loss function will provide more details and thus a more informative gradient can be back propagated.

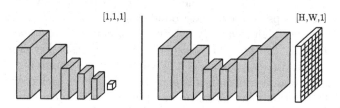

Fig. 3. (Left) Vanilla adversarial loss structure. (Right) Pixel-wise adversarial loss.

3.4 Averaging Weights

Stochastic Weight Averaging (SWA) [15] is a simple but effective algorithm for training any kind of neural network independently of its topology or loss function. The main idea consists of averaging of multiple points proposed by an SGD optimizer. In this way, it is possible to encounter a broader optima, which produces better generalization than conventional training methods.

Implementing SWA is rather straightforward and and not very compute intensive, we only need to keep updating the stochastic weight average θ_{swa}, written as

$$\theta_{\text{swa}} \leftarrow \frac{\theta_{\text{swa}} \cdot n + \theta_{\text{gen}}}{n+1}, \tag{7}$$

being n the number of skipped iterations of the SWA per generator iteration and θ_{gen} the generator parameters.

4 Experiments

In this section we present for a series of experiments evaluating the results on Pascal VOC 2012 and SegTrack-v2 datasets. We first give a detailed introduction of the experimental set up. Then, we discuss independently the results on the aforementioned dataset.

4.1 Experimental Settings

In the experiments, we use a model pre-trained on the ImageNet dataset [5] and Microsoft COCO [20] as our segmentation baseline network. After initializing our model with these pre-trained parameters, we train on Pascal VOC 2012 [6] and SegTrack-v2 [17] datasets. Our main evaluation metric is the mean Intersection-over-Union (mIoU) also known as Jaccard index and it is computed as

$$\text{mIoU} = \frac{1}{n} \sum_n \frac{|A_1 \bigcap A_2|}{|A_1 \bigcup A_2|}, \tag{8}$$

being n the number of input samples, and A_1 and A_2 the ground-truth and predicted label maps respectively. All the experiments have been implemented in a single NVIDIA GeForce GTX 1080 GPU.

We conducted the experiments adopting a segmentation network based on [12]. It integrates a modified version of DeepLabv2 [3] framework with ResNet-101 [10], where no multi-scale layer is used and the atrous spatial pyramid pooling (ASPP) substitutes the last classification layer. Moreover, the strides from the last two convolutional layers are modified, so that, the output feature maps size are exactly 1/8 of the input image size. Finally, dilated convolution in conv4 and conv5 layers are applied. Regarding the implementation of SWA, we maintain θ_{swa} (only used in the generator) and θ_{gen} separately, and we use the θ_{swa} at testing time. Algorithm 1 summarizes the training of the proposal model.

Algorithm 1. Training of the proposed architecture. All PASCAL VOC 2012 experiments in the paper used the default value $n_{\text{iter}} = 20000$, $n = 100$, $\alpha_{\text{gen}} = \alpha_{\text{disc}} = 0.00025$, $m = 16$.* (In Section SegTrack-v2 Dataset are further hyper-parameters introduced.)

1: Require: n_{iter}, number of iterations. n, number of skipped iterations of the SWA per generator iteration. α's, learning rate. m, batch size. $\hat{y}$, output from the generator.
2: Require: θ_{gen}^0 , initial generator parameters. θ_{disc}^0, initial discriminator parameters. $\theta_{\text{swa}}^0 = \theta_{\text{disc}}^0$, initial SWA parameters.
3: **for** $i < n_{\text{iter}}$ **do**
4:    Sample $\{\mathbf{x}^{(j)}\}_{j=0}^m$ a batch from images
5:    Sample $\{y^{(j)}\}_{j=0}^m$ a batch from masks
6:    # Train generator G
7:    $\theta_{\text{gen}} \leftarrow \theta_{\text{gen}} + \alpha_{\text{gen}}\nabla\mathcal{L}_{\text{gen}}(\mathbf{x}, y; \theta_{\text{gen}}, \theta_{\text{disc}})$
8:    **if** $mod(i, n) = 0$ **then**
9:       $\theta_{\text{swa}} \leftarrow \dfrac{\theta_{\text{swa}} \cdot n + \theta_{\text{gen}}}{n + 1}$
10:   **end if**
11:   # Train discriminator D
12:   $\theta_{\text{disc}} \leftarrow \theta_{\text{disc}} + \alpha_{\text{disc}}\nabla\mathcal{L}_{\text{disc}}(\hat{y}, y; \theta_{\text{disc}})$
13: **end for**

4.2   Training

Since our model is divided into two distinguishable parts, also two independent optimizers with their hyper-parameters are used during training.

Generator. The generator network integrates the SWA as optimization method. The learning rate used in the implementation has a polynomial decay in accordance with the number of iterations k, $\alpha_{gen}^k = \alpha_{gen}^0 \, (1 - \dfrac{k}{\text{max\_iter}})^p$, where the power decay $p = 0.9$ and the initial learning rate $\alpha_{gen}^0 = 0.00025$. The momentum is set to 0.9 and the weight decay is 0.00005.

Discriminator. The discriminator uses Adam optimizer with learning rate starting at 10^{-4}, $\beta_1 = 0.9$, $\beta_2 = 0.99$ and same annealing strategy as in the segmentation network. The adversarial loss $\mathcal{L}_{adv}$ is weighted by the hyper-parameter $\lambda = 0.01$, which gives its best result (see Fig. 4).

Hyper-Parameter Analysis

In order to determine the optimal hyper-parameters, we have conducted an independent grid search for each one of them. On one hand, we have investigated the effects of λ. It is responsible to determine how much $\mathcal{L}_{adv}$ will contribute to $\mathcal{L}_{gen}$. However, it does not exist a unique solution. We have found that λ is quite critical, since small modifications lead to big changes in mIoU score.

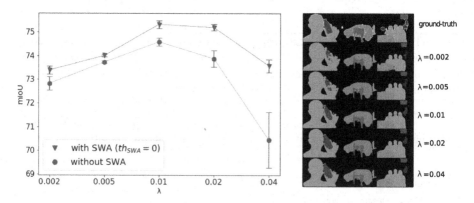

Fig. 4. The evolution of mIoU score behaves in a similar manner for both systems (with and without SWA). Having a peak performance when $\lambda = 0.01$. Results on Pascal VOC 2012 validation set.

On the other hand, n and th_{swa} hyper-parameters control the effect of SWA. First we look for the optimal threshold percentage of iterations that should be used for the weight averaging th_{swa}. We achieved best results when the weight averaging is applied from the beginning. Having a maximum score up to 73.1%, which is a gain of 1.0% with respect to the baseline. (Note that for this test

Table 1. Per-class validation test mIoU in Pascal VOC 2012 dataset.

Method	background	aeroplane	bicycle	bird	boat	bottle	bus	car	cat	chair	cow	dining table	dog	horse	motorbike	person	potted plant	sheep	sofa	train	tv monitor	mIoU
baseline	0.93	0.87	0.40	0.85	0.60	0.77	0.89	0.84	0.88	0.34	0.82	0.48	0.81	0.78	0.78	0.83	0.56	0.80	0.42	0.83	0.68	0.721
proposed	**0.94**	**0.88**	0.40	**0.88**	**0.69**	**0.78**	**0.93**	**0.86**	**0.89**	**0.37**	0.82	**0.60**	**0.83**	**0.79**	**0.83**	**0.85**	**0.63**	**0.82**	**0.49**	0.82	**0.74**	**0.754**

the discriminator is not involved). Second, after determining the optimum th_{swa} value, we have focused on the parameter n. This parameter has been found to have less fluctuations than th_{swa}, resulting in a maximum relative variation between different n's of 0.3%.

Pascal VOC 2012 Dataset

We evaluate our approach on the evaluation set from Pascal VOC 2012 dataset [6]. It is an extended benchmark for image segmentation that contains 1,464 and 1,449 images annotated with object instance contours for training and validation. These images have been slightly modified, by adding borders around the objects. Empirically, this procedure has been found beneficial for this dataset. With the further contribution of Segmentation Boundaries Dataset [9], we end up with 10,528 and 1,449 images for training and validation. The data augmentation is used; random scaling and cropping operations are applied while training. We train our model for 20K iterations with batch size 10 (see Fig. 5).

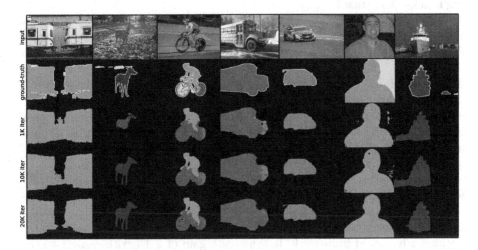

Fig. 5. Predicted masks at several stages of training in Pascal VOC 2012 dataset.

Our proposed framework clearly improves the baseline model, surpassing the mIoU among most of the classes and the overall. As can be seen in Table 1, when our proposed adversarial framework is fairly consistent, since it provides

Table 2. Validation results in Pascal VOC 2012 dataset. (Left) Proposed model compared to other adversarial approaches. (Right) Common segmentation metrics.

	Baseline	Adv.	Gain
[22]	71.8	72.0	0.2
[12]	73.6	74.9	1.3
[13]*	77.5	78.0	0.5
proposed	72.1	75.4	**3.3**

	Overall Acc.	mAcc.	fwIoU	mIoU
baseline	0.936	0.816	0.885	0.721
proposed	0.944	0.841	0.900	**0.754**

*Complete DeepLabv2 scheme used as a generative network.

a steady boost in almost all the classes from the dataset. Table 2 (right) reports in more detail the best result on the validation set and the improvement in the most common segmentation metrics respect to the baseline model.

We compare the proposed framework against other methods that also use adversarial training. Table 2 (left) shows how our approach has both a significant higher absolute gain and a higher mIoU. Note that both [12, 22] have the same baseline model as we have. However, we achieve a final score 3.4% higher than [22] and 0.5% than [12]. The model suggested in [13] uses a slightly different baseline version, since they do not remove the multi-scale fusion. As a result, their initial baseline is theoretically more advanced, therefore, stronger. Nevertheless, our method achieves a significant higher gain (2.8%) compared to [13].

SegTrack-v2 Dataset

We repeat the experiment, but this time we evaluate in SegTrack-v2 [17]. It is a video segmentation dataset with full pixel-level annotations on multiple objects at each frame within each video. It contains 14 video sequences with 24 objects and 947 frames. Every frame is annotated with a pixel-level object mask. As instance-level annotations are provided for sequences with multiple objects, each specific instance segmentation is treated as separate problem. In our implementation, we have 16 classes, since we were treating repeated classes as one. There are no extra images but the same sort of augmentation applied in Pascal VOC 2012 is present in that experiment during training. We train our model for 5K iterations with a batch size 10.

Figure 6 depicts the mIoU evolution during training. As it is expected, for both models the results get better over the training. However, using the adversarial set-up produces a boost on our model with respect to the baseline. Table 3 provides an overview of the best results observed on the validation set using the proposal adversarial framework. It achieves a gain of 2.3% with respect to the baseline. Some visual results are shown in Fig. 7, where top two rows belong to the Pascal VOC 2012 and bottom two rows to SegTrack-v2 validation set.

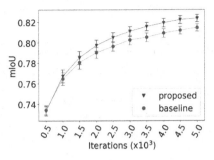

Table 3. Validation results in SegTrack-v2 dataset.

	Overall Acc.	mAcc.	fwIoU	mIoU
Baseline	0.989	0.871	0.980	0.812
Proposed	0.991	0.872	0.983	**0.831**

Fig. 6. Evolution of mIoU from the baseline and the adversarial proposal during training in SegTrack-v2 dataset.

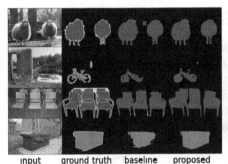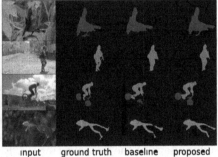

Fig. 7. Comparison of the predicted masks produced by the baseline and the proposed variant. (Left) Validation results in Pascal VOC 2012 dataset. (Right) Validation results in SegTrack-v2 dataset.

5   Ablation Study

In this last section, we present further experiments that support the proposed adversarial framework. First, we conduct a comparison study between pixel-wise and standard loss. And then, we evaluate different segmentation networks together with our framework.

5.1   Pixel-Wise vs Standard Loss

The usage of adversarial techniques to further improve the segmentation masks is still an open discussion. As mentioned above, standard loss [7] is by default the most widely extended. However, it is not always a reliable option. Empirically, we have observed the beneficial effects of pixel-wise loss (see Table 4). It offers more steady, general (independent of datasets) and accurate results. This is possible thanks to the capacity of producing better gradients which flow from the adversarial loss to the segmentation network.

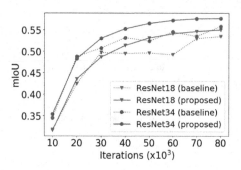

Table 4. Comparison of the different adversarial loss functions.

	Pascal VOC	SegTrackv2
Baseline	0.721	0.812
Standard	0.742	0.547
Pixel-wise	**0.754**	**0.831**

Fig. 8. Comparison of different segmentation networks architecture.

5.2 Flexibility Capacity of Our Approach

Finally, we have tested the versatility of our framework by using different architectures as a segmentation network. We replace our original segmentator topology with the DeepLabv3 [4]. In this newer version, the ASPP module has been augmented with image-level feature to capture longer range information. Furthermore, it includes batch normalization parameters to facilitate the training.

We have run the adversarial extension within DeepLabv3. Such architecture has been evaluated in ResNet18 and ResNet34, without pre-trained model and making usage of the improved ASPP. Figure 8 depicts the results.

6   Conclusion

In this paper, we present a novel end-to-end segmentation framework, making usage of a state-of-the-art pixel-wise adversarial loss for the discrimination network and the stochastic weight averaging. By training the discriminator in such an alternating fashion, all the experimental results get noticeably boosted, enhancing the final mIoU. Similar behaviour it is found on the ablation study, where we prove that our proposed adversarial scheme is effective and capable to lead to superior performances regardless of the segmentator.

References

1. Arjovsky, M., Chintala, S., Bottou, L.: Wasserstein GAN. arXiv preprint: arXiv:1701.07875 (2017)
2. Badrinarayanan, V., Kendall, A., Cipolla, R.: SegNet: a deep convolutional encoder-decoder architecture for image segmentation. arXiv preprint: arXiv:1511.00561 (2015)
3. Chen, L.C., Papandreou, G., Kokkinos, I., Murphy, K., Yuille, A.L.: DeepLab: semantic image segmentation with deep convolutional nets, atrous convolution, and fully connected CRFs. IEEE Trans. Pattern Anal. Mach. Intell. **40**(4), 834–848 (2018)

4. Chen, L.C., Papandreou, G., Schroff, F., Adam, H.: Rethinking atrous convolution for semantic image segmentation. arXiv preprint: arXiv:1706.05587 (2017)
5. Deng, J., Dong, W., Socher, R., Li, L.J., Li, K., Fei-Fei, L.: ImageNet: a large-scale hierarchical image database. In: IEEE Conference on Computer Vision and Pattern Recognition, CVPR 2009, pp. 248–255. IEEE (2009)
6. Everingham, M., Van Gool, L., Williams, C.K.I., Winn, J., Zisserman, A.: The PASCAL Visual Object Classes Challenge 2012 (VOC2012). Results http://www.pascal-network.org/challenges/VOC/voc2012/workshop/index.html
7. Goodfellow, I., et al.: Generative adversarial nets. In: Advances in Neural Information Processing Systems, pp. 2672–2680 (2014)
8. Gulrajani, I., Ahmed, F., Arjovsky, M., Dumoulin, V., Courville, A.C.: Improved training of Wasserstein GANs. In: Advances in Neural Information Processing Systems, pp. 5767–5777 (2017)
9. Hariharan, B., Arbelaez, P., Bourdev, L., Maji, S., Malik, J.: Semantic contours from inverse detectors. In: International Conference on Computer Vision (ICCV) (2011)
10. He, K., Zhang, X., Ren, S., Sun, J.: Deep residual learning for image recognition. In: Proceedings of the IEEE Conference on Computer Vision and Pattern Recognition, pp. 770–778 (2016)
11. Hoffman, J., et al.: CyCADA: cycle-consistent adversarial domain adaptation. arXiv preprint: arXiv:1711.03213 (2017)
12. Hung, W.C., Tsai, Y.H., Liou, Y.T., Lin, Y.Y., Yang, M.H.: Adversarial learning for semi-supervised semantic segmentation. arXiv preprint: arXiv:1802.07934 (2018)
13. Hwang, J.J., Ke, T.W., Shi, J., Yu, S.X.: Adversarial structure matching loss for image segmentation. arXiv preprint: arXiv:1805.07457 (2018)
14. Isola, P., Zhu, J.Y., Zhou, T., Efros, A.A.: Image-to-image translation with conditional adversarial networks. arXiv preprint (2017)
15. Izmailov, P., Podoprikhin, D., Garipov, T., Vetrov, D., Wilson, A.G.: Averaging weights leads to wider optima and better generalization. arXiv preprint: arXiv:1803.05407 (2018)
16. Karras, T., Aila, T., Laine, S., Lehtinen, J.: Progressive growing of GANs for improved quality, stability, and variation. arXiv preprint: arXiv:1710.10196 (2017)
17. Li, F., Kim, T., Humayun, A., Tsai, D., Rehg, J.M.: Video segmentation by tracking many figure-ground segments. In: Proceedings of the IEEE International Conference on Computer Vision, pp. 2192–2199 (2013)
18. Li, J., Liang, X., Wei, Y., Xu, T., Feng, J., Yan, S.: Perceptual generative adversarial networks for small object detection. In: IEEE CVPR (2017)
19. Lin, G., Milan, A., Shen, C., Reid, I.D.: RefineNet: multi-path refinement networks for high-resolution semantic segmentation. In: CVPR, vol. 1, p. 5 (2017)
20. Lin, T.-Y., et al.: Microsoft COCO: Common Objects in Context. In: Fleet, D., Pajdla, T., Schiele, B., Tuytelaars, T. (eds.) ECCV 2014, Part V. LNCS, vol. 8693, pp. 740–755. Springer, Cham (2014). https://doi.org/10.1007/978-3-319-10602-1_48
21. Long, J., Shelhamer, E., Darrell, T.: Fully convolutional networks for semantic segmentation. In: Proceedings of the IEEE Conference on Computer Vision and Pattern Recognition, pp. 3431–3440 (2015)
22. Luc, P., Couprie, C., Chintala, S., Verbeek, J.: Semantic segmentation using adversarial networks. arXiv preprint: arXiv:1611.08408 (2016)
23. Mathieu, M., Couprie, C., LeCun, Y.: Deep multi-scale video prediction beyond mean square error. arXiv preprint: arXiv:1511.05440 (2015)

24. Matthew, M.B.A.R.T., Blaschko, B.: The Lovász-Softmax loss: a tractable surrogate for the optimization of the intersection-over-union measure in neural networks (2018)
25. Peng, C., Zhang, X., Yu, G., Luo, G., Sun, J.: Large kernel matters–improve semantic segmentation by global convolutional network. In: 2017 IEEE Conference on Computer Vision and Pattern Recognition (CVPR), pp. 1743–1751. IEEE (2017)
26. Radford, A., Metz, L., Chintala, S.: Unsupervised representation learning with deep convolutional generative adversarial networks. arXiv preprint: arXiv:1511.06434 (2015)
27. Ronneberger, O., Fischer, P., Brox, T.: U-Net: convolutional networks for biomedical image segmentation. In: Navab, N., Hornegger, J., Wells, W.M., Frangi, A.F. (eds.) MICCAI 2015, Part III. LNCS, vol. 9351, pp. 234–241. Springer, Cham (2015). https://doi.org/10.1007/978-3-319-24574-4_28
28. Salimans, T., Goodfellow, I., Zaremba, W., Cheung, V., Radford, A., Chen, X.: Improved techniques for training GANs. In: Advances in Neural Information Processing Systems, pp. 2234–2242 (2016)
29. Souly, N., Spampinato, C., Shah, M.: Semi and weakly supervised semantic segmentation using generative adversarial network. arXiv preprint: arXiv:1703.09695 (2017)
30. Tsai, Y.H., Hung, W.C., Schulter, S., Sohn, K., Yang, M.H., Chandraker, M.: Learning to adapt structured output space for semantic segmentation. arXiv preprint: arXiv:1802.10349 (2018)
31. Tulyakov, S., Liu, M.Y., Yang, X., Kautz, J.: MoCoGAN: decomposing motion and content for video generation. arXiv preprint: arXiv:1707.04993 (2017)
32. Vondrick, C., Pirsiavash, H., Torralba, A.: Generating videos with scene dynamics. In: Advances in Neural Information Processing Systems, pp. 613–621 (2016)
33. Wang, X., Shrivastava, A., Gupta, A.: A fast R-CNN: hard positive generation via adversary for object detection. In: IEEE Conference on Computer Vision and Pattern Recognition (2017)
34. Xue, Y., Xu, T., Zhang, H., Long, L.R., Huang, X.: SegAN: adversarial network with multi-scale L_1 loss for medical image segmentation. Neuroinformatics **16**, 383–392 (2018)
35. Yu, F., Koltun, V.: Multi-scale context aggregation by dilated convolutions. arXiv preprint: arXiv:1511.07122 (2015)
36. Zhao, H., Shi, J., Qi, X., Wang, X., Jia, J.: Pyramid scene parsing network. In: IEEE Conference on Computer Vision and Pattern Recognition (CVPR), pp. 2881–2890 (2017)
37. Zhu, J.Y., Park, T., Isola, P., Efros, A.A.: Unpaired image-to-image translation using cycle-consistent adversarial networks. arXiv preprint (2017)

Visual Coin-Tracking: Tracking of Planar Double-Sided Objects

Jonáš Šerých$^{(\boxtimes)}$ and Jiří Matas

CMP Visual Recognition Group, Department of Cybernetics,
Faculty of Electrical Engineering, Czech Technical University in Prague,
Prague, Czech Republic
serycjon@cmp.felk.cvut.cz

Abstract. We introduce a new video analysis problem – tracking of rigid planar objects in sequences where both their sides are visible. Such *coin-like objects* often rotate fast with respect to an arbitrary axis producing unique challenges, such as fast incident light and aspect ratio change and rotational motion blur. Despite being common, neither tracking sequences containing coin-like objects nor suitable algorithm have been published.

As a second contribution, we present a novel *coin-tracking benchmark* containing 17 video sequences annotated with object segmentation masks. Experiments show that the sequences differ significantly from the ones encountered in standard tracking datasets. We propose a baseline coin-tracking method based on convolutional neural network segmentation and explicit pose modeling. Its performance confirms that coin-tracking is an open and challenging problem.

1 Introduction

Visual tracking is one of the fundamental problems in the field of computer vision. Given a video sequence and some defined object, e.g. by its location in the first frame, the task is to find its pose in each frame of the sequence. Until recently, standard visual tracking datasets like [17] or [23] have been only annotated using bounding boxes and subsequently, state-of-the-art trackers usually represented the objects pose as a rotated or axis-aligned bounding box. Recently, tracking-by-segmentation, also called video object segmentation, has gained on popularity, thanks to the introduction of segmentation-annotated datasets like DAVIS [20] and YouTube-VOS [24]. Here, object pose is a segmentation mask.

Visual tracking is an active research field; tracker performance improves significantly every year [15,16]. Nevertheless, a particular class of every-day objects remains challenging even for state-of-the-art methods, namely, rigid flat double-sided objects like cards, books, smartphones, magazines, coins[1], tools like knives, hand saws, sport equipment like table tennis rackets, paddles etc. Such objects often rotate fast producing unique challenges for trackers like fast incident light and aspect ratio change and rotational motion blur.

---

[1] Hence the problem name.

© Springer Nature Switzerland AG 2019
G. A. Fink et al. (Eds.): DAGM GCPR 2019, LNCS 11824, pp. 317–330, 2019.
https://doi.org/10.1007/978-3-030-33676-9_22

In this paper, we introduce an annotated *coin-tracking dataset*[2], CTR dataset in short, containing video sequences of coin-like objects. We then show that the proposed dataset is fundamentally different from the standard ones [15,23]. Finally, we propose a baseline coin-tracking method, called CTR-BASE, that outperforms classical state-of-the-art trackers in experiments on the CTR dataset.

2   Coin-Tracking Dataset

We define coin-tracking as tracking of rigid, approximately planar objects in video sequences. This means that at any time only one of the two sides - *obverse* (front) and *reverse* (back) - is visible. Unlike general objects, the rigidity and planarity of the coin-like objects means that the boundary between their two sides is always visible, except for occlusions by another object and position partially outside of the camera field of view. In this settings, the currently invisible side is fully occluded by the visible side and the visible side does not occlude itself at all. The state of a coin-like object is thus fully characterized by a visible side identification and a homography transformation to a canonical frame together with a possible partial occlusion mask.

However, because the objects in the CTR dataset are often symmetric, reflecting the real world coin-like object properties, the homography transformation might not be uniquely identifiable and thus we characterize the object state by a segmentation mask instead. Notice that unlike in standard general tracking sequences, where the exact extend of the tracked object is often not well defined due to the ambiguity of the initialization bounding box or segmentation, there is an unambiguous correspondence between a segmentation mask and a physical object in the case of coin-tracking.

Recent video object segmentation datasets [20,24] represent the object pose by segmentation as well, nevertheless, they contain mostly outdoor sequences of animals, people and vehicles. Therefore, there is a significant domain gap between these datasets and the proposed coin-tracking problem. Other datasets for tracking planar object exist, such as [5,18], but they only contain sequences with single side of the planar object visible. Moreover, in most cases the objects are fixed and the camera moves around them. This induces both different dynamics and appearance changes in the sequences as discussed in Sect. 2.1.

The are multiple levels of tracking of coin-like objects. In the simplest form, the tracker is initialized by a template of each side of the object and the object pose on the first frame of the sequence. One could also initialize the tracker on the first side only and require it to discover the reverse side without supervision. Moreover, a full 6D pose output (rotation and translation) together with a complete object surface reconstruction (including even the initially occluded parts of the object) could be required for sequences with known camera calibration.

The introduced CTR dataset contains 17 video sequences of coin-like objects, with total of 9257 frames and segmentation ground truth masks on every fifth frame. See Fig. 1 for examples of the sequences in the CTR dataset.

---

[2] Available at http://cmp.felk.cvut.cz/coin-tracking.

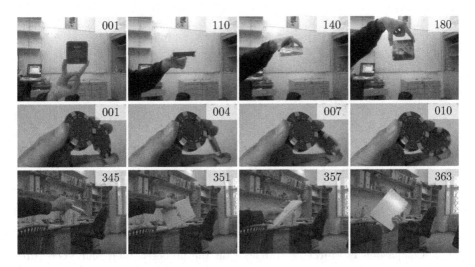

Fig. 1. Examples from the coin-tracking dataset (frame number in the top-right corner). Notice the effects of the out-of-plane rotation – fast illumination change, blur and significant aspect ratio change of the objects.

2.1 A Comparison with Other Datasets

The main motivation for introducing a new tracking dataset is its difference from the currently available tracking sequences. In this section we show some of the novel aspects of the proposed dataset.

The planar object tracking datasets [5, 18] are the closest to the CTR dataset, but they only contain a single sided view of the object; the viewing angle range is limited. In most of the sequences the tracked object is fixed to the background behind it, e.g. a poster fixed on a wall and the object motion in the sequence is induced by the camera motion only. On the contrary, the camera is static or close to static in many of the CTR sequences and it is the object that causes the motion. This difference is important since the two situations introduce different challenges to the visual tracking task.

When a planar object is fixed and a camera moves around it, the perceived out-of-plane rotation is relatively slow as the camera needs to move along a long arc in order to change the viewing angle significantly. On the other hand, when the main part of the perceived motion of the object in the sequence is caused by the physical motion of the object itself, as it is the case in the proposed sequences, the object out-of-plane rotation happens faster as it is physically easy to rotate coin-like objects.

Most state-of-the-art trackers, e.g. the winners of the VOT2018 tracking challenge [15] – MFT [1] and UPDT [2], represent the object pose as axis-aligned or rotated bounding box, while the aspect ratio change modeling is not common. Later in this section, we show that both the range and the speed of aspect ratio change in the CTR sequences is higher than in the VOT [14] and OTB [23] tracking datasets. Besides causing significant aspect ratio changes, the 3D rotation

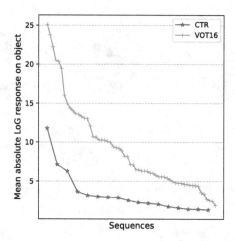

Fig. 2. Comparison of object "textureness" in the proposed CTR and VOT 2016 datasets, measured by the absolute value of Laplacian of Gaussian $\sigma = 0.8$ averaged over the tracked object pixels.

of the coin-like objects often induces fast changes of illumination as the object plane normal direction relative to the light sources changes rapidly. Apart from these differences, the objects in the CTR dataset are also less textured than the ones appearing in standard visual tracking datasets as discussed in the next section.

Textureness. As a measure of object textureness, we computed the Laplacian of Gaussian (LoG) responses and averaged their absolute values over the object pixels and all frames. Figure 2 shows that the typical object textureness in the CTR dataset is significantly lower than on the VOT 2016 dataset [14]. The lack of texture prevents tracking to be implemented by classical methods for homography estimation based on key-point correspondences.

Aspect Ratio Change. One of the unique properties of the coin-tracking dataset is the presence of strong changes in object aspect ratios, not usually encountered in the standard visual tracking datasets as shown in the following two experiments. In order to compute the aspect ratio statistics, we first compute minimal (rotated) rectangle bounding the ground truth segmentation mask on each frame. The aspect ratio (1) of the resulting rectangle with sides a, b is defined as

$$r(a,b) = \max\left(\frac{a}{b}, \frac{b}{a}\right) \tag{1}$$

We define the relative change in aspect ratios of two rectangles A, B with sides a_1, a_2 and b_1, b_2, respectively, as (2)

$$\Delta r(A, B) = \max\left(\frac{r(a_1, a_2)}{r(b_1, b_2)}, \frac{r(b_1, b_2)}{r(a_1, a_2)}\right) \tag{2}$$

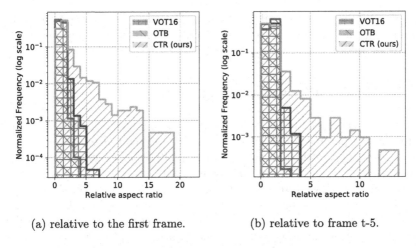

(a) relative to the first frame.   (b) relative to frame t-5.

Fig. 3. Histogram of aspect ratio changes

The maximum of the two ratios is chosen because only the magnitude of the aspect ratio change matters.

Aspect Ratio Change Relative to the First Frame. We have computed aspect ratio changes $\Delta r(R_1, R_t)$ between the bounding rectangle on the first frame and each of the other annotated frames in the sequence. We then represent each tested dataset (VOT2016, OTB, CTR) by a histogram of these aspect ratio changes in all the dataset sequences as shown in Fig. 3a. Notice that although the VOT2016 and OTB datasets are not restricted to rigid objects, i.e. their segmentation masks can change shape arbitrarily during the sequences, the CTR dataset contains significantly bigger changes in the aspect ratios.

Aspect Ratio Change Speed. In the proposed CTR dataset, the change in object aspect ratio is also faster than in the other compared datasets as shown in Fig. 3b. Instead of computing the aspect ratio change with respect to the first frame, the change is computed relative to the previous frame. Notice that because the CTR dataset does not contain ground truth segmentation masks on every frame, but only on every fifth, we measure $\Delta r(R_{t-5}, R_t)$ on all three datasets.

2.2 Evaluation Metric

We address the simplest form of the coin-tracking task, in which the tracker is initialized by an image of the front side of the tracked object on the first frame and an image of the back side later in the sequence, together with the respective ground truth segmentation masks.

We use *intersection over union* (IoU) as the evaluation metric – it is the standard metric for evaluating both segmentation and bounding box quality. In order to deal with frames with empty ground truth segmentation, i.e. with the object fully occluded or fully outside of the view, we augment the scoring function such that these frames do not contribute into the per-sequence total as proposed in [15].

3 The Baseline Coin-Tracking Method

Standard trackers represent the object by a bounding box and are thus unable to capture the perspective transformations common for coin-like objects. Trackers based on key-point correspondences can estimate homographies, but the low textureness of CTR objects prevents their use. Convolutional neural networks recently used for video object segmentation, e.g. [3,12,22], classify pixels as object or background taking into account large context thanks to large receptive fields of the neurons in the final layers. They do not consider the underlying homography transformations, but the segmentations capture the object extent in the image with high granularity.

Most video object segmentation methods use a deep neural network trained offline for general object segmentation. The network is then fine-tuned for tracking of a particular object at the initialization. One of the significant challenges in visual tracking is object appearance change and changes in the background in the video sequence. Because of this, trackers usually have to perform some kind of *online adaptation* to prevent performance deterioration soon after initialization. A simple adaptation scheme for video object segmentation has been proposed in ONAVOS [22], where the pixels classified as object with high confidence are treated as new object appearance examples. Background examples are taken from the parts of the image over a certain distance from the object. However, the online adaptation requires lengthy fine-tuning of the segmentation neural network on each frame, making the method slow.

An alternative approach has been proposed in FAST-VOS [6], where the segmentation is done by k-nearest neighbor search in an embedding space learned offline by a CNN. Instead of fine-tuning the embedding network on the first frame or later during online adaptation, the FAST-VOS method inserts dense embeddings into a k-NN classifier index. This makes the adaptation to a particular object faster and easier to interpret, compared to the network fine-tuning methods. The online adaptation proposed in [6] is similar to the original method in [22], selecting high confidence pixels – all of their $k = 5$ neighbors agree with the label – for the model update.

With all this in mind, we propose a baseline tracking method CTR-BASE, which is based on the tracking-by-segmentation FAST-VOS [6] method. After an input frame is segmented using the k-NN classifier, we explicitly model the object pose and possibly perform online adaptation.

3.1 Object Pose Estimation

We have performed experiments with the adaptation scheme of FAST-VOS but it did not work well on the coin-tracking sequences. The adaptation has quickly drifted and led to a complete failure of the tracker, either segmenting almost all of the background as the object or vice versa. Our experiments with distance-threshold based background adaptation as in [22] as well as experiments with other heuristics based on analysis of the connected components and other properties of the segmentation mask were not successful either. We hypothesize that one of the reasons that those adaptation techniques work reasonably well on the DAVIS dataset, but fail on the coin-tracking task, might be the length of the sequences. The mean number of frames in the DAVIS 2017 sequences is only 69.7 [21] while the mean number of frames in the coin-tracking sequence in the CTR dataset is 544, with several sequences as long as 1000 frames. The robustness of the online adaptation scheme is crucial on sequences of such length.

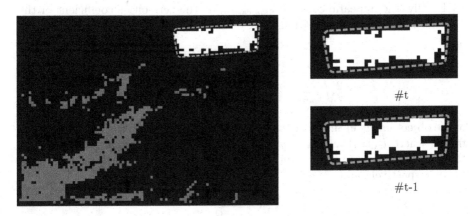

Fig. 4. Homography score computation. Left: the segmentation mask split into pixels inside (white) the object pose hypothesis (dashed green) and the rest (red). Right: Object visibility mask for the current and the last frames. (Color figure online)

In order to address the online adaptation in coin-tracking more robustly, we explicitly model the object pose using the homography to the ground-truth canonical frame. Both the object and the background pixel online adaptation is controlled by the agreement between the segmentation output by the k-NN classifier and the estimated pose model.

Objective Function. In each video frame, we search for the homography $\mathbf{H}_{*\to t}$ mapping the object on a ground truth frame into the current one, optimizing the objective function s, Eq. 5, composed of four parts computed as follows. First, we map the segmentation mask from the ground truth frame into the current frame using the homography. This splits the segmentation mask in the current frame into two parts, one inside and the other one outside of the hypothesized object contour as shown in Fig. 4. The s_{obj} part of the score function is set to the fraction of the segmentation mask located inside the contour, indicating the fraction of the segmentation explained by the object. This part of the score function penalizes segmentation outside of the object with the pose given by $\mathbf{H}_{*\to t}$.

The s_{cover} part of the score function s is the fraction of the pixels inside the hypothesized object contour being classified as the object. This part penalizes homographies mapping the object contour such that it is not well covered by the segmentation. Notice, however, that in the case of partial occlusion by other object, the segmentation should not cover the whole object. Since the occlusion mask is changing relatively slowly in CTR sequences, the s_{occl} component of the score function s is the IoU overlap of the current and last visibility mask, which is transformed to the current frame by $\mathbf{H}_{t-1\to t} = \mathbf{H}_{*\to t}\mathbf{H}_{*\to t-1}^{-1}$. This prefers homographies with a small occlusion change with respect to the previous frame.

Finally, the appearance score $s_{\text{appearance}}$ is the zero-offset coefficient of the zero-normalized cross-correlation (ZNCC) score

$$s_{\text{appearance}} = \frac{1}{2} + \frac{\sum\limits_{x,y\in O} (I_t(x,y) - \mu(I_t))(I_*(x,y) - \mu(I_*))}{2\sqrt{\sum\limits_{x,y\in O}(I_t(x,y) - \mu(I_t))^2 \sum\limits_{x,y\in O}(I_*(x,y) - \mu(I_*))^2}} \tag{3}$$

of the object image in the current frame and the template from the ground-truth frame, where $I_t(x,y)$ and $I_*(x,y)$ are the image values at coordinates $[x,y]$ in the current frame and the ground truth frame projected using the homography $\mathbf{H}_{*\to t}$ respectively and

$$\mu(I) = \frac{1}{|O|} \sum_{x,y\in O} I(x,y) \tag{4}$$

with O being the set of points segmented as object in both the ground truth and the current frame. The rationale behind introducing the appearance score is that it helps distinguishing a correct homography in case of objects with symmetric shape or partial occlusions. The final score, Eq. 5, of the homography is the product of these four components giving a number in 0–1 range:

$$s = s_{obj} \cdot s_{cover} \cdot s_{occl} \cdot s_{appearance} \tag{5}$$

Notice that compared to summing the score components, taking their product highlights drops in any of the score components and thus it is preferable for making our adaptation method conservative.

Optimization. Since the cost function described above is not differentiable, we use a probabilistic optimization procedure based on simulated annealing for finding $\mathbf{H}_{*\to t}$ for each frame. The optimization is initialized using either the homography found in the previous frame or using optical flow from the previous frame, in which case we uniformly sample 4 points from inside the object and transform them by the flow field to get 4 correspondences necessary for estimating the inter-frame homography. This is repeated 50 times and the $\mathbf{H}_{*\to t}$

maximizing the score function is chosen as the initialization of the following iterative optimization procedure.

In each step of the optimization a random homography matrix is sampled by randomly perturbing 4 control points at the corners of the object bounding box and computing the homography from the resulting 4 correspondences. Next, the homography score s is computed and compared to the current best score, s^*. The $H_{*\to t}$ hypothesis is accepted as the current estimate of the optimum with probability

$$p(s, s^*, T) = \begin{cases} 1 & \text{if } s > s^*, \\ e^{-\frac{s^*-s}{T}} & \text{otherwise,} \end{cases} \qquad (6)$$

where the T is decreasing in each iteration, allowing jumps from local minima but with decreasing probability during the optimization procedure. We also decrease the control point perturbation σ in each of the 350 iterations.

Depending on the ratio of pixels being classified as belonging to the obverse or the reverse side of the object, the optimization procedure is run against the respective ground truth frame. Finally, when the score of the best found homography is low, the tracker switches into a *lost* state and stays in it until a successful re-detection of the object.

The re-detection procedure is the same as the optimization described above, except for spending more time (400 iterations) sampling for the initialization pose and not using the information from the previous frame. The previous visibility mask used in computation of s_{occl} is replaced by the full object mask.

3.2 Online Adaptation

The proposed homography optimization procedure reduces the overall speed of the tracker, but we have observed that it finds a good solution reliably, unless the segmentation is grossly incorrect, enabling us to use online-adaptation on the long sequences in the CTR dataset. In particular, no online adaptation is attempted when the tracker is in the *lost* state, reducing the probability of making incorrect adaptation.

If the tracker is in the *tracking* state, new background and object embedding examples are added into the segmentation k-NN classifier. To stay on the safe side, only the pixels that are far from the object boundary and were incorrectly classified (with respect to the hypothesized object pose) are used as new background examples. Moreover, these pixels must not be connected to the object by the segmentation mask, otherwise they are not used for adaptation even if they are very far from the image.

For the new object examples, we select the pixels classified as background by the segmentation k-NN classifier that are not connected to the object edges, in other words only closed 'holes' in the object segmentation are adapted.

Altogether, the proposed online adaptation technique allows for conservative online adaptation, not making severe mistakes that would lead to complete failure of the tracker, as shown in the experiments in Sect. 4.2.

3.3   Implementation Details

We use a DeepLabv3+ [4] segmentation head on top of MobileNetv1 [10] backbone architecture. The MobileNet backbone was pretrained[3] on ImageNet [7], then trained for semantic segmentation on PASCAL VOC 2012 [8] enriched by the *trainaug* augmentations by [9]. We have used the Adam [13] optimizer with batch size 5 and initial learning rate of 7×10^{-4} decaying to 10^{-6} according to the *poly* schedule with decay power 0.9 for 53000 iterations. Finally, using the augmented triplet loss proposed by [6], we have fine-tuned the network for 492000 iterations on the YouTubeVOS dataset [24] to output dense 128-dimensional embeddings useful for segmentation by k-NN classifier. Given an $H \times W$ image, the network produces a per-pixel 128-D embeddings with output stride 4 (resolution $\frac{H}{4} \times \frac{W}{4}$). We use FAISS [11] library[4] with a flat L2 index for speeding up the nearest neighbor searches used in the segmentation. For the optical flow computation, we use ContinualFlow [19].

The method runs at around 7 s per frame at 1280×720 resolution with the majority of time spent optimizing the pose. The runtime drops without losing much performance when the pose optimization is done on lower resolution.

4   Experiments

In this section we show that the proposed CTR-BASE method outperforms general state-of-the-art trackers on the CTR dataset and retains good performance on the POT-210 [18] dataset. Then we demonstrate that the homography-based pose modeling prevents the CTR-BASE tracker from making fatal mistakes.

4.1   Baseline Experiment

In the standard visual tracking formulation, the tracker is initialized by the ground truth object pose, which can be represented by axis-aligned bounding box, rotated bounding box or segmentation mask [15,20,24]. This means that standard state-of-the-art trackers cannot be directly evaluated on the coin-tracking task in which the tracker is initialized on one frame from each side of the object. On the other hand, the coin-tracking task can be viewed as a long-term tracking on single side, enabling us to evaluate state-of-the-art long term trackers MBMD [25] and DASIAM_LT [26] – the winners of the VOT 2018 [15] long-term tracking challenge on the CTR dataset. Moreover, the VOT long-term tracking challenge requires a tracker confidence output on each frame, which allows us to run each tracker two times - once initialized from the obverse and once from the reverse side, merging the results by picking the one with higher tracker confidence. We have represented the axis-aligned bounding box outputs of the long-term trackers as segmentation masks and evaluated using the IoU metric. The results are shown in Table 1.

---

[3] Code and weights available at https://github.com/tensorflow/models/.

[4] Available at https://github.com/facebookresearch/faiss.

The proposed CTR-BASE method significantly outperforms both state-of-the-art bounding box trackers and a bounding box oracle, which outputs the bounding boxes of the ground truth segmentation masks. Computing IoU from the bounding boxes might not seem fair, but the performance gap demonstrates the need of representing the tracked object by segmentation, even with relatively compact objects present in the CTR dataset.

Table 1. The evaluation of the IoU overlap metric on the proposed CTR dataset. Notice that the CTR-BASE method outperforms both state-of-the-art long-term trackers and the bounding box oracle.

Sequence	MBMD	DASIAM_LT	bbox oracle	CTR-BASE (ours)
beermat	0.70	0.18	0.78	**0.83**
card1	0.72	0.71	0.73	**0.79**
card2	0.71	0.68	0.79	**0.93**
coin1	0.60	0.62	0.71	**0.80**
coin3	0.32	**0.46**	0.63	0.38
coin4	0.33	0.41	0.56	**0.65**
husa	0.35	0.40	0.51	**0.73**
iccv_bg_handheld	0.27	0.31	0.54	**0.33**
iccv_handheld	0.32	0.39	0.55	**0.50**
iccv_simple_static	0.37	0.31	0.51	**0.65**
iccv_static	0.34	0.40	0.55	**0.67**
pingpong1	**0.42**	0.38	0.64	0.33
plain	0.44	0.50	0.60	**0.74**
statnice	0.53	0.57	0.67	**0.87**
tatra	0.47	0.54	0.66	**0.86**
tea_diff_2	0.54	0.57	0.61	**0.87**
tea_same	0.53	0.52	0.63	**0.85**
Mean over all frames	0.47	0.44	0.63	**0.70**

In order to further test the CTR-BASE method, we evaluated it on the POT-210 [18] dataset, converting the ground – object corners – to segmentation (not modeling occlusions). The mean IoU (mIoU) is 0.81, showing that our method generalizes to POT-210 well. The best results were achieved on the *out-of-view* and the *perspective distortion* subsets of [18] with mIoU 0.89 and 0.88 respectively, while the worst on the *motion blur* subset with mIoU of 0.71.

4.2 Results on Confident Frames

The mean IoU score computed only on the frames where the CTR-BASE method is in the *tracking* state, i.e. online adaptation is allowed, improves from 0.70 to

Table 2. The IoU score of the CTR-BASE tracker evaluated only on the frames, where it is in the confident *tracking* state and the online adaptation is enabled. Notice that indeed the tracker is confident on the frames, where it performs well.

sequence	beermat	card1	card2	coin1	coin3	coin4	husa	iccv_bg_handheld	iccv_handheld	iccv_simple_static	iccv_static	pingpong1	plain	statnice	tatra	tea_diff_2	tea_same	average
IoU ×100	89	89	96	82	94	84	87	90	85	85	83	67	88	89	92	92	86	88
frames in *tracking* state %	89	68	93	64	02	21	69	17	15	29	28	17	42	46	34	87	47	47

0.88. This shows that the proposed tracker can correctly detect its own failures and only adapt when tracking reliably. Overall the tracker spends 47% of the frames in the *tracking* state as shown in Table 2.

5   Conclusion

We have introduced a novel video analysis problem – coin tracking – and presented a novel tracking CTR dataset consisting of 17 sequences of *coin-like* objects and ground truth segmentations. We have shown its dissimilarity to other tracking datasets. Besides studying the special properties of coin-like objects, the CTR dataset may benefit both training and the evaluation of general trackers, including video object segmentation methods, because it contains objects classes different from the ones encountered in the available datasets. Sequences in CTR are long, making online adaptation more challenging.

We have proposed a baseline CTR-BASE tracking method that enables robust online adaptation through explicit modeling of the tracked object pose and failure detection. The proposed CTR-BASE method outperforms state-of-the-art long-term trackers on the CTR dataset in terms of the IoU while generalizing well to the POT-210 dataset [18].

Finally, the advanced variants of the coin-tracking task described in Sect. 2, like the unsupervised back side discovery or full surface reconstruction, are challenging and open topics left for future research.

Acknowledgements. This work was supported by Toyota Motor Europe HS, by CTU student grant SGS17/185/OHK3/3T/13 and Technology Agency of the Czech Republic project TH0301019.

References

1. Bai, S., He, Z., Xu, T.B., Zhu, Z., Dong, Y., Bai, H.: Multi-hierarchical independent correlation filters for visual tracking. arXiv preprint: arXiv:1811.10302 (2018)
2. Bhat, G., Johnander, J., Danelljan, M., Khan, F.S., Felsberg, M.: Unveiling the power of deep tracking. In: Ferrari, V., Hebert, M., Sminchisescu, C., Weiss, Y. (eds.) ECCV 2018, Part II. LNCS, vol. 11206, pp. 483–498. Springer, Cham (2018). https://doi.org/10.1007/978-3-030-01216-8_30
3. Caelles, S., Maninis, K.K., Pont-Tuset, J., Leal-Taixé, L., Cremers, D., Van Gool, L.: One-shot video object segmentation. In: Proceedings of the IEEE Conference on Computer Vision and Pattern Recognition, pp. 221–230 (2017)
4. Chen, L.-C., Zhu, Y., Papandreou, G., Schroff, F., Adam, H.: Encoder-decoder with atrous separable convolution for semantic image segmentation. In: Ferrari, V., Hebert, M., Sminchisescu, C., Weiss, Y. (eds.) ECCV 2018, Part VII. LNCS, vol. 11211, pp. 833–851. Springer, Cham (2018). https://doi.org/10.1007/978-3-030-01234-2_49
5. Chen, L., et al.: Robust visual tracking for planar objects using gradient orientation pyramid. J. Electron. Imaging **28**(1), 1–16 (2019)
6. Chen, Y., Pont-Tuset, J., Montes, A., Van Gool, L.: Blazingly fast video object segmentation with pixel-wise metric learning. In: Proceedings of the IEEE Conference on Computer Vision and Pattern Recognition, pp. 1189–1198 (2018)
7. Deng, J., Dong, W., Socher, R., Li, L.J., Li, K., Fei-Fei, L.: ImageNet: a large-scale hierarchical image database. In: 2009 IEEE Conference on Computer Vision and Pattern Recognition, pp. 248–255, June 2009
8. Everingham, M., Van Gool, L., Williams, C.K.I., Winn, J., Zisserman, A.: The PASCAL Visual Object Classes Challenge 2012 (VOC2012) Results. http://www.pascal-network.org/challenges/VOC/voc2012/workshop/index.html
9. Hariharan, B., Arbelaez, P., Bourdev, L., Maji, S., Malik, J.: Semantic contours from inverse detectors. In: International Conference on Computer Vision (ICCV) (2011)
10. Howard, A.G., et al.: MobileNets: efficient convolutional neural networks for mobile vision applications. arXiv preprint: arXiv:1704.04861 (2017)
11. Johnson, J., Douze, M., Jégou, H.: Billion-scale similarity search with GPUs. IEEE Trans. Big Data (2019). https://doi.org/10.1109/TBDATA.2019.2921572
12. Khoreva, A., Benenson, R., Ilg, E., Brox, T., Schiele, B.: Lucid data dreaming for object tracking. In: The DAVIS Challenge on Video Object Segmentation (2017)
13. Kingma, D.P., Ba, J.: Adam: a method for stochastic optimization. In: Proceedings of the 3rd International Conference on Learning Representations (ICLR) (2014)
14. Kristan, M., et al.: The visual object tracking VOT2016 challenge results. In: Hua, G., Jégou, H. (eds.) ECCV 2016, Part II. LNCS, vol. 9914, pp. 777–823. Springer, Cham (2016). https://doi.org/10.1007/978-3-319-48881-3_54
15. Kristan, M., et al.: The sixth visual object tracking VOT2018 challenge results. In: Leal-Taixé, L., Roth, S. (eds.) ECCV 2018, Part I. LNCS, vol. 11129, pp. 3–53. Springer, Cham (2019). https://doi.org/10.1007/978-3-030-11009-3_1
16. Kristan, M., et al.: The visual object tracking VOT2015 challenge results. In: Proceedings of the IEEE International Conference on Computer Vision Workshops, pp. 1–23 (2015)
17. Kristan, M., et al.: A novel performance evaluation methodology for single-target trackers. IEEE Trans. Pattern Anal. Mach. Intell. **38**(11), 2137–2155 (2016)

18. Liang, P., Wu, Y., Lu, H., Wang, L., Liao, C., Ling, H.: Planar object tracking in the wild: a benchmark. In: 2018 IEEE International Conference on Robotics and Automation (ICRA), pp. 651–658. IEEE (2018)
19. Neoral, M., Šochman, J., Matas, J.: Continual occlusion and optical flow estimation. In: Jawahar, C.V., Li, H., Mori, G., Schindler, K. (eds.) ACCV 2018, Part IV. LNCS, vol. 11364, pp. 159–174. Springer, Cham (2019). https://doi.org/10.1007/978-3-030-20870-7_10
20. Perazzi, F., Pont-Tuset, J., McWilliams, B., Van Gool, L., Gross, M., Sorkine-Hornung, A.: A benchmark dataset and evaluation methodology for video object segmentation. In: Computer Vision and Pattern Recognition (2016)
21. Pont-Tuset, J., Perazzi, F., Caelles, S., Arbeláez, P., Sorkine-Hornung, A., Van Gool, L.: The 2017 davis challenge on video object segmentation. arXiv preprint: arXiv:1704.00675v2 (2017)
22. Voigtlaender, P., Leibe, B.: Online adaptation of convolutional neural networks for video object segmentation. In: British Machine Vision Conference (BMVC) (2017)
23. Wu, Y., Lim, J., Yang, M.H.: Object tracking benchmark. IEEE Trans. Pattern Anal. Mach. Intell. **37**(9), 1834–1848 (2015)
24. Xu, N., et al.: YouTube-VOS: sequence-to-sequence video object segmentation. In: Ferrari, V., Hebert, M., Sminchisescu, C., Weiss, Y. (eds.) ECCV 2018, Part V. LNCS, vol. 11209, pp. 603–619. Springer, Cham (2018). https://doi.org/10.1007/978-3-030-01228-1_36
25. Zhang, Y., Wang, D., Wang, L., Qi, J., Lu, H.: Learning regression and verification networks for long-term visual tracking. arXiv preprint: arXiv:1809.04320 (2018)
26. Zhu, Z., Wang, Q., Li, B., Wu, W., Yan, J., Hu, W.: Distractor-aware siamese networks for visual object tracking. In: Ferrari, V., Hebert, M., Sminchisescu, C., Weiss, Y. (eds.) ECCV 2018, Part IX. LNCS, vol. 11213, pp. 101–117. Springer, Cham (2018). https://doi.org/10.1007/978-3-030-01240-3_7

Exploiting Attention for Visual Relationship Detection

Tongxin Hu[1(✉)], Wentong Liao[1], Michael Ying Yang[2], and Bodo Rosenhahn[1]

[1] Leibniz University Hannover, Hanover, Germany
hutong@tnt.uni-hannover.de
[2] University of Twente, Enschede, Netherlands

Abstract. Visual relationship detection targets on predicting categories of predicates and object pairs, and also locating the object pairs. Recognizing the relationships between individual objects is important for describing visual scenes in static images. In this paper, we propose a novel end-to-end framework on the visual relationship detection task. First, we design a spatial attention model for specializing *predicate* features. Compared to a normal ROI-pooling layer, this structure significantly improves Predicate Classification performance. Second, for extracting relative spatial configuration, we propose to map simple geometric representations to a high dimension, which boosts relationship detection accuracy. Third, we implement a feature embedding model with a bi-directional RNN which considers *subject, predicate* and *object* as a time sequence. We evaluate our method on three tasks. The experiments demonstrate that our method achieves competitive results compared to state-of-the-art methods.

1 Introduction

In recent years, deep learning technology has achieved great success in computer vision tasks, such as object detection techniques [13, 26, 27], pose estimation [32], tracking [10], AI games [1, 29]. However, visual scene understanding remains open challenging tasks. Particularly, recognizing the relationships between objects is important for describing visual scenes in static images. It provides rich information for other visual tasks, such as Visual Turing Test [9]. Reasoning about the pair-wise interactions between objects is a visual-language task which builds the connection between visual images and human natural languages. A visual relationship is generally defined as two interacting objects combined together via a predicate, as illustrated in Fig. 1. The interacting objects are divided into *subject* and *object*. Following the definition in [20], we represent the visual relationship as a triplet *<subject, predicate, object>*.

Traditional methods [6, 28] consider this problem as a pure classification task which treats the combination of *<subject, predicate, object>* as a single category. Due to a large number of different possible combinations, such method requires a huge amount of training samples. It is difficult to collect enough samples of phrase combinations for training a reliable model, especially the unusual

© Springer Nature Switzerland AG 2019
G. A. Fink et al. (Eds.): DAGM GCPR 2019, LNCS 11824, pp. 331–344, 2019.
https://doi.org/10.1007/978-3-030-33676-9_23

< logo, on, shirt >
< man, holding, plate >
< man, has, hand>
< sign, with, pole>
...

(a) object detection   (b) visual relationship detection

Fig. 1. The ground truth of visual relationship detection for a given image. With the localized objects, relationships of pair-wise objects are represented.

phrases which might appear rarely in images (*i.e.* long-tail problem). For example, the phrase <*man, ride, horse*> is usual but combination <*kid, ride, dog*> is rare in the dataset. Another approach is to separately detect the object and predicate classes, which treats predicates as individual categories [4,20,37]. Our approach adopts such a strategy to reduce the dimensional complexity and avoid the long-tail problem caused by unusual phrases. Objects and predicates provide supplementary information to each other [17,18,34]. To leverage the dependencies, many recent works [17,18,34] propose to recognize objects and predicate jointly.

Based on the observation that objects and predicates affect each other, we propose a feature embedding model in our network. In the relationship triplet <*subject, predicate, object*>, as shown in Fig. 1, each element has semantic correlations with the next one. For each relationship triplet, we consider that the three elements are in a time sequence. The feature embedding process encodes the semantic correlations among three branches. Since the recurrent neural network is mostly adopted to deal with time sequence input, we apply a bi-directional RNN to compute the feature embedding for three branches. By observing the previous approaches, we find two problems: (1) Current strategies group the detected objects or object proposals to object pairs and use the union bounding boxes to extract union features, which are leveraged as the fundamental feature expressions of predicates [4,17,18,20,34]. Since union features are extracted using the union boxes of object pairs, background information is also included. The background information may distract the model's attention from the interaction between two objects, since the background is normally very complex and contains noise. However, the background also provides local contextual information which is useful for understanding interactions. Motivated by this observation, we propose a spatial attention model for specializing predicate features. (2) Spatial information, including relative locations and relative scales, is important for understanding the interactions between objects. However, using simple geometric representations [22,37,40] is not so effective. To solve this problem, we propose a new spatial feature extraction structure which maps the simple geometric representation to a high dimension.

Contributions. In this work, we propose a novel end-to-end model to incorporate attention and semantic correlations for visual relationship detection. The novelties of our work are: (1) We design a spatial attention model which constrains the network focusing more on the most important regions. (2) We introduce a new spatial feature extraction model which significantly improves the detection performance. (3) We implement a feature embedding model which encodes the semantic correlations among *subject, predicate* and *object* branches. Experimental results display that our method achieves competitive performance, compared to state-of-the-art methods.

2 Related Work

Over the decade, a number of researches [4,17,18,35,37–39] investigate the visual relationship detection task. In earlier days, efforts focused on learning specific relationships, *e.g.* spatial relations [3,15], physical support relations [12,36] or actions [8,25,33]. Many previous works proposed to use the visual relationship as a complementary tool for other visual tasks, such as image retrieval [21,24], image captioning [2,7] and scene understanding [11,41]. Fundamentally different from these previous works, our approach targets on generic visual relationship detection. Our method extends the variety of relationships. It can not only recognize positional relations (*"above"*) and verbs (*"walk on"*) but also prepositions (*"with"*) and functional relations (*"of"*).

Contemporary works pay more attention to recognize more general relationships. In [5,6,28], the visual task is considered as a pure classification task through recognizing visual phrases, which are the alliance of object and predicate categories. Such methods face difficulties because of the large combination space and long-tail problem. Another strategy is to implement object and predicate classifiers separately [19,23,39,40]. Lu *et al.* leverage semantic word embeddings (*i.e.* language priors) for recognizing predicates in [20]. Dai *et al.* [4] introduce Deep Relational Network for exploring statistical relations between object and predicate categories. Yu *et al.* [37] leverage both internal and external linguistic knowledge to regularize training process. In [17], Li *et al.* converge several subgraphs whose feature information was exchanged with object features. In [35], Yang *et al.* exploit the contextual information between objects and predicates through Graph Convolutional Network. Zellers *et al.* [38] analyze repeated substructures in the dataset and design to let the model learn from scene graph priors.

The most relevant works are [18,34], which propose to jointly detect objects and pair-wise relationships. In [34], messages are passed iteratively between object and predicate branches through the construction of the scene graph. In [18], Li *et al.* additionally introduce new convolutional features (*i.e.* region captions), features of three semantic branches are jointly refined. Different from their methods, we propose a feature embedding model which encodes the time dependencies and semantic correlations between objects and relationships. We also design a spatial attention model which constrains a higher attention for predicates. Experiments show that our proposed method performs better.

3   Framework

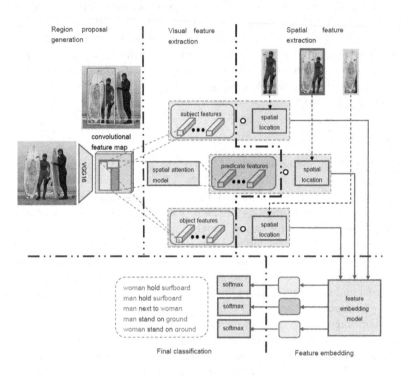

Fig. 2. An overview of our proposed framework.

An overview of our proposed framework is illustrated in Fig. 2. It contains object and predicate branches, where the object branch is divided into *subject* and *object* branch. Our overall network consists of five parts: (1) Object proposal generation. It aims to generate Region of Interests for objects and predicates. (2) Visual feature extraction. It targets on obtaining feature vectors based on obtained convolutional feature maps. (3) Spatial configurations. In addition to visual feature information, we also extract relative spatial information. (4) Feature embedding. Feature vectors of parallel branches are fused to generate an embedded feature vector, which indicates the semantic correlations of *subject*, *predicate* and *object*. (5) Final classification. Categories of *subject*, *predicate* and *object* are predicted, which are the final outputs of our network. In the following, we describe the involved parts in more detail.

3.1   Object Proposal Generation

The input of our entire network is an original image without any preprocessing. The foundation of visual relationship detection is object recognition. Therefore, we remove the last three fully connected layers and the last max pooling layer of

VGG-16 [30], and use 13 convolutional layers to generate convolutional feature map $X \in \mathbb{R}^{W \times H \times K}$, where K is the channel size. Then we apply the Region Proposal Network [27] to generate object ROIs (Region of Interests) [17,18]. We randomly group the obtained object proposals into object pairs. If we retain N object proposals from RPN, in this step we group them into $N \times (N - 1)$ object pairs, which are considered as *predicate* proposals in the following detection procedure. We split the object proposals into two subsets, i.e. *subject* and *object* proposals. These two subsets share the same layers and the same parameters.

3.2   Visual Feature Extraction

For different branches in our network, we require their corresponding features. For *subject* and *object* branches, we feed the shared convolutional feature map and the generated object proposals to a ROI-pooling layer. We acquire the *subject* and *object* visual feature vectors of size $512 \times 7 \times 7$ and flatten them. Through two 512-dimensional FC layers, we obtain 512-dimensional *subject* and *object* visual feature vectors.

A different feature specialization structure is implemented for the *predicate* branch. The grouped object pairs, i.e. *predicate* ROIs, contain background information. The most important parts of each *predicate* ROI are the object parts which form the specific *predicate* ROI. On the one hand, the background information may distract the network's attention on *subject* and *object*; on the other hand, it may be the supplemental information for *predicate* branch. So we wish to strengthen the information of object parts and also weaken the background information. In [16], Laskar *et al.* propose a model which combines background information and object proposals' features in a single feature representation for image retrieval task. Motivated by this observation, we propose a spatial attention model for *predicate* branch in our visual relationship detection task.

Spatial Attention Mechanism. We develop the spatial attention model for specializing *predicate* features. The grouped object pair, i.e. the *predicate* ROI $\mathcal{R}_{pr}$ is mapped to the convolutional feature map $X \in \mathbb{R}^{W \times H \times K}$. The mapped *predicate* ROI is represented as $\mathcal{R}'_{pr} \in \mathbb{R}^{W_{pr} \times H_{pr}}$. We define an attention map $A \in \mathbb{R}^{W_{pr} \times H_{pr}}$. This attention map is computed for all the K channels. The two mapped objects, which are employed to form *predicate* ROI, are denoted as $\mathcal{R}'_s$ and $\mathcal{R}'_o$. For each spatial position p on attention map A:

$$A_p = \begin{cases} 1, & \text{if } p \in \mathcal{R}'_s \cup \mathcal{R}'_o \\ M_p, & \text{if } p \in \mathcal{R}'_{pr} \text{ and } p \notin \mathcal{R}'_s \cup \mathcal{R}'_o \end{cases} \tag{1}$$

$p \in \mathcal{R}'_s \cup \mathcal{R}'_o$ denotes that the location point p lies inside the mapped *subject* ROI $\mathcal{R}'_s$ or *object* ROI $\mathcal{R}'_o$. $p \in \mathcal{R}'_{pr}$ and $p \notin \mathcal{R}'_s \cup \mathcal{R}'_o$ means that p lies in the background region of mapped *predicate* ROI $\mathcal{R}'_{pr}$. The saliency map M is defined as:

$$M_p = \sum_{k=1}^{K} X_{k,p}, \text{for } p \in \mathcal{R}'_{pr} \tag{2}$$

where $X_k \in X, k = 1...K$. We compute the max-normalization to ensure $M_p \in [0,1]$. For each $X_k \in X$, activation occurs:

$$\tilde{X}_{k,p} = \begin{cases} A_p X_{k,p}, & \text{if } p \in \mathcal{R}'_s \cup \mathcal{R}'_o \\ g(A_p) X_{k,p}, & \text{if } p \in \mathcal{R}'_{pr} \text{ and } p \notin \mathcal{R}'_s \cup \mathcal{R}'_o \end{cases} \tag{3}$$

The applied $g(\cdot)$ function is:

$$g(a) = \lambda_1 + \lambda_2 a^\phi \tag{4}$$

Constants $\lambda_1, \lambda_2 \in (0,1)$ are selected to satisfy the constraint $g(\cdot) < 1$.

Through this method, for each *predicate* ROI, the feature values of object pairs are activated by 1. The background information on *predicate* ROI is activated by values smaller than 1. So the effectiveness of background information for *predicate* branch is weakened.

After the computation with the attention map, max-pooling is implemented for *predicate* ROI as in normal ROI-pooling operation. The following process is the same as for *subject* and *object* branch, we use another two 512-dimensional FC layers for obtaining *predicate* visual feature vector.

3.3 Spatial Configurations

Previous attempts have proven that relative spatial configuration is important to the visual relationship detection task. We implement and compare two approaches for extracting spatial features.

Dual Mask. For each object pair, we crop the *subject* bounding box on the original image and define a binary mask for *subject*, where the pixels inside this bounding box are set to 1 and the others are 0. We perform the same process for the *object* bounding box, too. The two binary masks for *subject* and *object* are down-sampled and stacked to form the dual mask $M_D \in \mathbb{R}^{32 \times 32 \times 2}$. Through three convolutional layers and an FC layer, we obtain the *predicate* spatial feature vector. We concatenate this spatial feature vector with the *predicate* visual feature vector obtained from spatial attention model. The concatenated feature vector passes through a 512-dimensional FC layer and we obtain the new *predicate* feature.

Mapping Geometric Representation to a High Dimension. In another method, we first use 6-dimensional, 8-dimensional, and 6-dimensional vectors to express spatial information for three branches and then map the location information to a high dimension. From the object detector, we obtain *subject* $o_s = [x_s, y_s, w_s, h_s]$, *object* $o_o = [x_o, y_o, w_o, h_o]$ and also *predicate* bounding boxes $o_{pr} = [x_{pr}, y_{pr}, w_{pr}, h_{pr}]$. For *subject*, the geometric representation is:

$$\left[\frac{x_s - x_o}{w_o}, \frac{y_s - y_o}{h_o}, \log \frac{w_s}{w_o}, \log \frac{h_s}{h_o}, x_{s,central}, y_{s,central} \right] \tag{5}$$

where $[x_{s,central}, y_{s,central}]$ is the central point coordinate of the *subject* bounding box. $\frac{x_s - x_o}{w_o}$ and $\frac{y_s - y_o}{h_o}$ encode the normalized translation between *subject* and *object* bounding box. $\log \frac{w_s}{w_o}$ and $\log \frac{h_s}{h_o}$ represent the weight and height ratio of two boxes.

For *object*, the representation is:

$$\left[\frac{x_o - x_s}{w_s}, \frac{y_o - y_s}{h_s}, \log \frac{w_o}{w_s}, \log \frac{h_o}{h_s}, x_{o,central}, y_{o,central} \right] \tag{6}$$

And for *predicate* branch:

$$\left[\frac{x_s - x_{pr}}{w_{pr}}, \frac{y_s - y_{pr}}{h_{pr}}, \log \frac{w_s}{w_{pr}}, \log \frac{h_s}{h_{pr}}, \frac{x_o - x_{pr}}{w_{pr}}, \frac{y_o - y_{pr}}{h_{pr}}, \log \frac{w_o}{w_{pr}}, \log \frac{h_o}{h_{pr}} \right] \tag{7}$$

All three geometric representations are embedded in a high dimension. Sine and cosine calculations with different wavelengths [31] are calculated to compute the embedding:

$$E_{(g,2i)} = \sin\left(\frac{g}{10000^{\frac{2i}{D}}} \right), i = 0, ..., \left(\frac{D}{2} - 1 \right), i \in \mathbb{N} \tag{8}$$

$$E_{(g,2i+1)} = \cos\left(\frac{g}{10000^{\frac{2i+1}{D}}} \right), i = 0, ..., \left(\frac{D}{2} - 1 \right), i \in \mathbb{N} \tag{9}$$

where E denotes the embedded features in high dimension. g means the current spatial representation. D is the dimension of this mapping model and we select $D = 32$.

After the embedding process, we concatenate the spatial feature vectors respectively with the *subject*, *predicate*, and *object* visual feature vectors. We use one 512-dimensional FC layer for *subject* and *object* branches, and another 512-dimensional FC layer for *predicate* branch, to obtain new feature vectors for these three branches.

3.4   Feature Embedding

Information for objects and relationships is correlated. Through the iterative message processing among different branches, prediction performances for three branches will all be improved. Motivated by this thought, we add a feature embedding architecture after our feature extraction structure.

In our feature embedding model, we consider *subject*, *predicate* and *object* features as a time sequence. We apply the bi-directional RNN to compute the feature embedding for three branches. Our bi-RNN network accepts *subject* feature as the input of a sequence at the first time point t_1. *Predicate* feature is the input at the second time point t_2 of the time sequence and *object* feature the input at the third time point t_3. For our visual relationship detection task, the order of input features is really important for the final predictions. We take the hidden states in the forward and backward directions at the last time point, i.e. the third time point, as the embedded feature. It embeds the time dependency

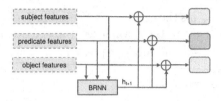

Fig. 3. Feature embedding model with a bi-directional recurrent neural network. We take the hidden states at the last time point as the embedded feature and then concatenate it respectively with *subject, predicate* and *object* features obtained from the third step.

of three branches. We concatenate this time-sequence-based embedded feature respectively with the previous *subject, predicate* and *object* features. The concatenated features are directly used for the final classification task. The feature embedding procedure using Bi-RNN is illustrated in Fig. 3.

4   Experiments

4.1   Implementation Details

Model Details. We initialize our model by a pre-trained VGG-16 [30] network on ImageNet. Instead of using original 4096, we employ 512 neurons in the fully connected layers, and the weights are initialized using the weights of the pre-trained model. The other parameters are initialized randomly.

Training Details. At first, we train the Region Proposal Network. Then we train the complete network with a mini-batch which contains only one image. After RPN, we use NMS with a threshold of 0.7 and keep at most 2000 object proposals (In testing, we set the threshold to 0.3 and keep at most 300 object proposals). Then we sample 256 object ROIs per image. We sample 512 predicate ROIs, of which 25% are positive. Our loss is the weighted sum of the cross-entropy for objects, the cross-entropy for predicates and the smooth L1 loss for box regression, the ratio is 1:1:0.2. We optimize using SGD with gradient clipping on GTX 1080, with a learning rate of $lr = 0.01$ which will be divided by 10 after every three epochs. The training process stops after 15 epochs and the running time is about three days.

4.2   Dataset and Evaluation

Dataset. We evaluate our proposed method on the cleansed Visual Genome [14] dataset. In previous works, there are different ways of data cleaning and dataset splitting. We use the filtered data from [34] where the most frequent 150 object and 50 predicate categories are chosen. We follow the train/test dataset splits in [34], where the training set contains 57723 and the testing set 26223 images.

Performance Metric. We adopt the same performance metric reported in [20], i.e. the *Top-K recall*, or represented as Rec@K. Rec@K denotes the number of correctly detected relationships in the top K relationship predictions. Following [20], we apply Rec@50 and Rec@100 for evaluation. We use this metric instead of using *mean average precision* mAP because the ground truth annotations applied for evaluation are incomplete.

Task Settings. We evaluate our methods on three tasks: (1) Predicate Classification(PredCls): The inputs are the object ground truth boxes and labels together with the image. We only evaluate the classification performance of *predicate* in this task. (2) Phrase Recognition(PhrRecog): Taken the image as input only, the model predicts *subject, predicate, object* together, and also the union bounding boxes of object pairs. If the overlap between the predicted union box and the ground truth box is larger than 0.5, the prediction will be considered as correct. (3) Relationship Recognition(RelRecog): The input is an image only. This task targets on localizing object pairs and predicting categories of *predicate* together with object pairs. Both two bounding boxes are required to have an overlap larger than 0.5 with ground truth boxes, for correct recognition.

4.3 Ablation Study

In our network, we propose a spatial attention model, a spatial feature extraction structure which embeds simple geometric representations in a higher dimension, and a feature embedding model. To evaluate how these parts influence the predictive performance of our final model, we perform ablation studies. The left columns of Table 1 display whether the spatial attention model (SA), the spatial feature extraction network (G or DM) and the feature embedding model (bi-RNN) is used or not.

In Table 1, we find that with the spatial attention model, the prediction performances on three tasks are all improved, especially on Predicate Classification. With SA, our network focuses more on the most important parts for *predicate* branch and it is not distracted by the other regions. This proves the effectiveness of 'attention'. The relative spatial configuration boosts prediction performances significantly. It provides supplementary information to simple visual feature representations. Comparing the two spatial feature extraction methods, we find that DM is slightly better than G. So we adopt DM to distill relative spatial information in our final network. Adding the feature embedding model to our network further improves the prediction performance. The feature embedding model is implemented to encode the dependencies of different branches. The improvement indicates that the features of different branches affect each other.

4.4 Comparison with Existing Methods

Previous works use different dataset splitting methods. Since we follow the data cleaning and train/test splitting in [34], we compare our results with those computed using the same dataset splitting. The comparison is listed in Table 2. In

Table 1. Ablation studies on our proposed network. We evaluate our method on the cleansed Visual Genome dataset and report the results for three evaluation tasks. All numbers in %. 'SA' represents the spatial attention model. 'G' indicates the spatial feature extraction structure which maps the geometric representation to a high dimension. 'DM' means the dual mask for extracting spatial features. 'bi-RNN' denotes the feature embedding model with the bi-directional recurrent neural network.

SA	G	DM	bi-RNN	PredCls		PhrRecog		RelRecog	
				Rec@50	Rec@100	Rec@50	Rec@100	Rec@50	Rec@100
–	–	–	–	29.0	40.0	7.3	10.1	3.0	4.8
✓	–	–	–	32.1	44.0	8.3	11.6	3.7	6.0
✓	✓	–	–	44.7	57.1	11.8	14.9	7.3	10.9
✓	–	✓	–	45.7	58.3	13.0	16.4	8.2	12.2
–	–	–	✓	47.5	60.5	17.4	20.9	**10.4**	**14.1**
✓	–	✓	✓	**48.9**	**61.5**	**17.5**	**21.1**	10.2	13.8

Table 2. Comparison of our proposed framework with the existing methods. The results of LP [20] are taken from [18]. The results of ISGG [34], MSDN [18], Factorizable Net [17] are taken from [17]. ours* reports the results where the network is first trained with ground truth boxes and then fine-tuned using pre-trained RPN.

Comparison	PredCls		PhrRecog		RelRecog	
	Rec@50	Rec@100	Rec@50	Rec@100	Rec@50	Rec@100
LP [20]	26.6	33.3	10.1	12.6	0.08	0.14
ISGG [34]	–	–	15.9	19.5	8.2	10.9
MSDN [18]	–	–	20.0	24.9	10.7	14.2
Factorizable Net [17]	–	–	22.8	28.6	13.1	16.5
Graph R-CNN [35]	54.2	59.1	–	–	11.4	13.7
Ours	48.9	61.5	17.5	21.1	10.2	13.8
Ours*	**58.2**	**60.7**	**29.4**	**34.5**	**19.4**	**22.7**

our original experiments (*i.e.* ours), we train RPN first and then apply the pre-trained model to train the entire network. From Table 2 we find that our model improves the Predicate Classification performance on Rec@100, and achieves comparative results on the Relationship Recognition, but performs not so well on the Phrase Recognition task. In an additional experiment (*i.e.* ours*), we first train our network using ground truth bounding boxes, and then fine-tune it using the pre-trained RPN. The object detector (*i.e.* RPN) is also fine-tuned. In this way, the performance improves significantly, especially on Phrase Recognition and Relationship Recognition tasks.

4.5   Qualitative Results

We show the qualitative results of our final network in Fig. 4, which displays the correct predictions, and Fig. 5, which illustrates the incorrect ones. The input of our network is an original image. Our network predicts *subject* and *object* bounding boxes and categories of *subject, predicate* and *object*. In the actual recognition process, the model attempts to find out all the possible relationship triplets for each image. For illustration in a simpler way, we only display one primal relationship triplet for one image.

Fig. 4. Qualitative results of our final network. The green and blue bounding boxes correspond to *subjects* and *objects* respectively. (Color figure online)

In Fig. 4, the green and blue boxes represent predicted *subject* and *object* respectively. It displays the effectiveness of our network on the visual relationship detection task. However, there are also some false predictions. In the left sub-image of Fig. 5, *shadow* is falsely detected as *light*, this might be caused by the predicted object bounding box which contains both shadow and light region. In the middle sub-image of Fig. 5, the correct category for *predicate* should be *beside* since there is no physical contact between *man* and *bike*. However, the network might consider that there exists physical contact between them. In the right sub-image of Fig. 5, the two glasses are close to each other and their colors are quite similar, which may lead to the mistake.

<light, on, sidewalk> ×   <man, hold, bike> ×   <glass, in, bottle> ×

Fig. 5. Incorrect results. In the left image, *shadow* is falsely detected as *light*. In the middle one, the correct label for *predicate* should be *beside*. And for the right one, the ground truth label is *<glass, next to, glass>*.

5   Conclusion

In this work, we propose a new framework for precise visual relationship detection. The proposed framework learns the predicate features between two objects by using a spatial attention module. To capture the contextual information between two objects which are involved in a likely relationship, an RNN module is utilized, which also integrates the spatial information with the visual features together. The framework is trained in an end-to-end fashion. The proposed method outperforms the previous works in the experiments w.r.t. the task of visual relationship detection. There remain some directions for improvement. Instead of using spatial attention module, another way is to exclude background information and only feed the features of two objects to the network. Another interesting direction is to replace the RNN embedding structure with other effective modules.

Acknowledgements. The work is funded by DFG (German Research Foundation) YA 351/2-1 and RO 4804/2-1 within SPP 1894. The authors gratefully acknowledge the support. The authors also acknowledge NVIDIA Corporation for the donated GPUs.

References

1. Awiszus, M., Rosenhahn, B.: Markov chain neural networks. In: CVPR Workshops, pp. 2180–2187 (2018)

2. Berg, A.C., et al.: Understanding and predicting importance in images. In: CVPR, pp. 3562–3569. IEEE (2012)
3. Choi, W., Chao, Y.W., Pantofaru, C., Savarese, S.: Understanding indoor scenes using 3D geometric phrases. In: CVPR, pp. 33–40 (2013)
4. Dai, B., Zhang, Y., Lin, D.: Detecting visual relationships with deep relational networks. In: CVPR, pp. 3076–3086 (2017)
5. Das, P., Xu, C., Doell, R.F., Corso, J.J.: A thousand frames in just a few words: lingual description of videos through latent topics and sparse object stitching. In: CVPR, pp. 2634–2641 (2013)
6. Divvala, S.K., Farhadi, A., Guestrin, C.: Learning everything about anything: Webly-supervised visual concept learning. In: CVPR, pp. 3270–3277 (2014)
7. Fang, H., et al.: From captions to visual concepts and back. In: CVPR, pp. 1473–1482 (2015)
8. Farhadi, A., et al.: Every picture tells a story: generating sentences from images. In: Daniilidis, K., Maragos, P., Paragios, N. (eds.) ECCV 2010, Part IV. LNCS, vol. 6314, pp. 15–29. Springer, Heidelberg (2010). https://doi.org/10.1007/978-3-642-15561-1_2
9. Geman, D., Geman, S., Hallonquist, N., Younes, L.: Visual turing test for computer vision systems. Proc. Natl. Acad. Sci. **112**(12), 3618–3623 (2015)
10. Henschel, R., von Marcard, T., Rosenhahn, B.: Simultaneous identification and tracking of multiple people using video and IMUs. In: CVPR Workshops (2019)
11. Izadinia, H., Sadeghi, F., Farhadi, A.: Incorporating scene context and object layout into appearance modeling. In: CVPR, pp. 232–239 (2014)
12. Jia, Z., Gallagher, A., Saxena, A., Chen, T.: 3D-based reasoning with blocks, support, and stability. In: CVPR, pp. 1–8 (2013)
13. Kluger, F., et al.: Region-based cycle-consistent data augmentation for object detection. In: 2018 IEEE International Conference on Big Data (Big Data), pp. 5205–5211. IEEE (2018)
14. Krishna, R., et al.: Visual genome: connecting language and vision using crowd-sourced dense image annotations. Int. J. Comput. Vis. **123**(1), 32–73 (2017)
15. Kulkarni, G., et al.: Baby talk: understanding and generating image descriptions. In: CVPR. Citeseer (2011)
16. Laskar, Z., Kannala, J.: Context aware query image representation for particular object retrieval. In: Sharma, P., Bianchi, F.M. (eds.) SCIA 2017, Part II. LNCS, vol. 10270, pp. 88–99. Springer, Cham (2017). https://doi.org/10.1007/978-3-319-59129-2_8
17. Li, Y., Ouyang, W., Zhou, B., Shi, J., Zhang, C., Wang, X.: Factorizable net: an efficient subgraph-based framework for scene graph generation. In: Ferrari, V., Hebert, M., Sminchisescu, C., Weiss, Y. (eds.) ECCV 2018, Part I. LNCS, vol. 11205, pp. 346–363. Springer, Cham (2018). https://doi.org/10.1007/978-3-030-01246-5_21
18. Li, Y., Ouyang, W., Zhou, B., Wang, K., Wang, X.: Scene graph generation from objects, phrases and region captions. In: ICCV, pp. 1261–1270 (2017)
19. Liao, W., Rosenhahn, B., Shuai, L., Ying Yang, M.: Natural language guided visual relationship detection. In: Proceedings of the IEEE Conference on Computer Vision and Pattern Recognition Workshops (2019)
20. Lu, C., Krishna, R., Bernstein, M., Fei-Fei, L.: Visual relationship detection with language priors. In: Leibe, B., Matas, J., Sebe, N., Welling, M. (eds.) ECCV 2016, Part I. LNCS, vol. 9905, pp. 852–869. Springer, Cham (2016). https://doi.org/10.1007/978-3-319-46448-0_51

21. Mensink, T., Gavves, E., Snoek, C.G.: Costa: co-occurrence statistics for zero-shot classification. In: CVPR, pp. 2441–2448 (2014)
22. Nagaraja, V.K., Morariu, V.I., Davis, L.S.: Modeling context between objects for referring expression understanding. In: Leibe, B., Matas, J., Sebe, N., Welling, M. (eds.) ECCV 2016, Part IV. LNCS, vol. 9908, pp. 792–807. Springer, Cham (2016). https://doi.org/10.1007/978-3-319-46493-0_48
23. Peyre, J., Sivic, J., Laptev, I., Schmid, C.: Weakly-supervised learning of visual relations. In: ICCV, pp. 5179–5188 (2017)
24. Prabhu, N., Venkatesh Babu, R.: Attribute-graph: a graph based approach to image ranking. In: ICCV, pp. 1071–1079 (2015)
25. Ramanathan, V., et al.: Learning semantic relationships for better action retrieval in images. In: CVPR, pp. 1100–1109 (2015)
26. Reinders, C., Ackermann, H., Yang, M.Y., Rosenhahn, B.: Object recognition from very few training examples for enhancing bicycle maps. In: 2018 IEEE Intelligent Vehicles Symposium (IV), pp. 1–8. IEEE (2018)
27. Ren, S., He, K., Girshick, R., Sun, J.: Faster R-CNN: towards real-time object detection with region proposal networks. In: Advances in Neural Information Processing Systems, pp. 91–99 (2015)
28. Sadeghi, M.A., Farhadi, A.: Recognition using visual phrases. In: CVPR 2011, pp. 1745–1752. IEEE (2011)
29. Silver, D., et al.: Mastering the game of go without human knowledge. Nature 550(7676), 354 (2017)
30. Simonyan, K., Zisserman, A.: Very deep convolutional networks for large-scale image recognition. arXiv preprint: arXiv:1409.1556 (2014)
31. Vaswani, A., et al.: Attention is all you need. In: Advances in Neural Information Processing Systems, pp. 5998–6008 (2017)
32. Wandt, B., Rosenhahn, B.: RepNet: weakly supervised training of an adversarial reprojection network for 3D human pose estimation. In: CVPR, pp. 7782–7791 (2019)
33. Xiong, Y., Zhu, K., Lin, D., Tang, X.: Recognize complex events from static images by fusing deep channels. In: CVPR, pp. 1600–1609 (2015)
34. Xu, D., Zhu, Y., Choy, C.B., Fei-Fei, L.: Scene graph generation by iterative message passing. In: CVPR, pp. 5410–5419 (2017)
35. Yang, J., Lu, J., Lee, S., Batra, D., Parikh, D.: Graph R-CNN for scene graph generation. In: Ferrari, V., Hebert, M., Sminchisescu, C., Weiss, Y. (eds.) ECCV 2018, Part I. LNCS, vol. 11205, pp. 690–706. Springer, Cham (2018). https://doi.org/10.1007/978-3-030-01246-5_41
36. Yang, M.Y., Liao, W., Ackermann, H., Rosenhahn, B.: On support relations and semantic scene graphs. ISPRS J. Photogramm. Remote Sens. 131, 15–25 (2017)
37. Yu, R., Li, A., Morariu, V.I., Davis, L.S.: Visual relationship detection with internal and external linguistic knowledge distillation. In: ICCV, pp. 1974–1982 (2017)
38. Zellers, R., Yatskar, M., Thomson, S., Choi, Y.: Neural motifs: scene graph parsing with global context. In: CVPR, pp. 5831–5840 (2018)
39. Zhang, H., Kyaw, Z., Chang, S.F., Chua, T.S.: Visual translation embedding network for visual relation detection. In: CVPR, pp. 5532–5540 (2017)
40. Zhuang, B., Liu, L., Shen, C., Reid, I.: Towards context-aware interaction recognition for visual relationship detection. In: ICCV, pp. 589–598 (2017)
41. Zitnick, C.L., Parikh, D., Vanderwende, L.: Learning the visual interpretation of sentences. In: ICCV, pp. 1681–1688 (2013)

Learning Task-Specific Generalized Convolutions in the Permutohedral Lattice

Anne S. Wannenwetsch[1]([✉])[iD], Martin Kiefel[2][iD], Peter V. Gehler[2][iD], and Stefan Roth[1][iD]

[1] TU Darmstadt, Darmstadt, Germany
anne.wannenwetsch@visinf.tu-darmstadt.de
[2] Amazon, Tübingen, Germany

Abstract. Dense prediction tasks typically employ encoder-decoder architectures, but the prevalent convolutions in the decoder are not image-adaptive and can lead to boundary artifacts. Different generalized convolution operations have been introduced to counteract this. We go beyond these by leveraging guidance data to redefine their inherent notion of *proximity*. Our proposed network layer builds on the *permutohedral lattice*, which performs sparse convolutions in a high-dimensional space allowing for powerful non-local operations despite small filters. Multiple features with different characteristics span this permutohedral space. In contrast to prior work, we *learn* these features in a task-specific manner by generalizing the basic permutohedral operations to learnt feature representations. As the resulting objective is complex, a carefully designed framework and learning procedure are introduced, yielding rich feature embeddings in practice. We demonstrate the general applicability of our approach in different joint upsampling tasks. When adding our network layer to state-of-the-art networks for optical flow and semantic segmentation, boundary artifacts are removed and the accuracy is improved.

1 Introduction

Deep learning approaches are the backbone of many state-of-the-art methods across computer vision [7,36,39]. Convolutional neural networks (CNNs) are particularly common as they greatly lower the number of parameters compared to fully-connected networks and thus scale to practically relevant image sizes. While early CNNs employed large filters [28], it is now common to use small kernels stacked into deep networks [16,35]. Chaining several smaller filters requires

---

A. S. Wannenwetsch—This project was mainly done during an internship at Amazon, Germany.

Electronic supplementary material The online version of this chapter (https://doi.org/10.1007/978-3-030-33676-9_24) contains supplementary material, which is available to authorized users.

G. A. Fink et al. (Eds.): DAGM GCPR 2019, LNCS 11824, pp. 345–359, 2019.
https://doi.org/10.1007/978-3-030-33676-9_24

fewer parameters for the same receptive field of a single large filter, and leads to more discriminative features by virtue of having more non-linearities [35].

While convolutions build a fundamental block of deep learning, they are not without drawbacks. First, they are not image-adaptive, *i.e.* content boundaries in a feature map are not respected but smoothed over. This is especially disadvantageous for dense prediction tasks, *e.g.* semantic segmentation or optical flow, leading to accuracy loss at boundaries [14,46]. Moreover, convolutions have a limited and predefined receptive field, which connects spatially close regions but cannot leverage similar, but more distant image structures. Here, a new definition of *pixel proximity* is needed that goes beyond two-dimensional (2D) spatial distance. For instance, image values themselves or abstract properties such as object classes could be used to define similarity in a more general setting.

Several methods have been proposed to counteract the named disadvantages. Sampling-based approaches [19,33] rearrange the image content but remain restricted to the 2D concept of proximity. Location specific networks [22,46] predict pixelwise filter kernels, but require many additional parameters. Other methods [8,40] determine neighboring pixels in an image-adaptive manner. However, the convolutional structure is fixed and only the position of neighbors is adjustable.

Image-adaptive filters, *e.g.* [15,41], have been used in traditional computer vision for years. The bilateral filter [41] adapts a Gaussian kernel according to the spatial distance and color difference of neighboring pixels. In [20,24], this concept is leveraged to construct bilateral convolution layers (BCLs) based on the *permutohedral lattice* [1] – a fast approximation of the bilateral filter. Filtering corresponds to a sparse convolution in a high-dimensional space, which is spanned by different features, *e.g.* spatial location and color. Jampani *et al.* [20,24] extend the Gaussian kernel to a general, image-adaptive convolution and learn the kernels from data. However, the features constituting the lattice space remain fixed. Feature parameters are not adjustable during training, which complicates integration into end-to-end learning. More importantly, relying on predefined features without further processing omits a possible source of improvements.

To counteract this disadvantage of BCLs, we present the *semantic lattice layer*. We rely on the permutohedral lattice as a backbone and show how to generalize its operations w.r.t. features with learnable parameters. The resulting computations are involved and may lead to practical challenges. We hence propose a specific setting in which basic features – as used in [20,24] – are processed by a CNN. This greatly simplifies the optimization since it allows to combine and especially refine features that are known to be beneficial for image-adaptive filtering. We further present various measures to avoid difficulties during learning. For instance, as the sparsity of the semantic lattice may avoid propagation of information if pixels are too distant, we restrict the output range of the embedded features. This rather simple measure has a large effect in practice.

Our setup enables us to learn meaningful feature embeddings from data. It allows to integrate feature parameters into training and effectively leverages guidance data to connect pixels due to their similar characteristics. As such, the semantic lattice is able to perform non-local operations while keeping the filter kernels and consequently the number of learnt parameters small and manageable. We show the benefits of the semantic lattice in different areas for image-adaptive upsampling. For the task of color upsampling, the semantic lattice outperforms previous approaches by a large margin. We further replace bilinear upsampling in state-of-the-art networks for optical flow and semantic segmentation. Here, the semantic lattice leads to better aligned and crisper content boundaries and also improves the accuracy, especially at discontinuities.

2 Related Work

Generalized Convolutions. We begin by reviewing work that generalizes convolution operations. Jaderberg et al. [19] introduce Spatial Transformers (STs), which transform feature maps depending on the data itself. Similar to warped convolutions [17], STs aim for invariance to certain transformations, e.g. rotation or scaling. [29] applies STs to allow for irregular patches in dense prediction tasks. In [33], saliency-based sampling emphasizes regions of high interest. These methods rearrange data in 2D space. In contrast, we can leverage additional feature dimensions to redefine the concept of pixel proximity.

Filter-weight networks [22] generate location-specific filters dependent on the input image. In [23], adaptive weights incorporate side information about the scene context. However, adaptive filters introduce many additional parameters in comparison to location-invariant networks and remain restricted to local transformations due to a fixed receptive field. Wu et al. [46] apply location-specific convolutions not only to the position itself but to several sampled neighboring regions, which extends their receptive field but requires additional computations.

Dilated convolutions use a fixed spacing between considered pixels to extend the spatial resolution [6,47]. It is possible to learn offsets for the input locations of each filter [21] or have them depend on the input and spatial location [8]. When using mixtures of Gaussians as filters, size and location of the receptive fields are learnable [40]. Structure-aware convolutions [5] use univariate functions as filters and are also applicable to non-Euclidean data. We do not learn individual neighborhoods for all filters but convolutions are instead performed consistently in a learnt feature space. Moreover, our convolution structure is not fixed; the number of neighbors is flexible and homogenous areas can be compressed.

Permutohedral Lattice. Adams et al. [1] propose the permutohedral lattice as a fast method for high-dimensional Gaussian filtering. It found widespread application, especially for fast inference in dense Conditional Random Fields (CRFs) [26,32,48] and upsampling or densification of data [10,34]. In contrast to our work, these approaches use fixed Gaussian filters and predefined features. [27] extends the fast inference method of [26] to learn parameters of dense CRFs, but the setup is restricted to Gaussian filters and customized to its application.

In [20,24], the high-dimensional filtering in permutohedral space is generalized by learnable convolution parameters. The proposed BCLs are beneficial in neural networks as they allow to redefine proximity of pixels w.r.t. different characteristics [12,20,30]. Moreover, BCLs can inherently cope with sparse data [24], *e.g.* in 3D point cloud processing [38]. Again, all methods rely on predefined features and thus restrict the flexibility of the generalized convolutions. We will show that a general setup with learnt features leads to better results in practice.

Another line of research aims for further speed-up of the permutohedral lattice. For instance, [9] proposes to encode its operations in a deep neural net.

Learnt Representations. Our embedding network aims to encode guidance data as discriminatively as possible for the task at hand. As such, our work is related to general embedding or metric learning; see [37,44] for an overview.

Image-Adaptive Filtering. We leverage additional properties for our generalized convolutions, which closely relates our approach to image-adaptive filtering methods such as bilateral filtering [41], non-local means [3], and guided image filtering [15]. All of these filters have been included into deep networks, *e.g.* for semantic segmentation [12,14], image processing [45], or video classification [42].

Only few approaches aim to learn guidance features for the filtering step in a general context. Harley *et al.* [14] propose segmentation-aware convolutions, which leverage image-adaptive masks from an embedding network. Object class labels are required for pre-training and large filter kernels increase the risk of overfitting. Deep joint image filtering (DJIF) [31] uses two individual networks to preprocess guidance and data features and subsequently merges the two branches for joint filtering. However, explicit knowledge about the relation between guidance and target data is not leveraged. Gharbi *et al.* [13] reproduce image enhancement operators with locally-affine models and upsample the low-resolution outputs guided by a learnt feature channel. Here, the offline learning of the models puts strong restrictions on the approximated operators. Deep guided filters [45] allow to learn a guidance image but restrict its dimensionality to a one-dimensional signal per output channel.

In contrast to previous work, the semantic lattice is applicable to a large variety of tasks and puts no restrictions on the guidance data. Moreover, the rich feature representations allow us to keep the applied filter kernels small.

3   The Semantic Lattice

To allow for the non-local combination of data, we build on the permutohedral lattice [1] to redefine the notion of *proximity* between the pixels of an image. The permutohedral lattice assumes that each input point is characterized by two properties – *features* and *data*. The feature value $\mathbf{f} \in \mathbb{R}^d$ indicates the location of the respective pixel in the d-dimensional permutohedral space, while the data value $\mathbf{v} \in \mathbb{R}^c$ describes the information stored at this location. In a first step, the data is projected into the lattice grid using the features to determine its position. Convolutions can then be performed in permutohedral space, considering a neighborhood defined by the feature dimensions. For instance, color values can be considered to connect visually similar areas and respect object boundaries

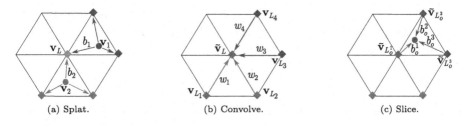

(a) Splat.   (b) Convolve.   (c) Slice.

Fig. 1. Basic operations in the permutohedral lattice.

[20,24]. This is in contrast to regular convolutions where the spatial location is used as the only feature to determine neighboring pixels. Finally, the convolved output is extracted at certain feature positions, which can but do not have to coincide with the input locations depending on the task at hand.

In the following, we introduce the permutohedral lattice and its properties more formally. We then extend the work in [20,24] to eliminate the usage of fixed, hand-crafted features. In particular, we show how to learn an appropriate feature space based on spatial positions as well as guidance data. As this approach allows to leverage semantically meaningful properties that go beyond the concept of predefined features, we refer to our proposed setup as the *semantic lattice*.

3.1 Permutohedral Lattice

Following [1], the permutohedral lattice is defined as the projection of the regular grid $\mathbb{Z}^{d+1}$ onto the hyperplane $\mathcal{H} : \mathbf{h} \cdot \mathbf{1} = 0 \subseteq \mathbb{R}^{d+1}$. The projected grid points thus represent the corners of permutohedral simplices, which split the hyperplane $\mathcal{H}$ into uniform cells. We refer to [1] for further details of the lattice structure.

The operation to read data into the lattice grid is denoted as *splatting*, see Fig. 1a. The feature vector $\mathbf{f}_i$ is used to place an input point $\mathbf{i} = (\mathbf{f}_i, \mathbf{v}_i)$ into the permutohedral lattice. Then, the data value is splat onto the enclosing lattice points according to its barycentric coordinates. The data value of a lattice point L is given as

$$\mathbf{v}_L = \sum_{i \in \mathcal{I}(L)} b_i \cdot \mathbf{v}_i, \tag{1}$$

where b_i denote the barycentric coordinates of input points $\mathcal{I}(L)$ splatting on L.

The *convolution* step is subsequently performed on the permutohedral grid points considering corners in a neighborhood $\mathcal{N}(L)$, *c.f.* Fig. 1b. If a neighboring corner was not set during splatting, its value is assumed to be zero. Using a kernel $\mathbf{W} = (w_1, \ldots, w_N)$, the convolution results in the updated lattice data

$$\tilde{\mathbf{v}}_L = \sum_{L_n \in \mathcal{N}(L)} w_n \cdot \mathbf{v}_{L_n}. \tag{2}$$

Figure 1c illustrates the final *slicing* operation, which interpolates the data from lattice points to an output pixel **o**. The value at pixel position $\mathbf{f}_o$ is obtained as

$$\tilde{\mathbf{v}}_o = \sum_{k=1}^{d+1} b_o^k \cdot \tilde{\mathbf{v}}_{L_o^k}, \tag{3}$$

with enclosing simplex corners L_o^k and barycentric coordinates b_o^k, $1 \leq k \leq d+1$.

In [20,24], the permuthedral lattice is integrated into deep learning by providing partial derivatives of the permutohedral operations w.r.t. the input data **v** and the kernel **W**. As such, the original Gaussian kernel [1] is transformed into a general convolution with a flexible filter **W** learnt from data. As the filter operation is performed in lattice space, the convolution respects the notion of proximity introduced by the features **f** that span the permutohedral lattice.

3.2 Generalized Features in the Semantic Lattice

To define the permutohedral space, [20,24] resort to predefined features, which are usually taken as $\mathbf{f} = (x, y, r, g, b)$. Here, x and y describe the spatial x- and y-coordinates of a pixel, which are concatenated with corresponding RGB values.

Our semantic lattice instead aims to learn feature embeddings from data to leverage the full capacity of the lattice. To that end, we introduce generalized input features $\mathbf{f}(\mathbf{i}; \boldsymbol{\theta}_I)$ that depend on each pixel **i** as well as a global set of parameters $\boldsymbol{\theta}_I$. The splatting operation in Eq. (1) then generalizes to

$$\mathbf{v}_L(\boldsymbol{\theta}_I) = \sum_{i \in \mathcal{I}(L; \theta_I)} b_i(\boldsymbol{\theta}_I) \cdot \mathbf{v}_i, \tag{4}$$

since the splatting points as well as the corresponding barycentric coordinates depend on the feature values and thus also on $\boldsymbol{\theta}_I$. Due to the fixed lattice structure, the set of neighbors for the convolution remains unchanged. However, the data value $\mathbf{v}_L$ at each lattice point depends on the inputs that splatted to this exact corner such that we rewrite the convolution in Eq. (2) as

$$\tilde{\mathbf{v}}_L(\boldsymbol{\theta}_I) = \sum_{L_n \in \mathcal{N}(L)} w_n \cdot \mathbf{v}_{L_n}(\boldsymbol{\theta}_I). \tag{5}$$

Finally, the set of lattice points surrounding an output pixel **o** and its barycentric coordinates are again dependent on its features $\mathbf{f}(\mathbf{o}, \boldsymbol{\theta}_O)$, which are parametrized by a set $\boldsymbol{\theta}_O$. This definition results in a generalized slicing operation given as

$$\tilde{\mathbf{v}}_o(\boldsymbol{\theta}_I, \boldsymbol{\theta}_O) = \sum_{k=1}^{d+1} b_o^k(\boldsymbol{\theta}_O) \cdot \tilde{\mathbf{v}}_{L_o^k(\theta_O)}(\boldsymbol{\theta}_I). \tag{6}$$

As operations in the lattice require specific computations, common automatic differentiation packages cannot be easily applied. Instead, we rely on customized

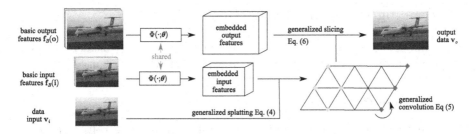

Fig. 2. Visualization of generalized feature learning in the semantic lattice; illustrated for the task of guided color upsampling.

functions for the above generalized operations as well as their parameter gradients. The derivatives then allow us to apply gradient based optimizers to learn task-specific feature representations $\mathbf{f}(\mathbf{i}; \boldsymbol{\theta}_I)$ and $\mathbf{f}(\mathbf{o}; \boldsymbol{\theta}_O)$ from data.

However, the nested occurrence of the parameter sets $\boldsymbol{\theta}_I$ and $\boldsymbol{\theta}_O$ already suggests that learning these generalized features may not be straightforward. Reconsidering the generalized operations in Eqs. (4)–(6), we observe that information between input and output pixels only propagates via a set of lattice corners defined by the neighborhood size of the convolution step. It is thus essential that input and output feature positions are sufficiently close in lattice space when starting the learning process. Otherwise, the loss gradient does not affect the input feature parameters $\boldsymbol{\theta}_I$ and no learning occurs.

To avoid this situation, we propose a specific framework as illustrated in Fig. 2 for the sample task of color upsampling. For given input and output points $\mathbf{p}$, we first generate several *basic features* $\mathbf{f}_B(\mathbf{p}) \in \mathbb{R}^{d'}$, *i.e.* hand-crafted features that we assume to be helpful for the task of interest. In the example case, the spatial location of each pixel and the corresponding grayscale image are chosen as basic features. Here, the additional grayscale information needs to be available for the input as well as output pixels. We denote it more generally as *guidance data* in the following. Then, a parametric function $\Phi : \mathbb{R}^{d'} \to \mathbb{R}^{d}$ is defined, which takes the basic features $\mathbf{f}_B$ as an input and returns a learnt feature embedding $\Phi(\mathbf{f}_B(\mathbf{p}); \boldsymbol{\theta})$ in $\mathbb{R}^d$. The parameter set $\boldsymbol{\theta}$ is shared across input and output points, *i.e.* $\boldsymbol{\theta} = \boldsymbol{\theta}_I = \boldsymbol{\theta}_O$, to ensure the necessary consistency of the feature embedding. We propose to use a multi-layer CNN for the embedding function Φ and refer to this network in the following as *feature* or *embedding network*. The parameter set $\boldsymbol{\theta}$ thus corresponds to the network weights. Embedded features as well as data inputs $\mathbf{v}_i$ are then used for the generalized operations in Eqs. (4)–(6).

As there are no restriction on the basic features, the semantic lattice is able to learn different kinds of non-local operations. Due to the characteristics of the permutohedral lattice, input and output positions are rearranged according to the learnt features and spatially far pixels are connected if they share the same characteristics. With this redefinition of proximity, the number of weight parameters remains limited while the semantic lattice yet operates globally.

4   Training the Semantic Lattice

The training and setup of the semantic lattice requires careful consideration. We detail this in the following and provide an experimental analysis in Sect. 5.2.

4.1   Training Procedure

Feature Scaling. As the size of the permutohedral lattice cells is fixed, a scaling factor applied to the individual features determines the importance of the different dimensions as well as the number of pixels that fall into one lattice cell. These scaling factors thus constitute important hyperparameters. Following [20, 24], we determine factors for our basic features via grid search. While with the semantic lattice it is possible to refine these factors in end-to-end training through backpropagation, we found little benefit in our experiments. Hence, we use the scaled features from the grid search as inputs to our embedding network.

Data Centering. If predefined features are used to map to the lattice space, the output is largely invariant to a global translation of the features. In contrast, we found feature network training to be more stable with zero mean input. We thus subtract the dataset mean from the basic features before feature scaling.

Explicit Spatial Features. As the embedding network combines basic features with various scale factors, we find that a random initialization may lead to a poor initial accuracy. While the feature network is able to recover a reasonable embedding starting from a random initialization, we observe long training times in practice as well as occasional convergence to poor local minima (inferior to the scaled basic features themselves). We find that this is mainly caused by the absence of reliable spatial coordinate features in the initial embedding network. Hence, we do not input the spatial coordinates into the embedding network, and instead explicitly concatenate the scaled spatial features and the learnt feature embedding to jointly define the lattice space for the subsequent convolutions.

Normalization Weights. The number of points per lattice cell can vary considerably, resulting in differing ranges of absolute data values at corner points (Eq. 4). Moreover, the flexible structure of the lattice results in a variable number of non-zero neighbors for the convolution in Eq. (5). For this reason, computations in permutohedral space require a normalization step on the slice result in Eq. (6). We divide by a normalization value, which is obtained by performing all lattice operations with a placeholder input with the same features as the regular input and $\mathbf{v}_i = 1$. This implies that an all-one input remains unchanged by the lattice operations. Note that this normalization becomes invalid as convolution weights turn negative. [20, 24] resolve this by introducing a separate set of convolution weights for the normalization. They rely on a fixed Gaussian filter, which reduces the flexibility. In contrast, we explicitly learn separate convolution weights for the normalization step and constrain them to be non-negative.

Learning Rates. If the feature network and permutohedral kernels are learnt simultaneously, individual learning rates are applied to both parameter sets.

4.2   Architecture

We use a CNN with 3×3 filters and leakyReLU activations as our feature embedding network. The non-linearities are omitted after the last convolution to allow for positive and negative features.[1] We experimented with ResNet-like feature networks [16], but observed little benefit. In contrast, we found it essential to add a batch normalization layer [18] at the end of the embedding network, *c.f.* Sect. 5.2. This can be understood as follows: Even in our carefully designed semantic lattice, it is possible that no data is splat to the lattice cells surrounding a specific output location. In such a case, the slice operation returns zero and the corresponding gradient with respect to the output location turns zero as well. Without further gradient signals from such pixels, learning keeps pushing more pixels into this disadvantageous state and the accuracy starts to degrade. Consequently, it is necessary to restrict the output range of the feature network, which batch normalization admits. While other normalization methods are possible, *e.g.* a simple min-max normalization, they show no clear benefit over batch normalization, which is commonly available in deep learning libraries.

Table 1. PSNR for *color upsampling* on the Pascal VOC 2012 Segmentation test set.

	PSNR [dB]		PSNR [dB]
Semantic lattice (*scaled basic features*)	36.55	Nearest neighbors	22.17
Semantic lattice (*learnt kernels*)	36.62	Bicubic upsampling	23.45
Semantic lattice (*learnt embedding*)	36.81	DGF [45]	35.17
Semantic lattice (*both learnt*)	**36.83**	DJIF [31]	23.99

In permutohedral space, we use a single kernel per input channel with a neighborhood of size one, *c.f.* supplemental material. For upsampling tasks as in Sect. 5.1, transitions of the sparse inputs between lattice cells may cause sudden changes of training loss. For this reason, we apply a nearest neighbor upsampling to the low-resolution guidance and input data before feeding them into the feature network and lattice, respectively. The spatial features are adapted to the upsampled input, which spreads the data more evenly over the lattice and leads to more reliable gradients w.r.t. the features.

---

[1] Details of the network architecture are provided in the supplemental material.

5   Experiments

5.1   Color Upsampling

Guided upsampling is a common application of image-adaptive filters [2,25,31, 45]. Here, guidance data is available at a higher resolution than the data of interest. This is particularly interesting if sensor data is available at different resolutions.

We evaluate our approach on the the task of joint color upsampling in which a grayscale image guides the upsamling of a low-resolution color image. Following [20], we use images of the Pascal VOC Segmentation splits [11] for training, validation, and test from which we removed grayscale images for fair comparison. Bilinear interpolation is used to downsample color and grayscale images by 4×.

The semantic lattice is applied to learn the offset between grayscale images and the RGB data. We use spatial coordinates and grayscale values as basic features. The semantic lattice is trained for 100 epochs on random crops of size 200 × 272 with learning rates of 0.001 and 0.01 for the feature network and permutohedral kernels, respectively. For comparison, we also train the deep guided filter (DGF) [45] in the same setting for 150 epochs using their procedure for image processing tasks. Again, the DGF predicts the offset between RGB and grayscale images as this slightly improves the results. We also compare with Deep Joint Image Filtering (DJIF) [31] by applying their residual network trained for the task of depth upsampling to predict color offsets.

Table 1 summarizes color upsampling results on Pascal VOC Segmentation test. When learning the permutohedral kernels (*learnt kernels*), we observe only a small benefit in comparison to the usage of a Gaussian filter (*scaled basic features*). In contrast, our learnt feature embedding (*learnt embedding*) leads to a significant improvement, highlighting the importance of using task-specific features. Combining both leads to another (minor) gain. Overall, we outperform the baselines of nearest neighbor and bicubic upsampling as well as related work [31,45] by a large margin. Please see supplemental material for visualizations.

5.2   Validation of Architectural Choices

We now compare different settings for feature learning to validate our proposed lattice setup. Table 2 summarizes results obtained with fixed Gaussian kernels. First, we train an embedding network without batch normalization to evaluate the importance of restricting its output range. We observe a significant drop in PSNR with a result only slightly better than that with scaled basic features. This is due to the fact that input and output locations do not necessarily coincide, which may lead to empty cells without gradients, *c.f.* Sect. 4.2. If the output range of the network is restricted, the number of such pixels can be kept small.

Next, we validate feeding our embedding network with guidance data and concatenating its output with spatial features. We first learn the scale factor of x- and y-coordinates jointly with the embedding. As this yields a negligible improvement over our baseline, we generally do not refine the scale factors. How-

(a) Ground truth flow   (b) RGB guidance image   (c) Learnt feature embedding

(d) Output PWC-Net [39]   (e) Output DGF [45]   (f) Output semantic lattice

Fig. 3. Flow fields and corresponding guidance data for a Sintel sequence.

ever, note that bigger benefits may be obtained from scale refinement if the initial scale factors are estimated only coarsely. In a second experiment, we apply the embedding network to all features, *i.e.* spatial coordinates and grayscale values. The network learns reasonable features from random initialization, but the PSNR is clearly lower than our baseline despite training 9× longer.

Finally, we evaluate our new normalization approach and learn kernels using scaled basic features. Applying a fixed Gaussian filter rather than a flexible, positive kernel for normalization reduces the PSNR by 0.04 dB.

Table 2. Validation of architectural choices for color upsampling on Pascal VOC test.

	PSNR [dB]
Baseline (*learnt embedding*)	36.81
W/o batch normalization layer	36.61
Learnt spatial scale factor	**36.82**
Spatial features embedded	36.55
Baseline (*learnt kernels*)	**36.62**
Gaussian normalization	36.58

5.3 Dense Prediction Tasks

We next apply our semantic lattice in deep networks for challenging dense prediction tasks, where networks typically operate on downsampled images and use bilinear upsampling as a last step, *e.g.* [7,39].

Optical Flow. We first consider optical flow for which PWC-Net [39] performs competitively on different benchmarks, *e.g.* [4]. However, the calculated flow looks blurry and boundary details are oversmoothed, see Fig. 3. We attribute this to the non-adaptive upsampling that enlarges the estimated flow by ∼ 4×.

To obtain sharper and more detailed flow, we replace the bilinear upsampling with a single convolution in the semantic lattice. As basis, we use the so-called *PWC-Net_ROB* model trained on a variety of datasets. For fair comparison, we do not backpropagate into the network itself but only update the parameters of the semantic lattice, since bilinear upsampling cannot benefit from learning. Spatial coordinates and color values of the first image are leveraged as basic features. The high-resolution guidance image is equally used for input and output features. Our setup is trained on the Sintel dataset [4], which we split randomly

Table 3. Average-end-point error (AEE) and boundary AEE (bAEE) on our Sintel test split (ours) and the official Sintel test set (off.). Semantic lattice abbreviated to SL.

	clean (ours)		final (ours)		clean (off.)	final (off.)
	AEE	bAEE	AEE	bAEE	AEE	AEE
SL (*scaled basic features*)	1.27	7.84	1.66	8.65	–	–
SL (*learnt embedding*)	1.26	7.50	1.66	8.61	–	–
SL (*both learnt*)	**1.25**	**7.49**	**1.65**	**8.56**	**3.84**	**4.89**
PWC-Net [39]	1.30	8.52	1.67	8.98	3.90	4.90
DGF [45]	1.29	8.31	1.67	8.91	–	–

into 862 training, 80 validation, and 99 test images. We use the average end-point error (AEE) as loss function and train all configurations for 100 epochs on random 281×512 crops. Learning rates are set to $1e - 3$ and $1e - 7$ for embedding parameters and permutohedral kernels, respectively. We again compare our approach to DGF [45], which we trained for 500 epochs using their setup for computer vision tasks and hyperparameters tuned on validation.

Table 3 shows results on our own test split of Sintel clean and final as well as on the official test images of the benchmark. Our proposed semantic lattice layer leads to a moderate AEE improvement on both sets. This is to be expected as our experimental setup can only refine the flow estimates. However, sharper flow boundaries are clearly visible when considering the results in Fig. 3. As the AEE is known to be insensitive towards boundary accuracy, we also evaluate a boundary average end-point error (bAEE). It focuses on accuracy close to motion discontinuities, which are determined from ground truth flow by applying a threshold to the flow gradient norm, *c.f.* [43]. As the varying motion ranges require different thresholds [4,43], we follow Weinzaepfel *et al.* [43] and generate multiple masks using values in $\{1, 3, 7, 10\}$. These masks are subsequently dilated with a structuring element of size 3. We finally calculate the bAEE by evaluating flow on boundary regions only and averaging over the different boundary masks. Our proposed approach shows a clear benefit for boundary regions, improving the bAEE much more significantly than DGF [45] on Sintel clean and final.

Semantic Segmentation. We finally consider the task of semantic segmentation and replace the bilinear upsampling of the recent DeepLabv3+ [7] with our semantic lattice. Again, we only update parameters of the semantic lattice and keep the remaining network fixed to an XCeption65 model trained on COCO and Pascal VOC augmented, *c.f.* [7]. Basic features and the setup of our lattice layer remain the same as for optical flow. We train the semantic lattice with random crops of size 200×272 on the training set of Pascal VOC 2012 [11], which we further split into training and validation. The embedding network is trained for 25 epochs with a learning rate of $1e - 3$, which we reduce by $10\times$ for the remaining 75 epochs. The learning rate for permutohedral kernels is fixed to $1e - 8$. DGF is trained as for optical flow with hyperparameters used in [45].

While the semantic lattice without learnt embedding performs slightly worse than the original implementation, the full semantic lattice and DGF outperform DeepLabv3+. Table 4 summarizes results on Pascal VOC 2012 validation; see supplemental for visualizations. The overall improvement is rather small, which we attribute mainly to DeepLabv3+ being highly engineered, with particular focus on the decoder (unlike the previous DeepLabv3). Nevertheless, image-adaptive filters may benefit further from jointly training with the entire network.

Table 4. Mean intersection over union (mIoU) for *semantic segmentation* on our Pascal VOC 2012 test set.

	mIoU
Semantic lattice (*scaled basic features*)	82.17%
Semantic lattice (*learnt embedding*)	82.24%
Semantic lattice (*both learnt*)	82.25%
DeepLabv3+ [7]	82.20%
DGF [45]	**82.26%**

6 Conclusion

We introduced the semantic lattice layer, a task-specific, generalized convolution. Our approach is built on the permutohedral lattice that rearranges input data according to different features and thus performs non-local operations with small filter kernels. First, we generalized the operations in permutohedral space to feature representations that can be learnt from data. We then showed how rich feature embeddings can be learnt in practice and validated the proposed architecture. When applying the semantic lattice to color upsampling, learning task-specific features showed a clear benefit. Adding the semantic lattice to decoders in deep neural networks for optical flow and semantic segmentation allowed to reduce boundary artifacts and improved the accuracy for both tasks.

References

1. Adams, A., Baek, J., Davis, M.A.: Fast high-dimensional filtering using the permutohedral lattice. Comput. Graph. Forum **29**(2), 753–762 (2010)
2. Barron, J.T., Poole, B.: The fast bilateral solver. In: Leibe, B., Matas, J., Sebe, N., Welling, M. (eds.) ECCV 2016, Part III. LNCS, vol. 9907, pp. 617–632. Springer, Cham (2016). https://doi.org/10.1007/978-3-319-46487-9_38
3. Buades, A., Coll, B., Morel, J.M.: A non-local algorithm for image denoising. In: CVPR (2005)
4. Butler, D.J., Wulff, J., Stanley, G.B., Black, M.J.: A naturalistic open source movie for optical flow evaluation. In: Fitzgibbon, A., Lazebnik, S., Perona, P., Sato, Y., Schmid, C. (eds.) ECCV 2012, Part VI. LNCS, vol. 7577, pp. 611–625. Springer, Heidelberg (2012). https://doi.org/10.1007/978-3-642-33783-3_44
5. Chang, J., Gu, J., Wang, L., Meng, G., Xiang, S., Pan, C.: Structure-aware convolutional neural network. In: NeurIPS*2018 (2018)
6. Chen, L., Papandreou, G., Kokkinos, I., Murphy, K., Yuille, A.L.: Semantic image segmentation with deep convolutional nets and fully connected CRFs. In: ICLR (2015)

7. Chen, L.-C., Zhu, Y., Papandreou, G., Schroff, F., Adam, H.: Encoder-decoder with atrous separable convolution for semantic image segmentation. In: Ferrari, V., Hebert, M., Sminchisescu, C., Weiss, Y. (eds.) ECCV 2018, Part VII. LNCS, vol. 11211, pp. 833–851. Springer, Cham (2018). https://doi.org/10.1007/978-3-030-01234-2_49

8. Dai, J., et al.: Deformable convolutional networks. In: ICCV (2017)

9. Dai, L., Tang, L., Xie, Y., Tang, J.: Designing by training: acceleration neural network for fast high-dimensional convolution. In: NeurIPS*2018 (2018)

10. Dolson, J., Baek, J., Plagemann, C., Thrun, S.: Upsampling range data in dynamic environments. In: CVPR (2010)

11. Everingham, M., Eslami, S.M.A., Gool, L.V., Williams, C.K.I., Winn, J., Zisserman, A.: The PASCAL visual object classes challenge: a retrospective. Int. J. Comput. Vis. 111(1), 98–136 (2015)

12. Gadde, R., Jampani, V., Kiefel, M., Kappler, D., Gehler, P.V.: Superpixel convolutional networks using bilateral inceptions. In: Leibe, B., Matas, J., Sebe, N., Welling, M. (eds.) ECCV 2016, Part I. LNCS, vol. 9905, pp. 597–613. Springer, Cham (2016). https://doi.org/10.1007/978-3-319-46448-0_36

13. Gharbi, M., Chen, J., Barron, J.T., Hasinoff, S.W., Durand, F.: Deep bilateral learning for real-time image enhancement. In: SIGGRAPH (2017)

14. Harley, A.W., Derpanis, K.G., Kokkinos, I.: Segmentation-aware convolutional networks using local attention masks. In: ICCV (2017)

15. He, K., Sun, J., Tang, X.: Guided image filtering. In: Daniilidis, K., Maragos, P., Paragios, N. (eds.) ECCV 2010, Part I. LNCS, vol. 6311, pp. 1–14. Springer, Heidelberg (2010). https://doi.org/10.1007/978-3-642-15549-9_1

16. He, K., Zhang, X., Ren, S., Sun, J.: Deep residual learning for image recognition. In: CVPR (2017)

17. Henriques, J.F., Vedaldi, A.: Warped convolutions: efficient invariance to spatial transformations. In: ICML (2017)

18. Ioffe, S., Szegedy, C.: Batch normalization: accelerating deep network training by reducing internal covariate shift. In: ICML (2015)

19. Jaderberg, M., Simonyan, K., Zisserman, A., Kavukcuoglu, K.: Spatial transformer networks. In: NIPS*2015 (2015)

20. Jampani, V., Kiefel, M., Gehler, P.V.: Learning sparse high dimensional filters: image filtering, dense CRFs and bilateral neural networks. In: CVPR (2016)

21. Jeon, Y., Kim, J.: Active convolution: learning the shape of convolution for image classification. In: CVPR (2017)

22. Jia, X., Brabandere, B.D., Tuytelaars, T., Gool, L.V.: Dynamic filter networks. In: NIPS*2016 (2016)

23. Kang, D., Dhar, D., Chan, A.B.: Incorporating side information by adaptive convolution. In: NIPS*2017 (2017)

24. Kiefel, M., Jampani, V., Gehler, P.V.: Permutohedral lattice CNNs. In: ICLR Workshop Track (2016)

25. Kopf, J., Cohen, M.F., Lischinski, D., Uyttendaele, M.: Joint bilateral upsampling. ACM Trans. Graph. 26(3), 96 (2007)

26. Krähenbühl, P., Koltun, V.: Efficient inference in fully connected CRFs with Gaussian edge potentials. In: NIPS*2011 (2011)

27. Krähenbühl, P., Koltun, V.: Parameter learning and convergent inference for dense random fields. In: ICML (2013)

28. Krizhevsky, A., Sutskever, I., Hinton, G.E.: ImageNet classification with deep convolutional neural networks. In: NIPS*2012 (2012)

29. Li, J., Chen, Y., Cai, L., Davidson, I., Ji, S.: Dense transformer networks. arXiv:1705.08881 [cs.CV] (2017)
30. Li, S., Seybold, B., Vorobyov, A., Lei, X., Kuo, C.-C.J.: Unsupervised video object segmentation with motion-based bilateral networks. In: Ferrari, V., Hebert, M., Sminchisescu, C., Weiss, Y. (eds.) ECCV 2018, Part III. LNCS, vol. 11207, pp. 215–231. Springer, Cham (2018). https://doi.org/10.1007/978-3-030-01219-9_13
31. Li, Y., Huang, J.B., Ahuja, N., Yang, M.H.: Joint image filtering with deep convolutional networks. IEEE Trans. Pattern Anal. Mach. Intell. **41**(8), 1909–1923 (2019)
32. Perazzi, F., Krähenbühl, P., Pritch, Y., Hornung, A.: Saliency filters: contrast based filtering for salient region detection. In: CVPR (2012)
33. Recasens, A., Kellnhofer, P., Stent, S., Matusik, W., Torralba, A.: Learning to zoom: a saliency-based sampling layer for neural networks. In: Ferrari, V., Hebert, M., Sminchisescu, C., Weiss, Y. (eds.) ECCV 2018, Part IX. LNCS, vol. 11213, pp. 52–67. Springer, Cham (2018). https://doi.org/10.1007/978-3-030-01240-3_4
34. Russell, C., Yu, R., Agapito, L.: Video pop-up: monocular 3D reconstruction of dynamic scenes. In: Fleet, D., Pajdla, T., Schiele, B., Tuytelaars, T. (eds.) ECCV 2014, Part VII. LNCS, vol. 8695, pp. 583–598. Springer, Cham (2014). https://doi.org/10.1007/978-3-319-10584-0_38
35. Simonyan, K., Zisserman, A.: Very deep convolutional networks for large-scale image recognition. In: ICLR (2015)
36. Singh, B., Najibi, M., Davis, L.S.: SNIPER: efficient multi-scale training. In: NeurIPS*2018 (2018)
37. Song, H.O., Xiang, Y., Jegelka, S., Savarese, S.: Deep metric learning via lifted structured feature embedding. In: CVPR (2016)
38. Su, H., et al.: SPLATNet: sparse lattice networks for point cloud processing. In: CVPR (2018)
39. Sun, D., Yang, X., Liu, M.Y., Kautz, J.: PWC-Net: CNNs for optical flow using pyramid, warping, and cost volume. In: CVPR (2018)
40. Tabernik, D., Kristan, M., Leonardis, A.: Spatially-adaptive filter units for deep neural networks. In: CVPR (2018)
41. Tomasi, C., Manduchi, R.: Bilateral filtering for gray and color images. In: ICCV (1998)
42. Wang, X., Girshick, R., Gupta, A., He, K.: Non-local neural networks. In: CVPR (2018)
43. Weinzaepfel, P., Revaud, J., Harchaoui, Z., Schmid, C.: Learning to detect motion boundaries. In: CVPR (2015)
44. Wu, C.Y., Manmatha, R., Smola, A.J., Krähenbühl, P.: Sampling matters in deep embedding learning. In: ICCV (2017)
45. Wu, H., Zheng, S., Zhang, J., Huang, K.: Fast end-to-end trainable guided filter. In: CVPR (2018)
46. Wu, J., Li, D., Yang, Y., Bajaj, C., Ji, X.: Dynamic filtering with large sampling field for ConvNets. In: Ferrari, V., Hebert, M., Sminchisescu, C., Weiss, Y. (eds.) ECCV 2018, Part X. LNCS, vol. 11214, pp. 188–203. Springer, Cham (2018). https://doi.org/10.1007/978-3-030-01249-6_12
47. Yu, F., Koltun, V.: Multi-scale context aggregation by dilated convolutions. In: ICLR (2016)
48. Zhang, Z., Fidler, S., Urtasun, R.: Instance-level segmentation for autonomous driving with deep densely connected MRFs. In: CVPR (2016)

Achieving Generalizable Robustness of Deep Neural Networks by Stability Training

Jan Laermann, Wojciech Samek, and Nils Strodthoff[(⊠)]

Fraunhofer Heinrich Hertz Institute, Einsteinufer 37, 10587 Berlin, Germany
{jan.laermann,wojciech.samek,nils.strodthoff}@hhi.fraunhofer.de

Abstract. We study the recently introduced stability training as a general-purpose method to increase the robustness of deep neural networks against input perturbations. In particular, we explore its use as an alternative to data augmentation and validate its performance against a number of distortion types and transformations including adversarial examples. In our image classification experiments using ImageNet data stability training performs on a par or even outperforms data augmentation for specific transformations, while consistently offering improved robustness against a broader range of distortion strengths and types unseen during training, a considerably smaller hyperparameter dependence and less potentially negative side effects compared to data augmentation.

1 Introduction

Deep neural networks (DNN) are complex learning systems, which have been used in a variety of tasks with great success in recent times. In some fields, like visual recognition or playing games, DNNs can compete with or even outperform their human counterparts [11,23], showcasing their utility and effectiveness.

In real-world applications, however, there are a number of quality criteria that go beyond single scalar performance metrics such as classification accuracy that are typically considered when comparing different classification algorithms. These quality criteria include interpretability [17], the quantification of uncertainty [8] but also robustness in a general sense. The aspect of robustness comprises both robustness against label noise, see [6] for a review, and robustness against any kind of input noise. In this work we are only concerned with robustness in the latter sense, which we further sub-categorize based on the kind of input perturbations under consideration. We distinguish on the one hand *noise distorsions* that include for example Gaussian noise, JPEG compression artifacts but also adversarial examples [25] and on the other hand *transformative*

Electronic supplementary material The online version of this chapter (https://doi.org/10.1007/978-3-030-33676-9_25) contains supplementary material, which is available to authorized users.

G. A. Fink et al. (Eds.): DAGM GCPR 2019, LNCS 11824, pp. 360–373, 2019.
https://doi.org/10.1007/978-3-030-33676-9_25

distorsions comprising image transformations such as rotations and crops. A particular challenge arises from the fact that the test data might exhibit distortions that have not been encountered by the network during training both in terms of distorsion strength as well as in terms of distorsion types. Therefore we strive to develop methods that ideally lead to *generalizable robustness* beyond distorsions seen during training.

One way of increasing the robustness against input perturbations is to use data augmentation (DA) [14]. In fact, DA by adding perturbed copies of existing data samples is by now an established method and has been shown to greatly increase the generalizability of a given model [27,30]. DA has two aspects: On the one hand, it enlarges the available training data to achieve a better generalization performance and on the other hand it increases the model's robustness against transformations used for DA. As we will see, this robustness, however, is highly specific to the kind and the particular characteristics of the perturbations used for DA. In particular, in the worst case DA can degrade the model performance for unperturbed inputs compared to the baseline model performance.

An alternative approach, which will be explored further in this work, was put forward under the name of stability training (ST) by Zheng et al. [33]. Instead of adding distortion instances to the training corpus, ST feeds the perturbed and the reference sample to the network simultaneously and introduces a consistency constraint as additional optimization objective that tries to align the network's outputs of the perturbed image and the reference sample. By extending the original work beyond Gaussian noise perturbation considered in the original work [33], we propose ST as a general-purpose alternative to DA that offers similar advantages with limited negative side effects. We also introduce modifications to the method, which mitigate weaknesses and extend its applicability. In particular, our contributions can be summarized as follows:

- We establish stability training as a competitive alternative to data augmentation, which produces comparable or superior robustness improvements across a wide range of distortion types, while exhibiting significantly lower risk to deteriorate performance compared to an unstabilized baseline model. To this end, we present a detailed analysis of the robustness of both data augmentation and stability training when trained/tested on specific distorsion types.
- We propose a symmetrical stability objective that increases the method's effectiveness in learning from data transformations, like rotations, that do not distinguish an unperturbed reference sample. The modified objective offers superior performance to data augmentation in scenarios that are likely to be encountered in real-world applications.
- We evaluate stability training as an alternative to adversarial training to increase robustness against adversarial examples generated via the fast gradient sign method [9].
- As an outlook we demonstrate the prospects of using multiple distorsion types simultaneously to further improve the robustness properties.

2 Stability Training

Stability training aims to stabilize predictions of a deep neural network in response to small input distortions. The idea behind this approach is that an input x' that is similar to x and semantically equivalent ought to produce similar outputs $f_\theta(x')$, where θ denotes the trainable parameters of the neural network. The full optimization objective is then defined as a composite loss function of the original task L_0, for example cross-entropy between the network's prediction $y = f_\theta(x)$ and the (one-hot encoded) ground truth label $\hat{y}$, and a separate stability objective L_{stab} which enforces the consistency constraint. More explicitly, given an original image x and a perturbed version x' of it, the combined training objective is then given by

$$L(x, x', \hat{y}; \theta) = L_0(x, \hat{y}; \theta) + \alpha L_{\mathrm{stab}}(x, x'; \theta), \tag{1}$$

where the stability loss is defined via

$$L_{\mathrm{stab}}(x, x'; \theta) = D(f_\theta(x), f_\theta(x')), \tag{2}$$

and the hyperparameter α adjusts the relative importance of the two loss components.

The choice of a distance function D is task-specific. Whereas for regression tasks the L_2-distance is a straightforward choice, in a classification setting with C classes, where

$$L_0(x, \hat{y}; \theta) = -\sum_{j=1}^{C} \hat{y}_j P(y_j | x; \theta), \tag{3}$$

the Kullback-Leibler (KL) divergence as considered in [33] represents a canonical way of comparing likelihoods of original and distorted inputs

$$D_{\mathrm{orig}}(y, y') = D_{\mathrm{KL}}(y \,\|\, y'). \tag{4}$$

The stability loss function is then given by

$$\begin{aligned} L_{\mathrm{stab}}(x, x'; \theta) &= D_{\mathrm{KL}}(f_\theta(x) \,\|\, f_\theta(x')) \\ &= -\sum_j P(y_j | x; \theta) \log\left(\frac{P(y_j | x; \theta)}{P(y_j | x'; \theta)}\right). \end{aligned} \tag{5}$$

As the KL-divergence is not symmetric with respect to its arguments, using it as distance measure is most appropriate in situations, where the reference sample can be clearly distinguished as undistorted from the modified copy, as it is the case for distortions we categorize as coming from the *noise* category. For *transformative* distorsions such as rotations it turns out to be beneficial to consider a symmetrized stability term, i.e.

$$D_{\mathrm{sym}}(y, y') = \tfrac{1}{2}\left(D_{\mathrm{KL}}(y \,\|\, y') + D_{\mathrm{KL}}(y' \,\|\, y)\right). \tag{6}$$

At this point it is worthwhile to point out a crucial difference between stability training and DA: In the DA-setting the neural network is trained on perturbed input samples while the loss is the original loss L_0 evaluated using the label of the reference image. On the contrary, stability training decouples solving the original task from stabilizing class predictions. This is achieved by evaluating the original loss L_0 only for the unperturbed samples while the perturbed samples only enter the consistency-enforcing stability loss term (2). This construction reduces the potential negative side-effects of DA, where for certain hyperparameter choices DA can worsen performance on the original unperturbed dataset compared to a baseline model. Note that stability training leads to increased memory requirements as the results for passing the original batch and the perturbed batch have to be held in memory simultaneously.

3   Related Work

This work builds on the original article on ST [33] that stands out from the literature as one of the few works that explicitly addresses increasing the robustness a neural network against generic input perturbations. We extend their work by considering train distorsions beyond Gaussian noise and a symmetric stability objective to increase the method's performance for transformative distorsions.

There is a large body of works on related methods in the context of semi-supervised learning, see [4,34] for reviews. The most relevant works for the present context can be subsumed as consistency/smoothness enforcing methods. The common idea in all cases is to impose a consistency constraint [19] to enforce similar classification behavior for the original and perturbed input. On the labeled subset of the data both the original loss and the consistency loss can be evaluated, whereas on the unlabeled subset only the consistency loss is imposed. The focus in these works lies on incorporating information from the unlabeled subset to increase the model performance but none of them considered the aspect of robustness with respect to input distorsions. The main difference between the different methods lies in the way how the consistency constraint is implemented [1,2,15,16,22,26,29].

In the domain of DA, Rajput et al. [21] recently presented a first theoretical investigation of the robustness properties of DA. On the practical side, there have been proposals for more elaborate implementations of DA that try to circumvent the need for dataset-specific hyperparameter searches by appropriate meta search algorithms [5,31], which focusing, however, on model performance rather than robustness. In fact, it would represent an interesting line of research to investigate also these techniques from the robustness point of view to see in detail how a far a DA strategy tailored for robustness can get. Mixup [32] can be seen as an extension to DA in the sense that not only on perturbed input samples but rather on convex combinations of input samples and the corresponding labels are used during training. Recent extensions such as [2,10,28] incorporate also a consistency constraint for stabilization.

4   Experimental Setup

4.1   Tiny ImageNet Full-Sized (TIFS) Dataset

We base our experiments on a dataset inspired by the Tiny ImageNet dataset [24]. The latter represents a reduced version of the original ImageNet dataset with only 200 instead of the original 1000 ImageNet classes and 500 samples per class downsized to resolution 64×64. As we wanted to keep the advantage of the reduced computational demands of Tiny ImageNet while working on full ImageNet resolutions, we decided to design our custom TIFS dataset along the lines of Tiny ImageNet but keeping the original samples from the ILSVRC2012 ImageNet dataset[1]. As no labels are provided for the official ImageNet test set, we used the images from the original validation set as the basis for the TIFS test set and split the original training set in a cross-validation fashion, such that for each class we randomly assigned 450 samples to the training set and 50 to the validation set.

Images contained in the ImageNet dataset and thus in the TIFS dataset come at varying sizes. We preprocess the dataset such that every image in the dataset is first resized, such that the shortest side is 256 pixels in length. Next, we crop out a 224 pixels wide quadratic area, such that the center points of the crop and the image coincide. The image is then converted from RGB integer color values ranging 0 to 255, to floating-point values ranging 0 to 1. Distortions are applied at this point. Finally, we normalize and whiten the (undistorted) images such that the channel-wise mean and variance across the entire dataset are 0 and 1, respectively.

4.2   Model Architecture and Optimization

In our experiments, we use a deep convolutional residual network (ResNet18) [12] as prototype for a state-of-the-art convolutional neural network that is presently used predominantly in computer vision applications. To optimize our model, we use mini-batch stochastic gradient descent with Nesterov accelerated momentum [18] and batch normalization [13]. We use the default *torchvision* implementation of ResNet18 as supplied with Pytorch [20] and use randomly initialized weights rather than pretrained weights that already include DA during pretraining.

We find that introducing the stability objective late during the training phase produces similar results to applying it from the beginning and therefore decided to use the following experimental procedure: We initially train a model for 30 epochs on the original training set with no distortions added to the preprocessing procedure. We save the model at each epoch and select the model with the highest performance on the undistorted validation set. This model serves as baseline model in the following experiments. All subsequent models are initialized with the weights of the baseline model. In an individual run using either ST or

---

[1] A corresponding preprocessing script is available at https://gist.github.com/nstrodt/bd270131160f02564f0165e888976471.

Table 1. Considered distortion types. "Type" denotes the assignment either to N(oise) or to T(ransformative) distorsions. The column "Practical" reflect a subjectively selected parameter value likely to be encountered for distorsions in real world applications.

Distortion (Type)	Parameter	Practical
Gaussian noise (N)	standard deviation σ	0.05
JPEG compression (N)	quality q	30
Thumbnail resizing (N)	pixel size A	150
FGSM Adversarial examples (N)	strength ϵ	0.001
Rotation (T)	max. rotation ρ	30
Random cropping (T)	pixel offset C	3

DA, the model is trained in the same fashion as the baseline model, except for a limited number of 10 epochs. For a selected distorsion we train a number of models according by varying distorsion hyperparameters. Similarly to the training of the baseline model we use the model performance on the undistorted validation set to perform early stopping, i.e. for a specific hyperparameter choice we select the model with the highest score on the undistorted validation set. We keep a fixed learning rate of 0.01 and a batch size of 128 for all experiments.

We consider a range of different distortion types that are summarized in Table 1. As already discussed above, we broadly categorize distortions as undirected noise distorsions or as transformative distortions arising from geometric transformations of the input image. For later reference we subjectively identified a parameter value for *practical* distorsions, that reflects a distorsion strength likely to be encountered in real world applications or in certain settings, like FGSM, a distorsion strength where the distortion is on the verge of being detectable by a human, but has not yet surpassed that threshold.

We consider the following distorsions: Gaussian noise adds pixel-wise independent Gaussian noise to the image such that $x'_k = x_k + \epsilon_k$, $\epsilon_k \sim \mathcal{N}(0, \sigma^2)$, where k indicates the index of the pixel in x and the standard deviation σ serves as hyperparameter. JPEG compression is an image compression algorithm that aims to minimize file size while maximizing retained semantic meaning. It offers a quality level $q \in [1, 100]$ indicating how much image quality is favored over file size. Thumbnail resizing crops the image down to a quadratic area with side-length A and afterwards resizes the image to its original dimensions. This introduces interpolation artifacts that increase in severity with lower values of A. We choose FGSM [9] as an example method to produce adversarial examples for its simplicity. An example is generated via $x' = x + \epsilon \operatorname{sign}(\nabla_x L(x, \hat{y}; \theta))$, where ϵ is a strength parameter and L is the full loss function. The rotation distortion represents a random rotation up to ρ degrees. Random cropping, unlike the other distortions considered here, changes the common preprocessing procedure. Usually the center point of the final crop and of the image coincide. This distortion

Table 2. Hyperparameter ranges used during training.

Hyperparameter	[start,end,# points]	Scale
ST: relative weight α	[0.01, 10.0, 3]	logarithmic
DA: transformation probability p	[0.5, 1.0, 2]	linear
Gaussian noise σ	[0.01, 1.0, 4]	logarithmic
JPEG compression q	[90, 10, 3]	linear
thumbnail resizing A	[20, 200, 3]	linear
FGSM Adversarial examples ϵ	[0.001, 1.0, 7]	logarithmic
rotation ρ	[0, 180, 3]	linear
random cropping C	[0, 15, 3]	linear

offers a parameter C such that these points are displaced by up to C pixels in all four directions.

For DA we introduce the probability p that the selected augmentation will be applied as an additional hyperparameter. This is the default setup in which DA is applied in practical applications and allows to mitigate effects of catastrophic forgetting [7], i.e. a performance deterioration on the original undistorted dataset that is observed for certain hyperparameter choices. The corresponding hyperparameter for ST is the coefficient α, see Eq. 1, that sets the relative scale of the consistency loss term compared to the original loss.

We conclude this section with a remark on the intricacies of comparing ST and DA. If one uses the same batch size in both cases and fixes the number of epochs to the same value in both settings, one the one hand ST is fed twice the amount of raw data. On the other hand, if DA is trained using the same number of examples i.e. by doubling the number of epochs compared to ST, it allows DA to make the double number of label uses compared to ST. Whereas the ST performance typically stabilizes rather quickly during training, increasing the number of training epochs in the DA setting has implications on the robustness properties of the model that will be discussed qualitatively below.

5   Results

In the following, we refer to the type of distortion to be used for regularization in conjunction with ST or DA during training(testing) as *training (test) distortion*. In our experiments we train models with a variety of training distortions from both distorsion types and evaluate their performance on various test distortions, see Table 2 for the hyperparameter ranges considered during training. The validation set is only used for early stopping based on the model performance on the undistorted validation set as described above. With the scenario of unknown test perturbation in mind, we present the corresponding test set performances for different hyperparameter choices. To guide the eye we typically report both for ST and for DA the performance of the model that performed best/worst at

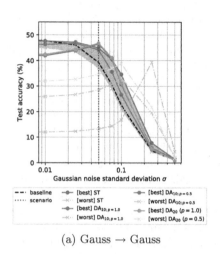

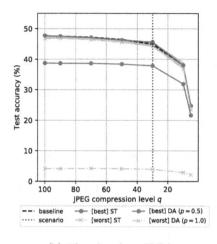

(a) Gauss → Gauss   (b) Thumbnail → JPEG

Fig. 1. Robustness properties of stability training (ST) vs. data augmentation (DA) for noise distorsions. The figure captions such as "Thumbnail → JPEG" refer to thumbnail resizing as training and JPEG as test distorsion. We typically report the performance of the best/worse model selected at the practical distorsion level. Subscripts refer to subsets of hyperparameters, i.e. [best] $DA_{10;p=0.5}$ refers to the best model among the set of all models with hyperparameter $p = 0.5$ trained for 10 epochs. On the contrary, values in parentheses denote hyperparameters of the selected best/worst model.

the specified practical distorsion level but we do not perform any form of model selection with respect to the distorsion hyperparameters. Finally, for ST we also report the performance range upper and lower bounds of any training setting at any test setting as a shaded area. This is used as an unbiased measure for the robustness of ST with respect to hyperparameter choices. In our results, we distinguish between those experiments where training and test distortion are of the same type and those where they differ. On the one hand, this allows us to investigate how well a method can increase robustness against a given distortion type and, on the other hand, it shows what side effects on other distortions this might induce.

In Figs. 1a, b, and 2a we compare the robustness properties of ST and DA for three different setups within the category of noise distorsions. Figure 1a shows the robustness using Gaussian noise as training distorsion, which corresponds to the setting considered in the original ST paper [33]. We observe in Fig. 1a that DA without reintroducing the reference image ($p = 1.0$) outperforms ST only with its peak performance at the chosen practical distorsion level but shows a worse performance compared to ST elsewhere. Even more importantly, an unfavorable hyperparameter choice for DA can lead to catastrophic forgetting, which can be seen quite drastically for the worst-performing DA models. This issue can be mitigated to some degree by the reintroduction of the reference image during training, here for $p = 0.5$, which, however results in worse performance (compared to DA with $p = 1.0$) at the practical distortion level. We also use this setting to illustrate the impact of an increased number of training epochs. Here we show results for DA trained for 20 epochs, which corresponds to the same number of batches seen during ST but double the number of labeled examples. Interestingly, increasing the number of training epochs does not result in a model with better performance or robustness. It only marginally improves the best-performing result found at 10 epochs. Even though the worst-performing model is improved by a sizable amount from 10 to 20 epochs, the ST range as illustrated by the area shaded in gray in Fig. 1a is still considerably smaller than the range of results obtained from models trained with DA. This leaves ST as the most favorable choice for stabilizing against Gaussian noise consistent with the claims in the original paper [33]. The qualitative findings concerning the impact of an increased number of epochs and the comparison of $p = 0.5$ and $p = 1.0$ represent a general pattern observed during all of our experiments. In the following plots we therefore conventionally show only the worst/best DA performance treating p as an additional hyperparameter and restrict ourselves to the setting of 10 training epochs for DA.

Figure 1b illustrates the cross-distorsion performance of both DA and ST. In this particular example, we trained with thumbnail rescaling and evaluated performance on JPEG compression. This setting resembles real-world applications where the model might encounter distorsion types unseen during training. As training and test distortion do not have many characteristics in common, we

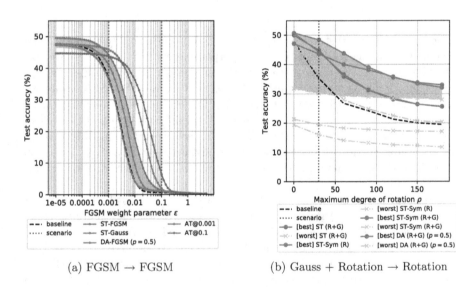

(a) FGSM → FGSM   (b) Gauss + Rotation → Rotation

Fig. 2. Robustness properties of stability training (ST) vs. data augmentation (DA) for FGSM adversarial examples and using multiple training distorsions. We use the same color-coding and nomenclature as in Fig. 1.

do not expect to see noticeable performance improvements via either method. Importantly, however, we can observe, that DA can severely harm the model's robustness against distortion types that were not present during training. Even the best possible model trained via data augmentation performed with a deficit of nearly 10% compared to baseline. ST, on the other hand, did not show any worsening impact. This example should not convey the impression that ST cannot acquire robustness from cross-category distortions. In fact, for any test distorsion in the noise category, ST performs best using Gaussian noise as training distorsion, while DA always favors coinciding training and test distorsions.

We also investigate the prospects of using ST to increase adversarial robustness. To this end, we dynamically generate adversarial examples via FGSM and feed them as the perturbed image via either ST, DA or adversarial training (AT) with $\mu = 0.5$ [9], where the latter corresponds to the optimization objective

$$L_{\mathrm{adv}}(x, x', \hat{y}) = \mu L_0(x, \hat{y}; \theta) + (1 - \mu)L_0(x', \hat{y}; \theta) \,, \tag{7}$$

where $\mu \in [0.1]$, x denotes the reference sample and x' the adversarial example and $\hat{y}$ is the ground truth label. In Fig. 2a, we observe that DA is unable to generalize at all, performing similar to baseline. ST offers a significant improvement compared to baseline performance across the entire intensity spectrum. Standard adversarial training offers no to marginal improvements at low intensity levels, but excels in mid-ranges, where it outperforms ST. To investigate this further, we also plot the results if we had selected the best-performing model for an extreme distorsion scenario ($\epsilon = 0.1$) instead of the regular practical scenario ($\epsilon = 0.001$). Here we see, that adversarial training sacrifices performance in the low-intensity domain while gaining in the mid- to high-intensity domains. The ST performance remains virtually unchanged comparing the best-performing models at extreme distorsion to that a practical distorsion level. As the gray ST band indicates, ST performance never drops below baseline performance. Interestingly, even ST with Gaussian noise leads to an increased adversarial robustness compared to the baseline performance. We are very well aware of the limitations of robustness against FGSM as indicator for general adversarial robustness [3] and merely see our findings as an indicator the general robustness properties of ST and a potential direction of future research.

Now we turn to the results on transformative distorsions as presented in Fig. 3. In particular, we compare the performance of the model trained using the symmetric stability objective from Eq. 6 to the performance of those trained with the standard stability objective. In fact, we observe in Fig. 3a that the symmetrized stability objective does remedy the shortcoming of the original stability objective when training with rotation. Across all intensity levels $\rho > 0$, the symmetrical objective can significantly increase the model's robustness towards rotation compared to regular ST. Even the increased performance of the original ST objective at $\rho = 0$ is consistent with expectations as the original ST loss distinguishes the reference image. We also show performance for DA ($p = 0.5$) with and without ($p = 1.0$) reintroducing the reference image. While the reintroduction of the reference image showed improvements in Fig. 1a, we observe

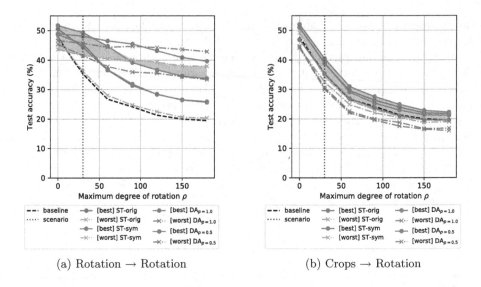

(a) Rotation → Rotation

(b) Crops → Rotation

Fig. 3. Robustness properties of stability training (ST) vs. data augmentation (DA) for transformative distorsions. We use the same color-coding and nomenclature as in Fig. 1.

the opposite effect in Fig. 3a. It is important to note, that the tested rotation range beyond the practical scenario is unrealistically large for real-world applications. In the range up to rotations in the practical scenario, the symmetrical stability loss offers the best performance of all configurations. However, it is interesting to note that the performance of the worst symmetrical ST model unlike that of the worst original ST model drops below the baseline performance in the undistorted case. Similarly to the noise category experiments, we evaluate the performance across distortion instances of the different type. This is shown exemplarily in Fig. 3b, where we trained models with varying crops of the input image and evaluated the resulting performance on rotated images. Again, we observe that symmetrical ST offers the best performance of all configurations across the entire intensity spectrum. Also, the gray area shows that no ST model drops below baseline performance, while DA does for unfavorable hyperparameter choices.

At this point we summarize the results of our single-distortion experiments: Even though we decided to present the results in the form of examples to illustrate the performance characteristics through the full range of distortion strengths, we want to stress that these examples just examplify the more general picture underlying our investigations, see also the figures in the supplementary material. For all considered distorsions in the setting of identical train and test distorsions ST outperformed DA in the practical distortion range in terms of best-model performance with a considerably smaller hyperparameter dependence. In particular, DA tends to optimize robustness by increasing the peak performance at the particular distorsion characteristics used during training whereas ST typically achieves a stable performance throughout the whole practical distorsion range, see e.g. Fig. 1a. ST also shows general robustness i.e. generalizes to unseen distorsions within the same noise/transformative distorsion category. We also investigated the use of cross-category training, i.e. training using a distorsion from the noise category while evaluating on the transformative category, but observed no noticeable improvements compared to baseline performance.

The more favorable setting and an interesting direction for future research turned out to be the combination of distorsions from both categories. As ST performs best for test distorsions of the noise categoy using Gaussian noise during training, we investigate the impact of using both Gaussian noise and rotation during training and compare its performance against models trained solely with the same distorsion as used for testing (rotation). As shown in Fig. 2b, regular ST offers some improvements across the entire intensity spectrum and shows no difference when adding Gaussian noise in addition to rotation during training. Data augmentation performs well when trained solely with rotation across the entire spectrum and can improve on its performance on mid to high intensity levels by adding Gaussian noise as an additional regularization. This comes, however, at the cost of a reduced performance in the practically relevant intensity range. The symmetrical stability loss offers the best performance across the entire spectrum of intensities, showcasing again how stability training is capable to utilize Gaussian noise a universal distorsion approximator to generally improve robustness. Also in this setting, the ST band is still considerably smaller than the performance range for DA applied using the two distorsions simultaneously.

6 Conclusion

In this work we investigated methods to increase the robustness of deep neural networks against various kinds of input distortions. To this end we thoroughly analyzed the prospects of using stability training [33] for this purpose, extending it beyond its original working domain of stabilization on Gaussian noise to arbitrary input distortions. We evaluated the proposed method on an ImageNet-scale image classification task and compared the robustness of models stabilized by stability training to those stabilized by data augmentation as predominantly used approach in practical applications to increase both generalization performance and robustness.

In our experiments we demonstrated that stability training performs on a par or even outperforms data augmentation in all investigated distortion settings ranging from noise distortions, including FGSM adversarial examples, to image transformations. Most importantly, stability training is considerably less sensitive to hyperparameter choices than data augmentation, whose performance on the original undistorted dataset may even deteriorate significantly compared to the baseline model for unfavorable hyperparameter values. Its generalizable robustness property makes stability training a particularly good choice for applications where the specific characteristics of the distortion to be encountered is unknown and general robustness is desired. The exploration of using multiple distortion types jointly for stabilization showed first promising results and represents an interesting direction for future research.

Acknowledgements. This work was supported by the Bundesministerium für Bildung und Forschung (BMBF) through the Berlin Big Data Center under Grant 01IS14013A and the Berlin Center for Machine Learning under Grant 01IS180371.

References

1. Bachman, P., Alsharif, O., Precup, D.: Learning with pseudo-ensembles. In: Ghahramani, Z., Welling, M., Cortes, C., Lawrence, N.D., Weinberger, K.Q. (eds.) NIPS, pp. 3365–3373. Curran Associates, Inc., New York (2014)
2. Berthelot, D., Carlini, N., Goodfellow, I., Papernot, N., Oliver, A., Raffel, C.: MixMatch: a holistic approach to semi-supervised learning (2019)
3. Carlini, N., et al.: On evaluating adversarial robustness. arXiv preprint: arXiv:1902.06705 (2019)
4. Chapelle, O., Schlkopf, B., Zien, A.: Semi-Supervised Learning. The MIT Press, Cambridge (2010)
5. Cubuk, E.D., Zoph, B., Mane, D., Vasudevan, V., Le, Q.V.: AutoAugment: learning augmentation policies from data. arXiv preprint: arXiv:1805.09501 (2018)
6. Frénay, B., Verleysen, M.: Classification in the presence of label noise: a survey. IEEE Trans. Neural Netw. Learn. Syst. **25**(5), 845–869 (2014)
7. French, R.M.: Catastrophic forgetting in connectionist networks. Trends Cogn. Sci. **3**(4), 128–135 (1994)
8. Gal, Y.: Uncertainty in deep learning. Ph.D. thesis, University of Cambridge (2016)
9. Goodfellow, I., Shlens, J., Szegedy, C.: Explaining and harnessing adversarial examples. In: International Conference on Learning Representations (2015)
10. Hataya, R., Nakayama, H.: Unifying semi-supervised and robust learning by mixup. In: ICLR the 2nd Learning from Limited Labeled Data (LLD) Workshop (2019)
11. He, K., Zhang, X., Ren, S., Sun, J.: Delving deep into rectifiers: surpassing human-level performance on ImageNet classification. In: CVPR, pp. 1026–1034 (2015)
12. He, K., Zhang, X., Ren, S., Sun, J.: Deep residual learning for image recognition. In: CVPR, pp. 770–778 (2016)
13. Ioffe, S., Szegedy, C.: Batch normalization: accelerating deep network training by reducing internal covariate shift. In: ICML, pp. 448–456 (2015)
14. Krizhevsky, A., Sutskever, I., Hinton, G.E.: ImageNet classification with deep convolutional neural networks. In: Pereira, F., Burges, C., Bottou, L., Weinberger, K. (eds.) NIPS, pp. 1097–1105. Curran Associates, Inc., New York (2012)
15. Laine, S., Aila, T.: Temporal ensembling for semi-supervised learning. In: ICLR (2017)
16. Miyato, T., Maeda, S.I., Koyama, M., Ishii, S.: Virtual adversarial training: a regularization method for supervised and semi-supervised learning. IEEE Trans. Pattern Anal. Mach. Intell. **41**(8), 1979–1993 (2018)
17. Montavon, G., Samek, W., Müller, K.R.: Methods for interpreting and understanding deep neural networks. Digit. Signal Process. **73**, 1–15 (2018)
18. Nesterov, Y.: A method for unconstrained convex minimization problem with the rate of convergence $O(1/k^2)$. Dokl. AN USSR **269**, 543–547 (1983)

19. Oliver, A., Odena, A., Raffel, C., Cubuk, E.D., Goodfellow, I.J.: Realistic evaluation of deep semi-supervised learning algorithms. arXiv preprint: arXiv:1804.09170 (2018)
20. Paszke, A., et al.: Automatic differentiation in PyTorch. In: NIPS Autodiff Workshop (2017)
21. Rajput, S., Feng, Z., Charles, Z., Loh, P.L., Papailiopoulos, D.: Does data augmentation lead to positive margin? arXiv preprint: arXiv:1905.03177 (2019)
22. Sajjadi, M., Javanmardi, M., Tasdizen, T.: Regularization with stochastic transformations and perturbations for deep semi-supervised learning. In: NIPS, pp. 1171–1179 (2016)
23. Silver, D., et al.: Mastering the game of Go with deep neural networks and tree search. Nature 529(7587), 484–489 (2016)
24. Stanford University's CS231 course: Tiny ImageNet. https://tiny-imagenet.herokuapp.com/. Accessed 7 May 2019
25. Szegedy, C., et al.: Intriguing properties of neural networks. arXiv preprint: arXiv:1312.6199 (2013)
26. Tarvainen, A., Valpola, H.: Mean teachers are better role models: weight-averaged consistency targets improve semi-supervised deep learning results. In: NIPS (2017)
27. Taylor, L., Nitschke, G.: Improving deep learning using generic data augmentation. arXiv preprint: arXiv:1708.06020 (2017)
28. Verma, V., Lamb, A., Kannala, J., Bengio, Y., Lopez-Paz, D.: Interpolation consistency training for semi-supervised learning. arXiv preprint: arXiv:1903.03825 (2019)
29. Xie, Q., Dai, Z., Hovy, E., Luong, M.T., Le, Q.V.: Unsupervised data augmentation. arXiv preprint: arXiv:1904.12848 (2019)
30. Yaeger, L.S., Lyon, R.F., Webb, B.J.: Effective training of a neural network character classifier for word recognition. In: Mozer, M.C., Jordan, M.I., Petsche, T. (eds.) NIPS, pp. 807–816. MIT Press, Cambridge (1997)
31. Zhang, C., Cui, J., Yang, B.: Learning optimal data augmentation policies via Bayesian optimization for image classification tasks (2019)
32. Zhang, H., Cisse, M., Dauphin, Y.N., Lopez-Paz, D.: mixup: Beyond empirical risk minimization. In: ICLR (2018)
33. Zheng, S., Song, Y., Leung, T., Goodfellow, I.: Improving the robustness of deep neural networks via stability training. In: CVPR, pp. 4480–4488 (2016)
34. Zhu, X.J.: Semi-supervised learning literature survey. Technical report, University of Wisconsin-Madison Department of Computer Sciences (2005)

2D and 3D Segmentation of Uncertain Local Collagen Fiber Orientations in SHG Microscopy

Lars Schmarje[1](✉)[iD], Claudius Zelenka[1][iD], Ulf Geisen[2][iD], Claus-C. Glüer[2][iD], and Reinhard Koch[1][iD]

[1] Multimedia Information Processing Group, Kiel University, Kiel, Germany
{las,cze,rk}@informatik.uni-kiel.de
[2] Molecular Imaging North Competence Center, Kiel University, Kiel, Germany
{ulf.geisen,glueer}@rad.uni-kiel.de

Abstract. Collagen fiber orientations in bones, visible with Second Harmonic Generation (SHG) microscopy, represent the inner structure and its alteration due to influences like cancer. While analyses of these orientations are valuable for medical research, it is not feasible to analyze the needed large amounts of local orientations manually. Since we have uncertain borders for these local orientations only rough regions can be segmented instead of a pixel-wise segmentation. We analyze the effect of these uncertain borders on human performance by a user study. Furthermore, we compare a variety of 2D and 3D methods such as classical approaches like Fourier analysis with state-of-the-art deep neural networks for the classification of local fiber orientations. We present a general way to use pretrained 2D weights in 3D neural networks, such as Inception-ResNet-3D a 3D extension of Inception-ResNet-v2. In a 10 fold cross-validation our two stage segmentation based on Inception-ResNet-3D and transferred 2D ImageNet weights achieves a human comparable accuracy.

Keywords: Comparison 2D and 3D · Weight transfer from 2D to 3D · Osteogenesis imperfecta · Second harmonic generation · Uncertain borders · Rough semantic segmentation

1 Introduction

In a variety of medical issues and research activities, computed tomography (CT) scans are used for bone examinations. However, most CT scans only have a resolution in the millimeter range. Special CT procedures allow resolutions of a few μm [4,17]. For this reason single collagen fiber bundles of about 2–3 μm [1] can not be detected well in CT scans. The structure and orientation of these

Electronic supplementary material The online version of this chapter (https://doi.org/10.1007/978-3-030-33676-9_26) contains supplementary material, which is available to authorized users.

© Springer Nature Switzerland AG 2019
G. A. Fink et al. (Eds.): DAGM GCPR 2019, LNCS 11824, pp. 374–386, 2019.
https://doi.org/10.1007/978-3-030-33676-9_26

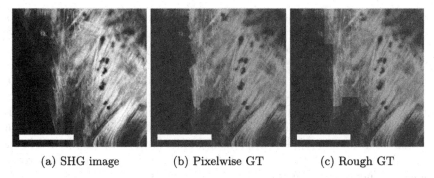

(a) SHG image   (b) Pixelwise GT   (c) Rough GT

Fig. 1. Example of a SHG input image and the corresponding ground-truth - Note that while (b) is a pixel-wise ground-truth annotation we are in a setting with uncertain borders. Hence we should try to recreate a rough segmentation as shown in (c). The white scale bar depicts a size of 100 μm. Color code: Similar orientation - red, Dissimilar orientation - green, Not of interest - blue (Color figure online)

bundles allow us to make conclusions about changes in the bone (e.g. by growth or disease) [1]. These characteristics of the inner bone structure are valuable for research in the fields of age determination, disease detection and cancer research.

Second harmonic generation (SHG) microscopy can visualize these structures of collagen due to its higher resolution. This methods allows us to generate large amounts of dense 3D scans of collagen fibers in bones. It is time-consuming to create statistics of fiber bundles orientations or to mark regions of interest by experts. Moreover, manual annotations for large datasets are not feasible due to time constraints, budget and subjective biases. These biases are results of the uncertain borders in local fiber orientations. Therefore, an automatic analysis of fiber bundles orientation in large amounts of SHG data would benefit a variety of medical research activities. Large scale studies are not practical without automatic analysis.

The disease osteogenesis imperfecta (OI), also known as brittle bone disease, changes the orientation of fiber bundles in the bones of affected people and animals [1]. Hence SHG data of healthy and diseased mice is predestined for the evaluation of new methods.

Consequently, we developed different automatic algorithms for fiber bundle orientation analysis. We considered the orientation of fiber bundles in a local region as a classification problem. We focused ourselves on three classes: Bundles with similar (S) and dissimilar (D) orientations and everything else or not of interest (N) (e.g. noise, background). Figure 1 shows an example input and the corresponding ground-truth segmentation images.

The classification of a local region can also be defined as a rough semantic segmentation of the entire image. Since borders of local orientations are not well defined and can be described as highly uncertain and fluent, the goal is not to create pixel-wise segmentation. Therefore, we are interested in rough localization of these regions and their classification. Due to large regions which are not of interest (N) a large class imbalance in favor of this class exists and must be addressed. We analyzed the effect of uncertain borders on human performance in the task of rough fiber orientation segmentation by a user study.

We investigated classical approaches like Fourier analysis and state-of-the-art methods like deep neural networks. Instead of reporting only the best results we present a complete overview and comparison for future research in rough semantic segmentation. Most of our neural networks use a state-of-the-art backbone and domain specific adaptions. We aimed to change as little as possible in the original backbones to allow interchangeability with other backbones in the future. We show how a state-of-the-art 2D backbone can be used in 3D rough semantic segmentation. We call this network Inception-ResNet-3D. Especially we present a way to transfer pretrained 2D weights into the 3D case. The code is publicly available for reproducibility.[1]

To sum up, the main contributions of our work are:

- We report a systematical comparison of algorithms for classification and segmentation in 2D and 3D with uncertain borders. We use a novel dense 3D SHG dataset with more than 4500 slices for method development and testing. Human performance to classify uncertain collagen fiber orientations on this dataset is also reported.
- We show a general way to convert weights from the 2D into 3D.
- Our two stage approach with Inception-ResNet-3D and transferred 2D weights achieves a performance comparable to humans for uncertain collagen fiber segmentation in a 10 fold cross-validation.

2   Related Work

Currently neural networks are state-of-the-art in the field of image data classification (e.g. ImageNet [18]). A variety of neural networks have emerged over the years [7,8,10,21,23,24]. These networks started with a simple architecture (e.g. VGG-16 [21]). They integrated new structure elements like residual [7] and inception blocks [24] as they were developed and proved their superior performance. This development led to an increase of the top1 accuracy on the ImageNet test set from 71.3% with VGG-16 to 80.3% with Inception-ResNet-v2. Parallel the depth and thereby the complexity increased from 23 to 572 layers[2].

Semantic segmentation gives a classification for every pixel in an image and is an extension of a classification problem. Shelhamer et al. [20] first proposed to use fully convolutional networks to solve semantic segmentation. U-Net [16] is a network for semantic segmentation which was designed for medical images. Often semantic segmentation networks consist of a down- and a upsampling part [16,20].

However, the current state-of-the-art approaches for image classification and semantic segmentation have two major drawbacks in the context of uncertain

---

[1] https://github.com/Emprime/uncertain-fiber-segmentation.
[2] Values are based on the reference implementation in Keras.

local fiber orientation classification. We have 3D data and a high uncertainty for the borders. Most research focuses on 2D data while Zhou et al. [26] showed that it is beneficial to use the 3D information for organ segmentation. Networks like PointNet [14] can classify 3D point clouds yet they do not consider dense 3D input as we have. The network 3D-U-Net [3] represents an expansion of U-Net to 3D data. It is typically used to segment 3D objects like organs [3]. This fixes the first drawback while the second one remains. Objects with uncertain borders like our fiber orientations are not well represented.

While 3D extensions of Inception-ResNet-v2 have been presented in [6,9] the usage of 2D pretraining is not so widely used. Parallel to our research Shan et al. proposed a 2D weight transfer strategy to 3D [19] which is most similar to ours (see Subsect. 4.1).

Collagen structures in SHG images have been analyzed in several publications [1,2,5,11,15,22,25]. They were analyzed in tissue [2] and bones [5,25]. Rao et al. [15] presented how Fourier analysis can be used to investigate the orientation of collagen fibers. The Fourier analysis was extended from small regions to the whole scan in [1,11,22]. The analysis classified small image parts as anisotropic, isotropic and dark. These classifications where used to calculate the distributions of classes over an image. In [22] these distributions where used to detect injured tendons. Moreover, Ambekar et al. [1] showed the change of distribution due to aging can be used to determine the age of pigs. Lau et al. [11] used the 3D information of SHG data and could show an increase in performance.

Nevertheless, their analysis is based on only few (<100) images. An analysis on larger amounts of data is not known. The data shown in the papers seems to be of overall of a good quality. Artifacts, noise and blurring and impact of performance was not reported.

Liang et al. [12] state to be the first to analyze SHG images with neural networks. They estimated the elastic properties of collagenous tissue. A classification or segmentation of fibers were not part of their investigation.

To our knowledge, we are the first who use neural networks to automatically classify and segment local collagen fiber orientation in large amounts of 2D or 3D data. In contrast to previous neural network literature we use 3D data and adapt our networks to uncertain borders. In comparison to earlier fiber analyses we utilize neural networks to process large amount of mixed quality data.

3 User Study

While we knew that we operated in a context with uncertain borders we did not know how this would impact performance. Therefore, we investigated this issue by a random sample user study. Our goal was to examine how well humans can classify and segment local fiber orientations. We compared 15 different people with each other (interpersonal) and 5 results of the same person over time (intrapersonal).

The participants were given two tasks. The first task was to chose one annotation out of 5 given example annotations for one image. This task was repeated for 10 different images. The second task was to create an annotation for 24 images.

For the first task we calculated the Pearson correlation coefficient between the annotation selections of all participants (interpersonal) or over time (intrapersonal). This leads to a mean absolute coefficient of 0.44 with a standard deviation of 0.26 for the intrapersonal comparison. The interpersonal comparison results in a mean absolute coefficient of 0.24 with a standard deviation of 0.2.

For the second task we calculated the accuracies of the created annotations with the ground-truth (see Subsect. 5.2 for the metric definition). The intrapersonal comparison reached a mean accuracy of 78.29% with a standard deviation of 2.40% over all 24 images. The interpersonal comparison resulted in a mean accuracy of 58.83% with a standard deviation of 7.44%.

All in all we see that it is more difficult for different people to select or create consistent annotations than for one person over time. However, even for a person over time the selection and creation is not perfect. We can state that humans achieve only about 78% accuracy consistency with themselves. If we train and evaluate a neural network on human created ground-truth with this consistency rate we can not expect that an algorithm performs significantly better.

4   Methods

All methods use the same datasets although the 2D methods ignore the inherent three-dimensional information. Therefore, 2D data will be referred to as scan slice or image and 3D data as scan. For all methods we investigated a variety of hyperparameters such as batchsize, backbones and loss variations. We will mention in the method description only important hyperparameter selections and specialties. For further details see the supplementary materials.

4.1   Weight Transfer 2D to 3D

We want to utilize the pretrained ImageNet weights in our 3D Networks and thus we have to transfer the 2D kernel weights into 3D kernel weights. Technically this is a function $I : \mathbb{R}^{w \times h \times c} \to \mathbb{R}^{w \times h \times d \times c}$ that transforms a 3D (width, height, channels) matrix M_1 into a 4D (width, height, depth, channels) matrix M_2 with $w, h, d, c \in \mathbb{N}$.

We investigated two methods for the weight transformation. We denote the set $\{1, .., N\}$ by $[n]$. The first approach is to divide M_1 by d and stack them d times to create M_2 for a given depth $d \in \mathbb{N}$:

$$M_{2(i,j,k,l)} = M_{1(i,j,l)}/d \text{ for all } i \in [w], j \in [h], k \in [d], \text{ and } l \in [c]. \tag{1}$$

The second approach is to insert the 3D matrix into the 4D matrix and fill the rest up with zeros. Shan et al. proposed in [19] a similar method. For given odd depth $d \in \mathbb{N}$ and center element $\hat{c} = \frac{(d-1)}{2} + 1$ this is defined as

$$M_{2(i,j,k,l)} = \begin{cases} M_{1(i,j,l)} & \text{for } k = \hat{c} \\ 0 & \text{for } k \in [d] \setminus \{\hat{c}\} \end{cases} \tag{2}$$

and all $i \in [w], j \in [h], k \in [d], m \in [c]$.

Henceforth, we refer to theses transformations if we talk about 2D weights in a 3D context or transferred weights. See Subsect. 4.4 for further details on the selected transfer strategies. We use this weight transformations in the network Inception-Resnet-3D a 3D extension of Inception-ResNet-v2 [23]. In general the architecture is the same but with 3D layers as done before by [6,9]. In the case of asymmetric input data we introduce asymmetric strides in the downsamplings in the stem block. These asymmetric strides create symmetric input for deeper layers.

4.2 Weighted Focal Loss

As mentioned before we have to address the issue of class imbalance in our training data and chose to investigate different loss variations. Lin et al. defined the novel loss function Focal Loss in [13] which should automatically balance the contribution of classes in skewed cases. As mentioned in [13] the loss L : $[0,1]^n \times \{0,1\}^n \rightarrow [0,1]$ can be extended to the non binary case as shown in Eq. 3 with $n \in \mathbb{N}$ being the number of classes and γ the Focal Loss parameter. Furthermore, we integrated weights $w \in \mathbb{R}^n$ for every prediction $\hat{y} \in [0,1]^n$ and ground-truth $y \in \{0,1\}^n$. In our case $n = 3$ and the values of y and $\hat{y}$ correspond to these three classes.

$$L(\hat{y}, y) = - \sum_{i \in [n]} w_i (1 - \hat{y_i})^\gamma y_i log(\hat{y_i}) \tag{3}$$

Keep in mind that Eq. 3 is equal to cross entropy if $\gamma = 0$ and $w = \{1\}^3$.

4.3 2D Methods

Fourier Analysis. As a reference we reimplemented a classification based on the Fourier analysis in small image patches [15]. We used thresholds like in [15] to discriminate different classes.

Classification. A straight forward approach for local region classification is to create such regions by splitting the images into smaller image parts each with the same width and height. An equal class distribution was enforced on these image regions and a graphical representation of the input is given in Fig. 2a. A rough segmentation for the image can be generated out of the classifications for all image parts.

During development we discovered that classification accuracy was higher if the image part size was larger. These larger sizes lead to a rougher segmentation and thus we used an ensemble and majority voting to combine the benefits of a smaller image part size and the higher accuracy of larger image parts. We used an Inception-ResNet-v2 [23] backbone with pretrained weights, $\gamma = 0$ and $w = \{1\}^3$.

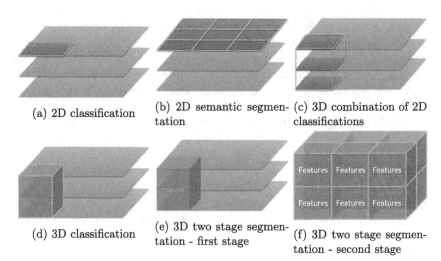

(a) 2D classification

(b) 2D semantic segmentation

(c) 3D combination of 2D classifications

(d) 3D classification

(e) 3D two stage segmentation - first stage

(f) 3D two stage segmentation - second stage

Fig. 2. Graphical representation of the used input and output for the different proposed methods - The orange slices represent the SHG images which form a scan together. The blue tiles or blocks are the inputs to the network while the green markings show the output format. For example (a) shows a 2D image part as an input and one value as output. While (f) takes features as a 3D matrix and outputs a 3D matrix. (Color figure online)

Semantic Segmentation. Classification of image parts has two major drawbacks. It is time consuming since a lot of image parts have to be processed and a post processing step is needed to combine the classifications to a segmentation. A parallel rough semantic segmentation of an image can overcome both these problems. In contrast to other literature [16,20] we use only a downscaling part and not an upsampling part in our segmentation network. As described earlier we are not interested in a fine segmentation and can drop the upsampling because of this (see Fig. 2b).

The segmentation networks differ from the original backbones mostly in the output. The architecture is shown in Fig. 3a. We use an average pooling layer and a 1×1 convolutional layer instead of a global average pooling layer and a fully connected layer for multiple reasons. Firstly, we want to create a matrix as an output which consists of softmax outputs for every row and column. Secondly, we can incorporate the neighborhood information through the pooling layer. Thirdly, we have to use a convolutional layer for the output because otherwise the number of parameters for the fully connected layer would have become unmanageable. In addition we can create a finer segmentation than the ensemble above (Subsect. 4.3) and also use neighborhood information due to average pooling layers. We used an Inception-ResNet-v2 [23] backbone with pretrained weights, $\gamma = 0$ and $w = (\frac{16/}{41}, \frac{24}{41}, \frac{1}{41})$. The weights are needed to account for the class imbalance in the input data.

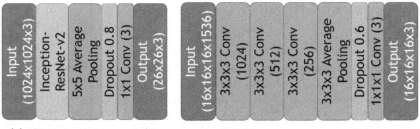

(a) 2D semantic segmentation   (b) 3D two stage segmentation

Fig. 3. Architecture of the 2D semantic segmentation network with backbone and the second stage network for the 3D two stage segmentation - Different layers have different colorings. The main part of Inception-ResNet-v2 up to the global average pooling layer is described as one block. The dimensions for in- and output and the number of feature maps for convolutional layers are given in brackets. The kernel size is given before the layer name.

4.4   3D Methods

Combination of 2D Classifications. This method is an extension of the 2D classification by combination. We use the 2D classifications and include 3D information by averaging over the classifications which are positioned next to each other. This simple aggregation yields a 3D classification but inherits the drawbacks of the 2D classification. A graphical representation is shown in Fig. 2c.

Classification. This method is a extension of the 2D classification in 3D. Instead of image parts (square) we use scan blocks (cuboid) for the classification. The graphical representation of the input and output is shown in Fig. 2d. However, we do not use an ensemble to combine different 3D classifications. We used our proposed Inception-ResNet-3D with transferred 2D weights based on ImageNet, $\gamma = 2$, $w = \{1\}^3$ and used the transfer strategy based on Eq. 1.

Two Stage Segmentation. In the 2D case parallel segmentation of a complete image could utilize the neighborhood information for every entry in the output matrix. In order to combine the information of a whole scan for an output and still fit in the memory of one GPU we had to take a two stage approach. The idea is to extract features with a pretrained network and then combine these features in a second network to create a 3D matrix where every entry correspondence to the three classes (graphical representation see Fig. 2e and f).

We used Inception-ResNet-3D as an extraction network with transferred ImageNet weights with the transfer strategy based on Eq. 1. Unlike in 3D classification we do not want one classification but the features as output. The second stage is a small network out of convolutional and average pooling layer to combine the 3D matrix of features to class predictions. The architecture is shown in Fig. 3b and was inspired by Fig. 3a.

5   Experimental Results

5.1   Dataset

We developed our methods on one dataset which was created by the MOIN CC[3]. The dataset consists of 4736 SHG images from 35 scans of 6 mice where 3 mice had the disease OI and the others do not. The scans were taken on different parts of the legs and had a resolution of 1000×1000 px or 1024×1024 px while capturing $250\,\mu m \times 250\,\mu m$ of the bone. We cannot downscale these images because we would loose the necessary resolution fine fiber structures. The depth of each scan was variable and ranged from 78 to 214 images while the distance in the bone between each image is $0.5\,\mu m$.

A main property of the data is the class imbalance. Roughly 2% of the data belongs to the class S (similar orientation) and 3% to the class D (dissimilar orientation). The remaining 95% belong to the class N (not of interest) and are, therefore, not interesting in medical research. The data was split in to a training, validation and test set. Figure 4 displays three example of used SHG images which represent the variety in the input data.

Moreover, investigations of selected background regions showed a high scanner noise. The average grey value (0–255) of the background should be zero but varied between 2.91 and 40.2. On average the registered grey values differ from the real values with a mean of 9.18 and a standard deviation of 8.79.

5.2   Evaluation Metrics

We use an adapted accuracy function to measure the performance of our results. In short we use the mean of accuracies per class as our accuracy measure. Our function $meanacc$ for prediction $\hat{y} \in [n]^k$ and ground-truth $y \in [n]^k$ with $n \in \mathbb{N}$ number of classes and $k \in \mathbb{N}$ entries is defined as follows

$$meanacc(\hat{y}, y) = \frac{1}{n} \sum_{j=1}^{n} \frac{\sum_{i=1}^{k} \mathbb{1}_{\hat{y}_i = y_i, \hat{y}_i = j}}{\sum_{i=1}^{k} \mathbb{1}_{y_i = j}}. \tag{4}$$

The function $meanacc$ has the benefit of being stable against class imbalance and is the same as the normal accuracy in the case of class balance. It allows an estimation of performance in a single value without tuning weights. In this paper accuracy on our data always refers to $meanacc$.

5.3   Method Comparison

We used a strict data separation during development to be able to compare methods. All hyperparameters were selected based on the validation set. The test set was only used during method comparison. In general we noticed two trends. Firstly, better network performance on ImageNet translates to improved

---

[3] Molecular Imaging North Competence Center.

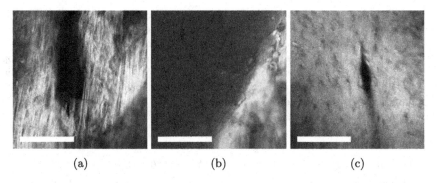

Fig. 4. Examples of used SHG images - (a) shows a desirable image. We have sharp and fine collagen structures while the noise ratio is low. (b) shows a noisy image where we can see collagen structures on the right hand side. Due to blurring and noise we can only detect rough shapes. (c) shows the macroscopic structure of the bone. We can detect the hole in the center but no single fibers or fiber bundles. The white scale bar depicts a size of 100 μm.

accuracies in all our methods. This isn't noteworthy for tasks like 2D classification but for improvements in segmentation and feature extraction tasks it is. Secondly, pretrained weights ensure a good initialization and lead to greater accuracies. This is expected and reported for 2D classification tasks but the fact that pretraining can be interpolated to a 3D case and still ensures greater performance is significant.

Table 1 compares all presented methods with regard to run-time, resolution and accuracy. The Fourier analysis results in the worst performance even on the validation set. Due to this inferior performance and the long run-time we did not evaluate the method further. We believe that the high variability in the data can not be captured from such a simple approach. The method of 2D semantic segmentation has the fastest run-time and the finest resolution. The accuracy is with about 65% the best for all 2D methods. The methods 3D classification and 3D two stage segmentation score a higher accuracy but have a rougher resolution and a longer run-time. The best accuracy of 72% is achieved by 3D two stage segmentation.

In general we see that it is beneficial to process as much data as possible simultaneously to achieve a high accuracy. This result can be explained due to the fact that simultaneous processing incorporates a larger neighborhood. Furthermore, we see that there is not one best method in all regards. Only a trade-off between different characteristics can be chosen.

It is remarkable that the features used in the second stage were extracted with transferred 2D ImageNet weights and still lead to the best results. Furthermore no adaption to domain specific weights is needed. In the context of a human consistency of about 78.29% in the user study (Sect. 3) a result of 72% is remarkable.

Table 1. Overview of the best results on the test set for each method - Run-time is the time it took to process the test set once which includes pre- and postprocessing. Resolution describes the number of pixels in the input that are mapped to one output value. Smaller resolutions result in finer segmentation but also in an accuracy drop for some methods and are, therefore, not reported here. The accuracy is reported on the test set. The best result of each column is marked bold. *Due to the inferior performance on the validation data and long run-time we did not evaluate the method Fourier analysis on the test set.

Method	Run-time	Resolution	Accuracy
2D Fourier analysis	N/A*	$16 \times 16 \times 1$	55.00%*
2D classification	101 min	$64 \times 64 \times 1$	59.54%
3D combination of 2D classifications	101 min	$64 \times 64 \times 16$	59.68%
2D semantic segmentation	**14 min**	$\mathbf{40 \times 40 \times 1}$	64.58%
3D classification	17 min	$128 \times 128 \times 64$	70.51%
3D two stage segmentation	72 min	$64 \times 64 \times 16$	**72.18%**

5.4   Cross-validation

We did 10 fold cross-validation on the complete dataset to verify that the chosen random split in different sets introduced no bias and represent the real data distribution. The data was split 10 times into a training (50%), a validation (25%) and a test (25%) set. We split randomly but kept only splits where at least 2% of the data had the class S and another 2% the class D. We put scans from the same bone region into the same set.

We trained the method two stage segmentation on the training set, used the best weights on the validation set and evaluated on the test set. The mean accuracy over 10 runs is 75.79%. Figure 5 shows that the accuracies for all runs are in a margin of about 10% around the mean. Some runs achieve an accuracy above the expected accuracy based on the user study.

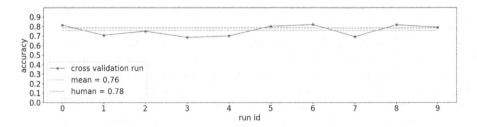

Fig. 5. Results of the cross-validation with mean and human performance based on the user study

6 Conclusion

We compared a variety of methods for rough semantic segmentation of collagen fiber orientation in 2D and 3D. As a dataset we used a novel collection of dense 3D SHG scans which is larger and more diverse as previously used datasets [1,11]. Our conducted user study implies that human can reach an average consistency of about 78.29% on the task of uncertain collagen fiber orientation segmentation. This results in a similar expected accuracy for trained algorithm due to the human annotated ground-truth. We showed how to use transformed 2D ImageNet weights in 3D networks in general and in Inception-ResNet-3D in particular. We proposed a two stage model that can simultaneously process large 3D inputs and use transformed 2D weights. This best method two stage segmentation achieves an average accuracy of 75.79% over 10 fold cross-validation. Based on the user study we can say that we created an algorithm with near human performance.

The presented user study led to great insights into possible performance of neural networks. It will be beneficial to repeat the user study at a larger scale. We are confident that two stage segmentation with transferred weights can be applied in different 3D classification and rough segmentation tasks. We will investigate these usages in the future. Furthermore, we will investigate how to create more objective ground-truth for example by leveraging pretrained features and reduced supervision.

References

1. Ambekar, R., Chittenden, M., Jasiuk, I., Toussaint, K.C.: Quantitative second-harmonic generation microscopy for imaging porcine cortical bone: comparison to sem and its potential to investigate age-related changes. Bone **50**(3), 643–650 (2012)
2. Campagnola, P.J., Loew, L.M.: Second-harmonic imaging microscopy for visualizing biomolecular arrays in cells, tissues and organisms. Nat. Biotechnol. **21**, 1356–1360 (2003)
3. Çiçek, Ö., Abdulkadir, A., Lienkamp, S.S., Brox, T., Ronneberger, O.: 3D U-Net: learning dense volumetric segmentation from sparse annotation. In: Ourselin, S., Joskowicz, L., Sabuncu, M.R., Unal, G., Wells, W. (eds.) MICCAI 2016, Part II. LNCS, vol. 9901, pp. 424–432. Springer, Cham (2016). https://doi.org/10.1007/978-3-319-46723-8_49
4. Genant, H., Engelke, K., Prevrhal, S.: Advanced CT bone imaging in osteoporosis. Rheumatology **47**(Suppl. 4), iv9–iv16 (2008)
5. Genthial, R., et al.: Label-free imaging of bone multiscale porosity and interfaces using third-harmonic generation microscopy. Sci. Rep. **7**(1), 3419 (2017)
6. Hassani, B., Mahoor, M.H.: Facial expression recognition using enhanced deep 3D convolutional neural networks. In: 2017 IEEE Conference on Computer Vision and Pattern Recognition Workshops (CVPRW), pp. 2278–2288 (2017)
7. He, K., Zhang, X., Ren, S., Sun, J.: Deep residual learning for image recognition. In: 2016 IEEE Conference on Computer Vision and Pattern Recognition (CVPR), pp. 770–778 (2016)

8. Huang, G., Liu, Z., van der Maaten, L., Weinberger, K.Q.: Densely connected convolutional networks. In: 2017 IEEE Conference on Computer Vision and Pattern Recognition (CVPR), pp. 2261–2269 (2017)
9. Kang, G., Liu, K., Hou, B., Zhang, N.: 3D multi-view convolutional neural networks for lung nodule classification. PloS ONE **12**(11), e0188290 (2017)
10. Krizhevsky, A., Sutskever, I., Hinton, G.E.: ImageNet classification with deep convolutional neural networks. Commun. ACM **60**, 84–90 (2012)
11. Lau, T.Y., Ambekar, R., Toussaint, K.C.: Quantification of collagen fiber organization using three-dimensional fourier transform-second-harmonic generation imaging. Opt. Exp. **20**(19), 21821–21832 (2012)
12. Liang, L., Liu, M., Sun, W.: A deep learning approach to estimate chemically-treated collagenous tissue nonlinear anisotropic stress-strain responses from microscopy images. Acta Biomater. **63**, 227–235 (2017)
13. Lin, T.Y., Goyal, P., Girshick, R.B., He, K., Dollár, P.: Focal loss for dense object detection. In: 2017 IEEE International Conference on Computer Vision (ICCV), pp. 2999–3007 (2017)
14. Qi, C.R., Su, H., Mo, K., Guibas, L.J.: PointNet: deep learning on point sets for 3D classification and segmentation. In: 2017 IEEE Conference on Computer Vision and Pattern Recognition (CVPR), pp. 77–85 (2017)
15. Rao, R.A.R., Mehta, M.R., Toussaint, K.C.: Fourier transform-second-harmonic generation imaging of biological tissues. Opt. Exp. **17**(17), 14534–14542 (2009)
16. Ronneberger, O., Fischer, P., Brox, T.: U-Net: convolutional networks for biomedical image segmentation. In: Navab, N., Hornegger, J., Wells, W.M., Frangi, A.F. (eds.) MICCAI 2015, Part III. LNCS, vol. 9351, pp. 234–241. Springer, Cham (2015). https://doi.org/10.1007/978-3-319-24574-4_28
17. Rueckel, J., Stockmar, M.K., Pfeiffer, F., Herzen, J.: Spatial resolution characterization of a X-ray microCT system. Appl. Radiat. Isot. **94**, 230–234 (2014)
18. Russakovsky, O., et al.: ImageNet large scale visual recognition challenge. Int. J. Comput. Vis. **115**, 211–252 (2015)
19. Shan, H., et al.: 3-D convolutional encoder-decoder network for low-dose CT via transfer learning from a 2-D trained network. IEEE Trans. Med. Imaging **37**, 1522–1534 (2018)
20. Shelhamer, E., Long, J., Darrell, T.: Fully convolutional networks for semantic segmentation. In: 2015 IEEE Conference on Computer Vision and Pattern Recognition (CVPR), pp. 3431–3440 (2015)
21. Simonyan, K., Zisserman, A.: Very deep convolutional networks for large-scale image recognition. CoRR abs/1409.1556 (2015)
22. Sivaguru, M., et al.: Quantitative analysis of collagen fiber organization in injured tendons using fourier transform-second harmonic generation imaging. Opt. Exp. **18**(24), 24983–24993 (2010)
23. Szegedy, C., Ioffe, S., Vanhoucke, V., Alemi, A.A.: Inception-v4, Inception-ResNet and the impact of residual connections on learning. In: Thirty-First AAAI Conference on Artificial Intelligence (2017)
24. Szegedy, C., et al.: Going deeper with convolutions. In: 2015 IEEE Conference on Computer Vision and Pattern Recognition (CVPR), pp. 1–9 (2015)
25. Thomas, B., et al.: Second-harmonic generation imaging of collagen in ancient bone. Bone Rep. **7**, 137–144 (2017)
26. Zhou, X., et al.: Performance evaluation of 2D and 3D deep learning approaches for automatic segmentation of multiple organs on CT images. In: Medical Imaging 2018: Computer-Aided Diagnosis, vol. 10575, p. 105752C. International Society for Optics and Photonics (2018)

Points2Pix: 3D Point-Cloud to Image Translation Using Conditional GANs

Stefan Milz[1]([✉]), Martin Simon[1]([✉]), Kai Fischer[1], Maximillian Pöpperl[1], and Horst-Michael Gross[2]

[1] Valeo Schalter und Sensoren GmbH, Kronach, Germany
martin.simon@valeo.com
[2] Ilmenau University of Technology, Ilmenau, Germany

Abstract. We present the first approach for 3D point-cloud to image translation based on conditional Generative Adversarial Networks (cGAN). The model handles multi-modal information sources from different domains, i.e. raw point-sets and images. The generator is capable of processing three conditions, whereas the point-cloud is encoded as raw point-set and camera projection. An image background patch is used as constraint to bias environmental texturing. A global approximation function within the generator is directly applied on the point-cloud (Point-Net). Hence, the representative learning model incorporates global 3D characteristics directly at the latent feature space. Conditions are used to bias the background and the viewpoint of the generated image. This opens up new ways in augmenting or texturing 3D data to aim the generation of fully individual images. We successfully evaluated our method on the KITTI and SunRGBD dataset with an outstanding object detection inception score.

1 Introduction

Domain translation is a well known and widely applied problem. It is typically treated in computer graphics or computer vision. Most research focuses on image-to-image translation [7,27,34]. Examples are Semantic-Labels to Image (e.g. Labels to Street-Scene, Labels to Facades) or Image conversions (e.g. Day to Night, Black-and-White to Color). Those techniques deal with real domain translation problems, since they convert semantic sensor-independent context into realistic RGB image data or vice versa. However, domain translation is performed on top of images. Both domains encode the information as RGB values in pictures with a spatial dependency. We call that single mode domain translation:

$$G_{x \to y} : x \to y \quad x, y \in \mathbb{R}^{w \times h \times 3}$$
$$G_{y \to x} : y \to x \tag{1}$$

Whereas, $G_{x \to y}, G_{y \to x}$ describe the translation functions between both image domains x, y with fixed image sizes: h (height), w (width).

S. Milz, M. Simon and K. Fischer—Equal contribution.

G. A. Fink et al. (Eds.): DAGM GCPR 2019, LNCS 11824, pp. 387–400, 2019.
https://doi.org/10.1007/978-3-030-33676-9_27

We propose a novel multi-modal domain translation model using the example of 3D point-cloud to image translation. The treated problem is formally known as:

$$G_{p \to y} : p \to y \quad p \in \mathbb{R}^{n \times 3} \quad y \in \mathbb{R}^{w \times h \times 3} \tag{2}$$

Here, n describes the number of points within the point-set. Our work is limited to $G_{p \to y}$ (not $G_{y \to p}$). Therefore an extensive new architecture is presented as combination of a typical encoder-decoder for image segmentation (UNet: [21]) as proposed by [7]. More important is the models second input, where the architecture incorporates the real point-set to add 3D characteristics into the global feature space for constraint based individual image generation. We put conditions as viewpoint dependent projection and background image patches for fully individual image generation in compliance with 3D specifications (conditions: background, shape, distance, viewpoint).

2   Related Work

2.1   Image Generation

Handcrafted Losses. As image generation could be reduced to per-pixel classification/regression with a wide application area it turns out to have a long tradition [6,23,30,31]. Those applications suppose a conditionally unstructured loss applied on the output space, i.e. a pixel independence in terms of semantic relationship is supposed. The performance of those approaches strongly depends on the loss design, e.g. semantic segmentation [15].

Conditional GANs. Conditional GANs (cGAN) instead learn structured losses that affect the overall output in form of a joint improvement [7]. In common, the cGAN is applied in a conditional setting. For image generation researchers were setting variable conditions: e.g. discrete labels [4,14], text [20] and images [7,27,34].

In general the cGAN performs a mapping function G, called generator, based on a condition c and a random noise vector z to generate an image y:

$$G : \{c, z\} \to y \quad y \in \mathbb{R}^{w \times h \times 3} \quad c = \begin{cases} \in \mathbb{R} & \to \text{label-to-image} \\ \in \mathbb{R}^t & \to \text{text-to-image} \\ \in \mathbb{R}^{w \times h \times 3} & \to \text{image-to-image} \end{cases} \tag{3}$$

For image-to-image translation [7] proposes a *U-Net* like structure for G. To create realistic images at higher resolutions (e.g. 1024×2048) [27] recommend a pyramidal approach for G similar to a *PSPNet* [32].

In general, the cGAN is composed by G and a competing discriminator D, which distinguishes between real images and created fake ones. A well-established discriminator network is the *Patchgan* [10] proposed by [7]. Derived from that the competing objective of the cGAN could be described by its loss L_{cGAN}:

$$L_{cGAN}(G, D) = \mathbb{E}_{c,y}\{\log(D(c, y))\} + \mathbb{E}_{c,z}\{\log(1 - D(c, G(c, z)))\} \tag{4}$$

2.2   Point-Cloud Processing

High requirements for perception tasks of robotic applications enforced the usage of 3D sensors, e.g. RGBD-cameras [26], Lidar (Valeo SCALA). Research progress in the field of 3D point-cloud processing received a boost in the recent years. In principle, point-clouds have specific properties that clearly distinguish them from images. Hence, specific processing models are needed. Points usually are not ordered, there is no grid that encodes the 3D position as an image does. The overall category of a point-set is influenced by the interaction of points among others. Only the global sum of the points forms a shape with a meaning. Last, point-sets are invariant to basic transformations like translation or rotation. Therefore the combination of 3D points clouds and machine learning is indispensable. The processing type could be categorized into the following three classes.

Real 3D Point-Cloud Processing.   [16] proposed the first neural network architecture *Point-Net* that handles natural points sets for classification and segmentation tasks with outperforming segmentation results on ShapeNet [2]: **mIoU 83.7.** The model does not use convolutional layers, but fully connected ones and directly processes the coordinates of the point-set (size n): $p = x_1..., x_n$ with $p \in \mathbb{R}^{n \times 3}$. A chain of local transformations h on the point-set followed by a global max-pooling layer is used to create an overall feature space, i.e. a global approximation function:

$$f(x_1, ..., x_n) \approx g(h(x_1), ..., h(x_n)) \qquad f : 2^{\mathbb{R}^{n \times 3}} \to \mathbb{R}$$
$$h : \mathbb{R}^{n \times 3} \to \mathbb{R}^K \qquad (5)$$
$$g : \{\mathbb{R}_1^K \times ... \times \mathbb{R}_n^K\} \to \mathbb{R}$$

I.e. The overall meaning f (e.g. object class) of a point set p is approximated by g. The advantage of the architecture is that it is robust against unordered point-clouds and transformations. The independence form the viewpoint variance helps to train with less training samples. Due to disadvantage for learning global features of large point sets the authors developed a second version *Point-Net++* [18].

Voxelization.   Voxelization approaches make use of the findings performing CNNs on images. Therefore, 3D data is converted to voxels or grid cells. After pre-processing standard machine learning architectures are applied. Unordered point-sets are avoided. Famous applications are 3D object detectors like [3,9,13,24].

Combined Models.   Combined models have often shown most robust results (e.g. 3D object detection) and mostly make use of different sensor types. [33] investigated a method based on many local *Point-Nets* followed by a global 3D

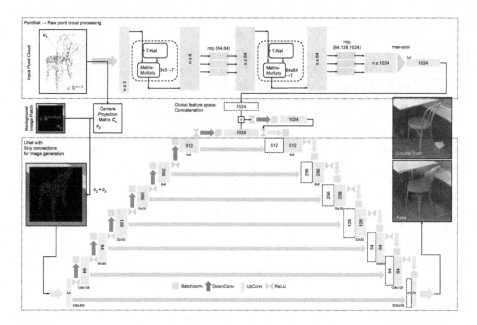

Fig. 1. Points2Pix Generator Architecture. The figure outlines the overall pipeline of the Points2Pix generator. In general we split the design into three areas: Top: the PointNet for a raw point-cloud processing; Bottom: Unet with skip connections for image generation; Middle: Global feature space concatenation from point-set (top) and image processing (bottom) pipeline. The model needs only a raw point-set as input, which acts as condition c_1. The point-sets coordinates will be directly processed by *PointNet*. A projection into the image plane is used for UNet as input, whereas as the camera projection matrix $\mathbf{C_c}$ works as condition c_2. Additionally an arbitrary background patch c_3 is used for background generation.

CNN. [17] architectures works the other way around. With the aid of a camera frustum points are filtered using a camera object detector. The filtered points are processed for 3D object detection with only one *Point-Net* [16] up to the last global max pooling layer ending in a 1×1024 general feature space. A 8 bit depth projection using the given camera projection matrix (c_2).

Generative Models. Point Cloud GAN by [11] is a famous approach for point-cloud generation. They do not perform any translation task, but they show that the common discriminator is not suitable for raw point-clouds. [1] performs label to point-cloud translation by using representative learning and introduce several 3D GAN derivatives. A similar study is published by [29] with focus on latent space analysis. However, learning 3D representations to generate viewpoint based images is missing within the research community. Therefore, we propose our novel technique Points2Pix.

3 Points2Pix

We propose a novel cGAN architecture for generating photo-realistic images from pure point-clouds. Additionally, we describe conditions to bias the viewpoint, distance, shape and the background within the latent space. Therefore, we introduce the network architecture consisting of a generator G (converting points to images), a discriminator D and the specific loss.

3.1 Generator

The objective of our generator $G(c_1, c_2, c_3)$ is to translate point-clouds into realistic-looking images, while using three conditions c_1, c_2, c_3. The whole architecture is shown in Fig. 1. The design is inspired by [7], which serves as base.

Condition One. First, c_1 as raw point-cloud $c_1 = \{x_1, ..., x_n\}$ is processed by *PointNet* [16]. The model samples $n = 1024$ points as input, applying an input transformation and aggregates global point features using fully connected layers and a generic max pooling (see Eq. 5):

$$f(c_1) \approx g(h(x_1), ..., h(x_n)) \qquad n = \{1...1024\} \tag{6}$$

However, in contrast to the basic *PointNet* pipeline, the proposed model incorporates the the global 3D feature space ($n \times 1024$) using concatenation at the innermost part within the Image encoder-decoder (*UNet*). Hence, $h(x_1), ..., h(x_n)$ are applied by the *PointNet* part, g is implicitly performed with the aid of *UNets* decoder (see Fig. 1).

Condition Two. The second condition denoted as $c_2 = \mathbf{C_c}$ is an image projection of the point-cloud using a perspective projection matrix $\mathbf{P}$

$$\mathbf{P} = \begin{bmatrix} s & 0 & 0 & 0 \\ 0 & s & 0 & 0 \\ 0 & 0 & -\frac{f_c}{f_c - n_c} & -1 \\ 0 & 0 & -\frac{f_c \cdot n_c}{f_c - n_c} & 0 \end{bmatrix} \quad s = \frac{1}{\tan(\frac{fov}{2} \cdot \frac{\pi}{180})} \quad \mathbf{x}_{\text{pixel}} = \underbrace{\mathbf{P} \cdot \mathbf{T}_{\text{pc}}^{\text{cam}}}_{\mathbf{C_c}} x_i \tag{7}$$

$$\mathbf{y}_g(\mathbf{x}_{\text{pixel}}) = \frac{|\mathbf{x}_{\text{cam}} - x_i|}{d_{\max}} \quad \mathbf{y}_b(\mathbf{x}_{\text{pixel}}) = I(x_i) \tag{8}$$

with a scaling s according to the horizontal field of view denoted as fov in degrees, near clipping plane denoted as n_c and far clipping plane f_c. We encode radial depth ($\mathbf{y}_g(\mathbf{x}_{\text{pixel}}) \rightarrow$ green channel) with a normalized depth $d_{\max}$ and intensities $I(x_i)$ of the measured reflectance for each point falling into the projection image ($\mathbf{y}_b(\mathbf{x}_{\text{pixel}}) \rightarrow$ blue channel). Before applying P, all points are transformed into the camera coordinate system using the extrinsic calibration $\mathbf{T}_{\text{pc}}^{\text{cam}}$. In this way we ensure the consistent viewpoint during training compared to the raw ground truth rgb image (Fig. 2).

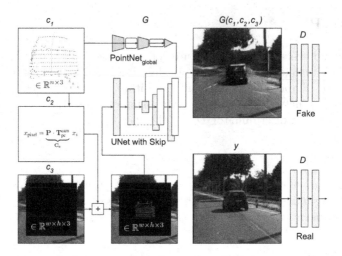

Fig. 2. Training Points2Pix: The figure outlines the competing training structure. The generators (G) output is a fake image based on its three conditions c_1, c_2, c_3. The discriminator D has to distinguish between fake $D\left[G(c_1, c_2, c_3)\right]$ and real images $D[y]$.

Condition Three. Finally, the third condition $c3$ is an arbitrary image background patch constraining environmental texturing. A surrounding image patch of the object cropped from the data set centered at the object origin up to a size of 256×256 is extracted. During training the image background patch is compliant to the ground truth. In test-mode, background patches can be randomly mixed with point-clouds.

Both, c_2 and c_3 are combined to an 256×256 input image, which is fed into a *UNet* with skip connections. At the innermost part, down sampled input features are concatenated with the global 3D feature space from c_1. After up-sampling the output is a generated image with 256×256 pixels. Since, we use a cGAN for training, there is no need for an unstructured Loss. The assessment of the output is performed by the discriminator. As a note, we do not use a random noise vector z (3). Noise is only incorporated as dropout similar to [7].

3.2 Discriminator

We use the Markovian discriminator *PatchGAN* [7] that tries to distinguish between fake $D\left[G(c_1, c_2, c_3)\right]$ and real images $D[y]$ at the scale of $N \times N$ patches as well as possible. In contrast to [7] we do not take the condition c_1, c_2, c_3 into account. The output depends only on the generated image. Therefore, it consists of an *L1* term to force low-frequency correctness [34] and is applied convolutionally across the image, averaging all responses. We only use 5 convolutional layers with batch and instance normalization. In this way, it effectively solves the problem to be able to model high- and low frequency structures at once.

3.3 Loss

The objective of a basic GAN can be explained by an additive combination of the generative network L_G loss and the discriminative network L_D loss. In order to iteratively improve results during training L_G should be reduced while L_D grows ideally. Consequently the basic cGAN loss can be described as follows assuming the three input conditions (c_1, c_2, c_3):

$$
L_{cGAN}(G, D) = \mathbb{E}_y[\log(D(c_2, c_3, y))] \\
+ \mathbb{E}_{c_1, c_2, c_3}[\log(1 - D(c_2, c_3, G(c_1, c_2, c_3)))]
\tag{9}
$$

Random noise z (3) is only realized using dropout. Compared to the typical cGAN loss L_{cGAN} (4), the model does not involve all conditions into the discriminator. However, we implicitly force conditions to be compliant within the output by using a weighted L_1 term [27] in the overall loss. This part describes the L_1 difference between the output and the ground truth. The final loss can be written as:

$$
L_{\text{Points2Pix}} = L_{cGAN}(G, D) \\
+ \lambda_{L1} \cdot \mathbb{E}_{c_1, c_2, c_3, y}[|||y - G(c_1, c_2, c_3)||_1]
\tag{10}
$$

4   Experiments

We conduct experiments on KITTI [5] for outdoor and SunRGBD [25] for indoor scenarios to explore the general validity of the method. Additionally, we show that the approach works for both, Lidar generated point-clouds and point-clouds coming from by RGB-D sensors. Following the recommendations of [7], the quality of the synthesized images is evaluated using an object based inception score. Furthermore, classification and diversity scores are added as additional assessment. Finally, we present some insights into our architecture decisions with additional ablation experiments.

4.1   Metrics

To assess the realism of the produced images, YOLOv3 [19] is used for validation. It is an off-the-shelf state of the art 2D object detector pre-trained on ImageNet and fine-tuned on the MS-Coco [12] data-set. This model includes overlapping classes in comparison to our experiments, e.g. cars (for KITTI) and chair (for SunRGBD). For the quantitative metrics we follow the instructions recommended by [28].

Classification Score. With the aid of YOLOv3 the number of correct detected classes is measured. This could be achieved due to object centered image patches in our experiments. The classification score S_c ratio is then given by the detection ratio of fake images and ground truth ($TP \rightarrow$ true positives). The score could be directly affected by adjusting the confidence rate of the 2D object detector: $S_c = TP_{\text{fake}}/TP_{real}$.

Object Based Inception Score[1]. For positive results in terms of classification we measure the intersection over union $IoU_{\text{Points2Pix}}$ of the predicted bounding box BB coming out of YOLOv3 for the ground truth and the accompanied fake image.

$$IoU_{\text{Points2Pix}} = \frac{BB_{\text{fake}} \cap BB_{\text{real}}}{BB_{\text{fake}} \cup BB_{\text{real}}} \mid S_c = 1 \tag{11}$$

Diversity Score. We measure the diversity ability of our cGAN to produce a wide spread of different output features using a diversity score. Our objective is to bias the shape, distance and 3D characteristics of the object. We collect randomly ten different background image patches, while keeping the point-cloud constant ($c1 = const$ and $c_2 = const$, $c_{3\rightarrow\{1...10\}}$). This leads to different output images that all should have the same 3D object inside. Therefore we compare the ground truth YOLOv3 results and all the fake images with the aid of calculating the mean S_c and the mean IoU.

4.2   Training Details

We train the network on both data sets separately for 100 epochs from scratch each, using the ADAM optimizer [8], with a learning rate of 0.0002 and momentum parameters $\beta_1 = 0.5$, $\beta_2 = 0.999$ such as $\lambda_{L1} = 100$. For our background condition c_3, we use image patches with a border width of 15 pixels. We found using objects containing at least 700 points in their point-cloud as a good trade-off for minimum point density as well as object size.

Kitti: In a pre-processing step, we split the 7481 training examples of the 3D object detection benchmark and use 3712 samples for training and 3769 for evaluation. Therefore, we generate more than $20k$ training images for the class *car* only using $d_{\text{max}} = 60$ m. Thus, each camera image is cropped centered at one labeled object with 256×256 pixels. At the same time, strongly occluded or truncated objects are skipped.

SunRGBD: We extract 3267 images from the SunRGBD data-set containing the following classes: *chair, table, desk, pillow, sofa* and *garbage bin*. The split for training and validation is a 90/10 ratio. Image patches are extracted at the object center from the cameras point of view with a size of 256×256 pixels with $d_{\text{max}} = 4$ m. The depth information comes from either MS kinect v1 or v2 and the Intel real-sense. Since, those sensors do not measure a reflectance, we only encode the radial depth inside the projection of c_2. Hence, the projection image contains one channel only.

4.3   Results

In Fig. 3 we show qualitative results for both data-sets and four different classes. Widely distributed output images are produced by alternating the background

---

[1] We call it inception score, because its similar to the proposal of [22]. We do not use an inception model.

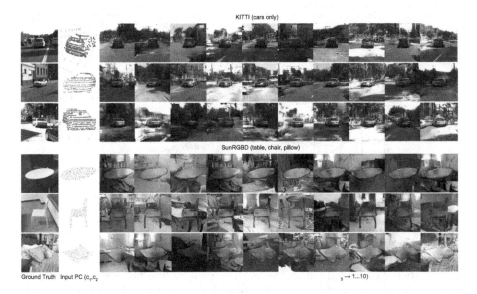

Fig. 3. Qualitative results of Points2Pix: The figure shows four different classes (cars (top) → 3 samples of KITTI; table, chair, pillow (bottom) → in each case one sample of SunRGBD). The results are taken from the test-set and never seen during training. The left column shows the ground truth image and the corresponding point-cloud in the second column. Fake images are generated based on a constant point-cloud $c_1, c_2 = const$ and ten alternating background patches c_3 (column 3–10). The model retains 3D characteristics of the objects.

while keeping the point-cloud constant. An interesting point is, that our model learns 3D characteristics. This could be proven with different outputs (backgrounds) where the objects geometry stays constant. Note, even the objects color stays the same apart from slight differences in reflections and illuminations. This means, the model associates a color with a specific 3D shape represented within the 3D latent feature space. Hence, alternating backgrounds do not affect the objects representation (geometry, color).

Tables 1 and 2, as well as Fig. 4 show quantitative results based on our metrics described in Sect. 4.1. We achieve extreme positive results for KITTI (S_c, IoU) and sufficient values for SunRGBD. SunRGBD includes a higher number of occlusions which drastically affects the scores. Additionally, there are far less samples on each class compared to *cars* in KITTI. Qualitative results of the inception score are shown in Fig. 5.

Ablation Study

Architectural Review. For completeness, we test two derivative architectures of our full pipeline (Fig. 6). In this way, we successfully show a point-cloud to image translation only based on the point cloud itself (*PointNet only*). Doing this, the

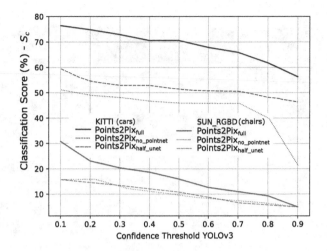

Fig. 4. Points2Pix classification score. The plot shows classification scores S_c for KITTI and SUN-RGBD of our full Points2Pix architecture as well as two derivative architectures (see Fig. 6) over confidence thresholds used for object detection with YOLOv3. The full architecture outperforms for KITTI as well as for SunRGBD.

Table 1. The object based inception score $IoU_{\text{Points2Pix}}$ is calculated on the test set for both data-sets. We show results for varying confidence thresholds, i.e. 0.3, 0.5, 0.7 for KITTI and 0.1, 0.2, 0.3 for SunRGBD.

Dataset	Class	$IoU_{\text{Points2Pix}}$		
		0.3	0.5	0.7
KITTI	car	0.76	0.77	0.77
		$IoU_{\text{Points2Pix}}$		
		0.1	0.2	0.3
SunRGBD	sofa	0.52	0.77	0.77
	table	0.70	–	–
	chair	0.60	0.58	0.58

Table 2. Diversity score is calculated on the test-set for both data-sets. Each sample is recomputed ten times with a random image background patches. A minus indicates no detections for the associated class.

Dataset	Class	$IoU_{\text{Points2Pix}}$		
		0.3	0.5	0.7
KITTI	car	0.71	0.70	0.68
		$IoU_{\text{Points2Pix}}$		
		0.1	0.2	0.3
SunRGBD	sofa	0.16	–	–
	table	0.24	0.22	–
	chair	0.45	0.37	0.33

whole training procedure runs much faster due to far less parameters to optimize. Nevertheless, sometimes a repeating noise with a high contrast similar to Moire effects appears, which indicates instabilities and uncertainties. Generated objects are in compliance with their 3D specifications, but in order to enlarge variance of the outputs and to control background conditions c_2 and c_3 are required. We found that the first part of the *UNet* and the view-point dependent projection c_2 especially help to reduce the mentioned noise effects. They provide additional information in 2D space and stabilize the network. As a fallback we

Fig. 5. Qualitative object based inception results. The figure shows several generated cars and chairs (left) together with their accompanied real images (right). Green bounding boxes indicate detections on the real rgb image patches and red boxes visualize the corresponding ones on the fake images. The blue value obtains the IoU of both. (Color figure online)

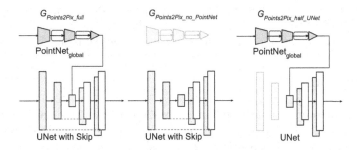

Fig. 6. Architectural review: Two derivatives from the basic Points2Pix $G(c_1, c_2, c_3)$ (left) generator are tested regarding their classification score (see Fig. 4). One on hand a *Unet only* version $G(c_2, c_3)$ (middle), on the other hand a *PointNet only* $G(c_1)$ (right) version is tested. The full model outperforms the others.

Fig. 7. Learning 3D representations: The full Points2Pix architecture learns 3D representations. The model offers a high flexibility in generation of different view points by adjusting condition c_2. The left part shows two examples of KITTI when rotating the point-cloud slightly by 20° around the y-axis. The right (SunRGBD) shows the results when flipping the projection by 180° around the x-axis.

additionally test a *Unet only* version (Fig. 6). However, our full pipeline significantly outperforms the derivative architectures in terms of classification (Fig. 4).

Rotations. To further emphasize the influence of c_2 and to show our models ability to constrain object view-points, we rotate all input points x_i for c_2. We test that for KITTI with a rotation of 20° around the y-axis and for SunRGBD with a rotation of 180° around the x-axis (see Fig. 7). Note, that our point-cloud condition c_1 stays unmodified, because *PointNet* approximates a symmetric function to be invariant of rotations. The test shows that rotations can be implicitly learned. This offers many opportunities in generating 3D data.

5   Conclusion

In this work, we propose a novel approach for 3D point-cloud to image translation based on conditional GANs. Our network handles multi-modal sources from different domains and is capable of the translating unordered point-clouds to regular image grids. We use three conditions to generate a high diversity, while being flexible and keeping 3D characteristics. We prove that the model learns 3D characteristics, what even makes it possible to sample images from different viewpoints. Those networks are applicable in a wide variety of applications, especially 3D texturing.

References

1. Achlioptas, P., Diamanti, O., Mitliagkas, I., Guibas, L.J.: Representation learning and adversarial generation of 3D point clouds. CoRR abs/1707.02392 (2017). http://arxiv.org/abs/1707.02392
2. Chang, A.X., et al.: ShapeNet: an information-rich 3D model repository. CoRR abs/1512.03012 (2015). http://arxiv.org/abs/1512.03012
3. Chen, X., Ma, H., Wan, J., Li, B., Xia, T.: Multi-view 3D object detection network for autonomous driving. CoRR abs/1611.07759 (2016). http://arxiv.org/abs/1611.07759
4. Denton, E.L., Chintala, S., Szlam, A., Fergus, R.: Deep generative image models using a Laplacian pyramid of adversarial networks. CoRR abs/1506.05751 (2015). http://arxiv.org/abs/1506.05751
5. Geiger, A.: Are we ready for autonomous driving? The Kitti vision benchmark suite. In: Proceedings of the 2012 IEEE Conference on Computer Vision and Pattern Recognition, CVPR 2012, Washington, DC, USA, pp. 3354–3361. IEEE Computer Society (2012). http://dl.acm.org/citation.cfm?id=2354409.2354978
6. Iizuka, S., Simo-Serra, E., Ishikawa, H.: Let there be color!: joint end-to-end learning of global and local image priors for automatic image colorization with simultaneous classification. ACM Trans. Graph. (Proc. of SIGGRAPH 2016) 35(4), 110:1–110:11 (2016)
7. Isola, P., Zhu, J., Zhou, T., Efros, A.A.: Image-to-image translation with conditional adversarial networks. CoRR abs/1611.07004 (2016). http://arxiv.org/abs/1611.07004
8. Kingma, D.P., Ba, J.: Adam: a method for stochastic optimization. CoRR abs/1412.6980 (2014). http://arxiv.org/abs/1412.6980
9. Ku, J., Mozifian, M., Lee, J., Harakeh, A., Waslander, S.: Joint 3D proposal generation and object detection from view aggregation. IROS (2018)
10. Li, B.: 3D fully convolutional network for vehicle detection in point cloud. CoRR abs/1611.08069 (2016). http://arxiv.org/abs/1611.08069
11. Li, C., Zaheer, M., Zhang, Y., Póczos, B., Salakhutdinov, R.: Point cloud GAN. CoRR abs/1810.05795 (2018). http://arxiv.org/abs/1810.05795
12. Lin, T., et al.: Microsoft COCO: common objects in context. CoRR abs/1405.0312 (2014). http://arxiv.org/abs/1405.0312
13. Luo, W., Yang, B., Urtasun, R.: Fast and furious: real time end-to-end 3D detection, tracking and motion forecasting with a single convolutional net. In: The IEEE Conference on Computer Vision and Pattern Recognition (CVPR), June 2018
14. Mirza, M., Osindero, S.: Conditional generative adversarial nets. CoRR abs/1411.1784 (2014). http://arxiv.org/abs/1411.1784
15. Paszke, A., Chaurasia, A., Kim, S., Culurciello, E.: ENet: a deep neural network architecture for real-time semantic segmentation. CoRR abs/1606.02147 (2016). http://arxiv.org/abs/1606.02147
16. Qi, C.R., Su, H., Mo, K., Guibas, L.J.: PointNet: deep learning on point sets for 3D classification and segmentation. arXiv preprint: arXiv:1612.00593 (2016)
17. Qi, C.R., Liu, W., Wu, C., Su, H., Guibas, L.J.: Frustum PointNets for 3D object detection from RGB-D data. CoRR abs/1711.08488 (2017). http://arxiv.org/abs/1711.08488
18. Qi, C.R., Yi, L., Su, H., Guibas, L.J.: Pointnet++: deep hierarchical feature learning on point sets in a metric space. CoRR abs/1706.02413 (2017). http://arxiv.org/abs/1706.02413

19. Redmon, J., Farhadi, A.: YOLOv3: an incremental improvement. CoRR abs/1804.02767 (2018). http://arxiv.org/abs/1804.02767
20. Reed, S.E., Akata, Z., Yan, X., Logeswaran, L., Schiele, B., Lee, H.: Generative adversarial text to image synthesis. CoRR abs/1605.05396 (2016). http://arxiv.org/abs/1605.05396
21. Ronneberger, O., Fischer, P., Brox, T.: U-Net: Convolutional networks for biomedical image segmentation. CoRR abs/1505.04597 (2015). http://arxiv.org/abs/1505.04597
22. Salimans, T., Goodfellow, I.J., Zaremba, W., Cheung, V., Radford, A., Chen, X.: Improved techniques for training GANs. CoRR abs/1606.03498 (2016). http://arxiv.org/abs/1606.03498
23. Shelhamer, E., Long, J., Darrell, T.: Fully convolutional networks for semantic segmentation. IEEE Trans. Pattern Anal. Mach. Intell. **39**(4), 640–651 (2017). https://doi.org/10.1109/TPAMI.2016.2572683
24. Simon, M., Milz, S., Amende, K., Gross, H.: Complex-YOLO: real-time 3D object detection on point clouds. CoRR abs/1803.06199 (2018). http://arxiv.org/abs/1803.06199
25. Song, S., Lichtenberg, S.P., Xiao, J.: SUN RGB-D: a RGB-D scene understanding benchmark suite. In: Proceedings of the IEEE Conference on Computer Vision and Pattern Recognition, 7–12 June 2015, pp. 567–576 (2015). https://doi.org/10.1109/CVPR.2015.7298655
26. Song, S., Xiao, J.: Deep sliding shapes for amodal 3D object detection in RGB-D images. CoRR abs/1511.02300 (2015). http://arxiv.org/abs/1511.02300
27. Wang, T.C., Liu, M.Y., Zhu, J.Y., Tao, A., Kautz, J., Catanzaro, B.: High-resolution image synthesis and semantic manipulation with conditional GANs. In: Proceedings of the IEEE Conference on Computer Vision and Pattern Recognition (2018)
28. Wang, X., Gupta, A.: Generative image modeling using style and structure adversarial networks. CoRR abs/1603.05631 (2016). http://arxiv.org/abs/1603.05631
29. Wu, J., Wang, Y., Xue, T., Sun, X., Freeman, W.T., Tenenbaum, J.B.: MarrNet: 3D shape reconstruction via 2.5D sketches. In: Advances in Neural Information Processing Systems (2017)
30. Xie, S., Tu, Z.: Holistically-nested edge detection. CoRR abs/1504.06375 (2015). http://arxiv.org/abs/1504.06375
31. Yoo, D., Kim, N., Park, S., Paek, A.S., Kweon, I.: Pixel-level domain transfer. CoRR abs/1603.07442 (2016). http://arxiv.org/abs/1603.07442
32. Zhao, H., Shi, J., Qi, X., Wang, X., Jia, J.: Pyramid scene parsing network. CoRR abs/1612.01105 (2016). http://arxiv.org/abs/1612.01105
33. Zhou, Y., Tuzel, O.: VoxelNet: end-to-end learning for point cloud based 3D object detection. CoRR abs/1711.06396 (2017). http://arxiv.org/abs/1711.06396
34. Zhu, J., Park, T., Isola, P., Efros, A.A.: Unpaired image-to-image translation using cycle-consistent adversarial networks. CoRR abs/1703.10593 (2017). http://arxiv.org/abs/1703.10593

MLAttack: Fooling Semantic Segmentation Networks by Multi-layer Attacks

Puneet Gupta[1]($\boxtimes$) and Esa Rahtu[2]

[1] IIT Indore, Indore, India
puneet@iiti.ac.in
[2] Tampere University, Tampere, Finland
esa.rahtu@tuni.fi

Abstract. Despite the immense success of deep neural networks, their applicability is limited because they can be fooled by adversarial examples, which are generated by adding visually imperceptible and structured perturbations to the original image. Semantic segmentation is required in several visual recognition tasks, but unlike image classification, only a few studies are available for attacking semantic segmentation networks. The existing semantic segmentation adversarial attacks employ different gradient based loss functions which are defined using only the last layer of the network for gradient backpropagation. But some components of semantic segmentation networks implicitly mitigate several adversarial attacks (like multiscale analysis) due to which the existing attacks perform poorly. This provides us the motivation to introduce a new attack in this paper known as $MLAttack$, i.e., Multiple Layers Attack. It carefully selects several layers and use them to define a loss function for gradient based adversarial attack on semantic segmentation architectures. Experiments conducted on publicly available dataset using the state-of-the-art segmentation network architectures, demonstrate that $MLAttack$ performs better than existing state-of-the-art semantic segmentation attacks.

1 Introduction

Deep learning algorithms have shown excellent performance in solving several artificial intelligence problems that are indispensable for humans like autonomous navigation, scene understanding, natural language processing, robotics, sound processing [11]. Despite their excellent performance, one important factor that limits its applicability is that these algorithms performs notoriously in the presence of adversarial examples [18]. An adversarial example is fabricated by adding human imperceptible perturbations in the input image. The perturbations are carefully generated such that the deep learning architecture provides incorrect results such as it provides incorrect classification for the task of image classification [3]. Such inappropriate existence of adversarial examples can induce catastrophic consequences in security critical applications like autonomous driving [6]. Thorough understanding of the adversarial example generation mechanisms is helpful in designing robust deep learning algorithms like several adversarial attacks can be mitigated by utilizing proper image preprocessing, adding random noise to input images and classifier retraining [16]. Thus, active research is proliferating in designing adversarial attack for the artificial intelligence problems [1].

© Springer Nature Switzerland AG 2019
G. A. Fink et al. (Eds.): DAGM GCPR 2019, LNCS 11824, pp. 401–413, 2019.
https://doi.org/10.1007/978-3-030-33676-9_28

Semantic segmentation is a prime requirement in several artificial intelligence applications like autonomous navigation and scene understanding. Unlike image classification where one class label is provided to one full image by analyzing only a few patches [16], semantic segmentation analyzes spatial context of each pixel and provide each pixel a class label (i.e., it localizes each class pixel) [12]. The problem of semantic segmentation is more complex than the image classification and several state-of-the-art semantic segmentation models utilize standard image classification models followed by additional components like dilated convolutions and multiscale analysis [2].

Attacking a semantic segmentation network is more difficult than attacking a classification network because: (i) unlike image classification, semantic segmentation considers spatial location of each pixel for the prediction [12]; (ii) differentiable surrogate loss function can be easily defined for the image classification task, but it is difficult in the case of semantic segmentation because consistency guarantee for their surrogate losses are unknown [4]; and (iii) several components in the semantic segmentation architectures implicitly provide the adversarial defense mechanisms [2]. Due to these factors, only a few studies are conducted that successfully perform adversarial attacks on semantic segmentation networks, despite being highly relevant in real-world scenarios. These factors motivates us to introduce a novel adversarial attack for the semantic segmentation.

Existing semantic segmentation adversarial attacks are performed by matching the responses of the last layers of source and target image. Thus, these attacks are easily mitigated when several components of semantic segmentation networks implicitly provide gradient masking [2]. It is observed that even when the actual gradients are masked by the semantic segmentation network, some useful gradient information can still be inferred by matching the intermediate layer responses of source and target images. To design a better adversarial attack, we leverage this observation in the proposed attack known as $MLAttack$, i.e., Multiple Layers Attack. To the best of our knowledge, we are the first one to define the loss functions for semantic segmentation which try to increase the similarity between the responses of source and target images at the multiple layers. Further, we experimentally demonstrate that the proposed attack $MLAttack$ outperforms the existing state-of-the-art semantic segmentation attacks.

2   Preliminaries

2.1   Adversarial Attacks

Most of the basic concepts of adversarial attacks are similar in image classification and semantic segmentation. For provide better understanding, we will refer to the case of image classification rather than semantic segmentation in this subsection. Adversarial attacks can be performed in either targeted or non-targeted manner. Targeted adversarial attacks require specific target and the input image is modified such that the final output corresponds to the provided target. In contrast, non-targeted adversarial attacks are performed by modifying the input image such that the model predictions are just different than the ground-truth prediction. Assume that X, y_c, $f(\cdot)$, δ and $f(X)_i$ denote clean image, predicted class, classifier, adversarial perturbations and the probability that X

belongs to class i respectively. Then, $f(\cdot)$ will classify X by $y_c = \underset{i}{\mathrm{argmax}} f(X)_i$. An adversary will generate an adversarial image X_a by adding δ in X where δ is defined such that: (i) δ is visually imperceptible, i.e., small; and (ii) the classification of X_a, y_a is given by the target label for targeted adversarial attacks while y is any other label except y_c for non-targeted attacks.

One of the most powerful and simplest adversarial attack is Fast Gradient Sign Method (FGSM) [7]. It defines δ using the sign of gradients. The gradients are evaluated by differentiating loss function l with respect to the clean image. Hence,

$$X_a = clip\left(X + \varepsilon \cdot sign\left(\nabla l\left(f\left(X\right), y_c\right)\right)\right) \tag{1}$$

where ε, $sign$, $clip$ and ∇ denote a fixed value to increment or decrement the image intensities, operation to get the sign, clipping operation to maintain range of image intensities and gradient operation respectively. This process is a one-step process, but better adversarial image can be obtained when this process is applied iteratively [9]. This iterative version of FGSM is known as Iterative Gradient Sign Method (IGSM) [9].

2.2 Semantic Segmentation

Current deep learning architectures can outperform the traditional segmentation systems and thus, they pave their way for deployment in real-world applications [22]. For instance, fully convolutional network proposed in [12], provides better semantic segmentation for the arbitrary size input image than the traditional systems. It utilizes the existing well-known classification networks to solve the problem of semantic segmentation. Further, it employs a skip architecture to consolidate the response from earlier layers (containing finer details) with the response from later layers (containing appearance information). Most of the existing state-of-the-art segmentation networks employ dilated convolutions and skip connections to provide correct segmentation like FCN-8s [12], PSPNet [23] and ICNet [22].

The performance of semantic segmentation networks is usually evaluated by per-pixel accuracy, per-class accuracy and mean Intersection over Union (mIoU). The mIoU is given by averaging IoU of all the classes and IoU of ith class, IOU_i is given by:

$$IOU_i = \frac{TP_i}{TP_i + FP_i + FN_i} \tag{2}$$

where TP_i, FP_i and FN_i denote the total number of true positives, false positives and false negatives for i^{th} class respectively.

2.3 Adversarial Attacks in Semantic Segmentation

Few studies have been conducted in the literature to perform adversarial attacks on semantic segmentation networks. Adversarial examples can be generated by adding either universal or image-dependent perturbations in the input image [13]. Universal perturbations are obtained by incorporating the pre-trained network and the full image dataset rather than the individual input image, hence, it models the entire dataset images and remain fixed for the dataset [14]. In contrast, image-dependent perturbations vary according to the input images and are generated by considering only the input image rather than the full dataset. Since it considers the image characteristics rather than full dataset behavior, image-dependent perturbations provide better adversarial examples than universal perturbations [15].

Adversarial image-dependent perturbations are generated in [15] by training a deep learning network and simultaneously satisfying the criteria of imperceptibility. In contrast, the gradient based approaches are utilized in [21] to obtain the adversarial image-dependent perturbations. [10] proposed an algorithm to attack only those segmentation networks, which constitute of Region Proposal Network (RPN) like Faster-RCNN [17]. It defines a loss function to attack the RPN rather than the entire network because if RPN cannot generate correct proposals, the entire process of segmentation pipeline will behave erroneously. Unfortunately, this algorithm is not generalized and cannot be applied to the segmentation networks that doesn't require RPN like PSPNet.

Ideally, adversarial examples should be obtained by defining a loss function using the metric corresponding to semantic segmentation, which is mIoU but unfortunately such a metric will be non-differentiable. Direct minimization approaches [8] can be used to solve such a non-differentiable loss function but it requires high computations due to solving a computationally expensive inference for each parameter update. Further, they are highly sensitive to the hyperparameter initialization. Alternatively, one can utilize those differentiable surrogate loss functions [19] instead of the actual task loss (i.e., mIoU in case semantic segmentation), that closely approximate the actual task loss. One such surrogate loss function is defined in [21] which aims to iteratively attack all the image pixels such that the modified pixels will be misclassified into the target class. This attack is known as dense adversary generation (DAG). Likewise, another surrogate loss function, Houdini is introduced in [4] which consists of two parts: the first part denotes the confidence of model prediction wile the second part corresponds to actual task loss.

One crucial factor that mitigates the adversarial attacks in the well known semantic segmentation architectures is that some of its components implicitly provide gradient masking. It is shown in [2] that adversarial attacks are difficult when the network employs multi-scale analysis. Even input images are analyzed at multiple scales for detecting the adversarial examples in [20].

3   Proposed System

In this section, we introduce $MLAttack$ to fool the semantic segmentation networks. This attack is an iterative gradient-based attack where gradients are iteratively computed to minimize the loss functions and the input image is modified according to these gradients such that the predictions of the adversarial image correspond to the predictions of target image. Various components of semantic segmentation networks implicitly offer gradient masking and in turn, provide adversarial defenses [2]. We try to make the correct gradient accessible by considering the responses of intermediate layers to define our loss function. It is based on the assumption that when actual gradients are masked by the semantic segmentation network, we can still obtain some useful gradient information by

---

Algorithm 1. The proposed attack $MLAttack$

Input: $f\left(\cdot\right)$, I_s and I_t denote the network, source image and target image respectively
Parameter: itr denotes the number of iterations
Output: Adversarial image, I_A

 1: Select the intermediate layers of $f\left(\cdot\right)$ required for the attack as described in Section 3.1.
 2: Let $d = 0$.
 3: **while** $d < itr$ **do**
 4:    Compute losses of intermediate layers using Equation (3) and compute the corresponding gradients, G^i_{int}.
 5:    Compute losses of final layer using Equation (4) and compute the corresponding gradient, G^i_f.
 6:    Consolidate all the gradients using Equation (6).
 7:    Compute the adversarial image for i^{th} iteration, I^d_a using Equation (7) .
 8:    Compute mIoU between I^d_a and I_t. Store it in $M[d]$
 9:    $d = d + 1$
10: **end while**
11: Store the index containing maximum mIoU in s, i.e., $s = \operatorname*{argmax}_{d} M[d]$
12: $I_A = I^s_a$
13: **return** I_A

---

matching the intermediate layer responses of source and target images. It consists of the following three stages: layer selection, gradient calculation and generating adversarial example. In the first stage, a few intermediate layers which can provide useful gradient information are selected. In the next stage, loss function is defined for each selected intermediate layer. The gradient is computed using each loss and eventually consolidated. In the last stage, adversarial attack is performed using the consolidated gradient. The steps involved in the proposed attack, $MLAttack$ are outlined in Algorithm 1.

3.1 Layers Selection

$MLAttack$ is applied to a few intermediate layers. Most of the segmentation networks are based on encoder-decoder architecture where encoder provides the low resolution semantic information from the image while decoder improves the localization by utilizing the responses of lower layers [12]. In such cases, we choose the last encoder layer for intermediate attack. For instance, we choose the responses given by $'conv5\_3/relu'$ in PSPNet, which is the last encoder layer. Similarly, we choose those layers in a network which combines information from several resolutions because it can lead to adversarial defenses by performing multi-scale analysis [2]. As an instance, we also choose the $'conv5\_3\_pool6\_interp'$, $'conv5\_3\_pool3\_interp'$, $'conv5\_3\_pool2\_interp'$ and $'conv5\_3\_pool1\_interp'$ layers in PSPNet which consolidates information from several resolutions. One can also utilize all the network layers for the attack but it is experimentally demonstrated that the achieved performance is not satisfactory in such a scenario (refer Sect. 4.4).

3.2   Gradient Calculation

After selecting the proper network layers, we aim to define loss functions which tries to increase the similarity between the responses of source and target images at the selected layers. The loss functions and gradient are iteratively computed. The total gradient information in an iteration for $MLAttack$ is obtained by combining the gradients obtained from the losses of the final layer and selected intermediate layers.

The loss of ith selected intermediate layer, L_{int}^i is obtained by computing the softmax cross entropy loss between the responses of ith layer of the network for source and target images. Mathematically, this loss is given by:

$$L_{int}^i = - \sum_{j \in \mathcal{J}} F_i^j \left(I_t \right) \cdot \log F_i^j \left(I_s \right) \tag{3}$$

where $F_i^j \left(\cdot \right)$ denotes classifier response of jth node for i^{th} layer after applying softmax function; I_s and I_t represent the source and target image respectively; and $\mathcal{J}_i$ denotes the nodes of ith layer. As in FGSM, intermediate loss, L_{int}^i is used to compute the gradient, G_{int}^i by differentiating the loss with respect to image pixels [7].

Similarly, the loss at the final layer is computed by softmax cross entropy loss. The last layer provides the final prediction of each pixel. Some of the predictions correspond to target labels and we do not want to penalize them hence they are not considered in the loss function. Hence, we define the loss on last layer, L_f using:

$$L_f = - \sum_{j \in \mathcal{J}} \left[F_i^j \left(I_t \right) \cdot \log F_i^j \left(I_s \right) \cdot A^j \right] \tag{4}$$

where A^j is given by:

$$A^j = \begin{cases} 0, & \text{if } F_i^j \left(I_t \right) = F_i^j \left(I_s \right) \\ 1, & \text{otherwise} \end{cases} \tag{5}$$

Subsequently, gradient, G_f^i is computed by differentiating L_f with respect to image pixels [7].

The final gradient, G is computed by combining G_{int}^i and G_f in the following manner:

$$G = \frac{\alpha \cdot G_f + \sum_{i=1}^n G_{int}^i}{\alpha + n} \tag{6}$$

where n and α denote the number of selected layers and the weight of G_f in the combination respectively.

3.3   Generating Adversarial Example

We perform iterative generation of adversarial example [9]. In the first iteration (which is 0th iteration in our case), adversarial perturbations are added to the source image. After that, adversarial perturbations are added in the previous perturbed image. Moreover, we apply the image clipping operation after each iteration for restricting image intensities from 0 to 255. Hence, the adversarial image obtained in d^{th} iteration, I_a^d is given by:

$$I_a^d = clip\left(I_a^{d-1} - \varepsilon \cdot sign\left(G\right)\right) \qquad (7)$$

where $clip$ and ε denote the image clipping operation and maximum allowable perturbations in an iteration respectively. Also, the adversarial image in 0th iteration, I_a^0 is given by the source image, I_s. Since surrogate loss functions can only be utilized for performing the attacks rather than actual loss [4], it is possible that loss may increase in the next iteration. Thus, we choose the iteration, which provides the maximum mIoU between source and target image to define the adversarial example. Mathematically, if M_d denote the mIoU between I_a^d and target image I_t then the adversarial image, I_A is given by:

$$I_A = I_a^s \quad where \quad s \;=\; \underset{d}{\mathrm{argmax}} M_d \qquad (8)$$

4 Experiments

4.1 Experimental Settings

We conduct the experiments on the Cityscapes test dataset [5] which is widely used as a semantic segmentation benchmark. It contains 1525 road-scene images which are categorized into 19 classes. This dataset contains high-resolution images of size 2048×1024 pixels. To reduce the memory requirements, just like other existing systems, we also resized all the images to 1024×512 for conducting the experiments. State-of-the-art semantic segmentation architectures are used for conducting the experiments. We used publicly available pre-trained models of FCN-8s [12] with backbone consists of VGG-16, PSPNet [23] and ICNet [22][1]. With backbone consists of VGG-16, PSPNet [23] and ICNet [22][1].

We perform both targeted and non-targeted adversarial attacks for the performance evaluation. In case of targeted attacks, the performance is evaluated by attacking each image using all the remaining images in the dataset as target images. Hence, we apply $MLAttack$ 1525×1524 times for the evaluation of targeted attacks. For non-targeted attacks, we create the target labels corresponding to a source image by considering the second most probable class for each pixel. Since intermediate layer responses are unavailable for these created target labels, we attack each source image in non-targeted attack by considering only the loss of the final layer (i.e., L_f).

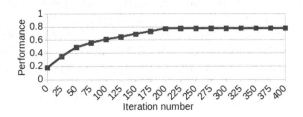

Fig. 1. Performance of $MLAttack$ at different itr

---

[1] https://github.com/hellochick/semantic-segmentation-tensorflow.

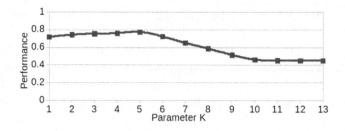

Fig. 2. Performance of $MLAttack$ at different values of k

4.2 Evaluation Metrics

Just like other existing semantic segmentation adversarial attacks, we employ mIoU for the performance evaluation because per-pixel accuracy behaves overoptimistic for highly unbalanced datasets and per-class accuracy does not sufficiently penalizes the false negatives for object classes but mIoU correctly evaluates accurate object localization [4]. We use mIoU to evaluate the performance in the following two ways: (i) $mIoU_s$ which evaluates the mIoU between the predicted labels and ground-truth, hence $mIoU_s$ decreases when adversarial attacks successfully fool the network, and (ii) $mIoU_t$ which evaluates the mIoU between the predicted labels and target labels, hence $mIoU_t$ increases when adversarial attacks successfully fool the network and forces the network to match the predicted and target labels.

4.3 Parameter Selection

The performance of $MLAttack$ can only increase as the number of iterations increases because the subspace of adversarial perturbation increases. But the increase in performance is marginal as the number of iterations increases. It can be observed from Fig. 1 which utilize Cityscapes validation dataset of 500 images to evaluate the performance in terms of $mIoU_t$ for targeted attacks on PSPNet. Moreover, one cannot expect the attack to run indefinitely and thus, we restrict the number of iterations to a sufficiently high number, which is 200. Further, we set $|L_\infty|$ to be 5 and ε to be 0.025. Another important parameter which impact the performance of $MLAttack$ is α. It is used in consolidating the gradients obtained from final layers and intermediate layers. Eventually the performance will be evaluated on the final layer only hence, better performance can be expected when weight of G_f increases with the number of iterations. This is leveraged by setting α equal to itr/k, where itr denotes the number of iterations and k is a hyperparameter. The performance of $MLAttack$ according to k is shown in Fig. 2. Since best performance is observed when k is equal to 5, α is set equal to $itr/5$ in the experiments.

Table 1. Performance of semantic segmentation adversarial attacks. $mIoU_t$ the higher, the better; $mIoU_s$: the lower, the better.

	Attack algorithm	Targeted		Non-targeted	
		$mIoU_t$	$mIoU_s$	$mIoU_t$	$mIoU_s$
FCN−8s[a]	[15]	0.623	0.124	0.772	0.099
	[21]	0.708	0.093	0.834	0.076
	[4]	0.725	0.088	0.847	0.071
	$ILAttack$[b]	0.461	0.456	NA	NA
	$FLAttack$[c]	0.726	0.089	0.848	0.071
	$MLAttack$ (ours)	**0.792**	**0.057**	**0.853**	**0.057**
PSPNet[a]	[15]	0.608	0.145	0.702	0.113
	[21]	0.683	0.104	0.785	0.082
	[4]	0.699	0.096	0.801	0.078
	$ILAttack$[b]	0.428	0.489	NA	NA
	$FLAttack$[c]	0.698	0.097	0.804	0.077
	$MLAttack$ (ours)	**0.774**	**0.048**	**0.816**	**0.045**
ICNet[a]	[15]	0.616	0.132	0.735	0.107
	[21]	0.698	0.098	0.807	0.079
	[4]	0.714	0.091	0.828	0.071
	$ILAttack$[b]	0.417	0.474	NA	NA
	$FLAttack$[c]	0.714	0.090	0.829	0.070
	$MLAttack$ (ours)	**0.783**	**0.059**	**0.839**	**0.053**

[a] Name of the semantic segmentation network.
[b] $ILAttack$ utilizes only L_{int}^i loss but avoids L_f loss. Thus, it is not applicable (NA) for non-targeted attacks.
[c] $FLAttack$ is similar to $MLAttack$ but it does not incorporate the loss employing intermediate layers, i.e., L_{int}^i loss.

4.4 Comparative Analysis

To understand the efficacy of the proposed attack, $MLAttack$, this subsection provides the performance comparison between $MLAttack$ and the existing state-of-art adversarial attacks for semantic segmentation which are [4, 15, 21]. Moreover, we conducted an ablation study to rigorously analyze the importance of utilizing different loss functions in $MLAttack$. For this, we compare $MLAttack$ with $FLAttack$ and $ILAttack$ which are obtained by modifying $MLAttack$. $FLAttack$ employ only the loss at the final layer (i.e., L_f) while $ILAttack$ employ only the losses at the intermediate layers (i.e., L_{int}^i). Thus, $MLAttack$ and $ILAttack$ are same in case of non-targeted attacks because both avoids L_{int}^i for non-targeted attacks. Also, the responses of only last layer are available in non-targeted attacks hence $ILAttack$ cannot be used in case of non-targeted attacks which require responses of intermediate layers.

The comparative analysis is presented in Table 1 and Fig. 3. An example of semantic segmentation is presented in the figure where error images highlight the pixels

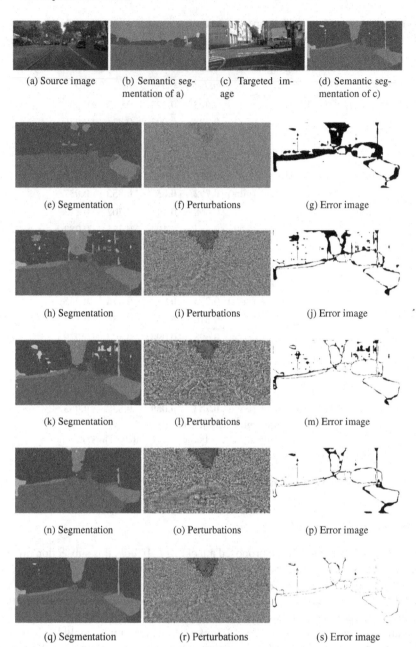

(a) Source image   (b) Semantic seg-   (c) Targeted im-   (d) Semantic seg-
                    mentation of a)   age   mentation of c)

(e) Segmentation   (f) Perturbations   (g) Error image

(h) Segmentation   (i) Perturbations   (j) Error image

(k) Segmentation   (l) Perturbations   (m) Error image

(n) Segmentation   (o) Perturbations   (p) Error image

(q) Segmentation   (r) Perturbations   (s) Error image

Fig. 3. Visualization of Semantic Segmentation performed by well known attacks: (a) to (d) depicts the source and target images along with their semantic segmentation; (e)–(g), (h)–(j), (k)–(m), (n)–(p) and (q)–(s) denote the predicted segmentation, adversarial perturbations and error images obtained by applying [15], [21], [4], $ALLAttack$ and $MLAttack$ respectively. Further, the images depicting adversarial perturbations are normalized for visualization and error images contain 1 when predicted and target labels are same while 0 otherwise.

containing different predicted and target labels. It can be observed from the table and figure that:

1. The proposed attack, $MLAttack$ exhibit better fooling capability than the state-of-art adversarial attacks for both targeted and non-targeted attacks. Also, it can be seen that non-targeted attack performs better than its corresponding targeted attack. It is because the difference of logits between source and predicted labels are less in case of non-targeted attacks than targeted attacks.
2. It can be seen from the table that $FLAttack$ which does not incorporate the loss at the intermediate layers, (that is, L_{int}^i), performs similar to the state-of-the-art semantic segmentation attack [4]. But the performance of $FLAttack$ increases significantly when it is used along with $ILAttack$ in the proposed attack, $MLAttack$.
3. It can be analyzed from the table that $ILAttack$ utilizing only intermediate loss, L_{int}^i has the potential to attack semantic segmentation. It clearly delineates the applicability of our novel loss function, L_{int}^i in attacking the semantic segmentation networks.
4. Upon inspecting the error images, it can be seen that just like other attacks, $MLAttack$ can fail for the edge pixels of the source image. It is because some edge pixels contain high frequency information and they require large intensity variations to change the labels.

We have also conducted another experiment using PSPNet network where all the layers are utilized in targeted attack of $MLAttack$ instead of a few selected layers. In such a case, $mIoU_t$ and $mIoU_s$ are found to be 0.213 and 0.134 respectively for the PSPNet. Based on this poor performance, it can be inferred that proper layers should be selected for attacking the semantic segmentation networks.

5   Conclusions and Future Work

The proposed attack known as $MLAttack$, i.e., Multiple Layers Attack, has successfully generated the adversarial examples to fool the well known semantic segmentation networks and force them to provide erroneous target labels. The existing semantic segmentation adversarial attacks aim to increase the similarity between the responses of the last layers of source and target image. These can be mitigated by the well known semantic segmentation networks because some of their components implicitly provide gradient masking. Even in such cases, $MLAttack$ has successfully attacked the networks because it is capable to infer some useful gradient information by matching the intermediate layer responses of source and target images. Due to this, experiments conducted on publicly available dataset using the state-of-the-art segmentation network architectures, have demonstrated that $MLAttack$ performs better than existing state-of-the-art semantic segmentation attacks.

In the future, we will improve $MLAttack$ by providing a better combining mechanism for the gradients. Moreover, we will work to improve the $MLAttack$ so that it can successfully attack the edge pixels of the source image.

References

1. Akhtar, N., Mian, A.: Threat of adversarial attacks on deep learning in computer vision: a survey. IEEE Access **6**, 14410–14430 (2018)
2. Arnab, A., Miksik, O., Torr, P.H.: On the robustness of semantic segmentation models to adversarial attacks. In: Proceedings of the IEEE Conference on Computer Vision and Pattern Recognition, pp. 888–897 (2018)
3. Chen, P.Y., Sharma, Y., Zhang, H., Yi, J., Hsieh, C.J.: EAD: elastic-net attacks to deep neural networks via adversarial examples. In: Thirty-second AAAI conference on Artificial Intelligence (2018)
4. Cisse, M.M., Adi, Y., Neverova, N., Keshet, J.: Houdini: fooling deep structured visual and speech recognition models with adversarial examples. In: Advances in Neural Information Processing Systems, pp. 6977–6987 (2017)
5. Cordts, M., et al.: The cityscapes dataset for semantic urban scene understanding. In: Proceedings of the IEEE Conference on Computer Vision and Pattern Recognition, pp. 3213–3223 (2016)
6. Evtimov, I., et al.: Robust physical-world attacks on deep learning models. In: Proceedings of the IEEE Conference on Computer Vision and Pattern Recognition, pp. 1625–1634 (2018)
7. Goodfellow, I.J., Shlens, J., Szegedy, C.: Explaining and harnessing adversarial examples. arXiv preprint: arXiv:1412.6572 (2014)
8. Hazan, T., Keshet, J., McAllester, D.A.: Direct loss minimization for structured prediction. In: Advances in Neural Information Processing Systems, pp. 1594–1602 (2010)
9. Kurakin, A., Goodfellow, I., Bengio, S.: Adversarial examples in the physical world. arXiv preprint: arXiv:1607.02533 (2016)
10. Li, Y., Tian, D., Bian, X., Lyu, S., et al.: Robust adversarial perturbation on deep proposal-based models. arXiv preprint: arXiv:1809.05962 (2018)
11. Liu, W., Wang, Z., Liu, X., Zeng, N., Liu, Y., Alsaadi, F.E.: A survey of deep neural network architectures and their applications. Neurocomputing **234**, 11–26 (2017)
12. Long, J., Shelhamer, E., Darrell, T.: Fully convolutional networks for semantic segmentation. In: Proceedings of the IEEE Conference on Computer Vision and Pattern Recognition, pp. 3431–3440 (2015)
13. Metzen, J.H., Kumar, M.C., Brox, T., Fischer, V.: Universal adversarial perturbations against semantic image segmentation. In: 2017 IEEE International Conference on Computer Vision (ICCV), pp. 2774–2783. IEEE (2017)
14. Moosavi-Dezfooli, S.M., Fawzi, A., Fawzi, O., Frossard, P.: Universal adversarial perturbations. In: Proceedings of the IEEE Conference on Computer Vision and Pattern Recognition, pp. 1765–1773 (2017)
15. Poursaeed, O., Katsman, I., Gao, B., Belongie, S.: Generative adversarial perturbations. In: Proceedings of the IEEE Conference on Computer Vision and Pattern Recognition, pp. 4422–4431 (2018)
16. Prakash, A., Moran, N., Garber, S., DiLillo, A., Storer, J.: Deflecting adversarial attacks with pixel deflection. In: Proceedings of the IEEE Conference on Computer Vision and Pattern Recognition, pp. 8571–8580 (2018)
17. Ren, S., He, K., Girshick, R., Sun, J.: Faster R-CNN: towards real-time object detection with region proposal networks. In: Advances in Neural Information Processing Systems, pp. 91–99 (2015)
18. Szegedy, C., et al.: Intriguing properties of neural networks. arXiv preprint: arXiv:1312.6199 (2013)
19. Tewari, A., Bartlett, P.L.: On the consistency of multiclass classification methods. J. Mach. Learn. Res. **8**(May), 1007–1025 (2007)

20. Xiao, C., Deng, R., Li, B., Yu, F., Liu, M., Song, D.: Characterizing adversarial examples based on spatial consistency information for semantic segmentation. In: Ferrari, V., Hebert, M., Sminchisescu, C., Weiss, Y. (eds.) ECCV 2018, Part X. LNCS, vol. 11214, pp. 220–237. Springer, Cham (2018). https://doi.org/10.1007/978-3-030-01249-6_14

21. Xie, C., Wang, J., Zhang, Z., Zhou, Y., Xie, L., Yuille, A.: Adversarial examples for semantic segmentation and object detection. In: Proceedings of the IEEE International Conference on Computer Vision, pp. 1369–1378 (2017)

22. Zhao, H., Qi, X., Shen, X., Shi, J., Jia, J.: ICNet for real-time semantic segmentation on high-resolution images. In: Ferrari, V., Hebert, M., Sminchisescu, C., Weiss, Y. (eds.) ECCV 2018, Part III. LNCS, vol. 11207, pp. 418–434. Springer, Cham (2018). https://doi.org/10.1007/978-3-030-01219-9_25

23. Zhao, H., Shi, J., Qi, X., Wang, X., Jia, J.: Pyramid scene parsing network. In: Proceedings of the IEEE Conference on Computer Vision and Pattern Recognition, pp. 2881–2890 (2017)

Not Just a Matter of Semantics: The Relationship Between Visual and Semantic Similarity

Clemens-Alexander Brust[1]([✉])[iD] and Joachim Denzler[1,2]

[1] Computer Vision Group, Friedrich Schiller University Jena, Jena, Germany
clemens-alexander.brust@uni-jena.de
[2] Michael Stifel Center Jena, Jena, Germany

Abstract. Knowledge transfer, zero-shot learning and semantic image retrieval are methods that aim at improving accuracy by utilizing semantic information, *e.g.*, from WordNet. It is assumed that this information can augment or replace missing visual data in the form of labeled training images because semantic similarity correlates with visual similarity.

This assumption may seem trivial, but is crucial for the application of such semantic methods. Any violation can cause mispredictions. Thus, it is important to examine the visual-semantic relationship for a certain target problem. In this paper, we use five different semantic and visual similarity measures each to thoroughly analyze the relationship without relying too much on any single definition.

We postulate and verify three highly consequential hypotheses on the relationship. Our results show that it indeed exists and that WordNet semantic similarity carries more information about visual similarity than just the knowledge of "different classes look different". They suggest that classification is not the ideal application for semantic methods and that wrong semantic information is much worse than none.

1 Introduction

There exist applications in which labeled training data cannot be acquired in sufficient amounts to reach the high accuracy associated with contemporary convolutional neural network (CNNs) with millions of parameters. These include industrial [14,18] and medical [15,27,31] applications as well as research in other fields like wildlife monitoring [4,5,7]. *Semantic methods* such as knowledge transfer and zero-shot learning often process information about the semantic relationship between classes from databases like WordNet [19] to allow high-accuracy classification even when training data is insufficient or missing entirely [24]. *They can only function when the unknown visual relationships between classes are predictable from the given semantic relationships.*

In this paper, we analyze and test this crucial assumption by evaluating the relationship between visual and semantic similarity in a detailed and systematic manner.To guide our analysis, we formulate three highly consequential, non-trivial hypotheses around the visual-semantic relationship. The exact nature of

© Springer Nature Switzerland AG 2019
G. A. Fink et al. (Eds.): DAGM GCPR 2019, LNCS 11824, pp. 414–427, 2019.
https://doi.org/10.1007/978-3-030-33676-9_29

(a) A deer and a forest. By taxonomy only, their semantic similarity is weak. Visual similarity however is strong.

(b) An orchid and a sunflower. Their semantic similarity very strong due to them both being flowers. The visual similarity between them is weak.

Fig. 1. Examples of semantic-visual disagreement.

the links and the similarity terms is specified in Sect. 4. Our first hypothesis concerns the relationship itself:

$\mathcal{H}_1$: *There is a link between visual and semantic similarity.* It seems trivial on the surface, but each individual component requires a proper, nontrivial definition to ultimately make the hypothesis verifiable (see Sect. 4). The observed effectiveness of semantic methods suggests that knowledge about semantic relationships is somewhat applicable in the visual domain. However, counter-examples are easily found, *e.g.,* Figs. 1 and 4. Furthermore, a crude approximation of semantic similarity is already given by the expectation that "different classes look different" (see Sect. 2.1). A similarity measure based on actual semantic knowledge should be a stronger predictor of visual similarity than this simple baseline.

Semantic methods seek to improve accuracy and in turn reduce model confusion, but the relationship between confusion and visual similarity is non-trivial. Insights about the low-level visual similarity may not apply to the more abstract confusion. To cover not only largely model-free, but also model-specific notions of visual similarity, we formulate our second and third hypotheses:

$\mathcal{H}_2$: *There is a link between visual similarity and model confusion.* Low inter-class distance in a feature space correlates with confusion, but it could also indicate strong visual similarity. This link depends on the selected features and classifier. It is also affected by violations of "different classes look different" in the dataset.

$\mathcal{H}_3$: *There is a link between semantic similarity and model confusion.* This link should be investigated because it directly relates to the goal of semantic methods, which is to reduce confusion by adding semantic information. It "skips" the low-level visual component and as such is interesting on its own. However, the expectation that "different classes look different" can already explain the complete confusion matrix of a perfect classifier. We also expect it to partly explain a real classifier's confusions. So, to consider $\mathcal{H}_3$ verified, we require semantic similarity to show an even stronger correlation to confusion than given by this expectation.

Our main contribution is an extensive and insightful evaluation of this relationship across five different semantic and visual similarity measures respectively. It is based on the three aforementioned hypotheses around the relationship. We show quantitative results measuring the agreement between individual measures and across visual and semantic similarities as rank correlation. Moreover, we analyze special cases of agreement and disagreement qualitatively. The results and their various implications are discussed in Sect. 5.5. They suggest that, while the relationship exists even beyond the "different classes look different" baseline, tasks different from classification need further research. The semantically reductive nature of class labels suggests that semantic methods may perform better on more complex tasks.

1.1 Related Work

The relationship between visual and semantic similarity has been subject of previous investigation. In [6], Deselaers and Ferrari consider a semantic similarity measure by Jiang and Conrath (see Sect. 2.4 and [11]) as well as category histograms, in conjunction with the ImageNet dataset. They propose a novel distance function based on semantic as well as visual similarity to use in a nearest neighbor setting that outperforms purely visual distance functions. The authors also show a positive correlation between visual and semantic similarity for their choice of similarity measures on the ImageNet dataset. Their selections of Jiang-Conrath distance and the GIST feature descriptor are also evaluated in our work, where we add several different methods to compare.

Bilal *et al.* observe the confusion matrix of a convolutional network trained on the ImageNet-1k dataset [26] in [2]. They use visual analytics to show that characteristics of the class hierarchy can be found in the confusion matrix, a result related to our hypothesis $\mathcal{H}_3$.

2 Semantic Similarity

The term *semantic similarity* describes the degree to which two concepts interact semantically. A common definition requires taking into account only the taxonomical (hierarchical) relationship between the concepts [9, p. 10]. A more general notion is *semantic relatedness*, where any type of semantic link may be considered [9, p. 10]. Both are *semantic measures*, which also include distances and dissimilarities [9, p. 9]. We adhere to these definitions in this work, specifically the hierarchical restriction of semantic similarity.

2.1 Prerequisites

In certain cases, it is easier to formulate a semantic measure based on hierarchical relationships as a distance first. Such a distance d between two concepts x, y can be converted to a similarity by $1/(1+d(x,y))$ [9, p. 60]. This results in a measure bounded by $(0,1]$, where 1 stands for maximal similarity, *i.e.*, the distance is zero. We will apply this rule to convert all distances to similarities in our experiments. We also apply it to dissimilarities, which are comparable to distances, but do not fulfill the triangle inequality.

Semantic Baseline. When training a classifier without using semantic embeddings [1] or hierarchical classification techniques [29], there is still prior information about semantic similarity given by the classification problem itself. Specifically, it is postulated that "classes that are different look different" (see Sect. 4). Machine learning can not work if this assumption is violated, *i.e.*, different classes look identical. We encode this "knowledge" in semantic similarity measure, defined as 1 for two identical concepts and zero otherwise. It will serve as a baseline for comparison with all other similarities.

2.2 Graph-Based Similarities

We can describe a directed acyclic graph $G(C, \textbf{is-a})$ using the taxonomic relation **is-a** and the set of all concepts C. The notions of semantic similarity described in this section can be expressed using properties of G. The graph distance $d_G(x,y)$ between two nodes x, y, which is defined as the length of the shortest path xPy, is an important example. If required, we reduce the graph G to a rooted tree T with root r by iterating through all nodes with multiple ancestors and successively removing the edges to ancestors with the lowest amount of successors. In a tree, we can then define the depth of a concept x as $\mathfrak{d}_T(x) = d_T(r,x)$. This simple, greedy approach make very few cuts in practice and does not strongly affect results.

A simple approach is presented by Rada *et al.* in [22, p. 20], where the semantic distance between two concepts x and y is defined as the graph distance $d_G(x,y)$ between one concept and the other in G.

To make similarities comparable between different taxonomies, it may be desirable to take the overall depth of the hierarchy into account. Resnik presents such an approach for trees in [23], considering the maximal depth of T and the *least common ancestor* $\mathcal{L}(x,y)$. $\mathcal{L}$ is the uniquely defined node in the shortest path between two concepts x and y that is an ancestor to both [9, p. 61]. The similarity between x and y is then given as [23, p. 3]:

$$2 \cdot \max_{z \in C} \mathfrak{d}_T(z) - d_T(x, \mathcal{L}(x,y)) - d_T(y, \mathcal{L}(x,y)). \tag{1}$$

2.3 Feature-Based Similarities

The following approaches use a set-theoretic view of semantics. The set of *features* $\phi(x)$ of a concept x is usually defined as the set of ancestors $A(x)$ of x [9]. We also include x itself, such that $\phi(x) = A(x) \cup \{x\}$ [28].

Inspired by the Jaccard coefficient, Maedche and Staab propose a similarity measure defined as the intersection over union of the concept features of x and y

respectively [17, p. 4]. This similarity is bounded by $[0, 1]$, with identical concepts always resulting in 1.

Sanchez *et al.* present a dissimilarity measure that represents the ratio of distinct features to shared features of two concepts. It is defined by [28, p. 7723]:

$$\log_2 \left(1 + \frac{|\phi(x)\backslash\phi(y)| + |\phi(y)\backslash\phi(x)|}{|\phi(x)\backslash\phi(y)| + |\phi(y)\backslash\phi(x)| + |\phi(y) \cap \phi(x)|} \right). \tag{2}$$

2.4   Information-Based Similarities

Semantic similarity is also defined using the notion of informativeness of a concept, inspired by information theory. Each concept x is assigned an *Information Content* (IC) $\mathcal{I}(x)$ [23,25]. This can be defined using only properties of the taxonomy, *i.e.*, the graph G (intrinsic IC), or using the probability of observing the concept in corpora (extrinsic IC) [9, p. 54].

We use an intrinsic definition presented by Zhou *et al.* in [36], based on the descendants $D(x)$:

$$\mathcal{I}(x) = k \cdot \left(1 - \frac{|D(x)|}{|C|} \right) + (1 - k) \cdot \left(\frac{\log(\mathfrak{d}_T(x))}{\log(\max_{z \in C} \mathfrak{d}_T(z))} \right). \tag{3}$$

With a definition of IC, we can apply an information-based similarity measure. Jiang and Conrath propose a semantic distance in [11] using the notion of *Most Informative Common Ancestor* $\mathfrak{M}(x, y)$ of two concepts x, y. It is defined as the element in $(A(x) \cap A(y)) \cup (x \cap y)$ with the highest IC [9, p. 65]. The distance is then defined as [11, p. 8]:

$$\mathcal{I}(x) + \mathcal{I}(y) - 2 \cdot \mathcal{I}(\mathfrak{M}(x, y)). \tag{4}$$

3   Visual Similarity

Assessing the similarity of images is not a trivial task, mostly because the term "similarity" can be defined in many different ways. In this section, we look at two common interpretations of visual similarity, namely perceptual metrics and feature-based similarity measures.

3.1   Perceptual Metrics

Perceptual metrics are usually employed to quantify the distortion or information loss incurred by using compression algorithms. Such methods aim to minimize the difference between the original image and the compressed image and thereby maximize the similarity between both. However, perceptual metrics can also be used to assess the similarity of two independent images.

An image can be represented by an element of a high-dimensional vector space. In this case, the Euclidean distance is a natural candidate for a dissimilarity measure. With the rule $1/(1 + d)$ from Sect. 2.1, the distance is transformed into a visual similarity measure. To normalize the measure *w.r.t.* image dimensions and to simplify calculations, the mean squared error (MSE) is used. Applying the MSE to estimate image similarity has shortcomings. For example, shifting an image by one pixel significantly changes the distances to other images, and even its unshifted self. An alternative, but related measure is the mean absolute difference (MAD), which we also consider in our experiments.

In [34], Wang *et al.* develop a perceptual metric called *Structural Similarity Index* to address shortcomings of previous methods. Specifically, they consider properties of the human visual system such that the index better reflects human judgement of visual similarity.

We use MSE, MAD and SSIM as perceptual metrics to indicate visual similarity in our experiments. There are better performing methods when considering human judgement, *e.g.,* [35]. However, we cannot guarantee that humans always treat visuals and semantics as separate. Therefore, we avoid further methods that are motivated by human properties [3,33] or already incorporate semantic knowledge [8,16].

3.2   Feature-Based Measures

Features are extracted to represent images at an abstract level. Thus, distances in such a feature space of images correspond to visual similarity in a possibly more robust way than the aforementioned perceptual metrics. Features have inherent or learned invariances *w.r.t.* certain transformations that should not affect the notion of visual similarity strongly. However, learned features may also be invariant to transformations that do affect visual similarity because they are optimized for semantic distinction. This behavior needs to be considered when selecting abstract features to determine visual similarity.

GIST [21] is an image descriptor that aims at describing a whole scene using a small number of estimations of specific perceptual properties, such that similar content is close in the resulting feature space. It is based on the notion of a *spatial envelope*, inspired by architecture, that can be extracted from an image and used to calculate statistics.

For reference, we observe the confusions of five ResNet-32 [10] models to represent feature-based visual similarity on the highest level of abstraction. Because confusion is not a symmetric function, we apply a transform $(M + M^T)/2$ to obtain a symmetric representation of the confusion matrix.

4   Evaluating the Relationship

Visual and semantic similarity are measures defined on different domains. Semantic similarities compare concepts and visual similarities compare individual images. To analyze a correlation, a common domain over which both can be evaluated is essential. We propose to calculate similarities over all pairs of classes in an image classification dataset, which can be defined for both visual and semantic similarities. These pairwise similarities are then tested for correlation. The process is clarified in the following:

1. **Dataset.** We use the CIFAR-100 dataset [13] to verify our hypotheses. This dataset has a scale at which all experiments take a reasonable amount of time. Our computation times grow quadratically with the number of classes as well as images. Hence, we do not consider ImageNet [26] or 80 million tiny images [32] despite their larger coverage of semantic concepts.

2. **Semantic similarities.** We calculate semantic similarity measures over all pairs of classes in the dataset. The taxonomic relation **is-a** is taken from WordNet [19] by mapping all classes in CIFAR-100 to their counterpart concepts in WordNet, inducing the graph $G(C, \textbf{is-a})$. Some measures are defined as distances or dissimilarities. We use the rule presented in Sect. 2.1 to derive similarities. The following measures are evaluated over all pairs of concepts $(x, y) \in C \times C$ (see Sect. 2):

   (S1) Graph distance $d_G(x, y)$ as proposed by Rada *et al.*, see [22, p. 20].
   (S2) Resnik's maximum depth bounded similarity, see Eq. (1) and [23, p. 3].
   (S3) Maedche and Staab similarity based on intersection over union of concept features [17, p. 4].
   (S4) Dissimilarity proposed by Sanchez *et al.* using distinct to shared features ratio, see Eq. (2) and [28, p. 7723].
   (S5) Jiang and Conrath's distance [11, p. 8], Eq. (4), using intrinsic Information Content from [36], see Eq. (3).

3. **Visual similarities.** To estimate a visual similarity between two classes x and y, we calculate the similarity of each test image of class x with each test image of class y and use the average as an estimate. Again we apply the rule from Sect. 2.1 for distances and dissimilarities. The process of comparing all images from one class to all from another is performed for the following measures (see Sect. 3):

   (V1) The mean squared error (MSE) between two images.
   (V2) The mean absolute difference (MAD) between two images.
   (V3) Structural Similarity Index (SSIM), see [34].
   (V4) Distance between GIST descriptors [21] of images in feature space.
   (V5) Observed symmetric confusions of five ResNet-32 [10] models trained on the CIFAR-100 training set.

4. **Aggregation.** For both visual and semantic similarity, there is more than one candidate method, *i.e.*, (S1)–(S5) and (V1)–(V5). For the following steps, we need a single measure for each type of similarity, which we aggregate from (S1)–(S5) and (V1)–(V5) respectively. Since each method has its merits, selecting only one each would not be representative of the type of similarity. The output of all candidate methods is normalized individually, such that its range is in $[0, 1]$. We then calculate the average over each type of similarity, *i.e.*, visual and semantic, to obtain two distinct measures (S) and (V).

5. **Baselines.** A basic assumption of machine learning is that "the domains occupied by features of different classes are separated" [20, p. 8]. Intuitively, this should apply to the images of different classes as well. We can then expect to predict at least some of the visual similarity between classes just by knowing whether the classes are identical or not. This knowledge is encoded in

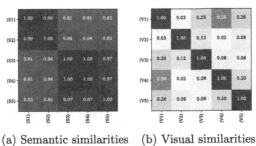

(a) Semantic similarities   (b) Visual similarities

Fig. 2. Rank correlation coefficient between different similarities, grouped by semantic and visual. $p < 0.05$ for all correlations.

the *semantic baseline* (SB), defined as 1 for identical concepts and zero otherwise (see also Sect. 2.1). We propose a second baseline, the *semantic noise* (SN), where the aforementioned pairwise semantic similarity (S) is calculated, but the concepts are permuted randomly. This baseline serves to assess the informativeness of the taxonomic relationships.

6. **Rank Correlation.** The similarity measures mentioned above are useful to define an order of similarity, *i.e.*, whether a concept x is more similar to z than concept y. However, it is not reasonable in all cases to interpret them in a linear fashion, especially since many are derived from distances or dissimilarities and all were normalized from different ranges of values and then aggregated. We therefore test the similarities for correlation *w.r.t.* ranking, using Spearman's rank correlation coefficient [30] instead of looking for a linear relationship.

5   Results

In the following, we present the results of our experiments defined in the previous section. We first examine both types of similarity individually, comparing the five candidate methods each. Afterwards, the hypotheses proposed in Sect. 1 are tested. We then investigate cases of (dis-)agreement between both types of similarity.

5.1   Semantic Similarities

We first analyze the pairwise semantic similarities over all classes. Although we consider semantic similarity to be a single measure when verifying our hypotheses, studying the correlation between our candidate methods (S1)-(S5) is also important. While of course affected by our selection, it reflects upon the degree of agreement between several experts in the domain. Figure 2(a) visualizes the correlations. The graph-based methods (S1) and (S2) agree more strongly with each other than with the rest. The same is true of feature-based methods (S3) and (S4), which show the strongest correlation. The *inter-agreement* R, calculated by taking the average of all correlations except for the main diagonal, is **0.89**.

This is a strong agreement and suggests that the order of similarity between concepts can be, for the most part, considered representative of a universally agreed upon definition (if one existed). At the same time, one needs to consider that all methods utilize the same WordNet hierarchy.

Baselines. Our semantic baseline (SB, see Sect. 4) encodes the basic knowledge that different classes look different. This property should also be fulfilled by the average semantic similarity (S, see Sect. 4). We thus expect there to be at least some correlation. The rank correlation between our average semantic similarity (S) and the semantic baseline (SB) is 0.17 with $p < 0.05$. This is a weak correlation compared to the strong inter-agreement of 0.89, which suggests that the similarities (S1)–(S5) are vastly more complex than (SB), but at the same time have a lot in common. As a second baseline we test the semantic noise (SN, see Sect. 4). It is not correlated with (S) at $\rho = 0.01, p > 0.05$, meaning that the taxonomic relationship strongly affects (S). If it did not, the labels could be permuted without changing the pairwise similarities.

5.2   Visual Similarities

Intuitively, visual similarity is a concept that is hard to define clearly and uniquely. Because we selected very different approaches with very different ideas and motivations behind them, we expect the agreement between (V1)–(V5) to be weak. Figure 2b shows the rank correlations between each candidate method. The agreement is strongest between the mean squared error (V1) and the GIST feature distance (V4). Both are L2 distances, but calculated in separate domains, highlighting the strong nonlinearity and complexity of image descriptors. The inter-agreement is very weak at $R = \mathbf{0.17}$. The results confirms our intuitions that visual similarity is very hard to define in mathematical terms. There is also no body of knowledge that all methods use in the visual domain like WordNet provides for semantics.

5.3   Hypotheses

To give a brief overview, the rank correlations between the different components of $\mathcal{H}_1$–$\mathcal{H}_3$ are shown in Fig. 3. In the following, we give our results *w.r.t.* the individual hypotheses. They are discussed further in Sect. 5.5.

$\mathcal{H}_1$: *There is a link between visual and semantic similarity.* Using the definitions from Sect. 4 including the semantic baseline (SB), we can examine the respective correlations. The rank correlation between (V) and (S) is $\mathbf{0.23}$, $p < 0.05$, indicating a link. Before we consider the hypothesis verified, we also evaluate what fraction of (V) is already explained by the semantic baseline (SB) as per our condition given in Sect. 4. The rank correlation between (V) and (SB) is 0.17, $p < 0.05$, which is a weaker link than between (V) and (S). Additionally, (V) and (SN) are not correlated, illustrating that the wrong semantic knowledge can be worse than none. Thus, we can **verify** $\mathcal{H}_1$.

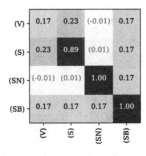

Fig. 3. Rank correlation coefficient between different types of similarities, grouped by semantic and visual. $p < 0.05$ except for numbers in parentheses. Main diagonal represents inter-agreement R. Similarities: (V) – visual, (S) – semantic, (SN) – semantic noise, (SB) – semantic baseline.

$\mathcal{H}_2$: *There is a link between visual similarity and model confusion.* Since model confusion as (V5) is a contributor to average visual similarity (V), we consider only (V-), comprised of (V1)–(V4) for this hypothesis. The rank correlation between (V-) and the symmetric model confusion (V5) is **0.21**, $p < 0.05$. Consequently, $\mathcal{H}_2$ is also **verified**.

$\mathcal{H}_3$: *There is a link between semantic similarity and model confusion.* Here we evaluate the relationship between (S) and the symmetric confusion matrix (V5) as defined in Sect. 4. (S) should offer more information about where confusions occur than the baseline (SB) to consider $\mathcal{H}_3$ verified. The rank correlation between (V5) and (S) is **0.39**, $p < 0.05$, while (V5) and (SB) are only correlated at $\rho = 0.21$, $p < 0.05$, meaning that $\mathcal{H}_3$ is **verified**, too.

See Sect. 5.5 for a discussion of possible consequences.

5.4   Agreement and Disagreement

To further analyze the correlation, we examine specific cases of very strong agreement or disagreement. Figure 4 shows these extreme cases. We determine agreement based on ranking, so the most strongly agreed upon pairs (see Fig. 4a) still show different absolute similarity numbers. Interestingly, they are not cases of extreme similarities. It suggests that even weak disagreements are more likely to be found at similarities close to the boundaries. When investigating strong disagreement as shown in Fig. 4b, there are naturally extreme values to be found. All three pairs involve `forest.n.01`, which was also a part of the second least semantically similar pair. Its partners are all animals which usually have a background visually similar to a forest, hence the strong disagreement. However, the low semantic similarity is possibly an artifact of reducing a whole image to a single concept.

424   C.-A. Brust and J. Denzler

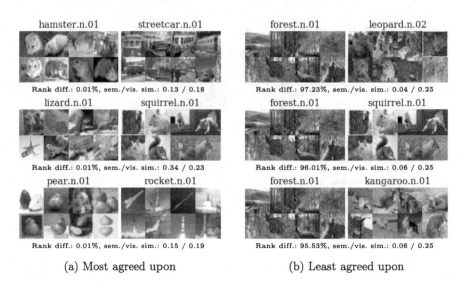

(a) Most agreed upon   (b) Least agreed upon

Fig. 4. CIFAR-100 classes selected by highest and lowest ranking agreement between visual and semantic similarity measures as defined in Sect. 4.

5.5   Discussion

$\mathcal{H}_1$: *There is a link between visual and semantic similarity.* The relationship is stronger than a simple baseline, but weak overall at $\rho = 0.23$ vs $\rho = 0.17$. This should be considered when employing methods where visuals and semantics interact, *e.g.,* in knowledge transfer. Failure cases such as in Fig. 4b can only be found when labels are known, which has implications for real-life applications of semantic methods. As labels are unknown or lack visual examples, such cases are not predictable beforehand. This poses problems for applications that rely on accurate classification such as safety-critical equipment or even research in other fields consuming model predictions. A real-world example is wildlife conservationists relying on statistics from automatic camera trap image classification to draw conclusions on biodiversity. That the semantic similarity of randomly permuted classes is not correlated with visual similarity at all, while the baseline is, suggests that wrong semantic knowledge can be much worse than no knowledge.

$\mathcal{H}_2$: *There is a link between visual similarity and model confusion.* Visual similarity is defined on a low level for $\mathcal{H}_2$. As such, it should not cause model confusion by itself. On the one hand, the model can fail to generalize and cause an avoidable confusion. On the other hand, there may be an issue with the dataset. The test set may be sampled from a different distribution than the training set. It may also violate the postulate that different classes look different by containing the same or similar images across classes.

$\mathcal{H}_3$: *There is a link between semantic similarity and model confusion.* Similar to $\mathcal{H}_1$, it suggests that semantic methods could be applied to our data, but maybe not in general because failure cases are unpredictable. However, it implies a stronger effectiveness than $\mathcal{H}_1$ at $\rho = 0.39$ vs. the baseline at $\rho = 0.21$. We attribute this to the model's capability of abstraction. It aligns with the idea of taxonomy, which is based on repeated abstraction of concepts. Using a formulation that optimizes semantic similarity instead of cross-entropy (which would correspond to the semantic baseline) could help in our situation. It may still not generalize to other settings and any real-world application of such methods should be verified with at least a small test set.

Qualitative. Some failures or disagreements may not be a result of the relationship itself, but of its application to image classification. The example from Fig. 1 is valid when the whole image is reduced to a single concept. Still, the agreement between visual and semantic similarity may increase when the image is described in a more holistic fashion. While "deer" and "forest" as nouns are taxonomically only loosely related, the descriptions "A deer standing in a forest, partially occluded by a tree and tall grass" and "A forest composed of many trees and bushes, with the daytime sky visible" already appear more similar, suggesting that more complex tasks stand to benefit more from semantic methods.

6 Conclusion

We present results of a comprehensive evaluation of semantic similarity measures and their correlation with visual similarities. We measure against the simple prior knowledge of different classes having different visuals. Then, we show that the relationship between semantic similarity, as calculated from WordNet [19] using five different methods, and visual similarity, also represented by five measures, is more meaningful than that. Furthermore, inter-agreement measures suggest that semantic similarity has a more agreed upon definition than visual similarity, although both concepts are based on human perception.

The results indicate that further research, especially into tasks different from image classification is warranted because of the semantically reductive nature of image labels. It may restrict the performance of semantic methods unneccessarily. It is likely that the relationship between semantic and visual similarity is much stronger when the semantics of an image are better approximated.

Further work should focus on the experimental setup. Viable alternatives to the simple visual similarity measures that we currently use are ones based on image gradients as well as cross-correlation. Larger datasets with well established semantic groundings such as ImageNet could be used together with a stochastic approach to approximating similarity to make them computationally feasible. Additionally, not only nouns should be considered, but also adjectives, decompositions of objects into parts. Datasets like Visual Genome [12] offer more complex annotations mapped to WordNet concepts.

Acknowledgements. This work was supported by the DAWI research infrastructure project, funded by the federal state of Thuringia (grant no. 2017 FGI 0031), including access to computing and storage facilities.

References

1. Barz, B., Denzler, J.: Hierarchy-based image embeddings for semantic image retrieval. In: 2019 IEEE Winter Conference on Applications of Computer Vision (WACV), pp. 638–647. IEEE (2019)
2. Bilal, A., Jourabloo, A., Ye, M., Liu, X., Ren, L.: Do convolutional neural networks learn class hierarchy? **24**(1), 152–162. https://doi.org/10.1109/TVCG.2017.2744683
3. Van den Branden Lambrecht, C.J., Verscheure, O.: Perceptual quality measure using a spatiotemporal model of the human visual system. In: Digital Video Compression: Algorithms and Technologies 1996, vol. 2668, pp. 450–462. International Society for Optics and Photonics (1996)
4. Brust, C.A., et al.: Towards automated visual monitoring of individual gorillas in the wild. In: International Conference on Computer Vision Workshop (ICCV-WS) (2017)
5. Chen, G., Han, T.X., He, Z., Kays, R., Forrester, T.: Deep convolutional neural network based species recognition for wild animal monitoring. In: 2014 IEEE International Conference on Image Processing (ICIP), pp. 858–862. IEEE (2014)
6. Deselaers, T., Ferrari, V.: Visual and semantic similarity in ImageNet. In: 2011 IEEE Conference on Computer Vision and Pattern Recognition (CVPR), pp. 1777–1784. IEEE (2011)
7. Freytag, A., Rodner, E., Simon, M., Loos, A., Kühl, H., Denzler, J.: Chimpanzee faces in the wild: Log-Euclidean CNNs for predicting identities and attributes of primates. In: German Conference on Pattern Recognition (GCPR), pp. 51–63 (2016)
8. Frome, A., et al.: Devise: a deep visual-semantic embedding model. In: Burges, C.J.C., Bottou, L., Welling, M., Ghahramani, Z., Weinberger, K.Q. (eds.) Advances in Neural Information Processing Systems 26, pp. 2121–2129. Curran Associates, Inc. (2013)
9. Harispe, S., Ranwez, S., Janaqi, S., Montmain, J.: Semantic similarity from natural language and ontology analysis. Synth. Lect. Hum. Lang. Technol. **8**(1), 1–254 (2015)
10. He, K., Zhang, X., Ren, S., Sun, J.: Deep residual learning for image recognition. In: Computer Vision and Pattern Recognition (CVPR) (2016)
11. Jiang, J.J., Conrath, D.W.: Semantic similarity based on corpus statistics and lexical taxonomy. arXiv preprint arXiv:cmp-lg/9709008 (1997)
12. Krishna, R., et al.: Visual genome: connecting language and vision using crowdsourced dense image annotations. Int. J. Comput. Vis. (IJCV) **123**(1), 32–73 (2017)
13. Krizhevsky, A., Hinton, G.: Learning multiple layers of features from tiny images. Technical report 4, University of Toronto (2009)
14. Kumar, A.: Computer-vision-based fabric defect detection: a survey. IEEE Trans. Industr. Electron. **55**(1), 348–363 (2008)
15. Litjens, G., et al.: A survey on deep learning in medical image analysis. Med. Image Anal. **42**, 60–88 (2017)
16. Liu, Y., Zhang, D., Lu, G., Ma, W.Y.: A survey of content-based image retrieval with high-level semantics. Pattern Recogn. **40**(1), 262–282 (2007)
17. Maedche, A., Staab, S.: Comparing ontologies-similarity measures and a comparison study. Technical report, Institute AIFB, University of Karlsruhe (2001)
18. Malamas, E.N., Petrakis, E.G., Zervakis, M., Petit, L., Legat, J.D.: A survey on industrial vision systems, applications and tools. Image Vis. Comput. **21**(2), 171–188 (2003)

19. Miller, G.A.: WordNet: a lexical database for English. Commun. ACM **38**(11), 39–41 (1995). https://doi.org/10.1145/219717.219748
20. Niemann, H.: Pattern Analysis. Springer Series in Information Sciences. Springer, Heidelberg (2012). https://doi.org/10.1007/978-3-642-96650-7. https://books.google.de/books?id=mdOoCAAAQBAJ
21. Oliva, A., Torralba, A.: Modeling the shape of the scene: a holistic representation of the spatial envelope. Int. J. Comput. Vision **42**(3), 145–175 (2001)
22. Rada, R., Mili, H., Bicknell, E., Blettner, M.: Development and application of a metric on semantic nets. IEEE Trans. Syst. Man Cybern. **19**(1), 17–30 (1989)
23. Resnik, P.: Using information content to evaluate semantic similarity in a taxonomy. arXiv preprint arXiv:cmp-lg/9511007 (1995)
24. Rohrbach, M., Stark, M., Schiele, B.: Evaluating knowledge transfer and zero-shot learning in a large-scale setting. In: 2011 IEEE Conference on Computer Vision and Pattern Recognition (CVPR), pp. 1641–1648. IEEE (2011)
25. Ross, S.M.: A First Course in Probability. Macmillan, New York (1976)
26. Russakovsky, O., et al.: ImageNet large scale visual recognition challenge. Int. J. Comput. Vision (IJCV) **115**(3), 211–252 (2015)
27. Salem, M.A.M., Atef, A., Salah, A., Shams, M.: Recent survey on medical image segmentation. In: Computer Vision: Concepts, Methodologies, Tools, and Applications, pp. 129–169. IGI Global (2018)
28. Sánchez, D., Batet, M., Isern, D., Valls, A.: Ontology-based semantic similarity: a new feature-based approach. Expert Syst. Appl. **39**(9), 7718–7728 (2012)
29. Silla, C.N., Freitas, A.A.: A survey of hierarchical classification across different application domains. Data Min. Knowl. Disc. **22**(1), 31–72 (2011)
30. Spearman, C.: The proof and measurement of association between two things. Am. J. Psychol. **15**(1), 72–101 (1904)
31. Thevenot, J., López, M.B., Hadid, A.: A survey on computer vision for assistive medical diagnosis from faces. IEEE J. Biomed. Health Inform. **22**(5), 1497–1511 (2018)
32. Torralba, A., Fergus, R., Freeman, W.T.: 80 million tiny images: a large data set for nonparametric object and scene recognition. Trans. Pattern Anal. Mach. Intell. (PAMI) **30**(11), 1958–1970 (2008)
33. Tversky, A.: Features of similarity. Psychol. Rev. **84**(4), 327 (1977)
34. Wang, Z., Bovik, A.C., Sheikh, H.R., Simoncelli, E.P.: Image quality assessment: from error visibility to structural similarity. IEEE Trans. Image Process. **13**(4), 600–612 (2004)
35. Zhang, R., Isola, P., Efros, A.A., Shechtman, E., Wang, O.: The unreasonable effectiveness of deep features as a perceptual metric. arXiv preprint arXiv:1801.03924
36. Zhou, Z., Wang, Y., Gu, J.: A new model of information content for semantic similarity in WordNet. In: Second International Conference on Future Generation Communication and Networking Symposia, 2008, FGCNS 2008, vol. 3, pp. 85–89. IEEE (2008)

DynGraph: Visual Question Answering via Dynamic Scene Graphs

Monica Haurilet[(✉)], Ziad Al-Halah, and Rainer Stiefelhagen

Karlsruhe Institute of Technology, 76131 Karlsruhe, Germany
{haurilet,rainer.stiefelhagen}@kit.edu, ziadlhlh@gmail.com

Abstract. Due to the rise of deep learning, reasoning across various domains, such as vision, language, robotics, and control, has seen major progress in recent years. A popular benchmark for evaluating models for visual reasoning is Visual Question Answering (VQA), which aims at answering questions about a given input image by joining the two modalities: (1) the *text* representing the question, as well as, (2) the *visual information* extracted from the input image. In this work, we propose a *structured* approach for VQA that is based on dynamic graphs learned automatically from the input. Unlike the common approach for VQA that relies on an attention mechanism applied on a cell-structured global embedding of the image, our model leverages the rich structure in the image depicted in the object instances and their interaction. In our model, nodes in the graph correspond to object instances present in the image while the edges represent relations among them. Our model automatically constructs the scene graph and attends to the relations among the nodes to answer the given question. Hence, our model can be trained end-to-end and it does not require additional training labels in the form of predefined graphs or relations. We demonstrate the effectiveness of our approach on the challenging open-ended Visual Genome [14] benchmark for VQA.

1 Introduction

The challenging task of Visual Question Answering (VQA) has received increasing attention in recent years [3,8,16,37,38]. Models for VQA aim at inferring the correct answer of a question in natural language about a given image. Hence, this task requires an elaborate understanding of both the *visual and the linguistic modalities* along with their interaction. Thus, VQA is considered an important step towards having an AI-complete task [1].

The common approach in VQA is to learn a global representation of the image using a convolutional neural network (CNN) and process this visual representation along with the question in a multi-layered network to infer the desired answer [17,19,24]. However, since these models rely on a global visual representation, they are unable to attend to specific parts in the image depending on the input question. Consequently, it is difficult for these models to handle questions about fine-grained visual properties or individual objects. To counter this drawback, visual attention modules can be employed to enable the model to emphasize the importance of certain image areas for a given question [16,37,38]. While these modules usually lead to better VQA models, they still do not take full advantage of the complex semantic structure available in the image, such as the present object instances and the type of interactions among them.

© Springer Nature Switzerland AG 2019
G. A. Fink et al. (Eds.): DAGM GCPR 2019, LNCS 11824, pp. 428–441, 2019.
https://doi.org/10.1007/978-3-030-33676-9_30

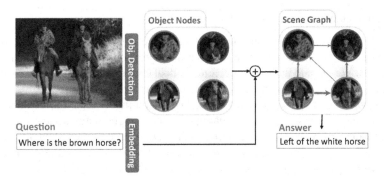

Fig. 1. Overview of the Dynamic Graph Architecture (DynGraph). Our model receives a set of nodes, which represent the object instances found in the image. Based on the current question, our model predicts the relationships among the objects to infer the correct answer. (Color figure online)

A possible representation of the semantic structure in the image are scene graphs [10]. In a scene graph, the object instances are mapped to nodes, while the edges represent certain type of pair-wise relations among the objects. For example, Fig. 1 shows a scene graph where the nodes represent the two horses and their riders along with their relations depicted in the edges. Leveraging this information can be very helpful for VQA, since most of the questions usually revolve around these object instances and their relations. Nonetheless, since the graph size in terms of both number of nodes and edges is variable and depends on the input image, it is especially difficult to employ such a representation in modern deep neural networks. One way to overcome this variability is to use recurrent neural networks (RNN). Here, the RNN iterates over the graph in a sequence of steps to encode the different parts of the graph [11]. However, this approach is quite sensitive to the order of encoding and the same graph can be represented differently given a different starting point. Recently, some methods were proposed to overcome the ordering issue by making use of edge pooling [25] or other graph-refinement techniques [12].

In this work, we propose a deep neural network (see Fig. 1) that leverages scene graphs as an intermediate representation for VQA. Our model does not require predefined graphs, but infers the scene graph automatically from the input image based on the detected objects. Moreover, our model inspects the scene graph in a dynamic fashion by attending to the edges based on the inferred relation from the question. We use thereafter this attention to create new embeddings for each node based on their neighbors. Thus, we obtain a representation that not only contains information about the current node, but also its connections. Furthermore, since a subset of the questions are about single objects (i.e. no relationship information is needed), we include residual connections to allow the network to easily skip unnecessary reasoning steps. Finally, we obtain a final global embedding of the image by attending over the nodes using the question to create the attention mechanism. In our previously mentioned example (Fig. 1), the green node (left bottom) would contain both the information about the brown horse as well as about the white horse. The attention mechanism picks the node that best matches the question and uses the information in the node to produce the answer.

To that end, our main contributions are:

1. A deep neural network that automatically infers the scene graph in a given image and dynamically attends to important relations among the object pairs based on the input question. We include in the architecture residual connections, to offer the model the possibility to easily skip unnecessary reasoning steps.
2. We demonstrate the effectiveness of the DynGraph model with a thorough evaluation on the Visual Genome benchmark [14], a challenging large-scale VQA dataset for open-ended answers. Furthermore, with qualitative results we show the *interoperability* of the graphs learned by our model by viewing example relations that were marked as relevant by the network for answering the current question.

2 Related Work

Attention-Based Methods for VQA. To combat the issue of lost information in the global representation (e.g. using the output of a fully connected layer of a pre-trained CNN), a form of attention mechanism can be applied to focus on local parts of the image that are relevant to the question [2,6,16,35,37]. Such an attention mechanism can be employed in various manners. For example, Yang et al. [37] argue that for answering a question about an image a multi-step reasoning is necessary. Thus, a stacked attention network is introduced that attends to different regions in the image in sequential steps, in such a way that at each step the attention map is refined with help of the question embedding. On the other hand, Lu et al. [16] propose a joint attention mechanism. Here, a co-attention model is used on both the image regions and the words in the question to emphasize important parts in both modalities. Moreover, [38] employs a multi-level attention over the image and predicted classes to incorporate information about semantic concepts in the scene. Finally, the module networks by Andreas et al. [3] leverage the structure of the question to compose multiple neural modules with customized attention maps.

While the attention-based embedding offers the VQA model the opportunity to focus on certain visual regions, the produced attention maps are usually hard to interpret since they are usually not aligned to salient objects in the scene. In contrast, our model attends to specific objects and relations in the image in a more controlled fashion. This, in turn, offers the possibility for better interpretation of the model decision by visualizing the learned graph.

Graph Neural Networks. A more efficient way to represent highly structured data are through graphs, which consist of a set of nodes and the corresponding set of edges using an adjacency matrix data structure. The use of neural networks on graphs was already considered in a wide range of applications, such as language [15], social interaction [13,26,36], knowledge representation [4,18,30] and chemistry [23]. Most of these approaches are either based on message passing through the graph either for better node representation [12,29,31] or they directly apply operations on edges [25,27]. A very popular technique for obtaining an efficient graph representation are graph-convolutions employed in many tasks e.g. zero-shot learning [34], video analysis [33], activity recognition [7] and co-author relationships [20].

In this work, we make use of graph convolution layer [12] to refine the node representations (i.e. object instances) using the structure of the visual scene. However, since we do not input any structural information about the scene, we let our network *dynamically* construct the graph based on our current question. More formally, we let the model link the object instances in such a way that this connection helps the network answer the question.

Graph-Based Models for VQA. Since information about the relations between objects can be useful for answering questions, there were some attempts in literature to leverage a graph-based representation for VQA. Teney et al. [29] introduce a model which represent both question and scene using undirected graphs over the synthetic Abstract Scene dataset [39]. Here, the words in the question are linked together based on dependency labels inferred by the Stanford NLP parser [21]. The scene, on the other hand, is represented with a simple fully connected graph where the nodes denote objects in the scene represented with one-hot encoding based on manually-defined ground truth annotation. Moreover, Santoro et al. [25] presented a VQA approach that leverages the relations among fixed image position over the CLEVR dataset [9]. Here, a pre-trained CNN is used to embed the entire image into a regular grid of feature cells, which can encode multiple objects, parts of objects or even simply background. Between each cell pair a relationship embedding vector is obtained based on the input question and then processed jointly to infer an answer. In comparison, the approaches proposed in [28,32] make use of object representation extracted from the objects' bounding boxes instead of simple taking features of a single grid. In [28,32] an attention mechanism was applied on each of the object instances (i.e. no relation information was used in the model).

Unlike [25], our model attends to salient semantic concepts in the scene offering better interpretable graphs. Additionally, we propose to infer the sought relation from the question which enables our model to dynamically generate a suitable graph rather than relying on a static fully connected one as in [29]. Finally, our model can be trained end-to-end and learn to infer the dynamic scene graph without the need of additional graph or relation labels.

3   Dynamic Graph Neural Network

We propose an approach for visual question answering that leverages scene graphs inferred automatically from the image. Starting with an image and a question, our approach consists of five main steps (see Fig. 2): (1) A *node encoder* will embed the extracted object instances of a scene and map them to nodes in the generated graph. (2) Then a language-based *question encoder* module will embed the relation among the objects that are subject to the query based on the input question. (3) Next, we create a scene graph using the *Dynamic Graph Module*, such that a connection between each pair of nodes is established in the context of the previously inferred relation and a new scene embedding is generated based on the learned scene graph. (4) Then, the model

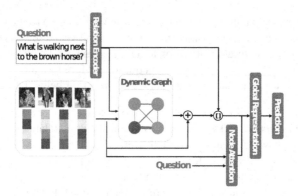

Fig. 2. Model overview. Our Dynamic Graph Network infers the scene graph depicted in the image using the predicted relation learned from the input question. The graph is employed to attend to the pairwise relations among all the nodes. Finally, our model attends to the nodes relevant to the question to predict the correct answer.

attends to the final node representations based on their correlation with the given question (*Node Attention Module*). Finally, (5) we compute the global graph representation and predict the answer using the *Answer Prediction Network*.

3.1   The Node Encoder

Given the input image, our Node Encoder produces a set of nodes that denotes the semantic objects present in the scene. For this, we employ two submodules: (1) an object detector network to detect objects location in the image represented with bounding boxes. (2) an object encoder where given the detected bounding boxes, the object instances are cropped from the image and fed to a CNN. We use the last fully connected layer output of a pre-trained ResNet-152 concatenated with the location of the object in the image as our node embedding. Thus, the node encoder output is a set of N nodes along with their D dimensional embedding: $I \in \mathbb{R}^{N \times D}$.

3.2   The Question Encoder

Our model learns to combine node representations in the context of the question in order to predict the correct answer. We enable this by using a Question Encoder which will encode the relevant information from the question needed to produce the necessary relations between the visual nodes. Thus, let the vector $Q \in \mathbb{R}^H$ be the question representation that is obtained by a recurrent neural network. The encoder takes as input the embedding Q and uses a fully connected layer with $W_Q \in \mathbb{R}^{E \times H}$ to extract the question encoding:

$$r(Q) = W_Q \cdot Q + b_Q.$$

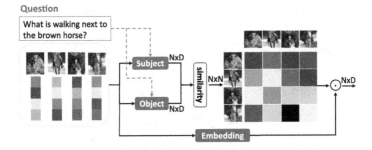

Fig. 3. The Dynamic Graph Module. We obtain in this step the graph-based embedding of N object instances. The probability of them to have a connection given the input question is calculated using the cosine similarity. The new embedding is obtained by multiplying the adjacency matrix with the node embeddings.

3.3   The Dynamic Graph Module

Given the nodes and relation embedding from previous step, the dynamic graph module produces the relevant scene graph. The module predicts an edge among two nodes in the graph if these nodes relation is deemed relevant to answer the input question as represented by the previous module (see Fig. 3).

We use the node representations I that we have obtained from the previous node encoding step to predict the graph adjacency matrix A. For this we jointly embed the relation encoding with each node using feed forward network. The model produces two different representations: the subject embedding (source nodes) and object embedding (target nodes):

$$subject_i = W_S \cdot [r(Q), I_i] + b_S \text{ and}$$

$$object_j = W_O \cdot [r(Q), I_j] + b_O,$$

where W_S and $W_O \in \mathbb{R}^{(D+E) \times F}$ and F the number of hidden units in the fully connected layers. We opt to use different embeddings for the source and target nodes (i.e. use a directed graph), since relations between object instances are not always commutative. A is inferred such that it has a high activation in the case that the subject and object nodes should form a connection depending on the question. We establish this connection by using a similarity measurement between each pair of subject-object nodes:

$$M_{i,j} = \text{similarity}(subject_i, object_j),$$

where the similarity function is the cosine-based similarity:

$$\text{similarity}(x, y) = \frac{x \cdot y}{\|x\| \cdot \|y\|}$$

Next, we normalize matrix M row-wise (i.e. values of a row sum to one) to a probability estimation over the connections of the nodes, such that the edge weights are normalized between zero and one:

$$A_{i,j} = \text{softmax}(M_{i,j}, M), \quad \text{where} \quad i, j \in V$$

with softmax defined as:

$$\text{softmax} : \mathbb{R} \times \mathbb{R}^N \to \mathbb{R}, \ \text{softmax}(x_{i,j}, x) = e^{x_{i,j}} / \sum_{k=1}^{N} e^{x_{i,k}}.$$

Thus, our module infers a scene graph representation:

$$G = (V, A), \text{where } V \in \mathbb{R}^{N \times D} \text{ and } A \in [0, 1]^{N \times N},$$

with V the set of nodes with the corresponding features $I \in N \times D$. Furthermore, these nodes are connected with a set of weighted directed edges represented by the adjacency matrix A.

Next, given A our module produces a new embedding for each node using graph convolutions. Depending on the strength of the connection we use information from the neighboring nodes to produce the new node representation. Thus, our new node embeddings I_Q are computed by multiplying the adjacency matrix with the representation of the nodes:

$$I^Q = relu(A \cdot (I \cdot W_A + b_A)).$$

Since not all questions require an elaborate processing of the scene graph, we add a skip connection to enable the model to select the best node representation based on the question difficulty.

$$I^R = I^Q + I.$$

3.4   Node Attention Module

We have now a set of nodes that contains in their representation also information from the neighbors. However, only a small set of these nodes contains relevant information to answer the question. We obtain the relevant nodes by using our previously extracted node embeddings I (before using any neighboring connections). The reason behind this is that we want our model to focus on the subject of the question. For example in Fig. 1 we want our model to pick the node with the brown horse since this node is the subject of the question. However, the person nodes might also have a connection to the brown horse node and therefore, have the representation of the brown horse embedded in the node. We attend to the individual nodes by measuring their similarity to the question embedding using cosine similarity:

$$e_i = \text{similarity}(W_Q \cdot Q + b_Q, W_I \cdot I_i + b_I)$$

Finally, we normalize the weights over all the nodes I using softmax:

$$\alpha_i = softmax(e_i, I).$$

3.5   Prediction Network

The Prediction Network composes the final representation of the scene graph. We filter the nodes based on the attention weights we obtained from the previous step.

Thus, we obtain the visual representation G, using the previously produced embeddings of the nodes from the dynamic graph and their attention weights:

$$G = \sum_{i \in V} \alpha_i \cdot I_i^R.$$

We jointly embed the question and the graph representation using their concatenation and their elementwise sum and product:

$$J = [G, Q, G + Q, G \cdot Q].$$

Finally, our model predict the answer in multi-way classification using two fully connected layers on the vector J:

$$\mathbf{a} = \text{softmax}(W_1 \cdot relu(W_2 \cdot J + b_2) + b_1).$$

where $\mathbf{a} \in \mathbb{R}^S$ is the predicted probability for all S possible answers in the data. The network is trained end-to-end with cross entropy loss and softmax normalization using solely ground truth question answer pairs.

4 Evaluation

We evaluate our model for answering questions in the open-ended VQA setting. Additionally, we provide a qualitative analysis of the generated dynamic scene graphs by our model.

4.1 Dataset

We opt to use the Visual Genome dataset for evaluating our model since it contains in addition to the question answer pairs, ground truth bounding boxes of the important object instances in the scene. Thus, we are able to evaluate the strength of the architecture on both *manually annotated* bounding boxes as well as the *predicted* ones which are produced by a pre-trained object detector.

Visual Genome. Visual Genome is currently the largest available dataset for VQA with manually annotated questions, containing over 100K images and over 1.7 million questions in an open-ended setting. Unlike, other datasets where there are multiple manually labeled correct answers per question, here we only have a single correct answer which makes it a very difficult task to predict the exact correct answer for the given question. In addition to the questions, Visual Genome contains manually annotated object instances, which can be useful for our model, as we can evaluate our approach on perfect bounding boxes without the errors caused by an object detector. As in [14] we take 40% of the data for testing, while we keep the remainder for training and validation. For validation, we use 10K images which we do not include in the training set. We report the results for all models on 75% of the questions, which have answers in the top 4K most frequent answers.

Metrics. As in [14], we use the accuracy as a measurement for evaluating our model i.e. an answer is considered correct it is equal to the ground truth answer.

Table 1. Comparison results on the Visual Genome Dataset presented by the accuracy over the test split. We report the results on the six different question types.

Approach	What	Where	When	Who	Why	How	Avg
Baseline [random]	0.0	0.0	0.0	0.0	0.0	0.0	0.0
Baseline [most-frequent]	0.2	0.0	0.0	0.0	0.0	25.1	3.3
FC [Infersent]	31.4	16.4	**55.5**	22.8	**31.2**	33.8	30.1
FC [Word2vec]	27.9	14.3	54.9	20.4	25.4	32.0	27.1
FC [gRes152]	4.7	0.2	6.6	0.4	0.2	0.0	5.0
FC [Infersent + gRes152]	35.6	20.8	51.5	24.5	27.7	31.9	33.1
DynGraph [mask-BB]	36.9	21.6	54.0	**27.0**	28.4	**34.5**	34.6
DynGraph [gt-BB]	**37.9**	**21.9**	50.0	26.7	29.8	34.1	**35.1**

4.2 Experimental Setting

Training Procedure. We use as an optimizer stochastic gradient descent, with an initial learning rate of 0.005 and a learning rate decay of 0.5, which we apply when the validation results stop improving. As a loss function we use cross entropy with softmax normalization and add a weight decay of 0.0001. The training process takes at most 20 epochs with early stopping based on the validation accuracy.

Question and Answer Representation. We investigate two different types of text embeddings in our model. The first is a sentence embedding scheme called InferSent [5] that has obtained state of the art results in a variety of tasks. In comparison with other text embedding approaches, this model is trained in a supervised setting by classifying the inference type between two sentences. The second embedding type we use for our model is the average embeddings of all words in the sentence as represented by word2vec [22].

4.3 Evaluation in an Open End Setting

In Table 1, we show the results of our model and our baselines on the Visual Genome Dataset. We have grouped here the methods by the input type: (1) no input, (2) question-only, (3) image-only and (4) using both the question and image to predict one of the 4K answers.

The random baseline, where we randomly pick one of the 4K answers, achieves a very low accuracy of only 0.03%. Our second baseline consists of always selecting the most frequent answer in the dataset, which in Visual Genome is the answer "One". This method slightly increases the accuracy to 2.6%. The baseline has a high performance in the "how" question type, as the answer "One" is a very frequent answer in counting-based questions.

What color is the wall? Answer: White. ✓

What are on the bookshelves? Answer: Books. ✓

What color is the closest car? Answer: Red. ✓

Who has on black clothing? Answer: A man. ✓

Where are the bricks? Answer: On the sidewalk. ✓

What is green? Answer: Trees. ✓

Fig. 4. Examples of correctly answered questions from the Visual Genome dataset. We also highlight the nodes with the highest activation in the node attention for answering each question.

In case of question-only, we have tested two different question embeddings: InferSent and word2vec. Both these models consists of using two fully connected layers, with an output layer with softmax normalization over the 4K answers. It is not surprising that InferSent outperforms word2vec, especially since the word2vec sentence representation is order invariant and in some cases it produces the same embedding for different questions.

For image-only, in a similar manner like in the previous case, we use two fully connected layers to produce the prediction, however, we use the global representation of the image instead of the question. We see that this model was able to use the image representation, such that it improved over the most frequent answer baseline.

The last baseline makes use of the question and additionally uses the global representation of the image. Both of these representations we embed using fully connected layers. The representations are thereafter concatenated, over which a fully connected layer is used to produce the final answer.

Finally, we show the results of our model for different object detection methods. We see that ground truth bounding boxes work the best, followed by our MaskRCNN object detections. In addition to the total accuracy we report also the accuracy for each type of the question. Our model improves over the baselines by a large margin in all question types except *when* and *why* questions. We see that the question-only baselines manage to get in these types of questions an improvement of around 1%. Since many when- and why-type questions can be answered using solely the question, the model focused only on the questions, and thus was able to improve the results.

  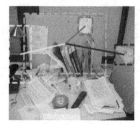

What color car is driving down the road? White. ✓

Who is about to cross the road?
A man. ✓

What is pinned to the board? Papers. ✓

  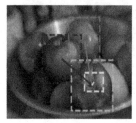

How many men are on horses?
Two. ✓

What color is the apple in the bowl? Red. ✓

How many apples are on top?
Three. ✓

Fig. 5. Examples of the predicted graphs for correctly answered questions. We show the top-3 highest connections (in order: dark blue, pink and yellow) to the source (blue). (Color figure online)

4.4   Qualitative Results

In this section we show qualitative examples of our model.

Node Attention. In Fig. 4, we see some examples of correctly answered questions. Additionally, we show in the image the bounding box of the object instance node, which produced the highest activation in the node attention weights. These example questions do not require a scene graph to produce an answer but rather an attention on the correct object suffices. Our model was able to attend correctly and predict the correct answer.

In comparison, in Fig. 6 we see a correctly answered question, with an incorrect attention. The network missed the drawers, however attended on the shelves with the same color. In the second image we show a miss of the network finding the correct node i.e. glass door, and produced an incorrect answer. The second row shows examples where the attention worked correctly, however the model was not able to produce the correct answer.

Dynamic Scene Graph. Next, we show some example graphs that our model produced for different questions, which require a relation understanding to be able to produce an answer. In Fig. 5, we show some questions that were correctly answered by our model. On each image we draw with light blue bounding boxes the instance with the

What color are the drawers?
GT: Brown.
Predicted: Brown. ✓

What is outside of the glass door?
GT: A balcony.
Predicted: A door. ✗

What is on the curtains?
GT: Sailboats.
Predicted: Shades. ✗

What is on the couch?
GT: Pillows.
Predicted: A teddy bear. (✗)

Fig. 6. Examples of incorrectly answered questions and incorrect node attention on the Visual Genome dataset.

highest activation in the node attention module. The other bounding boxes show its top-3 highest connection extracted from our dynamic scene graph (in the order: dark blue, pink and yellow). As we see our model has attended on both the correct source node and picked the correct connections between the source and target nodes.

5 Conclusion and Future Work

We presented a model for VQA which creates a dynamic scene graph of the image based on the question. Our model automatically predicts the relevant scene graph given a question and can be trained end-to-end using solely question answer pairs without additional nodes or relation annotations. We showed the effectiveness of our approach on the large-scale and realistic dataset Visual Genome for open-ended answers. Furthermore, we show in the qualitative results that our model learned reasonable dynamic scene graphs and attended to the proper nodes given the input query. In future work, we want to extend the model by using multiple relationship types by training the adjacency tensor using ground truth graphs.

References

1. Agrawal, A., et al.: VQA: visual question answering. In: Proceedings of the IEEE International Conference on Computer Vision, pp. 2425–2433 (2015)
2. Anderson, P., et al.: Bottom-up and top-down attention for image captioning and visual question answering. In: CVPR (2018)
3. Andreas, J., Rohrbach, M., Darrell, T., Klein, D.: Neural module networks. In: CVPR (2016)
4. Bouchard, G., Singh, S., Trouillon, T.: On approximate reasoning capabilities of low-rank vector spaces. In: AAAI (2015)
5. Conneau, A., Kiela, D., Schwenk, H., Barrault, L., Bordes, A.: Supervised learning of universal sentence representations from natural language inference data. In: EMNLP (2017)
6. Harzig, P., Eggert, C., Lienhart, R.: Visual question answering with a hybrid convolution recurrent model. In: Proceedings of the 2018 ACM on International Conference on Multimedia Retrieval, pp. 318–325. ACM (2018)
7. Deng, Z., Vahdat, A., Hu, H., Mori, G.: Structure inference machines: recurrent neural networks for analyzing relations in group activity recognition. In: CVPR (2016)
8. Hu, R., Andreas, J., Rohrbach, M., Darrell, T., Saenko, K.: Learning to reason: end-to-end module networks for visual question answering. In: ICCV (2017)
9. Johnson, J., Hariharan, B., van der Maaten, L., Fei-Fei, L., Zitnick, C.L., Girshick, R.: CLEVR: a diagnostic dataset for compositional language and elementary visual reasoning. In: CVPR (2017)
10. Johnson, J., et al.: Image retrieval using scene graphs. In: CVPR (2015)
11. Kembhavi, A., Salvato, M., Kolve, E., Seo, M., Hajishirzi, H., Farhadi, A.: A diagram is worth a dozen images. In: Leibe, B., Matas, J., Sebe, N., Welling, M. (eds.) ECCV 2016. LNCS, vol. 9908, pp. 235–251. Springer, Cham (2016). https://doi.org/10.1007/978-3-319-46493-0_15
12. Kipf, T.N., Welling, M.: Semi-supervised classification with graph convolutional networks. In: ICLR (2017)
13. Kok, S., Domingos, P.: Statistical predicate invention. In: ICML (2007)
14. Krishna, R., et al.: Visual genome: connecting language and vision using crowdsourced dense image annotations. Int. J. Comput. Vision 123(1), 32–73 (2017)
15. Kuhlmann, M., Oepen, S.: Towards a catalogue of linguistic graph banks. Computational Linguistics (2016)
16. Lu, J., Yang, J., Batra, D., Parikh, D.: Hierarchical question-image co-attention for visual question answering. In: NIPS (2016)
17. Ma, L., Lu, Z., Li, H.: Learning to answer questions from image using convolutional neural network. In: AAAI (2016)
18. Mahdisoltani, F., Biega, J., Suchanek, F.M.: YAGO3: a knowledge base from multilingual wikipedias. In: CIDR (2013)
19. Malinowski, M., Rohrbach, M., Fritz, M.: Ask your neurons: a deep learning approach to visual question answering. Int. J. Comput. Vision 125(1–3), 110–135 (2017)
20. Manessi, F., Rozza, A., Manzo, M.: Dynamic graph convolutional networks. arXiv preprint arXiv:1704.06199 (2017)
21. Manning, C., Surdeanu, M., Bauer, J., Finkel, J., Bethard, S., McClosky, D.: The Stanford CoreNLP natural language processing toolkit. In: Proceedings of 52nd Annual Meeting of the Association for Computational Linguistics: System Demonstrations (2014)
22. Mikolov, T., Sutskever, I., Chen, K., Corrado, G.S., Dean, J.: Distributed representations of words and phrases and their compositionality. In: NIPS (2013)
23. Radivojac, P., et al.: A large-scale evaluation of computational protein function prediction. Nat. Methods 10, 221–227 (2013)

24. Ren, M., Kiros, R., Zemel, R.: Exploring models and data for image question answering. In: NIPS (2015)
25. Santoro, A., et al.: A simple neural network module for relational reasoning. In: NIPS (2017)
26. Sen, P., Namata, G., Bilgic, M., Getoor, L., Galligher, B., Eliassi-Rad, T.: Collective classification in network data. AI Mag. **29**(3), 93–106 (2008)
27. Simonovsky, M., Komodakis, N.: Dynamic edge-conditioned filters in convolutional neural networks on graphs. arXiv (2017)
28. Teney, D., Anderson, P., He, X., van den Hengel, A.: Tips and tricks for visual question answering: learnings from the 2017 challenge. In: CVPR (2018)
29. Teney, D., Liu, L., van den Hengel, A.: Graph-structured representations for visual question answering. In: CVPR (2016)
30. Toutanova, K., Chen, D., Pantel, P., Poon, H., Choudhury, P., Gamon, M.: Representing text for joint embedding of text and knowledge bases. In: EMNLP (2015)
31. Veličković, P., Cucurull, G., Casanova, A., Romero, A., Lio, P., Bengio, Y.: Graph attention networks. arXiv preprint arXiv:1710.10903 (2017)
32. Wang, P., Wu, Q., Shen, C., van den Hengel, A.: The VQA-machine: learning how to use existing vision algorithms to answer new questions. In: CVPR (2017)
33. Wang, X., Gupta, A.: Videos as space-time region graphs. In: Ferrari, V., Hebert, M., Sminchisescu, C., Weiss, Y. (eds.) ECCV 2018. LNCS, vol. 11209, pp. 413–431. Springer, Cham (2018). https://doi.org/10.1007/978-3-030-01228-1_25
34. Wang, X., Ye, Y., Gupta, A.: Zero-shot recognition via semantic embeddings and knowledge graphs. In: CVPR (2018)
35. Xu, H., Saenko, K.: Ask, attend and answer: exploring question-guided spatial attention for visual question answering. In: Leibe, B., Matas, J., Sebe, N., Welling, M. (eds.) ECCV 2016. LNCS, vol. 9911, pp. 451–466. Springer, Cham (2016). https://doi.org/10.1007/978-3-319-46478-7_28
36. Yang, S.H., Long, B., Smola, A., Sadagopan, N., Zheng, Z., Zha, H.: Like like alike: joint friendship and interest propagation in social networks. In: Proceedings of the 20th International Conference on World Wide Web (2011)
37. Yang, Z., He, X., Gao, J., Deng, L., Smola, A.: Stacked attention networks for image question answering. In: CVPR (2016)
38. Yu, D., Fu, J., Mei, T., Rui, Y.: Multi-level attention networks for visual question answering. In: CVPR (2017)
39. Zitnick, C.L., Parikh, D.: Bringing semantics into focus using visual abstraction. In: CVPR (2013)

Training Invertible Neural Networks
as Autoencoders

The-Gia Leo Nguyen$^{(\boxtimes)}$ ⓘ, Lynton Ardizzone, and Ullrich Köthe ⓘ

Visual Learning Lab Heidelberg, Heidelberg, Germany
Leo.Nguyen@gmx.de,{lynton.ardizzone,ullrich.koethe}@iwr.uni-heidelberg.de

Abstract. Autoencoders are able to learn useful data representations in an unsupervised matter and have been widely used in various machine learning and computer vision tasks. In this work, we present methods to train Invertible Neural Networks (INNs) as (variational) autoencoders which we call *INN (variational) autoencoders*. Our experiments on MNIST, CIFAR and CelebA show that for low bottleneck sizes our INN autoencoder achieves results similar to the classical autoencoder. However, for large bottleneck sizes our INN autoencoder outperforms its classical counterpart. Based on the empirical results, we hypothesize that INN autoencoders might not have any intrinsic information loss and thereby are not bounded to a maximal number of layers (depth) after which only suboptimal results can be achieved (Code available at https://github.com/Xenovortex/Training-Invertible-Neural-Networks-as-Autoencoders.git).

1 Introduction

In machine learning and computer vision, CNNs[1] have been proven to be effective for various tasks, such as object detection [13], image captioning [22], semantic segmentation [27], object recognition [29] or scene classification [36]. However, all these approaches are based on supervised learning methods and require tremendous amounts of manually labeled data. This can be a limitation, since labeling images commonly involves human effort, which is impractical, expensive and not realizable on a large scale.

As a result, current research has moved more towards unsupervised learning methods. In particular, autoencoders and VAEs (see [5,9,25]) play a fundamental role in learning encoded representations of the data in an unsupervised manner.

The idea of INNs[2] goes back to the works of Dinh et al. [7,8], which introduced tractable invertible coupling layers. Since then, the research of INNs has seen some relevant advances in further understanding the characteristics of INNs, their relation to classical models and applying INNs to common deep learning tasks. Recent works on INNs include the RevNet[3] from Gomez et al. [14].

---

[1] Convolutional Neural Networks.
[2] Invertible Neural Networks.
[3] Reversible Residual Network, a variant of ResNet that does not require storage of activations during backpropagation.

© Springer Nature Switzerland AG 2019
G. A. Fink et al. (Eds.): DAGM GCPR 2019, LNCS 11824, pp. 442–455, 2019.
https://doi.org/10.1007/978-3-030-33676-9_31

They show that RevNets can achieve the same performance as traditional ResNets [19] of equal size on classification tasks. Jacobsen et al. [21] introduced the iRevNet, a fully invertible network that can reproduce the input based on the output of the last layer. They additionally show that the lack of information reduction does not affect the performance negatively. Impressive results have been achieve with Glow-type networks[4] as proposed by Kingma et al. [24]. The application of INNs on generative tasks has been done by Danihelka et al. [6], Schirrmeister et al. [32] and Grover et al. [18]. Ardizzone et al. [2] have successfully applied INNs on real world problems while proposing their own version of INNs, which allow for bi-directional training. Jacobson et al. [21] and Grathwohl et al. [16] have observed similar behaviors between ResNets and INNs such as iRevNets and Glow-type networks. Leveraging the similarities between ResNets and INNs, Behrmann et al. [4] were able to train the standard ResNet architecture to learn an invertible bijective mapping by adding a normalization step. A ResNet trained this way can be used for classification, generation and density estimation. Much of how INNs learn and their relation to traditional neural networks are still unknown and subject to current research endeavors. However, recent works on excessive invariance have given some insights in further understanding INNs such as [3,12,20].

In this work, we propose methods to train INNs as (variational) autoencoders which we call *INN (variational) autoencoder*. We compared their performance to conventional autoencoders for different bottleneck sizes on MNIST, CIFAR and CelebA. For all experiments, we made sure that the INN autoencoders and their classical counterparts have similar number of trainable parameters, where all classical models were given an advantage in number of trainable parameters. Our main contributions are:

- We propose a method to train INNs as (variational) autoencoders.
- We compare the performance of INN autoencoders and classical autoencoders for different bottleneck sizes on MNIST, CIFAR and CelebA.
- We demonstrate through experiments that INN autoencoders can achieve similar or better reconstruction results than classical autoencoders with comparable number of trainable parameters.
- We show that the architecture restrictions on INN autoencoders to ensure invertibility does not negatively affect the performance, while the advantages of INNs are still preserve (such as tractable Jacobian for both forward and inverse mapping as well as explicit computation of posterior probabilities).
- We provide an explanation for the saturation in reconstruction loss for large bottleneck sizes in classical autoencoders.
- Based on our experimental results, we propose the hypothesis that INNs might not have any intrinsic information loss and thereby are not bounded to a maximal number of layers (depth) after which only suboptimal results can be achieved.

---

[4] A likelihood-based model that improved on respective benchmarks and can synthesize new images.

2 Training INNs as Autoencoders

2.1 Invertible Neural Network (INN)

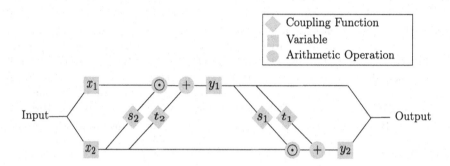

Fig. 1. Visualization of the invertible coupling layer

The building blocks of INNs are invertible *coupling layers* as proposed by Dinh et al. [7,8]. In this work, we use the modified version from Ardizzone et al. [2] as shown in Fig. 1. The coupling layer takes the input x and splits it into x_1 and x_2. The neural networks s_2 and t_2, also called *coupling functions* in the setting of coupling layers, take x_2 as input and scale/translate x_1 by their outputs. Afterwards, x_2 will be scaled and translated by the same approach. The output y will be the concatenation of y_1 and y_2. Mathematically, the forward process can be described as:

$$y_1 = x_1 \odot exp(s_2(x_2)) + t_2(x_2) \tag{1}$$
$$y_2 = x_2 \odot exp(s_1(y_1)) + t_1(y_1) \tag{2}$$

where s_i (*scale*) and t_i (*translation*) are arbitrarily complicated coupling functions represented by classical neural networks and $\odot$ is the Hadamard product[5]. In practice, we use the exponential function and clip extreme values to avoid numerical problems. The coupling layer is fully invertible, meaning the input $x = [x_1, x_2]$ can be reconstructed by the output $y = [y_1, y_2]$ with:

$$x_1 = (y_1 - t_2(x_2)) \odot exp(-s_2(x_2)) \tag{3}$$
$$x_2 = (y_2 - t_1(y_1)) \odot exp(-s_1(y_1)) \tag{4}$$

By stacking those coupling layers, we obtain an INN[6]. In contrast to deep Bayesian neural networks (DNN), which can learn any function, an INN will always learn a bijective mapping[7]. Generally, DNNs learn a non-bijective

---

[5] Element-wise product.

[6] FrEIA framework was used to implement INNs: https://github.com/VLL-HD/FrEIA

[7] Otherwise inverse mapping would not exists.

mapping causing an inherent *information loss* during the forward process, which makes the *inverse process* ambiguous (see Fig. 2). As presented in [2], this problem can be solved by adding latent output variables z in addition to y. The INN is then trained to put the information lost during the forward process $x \rightarrow y$ into the latent variables z. In other words, the latent variables z contain all the information that is not contained in y, but was originally part of the input x. As a result, the INN will learn a bijective mapping $x \leftrightarrow [y, z]$ (see Fig. 4).

Forward Process   Inverse Process

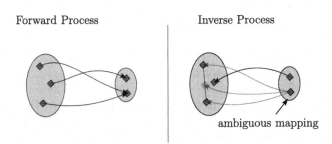

ambiguous mapping

Fig. 2. Visualization of information loss during the forward process and ambiguity of the inverse problem

INNs allow for *bi-directional training* (see [2]). For every training iteration, the forward as well as the inverse process will be performed. This enables us to compute the gradients in both directions and optimize losses on both the input and output domains with every iteration. Bi-directional and cyclic training have improved performance of GANs [15, 28] and autoencoders as demonstrated by [10, 11, 31, 37].

2.2   Artificial Bottleneck and INN Autoencoder

For INN mappings to be bijective, the dimensions of inputs x and outputs $[y, z]$ have to be identical. In contrast, the classical autoencoder has a bottleneck, which allows useful representations to be learned. Without this bottleneck restriction, learning to reconstruct an image would be a trivial task.

In order to build an INN autoencoder, we need to introduce an artificial bottleneck, that emulates its classical counterpart. This is achieved by zero-padding z at all times. With zero-padding, we ensure the extra dimensions given by z can not be used for representation learning. As a result, the forward process of INN autoencoders is given by $x \rightarrow [y, z \neq 0]$ and the inverse by $[y, z = 0] \rightarrow \hat{x}$ (see Fig. 3). The length of y defines the bottleneck dimension of INN autoencoders. The forward process of the INN can then be interpreted as the encoder and the inverse process as the decoder.

We train INNs as autoencoders by combining the artificial bottleneck with a reconstruction loss $L(x, \hat{x})$. The artificial bottleneck and the reconstruction loss will enforce the INN to put as much information as possible into y and reduce

Fig. 3. Visualization of zero-padding: zero-padding will be applied at all times. This ensures that the information in z is not available, hence creating an artificial bottleneck.

the information contained in z. The information loss through zero-padding is minimized, if z is the zero vector in the first place. Therefore, we add a zero-padding loss $\Omega(z, \mathbf{0})$ which compares z to the zero vector. The zero-padding loss Ω is not essential for the INN autoencoder, since the reconstruction loss L alone with the artificial bottleneck will enforce z to converge against the zero vector. However, we observed that the zero-padding loss Ω slightly improves convergence rate and stability during training without negatively affecting the reconstruction quality, since its objective is aligned with the reconstruction loss. We want to emphasize that the INN autoencoder can be successfully trained without using the zero-padding loss Ω. We only add the zero-padding loss Ω for technical reasons, because it does not affect reconstruction quality while making training more comfortable. The total loss function for training an INN autoencoder is given by:

$$L(x, \hat{x}) + \Omega(z, \mathbf{0}) \tag{5}$$

We can extend the INN autoencoder to an INN VAE by adding a distribution loss D to the loss function (5) which compares the learned latent distribution loss $q(y)$ with the true prior distribution $p(y)$:

$$L(x, \hat{x}) + \Omega(z, \mathbf{0}) + D_{MMD}(q(y) \parallel p(y)) \tag{6}$$

However, instead of using KL-divergence [26] as commonly used for classical VAEs to compare distributions, we will use maximum mean discrepancy (MMD) [17] as proposed by Ardizzone et al. [2] to compare distributions for INNs. Figure 4 visualizes the loss terms in Eq. (6) for INN VAEs.

3   Experimental Setup

The goal of our experiments is to examine how our proposed INN autoencoder trained with the artificial bottleneck performs in comparison to its classical counterpart with similar number of trainable weights. We trained our models until convergence for different bottleneck sizes and accessed the reconstruction loss on the testset. This will indicate how well our models have learned the representation of a given dataset.

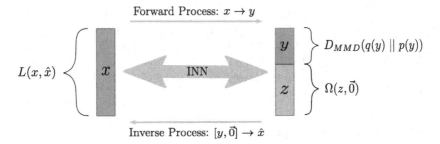

Fig. 4. Visualization of training a INN variational autoencoder with reconstruction loss L, zero-padding loss Ω and distribution loss D_{MMD} (For the simple INN autoencoder the distribution loss D_{MMD} is omitted.)

3.1 Architecture

For MNIST, we trained four different classical models. The encoder of model *classic* consists of four fully-connected layers (hidden size: 512, 256, 128 and bottleneck size) followed by ReLUs. The encoder of model *classic 1024* and *classic 2048* follow the same architecture, however the hidden size are modified to be 1024, 1024, 1024, bottleneck size and 2048, 2048, 2048, bottleneck size respectively. The model *classic deep* follows the same architecture as model *classic 1024*, however it has two additional fully-connected layers of size 1024. For CIFAR-10 and CelebA, the encoder consists of five convolutional layers (CIFAR-10: kernel size 3, stride 1 / CelebA: kernel size 4, stride 2) and one fully-connected layer. For all models the decoder mirrors the encoder, whereby the last activation function is replaced by a tanh function.

The INN autoencoder on MNIST consists of three coupling layers with convolutional coupling functions (hidden channel size: 100, kernel size: 3 and leaky ReLU slope: 0.1) and one coupling layer with fully-connected coupling functions (hidden layer size: 180). On CIFAR-10, we use the same architecture as for MNIST. However, the convolutional coupling functions have hidden channel size 128 and the fully-connected coupling functions have hidden layer size 1000. For CelebA, our INN model consists of six convolutional coupling layers with same coupling functions as for CIFAR-10 and one fully-connected coupling layer with hidden layer size 200.

3.2 Training

For both classical and INN models, we used L1-norm as reconstruction loss. The zero-padding loss Ω is chosen to be L2-norm. All models are trained with adaptive learning using Adam optimization [23] (weight decay $\to$ classic: 1×10^{-5}, INN: 1×10^{-6}).

The classical models were trained for (MNIST/CIFAR-10: 100, CelebA: 10) epochs with a batch size of (MNIST/CIFAR-10: 128, CelebA: 32). The learning rate started at 1×10^{-3} and was decreased by a factor of 10 at (MNIST: every 10th, CIFAR-10: 60th and 85th, CelebA: 8th and 9th) training epoch.

The INN models was trained for (MNIST: 10, CIFAR-10: 15, CelebA: 8) epochs with batch size (MNIST/CIFAR-10: 128, CelebA: 32). The learning rate started at 1×10^{-3} and was decreased by a factor of 10 at the (MNIST: 8th, CIFAR-10: 10th, CelebA: 6th and 7th) epoch.

4 Results and Discussion

In Fig. 5, we summarized our results by plotting the test reconstruction loss and the corresponding number of parameters in our models against the bottleneck size for MNIST, CIFAR-10 and CelebA.

We observe that across all three datasets, the INN autoencoder delivers results comparable to its classical counterpart for small bottleneck sizes.

Initially, we expected the reconstruction loss to further decrease for larger bottleneck sizes for both classical and INN models. However, the reconstruction loss for classical autoencoders seems to saturate for larger bottleneck sizes showing no further improvement despite increasing the bottleneck (see Fig. 5). The saturation sets in at about bottleneck sizes of 12 (MNIST), 250 (CIFAR-10) and 200–250 (CelebA)[8]. Based on the results, it seems, that saturation sets in at the approximate intrinsic dimension of the datasets.

In contrast, the INN autoencoder reconstruction loss resembles the expected exponential decay curve with better performance for larger bottleneck sizes. Since the INN autoencoder reconstruction loss does not saturate, it performs significantly better for larger bottleneck sizes than the classical autoencoder. In Fig. 6, we show examples of randomly reconstructed MNIST images by our INN and classical model with bottleneck size 32. Especially the difference between original and reconstructed image shows that the INN autoencoder produces better reconstructions than the classical autoencoder.

Besides the reconstruction loss, we additionally compared the number of trainable parameters in our models for different bottleneck sizes (see Fig. 5). The INN autoencoder architecture does not have to be changed for varying bottleneck sizes, only the split between y and z needs to be redefined. For the classical autoencoder, at least the bottleneck layer has to be changed, resulting in a higher number of trainable parameters for larger bottleneck sizes.

Since the saturation in reconstruction loss for our classical models was quite unexpected, we conducted additional experiments to further investigate the cause of observed saturation. For MNIST, we trained three additional models: *classic 1024*, *classic 2048* and *classic deep*.

Even though the reconstruction loss of model *classic 1024* and *classic 2048* improves for larger bottleneck sizes compared to model *classic*, it still does not reach the same performance as our INN model. The difference in performance

---

[8] Due to hardware/GPU limitations, we only trained our CelebA models for a sparse number of bottleneck sizes. This makes it more difficult to determine the exact point at which saturation sets in.

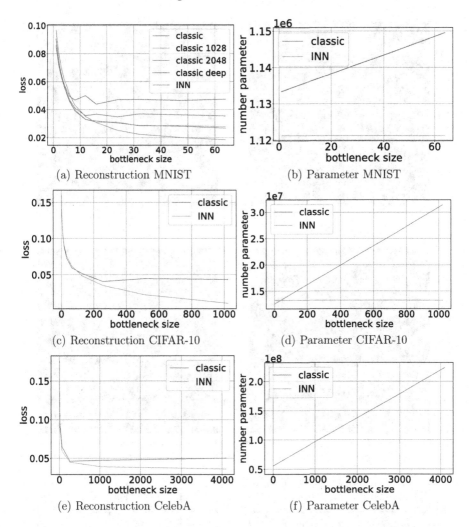

Fig. 5. Comparison of test reconstruction loss between our classical and INN models (a, c, e) and corresponding number of trainable parameters (b, d, f) for different bottleneck sizes on MNIST, CIFAR-10 and CelebA. Note that the y-axis of b, d and f does not necessary start at zero.

between model *classic 1024* and *classic 2048* is relatively small taking into account that model *classic 2048* has twice the hidden layer size of model *classic 1024*. This indicates that further increasing the hidden layer size would not yield significant improvements.

Model *classic deep* saturates at an even higher reconstruction loss than all other models, despite being deeper. This lets us conclude that model *classic* was already deep and complex enough for the given task on MNIST. This eliminates

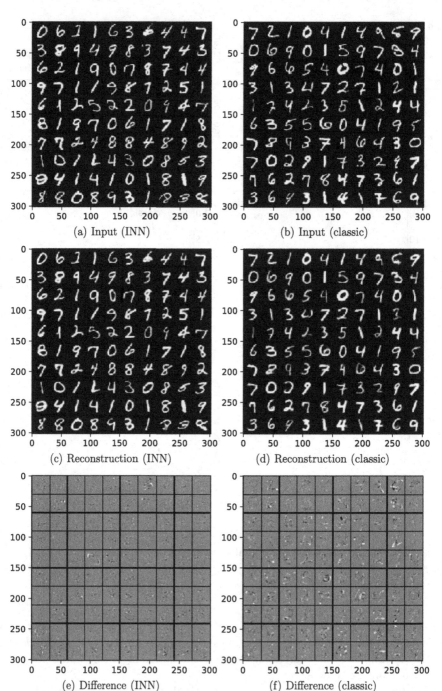

Fig. 6. Example of random reconstructed MNIST Images by our INN (left) and classical (right) autoencoder with bottleneck size 32: *Input* shows the original input images from the MNIST testset, *Reconstruction* shows the reconstructed images, *Difference* shows the difference between original and reconstructed image.

the possibility that our model *classic* fails to achieve the same reconstruction performance as our INN model simply because it was not deep enough.

Despite all the models being different, the saturation still sets in at about the same bottleneck size of 12 for all four classical models (see Fig. 5).

It is important to note that the hyperparameters for our models were only optimized for bottleneck sizes of 12 (MNIST) and 300 (CIFAR-10, CelebA). For all other bottleneck sizes, we trained our models with the same hyperparameters. However, for our MNIST classical models, we additionally optimized the hyperparameters for bottleneck size 64. Even with optimal hyperparameters, we could not reach the same performance as with our INN model. We also checked the reconstruction loss of our classical models on both the train- and testset and found no significant divergence which rules out the possibility of overfitting.

Given the results outlined above, we hypothesize that the cause of observed saturation leads back to the fundamental difference in network architecture of classical and INN autoencoders. Our hypothesis builds upon recent works of Yu et al. They applied information theory to CNNs [35] and specifically to autoencoders in [34]. By measuring the mutual information between input and feature maps of various layers within a DNN[9], they found that the mutual information decreases for deeper layers. Therefore, they concluded: *"However, from the DPI perspective validated in this work ([...]), the deeper the neural networks, the more information about the input is lost, thus the less information the network can manipulate. In this sense, one can expect an upper bound on the number of layers in DNNs that achieves optimal performance."* (cited from [34]). We believe that this is exactly what we observe with our model *classic deep*. It would also explain why the model *classic deep* performs worse than the other three models. Due to its depth, it loses more information about the input than all the other classical models. Further works that take an information-theoretic view and investigated the information bottleneck are [1, 30, 33].

This leads us back to the ambiguity problem of DNNs. We already established, that if a DNN does not learn a bijective function[10], information loss occurs during the forward process making the inverse process ambiguous. The INN solves this ambiguity problem by introducing latent variables z containing all the information lost during the forward process (see [2]). Therefore, we hypothesize that INNs have no intrinsic information loss contrary to DNNs and the findings of Yu et al. [34,35] do not apply to INNs. In other words, INNs are not bound to a maximal number of layers (depth) after which only suboptimal results can be achieved.

Furthermore, we believe that the intrinsic information loss of DNNs causes the saturation. In reverse, we could interpret the threshold at which the reconstruction loss saturates as a quantification for the intrinsic information loss of our classical models. This would explain why our deepest model *classic deep* saturates at the highest reconstruction loss threshold, since it has the highest intrinsic information loss.

---

[9] Deep Neural Network.

[10] Which we assume to be the case in general.

Increasing the hidden layer size as done with model *classic 1024* and *classic 2048*, seems to reduce the intrinsic information loss of the architecture. This makes intuitive sense, since a fully-connected layer of larger size is able to extract more information and minimize the information loss between its input and output. However, our experiments suggest that there is a lower bound for the information loss of DNNs at which increasing the hidden layer size will not further decrease its intrinsic information loss.

Since INN autoencoders do not have any intrinsic information loss according to our hypothesis, we expect the reconstruction loss threshold[11] of INN autoencoders to be at zero.

Despite INNs having no intrinsic information loss and thereby allowing arbitrary deep designs, in the application of autoencoders this might be a disadvantage. The main idea of autoencoders is to extract the essential information of the dataset and discard the rest to achieve a dimensionality reduction. Bounded to an information loss, a DNN has to get rid of information within its input. Most likely, it will choose to remove the noise in the dataset and keep the most essential information. This explains why the saturation sets in at approximately the intrinsic dimension of the datasets. At this bottleneck size the whole essential information of the dataset is already encoded. Further increasing the bottleneck would not yield any improvement, since the noise was already removed during the forward process. In contrast, the INN keeps all the noise within the latent variables z. Further increasing the bottleneck would add noise to the y-latent space in addition to the essential information and further improve the reconstruction quality. In case of dimensionality reduction, this might be an undesirable characteristic, since the goal is to remove the noise.

We conclude, that in order to use INN autoencoders for dimensionality reduction, the intrinsic dimension of the dataset has to be known or estimate appropriately. Nevertheless, if the bottleneck size is chosen accordingly, the INN autoencoder is capable of just learning the essential information of the dataset, but at the same time leaves the option to additionally learn the noise if needed. Furthermore, the INN autoencoder preserve all the advantages of INNs.

5   Conclusion

In conclusion, the experiments show that our proposed method of training INNs as autoencoders does indeed work. For small bottleneck sizes, the INN autoencoder performs equally well as the classical autoencoder. It is capable of extracting the essential information of a dataset and learning useful representations. For large bottleneck sizes, greater than the intrinsic dimension of the dataset, the INN autoencoder outperforms its classical counterpart. In summary, we demonstrated that the architecture restrictions cause by the invertibility constraint does not negatively affect the performance, while all the advantages of INNs such as tractable Jacobian for both forward and inverse mapping as well as

---

[11] At which saturation occurs.

explicit computation of posterior probabilities are still preserved. We hypothesize that INNs do not have any intrinsic information loss. This would allow the INN autoencoder to additionally learn the noise of the dataset, if the bottleneck size is chosen larger than the intrinsic dimension of the dataset. Furthermore, INNs might not be bounded to a maximal number of layers (depth) after which only suboptimal results can be achieved. However, further research is necessary to validate these hypotheses. Another advantage of INN autoencoders is that they are more versatile across different bottleneck sizes. The architecture does not need to be changed, only the split between y and z has to be redefined. There are both advantages as well as disadvantages in using INN autoencoders compared to the classical approach which we have outlined in this work. However, we believe that our results have shown interesting properties of INNs and their innate differences from classical DNNs. At the moment, INNs are still not fully understood which leaves room for further research. We hope that our findings can help towards uncovering the properties of INNs and encourage further research in this direction.

References

1. Alemi, A.A., Fischer, I., Dillon, J.V., Murphy, K.: Deep variational information bottleneck. arXiv e-prints arXiv:1612.00410, December 2016
2. Ardizzone, L., et al.: Analyzing inverse problems with invertible neural networks. arXiv e-prints arXiv:1808.04730, August 2018
3. Behrmann, J., Dittmer, S., Fernsel, P., Maaß, P.: Analysis of invariance and robustness via invertibility of ReLU-networks. arXiv e-prints arXiv:1806.09730, June 2018
4. Behrmann, J., Grathwohl, W., Chen, R.T.Q., Duvenaud, D., Jacobsen, J.H.: Invertible residual networks. arXiv e-prints arXiv:1811.00995, November 2018
5. Blei, D.M., Kucukelbir, A., McAuliffe, J.D.: Variational inference: a review for statisticians. arXiv e-prints arXiv:1601.00670, January 2016
6. Danihelka, I., Lakshminarayanan, B., Uria, B., Wierstra, D., Dayan, P.: Comparison of maximum likelihood and GAN-based training of Real NVPs. arXiv e-prints arXiv:1705.05263, May 2017
7. Dinh, L., Krueger, D., Bengio, Y.: NICE: non-linear independent components estimation. arXiv e-prints arXiv:1410.8516, October 2014
8. Dinh, L., Sohl-Dickstein, J., Bengio, S.: Density estimation using Real NVP. arXiv e-prints arXiv:1605.08803, May 2016
9. Doersch, C.: Tutorial on variational autoencoders. arXiv e-prints arXiv:1606.05908, Jun 2016
10. Donahue, C., Lipton, Z.C., Balsubramani, A., McAuley, J.: Semantically decomposing the latent spaces of generative adversarial networks. arXiv e-prints arXiv:1705.07904, May 2017
11. Dumoulin, V., et al.: Adversarially learned inference. arXiv e-prints arXiv:1606.00704, June 2016
12. Gilmer, J., et al.: Adversarial spheres. arXiv e-prints arXiv:1801.02774, January 2018
13. Girshick, R.: Fast R-CNN. arXiv e-prints arXiv:1504.08083, April 2015

14. Gomez, A.N., Ren, M., Urtasun, R., Grosse, R.B.: the reversible residual network: backpropagation without storing activations. arXiv e-prints arXiv:1707.04585, July 2017

15. Goodfellow, I.J., et al.: Generative adversarial networks. arXiv e-prints arXiv:1406.2661, June 2014

16. Grathwohl, W., Chen, R.T.Q., Bettencourt, J., Sutskever, I., Duvenaud, D.: FFJORD: free-form continuous dynamics for scalable reversible generative models. arXiv e-prints arXiv:1810.01367, October 2018

17. Gretton, A., Borgwardt, K.M., Rasch, M.J., Schölkopf, B., Smola, A.: A kernel two-sample test. J. Mach. Learn. Res. **13**, 723–773 (2012). http://dl.acm.org/citation.cfm?id=2188385.2188410

18. Grover, A., Dhar, M., Ermon, S.: Flow-GAN: combining maximum likelihood and adversarial learning in generative models. arXiv e-prints arXiv:1705.08868, May 2017

19. He, K., Zhang, X., Ren, S., Sun, J.: Deep residual learning for image recognition. arXiv e-prints arXiv:1512.03385, December 2015

20. Jacobsen, J.H., Behrmann, J., Zemel, R., Bethge, M.: Excessive invariance causes adversarial vulnerability. arXiv e-prints arXiv:1811.00401, November 2018

21. Jacobsen, J.H., Smeulders, A., Oyallon, E.: i-RevNet: deep invertible networks. arXiv e-prints arXiv:1802.07088, February 2018

22. Karpathy, A., Fei-Fei, L.: Deep visual-semantic alignments for generating image descriptions. arXiv e-prints arXiv:1412.2306, December 2014

23. Kingma, D.P., Ba, J.: Adam: a method for stochastic optimization. arXiv e-prints arXiv:1412.6980, December 2014

24. Kingma, D.P., Dhariwal, P.: Glow: generative flow with invertible 1×1 convolutions. arXiv e-prints arXiv:1807.03039, July 2018

25. Kingma, D.P., Welling, M.: Auto-encoding variational Bayes. arXiv e-prints arXiv:1312.6114, December 2013

26. Kullback, S., Leibler, R.A.: On information and sufficiency. Ann. Math. Statist. **22**(1), 79–86 (1951)

27. Long, J., Shelhamer, E., Darrell, T.: Fully convolutional networks for semantic segmentation. arXiv e-prints arXiv:1411.4038, November 2014

28. Mirza, M., Osindero, S.: Conditional generative adversarial nets. arXiv e-prints arXiv:1411.1784, November 2014

29. Russakovsky, O., et al.: ImageNet large scale visual recognition challenge. arXiv e-prints arXiv:1409.0575, September 2014

30. Shwartz-Ziv, R., Tishby, N.: Opening the black box of deep neural networks via information. arXiv e-prints arXiv:1703.00810, March 2017

31. Teng, Y., Choromanska, A., Bojarski, M.: Invertible autoencoder for domain adaptation. arXiv e-prints arXiv:1802.06869, February 2018

32. Schirrmeister, R.T., Chrabąszcz, P., Hutter, F., Ball, T.: Training generative reversible networks. arXiv e-prints arXiv:1806.01610, June 2018

33. Tishby, N., Zaslavsky, N.: Deep learning and the information bottleneck principle. arXiv e-prints arXiv:1503.02406, March 2015

34. Yu, S., Principe, J.C.: Understanding autoencoders with information theoretic concepts. arXiv e-prints arXiv:1804.00057, March 2018

35. Yu, S., Wickstrøm, K., Jenssen, R., Principe, J.C.: Understanding convolutional neural networks with information theory: an initial exploration. arXiv e-prints arXiv:1804.06537, April 2018
36. Zhou, B., Lapedriza, A., Xiao, J., Torralba, A., Oliva, A.: Learning deep features for scene recognition using places database. In: Ghahramani, Z., Welling, M., Cortes, C., Lawrence, N.D., Weinberger, K.Q. (eds.) Advances in Neural Information Processing Systems, vol. 27, pp. 487–495. Curran Associates, Inc. (2014). http://papers.nips.cc/paper/5349-learning-deep-features-for-scene-recognition-using-places-database.pdf
37. Zhu, J.Y., Park, T., Isola, P., Efros, A.A.: Unpaired image-to-image translation using cycle-consistent adversarial networks. arXiv e-prints arXiv:1703.10593, March 2017

Weakly Supervised Learning of Dense Semantic Correspondences and Segmentation

Nikolai Ufer$^{(\boxtimes)}$, Kam To Lui, Katja Schwarz, Paul Warkentin, and Björn Ommer

Heidelberg University, HCI/IWR, Heidelberg, Germany
nikolai.ufer@iwr.uni-heidelberg.de

Abstract. Finding semantic correspondences is a challenging problem. With the breakthrough of CNNs stronger features are available for tasks like classification but not specifically for the requirements of semantic matching. In the following we present a weakly supervised learning approach which generates stronger features by encoding far more context than previous methods. First, we generate more suitable training data using a geometrically informed correspondence mining method which is less prone to spurious matches and requires only image category labels as supervision. Second, we introduce a new convolutional layer which is a learned mixture of differently strided convolutions and allows the network to encode much more context while preserving matching accuracy at the same time. The strong geometric encoding on the feature side enables us to learn a semantic flow network, which generates more natural deformations than parametric transformation based models and is able to predict foreground regions at the same time. Our semantic flow network outperforms current state-of-the-art on several semantic matching benchmarks and the learned features show astonishing performance regarding simple nearest neighbor matching.

1 Introduction

Estimating correspondences between images is one of the main problems in computer vision with applications in stereo matching [14], structure from-motion [15], image stitching [41] and segmentation [39]. Early approaches have focused on finding correspondence between images depicting identical objects or scenes from different viewpoints [14,41]. With increasingly better feature representations, recent work focuses on estimating correspondences between different instances of the same semantic category [20,30]. This problem is denoted as semantic matching or semantic flow estimation in the case of dense correspondences.

N. Ufer and K. T. Lui—Both authors contributed equally.

Electronic supplementary material The online version of this chapter (https://doi.org/10.1007/978-3-030-33676-9_32) contains supplementary material, which is available to authorized users.

© Springer Nature Switzerland AG 2019
G. A. Fink et al. (Eds.): DAGM GCPR 2019, LNCS 11824, pp. 456–470, 2019.
https://doi.org/10.1007/978-3-030-33676-9_32

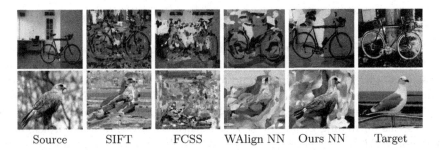

Source   SIFT   FCSS   WAlign NN   Ours NN   Target

Fig. 1. Nearest neighbor matching visualization. Previous learned features encode too little context information. While they allow to find correspondences, they ignore larger context like the shape of the object, see the results of SIFT [33], FCSS [23] and fine-tuned ResNet-101 features from Rocco et al. [37] (WAlign NN). In contrast our features (Ours NN) are able to encode larger context and resolve matching ambiguities.

In general, matching approaches consist of two main parts: First, a feature extraction method, usually a convolutional network, and second, a geometric model, which estimates a global transformation using local feature similarities. Current state-of-the-art methods [13,21,38] try to learn both parts jointly but suffer from three limitations: (1) The feature representation is often based on standard image classification networks, which are not well suited for finding semantic correspondences. One important reason is that these networks have only a small effective receptive field [34] and cannot resolve matching ambiguities by using larger context, see Fig. 1. (2) The majority of approaches [13,37,38] utilize parametric alignment models, like a TPS [1], which aggregate local feature similarities and provide a strong spatial regularization. However, these models are not able to cope with complex non-linear deformations. In contrast non-parametric transformation models try to estimate pixel-wise accurate flow fields [21,49]. But learning these models requires a large amount of data due to their many degrees of freedom. (3) A lot of progress has been made in the area of image co-segmentation [29] where the foreground objects in two or more images are predicted. Recent semantic matching algorithms [21,38] completely neglect this aspect: they find pixel-wise correspondences but do not predict which pixels in the two images belongs to the foreground object.

To address these limitations we introduce the following innovations. First, we propose a geometrically informed correspondence mining procedure, which circumvents tedious manual labeling. Second, we introduce a new layer which allows the network to propagate information from different spatial resolutions through the network, see Fig. 1. Based on these features the loose geometric regularization of local transformation models can be resolved and we are able to train a semantic flow network in a weakly supervised way which provides more natural warps compared to previous parametric models and in addition is able to provide pixel-wise foreground predictions.

2   Related Work

The pioneering work in semantic matching was done by Liu et al. with the development of SIFT Flow [30] and its extension of Kim et al. [20]. They densely sampled SIFT descriptors and formulated a discrete optimization problem for finding an optimal flow field. Due to the success of CNNs more recent approaches replaced hand engineered [6,30] with learned descriptors. First, there was a focus on finding geometric sensitive feature representations for semantic matching [4,22]. Choey et al. [4] introduced a fully convolutional Siamese architecture using contrastive loss and Kim et al. [22] proposed an approach based on the principle of local self-similarity. However, in these works the final geometric alignment was still estimated using hand-engineered models. More recent approaches learned descriptors and geometric alignment models jointly. [12,37]. Inspired by Proposal Flow [12] Han et al. [13] formulated a convolutional neural network architecture based on probabilistic Hough matching. And Roccoco et al. [37,38] regressed the parameters of a thin plate spline [1] based on feature correlation maps. However, these methods estimate parametric transformation models, which provide a strong geometric regularization and poor spatial alignments. There exist only a few exceptions where trainable networks for estimating semantic flow fields are examined [49]. Zhou et al. [49] proposed an encoder-decoder network for dense semantic flow, but they require 3D CAD models to synthesize a large set of pixel-wise accurate ground truth flow. Just recently Kim et al. [21] introduced a recurrent network for learning semantic flow fields, however they require image pairs of similar objects and are not able to estimate object segmentation masks.

Weakly Supervised Training. The majority of semantic matching methods are trained on strong supervision in form of keypoint annotations [4,13], 3D models [49], bounding box annotations [9,22,35,46] or image segmentation masks [17]. There are only few exceptions, like Novotny and Lorenz et al. [32,36], which use image-level labels to learn discriminative part filters. However, the accuracy of these filters are rather limited and restricted to specific object categories. Another popular approach is the generation of synthetic training data [19,37,38]. For example WarpNet [19] and Rocco et al. [37] estimate the parameters of a thin plate spline using a large set of synthetically warped image pairs. Other approaches generate training data by estimating correspondences using a simple one-cycle consistency constraint [17,22]. However, this approach is prone to background clutter and therefore, require strong supervision in form of bounding boxes or segmentation masks. In contrast our method does not require labeled image pairs [17,21,38], synthetic training data [37,38], segmentation masks [17] or bounding boxes [22]. It only relies on image category labels as source of supervision and hence, it is applicable on a large-scale dataset like ImageNet [7].

Context Aware Feature Representation. To incorporate more contextual information various approaches have been proposed. For semantic segmentation Long et al. [31] proposed a skip-connection architecture to aggregate multiple scales of deep feature hierarchies. Yu et al. [47] introduced dilated convolutions,

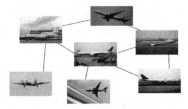 

Fig. 2. Overview of our correspondence mining approach. Based on global image features we generate an image graph to find similar image pairs (left). On these pairs we apply our graph matching approach to find consistent correspondences (right).

also known as atrous convolution, which increases the internal filter's stride. Dai et al. [5] proposed an extension, where the grid like sampling pattern was resolved and augmented with an additional offset module. For estimating visual correspondences Wang et al. [45] propose a multi-scale pyramid approach, where multi-scale features maps are combined using an attention module. In contrast we learn a mixture of dilated convolutions for each layer, which enables the network to propagate information of different scales through the network.

Contributions. There are four main contributions. (1) We propose an efficient correspondence mining procedure which requires only image labels and generates better training data then sparsely annotated keypoints. (2) We propose a new convolutional layer, which produces highly context aware feature representations. Simple nearest neighbor matching with these 128 dimensional features show competitive performance compared to state-of-the-art matching methods with sophisticated and optimized transformation models. (3) Our semantic flow network is not only capable to predict accurate semantic flow but also to provide foreground segmentation. (4) We outperform state-of-the-art methods on challenging benchmark datasets.

3   Approach

In the following we present the details of our feature learning approach and demonstrate that this representation can be used to learn a flow network without additional supervision. Our approach consists of three major stages: (1) We mine correspondences in a weakly supervised manner using only image category labels. (2) Based on these correspondences we train a feature encoder network using contrastive loss and introduce a new layer, which is a mixture of differently strided convolutions. (3) Based on the feature encoder we learn a semantic flow network using the mined correspondences and their endpoints as proxy segmentation mask to predict dense semantic correspondences and object segmentation.

3.1   Weakly Supervised Correspondence Mining

Given a set of images $\mathcal{I}$ from the same category, our weakly supervised mining approach consists of two main steps, see Fig. 2 for an illustration. First, using a similarity graph, we identify images depicting semantically similar objects from the same viewpoint. Second, we utilize a sparse graph matching approach, which finds corresponding regions between a given image pair.

Choosing Image Pairs to Match. Mining correspondences between all image pairs is not feasible and not desirable since objects from different viewpoints and types would lead to spurious matches. Therefore, we use a simple, yet effective heuristic and construct a k-nearest neighbor graph $\mathcal{G}(\mathcal{I}, \mathcal{N})$ based on conv4 features of AlexNet [28] pre-trained on ImageNet [7], where an edge $(i, j) \in \mathcal{N}$ exists if image I_j is among the k nearest neighbors of image I_i. We assume that neighboring images are semantically close and depict objects from similar viewpoints. By selecting all edges we obtain a large set of image pairs on which we apply the graph matching approach for finding corresponding regions.

Finding Corresponding Regions. For finding matching regions we utilize a modified version of the sparse graph matching approach of Ufer et al. [44]. Given an image pair (I_i, I_j) we extract conv4 features of AlexNet [66] pre-trained on ImageNet [7] on 6 different image resolutions for both images. Based on this image representation we select a fixed number of salient features as query features using non-maximum suppression on the overall feature activation. The selected query features are matched densely in a sliding-window manner at every scale using cosine similarity in the feature space of the other image. For each query feature we select the k best matches as matching candidates. Since each query patch has at most one corresponding patch in the other image the resulting problem of assigning each query feature to its geometric most consistent matching candidate is a one-to-one matching problem. Analogously to [43,44] we formulate this as a second order graph matching problem with an additional outlier class. The outlier class allows a query feature not to be assigned to any of its candidates but to be declared as an outlier. This is important since a query patch might be in the background without any correspondence in the other image or its matching candidates might be wrong and violate the overall geometry of all other matches. For more details regarding the graph matching formulation we refer the reader to [44]. The assignment problem is solved with the approximate inference method TRWS [26] and results in our final set of patch correspondences on different scales. Please see the supplementary material for qualitative results.

3.2 Feature Learning Using Multi-scale Convolutions

We follow a standard metric learning approach with a Siamese network [3]. Given two images we extract features from intermediate convolutional layers at the centers of the corresponding patches and penalize their Euclidean distance using contrastive loss [4,22]. The set of matching pairs is given by our mined correspondences and non-matching pairs are generated by hard negative mining. We adopt the hard negative mining approach of UCN [4] by searching for nearest neighbors outside a certain radius of corresponding points in the target image.

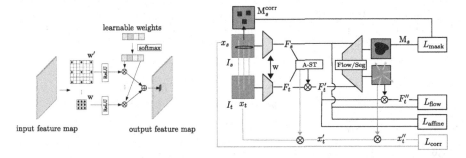

Fig. 3. Illustration of the proposed multi-scale convolution layer (left) and the semantic flow network architecture (right). The new layer consists of a combination of differently strided dilated convolutions. The proposed semantic flow network utilizes the mined sparse correspondences and their endpoints as proxy segmentation masks to learn dense semantic correspondences and segmentation at the same time. It consists of an encoder with the new multi-scale convolution layer, an affine spatial transformer (A-ST), which roughly registers the input features for the decoder, which estimates semantic flow and object segmentation masks jointly.

Multi-scale Convolutions. For learning context aware feature representations we replace all convolutional layers in the network with a combination of dilated convolutions with different strides, which we refer to as multi-scale convolutions, see Fig. 3. These dilated convolutions are combined in a weighted sum, where the weights are also learned during back propagation. To obtain the same dimensions of the output feature maps we adjust the zero padding on the input feature map for each scale separately. Each dilated convolution implies a specific receptive field and by optimizing the weighted sum the network learns how to adjust its effective receptive field in each layer for the matching task. This is important since the network can use the wider context to resolve ambiguities in semantic matching while a smaller receptive field is still available to maintain localization accuracy. In the following experiments we will show that adjusting the weights for each layer is crucial since each layer requires a different amount of contextual information. Our experiments have also shown that applying the non-linear activation before the fusion step provides better results since it prevents the signal of a single scale to suppress all others.

3.3 Semantic Flow Network

Based on the previously described encoder we train a semantic flow network which provides dense correspondences and object foreground predictions at the same time. It consists of three main parts, see Fig. 3, which are an affine spatial transformer (A-ST), a flow network and an auxiliary segmentation network.

Affine Transformer. After extracting the feature maps we fist try to get a rough alignment of the images. Inspired by the spatial transformer [16] we concatenate the features F_s and F_t and regress the parameters of an affine transformation from source image I_s to the target image I_t using a localization network. It is trained by minimizing the $L2$ loss between features F_s and the transformed target feature F_t',

$$L_{\text{affine}} = \frac{1}{h_s w_s} \sum_{y=1}^{h_s} \sum_{x=1}^{w_s} \|F_s(x,y) - F_t'(x,y)\|_2, \tag{1}$$

where h_s and w_s are the height and width of the source image.

Flow Network. To get pixel-wise accurate correspondences we utilize a flow network on top. We follow a similar network architecture as the popular FlowNet Simple model [8]. The input of the network are the concatenated features F_s and F_t', and the output is the flow from source to the affine transformed target image. The warped target feature F_t'' is constructed from F_t' via grid sampling and the final loss between features F_s and F_t'' is computed by the $L2$ distance

$$L_{\text{flow}} = \frac{1}{h_s w_s} \sum_{y=1}^{h_s} \sum_{x=1}^{w_s} \|F_s(x,y) - F_t''(x,y)\|_2. \tag{2}$$

Correspondence Loss. Despite the previously introduced unsupervised feature losses which try to find transformations by mapping similar feature on top of each other, we utilize the mined correspondences as proxy ground truth and minimize their $L2$ loss,

$$L_{\text{corr}} = \frac{1}{\sqrt{h_s^2 + w_s^2}} \frac{1}{|\Omega|} \sum_{i \in \Omega} \|x_{s,i} - x_{t,i}''\|_2, \tag{3}$$

where $(x_{s,i}, x_{t,i})$ are the mined correspondences between the source and target image and the $x_{t,i}''$ is the transformed target point $x_{t,i}$ w.r.t. to the predicted affine transformation and the flow field.

Auxiliary Segmentation Network. The majority of correspondences are localized on the foreground. By aggregating this information over a large set of image pairs we should be able to identify foreground objects. Therefore, we create an auxiliary network for pixel-wise foreground classification. The network shares the architecture and weights of the flow network except the last layer and a sigmoid function which produces the segmentation mask. As our model is trained in an weakly supervised manner, we approximate the ground truth segmentation mask using neighboring pixels of the correspondence endpoints M_s^{corr}. We minimize the pixel-wise cross-entropy loss

$$L_{\text{mask}} = \frac{1}{h_s w_s} \sum_{y=1}^{h_s} \sum_{x=1}^{w_s} \left(M_s^{\text{corr}}(x,y) \log(M(x,y)) \right.$$

$$\left. + (1 - M_s^{\text{corr}}(x,y)) \log(1 - M(x,y)) \right) \tag{4}$$

of the predicted segmentation mask M and the segmentation mask extracted from our correspondences M_s^{corr}. Given two images our network produces two probability maps which predict how likely each pixel belongs to the foreground. As postprocessing step we normalize the output of the softmax function to the unit interval and apply the fully-connected CRF of Krähenbühl et. al [27], which results in our final binary segmentation mask.

Final Loss. We train the semantic flow network by taking a weighted average of the individual losses:

$$L_{total} = L_{aff} + \gamma L_{flow} + \mu L_{corr} + \nu L_{mask} \qquad (5)$$

where γ, μ and ν are hyperparameters.

Table 1. Influence of different dilation values on PF-PASCAL [12] using NN matching. We compare our learned mixture (MSConv Learn) with a simple averaging (MSConv Avg.) and deformable convolutions (DeformConv) [5].

Methods	PCK		
	@0.05	@0.1	@0.15
Dilation 1	49.0	68.4	75.6
Dilation 3	48.4	73.5	82.7
Dilation 5	45.9	73.9	84.8
DeformConv [5]	48.6	65.8	71.8
MSConv - Avg.	48.7	74.5	83.7
MSConv - Learn	**53.1**	**77.2**	**86.0**

Table 2. Learned dilation weights for VGG-16 [40] on the PF-PASCAL benchmark [12], where we averaged the multi-scale convolution weights over each layer for a compact representation.

Layer	Dilation				
	1	2	3	4	5
Conv1	0.58	0.24	0.07	0.05	0.06
Conv2	0.24	0.34	0.18	0.12	0.12
Conv3	0.18	0.25	0.20	0.17	0.19
Conv4	0.14	0.14	0.14	0.16	0.17

4 Experiments

4.1 Experimental Details

We train on the PF-PASCAL dataset [12], where we do not use the subdivision into image pairs and apply the correspondence mining algorithm on each object class separately. We exclude test image pairs from training. In the supplementary material we also provide experiments for training on the Caltech-101 dataset [11].

Weakly Supervised Correspondence Mining. For the nearest neighbor graph we set $k = 10$ and select 80 query features per image with two matching candidates. Overall our mining procedure selects around 7k image pairs and generates roughly 80 correspondences per pair.

Feature Encoder. As backbone architectures we use VGG-16 [40] truncated after the conv4 layer and initialized with pre-trained ImageNet [7] weights.

To reduce the feature dimension to 128 we append a 1×1 convolutional layer. For training we rescaled images to 224×224 pixels and augment the image pairs by mirroring, randomly padding, cropping and rotating. In each training iteration we update the network on one image pair and use the ADAM solver [25] with $\beta_1 = 0.9$, $\beta_2 = 0.999$ and a learning rate of 0.0001. For each correspondence we extract 60 hard negatives and set the radius of positive correspondences to 32 pixels. We set the contrastive loss margin to 1 and trained 12 epochs in total.

Semantic Flow Network. We followed the same training protocol as for the feature encoder. We computed the loss in forward and backward directions and determined the gradients based on their sum. The radius for generating segmentation masks from the endpoints of the mined correspondences is 5 pixels. In our experiments the training was stable regarding the weighting in Eq. 5, but we obtained slightly better results for $\gamma = 4$, $\mu = 1$ and $\nu = 1$. The network was trained for 40 epochs.

4.2   Evaluation Benchmarks

The following benchmark datasets were used for evaluation.

PF-PASCAL Benchmark [12]. We follow the evaluation protocol of [13] and use keypoint annotations of the same test pairs. The matching accuracy is measured using the percentage of correct keypoints (PCK) [31]. A keypoint is counted as transferred correctly, if its Euclidean distance to the ground truth annotation is smaller than α, where the coordinates are normalized in the range $[0, 1]$. Please see [13] for more details about this dataset.

PASCAL-Part Benchmark [48]. We follow the evaluation protocol of [48] and evaluate on two different tasks, which are part segment matching and keypoint matching. For part segment matching, the flow field accuracy is measured based on the transformation of part segmentation masks. We use the weighted intersection over union (IoU) as quantitative measure, where the weights are determined by the area of each part. Please see [48] for more details.

Taniai Benchmark [42]. We follow the evaluation protocol of [37, 42] and measure the flow accuracy by computing PCK densely over the whole flow field of the source object. The misalignment threshold is set to 5 pixels after resizing images so that their larger dimension is 100 pixels. For the NN matching we randomly sample 1000 points on the object. To account for different orientations in this dataset we flip the second image based on the feature loss of the flipped and unflipped version. Please see [42] for more details of this dataset.

4.3   Ablation Study: Multi-scale Convolution

We investigate the influence of dilation levels and fusion methods. From Table 1 we see that by increasing the dilation stride the matching accuracy increases, although the theoretical receptive field already covers the whole image, which is in accordance with Luo et al. [34]. For a visualization of the effective receptive field we refer to the supplementary material. In Table 2 we provide the learned weights for each layer after training on our mined correspondences. It shows that in the first few layers the network prefers convolutions with small dilation levels, but with higher layers this preference is reversed. This is reasonable, since in early layers the network learns low-level concepts which require a high spatial resolution while later layers tend to learn more semantic and contextual relations where a large receptive field is beneficial. Therefore, by adjusting the dilation weight for each multi-scale convolution during the training process we obtain a clear improvement compared to a simple averaging.

4.4   Ablation Study: Correspondence Mining

We evaluate our correspondence mining approach by comparing NN matching accuracy using features trained on our mined correspondences against features trained on ground truth annotations, see Table 3. First, we trained each method on the whole training set and evaluated on the test set using all classes, see the upper part of Table 3. It shows that by training on our mined correspondences we obtain almost identical matching accuracy without any keypoint or image pair labels. This is remarkable since our mining generates a lot of inconsistent image pairs with many false correspondences, see the supplementary material for some examples. To compare the generalization capabilities of the learned features we select random splits of the dataset classes (class split) and train on one half and test on the other half. From the bottom part of Table 3 we observe that our mining procedure generates feature encodings which generalize better to unseen objects compared to ground truth annotations.

Table 3. Comparison of our correspondence mining (Ours) against ground truth data (GT) for NN matching on PF-PASCAL [12]. In addition we split classes and trained on one half and tested on the other half (class split).

Methods	PCK		
	@0.05	@0.1	@0.15
GT	53.1	78.1	87.4
Ours	53.1	77.2	86.0
GT (class split)	28.7	54.9	69.5
Ours (class split)	39.0	61.8	73.5

Table 4. Ablation study of our semantic flow network on the PF-PASCAL benchmark [12] using NN matching, where we removed the affine and flow network and also disabled the feature losses L_{aff} and L_{flow} and correspondence loss L_{corr}.

Methods	PCK@0.1
Ours w/NN	77.2
Ours wo/Flow Network	75.8
Ours wo/Affine Network	77.4
Ours wo/(L_{aff} & L_{flow})	77.0
Ours wo/L_{corr}	76.7
Ours	**78.5**

4.5   Ablation Study: Semantic Flow Network

From Table 4 it can be seen that the consecutive execution of an affine transformation with a flow field clearly improves the performance. This is conceptually similar to [21] but circumvents the expensive training of a recurrent network. The affine transformation model alone is not sufficient since it is not capable to recover non-linear deformations. Furthermore, the introduction of the feature losses L_{aff} and L_{flow} improve the results since they favor transformations where similar features are mapped on top of each other and thus, provide an additional training signal in regions where no correspondence predictions are available.

4.6   Results on Benchmark Datasets

Qualitative Results. Figure 4 shows qualitative results on the PF-PASCAL dataset [12] with our features using nearest neighbor matching. It can clearly be seen that our matching provides more natural warps and is able to capture difficult non-linear transformations. Please notice the difficulty of this task as demonstrated in Fig. 1. Examples on the Taniai dataset [42] can be seen in Fig. 5.

Source   WAlign   Ours NN   Target   Source   WAlign   Ours NN   Target

Fig. 4. Qualitative examples on the PF-PASCAL dataset [13], which shows a source, target and the warped images using NN matching with our features (Ours NN) and the weak alignment method (WAlign) [37].

Source   WAlign   Ours Prob.   Ours   Target Seg.   Target

Fig. 5. Qualitative examples on the Taniai dataset [42], which shows a source image, the warped images with the weak alignment method (WAlign) [37], the probability map of our segmentation network (Ours Prob.), the transformation of our semantic flow network with segmentation (Ours), the ground truth segmentation of the target (Target Seg.) and the target image.

Source   Source Parts   DSP   Ours   Target Parts   Target

Fig. 6. Visualization of part segment transformations on the PASCAL Parts dataset [2], which shows a source image, the color-coded part masks, part segment transformations with DSP [20] and with our semantic flow network (Ours), target masks and the target.

In contrast to recent deep learning based approaches our network is also capable to predict foreground segmentation masks. In Fig. 6 we provide an example of part matchings on the PASCAL Parts dataset [2]. See the supplementary material for more qualitative examples.

Quantitative Results. In Table 5 we present quantitative comparisons. Due to space limitations we compare only with most recent results. We observe that nearest neighbor matching with our features outperform all existing semantic matching methods on the PF-PASCAL dataset [12], including supervised methods like [12]. Furthermore, our semantic flow network outperforms current benchmarks on PF-PASCAL [12], Taniai [42] and PASCAL Parts [2]. We evaluate our auxiliary segmentation network also for the task of co-segmentation and obtain superior results compared to the state-of-the-art on the Taniai dataset [42], see Table 6.

Table 5. Evaluation results on the PF-PASCAL, Taniai and PASCAL Parts dataset.

Methods	Feat. Extr.	Superv.	PF-PASCAL PCK@0.1	Taniai Avg.	PASCAL Parts IoU	@0.05	@0.1
DSP [20]	SIFT	–	37	44.5	0.39	17	–
PF [12]	HOG	–	62.5	65.7	0.41	17	36
DCTM [24]	VGG-16	–	69.6	74.0	0.48	32	50
UCN-ST [4]	Inception-v1	keyPts	55.6	67.9	–	26	44
FCSS-LOM [22]	VGG-16	bbox	68.9	66.8	0.44	28	47
SCNet-AG+ [13]	VGG-16	keyPts	72.2	61.9	0.48	18	–
CNNGeo [38]	VGG-16	synth	62.6	67.3	0.51	22.1	46.6
CNNGeo [38]	ResNet-101	synth	69.5	73.5	0.54	25.8	49.5
WAlign [37]	ResNet-101	synth & imgPairs	74.8	73.7	0.55	28.4	53.2
RTNs [21]	VGG-16	imgPairs	74.3	73.2	–	–	–
RTNs [21]	ResNet-101	imgPairs	75.9	77.2	–	–	–
Ours w/NN	VGG-16	classL	77.2	75.7	–	**37.2**	54.3
Ours	VGG-16	classL	**78.5**	**79.7**	**0.57**	34.7	**54.5**

Table 6. Evaluation of our network for co-segmentation on the Tania benchmark [42].

Methods	Joulin et al. [18]	Faktor et al. [10]	Tania et al. [42]	Ours
IoU	0.39	0.58	0.64	**0.72**

5 Conclusion

We have presented a new convolutional layer for semantic matching which learns highly context aware feature representations with a high localization accuracy. It clearly outperforms other methods like dilated and deformable convolutions. To alleviate tedious manual labeling, we have introduced a correspondence mining procedure which requires only class labels and is more effective than training on ground truth keypoints. Therefore, we require less supervision than the current best methods. Our semantic flow network produces more natural warps compared to parametric transformation based models and is also capable to provide reliable foreground segmentation masks at the same time. The presented approach demonstrated significant improvements on several challenging benchmark datasets for semantic matching and joint co-segmentation.

Acknowledgment. This work has been supported in part by the DFG grand OM81/1-1 and a hardware donation from NVIDIA Corporation.

References

1. Bookstein, F.L.: Principal warps: thin-plate splines and the decomposition ofdeformations. TPAMI **11**(6), 567–585 (1989)
2. Chen, X., Mottaghi, R., Liu, X., Fidler, S., Urtasun, R., Yuille, A.: Detect what you can: detecting and representing objects using holistic models and body parts. In: CVPR (2014)
3. Chopra, S., Hadsell, R., LeCun, Y.: Learning a similarity metric discriminatively, with application to face verification. In: CVRP (2005)
4. Choy, C.B., Gwak, J., Savarese, S., Chandraker, M.: Universal correspondence network. In: NeurIPS (2016)
5. Dai, J., et al.: Deformable convolutional networks. In: ICCV (2017)
6. Dalal, N., Triggs, W.: Histograms of oriented gradients for human detection. In: CVPR (2004)
7. Deng, J., Dong, W., Socher, R., Li, L.J., Li, K., Fei-Fei, L.: Imagenet: a large-scale hierarchical image database. In: CVPR (2009)
8. Dosovitskiy, A., et al.: Flownet: learning optical flow with convolutional networks. In: ICCV (2015)
9. Eigenstetter, A., Takami, M., Ommer, B.: Randomized max-margin compositions for visual recognition. In: CVPR (2014)
10. Faktor, A., Irani, M.: Co-segmentation by composition. In: ICCV (2013)
11. Fei-Fei, L., Fergus, R., Perona, P.: One-shot learning of object categories. TPAMI **28**(4), 594–611 (2006)
12. Ham, B., Cho, M., Schmid, C., Ponce, J.: Proposal flow. In: CVPR (2016)

13. Han, K., et al.: Scnet: learning semantic correspondence. In: ICCV (2017)
14. Hannah, M.J.: Computer matching of areas in stereo images (1974)
15. Hartley, R., Zisserman, A.: Multiple View Geometry in Computer Vision. Cambridge University Press, Cambridge (2003)
16. Jaderberg, M., Simonyan, K., Zisserman, A., et al.: Spatial transformer networks. In: NeurIPS (2015)
17. Jeon, S., Kim, S., Min, D., Sohn, K.: Parn: pyramidal affine regression networks for dense semantic correspondence. In: ECCV (2018)
18. Joulin, A., Bach, F., Ponce, J.: Discriminative clustering for image co-segmentation. In: CVPR (2010)
19. Kanazawa, A., Jacobs, D.W., Chandraker, M.: Warpnet: weakly supervised matching for single-view reconstruction. In: CVPR (2016)
20. Kim, J., Liu, C., Sha, F., Grauman, K.: Deformable spatial pyramid matching for fast dense correspondences. In: CVRP (2013)
21. Kim, S., Lin, S., Jeon, S.R., Min, D., Sohn, K.: Recurrent transformer networks for semantic correspondence. In: NeurIPS (2018)
22. Kim, S., Min, D., Ham, B., Jeon, S., Lin, S., Sohn, K.: Fcss: fully convolutional self-similarity for dense semantic correspondence. In: CVPR (2017)
23. Kim, S., Min, D., Ham, B., Lin, S., Sohn, K.: Fcss: fully convolutional self-similarity for dense semantic correspondence. In: TPAMI (2018)
24. Kim, S., Min, D., Lin, S., Sohn, K.: Dctm: discrete-continuous transformation matching for semantic flow. In: ICCV (2017)
25. Kingma, D.P., Ba, J.: Adam: a method for stochastic optimization. CoRR abs/1412.6980 (2014). http://arxiv.org/abs/1412.6980
26. Kolmogorov, V.: Convergent tree-reweighted message passing for energyminimization. TPAMI **28**(10), 1568–1583 (2006)
27. Krähenbühl, P., Koltun, V.: Efficient inference in fully connected CRFs with Gaussian edge potentials. In: NeurIPS (2011)
28. Krizhevsky, A., Sutskever, I., Geoffrey E., H.: Imagenet classification with deep convolutional neural networks. In: NeurIPS (2012)
29. Li, W., Hosseini Jafari, O., Rother, C.: Deep object co-segmentation. In: ACCV (2018)
30. Liu, C., Yuen, J., Torralba, A.: SIFT flow: dense correspondence across scenes and its applications. TPAMI **33**(5), 978–994 (2011)
31. Long, J.L., Zhang, N., Darrell, T.: Do convnets learn correspondence? In: NeurIPS (2014)
32. Lorenz, D., Bereska, L., Milbich, T., Ommer, B.: Unsupervised part-based disentangling of object shape and appearance. In: CVPR (2019)
33. Lowe, D.G.: Distinctive image features from scale-invariant keypoints. IJCV **60**(2), 91–110 (2004)
34. Luo, W., Li, Y., Urtasun, R., Zemel, R.: Understanding the effective receptive field in deep convolutional neural networks. In: NeurIPS (2017)
35. Monroy, A., Ommer, B.: Beyond bounding-boxes: learning object shape by model-driven grouping. In: Fitzgibbon, A., Lazebnik, S., Perona, P., Sato, Y., Schmid, C. (eds.) ECCV 2012. LNCS, vol. 7574, pp. 580–593. Springer, Heidelberg (2012). https://doi.org/10.1007/978-3-642-33712-3_42
36. Novotny, D., Larlus, D., Vedaldi, A.: Anchornet: a weakly supervised network to learn geometry-sensitive features for semantic matching. In: CVPR (2017)
37. Rocco, I., Arandjelovi, R., Inria, J.S.: Convolutional neural network architecture for geometric matching. In: CVPR (2017)

38. Rocco, I., Arandjelović, R., Sivic, J.: End-to-end weakly-supervised semantic alignment. In: CVPR (2018)
39. Rubio, J.C., Serrat, J., López, A., Paragios, N.: Unsupervised co-segmentation through region matching. In: CVPR (2012)
40. Simonyan, K., Zisserman, A.: Very deep convolutional networks for large-scale image recognition. arXiv preprint arXiv:1409.1556 (2014)
41. Szeliski, R., et al.: Image alignment and stitching: a tutorial. Found. Trends® Comput. Graph. Vis. **2**(1), 1–104 (2007)
42. Taniai, T., Sinha, S.N., Sato, Y.: Joint recovery of dense correspondence and cosegmentation in two images. In: CVPR (2016)
43. Torresani, L., Kolmogorov, V., Rother, C.: A dual decomposition approach to feature correspondence. TPAMI **35**(2), 259–271 (2013)
44. Ufer, N., Ommer, B.: Deep semantic feature matching. In: CVPR (2017)
45. Wang, S., Luo, L., Zhang, N., Li, J.: Autoscaler: scale-attention networks for visual correspondence. arXiv preprint arXiv:1611.05837 (2016)
46. Yarlagadda, P., Ommer, B.: From meaningful contours to discriminative object shape. In: ECCV (2012)
47. Yu, F., Koltun, V.: Multi-scale context aggregation by dilated convolutions. arXiv preprint arXiv:1511.07122 (2015)
48. Zhou, T., Lee, Y.J., Yu, S., Efros, A.: Flowweb: joint image set alignment by weaving consistent pixel-wise correspondences. In: CVPR (2015)
49. Zhou, T., Krahenbuhl, P., Aubry, M., Huang, Q., Efros, A.A.: Learning dense correspondences via 3D-guided cycle consistency. In: CVPR (2016)

A Neural-Symbolic Architecture for Inverse Graphics Improved by Lifelong Meta-learning

Michael Kissner[(✉)] and Helmut Mayer

Institute for Applied Computer Science, Bundeswehr University Munich,
Neubiberg, Germany
{michael.kissner,helmut.mayer}@unibw.de

Abstract. We follow the idea of formulating vision as inverse graphics and propose a new type of element for this task, a neural-symbolic capsule. It is capable of de-rendering a scene into semantic information feedforward, as well as rendering it feed-backward. An initial set of capsules for graphical primitives is obtained from a generative grammar and connected into a full capsule network. Lifelong meta-learning continuously improves this network's detection capabilities by adding capsules for new and more complex objects it detects in a scene using few-shot learning. Preliminary results demonstrate the potential of our novel approach.

1 Introduction

The idea of inverting grammar parse-trees to generate neural networks is not new [24,25], but has been largely abandoned. We revisit this idea and invert a generative grammar into a network of neural-symbolic capsules. Instead of labels, this capsule network outputs an entire scene-graph of the image, which is commonplace in modern game engines like Godot [22]. Our approach is an inverse graphics pipeline for the prospective idea of an inverse game-engine [2,27].

We begin by introducing the generative grammar and how to invert symbols and rules to obtain neural-symbolic capsules (Sect. 3). They are internally different to the ones proposed by Hinton et al. [4], as they essentially act as containers for regression models. Next, we present a modified routing-by-agreement and training protocol (Sect. 4), coupled to a lifelong meta-learning pipeline (Sect. 5). Through meta-learning, the capsule network continuously grows and trains individual capsules. We finally demonstrate the potential of the approach by presenting some results based on an "Asteroids"-like environment (Sect. 6) before ending with a conclusion.

2 Related Work

Capsule Networks. In [4] Hinton et al. introduced capsules, extending the idea of classical neurons by allowing them to output vectors instead of scalars. These vectors can be interpreted as attributes of an object and aim to reduce

© Springer Nature Switzerland AG 2019
G. A. Fink et al. (Eds.): DAGM GCPR 2019, LNCS 11824, pp. 471–484, 2019.
https://doi.org/10.1007/978-3-030-33676-9_33

information-loss between layers of convolutional neural networks (CNN) [6,8]. Capsules require specialized routing protocols, such as routing-by-agreement [20], where the activation probability of a capsule is dependent on the agreement of its real inputs with their expected values. Further extensions for capsules have been proposed, such as using matrices internally [5], using 3D input [32] and improving equivariance [9].

Neural-Symbolic Methods. There has been a strong effort to make a purely neural approach to vision more interpretable [10,13,16,19,21,31]. An alternative approach to interpretability has been to deeply intertwine symbolic methods into connectionist methods. For computer vision, this is proving fruitful for de-rendering and scene decomposition [7,11,12,23,26,28,34]. Many of these approaches use shape programs, a decomposition of the scene into a set of rendering instructions. The scene-graphs we construct can be viewed as such shape programs, but in a different representation. This symbolic information is well suited for more complex tasks, such as visual question answering (VQA) [14,30] and scene manipulation [29]. We follow many of the presented ideas in our work.

3   Generative Grammar

The neural-symbolic capsules are derived from a modified [15] generative attributed context-free grammar for image generation. We require that our grammar is non-recursive and has a finite number of symbols to avoid infinite productions. The following notation is used for our grammar G:

$$G = (S, V, \Sigma, R, A, C) \tag{1}$$

S: The axiom (starting) symbol S of our grammar is some object name (e.g., $[car]$ or $[house]$) for which we want to generate further, more detailed symbols.

V: The finite set of non-terminal symbols V represents parts of the axiom symbol (e.g., $[car\ door]$) or parts of parts (e.g., $[door\ handle]$). The further down the grammar parse-tree a symbol resides, the more primitive it becomes.

Σ: The set of terminal symbols Σ consists of graphical primitives. These may include elements such as $[edge]$ or $[sphere]$. Whichever terminal symbols are chosen will determine the possible complexity that can be represented by the non-terminal symbols.

R: A production rule $r \in R$ is of the form

$$\Omega \to \lambda \quad \text{with } \Omega \in V, \lambda \in \bigcup_{i \in \mathbb{N} \setminus \{0\}} (V \cup \Sigma). \tag{2}$$

The right-hand-side (RHS) of a rule r has the form $\lambda = \lambda_1 \cdots \lambda_{|\lambda|}$, where λ_i is either terminal or non-terminal and by $|\lambda|$ we denote the total number of produced symbols. There may be multiple rules in R that have the same left-hand-side (LHS) symbol. We also introduce a special function called *draw* that applies to terminal symbols, i.e., primitives, forcing them to produce a set of pixels corresponding to their graphical representation (cf. Fig. 1)

$$draw : \lambda \to [pixel\text{-}layer] \quad \lambda \in \Sigma. \tag{3}$$

A: Every terminal and non-terminal symbol λ_j with rule r, as well as each [*pixel-layer*], is associated with an attribute vector $\boldsymbol{\alpha}_j = (\alpha_j^1, \cdots, \alpha_j^n)$.

C: For r to produce meaningful attributes, they must be constrained by a set of realistic laws that allow for a wide spectrum of results. Particularly, we introduce a set of non-linear equations which constrain the attributes. Each attribute α_j^i of a symbol λ_j produced by rule $r : \Omega \to \lambda$ is associated with a constraint g_j^i and calculated using $\alpha_j^i = g_j^i(\boldsymbol{\alpha}_\Omega)$. By $A(r)$ we denote the set of attributes $\{\boldsymbol{\alpha}_j\}$ and by $C(r)$ the set of all constraints $\{g_j^i\}$ for r. The *draw* function is also considered to be such a constraint g.

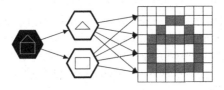

Fig. 1. Draw: a grammar producing an image from a [*house*] symbol.

The order of the symbols produced by a rule represents depth-sorting. For example, [*triangle*] [*square*] first draws the triangle, then the square. We interpret two rules with the same LHS symbol to be equivalent to either drawing different unique **viewpoints** (from the front, from the back) of the same object, drawing a primitive using different part **configurations** (chair with padding, chair without padding) or drawing it in different **styles** (sketch, photo).

4   Neural-Symbolic Capsules

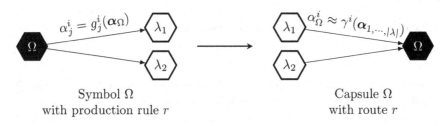

Symbol Ω Capsule Ω
with production rule r with route r

Fig. 2. Inversion of a symbol of the grammar parse-tree results in a capsule. We illustrate both the symbol and the capsule using a hexagon to avoid confusion with neurons.

In this section we introduce our neural-symbolic capsules. We "invert" a symbol of our grammar to create a capsule and connect it in reverse to the order in the parse-tree to form a capsule network. Our approach to the capsule's internals is different to [20]. The idea of routing-by-agreement and vectorized outputs remains unchanged, however, we replace the internal algorithm by a regression model and output an additional activation probability.

Terminal Symbols → Primitive Capsules. Each terminal symbol represents a renderable graphical primitive that is connected directly to a layer of pixels and we refer to its inversion as a **primitive capsule**. These capsules perform detection based on pixel inputs.

Non-Terminal Symbols → Semantic Capsules. We invert non-terminal symbols to form **semantic capsules**. By Ω we henceforth interchangeably refer to both the capsule and its corresponding symbol.

Rules → Routes. The constraints g of a rule r take the attributes α_Ω of symbol Ω and produce new attributes $\alpha_1, \cdots \alpha_{|\lambda|}$. After inversion, the capsule Ω takes those same attributes $\alpha_1, \cdots \alpha_{|\lambda|}$ as input to generate α_Ω using g^{-1}. However, g is not invertible in most cases and we instead introduce γ as our best approximation, such that

$$||g(\gamma(\boldsymbol{\alpha})) - \boldsymbol{\alpha}|| \tag{4}$$

is minimized (cf. Fig. 2). We refer to the inverted rule as a **route** and depending on context we denote by r both the rule and the route. This also holds true for primitive capsules, where detection means the inversion of its *draw* function.

4.1 Routing-By-Agreement

We use a modified routing-by-agreement protocol to find the best fitting route and attributes. Ω may appear on the RHS of multiple routes (i.e., LHS of a rule), but as only one route leads to the activation of the capsule, we introduce an activation probability p_r for each. Our goal is attribute equivariance and activation probability invariance under feature-preserving transformations. We propose the following internals of our capsule (cf. Fig. 3):

1. The output α_{Ω_r} for a route r is calculated using

$$\alpha_{\Omega_r} = \gamma_r(\boldsymbol{\alpha}_{1,\cdots,|\lambda|}). \tag{5}$$

2. For each input α_{j_r} for a route r, we estimate the expected input value $\tilde{\alpha}_{j_r}$ as if α_{j_r} were unknown, using the following equation:

$$\tilde{\alpha}_j = g_{r,j}(\alpha_{\Omega_r}). \tag{6}$$

3. The activation probability p_{Ω_r} of a route r is calculated as

$$p_{\Omega_r} = \frac{1}{|(\lambda)_r|} \sum_{(\lambda)_r} \frac{||Z(\boldsymbol{\alpha}_i, \tilde{\boldsymbol{\alpha}}_i)||_1}{|Z|} \cdot w\left(\frac{p_i}{\bar{p}_i} - 1\right), \tag{7}$$

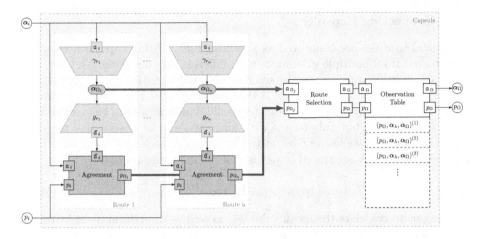

Fig. 3. The inner structure of a capsule Ω with inputs α_i, p_i and outputs α_Ω, p_Ω, representing our routing-by-agreement protocol (Eqs. 5 to 9). The outputs are stored in an observation table and individual routes are highlighted in yellow. (Color figure online)

where $(\lambda)_r$ denotes the set of all inputs that contribute to a route r, p_i the route's input capsule's probability of activation, Z an agreement-function with output vector of size $|Z|$, $\|\cdot\|_1$ the l_1-norm, w some window function with $w(0) = 1$, $\sup\{w\} = 1$ and $\bar{p}_i$ the past mean probability for that input.

4. Steps 1. - 3. are repeated for each $r \in R(\Omega)$.
5. Find the route that was most likely used

$$r_{final} = \min_r \{p_{\Omega_r}\} \tag{8}$$

and set the final output as

$$p_\Omega = p_{\Omega_{r_{final}}} \tag{9}$$

$$\alpha_\Omega = \alpha_{\Omega_{r_{final}}}. \tag{10}$$

Steps 1 and 2 correspond to an architecture equivalent to a de-rendering autoencoder, $g(\gamma(\alpha)) = \tilde{\alpha}$, but with known interpretation for the latent variables (attributes). Here, γ acts as encoder and g as decoder.

For now assume that $\bar{p}_i$ is known in step 3. The agreement-function Z measures how well the inputs of γ correspond to the outputs of g. For semantic capsules, we choose the agreement-function

$$Z(\alpha_i, \tilde{\alpha}_i) = \max\{w(\tilde{\alpha}_i - \hat{\alpha}_i) : \hat{\alpha}_i \in R_{\alpha_i}\}, \tag{11}$$

where w describes an n-dimensional window function and R_{α_i} the set of rotationally equivalent α_i. For primitive capsules finding an appropriate Z depends very much on the design and symmetries of the decoder g (*draw*-function).

4.2   Connecting Capsules

Individual capsules are connected as shown in Fig. 2. A full capsule network is constructed from multiple grammars with different axioms ([table], [chair], ...). To avoid multiple capsules for the same symbol in the network, we merge them and introduce an observation table Λ that stores all occurrences on a per-image basis (cf. Fig. 3). For instance, a [table] capsule does not need to connect to four [table-leg] capsules, but only to one with four entries in its observation table.

As these observations are reset at the beginning of each pass, we assume that all past entries in Λ are stored in permanent memory elsewhere as

$$\left((p_\lambda)^{(i)}, (\boldsymbol{\alpha}_\lambda)^{(i)}, (\boldsymbol{\alpha}_\Omega)^{(i)} \right)_r, \tag{12}$$

allowing us to calculate the mean value $\bar{p}_\lambda$, as well as to perform meta-learning.

During a forward pass the entries in all the observation tables form one or many tree structures, which we call the **observed parse-trees**. Their topmost symbol is not necessarily one of the axioms of the grammars the capsule network is based on (cf. left of Fig. 4). Each observed parse-tree, thus, induces its own **observed grammar** with the topmost symbol being its **observed axiom**.

For the multitude of observed grammars in the capsule network, we postulate that we can always define a higher-level grammar by simply taking their union and defining a new axiom with a rule that produces the previous axioms (cf. Fig. 4). For example, the grammars for [table] and [chair] allow us to define a meaningful higher-level grammar with [dining-room] as the axiom.

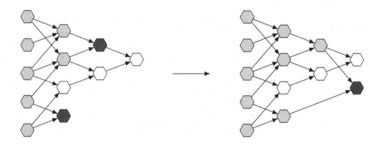

Fig. 4. A capsule network with all activated capsules in blue (left). Here, the topmost activated capsules (dark blue) do not have a common parent capsule that activated. In this case the meta-learning agent adds a common parent/axiom (right). (Color figure online)

4.3   Training Capsules

Training Primitive Capsules. We assume the decoder g (*draw*) for primitive capsules is known. Finding an analytical solution to γ is out of reach. Instead, we use a regression model for γ and synthesize training sets with g. We define the inputs to g using quantile functions $Q_j(p) = p$ for each attribute α_Ω^j, which we may refine according to our prior knowledge. Next, with $\chi_{i,j}$ some uniform random variable, $\chi_{i,j} \sim U([0,1])$ and f some function that applies random backgrounds, occlusions and special effects, we generate γ's virtually infinite training set using

$$\left((f(g(Q_j(\chi_{i,j}))))^{(i)}, (Q_j(\chi_{i,j}))^{(i)} \right). \tag{13}$$

Training Semantic Capsules. If only γ of a route is known and g unknown, we use a similar method to the case above. Ideally, we calculate α_Ω using γ and train g using the training sets

$$((\gamma(\alpha_\lambda))^{(i)}, (\alpha_\lambda)^{(i)}). \tag{14}$$

We must, however, first find a suitable γ. The initial output attributes of our semantic capsules consist of the distinct set of all input attributes $\bigcup_i A(r_i)$. We are free in our choice for γ, which is non-injective in most cases. It is expected that there will be collisions, i.e., different sets of inputs leading to the same output. These collisions are the main focus of our meta-learning pipeline. To minimize these collisions, we choose a γ that calculates the mean of inputs of the same type, weighted by their size (width, height, depth). This weighting by size is to ensure that, for example, a wooden chair with many metallic screws is still considered wooden instead of metallic. For a general kth attribute we have:

$$\alpha_\Omega^k = \gamma^k(\alpha_\lambda) = \frac{1}{\sum_\lambda \|\alpha_\lambda^{size}\|} \sum_\lambda \alpha_\lambda^k \cdot \|\alpha_\lambda^{size}\|. \tag{15}$$

However, we use special functions for size and position

$$\alpha_\Omega^{size} = \gamma^{size}(\alpha_\lambda) = \max_{\lambda,i} \left(R_\Omega^{-1} \cdot (\alpha_\lambda^{pos} + R_\lambda \cdot B_{\lambda,i}) \right) \\ - \min_{\lambda,i} \left(R_\Omega^{-1} \cdot (\alpha_\lambda^{pos} + R_\lambda \cdot B_{\lambda,i}) \right) \tag{16}$$

$$\alpha_\Omega^{pos} = \gamma^{pos}(\alpha_\lambda) = R_\Omega \cdot \frac{1}{2} \left[\max_{\lambda,i} \left(R_\Omega^{-1} \cdot (\alpha_\lambda^{pos} + R_\lambda \cdot B_{\lambda,i}) \right) \\ + \min_{\lambda,i} \left(R_\Omega^{-1} \cdot (\alpha_\lambda^{pos} + R_\lambda \cdot B_{\lambda,i}) \right) \right], \tag{17}$$

to ensure that they are in the correct reference frame. Here, $\alpha^{rot}, \alpha^{size}, \alpha^{pos}$ are the vectorized subsets of the attribute vector α for rotation, size and position, R_λ and R_Ω indicate the Euler rotation matrix calculated from the rotation attributes α_λ^{rot} and α_Ω^{rot} and $B_{\lambda,i}$ the ith corner position vector of the bounding box of λ (i.e., pairwise permutations of $\alpha_\lambda^{size}/2$ and $-\alpha_\lambda^{size}/2$).

We can't create arbitrary inputs for training. Instead we use observations from memory (cf. Eq. 12) for augmentation. Detection needs to be invariant under changes of the outputs α_Ω^{pos}, α_Ω^{rot} and $\alpha_\Omega^{size} > 0$ and we let $T_i(\cdot)$ denote transformation functions that rotate (acting on α_λ^{pos}, α_λ^{rot}), translate (acting on α_λ^{pos}) and scale (acting on α_λ^{pos}, α_λ^{size}) all parts, while leaving the relative rotation, position and size to each other unchanged.

For the other attributes α_λ^k we have little knowledge on how to perform feature-preserving transformations. However, if our original training set (cf. Eq. 14) contains an output attribute α_Ω^k for which all entries are smaller than some ϵ, we can safely assume that we have never encountered an object with this attribute and are free to "invent" possible values for this attribute type by simply setting all input α_λ^k uniformly to some constant. For example, if our training set is filled with real apples, for which the stem is brown and the body red or green, we can invent a metallic apple by simply assuming that both the stem and body are metallic, as we have no idea what it really would look like. By $U_i(\cdot)$ we denote a linear "style" transformation that sets a constant value in the range $[0, 1]$ to all unused attributes of the same type and either activates or deactivates it. We finally have our fully augmented set for training g:

$$((\gamma(T_i(U_i(\alpha_\lambda))))^{(i)}, (T_i(U_i(\alpha_\lambda)))^{(i)}). \tag{18}$$

A single example is sufficient for the above training regime to begin augmentation by translating, rotating and resizing the object (T_i), as well as trying out different styles (U_i).

New Attributes and Re-training. For semantic capsules, the set of attributes is not static and can grow. We differentiate between adding attributes due to inheritance and due to a trigger from the meta-learning agent.

Inheritance occurs automatically when one of the input capsules is extended by an attribute that is unknown to the current capsule. We simply expand the capsule's internals by said attribute and retrain it. This inheritance propagates down the network, forcing subsequent capsules to inherit them as well.

The more interesting case arises when the capsule is triggered by meta-learning to expand its attributes by adding α_Ω^{new}. First, we expand every attribute vector in memory for this capsule by the new attribute, but set to $\alpha_\Omega^{new} = 0$. Next, the internal attribute vector of the capsule and its γ and g functions are extended. We begin by replacing g with a new regression model of increased input width. The problem here is that we require γ to train it, which at this point has not been extended yet. Instead we split α and γ into two parts, one containing the newly added attribute $\alpha_\Omega^{new} = \gamma^{new}(\alpha_\lambda)$ as an output and one with the previous attributes as output $\alpha_\Omega^{old} = \gamma^{old}(\alpha_\lambda)$:

$$\gamma(\alpha_\lambda) = \left(\gamma^{old}(\alpha_\lambda) \oplus \gamma^{new}(\alpha_\lambda)\right), \tag{19}$$

where by $a \oplus b$ we mean the concatenation of two vectors. At this point γ^{old}, α_Ω^{new} and α_λ are known and this suffices to start training g using

$$\left((\gamma^{old}(T_i(U_i(\alpha_\lambda))) \oplus \alpha_\Omega^{new})^{(i)}, (T_i(U_i(\alpha_\lambda)))^{(i)}\right). \tag{20}$$

Finally we need to determine γ^{new}. We add a regression model with one output that runs in parallel to γ^{old} and train it using the new decoder g:

$$\left((g(\alpha_\Omega^{old} \oplus \alpha_\Omega^{new}))^{(i)}, (\alpha_\Omega^{new})^{(i)}\right). \tag{21}$$

5   Meta-learning

It is far too difficult to define the entire grammar with all rules and constraints from scratch to generate a complete capsule network. Instead, our approach works bottom-up and we only define the terminal symbols (primitive capsules), letting the meta-learning agent learn all semantic capsules and routes. This means that our initial set of primitive capsules limits what the network can eventually analyze and learn. Ideally, we would define primitive capsules for the most basic set of primitives from which we are able to construct every kind of object. We can, however, refine this set later on. A grammar with [square] as terminal symbol produces the same results, even if it is refined by [edge] terminal symbols with the rule [square] → [edge] [edge] [edge] [edge]. For the *draw* functions, we rely on the current state of computer graphics. Here we have access to a near endless supply of parameterizable primitives [18,33] and graphics pipelines capable of physically-based rendering [17]. By Eq. 4, if we can render, we can de-render it to some set of valid attributes.

We postulated above that there always exists a higher-level grammar with an axiom that includes all the symbols of the observed grammars. We go a step further and view the capsule network as incomplete if there is more than one observed axiom (cf. Fig. 4). There are four possible causes for this:

A.1 A non-activated parent capsule is lacking a route.
"What existing symbol best describes these parts?"
A.2 A parent capsule is missing.
"What new symbol best describes these parts?"
B.1 An attribute is lacking training data.
"What existing attribute best describes this style or pose?"
B.2 An attribute is missing.
"What new attribute best describes this style or pose?"

We may remedy these causes using one of two methods, either triggering the creation of a new route in an existing or new capsule ((**A.1**), (**A.2**)) or triggering the training of an existing or new attribute ((**B.1**), (**B.2**)).

However, deciding which of the four causes is responsible for the multiple observed axioms in the current forward pass is subjective even for humans. For example, consider a capsule network that has [leg], [panel] and [chair] capsules. It encounters a new scene and the observed parse-tree contains four [leg] activations and one [panel] activation. [chair], however, did not activate, triggering the meta-learning pipeline, due to multiple observed axioms. Is this just a [chair] with a previously unknown style (**B.2**)? Or is this a completely new capsule such as [stool] (**A.2**)?

We, thus, introduce a decision matrix (cf. Table 1). Akin to child development, we train this matrix by querying an oracle in the early stages of the capsule network's training process and update the entries. Decisions are made by summing up all rows of features that evaluate to true and finding the column with maximum value. We may remove the oracle at any point in time, as it does not

Table 1. Example of a trained decision matrix with an excerpt of features derived from the observed parse-trees and what cause they indicate (number of past oracle decisions). Here Ω is the capsule with the highest p_Ω that did not activate.

Feature	A.1	A.2	B.1	B.2
Observed Axioms have same Ω as parent	4	3	14	12
Observed Axioms don't have same Ω as parent	5	19	1	0
Parts tracked from previous scenes	14	1	17	12
$\Omega : Z(\alpha, \tilde{\alpha})$ indicates one attribute mismatch with no entry in memory $\alpha^i > \epsilon$	1	0	12	2
$\Omega : Z(\alpha, \tilde{\alpha})$ indicates attribute mismatch for (position, rotation, size) only	4	3	13	10
$\Omega : Z(\alpha, \tilde{\alpha})$ indicates attribute mismatch for more than half of all attributes	12	14	4	4
$\cdots$				

impair the learning capability of the network itself, only the ability of the agent to make human-like decisions and learn the correct names.

Lexical Interpretation. We interpret our grammar lexically. It is easy to see that each symbol represents a compound noun ($[chair]$ or $[dining\text{-}room]$). For attributes, this analysis is more involved. Note that we have three attributes which we treated differently in Eqs. 15–17: $\alpha^{rot}, \alpha^{size}$ and α^{pos}. We interpret these as prepositions. This becomes obvious, once we have multiple objects in a scene and are able to refer to their spatial relationship using words such as "on" or "near", based purely on these attributes.

For static scenes, we interpret all remaining attributes as adjectives, such as "wooden" or "red". Their magnitude is then related to adverbs, such as "very". However, in dynamic scenes, some attributes of an object change over time and describe new poses for the parts. Thus, we interpret these time-dependent attributes as verbs, such as "walk". Their value is equivalent to the normalized time evolution of an animation.

These interpretations are both interesting semantically, as well as for querying the oracle. Instead of presenting a choice between **(A.1)**–**(B.2)** and some values, an actual question can be formed from the activated features (cf. Table 1). Consider a capsule network that has thus far only seen a modern $[chair]$, made out of a blend of metal and wood. We now show it a chair made of the same parts, but with less metal and in a classical design. Even though the capsule was trained with basic style transformations U, the design is still too complex to grasp. Instead, meta-learning is triggered by cause **(B.2)**, because of a mismatch of attributes "metallic", "wooden" and "modern" in $Z(\alpha, \tilde{\alpha})$. As we have access to a lexical interpretation, we can make these abstract pieces of information easier to understand for a human oracle, by letting the meta-learning agent pose an actual question: "This object looks similar to a modern chair, but is very wooden instead. What adjective best describes this style?". The answer "classical" then adds a new attribute to the capsule.

6   Implementation, Results and Comparison

Implementation. We implement the renderer g of primitive capsules using signed distance fields [18] and their encoder γ using an AlexNet-like convolutional neural network [6] for regression. For semantic capsules we use Eqs. 15–17 for γ and a 4-layer deep dense regression neural network with tanh activation functions for g. The training data is generated synthetically using the process described in this paper and all hyperparameters, such as learning rate, are fine-tuned by hand. Our implementation called VividNet is found on Github at https://github.com/Kayzaks/VividNet.

Results. In the initial phase, our capsule network has three primitive capsules: $[square]$, $[triangle]$ and $[circle]$. We begin by showing it an image of a spaceship (LHS of Fig. 5), upon which it detects all the relevant graphical primitives, such as three triangles, one circle and one square, but has no semantic understanding of their relation. As this constellation leads to five activated capsules with no common parent, the meta-learning agent is called into action. In this case, it is obvious that (**A.2**) is triggered, as there are no semantic capsules yet. The exact split, however, is subjective and up to the oracle. We may treat these primitives as one space-ship (top row of Fig. 5) or group them into two independent parts, booster and shuttle, which make up the space-ship (bottom row of Fig. 5). In either case, the capsule network is extended by new capsules and trained using only this one example.

Now, the capsule network is shown a new scene, which includes an asteroid made up of three circles. The routes of the $[ship]$, $[booster]$ and $[shuttle]$ capsules find no agreement, as none of them have three circles as their parts. Again, the meta-learning agent queries the oracle, which concludes that a new $[asteroid]$ capsule is required (**A.2**). The asteroids, however, vary quite a bit. In a new scene with a different asteroid, three circles are detected. This time however, a parent capsule ($[asteroid]$) does exist, that admits all three circles as its parts, but due to the different configuration did not activate. This leads to a different set of activated features in our decision matrix and we find, after querying the oracle, that the $[asteroid]$ is merely missing a route (**A.1**). Alternatively, the agent could have concluded that the capsule is missing a style attribute (**B.2**).

In Fig. 5 we show two of the many possible timelines the training process could have taken, depending on the choice of features in the decision matrix, as well as the response by the oracle during the meta-learning process. It was sufficient to show the capsule network one spaceship (or its parts) and a few asteroids to construct the entire network and correctly identify these objects and all their attributes in a new scene.

Comparison. Our approach differs too much from current classification methods in order to make a direct numeric comparison. The neural symbolic capsule

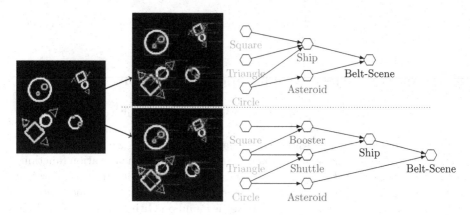

Fig. 5. Two of many possible capsule network configurations the meta-learning agent might end up with, depending on the oracle and decision matrix.

network can only express confidence, but has no notion of accuracy, as any inaccuracy is remedied by the meta-learning pipeline and its oracle. This does not mean it has perfect accuracy, but rather that it continues to learn forever. Further, the initial choice of primitive capsules is very important in the overall performance of the network. Any comparison would, thus, need to fixate the capsule network in a subjective configuration, eliminating the benefit of lifelong meta-learning.

7   Conclusion and Outlook

In this work we showed the internal workings of our neural-symbolic capsule network and how it extends itself through lifelong meta-learning. The proposed network is bi-directional: Feed-forward (i.e., the capsule network) it is a pattern recognition algorithm and feed-backward (i.e., the generative grammar) it is a procedural graphics engine. The ability to render allows us to generate a segmentation mask for all detected objects and their components. However, our reliance on rendering for primitive capsules as the underlying mechanism for inverse graphics also comes with the downside that we are limited by the current state of computer graphics for detection.

We also showed how the network is capable of learning to detect new objects using a few-shot approach and that the training process is very human-like. This allows it to grow indefinitely with less training data, but requires the presence of an oracle to provide nouns, adjectives or verbs for new discoveries, replacing the large amounts of hand labeled data found in the classical approach.

We believe that by next focusing on video data as input and coupling the system with intuitive physics [1,3], we may extend the inverse-graphics capabilities to inverse-simulation.

References

1. Battaglia, P., Pascanu, R., Lai, M., Rezende, D.J., Kavukcuoglu, K.: Interaction networks for learning about objects, relations and physics. In: NIPS (2016)
2. Battaglia, P.W., Hamrick, J.B., Tenenbaum, J.B.: Simulation as an engine of physical scene understanding. Proc. Nat. Acad. Sci. **110**(45), 18327–18332 (2013)
3. Hamrick, J.B., Ballard, A.J., Pascanu, R., Vinyals, O., Heess, N., Battaglia, P.W.: Metacontrol for adaptive imagination-based optimization. In: ICLR (2017)
4. Hinton, G.E., Krizhevsky, A., Wang, S.D.: Transforming auto-encoders. In: Honkela, T., Duch, W., Girolami, M., Kaski, S. (eds.) ICANN 2011. LNCS, vol. 6791, pp. 44–51. Springer, Heidelberg (2011). https://doi.org/10.1007/978-3-642-21735-7_6
5. Hinton, G.E., Sabour, S., Frosst, N.: Matrix capsules with EM routing. In: ICLR (2018)
6. Krizhevsky, A., Sutskever, I., Hinton, G.E.: ImageNet classification with deep convolutional neural networks. In: NIPS, pp. 1097–1105 (2012)
7. Kulkarni, T.D., Whitney, W.F., Kohli, P., Tenenbaum, J.B.: Deep convolutional inverse graphics network. In: NIPS (2015)
8. LeCun, Y., Bottou, L., Bengio, Y., Haffner, P.: Gradient-based learning applied to document recognition. Proc. IEEE **86**(11), 2278–2324 (1998)
9. Lenssen, J.E., Fey, M., Libuschewski, P.: Group equivariant capsule networks. In: NIPS (2018)
10. Lipton, Z.C.: The mythos of model interpretability. CoRR abs/1606.03490 (2017)
11. Liu, Y., Wu, Z., Ritchie, D., Freeman, W.T., Tenenbaum, J.B., Wu, J.: Learning to describe scenes with programs. In: ICLR (2019)
12. Liu, Z., Freeman, W.T., Tenenbaum, J.B., Wu, J.: Physical primitive decomposition. In: ECCV (2018)
13. Mahendran, A., Vedaldi, A.: Understanding deep image representations by inverting them. In: CVPR, pp. 5188–5196 (2015)
14. Mao, J., Gan, C., Kohli, P., Tenenbaum, J.B., Wu, J.: The neuro-symbolic concept learner: interpreting scenes, words, and sentences from natural supervision. In: ICLR (2019)
15. Martinovic, A., Gool, L.V.: Bayesian grammar learning for inverse procedural modeling. In: CVPR (2013)
16. Montavon, G., Samek, W., Müller, K.R.: Methods for interpreting and understanding deep neural networks. Digit. Signal Process. **73**, 1–15 (2018)
17. Pharr, M., Humphreys, G., Jakob, W.: Physically Based Rendering, 3rd edn. Morgan Kaufmann, Burlington (2016)
18. Quílez, I.: Rendering signed distance fields (2017). http://www.iquilezles.org
19. Ribeiro, M.T., Singh, S., Guestrin, C.: "Why should I trust you?" explaining the predictions of any classifier. In: Knowledge Discovery and Data Mining, pp. 1135–1144 (2016)
20. Sabour, S., Frosst, N., Hinton, G.E.: Dynamic routing between capsules. In: NIPS (2017)
21. Simonyan, K., Vedaldi, A., Zisserman, A.: Deep inside convolutional networks: visualising image classification models and saliency maps. arXiv:1312.6034 (2014)
22. Godot Engine Team: Godot engine (2019). https://godotengine.org
23. Tian, Y., et al.: Learning to infer and execute 3D shape programs. In: ICLR (2019)
24. Towell, G.G., Shavlik, J.W.: Extracting refined rules from knowledge-based neural networks. Mach. Learn. **13**(1), 71–101 (1993)

25. Towell, G.G., Shavlik, J.W.: Knowledge-based artificial neural networks. Artif. Intell. **70**(1), 119–165 (1994)
26. Tulsiani, S., Su, H., Guibas, L.J., Efros, A.A., Malik, J.: Learning shape abstractions by assembling volumetric primitives. In: CVPR (2017)
27. Ullman, T.D., Spelke, E., Battaglia, P., Tenenbaum, J.B.: Mind games: game engines as an architecture for intuitive physics. Trends Cogn. Sci. **21**(9), 649–665 (2017)
28. Wu, J., Tenenbaum, J.B., Kohli, P.: Neural scene de-rendering. In: CVPR (2017)
29. Yao, S., et al.: 3D-aware scene manipulation via inverse graphics. In: NIPS (2018)
30. Yi, K., Wu, J., Gan, C., Torralba, A., Kohli, P., Tenenbaum, J.B.: Neural-symbolic VQA: disentangling reasoning from vision and language understanding. In: NIPS (2018)
31. Zhang, Q., Wu, Y.N., Zhu, S.C.: Interpretable convolutional neural networks. In: CVPR, pp. 8827–8836 (2018)
32. Zhao, Y., Birdal, T., Deng, H., Tombari, F.: 3D point-capsule networks. arXiv:1812.10775 (2018)
33. Zhou, Y., Zhu, Z., Bai, X., Lischinski, D., Cohen-Or, D., Huang, H.: Non-stationary texture synthesis by adversarial expansion. In: SIGGRAPH (2018)
34. Zou, C., Yumer, E., Yang, J., Ceylan, D., Hoiem, D.: 3D-PRNN: generating shape primitives with recurrent neural networks. In: ICCV (2017)

Unsupervised Multi-source Domain Adaptation Driven by Deep Adversarial Ensemble Learning

Sayan Rakshit[1], Biplab Banerjee[1(✉)], Gemma Roig[2], and Subhasis Chaudhuri[1]

[1] Indian Institute of Technology Bombay, Mumbai, India
getbiplab@gmail.com
[2] Singapore University of Technology and Design, Singapore, Singapore

Abstract. We address the problem of multi-source unsupervised domain adaptation (MS-UDA) for the purpose of visual recognition. As opposed to single source UDA, MS-UDA deals with multiple labeled source domains and a single unlabeled target domain. Notice that the conventional MS-UDA training is based on formalizing independent mappings between the target and the individual source domains without explicitly assessing the need for aligning the source domains among themselves. We argue that such a paradigm invariably overlooks the inherent category-level correlation among the source domains which, on the contrary, is deemed to bring meaningful complementarity in the learned shared feature space. In this regard, we propose a novel approach which simultaneously (i) aligns the source domains at the class-level in a shared feature space, and (ii) maps the target domain data in the same space through an adversarially trained ensemble of source domain classifiers. Experimental results obtained on the Office-31, ImageCLEF-DA, and Office-CalTech dataset validate that our approach achieves a superior accuracy compared to state-of-the-art methods.

Keywords: Multi-source domain adaptation · Adversarial training · Object classification

1 Introduction

In statistical learning theory, it is commonly assumed that the training and test data distributions are constrained to be similar within a supervised learning framework. In practice, such a hard constraint is frequently violated considering the implicit differences in the data generating processes of different sources. In this scenario, it is found that a learning model trained on the samples of a given source hardly performs satisfactorily on the data obtained from a different source. This is primarily due to the inherent *domain-shift* between different data sources [2] that the learning module fails to adequately capture. Although this problem is prevalent in different application areas, we focus on the problem of cross-domain visual object classification.

© Springer Nature Switzerland AG 2019
G. A. Fink et al. (Eds.): DAGM GCPR 2019, LNCS 11824, pp. 485–498, 2019.
https://doi.org/10.1007/978-3-030-33676-9_34

Amongst different approaches to solving the supervised classification problem under domain-shift, the paradigm of domain adaptation (DA) [16] is highly popular. Nonetheless, note that the majority of the DA techniques reported in the literature tackle the problem of single-source DA within an unsupervised setting (UDA). By definition, UDA methods consider the presence of two related yet different data domains: a source domain $\mathcal{S}$ equipped with ample amount of labeled training samples, and a target domain $\mathcal{T}$, where the unlabeled test samples are present. It is assumed that the domain distributions are different, $P(\mathcal{S}) \neq P(\mathcal{T})$. In many cases, the class-conditional probabilities also differ between $\mathcal{S}$ and $\mathcal{T}$, thus complicating the problem drastically. The standard UDA approaches do not consider *category-shift*, meaning that both $\mathcal{S}$ and $\mathcal{T}$ share the same set of semantic categories.

In real-life applications, the training samples can also be obtained from several source domains, as opposed to the traditional single-source based UDA setup. Under this multi-source UDA (MS-UDA) framework, the goal is to incorporate the multi-domain training scenario, where multiple source domains ($\mathcal{S}_1$, $\mathcal{S}_2$, ...) with labeled training samples are available, and the task is to classify the samples of an unlabeled target domain ($\mathcal{T}$). Note that this is a more challenging setup as compared to traditional UDA concerning the fact that: $P(\mathcal{S}_k) \neq P(\mathcal{S}_l)$ for the given k^{th} and l^{th} source domains, respectively.

To develop the MS-UDA paradigm, an extension of the $\mathcal{H}\Delta\mathcal{H}$ distance [2], which was originally introduced to theoretically upper-bound the true risk on $\mathcal{T}$ in case of single-domain DA has been proposed [14]. This accounts for the consideration of a measure of divergence between a weighted combination of the source domains and the target domain, respectively. Yet, there are only a few MS-UDA endeavors which have been introduced within a deep learning framework [18,23] considering the inherent difficulties in practically implementing the MS-UDA algorithms. This is mainly because: (i) owing to the inherent distributions mismatch among the source domains, considering all of them as constituting a single source and subsequently applying any standard end-to-end single-source UDA approach may lead to sub-optimal model training, and (ii) since such approaches are constrained to learn separate mapping functions for each of the source domains and the target domain, they are not highly scalable in general.

We propose a novel neural network based MS-UDA framework to alleviate the aforementioned issues following two intuitive paradigms: (i) class-wise reconstruction based alignment of the source domains in a learned latent feature space. In the learned space, all the samples belonging to different source domains but sharing a common class label are coerced to be closely placed. Modeling such a domain invariant space for all the source domains in this way is rather intuitive than simply combining all the domains in the original feature space overlooking their differences. Furthermore, this alleviates the need for learning separate mappings for each of the source-target pairs. And (ii) a classifiers ensemble (of the source domains) driven adversarial training to project the target domain samples in the same latent space, thus mitigating the domain difference globally. In particular, while the source classifiers aim at maximizing their disagreement on the outcomes of the target samples, the feature extraction module, on the other hand, focuses on minimizing this discrepancy. Clearly, this approach allows fine-grained alignment of the target domain samples with the source domains in the latent space by leveraging the class information instead of asserting to a global distributions matching framework. Both the reconstruction based alignment loss for the source domains and the adversarial loss for sources-target alignment are simultaneously optimized. Once the model is trained, given that the source-specific classifiers ideally focus on non-overlapping regions within the support of each category in the shared feature space, the proposed classification framework resembles the paradigm of bagging based ensemble learning. Likewise, the classification of the target samples are based on the principle of decision fusion of the source-centric classifiers. Note that as opposed to the other adversarial approaches [17,23], we bypass the need of similarity weight learning for the source domains given the target domain data, thanks to our source domains alignment module. In short, we highlight our novel contributions as:

- We assess the advantages of explicitly aligning the source domains in a MS-UDA setup through a simple reconstruction based loss function.
- We follow an intuitive classifiers ensemble driven adversarial training strategy for aligning the target domain samples with the source domains in the shared feature space.
- We perform extensive experiments on the challenging Office-31, ImageCLEF-DA and Office-CalTech dataset for demonstrating the efficacy of our approach.

2   Related Works

Single-source UDA: The single-source UDA approaches are broadly feature transformation or classifier adaptation based. The feature transformation based techniques primarily learn a transformation matrix which either (i) projects the (source)target domain samples onto the distributions of other domain or model a shared latent space where samples from both the domains can simultaneously be projected. In this regard, techniques including transfer component analysis (TCA) [15], subspace alignment (SA) [5], domain matching in the manifold (geodesic flow kernel (GFK) [8], MEDA [22]) have been used extensively along with visual data. Similarly, the maximum mean discrepancy (MMD) [1] learns the shared space in the kernel induced Hilbert space. On a different note, CORAL [20] minimizes the domain-shift in terms of the Euclidean distance between the second-order statistics governing $\mathcal{S}$ and $\mathcal{T}$.

The deep neural network based approaches, on the other hand, learn domain invariant features by leveraging the data-driven representation learning techniques: supervised [19], self-supervised (encoder-decoder based) [3], unsupervised [25], to name a few. Majority of the recent techniques in this regard are in favor of adversarial loss functions to reduce the domain difference: learning a representation space that is simultaneously discriminative for source domain while being insensitive to individual domain properties [7,13]. Amongst the different adversarial training based UDA methods, cycle-GAN [27] endorses a cycle consistency loss to model the mapping $\mathcal{S} \rightarrow \mathcal{T} \rightarrow \mathcal{S}$ using identical functions, thus being robust to minute domain perturbations.

Multi-source UDA: Historically, the research on MS-UDA originated in [24] (A-SVM) which distills the advantages of source domain classifiers ensemble to tune the target domain classification module. Subsequently, there have been several ad-hoc approaches towards MS-UDA for visual and textual data [10]. From the perspective of deep learning or adversaial training, [17] proposes a moment-matching network for MS-UDA which is based on aligning higher-order moments between the domain specific features. On the other hand, [23] proposes deep cocktail network which considers that the target distribution can be described in terms of a weighted combination of the source domain distributions. In the same line, [9] introduces the idea of deploying a mixture of source experts for MS-UDA for the purpose of cross-domain sentiment analysis.

Additionally, there have been several theoretical advancements towards the development of tighter generalization bounds for MS-UDA. Apart from the multi-source extension of the $\mathcal{H}\Delta\mathcal{H}$ distance [14], [4] proposes to represent the true classification bound of $\mathcal{T}$ in terms of the nearest k source domains. As it is evident, the success of the MS-UDA strongly depends upon the proper exploration of the source domains.

How Are We Different?: We are different from the related literature in the sense that, (i) we do not learn separate mappings for each source and the target domains. While [23] performs the same in terms of the individual adversarial domain classifier training for each of the source-target pairs, (ii) [17] considers a pair of classifiers per source domain and minimizes their disagreement on the target samples for aligning the target to that particular source domain. (iii) [26] proposes an adversarial training with multiple domain shifts are available and one unlabeled target domain for average case generalization bound for both classification and regression, while we train our model adversarially with combining multiple source domain classifier. In contrast, we seek to align the source domains class-wise in a common latent space. In addition, we project the target samples in the same space through an adversarial classifiers ensemble based training strategy. As a whole, we sensibly tackle the MS-UDA problem as the standard bagging based classifiers ensemble problem in the shared feature space.

3   Proposed Method

We detail the proposed framework in the following. We deal with the model training first followed by the inference stage. A block diagram of our model can be found in Fig. 1.

3.1   Preliminaries

Let us consider $\mathcal{K}$ source domains $\{\mathcal{S}_k\}_{k=1}^{\mathcal{K}}$ each consisting of the domain specific training samples $\{\mathbf{x}_i^k, y_i^k\}_{i=1}^{|\mathcal{S}_k^{tr}|}$ where $\mathbf{x}_i^k \in \mathbb{R}^d$ and $y_i^k \in \{1, 2, \ldots, C\}$, respectively. Notice that $|\mathcal{S}_k^{tr}|$ denotes the size of the kth source domain training set. On the other hand, $\mathcal{T}$ indicates the sole unlabeled target domain with samples $\{\mathbf{x}_j^t\}_{j=1}^{|\mathcal{T}|}$.

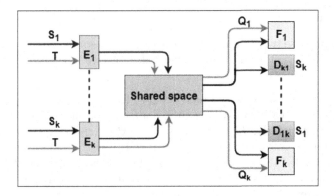

Fig. 1. A block diagram of the proposed model. The lines showcase the forward propagation of the samples. $\mathcal{S}$ and $\mathcal{T}$ denote the source and the target domains, respectively. E, D, and F denote the encoder, decoder, and the classifier modules. $\mathbf{Q}$ defines the logits for the target samples. The loss functions are detailed in Sect. 3.2.

Following the assumptions of MS-UDA, $P(\mathcal{S}_k) \neq P(\mathcal{S}_l)$ for $k, l \in \{1, 2, \ldots, \mathcal{K}\}$, $k \neq l$ and $P(\mathcal{S}_k) \neq P(\mathcal{T})$.

We propose an encoder-decoder based neural network model to carry out the MS-UDA task. Broadly, the proposed framework consists of three sub-modules: (i) the $\mathcal{K}$ feature extractors $\{E^k\}_{k=1}^{\mathcal{K}}$ where a given E^k is shared by the kth source domain and the target domain, respectively, (ii) $\{F^k\}_{k=1}^{\mathcal{K}}$ be the $\mathcal{K}$ source domain multi-class classifiers (on the learned feature representations) with each one producing a C-dimensional vector of class softmax probability scores, and (iii) the $\mathcal{K}(\mathcal{K}-1)$ decoders $\{D^{kl}\}$ where a given D^{kl} reconstructs the samples of $\mathcal{S}_l$ from the latent representations of the samples from $\mathcal{S}_k$ at the category level. All the modules are equipped with separate learnable set of parameters. Given that, we wish to model a common latent feature space where (i) the feature encodings for the source domains specific samples largely coincide at the class-level given the trained E^ks and (ii) the target domain data become indistinguishable from the source domains.

Precisely, our source domains alignment is majorly governed by a latent loss and a decoder loss. While the latent loss tries to make the class-level feature embeddings similar for the different source domains, the decoder loss performs cross domain sample reconstruction at the class level. As a result, the latent space is able to learn the shared feature representations at the class-scale while simultaneously ensuring class-wise compactness. Additionally, the source domains specific classifiers make the latent space more discriminative in nature. On the other hand, we judiciously utilize the disagreement among these classifiers while predicting the labels for the target domain data under an adversarial training strategy for sources-target alignment.

3.2   Training

Broadly, we propose two different loss measures for (i) source domains alignment, and (ii) sources-target alignment. In the following, we discuss each of the loss functions in detail.

Source Domains Alignment Loss: Let $\xi_i = \{\mathbf{x}_i^1, \mathbf{x}_i^2, \ldots, \mathbf{x}_i^{\mathcal{K}}\}$ denote the samples obtained from each of the $\mathcal{K}$ source domains but sharing a common class label $(y_i^k = c)$. Similarly, $E^k(\mathbf{x}_i^k)$ and $D^{kl}(E^k(\mathbf{x}_i^k))$ represent the encoded and l^{th} decoded representations of $\mathbf{x}_i^k$, respectively. Under this setup, we aim for: (i) making the encoded feature representations for all the samples in ξ_i consistent by minimizing a latent loss $(\mathcal{L}_1)$, (ii) ensuring that the latent representations can effectively capture the class-level shared features by encouraging cross-domain reconstruction at the decoder end $(\mathcal{L}_2)$, and (iii) learning separate classifiers for the source domain specific data given their encoded representations $(\mathcal{L}_3)$. They are elaborated below.

– **Latent loss**: First, we demand the encoded feature representations of the different source domain samples in ξ_i to be largely identical by minimizing the following loss measure:

$$\mathcal{L}_1 = \mathbb{E}[\frac{1}{\mathcal{K}(\mathcal{K}-1)}\sum_k \sum_{l, l \neq k} ||E^k(\mathbf{x}_i^k) - E^l(\mathbf{x}_i^l)||_2^2] \tag{1}$$

Notice that we obtain many ξ_is from $\{\mathcal{S}_k\}_{k=1}^{\mathcal{K}}$ following random sampling in this regard.

– **Decoder loss**: For a given $E^k(\mathbf{x}_i^k)$, each of the D^{kl}s is constrained to reconstruct $\mathbf{x}_i^l$ in the kl^{th} decoder output. This cross-domain class-specific sample reconstruction, in turn, directs the E^k to capture the shared features between the kth and l^{th} domains at the class-level. In this way, we consider to minimize all possible pairwise reconstruction loss measures simultaneously, thus making the encoded representations of all the source domains to be highly domain invariant. In particular, the respective loss measure can be formulated as:

$$\mathcal{L}_2 = \mathbb{E}[\frac{1}{\mathcal{K}(\mathcal{K}-1)}\sum_k \sum_{l, l \neq k} ||D^{kl}(E^k(\mathbf{x}_i^k)) - \mathbf{x}_i^l||_2^2] \tag{2}$$

– **Classification loss**: Finally, separate softmax classifiers are modeled based on the encoded feature representations given by the $E^k(\mathbf{x}_i^k)$s and the respective cross-entropy loss measure is minimized. Note that we have $\mathcal{K}$ different classifiers in this way. The average cross-entropy loss over all the classifiers is subsequently put as:

$$\mathcal{L}_3 = \frac{1}{\mathcal{K}}\mathbb{E}[\sum_c - y_i^{kc} \log F^{kc}(E^k(\mathbf{x}_i^k))], c \in [1, C] \tag{3}$$

where y_i^{kc} and F^{kc} denote the cth class ground-truth score (in binary) and the output of F^k for a given $\mathbf{x}_i^k$, respectively.

Minimization of Eqs. (1–3) jointly ensures feature independence among the source domains in the learned feature space. Next, we are interested into projecting samples from $\mathcal{T}$ in the same space in such a way that the target samples largely overlap with the source features.

Sources-Target Alignment Module: Ideally, we obtain $\mathcal{K}$ encoded representations of the target domain samples given the $\mathcal{K}$ E^ks. For a given $\mathbf{x}_j^t$ and its representation $E^k(\mathbf{x}_j^t)$ according to the kth source domain feature extractor, we propagate the sample further through F^k and consider the respective C-dimensional unnormalized logit scores. We subsequently aim for a consistency among these logit scores given the $\mathcal{K}$ classifiers. This will simultaneously serve two purposes: (i) since each feature extractor is shared between the respective source domain and the target domain together, the correlation between both the domains are better captured by the feature extractor implicitly, and (ii) the classifier's consistency constraint is expected to bring the target domain samples towards the generic source domains distributions in the latent feature space. Precisely, if $\mathbf{Q}_j^k$ defines the C-dimensional logit vector for $E^k(\mathbf{x}_j^t)$ corresponding to the kth source domain classifier where $k \in [1, \ldots, \mathcal{K}]$, we mention the logit consistency loss for the sources-target alignment as:

$$\mathcal{L}_4 = \mathbb{E}[\frac{1}{\mathcal{K}^2} \sum_k \sum_{l,l \neq k} ||\mathbf{Q}_j^k - \mathbf{Q}_j^l||_2^2] \tag{4}$$

We follow an adversarial training strategy for projecting $\mathcal{T}$ onto the shared feature space. While the classifiers (F^ks) try to maximize the logit consistency loss $\mathcal{L}_4$ on the target domain samples, the feature encoders (E^ks), on the other hand, focus on minimizing the same. Ideally, for the target domain samples which are closer to the support of the source domains in the latent space, $\mathcal{L}_4$ is already substantially small, whereas it is large for samples lying outside the support of the $\mathcal{S}_k$s. Maximization of $\mathcal{L}_4$ with respect to the classifiers tries to implicitly highlight such samples and the feature extractors subsequently bring them closer to the source distributions. Furthermore, since we deploy the class information of different source domains in aligning the target samples, our domain alignment is precisely fine-grained in nature and adhere the semantic meanings carefully in the latent representations.

Optimization: We follow the alternate optimization strategy for training the network. In particular, we follow an iterative process where Eqs. 5–7 are sequentially optimized in each iteration:

– First, the source domains centric loss measures are together minimized

$$\min_{\{E^k\}, \{D^{kl}\}, \{F^k\}} \mathcal{L}_1 + \mathcal{L}_2 + \mathcal{L}_3 + \lambda \mathcal{R} \tag{5}$$

where $\mathcal{R}$ defines the standard ℓ_2 regularizer on the parameters of E^ks and λ is the weight-decay hyper-parameter.

– Next, we train the classifier's parameters which simultaneously minimizes the $\mathcal{L}_3$ loss for the source domains and maximizes $\mathcal{L}_4$ given the target domain samples. This stage identifies target domain samples which are originally far from the source embeddings. Note that the inclusion of $\mathcal{L}_3$ in Eq. 6 is experimentally found to be useful than solely maximizing $\mathcal{L}_4$. This is mentioned as:

$$\min_{\{F^k\}} \mathcal{L}_3 - \mathcal{L}_4 \qquad (6)$$

– Finally, the feature extractors are updated solely based on the target domain samples through the minimization of $\mathcal{L}_4$ which brings the target data close to the source embeddings.

$$\min_{\{E^k\}} \mathcal{L}_4 \qquad (7)$$

For the maximization problem corresponding to the target samples related to Eq. 6 ($\mathcal{L}_4$), we make use of the RevGrad algorithm [6] which inserts a gradient reversal layer corresponding to $\mathcal{L}_4$.

3.3 Inference

During generalization, the target domain samples are progressively propagated through the feature encoders E^ks and the individual classifier modules F^ks, respectively. Next, we perform decision fusion considering the logit values of all the classifiers. Ideally, we apply a pointwise $max(\cdot)$ operation on the logit outputs of all the classifiers and the obtained vector representation is further normalized using $softmax(\cdot)$ function. Finally, the class with the highest softmax probability score is considered for label assignment to the respective $\mathbf{x}_j^t$.

Table 1. Multi-source UDA results on Office-31 (in %). * Note that the performance of ADDA on the W,D-A fluctuates very much over the epochs and does not stabilizes. We prefer not to report that.

Method	A,D - W	A,W - D	W,D - A	Average
Deep Cocktail Network [23]	96.9	**99.6**	54.9	83.8
Source only (Resnet-50) (source combine)	93.4	99.2	56.1	82.8
DAN (Resnet-50) (source combine) [12]	96.5	97.59	66.53	86.9
DANN (Resnet-50) (source combine) [6]	94.3	97.5	54.2	82.1
ADDA (Resnet-50) (source combine)[21]	91.1	96.4	-*	-*
MEDA (Resnet-50) (source combine) [22]	95.8	97.7	**69.0**	87.5
Ours (Resnet-50)	**97.3**	99.3	68.1	**88.3**

4 Experimental Results

Dataset and Base Features: We evaluate the performance of our model on the following cross-domain object recognition dataset: (i) Office-31[1] which consists of three domains representing a total of 4652 images from 31 categories: Amazon (A), Webcam (W), and DSLR (D), respectively. (ii) Office-CalTech which is an extension of the Office-31 dataset and consists of the 10 shared categories between Amazon (A), CalTech (C), DSLR (D), and Webcam (W). (iii) The ImageCLEF-DA[2] dataset is derived from the ImageClef-2014 challenge and is made up of images from the 12 shared categories among the Imagenet-2012 (I), Pascal-VOC (P), and CalTech-256 (C), respectively. Note that 50 images per category are considered leading to 600 images per domain. For all the three dataset, we rely on the fine-tuned Resnet-50 features with 2048 dimensions.

Model Architecture and Protocols: We design the entire network in terms of the fully-connected (fc) neural network layers coupled with $relu(\cdot)$ non-linearity. In particular, the E^ks and D^{kl}s are formed with two fc layers each with the dimensions of the latent feature space being 128. The F^ks, on the other hand, are directly derived from this latent representation space and each consists of a single fc layer. For optimizing $\mathcal{L}_1$, we randomly consider 1000 ξ_is in all the experimental

Table 2. Multi-source UDA results on Office-CalTech (in %).

Method	A,C,D - W	A,C,W - D	A,W,D - C	D,C,W - A	Average
Deep Cocktail Network [23]	99.4	99.0	90.2	92.7	95.3
Source only (Resnet-50) (source combine)	97.1	99.2	89.4	94.7	95.6
DAN (Resnet-50) (source combine) [12]	98.3	98.3	90.2	96.6	95.9
DANN (Resnet-50) (source combine) [6]	96.5	99.1	89.2	94.7	94.8
ADDA (Resnet-50) (source combine) [21]	96.0	96.7	90.1	92.6	93.9
MEDA (Resnet-50 (source combine)[22]	99.3	94.9	93.1	**98.7**	96.5
Moment matching MS-UDA (Resnet-101) [17]	99.5	99.2	92.2	94.5	96.3
Ours (Resnet-50)	**99.7**	**100.0**	**93.9**	96.7	**97.5**

Table 3. Multi-source UDA results on ImageCLEF-DA (in %).

Method	I,P - C	I,C - P	C,P - I	Average
Deep Cocktail Network [23]	90.0	68.8	83.5	80.8
Source only (Resnet-50) (source combine)	92.3	77.2	88.1	85.8
DAN (Resnet-50) (source combine) [12]	95.3	77.8	92.3	88.5
DANN (Resnet-50) (source combine) [6]	92.2	76.0	88.4	85.5
ADDA (Resnet-50) (source combine) [21]	94.0	76.5	93.2	87.9
MEDA (Resnet-50) (source combine) [22]	96.3	79.0	**96.5**	90.6
Ours (Resnet-50)	**97.1**	**80.3**	96.1	**91.2**

---

[1] https://people.eecs.berkeley.edu/~jhoffman/domainadapt/.
[2] https://www.imageclef.org/2014/adaptation.

cases. We set the weight decay parameter λ empirically by performing grid-search within the interval $[1, 0.0001]$ and we specifically look for the value which produces the maximum accuracy on a validation set. Besides, the learning rate is fixed at 0.0001. Adam optimizer [11] is used for training.

For Office-31 and ImageCLEF, we consider two source and a single target domains, thus leading to three possible sources-target combinations for each. Likewise, we consider three source and a target domains for the Office-CalTech dataset which results in four possible situations. Note that we report the target domain classification performance for all the scenarios as well as the overall average classification accuracy measures.

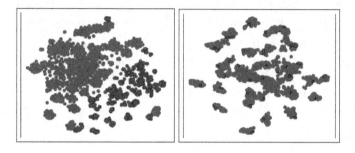

Fig. 2. t-SNE plots for the W,D - A (Office-31) - before and after the proposed domain adaptation. The colors signify different domains (left to right).

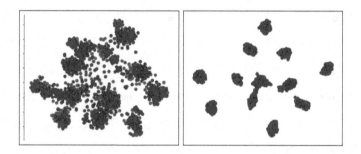

Fig. 3. t-SNE plots for the I,C - P (ImageCLEF) - before and after the proposed domain adaptation. The colors signify different domains (left to right).

As already discussed, the MS-UDA literature comprises of only a few dominant techniques. Following [17], we consider two comparative scenarios: (i) **source combine** where all the source domains are grouped to make a single source domain and is further used along with the single target setting. In this regard, we consider (a) simple multi-class classifier training without any explicit adaptation (b) single source adaptation using DANN [6], DAN [12], and

ADDA [21] (all adversarial), and (c) single source adaptation using MEDA [22] (non-adversarial). We found MEDA outputs the best performance among all the non-adversarial algorithms, and (ii) the **existing adversarial multi-source approaches**: deep cocktail network [23] and the moment matching based technique proposed in [17], respectively. However note that, while [23] considers an end-to-end training for task-specific feature extraction, [17] depends on the pretrained Resnet-101 features. In addition, we perform thorough ablation analysis to highlight the effects of (i) the classifiers ensemble, (ii) the individual loss terms, and (iii) the size of the target domain samples to be used during training.

4.1 Comparison to the Literature

Office-31: Note that this dataset is largely imbalanced as far as the number of samples per class over the domains is concerned. While the distributions gap between W and D is subtle, domain adaptation while A is the target domain is extremely challenging due to the dataset disparity. Table 1 mentions the performance comparison for Office-31. It can be found that the proposed method yields the best performance on this dataset with mean classification performance of 88.3%. Individually, note that a sharp improvement of 9–12% can be observed for the W,D - A case over [23] and [6].

Office-Caltech: All the methods produce comparatively high accuracy for this dataset (Table 2). This can be attributed to the presence of less number of categories (10) shared among the domains. The moment matching network [17] produces an mean classification accuracy of 96.3% in this case. On the other hand, our framework outperforms [17] both in terms of overall classification performance (by 1.2%) as well as the individual combinations, even using Resnet-50 features. Note that for both Office-31 and Office-Caltech, MEDA produces comparable performances with our approach.

ImageCLEF: We find that ADDA and MEDA produce very competent accuracy measures for this dataset: 87.9% and 90.0%, respectively. Our proposed method is able to outperform both of them substantially both in term of individual and overall classification performances (increase of 0.6–1%) (Table 3).

4.2 Critical Analysis

We consider two cases to extensively study the critical aspects of the proposed model: (i) W,D - A (Office-31) and I,C - P (ImageCLEF-DA).

Visualization: Here we plot the t-SNE for all the source and the target domains before and after adaptation. It can be observed that the feature extraction module encourages the learned features to be more compact, and largely overlapping given the domains. In particular, note that the domain denoted by the red color in Fig. 2 is entirely non-overlapping from the other two domains in the original feature space which is corrected substantially after adaptation by our model. Similar effects can be observed for Fig. 3 as well.

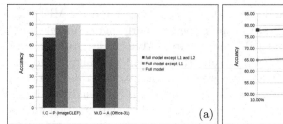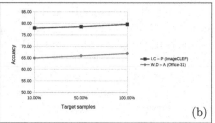

(a)   (b)

Fig. 4. (a)The ablation study on the loss terms, (b) The effect of size of the considered target samples during training.

Ablation Study on the Loss Terms: In order to analyze the effect of the cross-source domain reconstruction in the decoder, we train a different model where an auto-encoder structure is followed for the source domains in place of our cross-source domain mapping module. As a result, there are $\mathcal{K}$ decoder branches instead of $\mathcal{K}(\mathcal{K} - 1)$. In both the experimental scenarios, we find that the our full model with cross-source decoders outperforms the auto-encoder based setup sharply by 5–7%. While focusing on the proposed loss terms, we see from Fig. 4a that our base model without $\mathcal{L}_1$ and $\mathcal{L}_2$ loss measures performs comparatively poorly for both the cases. A sharp enhancement can be observed when $\mathcal{L}_2$ is introduced to the base model whereas the increase is rather marginal when $\mathcal{L}_1$ is further incorporated. In all the cases, we find that all the classifiers, once trained, start producing comparative accuracy measures and the ensemble improves the results of the individual classifiers by at least a margin of 1.5–2%.

Effect of the target domain sample size during training: We find that it is better to use more samples from $\mathcal{T}$ during training (for $\mathcal{L}_4$). In this regard, we consider 10%, 50%, and 100% samples from $\mathcal{T}$ during training. We observe steady enhancements for both the cases (W,D-A, and I,C-P) (Fig. 4b).

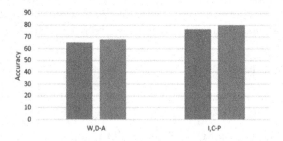

Fig. 5. Effect of the ensemble classification over single best source classifier.

Effect of the Ensemble Classification: In all the cases, we find that the classifiers ensemble approach sharply outperforms the performance of the individual classifiers by at least $3 - 5\%$ for both the cases. This can be attributed to the effectiveness of the source specific classifiers. Figure 5 shows the performance of the ensemble with respect to the single based source classifier for both W,D-A and I,C-P. Further, note that we perform simple unweighted decision fusion of the source classifiers, as opposed to the traditional weighted fusion generally followed in the MS-UDA literature. Although, we experimented with the weighted fusion approach, but found comparatively poor performance than the unweighted one by at least 3–4%.

5 Conclusions

We propose a novel MS-UDA model in this paper in terms of an end-to-end trainable system. As opposed to the few existing approaches in this domain, we align the labeled source domains while simultaneously projecting the target domain samples in the same space. Note that our method utilizes the advantages of ensemble learning judiciously during training and inference. We obtain sharp improvement in the performance with different sources-target combinations for the Office-31, ImageCLEF-DA, and Office-CalTech dataset. We are now interested in incorporating the notion of *category-shift* among the different source domains as a future endeavor.

References

1. Baktashmotlagh, M., Harandi, M.T., Lovell, B.C., Salzmann, M.: Unsupervised domain adaptation by domain invariant projection. In: Proceedings of the IEEE International Conference on Computer Vision, pp. 769–776 (2013)
2. Ben-David, S., Blitzer, J., Crammer, K., Kulesza, A., Pereira, F., Vaughan, J.W.: A theory of learning from different domains. Mach. Learn. **79**(1–2), 151–175 (2010)
3. Chen, M., Xu, Z., Weinberger, K., Sha, F.: Marginalized denoising autoencoders for domain adaptation. arXiv preprint arXiv:1206.4683 (2012)
4. Crammer, K., Kearns, M., Wortman, J.: Learning from multiple sources. In: Schölkopf, B., Platt, J.C., Hoffman, T. (eds.) Advances in Neural Information Processing Systems 19, pp. 321–328. MIT Press (2007). http://papers.nips.cc/paper/2972-learning-from-multiple-sources.pdf
5. Fernando, B., Habrard, A., Sebban, M., Tuytelaars, T.: Unsupervised visual domain adaptation using subspace alignment. In: Proceedings of the IEEE International Conference on Computer Vision, pp. 2960–2967 (2013)
6. Ganin, Y., Ustinova, E., Ajakan, H., Germain, P., Larochelle, H., Laviolette, F., Marchand, M., Lempitsky, V.: Domain-adversarial training of neural networks. J. Mach. Learn. Res. **17**(1), 2030–2096 (2016)
7. Ghifary, M., Kleijn, W.B., Zhang, M.: Domain adaptive neural networks for object recognition. In: Pham, D.-N., Park, S.-B. (eds.) PRICAI 2014. LNCS (LNAI), vol. 8862, pp. 898–904. Springer, Cham (2014). https://doi.org/10.1007/978-3-319-13560-1_76
8. Gong, B., Shi, Y., Sha, F., Grauman, K.: Geodesic flow kernel for unsupervised domain adaptation. In: 2012 IEEE Conference on Computer Vision and Pattern Recognition (CVPR), pp. 2066–2073. IEEE (2012)

9. Guo, J., Shah, D.J., Barzilay, R.: Multi-source domain adaptation with mixture of experts. arXiv preprint arXiv:1809.02256 (2018)
10. Jhuo, I.H., Liu, D., Lee, D., Chang, S.F.: Robust visual domain adaptation with low-rank reconstruction. In: 2012 IEEE Conference on Computer Vision and Pattern Recognition (CVPR), pp. 2168–2175. IEEE (2012)
11. Kingma, D.P., Ba, J.: Adam: A method for stochastic optimization. arXiv preprint arXiv:1412.6980 (2014)
12. Long, M., Cao, Y., Wang, J., Jordan, M.I.: Learning transferable features with deep adaptation networks. arXiv preprint arXiv:1502.02791 (2015)
13. Long, M., Zhu, H., Wang, J., Jordan, M.I.: Unsupervised domain adaptation with residual transfer networks. In: Advances in Neural Information Processing Systems, pp. 136–144 (2016)
14. Mansour, Y., Mohri, M., Rostamizadeh, A.: Domain adaptation with multiple sources. In: Koller, D., Schuurmans, D., Bengio, Y., Bottou, L. (eds.) Advances in Neural Information Processing Systems 21, pp. 1041–1048. Curran Associates, Inc. (2009). http://papers.nips.cc/paper/3550-domain-adaptation-with-multiple-sources.pdf
15. Pan, S.J., Tsang, I.W., Kwok, J.T., Yang, Q.: Domain adaptation via transfer component analysis. IEEE Trans. Neural Netw. 22(2), 199–210 (2011)
16. Patel, V.M., Gopalan, R., Li, R., Chellappa, R.: Visual domain adaptation: a survey of recent advances. IEEE Signal Process. Mag. 32(3), 53–69 (2015)
17. Peng, X., Bai, Q., Xia, X., Huang, Z., Saenko, K., Wang, B.: Moment matching for multi-source domain adaptation. arXiv preprint arXiv:1812.01754 (2018)
18. Redko, I., Courty, N., Flamary, R., Tuia, D.: Optimal transport for multi-source domain adaptation under target shift. arXiv preprint arXiv:1803.04899 (2018)
19. Saito, K., Ushiku, Y., Harada, T., Saenko, K.: Adversarial dropout regularization. arXiv preprint arXiv:1711.01575 (2017)
20. Sun, B., Feng, J., Saenko, K.: Return of frustratingly easy domain adaptation. In: AAAI, vol. 6, p. 8 (2016)
21. Tzeng, E., Hoffman, J., Saenko, K., Darrell, T.: Adversarial discriminative domain adaptation. In: Proceedings of the IEEE Conference on Computer Vision and Pattern Recognition, pp. 7167–7176 (2017)
22. Wang, J., Feng, W., Chen, Y., Yu, H., Huang, M., Yu, P.S.: Visual domain adaptation with manifold embedded distribution alignment. In: 2018 ACM Multimedia Conference on Multimedia Conference, pp. 402–410. ACM (2018)
23. Xu, R., Chen, Z., Zuo, W., Yan, J., Lin, L.: Deep cocktail network: multi-source unsupervised domain adaptation with category shift. In: Proceedings of the IEEE Conference on Computer Vision and Pattern Recognition, pp. 3964–3973 (2018)
24. Yang, J., Yan, R., Hauptmann, A.G.: Cross-domain video concept detection using adaptive SVMS. In: Proceedings of the 15th ACM International Conference on Multimedia, pp. 188–197. ACM (2007)
25. Zhang, L., He, Z., Liu, Y.: Deep object recognition across domains based on adaptive extreme learning machine. Neurocomputing 239, 194–203 (2017)
26. Zhao, H., Zhang, S., Wu, G., Moura, J.M., Costeira, J.P., Gordon, G.J.: Adversarial multiple source domain adaptation. In: Advances in Neural Information Processing Systems, pp. 8559–8570 (2018)
27. Zhu, J.Y., Park, T., Isola, P., Efros, A.A.: Unpaired image-to-image translation using cycle-consistent adversarial networks. arXiv preprint (2017)

Time-Frequency Causal Inference Uncovers Anomalous Events in Environmental Systems

Maha Shadaydeh[1(✉)] ⓘ, Joachim Denzler[1,4] ⓘ, Yanira Guanche García[2,4] ⓘ, and Miguel Mahecha[3,4] ⓘ

[1] Computer Vision Group, Friedrich Schiller University, Jena, Germany
maha.shadaydeh@uni-jena.de
[2] Institute of Data Science, German Aerospace Center, DLR, Jena, Germany
[3] Max Planck Institute for Biogeochemistry, Jena, Germany
[4] Michael Stifel Center for Data Driven and Simulation Science, Jena, Germany

Abstract. Causal inference in dynamical systems is a challenge for different research areas. So far it is mostly about understanding to what extent the underlying causal mechanisms can be derived from observed time series. Here we investigate whether anomalous events can also be identified based on the observed changes in causal relationships. We use a parametric time-frequency representation of vector autoregressive Granger causality for causal inference. The use of time-frequency approach allows for dealing with the nonstationarity of the time series as well as for defining the time scale on which changes occur. We present two representative examples in environmental systems: land-atmosphere ecosystem and marine climate. We show that an anomalous event can be identified as the event where the causal intensities differ according to a distance measure from the average causal intensities. The driver of the anomalous event can then be identified based on the analysis of changes in the causal effect relationships.

Keywords: Time-frequency causality analysis · Vector Autoregressive Granger Causality · Attribution of anomalous events

1 Introduction

Understanding causal effect relationships in dynamical systems is a challenging problem in different areas of research such as brain neural connectivity analysis, climatic attribution, psychology, among many others. These relationships are guided by the processes generating them. Hence, monitoring changes in the interaction patterns within the system variables can be used for simultaneous detection and diagnosis of changes in the underlying process. For visual illustration purpose, in Fig. 1 we present an example where we show that the time (date of occurrence) and the scale (duration of the event) of three historic hurricanes in the North Sea can be visualized using some correlation measure between

© Springer Nature Switzerland AG 2019
G. A. Fink et al. (Eds.): DAGM GCPR 2019, LNCS 11824, pp. 499–512, 2019.
https://doi.org/10.1007/978-3-030-33676-9_35

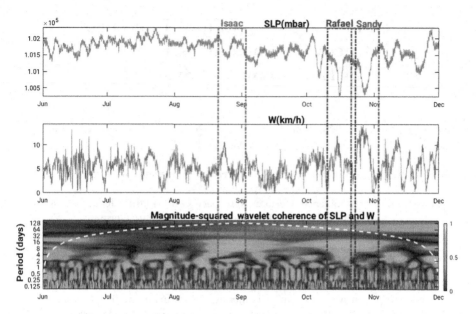

Fig. 1. Plots of sea level pressure (SLP), wind speed (W), and the magnitude-squared wavelet coherence of SLP and W. Data is extracted from the National Data Buoy Center for a buoy located near the Bahamas in the Atlantic Sea (23.838 N, 68.333 W). The high magnitude wavelet coherence correlates well with the time and duration of three historic hurricanes in year 2012: *Isaac*, *Rafael*, and *Sandy*. The white dashed line shows the cone of statistical significance.

two different marine variables namely: sea level pressure (SLP) and wind speed (W). This figure illustrates that, in a normal marine climate conditions, the wavelet coherence (a measure of the correlation between two variables in the time-frequency domain) is low, indicating that these variables are almost independent. However, during certain events, such as hurricanes, these variables start to show higher coherence that can be visualized on the time scale of 8 to 16 days.

To understand events in multivariate environmental time series, however, we need to go beyond monitoring correlation patterns and try to identify the driver of the event based on the analysis of the changes in the causal effect relationships between the variables. In this paper, we aim to build on this core idea for the detection and attribution of changes in environmental time series. To this end, we approach the problem in a way similar to fault detection and diagnosis in plants of automatic control systems [13,31]. That is, we try to estimate the underlying models of different time intervals, and define change or anomaly based on how far is the estimated model of a certain time interval from an estimation of the true one. The change is then attributed to the variable(s) responsible for this change and is defined based on the overall change in its causal effects on other variables in the system.

Various causality measures have been reported in literature [9,21]. Among many other linear regression-based models, Granger causality (GC) [15] is the most widely known method for causality analysis. GC is based on the idea that causes both precede and help predict their effects. Hence, GC mainly focuses on linear models which assumes that the causes and effects are separable. It has received intense research interest in neuroscience literature aiming to unravel the detailed circuitry underlying perception, cognition, and behaviour [25]. Several attempts in the literature have applied the concept of Granger causality to climatic attribution. The authors of [5] provide a review of the use of GC for the attribution of global warming. To overcome the shortcoming of the separability assumption in Granger causality, several causality analysis methods for nonlinear systems have been proposed so far. Examples include methods developed from transfer entropy, recurrence networks [12] and nonlinear extension of Granger causality [19,20].

Despite the abundance of environmental data, data-driven causal inference methods remain at its infancy compared to other areas of research [11]. A major challenge particular to environmental data is that causal effect interactions occur on multiple temporal and spatial scales. Recently, the importance of using deep learning approaches for understanding Earth and ecological processes has been addressed in [23]. While deep learning as well as other non-linear methods are continuously under development, linear methods remain of great interest mainly for being strictly connected to the frequency domain representation of multivariate time series [10], which is of great advantage in the analysis of environmental data. This is due to the fact that environmental time series most often contain trend and periodical components (diurnal and seasonal cycles) that can significantly mask the underling causality structure in time domain. Moreover, the impact of filtering and down sampling (the two necessary steps for time domain multiscale causality analysis in discrete systems) on causal inference has been only recently studied for linear discrete systems [7,27]; and it still presents a major challenge in nonlinear systems [27]. For the black box of deep learning structure, such impact is still far from being comprehensible.

In this paper we present a method for simultaneous detection and attribution of changes in multivariate environmental systems based on time-frequency causality analysis. The causal effect relationships are extracted using the parametric frequency domain representation of Vector AutoRegressive Granger causality (VAR-GC) [14,16] applied on a sliding time window. In particular we use the generalized partial directed coherence (gPDC) [6] method for causal inference which allows for causality analysis at different frequency components. After introducing the time-frequency causal inference method, we present two different examples in environmental systems, where we show that an anomalous event can be defined as this event where the causal intensities between the variables differ according to some statistical distance measure from the average dynamical behaviour, and such anomalous event can be directly attributed to the variable(s) causing such deviation assuming that there is no hidden drivers.

2 Methodology

2.1 Vector Autoregressive Granger Causality (VAR-GC)

Let $\mathcal{S} = \{X_k, 1 \leq k \leq N\}$ denote a discrete stationary stochastic process which constitutes of N real valued environmental variables. Given the length m time series $x_k(n), n = 1, \ldots, m$ as the realizations of $X_k, k = 1, \ldots, N$, these time series can be represented by a pth order vector autoregressive model (VAR(p)) of the form

$$
\begin{bmatrix} x_1(n) \\ \vdots \\ x_N(n) \end{bmatrix} = \sum_{r=1}^{p} A_r \begin{bmatrix} x_1(n-r) \\ \vdots \\ x_N(n-r) \end{bmatrix} + \begin{bmatrix} \epsilon_1(n) \\ \vdots \\ \epsilon_N(n) \end{bmatrix}, \tag{1}
$$

The residuals $\epsilon_k, k = 1, \ldots, N$ constitute a white noise stationary process with an $N \times N$ residual covariance matrix Σ. The model parameters at time lags $r = 1, \ldots, p$ are predefined by

$$
A_r = \begin{bmatrix} a_{11}(r) & \ldots & a_{1N}(r) \\ \vdots & \ddots & \vdots \\ a_{N1}(r) & \ldots & a_{NN}(r) \end{bmatrix}. \tag{2}
$$

The elements of the matrix A_r, $a_{ij}(r)$ quantify the causal link from x_j to x_i at time lag r. The model order p defines the maximum lag used to estimate causal interactions. It can be estimated using either Akaike [3] or Bayesian Criterion [24]. The model parameters $a_{ij}(r), i, j = 1, \ldots, N, r = 1, \ldots, p$ can then be estimated using for example the method of Least Squares (LS) [17].

It should be noted that the use of the VAR(p) model (1) makes no assumption on the mechanism that produced the data (for example whether it is a linear one) except that the model itself exists and is stable [4].

The time domain VAR-GC of x_i on x_j conditioned on all other variables is defined by the likelihood ratio [1,14]

$$
\gamma_{i \to j} = \ln \frac{|\Sigma_j^{i-}|}{|\Sigma_j|}, \tag{3}
$$

where Σ_j and Σ_j^{i-} are the covariance matrices of the residual ϵ_j associated to x_j using the full and reduced model (after eliminating x_i) respectively. The conditional MVAR GC (3) thus quantifies the degree to which the past of x_i helps predict x_j, over and above the degree to which x_j is already predicted by its own past and the past of variables other than x_i.

2.2 Frequency Domain VAR-GC: The Generalized Partial Directed Coherence (gPDC)

As noted above, environmental time series most often contain periodical components (diurnal and seasonal cycles) that can significantly mask the underlying causality structure in time domain. Removal of these periodic components might degrade causal inference [7]. In previous work [26] we have shown through comparison between time and frequency domain causality analysis of environmental time series that time-domain GC might result in several spurious causal links due to the presence of periodic components. Hence, the use of spectral-domain analysis enables change detection in certain frequency bands where for example the influence of trends (low frequency) or daily and seasonal cycle can be excluded.

The causal relation from x_i to x_j is described in the frequency domain via the generalized partial directed coherence (gPDC) [6]:

$$g\pi_{i\to j}(f) = \frac{\frac{1}{\sigma_{jj}}\overline{A}_{ji}(f)}{\sqrt{\sum_{k=1}^{m}\frac{1}{\sigma_{kk}^2}\left|\overline{A}_{ki}(f)\right|^2}}, \tag{4}$$

where $\overline{A}_{ij}(f), i, j = 1 \ldots N$ are the elements of the matrix $\overline{A}(f) = I - A(f)$ where $A(f)$ is the Fourier transform of $A(r), r = 1, \ldots, p$:

$$A(f) = \sum_{r=1}^{p} \mathbf{A}_r z^{-r}|_{z=e^{i2\pi f}}, \tag{5}$$

and σ_{ii}^2 are the diagonal entries of the residual covariance matrix Σ. The value of $g\pi_{i\to j}(f)$ represents the causality strength of x_i on x_j as compared to all of x_i's interactions to other variables. Nullity of $g\pi_{i\to j}(f)$ indicates absence of Granger causality from x_i to x_j at the normalized frequency f. Note that the normalizing term in the denominator in Eq. 4 is selected such that $0 \leq |g\pi_{i\to j}(f)| \leq 1$.

2.3 Event Detection and Attribution Based on Time-Frequency Causality Analysis

A major issue in causal inference in environmental data is that the underlying system is most often a time-varying one. To deal with this issue, one can use for example an adaptive system such as the Kalman filter [2] or a sliding time window approach where the system is assumed to be time-invariant. In this paper we use the latter solution, i.e. we extract changes in the causal intensities by calculating the gPDC on selected time windows where the stationarity assumption is assumed to hold. To this end, for each time window, the model order is first estimated using Bayesian criterion and the model parameters are estimated using the LS method. The spectral causal effect values are then calculated using Eq. 4. The estimated spectral causal effect intensities serve as an approximation of the pairwise sub-models. The accuracy of this approximation depends on several factors such as the sample size in the selected time window, the method used for model order estimation, as well as the procedure used for the identification of the model parameters.

The authors of [28] presented an extensive study on the asymptotic distribution of the partial directed coherence when applied to multichannel electroencephalographic data. They proved that for a stable stationary Gaussian VAR(p) process, the maximum likelihood estimator $|\pi_{i \to j}(f)|^2$ is consistent and asymptotically normally distributed if $|\pi_{i \to j}(f)|^2 \neq 0$, while $|\pi_{i \to j}(f)|^2 = 0$ indicates an absence of causal link between the time series. Hence the PDC measure provides means of comparing different strengths of connectivity between the observed time series. For non-zero values, the asymptotically normal behaviour degenerates into that of a mixture of χ variables allowing the computation of threshold for connectivity tests [28].

Under similar assumptions, the results of [28] can be directly extended to multivariate environmental data. Accordingly, comparison of the causal intensities in a certain time interval, and in the desired frequency band, with the average causal intensities (the mean value of the gPDC calculated over several realizations) can be utilized in principle to simultaneously detect and attribute anomalous events. The anomalous events here are meant to be those time windows where the causal effect intensities show, according to some distance measure, considerable deviation from the average causal intensities. The detected anomalous event can be then attributed to the variable(s) causing such deviation and is defined based on the change in its causal effect intensities on other variables.

Let us assume that we have L different realizations or different time intervals of the process $\mathcal{S}$ and let $g\pi_{i \to j}^l(f), i, j = 1, \ldots, N$ denote the causal intensities for realizations $l, l = 1, \ldots, L$. We define the average causal intensity of x_j on x_i at frequency f as

$$\overline{g\pi}_{i \to j}(f) = \frac{1}{L} \sum_{l=1}^{L} |g\pi_{i \to j}^l(f)|. \tag{6}$$

An event or time interval l is defined as anomalous if the causal intensities $g\pi_{i \to j}^l(f), i, j = 1, \ldots, N$ over a frequency band $f_1 \leq f \leq f_2$ is significantly higher than the average causal intensities $\overline{g\pi}_{i \to j}(f)$. In this paper we use the difference in the area under the two causal intensity curves for statistically significant values as a distance measure, however, other distance measures can be applied as well.

For statistical significance test against the null hypothesis of absence of a causal link, i.e. $|g\pi_{i \to j}(f)|^2 = 0$, we used two different tests. The first is the permutation test where we first generate permutations of the time series, calculate the gPDC values, and then take the maximum of the gPDC values over all permutations at each frequency. The second statistical significance test is the Fourier Transform (FT) surrogate method [29] where time series surrogates can be generated by substituting the phase of the FT of the time series with a realization of uniformly distributed random variable in the range $[0, \pi)$ while keeping the amplitude of the FT the same. The FT surrogate method gives a more strict confidence interval when compared to other statistical significance tests of gPDC [10].

Different anomaly detection methods can then be utilized to classify events as normal or anomalous. For example, a simple approach for anomalous event detection would be to use a fixed percentile of the χ^2 distribution of the distance measure as a threshold to detect anomalous events.

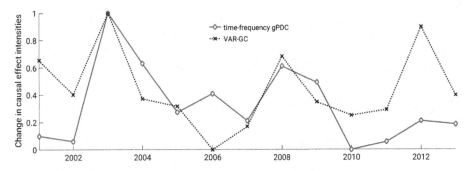

Fig. 2. The deviation of the causal effect intensities from the average ones during the months of August in years 2001–2013 summed over all variables and normalized to the [0–1] range. The peak in year 2003 correlates with the summer heatwave in France in August 2003.

3   Experimental Results

3.1   Event Detection and Attribution in Ecological Time Series

Understanding causal effect relationships are essential to understand ecosystem behaviour under climate change conditions. A particular cause of concern is the question of how ecosystem functioning (e.g. land-atmosphere exchange processes of CO2, water, and energy) are affected during unusual hydro-meteorological conditions [18]. This experiment aims to investigate the causal effect relationships between air temperature (T), vapour pressure deficit (VPD), latent energy (LE) and net ecosystem exchange (NEE). Experiments are performed on the real half-hourly meteorological observations and land flux eddy covariance data measured at the flux tower site of Puechabon-France spanning years 2001–2013 [22].

For the gPDC time-frequency analysis, we adopted a sliding time window approach of length 1440 (30 days by 48 samples/day) and followed the steps in Sect. 2.3: the model order and parameters are estimated for each time window, then the spectral causal effect values are calculated using Eq. 4. The summation of the absolute difference between the causal effect intensities of the system within the month of August over years 2001–2013 and the average causal intensities (average of the causal intensities in the month of August over 13 years) over all variables is calculated. Note that in the calculation of this change we excluded the values of gPDC that are not statistically significant.

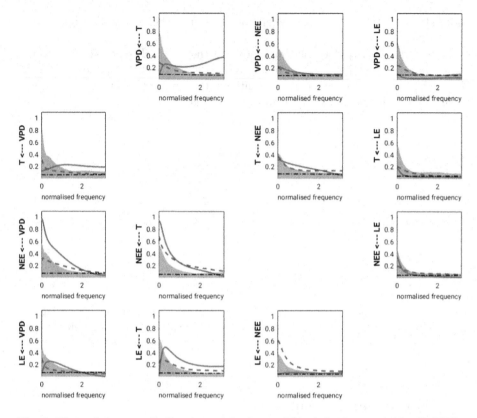

Fig. 3. Plots of the causal effect intensities $|g\pi_{i\rightarrow j}(f)|$ of the four variables T, VPD, NEE, LE measured at the flux tower site of Puechabon-France during the heatwave in August 2003 (solid blue line) when compared to the average causal intensities $\overline{g\pi}_{i\rightarrow j}(f)$ of similar summer period within years 2001–2013 (red dashed line). The threshold for statistical significance estimated using permutation test and the FT surrogate test is shown in the dashed-dotted line and gray area respectively. (Color figure online)

Similar experiment is performed using time domain VAR-GC as defined in Eq. 3. Figure 2 shows the comparison between the proposed time-frequency gPDC-based method and the time domain VAR-GC. Both approaches shows clear peak in August 2003 which correlates with the historic heatwave in France in August 2003. For the VAR-GC, however, we can notice another clear peak in year 2012. Although we have no ground truth to present quantitative comparison between the two methods, to the best of our knowledge, no historical event has been recorded in August 2012.

In Fig. 3, we compare the pairwise causal intensities of August 2003 with the average pairwise causal intensities of the months of August in years 2001–2013. It can be observed that there is considerable change in the causal intensity

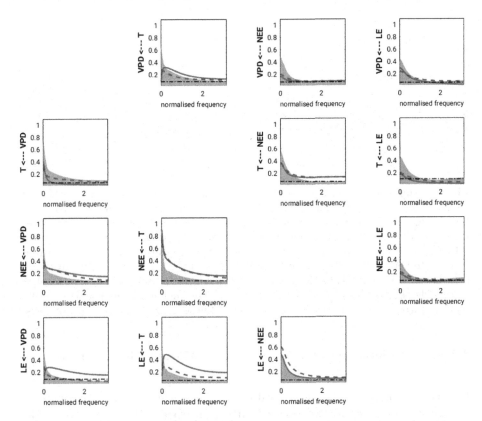

Fig. 4. Plots of the causal effect intensities $|g\pi_{i\to j}(f)|$ of the four variables T, VPD, NEE, LE measured at the flux tower site of Puechabon-France during August 2002 (blue solid line) when compared to the average causal intensities $\overline{g\pi}_{i\to j}(f)$ of similar summer period within years 2001–2013 (red dashed line). The threshold for statistical significance estimated using permutation test and the FT surrogate test is shown in the dashed-dotted line and gray area respectively. (Color figure online)

of T $\to$ VPD in the high frequency range which corresponds to a short term change (half an hour up to two hours); there is also clear increase in the causal intensity of VPD $\to$ NEE at the low frequency range (long term change) pointing towards an increase in water stress on ecosystem functioning; other causal effect intensities however remain the same. Comparing similar results for year 2002 (Fig. 4), shows that while in a normal summer, such as in year 2002, the causal intensities match well with the average behaviour of the system, the ones in 2003 show clear deviation in the system dynamics from the average behaviour with T being the main driving variable.

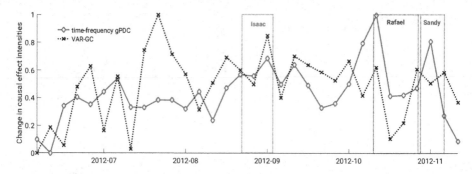

Fig. 5. Changes in the causal effect intensities of all the extracted segments within the six months period of the data (June 2012 until November 2012) when compared to the average causal intensities summed over all variables and normalized to the [0–1] range. For the time-frequency analysis using the generalized partial directed coherence (gPDC), the high change values correlate highly with the three hurricanes: Issac (from Aug. 21 to Sept. 03, 2012), Rafael (from Oct. 12 to Oct. 26, 2012), and Sandy (from Oct. 22 to Nov. 02, 2012). The peak on the first week of July is due to a tropical storm. The rectangles show the start and end dates of the hurricanes. The dates of the markers correspond to the dates of the center of the segments, each of length 20 days.

3.2   Event Detection and Attribution in Marine Climate Time Series

In this example we study the causal effect relationships within three climate marine variables: sea level pressure (SLP), wind speed (W), and wave height (Hs). Time series data of a buoy located near the Bahamas in the Atlantic Sea (23.838 N, 68.333 W) were extracted from the National Data Buoy Center (http://www.ndbc.noaa.gov/) and used in this experiment (same data used in Fig. 1). The time series comprises six months of hourly data, from June 2012 until November 2012. This period corresponds to the Atlantic hurricane season, which in that year was especially active [8].

For the gPDC spectral analysis, we used a sliding hamming window to extract segments of length 480 samples (20 days by 24 sample/day) with 25% overlap. Figure 5 shows the changes in the causal effect intensities of all extracted segments within the six months period of the data when compared to the average causal intensities for both the VAR-GC and the gPDC methods. The high change values of the proposed gPDC-based method correlate highly with the three historic hurricanes *Issac, Rafael* and *Sandy* of the year 2012 as shown in Fig. 1. The peak on the first week of July is due to a tropical storm.

It can be even visually verified that applying any fixed percentile threshold to the VAR-GC and gPDC-based causal intensities-change measures (Fig. 5) for the detection of anomalous events would reveal that the proposed method has higher detection accuracy of the hurricanes and less false positive detection.

Figure 6 shows the plots of the pairwise causal effect relationships at different time windows when compared to the average causal intensities. For a time

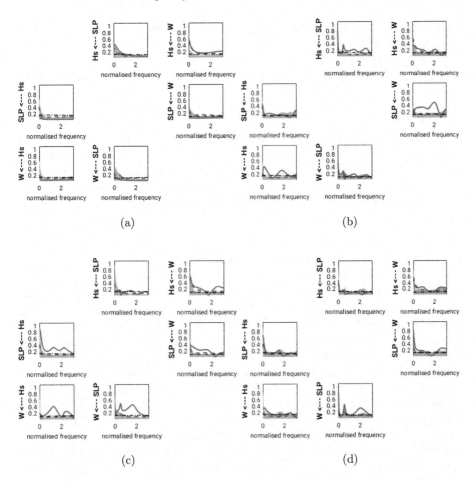

Fig. 6. Plots of the causal effect intensities $|g\pi_{i \to j}(f)|$ (solid blue line) of the three marine climate variables: sea level pressure (SLP), wave height (Hs), and wind speed (W) during normal sea conditions (a), hurricane *Issac* (from Aug. 21 to Sept. 03, 2012) (b), hurricane *Rafael* (from Oct. 12 to Oct. 26, 2012) (c), and hurricane *Sandy* (from Oct. 22 to Nov. 02, 2012) (d). The red dashed line shows the average causal intensities $\overline{g\pi}_{i \to j}(f)$ over all segments within the six months period of the data (June 2012 until November 2012). The threshold for statistical significance estimated using permutation test and the FT surrogate test is shown in the dashed-dotted line and gray area respectively. (Color figure online)

window with normal sea conditions, the causal effect relationships are either statistically insignificant or match well with the average causal intensities. For hurricane *Isaac* however, there is an increase in the causal effect intensities, particularly the causal effect of W on other variables. During hurricanes *Rafael* and *Sandy*, we can notice an increase in the causal effect of SLP on other variables. Interestingly, this increase is particularly high at the frequency that corresponds to the semi-diurnal (twice-daily) cycle of the atmospheric pressure. The differences in the causal effect patterns of these three hurricanes can be related to the trajectories of the hurricanes compared to the location of the buoy where the data were recorded: *Rafael* and *Sandy* passed much closer to the Bahamas than *Isaac*.

It should be noted that the proposed attribution method is based on the assumption that there are no unobserved drivers. To account for hidden drivers, the presented approach can be extended by using a state-space model with latent variables instead of the VAR model. For highly nonlinear causal effect relationship with hidden confounding, the concept of detecting anomalous event based on the changes in the causal effect relationships is currently being explored by the authors using deep learning approach along with domain knowledge integration [30].

4 Conclusions and Future Work

In this paper, we have presented an attribution scheme for changes in environmental data based on the analysis of the causal effect relationships in multivariate environmental time series. The coupling between the used variables is assumed to be well represented by a vector autoregressive (VAR) model. The causal effect relationships are extracted using the generalized partial directed coherence. Through some representative examples in environmental systems, we have shown that an anomalous event can be detected as the one where the causal intensities between the variables differ according to some statistical measure from the average causal intensities. Moreover, the analysis of the causal effect patterns allows for understanding these events and defining the time scale on which changes occur. Current research work is directed towards the development of methods that are able to integrate the presented approach with domain knowledge for improved anomalous event detection and classification in a spatiotemporal context as well as towards using adaptive time window selection instead of the fixed-size window used in this study.

Acknowledgments. The authors thank the Carl Zeiss Foundation for the financial support within the scope of the program line "Breakthroughs: Exploring Intelligent Systems" for "Digitization—explore the basics, use applications". This work used eddy covariance data acquired and shared by the FLUXNET community.

References

1. Barnett, L., Seth, A.K.: The MVGC multivariate Granger causality toolbox: a new approach to Granger-causal inference. J. Neurosci. Methods **223**, 50–68 (2014)
2. Wan, E.A., Nelson, A.T.: Dual Extended Kalman Filter Methods, pp. 123–173. Wiley-Blackwell (2002). https://doi.org/10.1002/0471221546.ch5. Chapter 5
3. Akaike, H.: A new look at the statistical model identification. IEEE Trans. Autom. Control **19**(6), 716–723 (1974). https://doi.org/10.1109/TAC.1974.1100705

4. Anderson, T.: The Statistical Analysis of Time Series. Wiley Classics Library. Wiley, New York (1994)
5. Attanasio, A., Pasini, A., Triacca, U.: Granger causality analyses for climatic attribution. Atmos. Clim. Sci. **3**(4), 515–522 (2013). https://doi.org/10.4236/acs.2013.34054
6. Baccalá, L.A., Sameshima, K., Takahashi, D.: Generalized partial directed coherence. In: 15th International Conference on Digital Signal Processing, pp. 163–166. IEEE (2007)
7. Barnett, L., Seth, A.K.: Behaviour of Granger causality under filtering: theoretical invariance and practical application. J. Neurosci. Methods **201**(2), 404–419 (2011). https://doi.org/10.1016/j.jneumeth.2011.08.010
8. Barz, B., Guanche, Y., Rodner, E., Denzler, J.: Maximally divergent intervals for extreme weather event detection. In: MTS/IEEE OCEANS Conference Aberdeen, pp. 1–9 (2017). https://doi.org/10.1109/OCEANSE.2017.8084569
9. Eichler, M.: Graphical modelling of multivariate time series. Probab. Theory Relat. Fields **153**(1), 233–268 (2012). https://doi.org/10.1007/s00440-011-0345-8
10. Faes, L., Porta, A., Nollo, G.: Testing frequency-domain causality in multivariate time series. IEEE Trans. Biomed. Eng. **57**(8), 1897–1906 (2010)
11. Faghmous, J.H., Kumar, V.: A big data guide to understanding climate change: the case for theory-guided data science. Big Data **2**(3), 155–163 (2014)
12. Feldhoff, J., Donner, R.V., Donges, J.F., Marwan, N., Kurths, J.: Detection of coupling directions by means of inter-system recurrence networks. Phys. Lett. A **376**, 3504–3513 (2012)
13. Frank, P.: Analytical and qualitative model-based fault diagnosis - a survey and some new results. Eur. J. Control **2**(1), 6–28 (1996). https://doi.org/10.1016/S0947-3580(96)70024-9
14. Geweke, J.: Measurement of linear dependence and feedback between multiple time series. J. Am. Stat. Assoc. **77**(378), 304–313 (1982)
15. Granger, C.W.J.: Investigating causal relations by econometric models and cross-spectral methods. Econometrica **37**(3), 424–438 (1969). http://www.jstor.org/stable/1912791
16. Granger, C.W.: Investigating causal relations by econometric models and cross-spectral methods. Econometrica J. Econometric Soc. **37**, 424–438 (1969)
17. Haykin, S.: Adaptive Filter Theory, 3rd edn. Prentice-Hall Inc., Upper Saddle River (1996)
18. Mahecha, M.D., et al.: Detecting impacts of extreme events with ecological in situ monitoring networks. Biogeosciences **14**(18), 4255–4277 (2017). https://doi.org/10.5194/bg-14-4255-2017
19. Marinazzo, D., Liao, W., Chen, H., Stramaglia, S.: Nonlinear connectivity by Granger causality. NeuroImage **58**(2), 330–338 (2011). https://doi.org/10.1016/j.neuroimage.2010.01.099
20. Papagiannopoulou, C., et al.: A non-linear Granger-causality framework to investigate climate-vegetation dynamics. Geoscientific Model Dev. **10**(5), 1945–1960 (2017). https://doi.org/10.5194/gmd-10-1945-2017
21. Peters, J., Janzing, D., Schölkopf, B.: Elements of Causal Inference - Foundations and Learning Algorithms. Adaptive Computation and Machine Learning Series. The MIT Press, Cambridge (2017)
22. Rambal, S., Joffre, R., Ourcival, J.M., Cavender-Bares, J., Rocheteau, A.: The growth respiration component in Eddy CO_2 flux from a *quercus ilex* mediterranean forest. Glob. Change Biol. **10**(9), 1460–1469 (2004). https://doi.org/10.1111/j.1365-2486.2004.00819.x

23. Reichstein, M., Camps-Valls, G., Stevens, B., Jung, M., Denzler, J., Carvalhais, N., Prabhat: Deep learning and process understanding for data-driven earth system science. Nature 195–204 (2019). https://doi.org/10.1038/s41586-019-0912-1

24. Schwarz, G.: Estimating the dimension of a model. Ann. Statist. **6**(2), 461–464 (1978). https://doi.org/10.1214/aos/1176344136

25. Seth, A.K., Barrett, A.B., Barnett, L.: Granger causality analysis in neuroscience and neuroimaging. J. Neurosci. **35**(8), 3293–3297 (2015). https://doi.org/10.1523/JNEUROSCI.4399-14.2015

26. Shadaydeh, M., Garcia, Y.G., Mahecha, M., Reichstein, M., Denzler, J.: Causality analysis of ecological time series: a time-frequency approach. In: Chen, C., Cooley, D., Runge, J., Szekely, E. (eds.) Climate Informatics Workshop 2018, pp. 111–114 (2018)

27. Solo, V.: State-space analysis of Granger-Geweke causality measures with application to fMRI. Neural Comput. **28**(5), 914–949 (2016). https://doi.org/10.1162/NECO_a_00828. pMID: 26942749

28. Takahashi, D.Y., Baccal, L.A., Sameshima, K.: Connectivity inference between neural structures via partial directed coherence. J. Appl. Stat. **34**(10), 1259–1273 (2007). https://doi.org/10.1080/02664760701593065

29. Theiler, J., Eubank, S., Longtin, A., Galdrikian, B., Farmer, J.D.: Testing for nonlinearity in time series: the method of surrogate data. Physica D **58**(1), 77–94 (1992). https://doi.org/10.1016/0167-2789(92)90102-S

30. Trifunov, V.T., Shadaydeh, M., Runge, J., Eyring, V., Reichstein, M., Denzler, J.: Nonlinear causal link estimation under hidden confounding with an application to time series anomaly detection. In: German Conference on Pattern Recognition (2019)

31. Zhong, M., Xue, T., Ding, S.X.: A survey on model-based fault diagnosis for linear discrete time-varying systems. Neurocomputing **306**, 51–60 (2018). https://doi.org/10.1016/j.neucom.2018.04.037

Tongue Contour Tracking in Ultrasound Images with Spatiotemporal LSTM Networks

Enes Aslan[1,2](✉) [ID] and Yusuf Sinan Akgul[1] [ID]

[1] Department of Computer Engineering, GIT Vision Lab, Gebze Technical
University, Kocaeli, Turkey
enesaslan92@gmail.com
[2] R&D Department, Kuveyt Turk Participation Bank, Kocaeli, Turkey

Abstract. Analysis of ultrasound images of the human tongue has many
applications such as tongue modeling, speech therapy, language education and speech disorder diagnosis. In this paper we propose a novel
ultrasound tongue contour tracker that enforces constraints of ultrasound imaging of the tongue such as spatial and temporal smoothness
of the tongue contours. We use 3 different LSTM networks in sequence
to satisfy these constraints. The first network uses only spatial image
information from each video frame separately. The second and third networks add temporal information to the results of the first spatial network. Our networks are designed by considering the ultrasound image
formation process of the human tongue. We use polar Brightness-Mode
of the ultrasound images, which makes it possible to assume that each
column of the image can contain at most one contour position. We tested
our system on a dataset that we collected from 4 volunteers while they
read written text. The final accuracy results are very promising and they
exceed the state of the art results while keeping the run times at very
reasonable levels (several frames per second). We provide the complete
results of our system as supplementary material.

1 Introduction

There is a very large amount of research on ultrasound tongue contour tracking [5]. It is used in areas such as tongue modeling [12], speech therapy [19],
language education [13,20–22], medical treatment [17,18], the identification of
some inherited diseases based on the structural disorder of the tongue can be
given as examples of applications in these areas.

Classically, studies on tracking the ultrasound tongue contour [3–6] generally
employ variants of active contours [8]. These methods attempt to minimize an
energy function consisting of parameters such as neighbor relations, contour

Electronic supplementary material The online version of this chapter (https://
doi.org/10.1007/978-3-030-33676-9_36) contains supplementary material, which is
available to authorized users.

G. A. Fink et al. (Eds.): DAGM GCPR 2019, LNCS 11824, pp. 513–521, 2019.
https://doi.org/10.1007/978-3-030-33676-9_36

slope, and proximity to the edges of the contour by using the image properties without any machine learning.

In recent years, deep-learning-based methods appeared to address this task. [1] uses Restricted Boltzmann Machines [10] (RBM) with a two-phase automatic encoder-decoder architecture for tongue contour extraction. In the first phase, the deep neural network is trained as an automatic encoder with both raw ultrasound image and the contour as an image. In the second phase, trained network is used as a decoder, only the raw image is given to the network and the contour image is taken as output. Another deep-learning based method [7] uses Convolutional Neural Network (CNN) based sU-Net architecture for the segmentation of ultrasound tongue contour images. Our earlier work [9] uses image parts for the training of CNN. A class is assigned to each image part according to its distance from the contour and the network is trained with these image parts. In the test phase the ultrasound tongue contour is extracted by using a sliding window method. [13] develops real time tongue contour tracker using SegNet [15] and U-net [16] but they consider the problem as a pixel segmentation task.

All these deep learning based studies handle ultrasound tongue contour tracking as a general contour tracking problem and they mostly consider the problem as a generic pixel classification task. We argue that the problem is very specialized and hence novel methods should be adopted to take advantage of problem specific constraints. Ultrasound tongue contours should be smooth and they also should move smoothly in time. Our proposed technique tracks the tongue contour by enforcing the above constraints using two types of LSTM networks: a spatial contour tracker and a spatiotemporal point tracker. Spatial contour tracker attempts to find smooth 2D tongue contours for each frame of an ultrasound tongue video. Spatiotemporal point tracker, on the other hand, uses the output of the spatial tracker and it attempts to track given tongue contour in time, enforcing temporal smoothness of the extracted contours. These two networks are trained in sequence to satisfy the expected spatial and temporal smoothness constraints at the same time. We collected data for this study to verify the final results which showed that the overall system exceeds state of the art accuracy rates and it is very fast at several frames per second.

The rest of this paper is organized as follows: Sect. 2 describes details the ultrasound visualization, Sect. 3 proposes spatial contour tracker and temporal point tracker, Sect. 4 includes experiments and Sect. 5 presents conclusion and feature studies.

2   Understanding the Ultrasound Visualization

In order enforce ultrasound image related tongue contour constraints in our tongue contour extraction task, we need to understand how the ultrasound images of the tongue is created. The ultrasound image is obtained by measuring time of return of the ultrasound waves that originate from ultrasound transducers. There are different ways of visualization of ultrasound data. Figure 1(a) shows a single wave of ultrasound transducer pointing to the tongue, Fig. 1(b) is

Amplitude-Mode ultrasound display, which shows the amplitude of the returned (echoed) ultrasound wave amplitude for a given time. Figure 1(c) is a single column of Brightness-Mode ultrasound display, which is equivalent to Amplitude-Mode display. Brightness-Mode shows the time of return values as image brightness values instead of amplitudes. If many ultrasound transducers are brought together as in Fig. 1(d) and their Brightness mode results are displayed in a single image, we obtain 2D B-Mode ultrasound display in polar coordinate system as shown in Fig. 1(f). Figure 1(e) is the rectangular coordinate system Brightness-Mode ultrasound image.

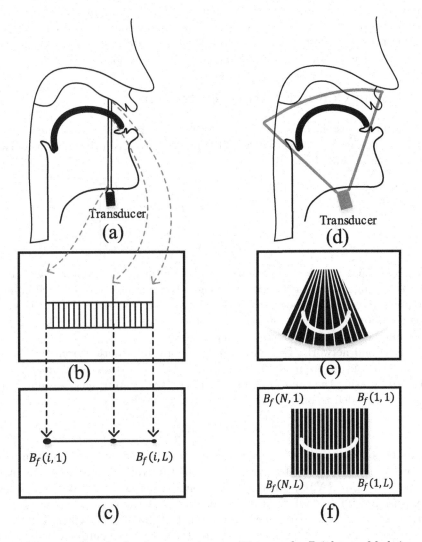

Fig. 1. Ultrasound modes for the tongue images. We use polar Brightness-Mode images (f) in our system. See Sect. 2 for details.

In this study, we use 2D Brightness-Mode ultrasound display images in polar coordinates. We formulate an ultrasound video image as $B_f(i, l)$ where f is the video frame index, i is the wave id that propagated from i^{th} transducer, l is the depth, i.e, the distance from the transducer. We consider minimum depth as 1 and maximum depth as L. Each columns of the polar Brightness-Mode image corresponds to a different single ultrasound transducer. Note that, the tongue surface can intersect with a single ultrasound wave at most once, which means each column of the polar Brightness-Mode image can contain only zero or one tongue contour point. This makes it possible to use a single column of this mode image as a feature vector input to an LSTM network. The output of this LSTM network would simply be the depth value of the tongue surface if that column intersects with the tongue surface. This type of design makes it very convenient to apply LSTM networks to the columns of Brightness-Mode ultrasound display images, which takes advantage of the overall ultrasound tongue image formation process.

3   Tongue Contour Extraction System

The proposed system uses 3 LSTM networks to enforce the constraints of the problem (see Fig. 2). The spatial S-LSTM network works on the columns of each video frame SF_f as shown by Eq. 1.

$$SF_f = \begin{bmatrix} B_f(1,1) & B_f(1,2) & \ldots & B_f(1,L) \\ B_f(2,1) & B_f(2,2) & \ldots & B_f(2,L) \\ \vdots & \vdots & \vdots & \vdots \\ B_f(N,1) & B_f(N,2) & \ldots & B_f(N,L) \end{bmatrix} \tag{1}$$

where each matrix row corresponds to one column in ultrasound image. During the training of this network, the tongue contour position for each column is represented as a one-hot vector. S-LSTM network works only on 2D video images without any time information. In other words, it can enforce smoothness constraints in 2D space but not in time dimension.

Our second network, TS-LSTM uses temporal information from the images by using the output from S-LSTM network. TS-LSTM trackers training data is obtained by using the same columns of consecutive video frames. Ground truth labels are encoded as one-hot vector, whose size is calculated as;

$$D = max(L) - min(L) \tag{2}$$

where D is the length of one-hot vector, $min(L)$ and $max(L)$ are minimum and maximum depths of tongue contours in the training data set. It can be represented as $H_f(N, D)$ where f is current frame, N is number of columns in ultrasound image and D is length of vector. If the corresponding element of this vector includes a tongue contour, then its value is 1, otherwise it is 0. As we mentioned previously, we know that the tongue contour can intersect with a given ultrasound beam at most once, which is reflected in the design of $H_f(N, D)$.

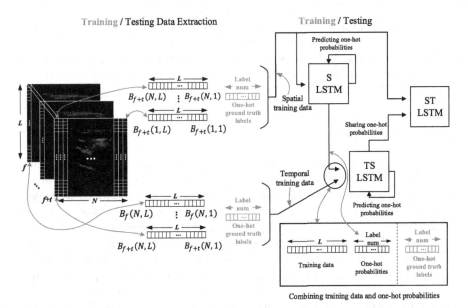

Fig. 2. Overall architecture of the proposed system.

The S-LSTM network is first trained with 2D image columns then one-hot probability vector is obtained by making prediction with the same data on model. Obtained vectors are appended at the end of temporal features, which is used for the training of TS-LSTM. For the column N, TS-LSTM's features can be represented as;

$$TSF_N = \begin{bmatrix} B_f(N,1) & \cdots & B_f(N,L) & H_f(N,1) & \cdots & H_f(N,D) \\ B_{f+1}(N,1) & \cdots & B_{f+1}(N,L) & H_{f+1}(N,1) & \cdots & H_{f+1}(N,D) \\ \vdots & \vdots & \vdots & \vdots & \vdots & \vdots \\ B_{f+t}(N,1) & \cdots & B_{f+t}(N,L) & H_{f+t}(N,1) & \cdots & H_{f+t}(N,D) \end{bmatrix} \quad (3)$$

Our systems final network is the spatiotemporal ST-LSTM network. TS-LSTM outputs are also one-hot vectors which are appended to ST-LSTM's input features. For frame f, spatial-temporal features are shown above.

$$STF_f = \begin{bmatrix} B_f(1,1) & \cdots & B_f(1,L) & H_f(1,1) & \cdots & H_f(1,D) \\ B_f(2,1) & \cdots & B_f(2,L) & H_f(2,1) & \cdots & H_f(2,D) \\ \vdots & \vdots & \vdots & \vdots & \vdots & \vdots \\ B_f(N,1) & \cdots & B_f(N,L) & H_f(N,1) & \cdots & H_f(N,D) \end{bmatrix} \quad (4)$$

During the testing phase, we follow the same steps as training phase without ground truth labels. The training data set is passed through the 3 bidirectional LSTM networks and a label is assigned to each column using temporal and spatial information. We fit a 3rd degree polynomial on the extracted points by using RANSAC algorithm [14] for continuous contours.

4   Experiments

The experiments were performed with 972 hand marked ultrasound tongue images that obtained from approximately 45 s of recording. 544 of the images were used for training, 428 for testing. The data set were obtained by making 2 sessions with 4 people. The images were converted to polar coordinates as 250×250 resolution image frames. All three LSTM networks parameters are 75 hidden nodes, 7 time steps and 20 batch size. Adam optimization algorithm was used for the optimization. The proposed method was implemented by using Keras [11] library with TensorFlow [2] back end. Two kinds of experiments were performed. First experiment was performed for observing temporal and spatial LSTM's effects of each others results. Table 1 shows that temporal info improves S-LSTM's results by 17.46%, spatial information improves T-LSTM's results by 59.3%. Although we did not use T-LSTM by itself in our system, we made experiments with it to show the importance of temporal and spatial information on the results. We also showed the effect of the two types of information on each other. In the first experiment, raw LSTM results are used, we did not apply RANSAC on found points. In our second experiment, we compared system results with the state of the art methods [1,4,13] (see Table 2). The MSD (Mean Sum of Distances) error measurement method that mentioned by [1] was used for making comparison. Our systems average MSD is 0.28 mm (1 px = 0.685 mm). For the DBN method, MSD is 1.0 mm (1 px = 0.295 mm) while the RT-Tracker achieved 0.91 mm (1 px = 0.638 mm). Active contour based methods MSD is 1.05 mm (1 px = 0.295 mm). We showed a few system outputs at Fig. 3.

Table 1. Network errors and improvements.

Network	MSD (mm)	MSD (px)	Improvement (%)
T LSTM (without one-hot features)	0.96	1.45	–
S LSTM (without one-hot features)	0.42	0.63	–
TS LSTM	0.39	0.59	59.3
ST LSTM	0.34	0.52	17.46

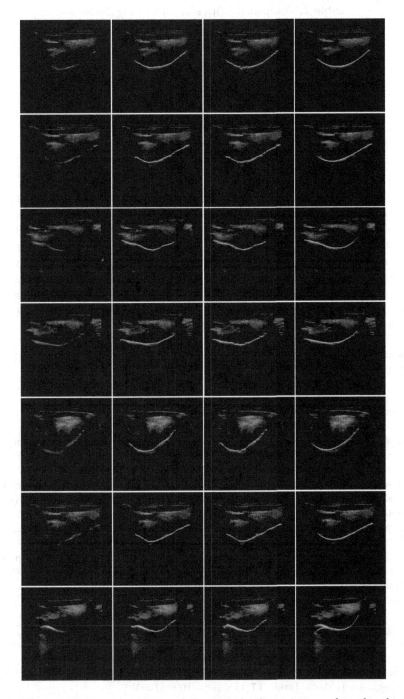

Fig. 3. The first column is raw images, the second column is ground truths, the third column is LSTM results, and the fourth column is RANSAC applied results.

Table 2. Comparison with state of the arts methods.

Method	MSD (mm)
Our System	0.28
R-T Tracker [13]	0.91
DBN [1]	1.0
Active Contour [4]	1.05

5   Conclusions

In this paper we proposed a specialized tongue contour tracker using ultrasound tongue contour characteristics. Unlike other methods based on deep learning, we did not consider the problem as a pixel classification task. We enforced some constraints directly from the ultrasound imaging. We defined three consecutive LSTM networks that consider the problem as spatially and temporally constrained. Our results achieved better results compared to the state of art deep learning based methods. The running time of the proposed system is promising for the applicability of real life employment. In future studies, we plan to make the system faster for real-time applications.

Acknowledgement. We like to thank Dr. Naci Dumlu of Pendik State Hospital, Istanbul for providing the experiment environment.

References

1. Fasel, I., Berry, J.: Deep belief networks for real-time extraction of tongue contours from ultrasound during speech. In: 20th International Conference on Pattern Recognition, pp. 1493–1496. IEEE, August 2010
2. Abadi, M., et al.: TensorFlow: a system for large-scale machine learning. In: 12th USENIX Symposium on Operating Systems Design and Implementation (OSDI 2016), pp. 265–283 (2016)
3. Akgul, Y.S., Kambhamettu, C., Stone, M.: Automatic extraction and tracking of the tongue contours. IEEE Trans. Med. Imaging **18**(10), 1035–1045 (1999)
4. Li, M., Kambhamettu, C., Stone, M.: Automatic contour tracking in ultrasound images. Clin. Linguist. Phonetics **19**(6–7), 545–554 (2005)
5. Stone, M.: A guide to analysing tongue motion from ultrasound images. Clin. Linguist. Phonetics **19**(6–7), 455–501 (2005)
6. Xu, K., et al.: Robust contour tracking in ultrasound tongue image sequences. Clin. Linguist. Phonetics **30**(3–5), 313–327 (2016)
7. Wen, S.: Automatic tongue contour segmentation using deep learning. Doctoral dissertation, Université d'Ottawa/University of Ottawa (2018)
8. Lai, K.F., Chin, R.T.: Deformable contours: modeling and extraction. IEEE Trans. Pattern Anal. Mach. Intell. **17**(11), 1084–1090 (1995)
9. Aslan, E., Dumlu, N., Akgul, Y.S.: Tongue contour extraction from ultrasound images using image parts. In: 26th Signal Processing and Communications Applications Conference (SIU), pp. 1–4. IEEE, May 2018

10. Hinton, G.E.: A practical guide to training restricted Boltzmann machines. In: Montavon, G., Orr, G.B., Müller, K.-R. (eds.) Neural Networks: Tricks of the Trade. LNCS, vol. 7700, pp. 599–619. Springer, Heidelberg (2012). https://doi. org/10.1007/978-3-642-35289-8_32

11. Chollet, F.: Keras: deep learning library for Theano and TensorFlow, GitHub Repos. (2015)

12. Gérard, J.M., Perrier, P., Payan, Y.: 3D biomechanical tongue modeling to study speech production, pp. 85–102 (2006)

13. Mozaffari, M.H., Wen, S., Wang, N., Lee, W.: Real-time automatic tongue contour tracking in ultrasound video for guided pronunciation training. In: Proceedings of the 14th International Joint Conference on Computer Vision, Imaging and Computer Graphics Theory and Applications, pp. 302–309 (2019)

14. Chum, O., Matas, J., Kittler, J.: Locally optimized RANSAC. In: Michaelis, B., Krell, G. (eds.) DAGM 2003. LNCS, vol. 2781, pp. 236–243. Springer, Heidelberg (2003). https://doi.org/10.1007/978-3-540-45243-0_31

15. Badrinarayanan, V., Kendall, A., Cipolla, R.: SegNet: a deep convolutional encoder-decoder architecture for image segmentation. IEEE Trans. Pattern Anal. Mach. Intell. 39(12), 2481–2495 (2017)

16. Ronneberger, O., Fischer, P., Brox, T.: U-Net: convolutional networks for biomedical image segmentation. In: Navab, N., Hornegger, J., Wells, W., Frangi, A. (eds.) MICCAI 2015. LNCS, vol. 9351, pp. 234–241. Springer, Cham (2015). https://doi. org/10.1007/978-3-319-24574-4_28

17. Makin, I.R.S., Dunki-Jacobs, R., Pellegrino, R.C., Slayton, M.H.: U.S. Patent No. 7,806,892. U.S. Patent and Trademark Office, Washington, DC (2010)

18. Makin, I.R., Avidor, Y., Barthe, P., Slayton, M.: U.S. Patent Application No. 10/847,209 (2005)

19. Bridal, S.L., Correas, J.M., Saied, A.M.E.N.A., Laugier, P.: Milestones on the road to higher resolution, quantitative, and functional ultrasonic imaging. Proc. IEEE 91(10), 1543–1561 (2003)

20. Abel, J., et al.: Ultrasound-enhanced multimodal approaches to pronunciation teaching and learning. Can. Acoust. 43(3), 124–125 (2015)

21. Bernhardt, M.B., et al.: Ultrasound as visual feedback in speech habilitation: exploring consultative use in rural British Columbia, Canada. Clin. Linguist. Phonetics 22(2), 149–162 (2008)

22. Preston, J.L., McCabe, P., Rivera-Campos, A., Whittle, J.L., Landry, E., Maas, E.: Ultrasound visual feedback treatment and practice variability for residual speech sound errors. J. Speech Lang. Hear. Res. 57(6), 2102–2115 (2014)

Localized Interactive Instance Segmentation

Soumajit Majumder[1]($\boxtimes$)(iD) and Angela Yao[2](iD)

[1] University of Bonn, Bonn, Germany
majumder@cs.uni-bonn.de
[2] National University of Singapore, Singapore, Singapore

Abstract. In current interactive instance segmentation works, the user is granted a free hand when providing clicks to segment an object; clicks are allowed on background pixels and other object instances far from the target object. This form of interaction is highly inconsistent with the end goal of efficiently isolating objects of interest. In our work, we propose a clicking scheme wherein user interactions are restricted to the proximity of the object. In addition, we propose a novel transformation of the user-provided clicks to generate a weak localization prior on the object which is consistent with image structures such as edges, textures etc. We demonstrate the effectiveness of our proposed clicking scheme and localization strategy through detailed experimentation in which we raise state-of-the-art on several standard interactive segmentation benchmarks.

1 Introduction

Interactive object selection or interactive instance segmentation allows users to select objects of interest down to a pixel level by providing inputs such as clicks, scribbles and bounding boxes. The selected results are useful for downstream applications such as image/video editing [3,23], medical diagnosis [39], image annotation tools [4] etc. GrabCut [37] is a pioneering example of interactive segmentation; other notable methods include Random Walk [15] and GeoS [10].

More recent methods [20,25,29,30,41] have approached the problem with deep learning architectures such as convolutional neural networks (CNNs). In deep interactive segmentation, the input consists of the RGB image as well as 'guidance' maps based on user-provided supervision. Users give 'positive' clicks on the object of interest and 'negative' clicks on the background or other objects in the scene. The guidance map helps the network to focus on the object instance to segment; in an iterative setting, it helps to correct errors from previous segmentations [3,25,28,29,41]. Typically, such guidance maps are generated via fixed rules and are not visible to the end user; only the image and intermediate and end segmentation results are visible to the interacting user.

For deep interactive segmentation, research efforts have predominantly been limited to introducing new architectures [3,28] and more sophisticated training

© Springer Nature Switzerland AG 2019
G. A. Fink et al. (Eds.): DAGM GCPR 2019, LNCS 11824, pp. 522–536, 2019.
https://doi.org/10.1007/978-3-030-33676-9_37

procedures [25, 28]. Yet minimizing user interaction and maintaining high quality segmentation requires a fine interplay between good specification of user interactions and careful leveraging of the provided inputs. Previous methods have ignored these aspects by allowing users to freely provide inputs [3, 28, 41] in any order and at any location in the scene. In addition, the guidance generated from the clicks are primitive and agnostic to structures present in the image [3, 28, 30].

In fact, the number and type of clicks to give, as well as how to encode user clicks are open research questions with enormous impact on the performance of the interactive system. For example, [29] showed that with improved click encodings, a simple base segmentation network such as the FCN-8s [27] can outperform methods [3, 28, 30] that use much deeper and stronger base networks such as ResNet-101 [18]. In this paper, we follow along this line of work in looking at how to cleverly specify and leverage user clicks to improve interactive instance segmentation. In this paper, our interest is in directing user clicks to weakly constrain the area of interest for interactive segmentation. Limiting the spatial extent is advantageous both for the network and the user, *i.e.* it tells the network which area to focus on for learning and also gives some indication of object scale; it also directs the user clicks to ambiguous locations which will most benefit from guidance.

Directing user clicks to specify the location may seem like an obvious way for interaction but few works on interactive segmentation have done so to date. Instead, they favour hard constraints enacted by directly cropping out the bounding boxes derived from user-given inputs [30] or object detections [40]. This hard crop relies on highly specific user inputs such as extreme points [30] which may slow down the user interaction, or having pre-trained object detectors for the object classes of interest for segmentation [40]. We favour a simple approach, where we ask users to first roughly localize objects with the first two interactions, *e.g.* on the two opposite corners in a bounding box, or clicking at the center of the object and one outside the object boundary. We propose using these first two interactions or clicks as the initial form of interaction. Ensuing corrective positive and negative clicks are constrained to be outside and within the enclosing boundary.

In addition, we propose a new transformation scheme for the user-provided clicks which provides a weak localization prior on the object of interest and is consistent with low-level structures such as edges, textures, etc in the scene. Unlike [40], this prior is generated without using class-specific bounding box detections. With the arrival of newer clicks, this proposed transformation gradually refines the localization prior. Our proposed approach can deal naturally with several types of guidance modalities, including superpixel-based guidances [29] and bounding box type guidances [40]. Our key contributions are:

- a simple yet efficient clicking scheme which focuses the user's attention to the object of interest and its vicinity,
- a novel transformation of the user clicks which provides a weak localization prior on the object; with the arrival of new user clicks the generated guidance map gradually refines to the object boundary.

- state-of-the-art performance on three interactive image segmentation bench-marks including the challenging MS COCO [26]; like other competing meth-ods in literature, through simulation of user clicks, we significantly reduce the amount of user input required to generate accurate segmentation.

2   Related Works

The development of automated semantic and instance segmentation frameworks is a rapidly growing area in computer vision [9,42,43]. Accompanying this line of work is *interactive* segmentation - where users give clicks, scribbles, or bounding boxes to adjust and improve the outputs of these fully automated methods. Early interactive image segmentation approaches include parametric active contours, snakes [22] and intelligent scissors [32]. Since these methods focus primarily on boundary properties, they suffer when edge evidence is weak. More recent methods are based on graph cuts [5,23,37,38], geodesics [2,10], or a combination of both [16,36]. However, since these methods try to separate foreground and background solely based on low-level features such as colour and texture, they are not robust and fare poorly when segmenting images with similar foreground and background appearances, intricate textures, and poor lighting.

Recently, deep convolutional neural networks (CNNs) have been incorporated into interactive segmentation frameworks. The initial work of [41] uses Euclidean distance maps to represent user-provided positive and negative clicks which are then concatenated with the original colour image and provided as input to a fully convolutional network [27]. Following works have focused primarily on making extensions with newer CNN architectures [3,28] and iterative training proce-dures [25,28]. Instead of training with fixed user clicks as input [41], iterative training algorithms [25,28] progressively add clicks based on the error of the network predictions.

In the majority of interactive segmentation frameworks, user guidance has been provided in the form of point-wise clicks [20,24,25,28,30,41] which are then transformed into a Euclidean distance map [20,24,41]. One observation made in [3,28,30] was that encoding the clicks as Gaussians led to performance improvement because it localizes the clicks better [28] and can encode both positive and negative click in a single channel [3]. A more recent work [4] observed encoding user clicks as small binary disks to be more effective than Gaussian and the Euclidean encoding.

Different to [3,4,25,28,30,41], we use guidance maps which are consistent with the low-level image structures. Additionally, we propose a superpixel box guidance map which provides weak localization cues to the network. This is similar in spirit to [4,30,40] in which object bounding boxes are cropped out from extreme points specified by the user [30], (loose) ground truth bounding boxes [4] or object detections [40]. Our work relaxes the hard constraint of [30], wherein clicks have to be placed on the four extremities of the object and on the object boundary. Furthermore, unlike [40], our proposed superpixel box guidance is class-agnostic and does not require having pre-trained object detectors available.

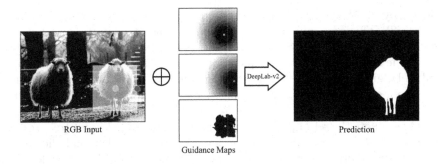

RGB Input   Prediction

Guidance Maps

Fig. 1. Outline. Given an image and user clicks, we transform the positive and negative clicks (denoted by the green and red circles respectively) into three separate channels - 2 channel superpixel-based (middle column, rows 1–2) and 1 superpixel-box (middle column, row 3) guidance map. These are concatenated (denoted by ⊕) with the 3-channel image input and is fed to our base segmentation network.

3 Proposed Method

We adopt the common approach for interactive segmentation that has been used in previous deep learning-based frameworks [3,25,28,29,41]. The user provides inputs on the original RGB image in the form of *'positive'* and *'negative'* clicks to indicate foreground and background respectively. The clicks are then encoded into guidance maps via transformations (Sects. 3.2 and 3.3).

Typically, pixel values on the guidance map are a function of the pixel distance on the image grid to the points of interaction (see Fig. 2). This includes Euclidean [20,41] and Gaussian guidance maps [3,28,30]. However, such guidance maps are generated in an image-agnostic manner with the assumption that pixels in an image are independent of one another. Alternative variants take image structures such as superpixels [7,29] and region-based object proposals [29] into consideration for generating guidance maps. Guidance maps are then concatenated as additional channels to the input image and passed through the network [7,25,29,30,41] (see Fig. 1).

3.1 Interaction Loop

In previous works [3,20,28,29,41], the user has the liberty to provide clicks anywhere in the scene. This includes clicking on object instances far from the one of interest. Intuitively, a user interested in recovering an object instance from the scene would primarily fixate in the vicinity of the object of interest and focus more on delineating the object from the nearby background. Additionally, unconstrained clicks on the background and other objects fail to provide hints on the whereabouts of the object which calls for additional click sampling strategies are proposed [3,28,41] to ensure negative clicks encompassing the object.

We propose a simple yet intuitive interaction framework. At the onset of interaction, the user provides a click at the center of the object of interest followed by another click on a background pixel in the vicinity of the object (see Fig. 2). This first pair of clicks is used to generate a coarse prior on the location of the object (see Sect. 3.3) in the form of an enclosing box. We then restrict the locations of user subsequent inputs. More specifically, negative clicks need to be given inside the estimated bounding box, while positive clicks need to be given outside. In turn, the new positive clicks are then used to update the location prior.

Let us denote the set of positive and negative clicks as $\{c_i^+\}$ and $\{c_i^-\}$ respectively for $i = \{1, \cdots, n\}$ and the initial foreground and background click as c_0^+ and c_0^- respectively. Based on $\{c_0^+, c_0^-\}$, a coarse prior $\mathcal{G}$ on the object location is generated (see Sect. 3.3) specified by the corners e_0 and e_1. We then restrict the locations of user subsequent inputs. More specifically, negative clicks need to be given inside the estimated object location, while positive clicks need to be given outside. The new positive clicks are used to update the enclosing corners $\tilde{e}_0$ and $\tilde{e}_1$, while all additional clicks, $c_{i\neq0}^+$ and $c_{i\neq0}^-$, are used to update $\mathcal{G}$.

3.2 Superpixel-Based Guidance Maps

Superpixels are known for their ability to group locally similar pixels [14,19,33]. For our guidance maps, we consider the superpixel-based variant of [29] which outperformed approaches using Euclidean and Gaussian guidance maps. In [29], user clicks given at single pixels are propagated to entire superpixels. Guidance values of other superpixels in the scene are then given by the minimum Euclidean distance from the centroid of each superpixel to the centroid of a user-selected superpixel.

More specifically, let $\{\mathcal{Z}\}$ denote the set of superpixels constituting an image and $f_{\mathcal{Z}}^p$ denote a function which maps every pixel p to its corresponding superpixel. Let $\{z^+\} = f_{\mathcal{Z}}^p(\{c^+\})$ and $\{z^-\} = f_{\mathcal{Z}}^p(\{c^-\})$ be the set of positive and negative superpixels based on the user-provided clicks. The value of each pixel for the guidance map $\mathcal{S}_{\mathcal{Z}}^+(p)$ corresponding to the set of positive clicks $\{c^+\}$ is given by,

$$\mathcal{S}_{\mathcal{Z}}^+(p) = \min_{z \in \{z^+\}} d_c^2(z, f_{\mathcal{Z}}^p(p)), \tag{1}$$

and likewise for $\mathcal{S}_{\mathcal{Z}}^-(\cdot)$ for $\{c^-\}$. In Eq. 1, $d_c^2(z_i, z_j)$ is the Euclidean distance between the centroids z_i^c and z_j^c of superpixels z_i and z_j respectively, where $z_i^c = (\sum_i x_i/|z_i|, \sum_i y_i/|z_i|)$ and $|z_i|$ is the number of superpixels in z_i. The values of the guidance maps are truncated to 255. Examples of positive and negative superpixel-based guidance maps are shown in Fig. 2, rows 3 and 4 respectively. We additionally experimented with guidance maps generated based on the CIE-LAB color difference between the annotated superpixels and the other superpixels as per [7] but we did not observe any promising results.

3.3 Superpixel-Box Guidance Map

Cropping images to exactly contain the object of interest has been shown to improve interactive segmentation performance [4,30]. However, such frameworks are limited by the placement of the additional clicks; [30] requires corrective clicks to be placed precisely on object boundaries. Besides, cropping leads to a set of unnatural training images dominated by the object of interest. This prevents the network from learning from the background regions. Unlike [30], we refrain from cropping the image to contain only the object of interest.

Instead, we provide, as an additional guidance channel, a weak prior on the whereabouts of the object in the scene based on the initial pair of clicks. With additional clicks, the guidance channel updates the prior. At the onset, it behaves like a weak rectilinear enclosing albeit consistent with low-level image features (*e.g.* edges). With the arrival of additional clicks, it gets further refined into sloppy contours [12], and provides the segmentation network with a strong cue on the location of the objects (see Fig. 2). Unlike object-based guidance maps [29] generated based on object proposals [35], our proposed guidance is more flexible and adapts more quickly to the user-provided inputs.

More formally, given the first pair of positive and negative click $c_0^+ = (x_0^+, y_0^+)$ and $c_0^- = (x_0^-, y_0^-)$ for an image, we obtain the top-left and the bottom-right co-ordinates of the object, e_0 and e_1 respectively. Let $\{\mathcal{Z}_b\} \subset \{\mathcal{Z}\}$ be the set of superpixels which lie on or inside the spatial extent defined by e_0 and e_1. The value of each pixel p of the superpixel-box based guidance map is given by,

$$\mathcal{G}(p) = \mathbf{1}[p \subset z] \cdot \mathbf{1}[z \subset \{\mathcal{Z}_b\}] \qquad (2)$$

where $\mathbf{1}[p \subset z]$ is an indicator function which returns 1 if pixel p lies belongs to superpixel z. $\mathbf{1}[z \subset \{\mathcal{Z}_b\}]$ returns 1 if superpixel z belongs to the set of superpixels $\{\mathcal{Z}_b\}$. For the additional set of clicks $\{c_{i\neq0}^+\}$ and $\{c_{i\neq0}^-\}$, we obtain the updated guidance map $\hat{\mathcal{G}}(p)$ as follows,

$$\{z_{i\neq0}^+\} = f_\mathcal{Z}^p(\{c_{i\neq0}^+\}) \qquad (3)$$

$$\{z_{i\neq0}^-\} = f_\mathcal{Z}^p(\{c_{i\neq0}^-\}) \qquad (4)$$

$$\{\hat{\mathcal{Z}}_b\} = \{\mathcal{Z}_b\} \cup \{z_{i\neq0}^+\} \setminus \{z_{i\neq0}^-\} \qquad (5)$$

$$\hat{\mathcal{G}}(p) = \mathbf{1}[p \subset z] \cdot \mathbf{1}[z \subset \{\hat{\mathcal{Z}}_b\}] \qquad (6)$$

3.4 Simulating User Interactions

To train and test our network, we simulate user interactions, as per previous works on interactive segmentation [3,28,41]. For simulating user interactions, we make use of the ground truth masks of PASCAL VOC 2012 [13] along with the additional masks from Semantic Boundaries Dataset (SBD) [17]. We use the centroid of the ground truth masks as our first positive click; for concave object masks, clicks falling outside the object mask are relocated to a point within the object. We then displace the click location by 20-50 pixels randomly; we ensure that the final click location remains within the object. This is done to introduce variation in the training data; the perturbation prevents center clicks to always fall on the same superpixel during each training iteration and also better approximates true user interactions which may not perfectly localize the

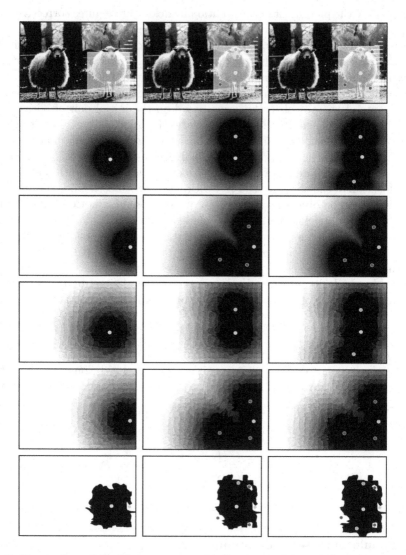

Fig. 2. Examples of Guidance maps: At the onset of interaction, our approach receives an initial pair of enclosing clicks (denoted by yellow and blue at the center of the object and on a background pixel respectively). These clicks are transformed into guidance maps. With each round of additional clicking, the guidance maps are updated by considering the positive clicks (shown in green) and negative clicks (shown in red). Examples of user click transformations are shown in rows 2 to 6; rows 2–3: positive and negative Euclidean distance maps, rows 4–5: positive and negative superpixel-based guidance maps, row 6: the superpixel-box guidance. The values of the superpixel-box guidance are inverted for ease of visualization. The image along with the guidance maps are used as input for the segmentation network. *Note that euclidean distance maps are not used as guidance maps in our approach.* (Color figure online)

object center. Next, we sample the first negative click which is at least d pixels away from the center click; in our experiments for a bounding box of height h and width w, we set d to be,

$$d = (r_1 - r_2) \cdot w + (1 + r_2) \cdot h \tag{7}$$

where r_1 is sampled from the uniform distribution $\mathcal{U}(0, 1)$ and r_2 is sampled from the normal distribution $\mathcal{N}(0, 1)$. We use the first pair of clicks to generate the enclosing superpixel box; we keep superpixel boxes with an intersection over union (IoU) of ≥ 0.7. For simulating additional positive and negative clicks, we randomly pick 2–5 superpixels from the set of superpixels lying outside the enclosing box and inside respectively.

4 Experimentation

4.1 Datasets and Evaluation

We evaluate the performance our proposed method on five publicly available datasets used for benchmarking interactive image and video segmentation [7,25,29,30,41]: PASCAL VOC 2012 [13], GrabCut [37], Berkeley [31], MS COCO [26] and DAVIS-2016 [34].

PASCAL VOC 2012 consists of 1464 training and 1449 validation images across 20 object classes; many images contain multiple objects. For training, we consider the 1464 images plus the additional instance annotations from SBD provided by [17] which results in around 20,000 instances across 20 object classes.

GrabCut is a small dataset (50 images) and is one of the simpler interactive segmentation benchmark. The images consist of a single foreground object mostly with a distinctive appearance.

Berkeley consists of 100 images with a single foreground object. The images in this dataset are representative of the typical challenges encountered in interactive segmentation such as heavily textured backgrounds, low contrast between the foreground object and the background, etc.

MS COCO is a large-scale image segmentation dataset with 80 different object categories, 20 of which are common with Pascal VOC 2012. For fair comparison with [25,29,41], we split the dataset into the 20 PASCAL VOC 2012 categories and the 60 additional categories, and randomly sample 10 images per category for evaluation.

DAVIS-2016 is a dataset for video object segmentation. It consists of 50 video sequences 20 from which are in the validation set. The sequences feature a single foreground object; the pixel mask of the object is provided for all frames.

Evaluation. The performance of fully automated instance segmentation algorithms is usually measured by the average mean intersection over union (mIoU) between the ground truth and the predicted object mask. In interactive segmentation, a user can always provide more positive and negative clicks to further improve the predicted segmentation. The established way of evaluating an interactive system is based on the number of clicks required for each object instance to achieve a fixed mIoU [3,28,29,41]. This fixed mIoU threshold is 90% for Grab-Cut and Berkeley and 85% for the more challenging Pascal VOC 2012 and MS COCO. Like [3,25,28,29,41], we threshold the maximum number of clicks per instance to 20 clicks. Unlike [3,25,41], we do not apply any post-processing with a conditional random field.

4.2 Implementation Details

Model Architecture. As our base segmentation network, we use DeepLab-v2 [8]; it consists of a ResNet-101 [18] backbone and a Pyramid Scene Parsing network [44] acting as the prediction head. The output of the CNN is a probability map representing whether a pixel belongs to the object. We initialize the weights from a network DeepLab-v2 model pre-trained on ImageNet [11], and fine-tuned on PASCAL VOC 2012 for semantic segmentation.

Training Data. We further tune the network for instance segmentation on the 1464 training images of PASCAL VOC 2012 [13] with the instance-level masks, along with the 10582 images of SBD [17]. We further augment the training samples with random scaling, flipping and rotation operations.

Superpixels. We use SLIC [1] as our superpixeling algorithm. We generate around 1000 superpixels on an average per image; using 1000 SLIC superpixels over 500 SLIC superpixels have been shown to improve performance [29]. Generating finer superpixels ($\geq$2000 superpixels per image) degrades the performance as the superpixel-based guidance map degenerates to the Euclidean distance map. During evaluation on the GrabCut [37], Berkeley [31], MS COCO [26] and DAVIS-2016 [34] dataset, we roughly generate 1000 SLIC superpixels [1] for each image.

Training Details. Our network is trained to minimize a pixel-wise binary cross-entropy loss between the ground truth mask and the predicted mask. For optimization, we use stochastic gradient descent with Nesterov momentum with its default value of 0.9. The learning rate is fixed at 10^{-7} across all epochs and weight decay is $5 \cdot 10^{-4}$. A mini-batch of size 5 is used. The implementation is done in PyTorch and built on top of the implementation provided by [30]. We train our network for 50 epochs.

Guidance Dropout. Dropout can be incorporated into the guidance inputs by introducing fixed-value maps into the training scheme with some probability. Guidance dropout has been shown to be effective for interactive segmentation [29] since it encourages the base segmentation network which is trained for semantic segmentation to switch over to instance segmentation without any user interaction. Following [29], during training, when the network receives an image with single object, we fix the value of 255 for the superpixel-based and the superpixel-box based guidance map with a probability of 0.1 to encourage good initial segmentations in absence of clicks. Additionally to make it robust to the number of user clicks, during training, we provide guidance maps with a single positive click (at the center) and the initial positive-negative click pair with a probability of 0.1.

4.3 Ablation Studies

We perform an ablation study to analyze the impact of different components in our interactive instance segmentation pipeline on the Berkeley dataset [31] (see Table 1). Similar to the observation in [29], using a superpixel-based guidance map leads to a significant improvement over its euclidean distance map counterpart (denoted by EU) as used in iFCN [41] (Table 1, rows 1–2). We observe additional gains from adopting the more recent ResNet-101 [18] as our backbone architecture w.r.t FCN-8s [27] as used in [29] (Table 1, row 3).

Table 1. Ablation study on the Berkeley dataset [31]

EU	SP	BBox	SPBox	DT	Base Network	Berkeley @90%
✓					FCN-8s [27]	8.65 [41]
	✓				FCN-8s [27]	6.67 [29]
	✓				ResNet-101 [18]	6.32
	✓	✓		✓	ResNet-101 [18]	5.49
	✓	✓			ResNet-101 [18]	5.26
	✓		✓		ResNet-101 [18]	5.18

Next, the benefits of having a weak localization prior on the object of interest as an additional mode of guidance Table 1, rows 4–6). BBox refers to the rectilinear box drawn between corner pixel locations e_0 and e_1 generated from user clicks $\{c_i^+\}$ and $\{c_i^-\}$. SPBox refers to the superpixel-box guidance generated from $\{c_i^+\}$ and $\{c_i^-\}$ (Sect. 3.3, Eq. 2–6). Having a weak localization prior is shown to improve results across the board; the improvement is higher when using the SPBox guidance. Additionally, we consider the distance transform (DT) of the BBox as guidance but the average number of clicks increase from 5.26 to 5.49. Throughout our experiments, we use the superpixel-based guidances and the superpixel-box guidance as our guidance maps.

4.4   Comparison to State of the Art

We compare the average number of clicks required to reach a required mIoU (see Table 2) against existing interactive segmentation approaches. We achieve the lowest number of clicks required for the GrabCut and for the challenging MS COCO (both seen and unseen categories) datasets, proving the benefits of restricting the interaction to only the object of interest. In Fig. 3, we show some qualitative results from the PASCAL VOC 2012 validation set.

As shown in Table 2, our full model needs the fewest number of clicks to reach the required mIoU threshold of 90% on GrabCut, with a relative improvement

Table 2. The average number of clicks required to achieve a particular mIoU. The best results are indicated in **bold**.

Method	GrabCut @90%	Berkeley @90%	VOC12 @85%	MS COCO seen@85%	MS COCO unseen@85%
iFCN [41]	6.04	8.65	6.88	8.31	7.82
RIS-Net [25]	5.00	6.03	5.12	5.98	6.44
ITIS [28]	5.60	-	3.80	-	-
DEXTR [30]	4.00	-	4.00	-	-
VOS-Wild [3]	3.80	-	5.60	-	-
FCTSFN [20]	3.76	6.49	4.58	9.62	9.62
IIS-LD [24]	4.79	-	-	12.45	12.45
MLG [29]	3.58	5.60	**3.62**	5.40	6.10
BRS [21]	3.60	**5.08**	-	-	-
Ours	**3.46**	5.18	3.70	**5.15**	**5.70**

Fig. 3. Qualitative Results Examples of high-quality object segmentations generated on PASCAL VOC 2012. *Note that final segmentation masks might not align to object boundaries as no CRF-based post-processing was performed.*

of 3.3%. For MS COCO, we observe an improvement of 4.6% and 6.5% over the 20 seen and 60 unseen object categories respectively. We also report a relative 7.5% improvement for PASCAL VOC 2012 *val* set w.r.t previous state-of-art algorithms using a fixed clicking scheme [30]. For MS COCO dataset, it should be noted that FCTSFN [20] and IIS-LD [24] report their result averaged over all the 80 object categories.

4.5   Correcting Masks for Video Object Segmentation

Fully automated video object segmentation techniques can generate object segmentation masks of unsatisfactory quality; such masks are unsuitable for their intended downstream application. These scenarios can benefit from interactive segmentation approaches. Given an unsatisfactory prediction, users can provide additional clicks to improve the mask. Following [3,28], we proceed to improve the worst segmentation masks per sequence as generated by OSVOS [6]. The changed mIoU is reported after the addition of 1, 4 and 10 clicks.

Table 3. Refinement of the worst predictions from OSVOS [6] on DAVIS-2016 [34] (performance measured in mIoU).

Method	OSVOS [6]	1-click	4-clicks	10-clicks
GrabCut [37]	50.4	46.6	53.5	68.8
iFCN [41]	50.4	55.7	71.3	79.9
VOS-Wild [3]	50.4	63.8	75.7	82.2
ITIS [28]	50.4	67.0	77.1	82.8
Ours	50.4	**72.2**	**80.1**	**84.3**

We initialize our enclosing area for the superpixel-box guidance map based on the initial segmentation by OSVOS. Superpixel-based guidance maps are set to a value of 255. We then provide additional positive and negative clicks to improve the mask quality which are then used to update the superpixel-based guidance maps. Our proposed algorithm reports a significant gain of over 5% in mIoU for a single click and also outperforms the reported results for 4 and 10 clicks (see Table 3).

5   Conclusion

In this paper, we demonstrate that limiting the extent of user interaction to only the object of interest can significantly reduce the amount of user interaction required to obtain satisfactory segmentations. Additionally, via experiments, we demonstrate the benefits of having a weak localization prior generated in the form of superpixel box guidance. Our proposed algorithm primarily faced difficulties when trying to segment occluded instances. In such cases, the superpixel box guidance overlaps significantly, making it difficult for the network to segment both the instances properly.

Acknowledgement. Research in this paper was partly supported by the Singapore Ministry of Education Academic Research Fund Tier 1. We also gratefully acknowledge NVIDIA's donation of a Titan X Pascal GPU.

References

1. Achanta, R., Shaji, A., Smith, K., Lucchi, A., Fua, P., Süsstrunk, S., et al.: SLIC superpixels compared to state-of-the-art superpixel methods. TPAMI **34**(11), 2274–2282 (2012)
2. Bai, X., Sapiro, G.: Geodesic matting: a framework for fast interactive image and video segmentation and matting. IJCV **82**(2), 113–132 (2009)
3. Benard, A., Gygli, M.: Interactive video object segmentation in the wild. arXiv preprint arXiv:1801.00269 (2017)
4. Benenson, R., Popov, S., Ferrari, V.: Large-scale interactive object segmentation with human annotators. In: CVPR, pp. 11700–11709 (2019)
5. Boykov, Y.Y., Jolly, M.P.: Interactive graph cuts for optimal boundary and region segmentation of objects in N-D images. In: ICCV, pp. 105–112 (2001)
6. Caelles, S., Maninis, K.K., Pont-Tuset, J., Leal-Taixé, L., Cremers, D., Van Gool, L.: One-shot video object segmentation. In: CVPR, pp. 221–230 (2017)
7. Chen, D.J., Chien, J.T., Chen, H.T., Chang, L.W.: Tap and shoot segmentation. In: AAAI (2018)
8. Chen, L.C., Papandreou, G., Kokkinos, I., Murphy, K., Yuille, A.L.: Deeplab: semantic image segmentation with deep convolutional nets, atrous convolution, and fully connected crfs. TPAMI **40**(4), 834–848 (2018)
9. Chen, L.-C., Zhu, Y., Papandreou, G., Schroff, F., Adam, H.: Encoder-decoder with atrous separable convolution for semantic image segmentation. In: Ferrari, V., Hebert, M., Sminchisescu, C., Weiss, Y. (eds.) ECCV 2018. LNCS, vol. 11211, pp. 833–851. Springer, Cham (2018). https://doi.org/10.1007/978-3-030-01234-2_49
10. Criminisi, A., Sharp, T., Blake, A.: GeoS: geodesic image segmentation. In: Forsyth, D., Torr, P., Zisserman, A. (eds.) ECCV 2008. LNCS, vol. 5302, pp. 99–112. Springer, Heidelberg (2008). https://doi.org/10.1007/978-3-540-88682-2_9
11. Deng, J., Dong, W., Socher, R., Li, L.J., Li, K., Fei-Fei, L.: Imagenet: a large-scale hierarchical image database. In: CVPR, pp. 248–255 (2009)
12. Dutt Jain, S., Grauman, K.: Predicting sufficient annotation strength for interactive foreground segmentation. In: ICCV, pp. 1313–1320 (2013)
13. Everingham, M., Van Gool, L., Williams, C.K., Winn, J., Zisserman, A.: The pascal visual object classes (voc) challenge. IJCV **88**(2), 303–338 (2010)
14. Faktor, A., Irani, M.: Video segmentation by non-local consensus voting. In: BMVC (2014)
15. Grady, L., Schiwietz, T., Aharon, S., Westermann, R.: Random walks for interactive organ segmentation in two and three dimensions: implementation and validation. In: Duncan, J.S., Gerig, G. (eds.) MICCAI 2005. LNCS, vol. 3750, pp. 773–780. Springer, Heidelberg (2005). https://doi.org/10.1007/11566489_95
16. Gulshan, V., Rother, C., Criminisi, A., Blake, A., Zisserman, A.: Geodesic star convexity for interactive image segmentation. In: CVPR, pp. 3129–3136 (2010)

17. Hariharan, B., Arbelaez, P., Bourdev, L., Maji, S., Malik, J.: Semantic contours from inverse detectors. In: ICCV, pp. 991–998 (2011)
18. He, K., Zhang, X., Ren, S., Sun, J.: Deep residual learning for image recognition. In: CVPR, pp. 770–778 (2016)
19. He, X., Zemel, R.S., Ray, D.: Learning and incorporating top-down cues in image segmentation. In: Leonardis, A., Bischof, H., Pinz, A. (eds.) ECCV 2006. LNCS, vol. 3951, pp. 338–351. Springer, Heidelberg (2006). https://doi.org/10.1007/11744023_27
20. Hu, Y., Soltoggio, A., Lock, R., Carter, S.: A fully convolutional two-stream fusion network for interactive image segmentation. Neural Netw. 109, 31–42 (2019)
21. Jang, W.D., Kim, C.S.: Interactive image segmentation via backpropagating refinement scheme. In: CVPR, pp. 5297–5306 (2019)
22. Kass, M., Witkin, A., Terzopoulos, D.: Snakes: Active contour models. IJCV 1(4), 321–331 (1988)
23. Li, Y., Sun, J., Tang, C.K., Shum, H.Y.: Lazy snapping. ACM Trans. Graph. (ToG) 23(3), 303–308 (2004)
24. Li, Z., Chen, Q., Koltun, V.: Interactive image segmentation with latent diversity. In: CVPR, pp. 577–585 (2018)
25. Liew, J., Wei, Y., Xiong, W., Ong, S.H., Feng, J.: Regional interactive image segmentation networks. In: ICCV, pp. 2746–2754 (2017)
26. Lin, T.-Y., et al.: Microsoft COCO: common objects in context. In: Fleet, D., Pajdla, T., Schiele, B., Tuytelaars, T. (eds.) ECCV 2014. LNCS, vol. 8693, pp. 740–755. Springer, Cham (2014). https://doi.org/10.1007/978-3-319-10602-1_48
27. Long, J., Shelhamer, E., Darrell, T.: Fully convolutional networks for semantic segmentation. In: CVPR, pp. 3431–3440 (2015)
28. Mahadevan, S., Voigtlaender, P., Leibe, B.: Iteratively trained interactive segmentation. In: BMVC (2018)
29. Majumder, S., Yao, A.: Content-aware multi-level guidance for interactive instance segmentation. In: CVPR, pp. 11602–11611 (2019)
30. Maninis, K.K., Caelles, S., Pont-Tuset, J., Van Gool, L.: Deep extreme cut: from extreme points to object segmentation. In: CVPR, pp. 616–625 (2018)
31. McGuinness, K., O'connor, N.E.: A comparative evaluation of interactive segmentation algorithms. Pattern Recogn. 43(2), 434–444 (2010)
32. Mortensen, E.N., Barrett, W.A.: Intelligent scissors for image composition. In: SIGGRAPH, pp. 191–198 (1995)
33. Papazoglou, A., Ferrari, V.: Fast object segmentation in unconstrained video. In: ICCV, pp. 1777–1784 (2013)
34. Perazzi, F., Pont-Tuset, J., McWilliams, B., Van Gool, L., Gross, M., Sorkine-Hornung, A.: A benchmark dataset and evaluation methodology for video object segmentation. In: CVPR, pp. 724–732 (2016)
35. Pont-Tuset, J., Arbelaez, P., Barron, J.T., Marques, F., Malik, J.: Multiscale combinatorial grouping for image segmentation and object proposal generation. TPAMI 39(1), 128–140 (2017)
36. Price, B.L., Morse, B., Cohen, S.: Geodesic graph cut for interactive image segmentation. In: CVPR, pp. 3161–3168 (2010)
37. Rother, C., Kolmogorov, V., Blake, A.: Grabcut: Interactive foreground extraction using iterated graph cuts. ACM Trans. Graph. (TOG) 23(3), 309–314 (2004)
38. Vezhnevets, V., Konouchine, V.: Growcut: Interactive multi-label nd image segmentation by cellular automata. Graphicon. 1, 150–156 (2005)
39. Wang, G., et al.: DeepIGeoS: a deep interactive geodesic framework for medical image segmentation. TPAMI 41, 1559–1572 (2018)

40. Xu, N., Price, B., Cohen, S., Yang, J., Huang, T.: Deep grabcut for object selection. In: BMVC (2017)
41. Xu, N., Price, B., Cohen, S., Yang, J., Huang, T.S.: Deep interactive object selection. In: CVPR, pp. 373–381 (2016)
42. Yu, C., Wang, J., Peng, C., Gao, C., Yu, G., Sang, N.: Learning a discriminative feature network for semantic segmentation. In: CVPR, pp. 1857–1866 (2018)
43. Zhang, H., et al.: Context encoding for semantic segmentation. In: CVPR, pp. 7151–7160 (2018)
44. Zhao, H., Shi, J., Qi, X., Wang, X., Jia, J.: Pyramid scene parsing network. In: CVPR, pp. 2881–2890 (2017)

Iterative Greedy Matching for 3D Human Pose Tracking from Multiple Views

Julian Tanke$^{(\boxtimes)}$ and Juergen Gall

University of Bonn, Bonn, Germany
{tanke,gall}@iai.uni-bonn.de

Abstract. In this work we propose an approach for estimating 3D human poses of multiple people from a set of calibrated cameras. Estimating 3D human poses from multiple views has several compelling properties: human poses are estimated within a global coordinate space and multiple cameras provide an extended field of view which helps in resolving ambiguities, occlusions and motion blur. Our approach builds upon a real-time 2D multi-person pose estimation system and greedily solves the association problem between multiple views. We utilize bipartite matching to track multiple people over multiple frames. This proofs to be especially efficient as problems associated with greedy matching such as occlusion can be easily resolved in 3D. Our approach achieves state-of-the-art results on popular benchmarks and may serve as a baseline for future work.

1 Introduction

3D human pose tracking has applications in surveillance [40] and analysis of sport events [7,23]. Most existing approaches [19,21,25–29,33,38] address 3D human pose estimation from single images while multi-view 3D human pose estimation [3,4,7,12,23] remains less explored, as obtaining and maintaining a configuration of calibrated cameras is difficult and costly. However, in sports or surveillance, calibrated multi-camera setups are available and can be leveraged for accurate human pose estimation and tracking. Utilizing multiple views has several obvious advantages over monocular 3D human pose estimation: ambiguities introduced by foreshortening as well as body joint occlusions or motion blurs can be resolved using other views. Furthermore, human poses are estimated within a global coordinate system when using calibrated cameras.

In this work we propose an iterative greedy matching algorithm based on epipolar geometry to approximately solve the k-partite matching problem of multiple human detections in multiple cameras. To this end we utilize a real-time 2D pose estimation framework and achieve very strong results on challenging multi-camera datasets. The common 3D space proves to be very robust for greedy tracking, resulting in a very efficient and well-performing algorithm. In contrast to previous works [7,13,23,34], our approach does not discretize the solution space but combines triangulation with an efficient pose association approach across camera views and time. Furthermore, our approach does not utilize individual shape models for each person [26].

© Springer Nature Switzerland AG 2019
G. A. Fink et al. (Eds.): DAGM GCPR 2019, LNCS 11824, pp. 537–550, 2019.
https://doi.org/10.1007/978-3-030-33676-9_38

Fig. 1. Qualitative results on the Shelf [3] dataset.

We make the following contributions: (i) we present a greedy approach for 3D multi-person tracking from multiple calibrated cameras and show that our approach achieves state-of-the-art results. (ii) We provide extensive experiments on both 3D human pose estimation and on 3D human pose tracking on various multi-person multi-camera datasets.

2   Related Work

Significant progress has been made in pose estimation and pose tracking in recent years [8,11,20,39] and our model is built on advancements in the field of 2D multi-person pose estimation [8,9,15,17,24,31,36,39]. For instance, part affinity fields [8] are 2D vector fields that represent associations between body joints which form limbs. It utilizes a greedy bottom-up approach to detect 2D human poses and is robust to early commitment. Furthermore, it decouples the runtime complexity from the number of people in the image, yielding real-time performance.

There is extensive research in monocular 3D human pose estimation [19,21, 25,27–29,33,38]. For instance, Martinez et al. [27] split the problem of inferring 3D human poses from single images into estimating a 2D human pose and then regressing the 3D pose on the low-dimensional 2D representation. Though 3D human pose estimation approaches from single images yield impressive results they do not generalize well to unconstrained data.

While multiple views are used in [34,35] to guide the training for monocular 3D pose estimation, there are also approaches that use multiple views for inference. A common technique to estimate a single 3D human pose from multiple views is to extend the well-known pictorial structure model [14] to 3D [2,5,7,23,34]. Burenius et al. [7] utilize a 2D part detector based on the HOG-descriptor [10] while Kazemi et al. [23] use random forests. Pavlakos et al. [34] outperform all previous models by utilizing the stacked hourglass network [32] to extract human joint confidence maps from the camera views. However, these models have to discretize their solution space resulting in either a very coarse result or a very large state space making them impractical for estimating 3D poses of multiple people. Furthermore, they restrict their solution space to a 3D bounding volume around the subject which has to be known in advance.

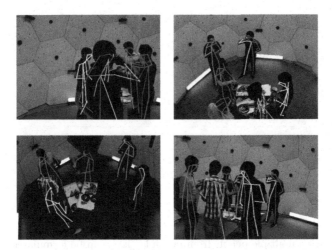

Fig. 2. Challenging 3D reconstruction of 6 persons in the *CMU Panoptic Dataset* [22] with significant occlusion and partial visibility of persons.

Estimating multiple humans from multiple views was first explored by Belagiannis et al. [3,4]. Instead of sampling from all possible translations and rotations they utilize a set of 3D body joint hypotheses which were obtained by triangulating 2D body part detections from different views. However, these methods rely on localizing bounding boxes using a person tracker for each individual in each frame to estimate the number of persons that has to be inferred from the common state space. This will work well in cases where individuals are completely visible in most frames but will run into issues when the pose is not completely visible in some cameras as shown in Fig. 2. A CNN-based approach was proposed by Elhayek et al. [12] where they fit articulated skeletons using 3D sums of Gaussians [37] and where body part detections are estimated using CNNs. However, the Gaussians and skeletons need to be initialized beforehand for each actor in the scene, similar to [26]. Fully connected pairwise conditional random fields [13] utilize approximate inference to extract multiple human poses where DeeperCut [18] is used as 2D human pose estimation model. However, the search space has to be discretized and a fully connected graph has to be solved, which throttles inference speed. Our approach does not suffer from any of the aforementioned drawbacks as our model works off-the-shelf without the need of actor-specific body models or discretized state space and uses an efficient greedy approach for estimating 3D human poses.

3   Model

Our model consists of two parts: First, 3D human poses are estimated for each frame. Second, the estimated 3D human poses are greedily matched into tracks which is described in Sect. 3.2. To remove outliers and to fill-in missing joints in

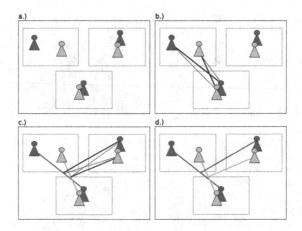

Fig. 3. Estimating multiple people from multiple views can be formulated as k-partite graph partitioning where 2D human pose detections must be associated across multiple views. We employ a greedy approach to make the partitioning tractable. Given a set of 2D human pose detections on multiple views (a) we greedily match all detections on two images (b) where the weight between two detections is defined by the average epipolar distance of the two poses. Other views are then integrated iteratively where the weight is the average of the epipolar distance of the 2D detections in the new view and the already integrated 2D detections (c). 2D detections with the same color represent the same person.

some frames, a simple yet effective smoothing scheme is applied, which is also discussed in Sect. 3.2.

3.1   3D Human Pose Estimation

First, 2D human poses are extracted for each camera separately. Several strong 2D multi-person pose estimation [8,9,15,17,24,31,36,39] models have been proposed but in our baseline we utilize OpenPose [8] as it is well established and offers real-time capabilities. We denote the 2D human pose estimations as

$$\left\{ h_{i,k} \right\}_{i \in [1,N]}^{k \in [1,K_i]} \tag{1}$$

where N is the number of calibrated cameras and K_i the number of detected human poses for camera i.

In order to estimate the 3D human poses from multiple cameras, we first associate the detections across all views as illustrated in Fig. 3. We denote the associated 2D human poses as $\mathcal{H}$ where $|\mathcal{H}|$ is the number of detected persons and $\mathcal{H}_m = \{ h_{i,k} \}$ is the set of 2D human poses that are associated to person m. Once the poses are associated, we estimate the 3D human poses for all detected persons m with $|\mathcal{H}| > 1$ by triangulating the 2D joint positions.

For the association, we select camera $i = 1$ as starting point and choose all 2D human pose detections $h_{1,k}$ in this camera view as person candidates,

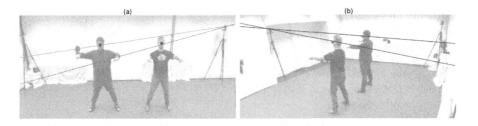

Fig. 4. Epipolar lines for two camera views of the UMPM Benchmark [1]. The blue and the red dot in image (a) are projected as blue (red) epipolar lines in the second image (b) while the orange and light-blue dot from image (b) are projected onto image (a). (Color figure online)

i.e., $\mathcal{H} = \{\{h_{1,k}\}\}$. We then iterate over the other cameras and greedily match their 2D detections with the current list of person candidates $\mathcal{H}$ using bi-partite matching [30].

The cost for assigning a pose $h_{i,k}$ to an existing person candidate $\mathcal{H}_m$ is given by

$$\Phi(h_{i,k}, \mathcal{H}_m) = \frac{1}{|\mathcal{H}_m||J_{kl}|} \sum_{h_{j,l} \in \mathcal{H}_m} \sum_{\iota \in J_{kl}} \phi(h_{i,k}(\iota), h_{j,l}(\iota)) \tag{2}$$

where $h_{i,k}(\iota)$ denotes the 2D pixel location of joint ι of the 2D human pose $h_{i,k}$ and J_{kl} is the set of joints that are visible for both poses $h_{i,k}$ and $h_{j,l}$. Note that the 2D human pose detections might not contain all J joints due to occlusions or truncations. The distance between two joints in the respective cameras is defined by the distance between the epipolar lines and the joint locations:

$$\phi(p_i, p_j) = |p_j^T F^{i,j} p_i| + |p_i^T F^{j,i} p_j| \tag{3}$$

where $F^{i,j}$ is the fundamental matrix from camera i to camera j. Figure 4 shows the epipolar lines for two joints.

Using the cost function $\Phi(h_{i,k}, \mathcal{H}_m)$, we solve the bi-partite matching problem for each image i:

$$X^* = \underset{X}{\arg\min} \sum_{m=1}^{|\mathcal{H}|} \sum_{k=1}^{K_i} \Phi(h_{i,k}, \mathcal{H}_m) X_{k,m} \tag{4}$$

where

$$\sum_k X_{k,m} = 1 \,\forall m \quad \text{and} \quad \sum_m X_{k,m} = 1 \,\forall k.$$

$X_{k,m}^* = 1$ if $h_{i,k}$ is associated to an existing person candidate $\mathcal{H}_m$ and it is zero otherwise. If $X_{k,m}^* = 1$ and $\Phi(h_{i,k}, \mathcal{H}_m) < \theta$, the 2D detection $h_{i,k}$ is added to $\mathcal{H}_m$. If $\Phi(h_{i,k}, \mathcal{H}_m) \geq \theta$, $\{h_{i,k}\}$ is added as hypothesis for a new person to $\mathcal{H}$. Algorithm 1 summarizes the greedy approach for associating the human poses across views.

Result: Associated 2D poses $\mathcal{H}$

$\mathcal{H} := \{\{h_{1,k}\}\}$;

for *camera* $i \leftarrow 2$ **to** N **do**
    for *pose* $k \leftarrow 1$ **to** K_i **do**
        for *hypothesis* $m \leftarrow 1$ **to** $|\mathcal{H}|$ **do**
            $\mid$ $C_{k,m} = \Phi(h_{i,k}, \mathcal{H}_m)$;
        end
    end
    $X^* = \underset{X}{\operatorname{argmin}} \sum_{m=1}^{|\mathcal{H}|} \sum_{k=1}^{K_i} C_{k,m} X_{k,m}$;
    for k, m *where* $X^*_{k,m} = 1$ **do**
        if $C_{k,m} < \theta$ **then**
            $\mid$ $\mathcal{H}_m = \mathcal{H}_m \bigcup \{h_{i,k}\}$;
        else
            $\mid$ $\mathcal{H} = \mathcal{H} \bigcup \{\{h_{i,k}\}\}$;
        end
    end
end
$\mathcal{H} = \mathcal{H} \setminus \mathcal{H}_m \ \forall m$ **where** $|\mathcal{H}_m| = 1$;

Algorithm 1: Solving the assignment problem for multiple 2D human pose detections in multiple cameras. $\Phi(h_{i,k}, \mathcal{H}_m)$ (2) is the assignment cost for assigning the 2D human pose $h_{i,k}$ to the person candidate $\mathcal{H}_m$. X^* is a binary matrix obtained by solving the bi-partite matching problem. The last line in the algorithm ensures that all hypotheses that cannot be triangulated are removed.

3.2   Tracking

For tracking, we use bipartite matching [30] similar to Sect. 3.1. Assuming that we have already tracked the 3D human poses until frame $t - 1$, we first estimate the 3D human poses for frame t as described in Sect. 3.1. The 3D human poses of frame t are then associated to the 3D human poses of frame $t - 1$ by bipartite matching. The assignment cost for two 3D human poses is in this case given by the average Euclidean distance between all joints that are present in both poses. In some cases, two poses do not have any overlapping valid joints due to noisy detections or truncations. The assignment cost is then calculated by projecting the mean of all valid joints of each pose onto the xy-plane, assuming that the z-axis is the normal of the ground plane, and taking the Euclidean distance between the projected points. As long as the distance between two matched poses is below a threshold τ, they will be integrated into a common track. Otherwise, a new track is created. In our experiments we set $\tau = 200$ mm.

Due to noisy detections, occlusions or motion blur, some joints or even full poses might be missing in some frames or noisy. We fill in missing joints by temporal averaging and we smooth each joint trajectory by a Gaussian kernel with standard deviation σ. This simple approach significantly boosts the performance of our model as we will show in Sect. 4.

Table 1. Quantitative comparison of methods for single human 3D pose estimation from multiple views on the KTH Football II [23] dataset. The numbers are the PCP score in 3D with $\alpha = 0.5$. Methods annotated with * can only estimate single human poses, discretize the state space and rely on being provided with a tight 3D bounding box centered at the true 3D location of the person. $Ours^+$ and $Ours$ describe our method with and without track smoothing (Sect. 3.2). ul and la show the scores for upper and lower arm, respectively, while ul and ll represent upper and lower legs.

	[7]*	[23]*	[34]*	[3]	[4]	[13]	Ours	Ours$^+$
ua	.60	.89	1.0	.68	.98	.97	.99	1.0
la	.35	.68	1.0	.56	.72	.95	.99	1.0
ul	1.0	1.0	1.0	.78	.99	1.0	.98	.99
ll	.90	.99	1.0	.70	.92	.98	.93	.997
avg	.71	.89	1.0	.68	.90	.98	.97	**.997**

4 Experiments

We evaluate our approach on two human pose estimation tasks, single person 3D pose estimation and multi-person 3D pose estimation, and compare it to state-of-the-art methods. Percentage of correct parts (PCP) in 3D as described in [7] is used for evaluation. We evaluate on the limbs only as annotated head poses vary significantly throughout various datasets. In all experiments, the order in which the cameras are processed is given by the dataset. We then evaluate the tracking performance. The source code is made publicly available[1].

4.1 Single Person 3D Pose Estimation

Naturally, first works on 3D human pose estimation from multiple views cover only single humans. Typical methods [7,23,34] find a solution over the complete discretized state space which is intractable for multiple persons. However, we report their results for completeness. All models were evaluated on the complete first sequence of the second player of the KTH Football II [23] dataset. Our results are reported in Table 1. Our model outperforms all other multi-person approaches and gets close to the state-of-the-art for single human pose estimation [34] which makes strong assumptions and is much more constrained. Our model has the lowest accuracy for lower legs (ll) which experience strong deformation and high movement speed. This can be mostly attributed to the 2D pose estimation framework which confuses left and right under motion blur, as can be seen in Fig. 7. When smoothing the trajectory (Sect. 3.2) this kind of errors can be reduced.

---

[1] https://github.com/jutanke/mv3dpose.

Table 2. Quantitative comparison of multi-person 3D pose estimation from multiple views on the evaluation frames of the annotated Campus [3, 16] and Shelf dataset [3]. The numbers are the PCP score in 3D with $\alpha = 0.5$. *Ours*$^+$ and *Ours* describe our method with and without track smoothing (Sect. 3.2). We show results for each of the three actors separately as well as averaged for each method (*average**).

Campus dataset ($\alpha = 0.5$)

	[3]			[4]			[13]			Ours			Ours$^+$		
Actor	1	2	3	1	2	3	1	2	3	1	2	3	1	2	3
ua	.83	.90	.78	.97	.97	.90	.97	.94	93	.86	.97	.91	.99	.98	.98
la	.78	.40	.62	.86	.43	.75	.87	.79	70	.74	.64	.68	.91	.70	.92
ul	.86	.74	.83	.93	.75	.92	.94	.99	88	1.0	.99	.99	1.0	.98	1.0
ll	.91	.89	.70	.97	.89	.76	.97	.95	81	1.0	.98	.99	1.0	.98	.99
avg	.85	.73	.73	.93	.76	.83	.94	.93	.85	.90	.90	.89	.98	.91	.98
avg*	.77			.84			.91			.90			**.96**		

Shelf dataset ($\alpha = 0.5$)

	[3]			[4]			[13]			Ours			Ours$^+$		
Actor	1	2	3	1	2	3	1	2	3	1	2	3	1	2	3
ua	.72	.80	.91	.82	.83	.93	.93	.78	.94	.99	.93	.97	.1.0	.97	.97
la	.61	.44	.89	.82	.83	.93	.83	.33	.90	.97	.57	.95	.99	.64	.96
ul	.37	.46	.46	.43	.50	.57	.96	.95	.97	.998	1.0	1.0	1.0	1.0	1.0
ll	.71	.72	.95	.86	.79	.97	.97	.93	.96	.998	.99	1.0	1.0	1.0	1.0
avg	.60	.61	.80	.73	.74	.85	.92	.75	.94	.99	.87	.98	.998	.90	.98
avg*	.67			.77			.87			.95			**.96**		

4.2   Multi-person 3D Pose Estimation

To evaluate our model on multi-person 3D pose estimation, we utilize the Campus [3, 16], Shelf [3], CMU Panoptic [22] and UMPM [1] dataset. The difficulty of the Campus dataset lies in its low resolution (360×288 pixel) which makes accurate joint detection hard. Furthermore, small errors in triangulation or detection will result in large PCP errors as the final score is calculated on the 3D joint locations. As in previous works [3, 4] we utilize frames 350–470 and frames 650–750 of the Campus dataset and frames 300–600 for the Shelf dataset. Clutter and humans occluding each others make the Shelf dataset challenging. Nevertheless, our model achieves state-of-the-art results on both datasets by a large margin which can be seen in Table 2. Table 3 reports quantitative results on video *p2_chair_2* of the UMPM [1] benchmark. A sample frame from this benchmark can be seen in Fig. 4. As the background is homogeneous and the human actors maintain a considerable distance to each other the results of our method are quite strong.

Table 3. Quantitative comparison of multi-person 3D pose estimation from multiple views on *p2_chair_2* of the UMPM benchmark [1].

	Ours⁺	
Actor	1	2
ua	.997	.98
la	.98	.996
ul	1.0	1.0
ll	.99	.997
avg	0.99	0.99

Table 4. Quantitative evaluation of multi-person 3D pose tracking on the CMU Panoptic dataset [22] using the MOTA [6] score. *Ours*⁺ and *Ours* describe our method with and without track smoothing (Sect. 3.2).

	Ours	Ours⁺
160422_ultimatum1 [22]	.89	.89
160224_haggling1 [22]	.92	.92
160906_pizza1 [22]	.92	.93

4.3 Tracking

For evaluating the tracking accuracy, we utilize the MOTA [6] score which provides a scalar value for the rate of false positives, false negatives, and identity switches of a track. Our model is evaluated on the CMU Panoptic dataset [22] which provides multiple interacting people in close proximity. We use videos *160224_haggling1* with three persons, *160422_ultimatum1* with up to seven person, and *160906_pizza1* with six persons. For the videos *160422_ultimatum1* we use frames 300 to 3758, for *160906_pizza1* we use frames 1000 to 4458 and for *160224_haggling1* we use frames 4209 to 5315 and 6440 to 8200. The first five HD cameras are used. Our results are reported in Table 4 which shows that our approach yields strong tracking capabilities.

4.4 Effects of Smoothing

As can be seen in Tables 1 and 2 the effects of smoothing can be significant, especially when detection and calibration are noisy as is the case with the Campus and the KTH Football II dataset. In both datasets 2D human pose detection is challenging due to low resolution (Campus) or strong motion blur (KTH Football II). Datasets with higher resolution and less motion blur like the Shelf dataset do not suffer from this problems as much and as such do not benefit the same way from track smoothing. However, a small gain can still be noted as smoothing also fills in joint detections that could not be triangulated. Figure 5 explores different σ values for smoothing on the KTH Football II, Campus, and Shelf dataset.

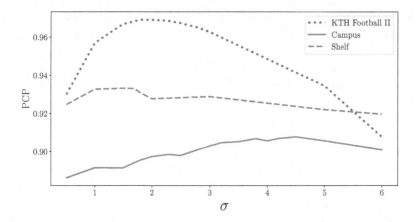

Fig. 5. PCP score for different smoothing values σ for tracking on KTH Football II, Campus, and Shelf. If σ is too small, the smoothing has little effect and coincides with the un-smoothed results. When the joint trajectories are smoothed too much, the PCP score drops as well as the trajectories do not follow the original path anymore. (Larger PCP scores are better)

It can be seen that smoothing improves the performance regardless of the dataset but that too much smoothing obviously reduces the accuracy. We chose $\sigma = 2$ for all our experiments except for the Campus dataset where we set $\sigma = 4.2$. The reason for the higher value of σ for the Campus dataset is due to the very low resolution of the images compared to the other datasets, which increases the noise of the estimated 3D joint position by triangulation.

4.5 Effects of Camera Order

So far we used the given camera order for each dataset, but the order in which views are greedily matched matters and different results might happen with different orderings. To investigate the impact of the camera order, we evaluated our approach using all 120 permutations of the 5 cameras of the Shelf dataset. The results shown in Fig. 6 show that the approach is very robust to the order of the camera views.

4.6 Early Commitment

A failure case happens due to the early commitment of our algorithm with regards to the 2D pose estimation, as can be seen in Fig. 7. When the pose estimation is unsure about a pose, it still fully commits to its output and disregards uncertainty. This problem occurs due to motion blur as the network has difficulties to decide between left and right in this case. As our pose estimation model has mostly seen forward-facing persons it will be more inclined towards predicting a forward-facing person in case of uncertainty. When left and right of

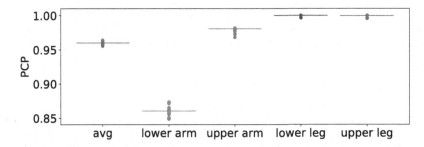

Fig. 6. PCP score averaged over all subjects for all 120 camera permutations of the Shelf dataset. The vertical line represents the mean value over all permutations while the dots represent each camera permutation.

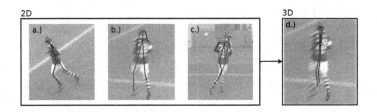

Fig. 7. Issues with early commitment. As we utilize the 2D pose estimations directly, our method suffers when the predictions yield poor results. In this example the pose estimation model correctly estimates (a) and (c) but confuses left and right on (b) due to motion blur. The resulting 3D pose estimation (d) collapses into the centre of the person. The red limbs represent the right body side while blue limbs represent the left body side. (Color figure online)

a 2D prediction are incorrectly flipped in at least one of the views, the merged 3D prediction will collapse to the vertical line of the person resulting in a poor 3D pose estimation.

5   Conclusion

In this work we presented a simple baseline approach for 3D human pose estimation and tracking from multiple calibrated cameras and evaluate it extensively on several 3D multi-camera datasets. Our approach achieves state-of-the-art results in multi-person 3D pose estimation while remaining sufficiently efficient for fast processing. Due to the models simplicity some common failure cases can be noted which can be build upon in future work. For example, confidence maps provided by the 2D pose estimation model could be utilized to prevent left-right flips. Our approach may serve as a baseline for future work.

Acknowledgement. The work has been funded by the Deutsche Forschungsgemeinschaft (DFG, German Research Foundation) GA 1927/5-1 (FOR 2535 Anticipating Human Behavior) and the ERC Starting Grant ARCA (677650).

References

1. Aa, N.v.d., Luo, X., Giezeman, G., Tan, R., Veltkamp, R.: Utrecht Multi-Person Motion (UMPM) benchmark: a multi-person dataset with synchronized video and motion capture data for evaluation of articulated human motion and interaction. In: Workshop on Human Interaction in Computer Vision (2011)
2. Amin, S., Andriluka, M., Rohrbach, M., Schiele, B.: Multi-view pictorial structures for 3D human pose estimation. In: British Machine Vision Conference (2013)
3. Belagiannis, V., Amin, S., Andriluka, M., Schiele, B., Navab, N., Ilic, S.: 3D pictorial structures for multiple human pose estimation. In: Conference on Computer Vision and Pattern Recognition (2014)
4. Belagiannis, V., Amin, S., Andriluka, M., Schiele, B., Navab, N., Ilic, S.: 3D pictorial structures revisited: multiple human pose estimation. Trans. Pattern Anal. Mach. Intell. **38**, 1929–1942 (2016)
5. Bergtholdt, M., Kappes, J., Schmidt, S., Schnörr, C.: A study ofparts-based object class detection using complete graphs. Int. J. Comput. Vis. **87**, 93 (2010)
6. Bernardin, K., Elbs, A., Stiefelhagen, R.: Multiple object tracking performance metrics and evaluation in a smart room environment. In: Workshop on Visual Surveillance (2006)
7. Burenius, M., Sullivan, J., Carlsson, S.: 3D pictorial structures for multiple view articulated pose estimation. In: Conference on Computer Vision and Pattern Recognition (2013)
8. Cao, Z., Simon, T., Wei, S.E., Sheikh, Y.: Realtime multi-person 2D pose estimation using part affinity fields. In: Conference on Computer Vision and Pattern Recognition (2017)
9. Chen, Y., Wang, Z., Peng, Y., Zhang, Z., Yu, G., Sun, J.: Cascaded pyramid network for multi-person pose estimation. In: Conference on Computer Vision and Pattern Recognition (2018)
10. Dalal, N., Triggs, B.: Histograms of oriented gradients for human detection. In: Conference on Computer Vision and Pattern Recognition (2005)
11. Doering, A., Iqbal, U., Gall, J.: JointFlow: temporal flow fields for multi person tracking. In: British Machine Vision Conference (2018)
12. Elhayek, A., et al.: Efficient ConvNet-based marker-less motion capture in general scenes with a low number of cameras. In: Conference on Computer Vision and Pattern Recognition (2015)
13. Ershadi-Nasab, S., Noury, E., Kasaei, S., Sanaei, E.: Multiple human 3D poseestimation from multiview images. Multimed. Tools Appl. **77**, 15573–15601 (2018)
14. Felzenszwalb, P.F., Huttenlocher, D.P.: Pictorial structures for objectrecognition. Int. J. Comput. Vis. **61**, 55–79 (2005)
15. Fieraru, M., Khoreva, A., Pishchulin, L., Schiele, B.: Learning to refine human pose estimation. In: Conference on Computer Vision and Pattern Recognition Workshops (2018)
16. Fleuret, F., Berclaz, J., Lengagne, R., Fua, P.: Multicamera people tracking with a probabilistic occupancy map. Pattern Anal. Mach. Intell. **30**, 267–282 (2007)

17. Guo, H., Tang, T., Luo, G., Chen, R., Lu, Y., Wen, L.: Multi-domain pose network for multi-person pose estimation and tracking. In: European Conference on Computer Vision (2018)
18. Insafutdinov, E., Pishchulin, L., Andres, B., Andriluka, M., Schiele, B.: DeeperCut: a deeper, stronger, and faster multi-person pose estimation model. In: Leibe, B., Matas, J., Sebe, N., Welling, M. (eds.) ECCV 2016. LNCS, vol. 9910, pp. 34–50. Springer, Cham (2016). https://doi.org/10.1007/978-3-319-46466-4_3
19. Iqbal, U., Doering, A., Yasin, H., Krüger, B., Weber, A., Gall, J.: A dual-source approach for 3D human pose estimation from single images. Comput. Vis. Image Underst. **172**, 37–49 (2018)
20. Iqbal, U., Milan, A., Gall, J.: PoseTrack: joint multi-person pose estimation and tracking. In: Conference on Computer Vision and Pattern Recognition (2017)
21. Iqbal, U., Molchanov, P., Breuel Jürgen Gall, T., Kautz, J.: Hand pose estimation via latent 2.5D heatmap regression. In: Proceedings of the European Conference on Computer Vision (2018)
22. Joo, H., et al.: Panoptic studio: a massively multiview system for social motion capture. In: International Conference on Computer Vision (2015)
23. Kazemi, V., Burenius, M., Azizpour, H., Sullivan, J.: Multi-view body part recognition with random forests. In: British Machine Vision Conference (2013)
24. Kocabas, M., Karagoz, S., Akbas, E.: MultiPoseNet: fast multi-person pose estimation using pose residual network. In: Ferrari, V., Hebert, M., Sminchisescu, C., Weiss, Y. (eds.) ECCV 2018. LNCS, vol. 11215, pp. 437–453. Springer, Cham (2018). https://doi.org/10.1007/978-3-030-01252-6_26
25. Kostrikov, I., Gall, J.: Depth sweep regression forests for estimating 3D human pose from images. In: British Machine Vision Conference (2014)
26. Liu, Y., Stoll, C., Gall, J., Seidel, H.P., Theobalt, C.: Markerless motion capture of interacting characters using multi-view image segmentation. In: Conference on Computer Vision and Pattern Recognition (2011)
27. Martinez, J., Hossain, R., Romero, J., Little, J.J.: A simple yet effective baseline for 3d human pose estimation. In: International Conference on Computer Vision (2017)
28. Mehta, D., et al.: Monocular 3D human pose estimation in the wild using improved CNN supervision. In: International Conference on 3D Vision (2017)
29. Mehta, D., et al.: Single-shot multi-person 3D pose estimation from monocular RGB. In: International Conference on 3D Vision (2018)
30. Munkres, J.: Algorithms for the assignment and transportation problems. J. Soc. Ind. Appl. Math. **5**, 32–38 (1957)
31. Newell, A., Huang, Z., Deng, J.: Associative embedding: End-to-end learning for joint detection and grouping. In: Advances in Neural Information Processing Systems (2017)
32. Newell, A., Yang, K., Deng, J.: Stacked hourglass networks for human pose estimation. In: Leibe, B., Matas, J., Sebe, N., Welling, M. (eds.) ECCV 2016. LNCS, vol. 9912, pp. 483–499. Springer, Cham (2016). https://doi.org/10.1007/978-3-319-46484-8_29
33. Pavlakos, G., Zhou, X., Derpanis, K.G., Daniilidis, K.: Coarse-to-fine volumetric prediction for single-image 3D human pose. In: Conference on Computer Vision and Pattern Recognition (2017)
34. Pavlakos, G., Zhou, X., Derpanis, K.G., Daniilidis, K.: Harvesting multiple views for marker-less 3D human pose annotations. In: Conference on Computer Vision and Pattern Recognition (2017)

35. Rhodin, H., et al.: Learning monocular 3D human pose estimation from multi-view images. In: Conference on Computer Vision and Pattern Recognition (2018)
36. Rogez, G., Weinzaepfel, P., Schmid, C.: LCR-Net++: multi-person 2D and 3D pose detection in natural images. Trans. Pattern Anal. Mach. Intell. (2019)
37. Stoll, C., Hasler, N., Gall, J., Seidel, H.P., Theobalt, C.: Fast articulated motion tracking using a sums of gaussians body model. In: International Conference on Computer Vision (2011)
38. Tome, D., Russell, C., Agapito, L.: Lifting from the deep: convolutional 3D pose estimation from a single image. In: Conference on Computer Vision and Pattern Recognition (2017)
39. Xiao, B., Wu, H., Wei, Y.: Simple baselines for human pose estimation and tracking. In: Ferrari, V., Hebert, M., Sminchisescu, C., Weiss, Y. (eds.) ECCV 2018. LNCS, vol. 11210, pp. 472–487. Springer, Cham (2018). https://doi.org/10.1007/978-3-030-01231-1_29
40. Zheng, L., Shen, L., Tian, L., Wang, S., Wang, J., Tian, Q.: Scalable person re-identification: a benchmark. In: International Conference on Computer Vision (2015)

Visual Person Understanding Through Multi-task and Multi-dataset Learning

Kilian Pfeiffer, Alexander Hermans[✉], István Sárándi, Mark Weber, and Bastian Leibe

Visual Computing Institute, RWTH Aachen University, Aachen, Germany
hermans@vision.rwth-aachen.de

Abstract. We address the problem of learning a single model for person re-identification, attribute classification, body part segmentation, and pose estimation. With predictions for these tasks we gain a more holistic understanding of persons, which is valuable for many applications. This is a classical multi-task learning problem. However, no dataset exists that these tasks could be jointly learned from. Hence several datasets need to be combined during training, which in other contexts has often led to reduced performance in the past. We extensively evaluate how the different task and datasets influence each other and how different degrees of parameter sharing between the tasks affect performance. Our final model matches or outperforms its single-task counterparts without creating significant computational overhead, rendering it highly interesting for resource-constrained scenarios such as mobile robotics.

1 Introduction

Humans are arguably the most important visual category that autonomous systems need to understand in detail. A multi-faceted understanding is especially critical for mobile robotics and autonomous driving to enable smooth human-robot interaction and pedestrian safety. However, these are also applications with tight constraints on computational resources for reasons of cost- and energy-efficiency. Sharing computation across tasks such as human pose estimation and attribute classification is therefore highly important. Synergies between person-centric tasks can also emerge, potentially resulting in more accurate models.

To gain a more holistic visual understanding of a person, we jointly approach the tasks of re-identification (ReID), attribute classification, pose estimation and body part segmentation, as shown in Fig. 1. We argue that ReID is especially important for person understanding, as it enables tracking and merging person information across longer timespans. Hence we place an emphasis on this task throughout our experiments.

Electronic supplementary material The online version of this chapter (https:// doi.org/10.1007/978-3-030-33676-9_39) contains supplementary material, which is available to authorized users.

© Springer Nature Switzerland AG 2019
G. A. Fink et al. (Eds.): DAGM GCPR 2019, LNCS 11824, pp. 551–566, 2019.
https://doi.org/10.1007/978-3-030-33676-9_39

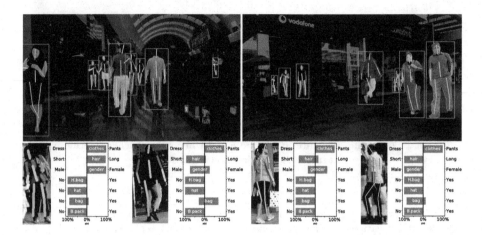

Fig. 1. Given person detections, we perform pose estimation, body part segmentation and attribute classification jointly with person re-identification (not visualized) using a shared CNN backbone with small task-specific heads. Box colors correspond to gender predictions (female, male). (Color figure online)

Given the great success of deep learning in computer vision, such multitask learning (MTL) can be realized by adding multiple output heads to a shared convolutional neural network (CNN) backbone [6,12,27]. Several prior works have addressed some person-centric tasks jointly in this fashion. ReID and attribute classification are known to work well together [18,19,34], similarly with pose estimation and body part segmentation [16,23], but so far no methods have tackled all these four tasks in a single CNN. Possibly because no publicly available dataset has annotations for all four of these tasks. While many interesting MTL approaches exist [12,30], only few of them approach multi-dataset learning, where task annotations are spread across datasets [15,21,42]. Different dataset biases make this very challenging, and it is not always possible to obtain improved results for multi-dataset learning [15], as opposed to single-dataset MTL, where synergies between tasks have proven beneficial [3,12].

The design space spanned by different task-specific tricks, learning schedules, architectures, and MTL techniques is extremely large. We therefore limit this empirical study to a single, widely used, CNN backbone with different degrees of hard parameter sharing and a simple loss weighting of the different tasks.

We first create a set of single-task baseline networks and validate their performance against state-of-the-art approaches. We then unify these into a shared-backbone network and evaluate multi-task learning, still on a single dataset, by augmenting a ReID+attribute dataset with automatically created pose and segmentation annotations. Finally, we evaluate how multi-dataset training affects performance. In this setting, we find that choosing the right type of backbone normalization layers is crucial for good performance. We consider three model variants with different degrees of parameter sharing. Even without the use of advanced MTL techniques, our final network is able to perform all four tasks with hard parameter sharing with similar, or better performance than the baseline, rendering it very useful for practical applications.

2 Related Work

Multi-task learning (MTL) has a long history [3] with the core idea that several source tasks can serve as a domain-specific inductive bias for a target task. Ruder [30] gives an overview of recent MTL network designs and loss or gradient merging techniques. These developments are largely orthogonal to our experiments, since we focus on hard parameter sharing with a simple loss summation and can thus likely benefit further from some of these MTL approaches.

Several multi-task approaches exist for visual person analysis using a single dataset. Some train pose estimation and part segmentation jointly [16,23]. Hyperface [27] performs face detection, landmark localization, gender classification, and headpose estimation in a single network, but does not consider ReID. He et al. [6] train their Mask-RCNN to jointly perform instance segmentation and human pose estimation. Other non-person-related MTL approaches include the recently proposed panoptic segmentation [14], merging instance and semantic segmentation. Zamir et al. [45] create a Taskonomy of indoor scene tasks, showing that many vision tasks can provide complementary supervision.

Fewer MTL approaches also learn different tasks from different datasets. Uber-Net by Kokkinos [15] is probably the most extensive MTL approach to date, being trained on seven tasks across six different datasets. However, they report decreased performance when trained on multiple datasets. Xiao et al. [42] perform several tasks on indoor scenes such as semantic, part, and texture segmentation, by pooling annotations from different datasets. Rebuffi et al. [28] introduce the visual decathlon challenge spanning ten rather different classification datasets. They propose a shared network with domain-specific adaptation modules that modify the backbone, depending on the dataset an image comes from. In contrast, we aim to use the same backbone on any image and perform several tasks. To the best of our knowledge, Luvizon et al. [21] are the first to tackle a person-centric multi-task problem by training on multiple datasets. They perform 2D/3D pose estimation and action recognition, but merge the tasks in a more complex way, whereas we simply attach task-specific network heads.

In the person ReID literature, MTL often refers to using several ReID losses, for example, Wang et al. [38] use a classification, triplet, and attention loss, which are all based on ReID annotations. Some MTL approaches use attribute classification to improve ReID [18,19,34]. Other ReID approaches use pose estimation [25,31,33] or part segmentation [11], but in the form of additional inputs, instead of producing them as outputs, like we do.

3 Network Architectures

We first introduce our single-task baseline architectures and then describe different options for merging these into multi-task architectures. All models are built

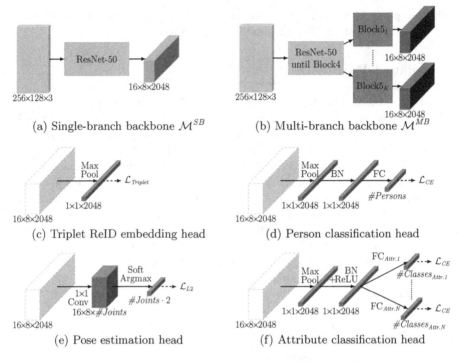

(a) Single-branch backbone $\mathcal{M}^{SB}$ (b) Multi-branch backbone $\mathcal{M}^{MB}$

(c) Triplet ReID embedding head   (d) Person classification head

(e) Pose estimation head   (f) Attribute classification head

Fig. 2. (a, b) Single and multi-branch backbones with a part shared across tasks (green), and a task-specific part (red). (c–f) Heads that can be attached to a branch output (shown as dashed outline). The segmentation head is not shown. (Color figure online)

on a ResNet-50 backbone [7], without the global pooling and later layers. We use a stride of one in the last block, doubling the output resolution.

Person Re-identification. We apply global max pooling on the backbone and directly use the 2048D output as an embedding vector, in line with recently suggested best practices [20] (see Fig. 2c). We minimize the batch hard triplet loss [8], and only use horizontal flip data augmentation.

When also applying the person classification loss for ReID, we attach a BatchNorm [9] and a fully-connected layer with softmax activation, reducing the dimensionality to the number of training persons. We minimize the cross-entropy loss (see Fig. 2d).

Attribute Classification. On top of the ReID architecture, we add a Batch-Norm layer and ReLU non-linearity, followed by separate fully-connected layers with softmax activations for every attribute, projecting the network output down to the number of classes per attribute (see Fig. 2f). The average of all attribute-specific cross-entropy losses is used, while again employing flip augmentation.

2D Pose Estimation. We follow the approach by Sun *et al.* [35] since it is one of the simplest 2D pose estimation methods only requiring a small network head. we predict a heatmap for every joint, from which a soft-argmax extracts 2D joint coordinates. However, in contrast to their customized multi-stage architecture, we directly generate joint heatmaps using a 1×1 convolution on top of the backbone output. We minimize the Euclidean loss between the predicted and ground-truth positions with no further heatmap-based losses (see Fig. 2e). Next to the random horizontal flipping, we also use rotation, translation, and scale augmentation, which is common practice for pose estimation [32,35].

Body Part Segmentation. For part segmentation, we use a recent panoptic segmentation model [14]. It builds a segmentation branch on top of the Feature Pyramid Network (FPN) [17], which extracts features from the backbone at several resolutions and merges them into a feature pyramid. The levels of the pyramid are converted to quarter-resolution feature maps, which are summed and converted to a full-resolution segmentation prediction. Since our last ResNet block has a stride of one, we omit one upsampling step in the segmentation branch. This lightweight segmentation network performs competitively on semantic segmentation benchmarks and is thus well-suited for our experiments. Since the FPN extracts information from the backbone without changing it, it is compatible with all other baseline networks. The segmentation is produced using a pixel-wise softmax and is trained using the bootstrapped cross-entropy loss [41] that only considers the hardest 25% of pixels. We apply rotation, translation and scaling augmentation during training.

Multi-task Architectures. Creating a multi-task architecture from the separate baselines described above is straightforward, since all are built on top of the same backbone. The simplest multi-task architecture merges all heads onto a common, single-branch backbone shown in Fig. 2a. This achieves maximal parameter sharing, since all but the final task-specific parameters are updated by every task. Sharing all parameters might not be beneficial for all tasks, thus we also investigate a multi-branch variant, where we duplicate block 5 of our backbone for every task (Fig. 2b).

4 Experimental Evaluation

4.1 Datasets

We use three datasets to cover annotations for the four considered tasks.

Market-1501. [2] is a ReID dataset with 32,668 images spanning 1,501 different persons. We use the default train/test split and the single-query evaluation protocol with the standard metrics: mean Average Precision (mAP) and Cumulative Matching Characteristic (CMC). Lin *et al.* [18] provide an attribute classification extension, which we evaluate using accuracy averaged over all attributes.

MPII. [1] is a 2D pose estimation dataset with 15,855 well-separated person instances for training and 3,330 for validation, following the split of [37]. The evaluation measure is the percentage of correct keypoints, which have to be closer to the ground truth than half the head size (PCKh@0.5 metric).

LIP. [16] provides body part segmentation and pose estimation annotations for 30,462 training and 10,000 validation images in the single-person setup. The part segmentation consists of 20 classes, which we evaluate using the standard mean intersection over union score (mIoU). The pose annotations and evaluation are consistent with MPII.

Automatic Annotations. To isolate the effect of multi-dataset learning, we first perform multi-task training on a single dataset. Since no dataset provides annotations for all the tasks we consider, we extend the Market training set with automatic annotations for pose estimation and part segmentation. To achieve this, we train baseline models on the respective datasets and use their predictions. Visual examples are shown in the supplementary material. Even though such annotations are of significantly lower quality than hand-annotated data, they result in interesting multi-task training results. To reduce annotation failures, we merge several segmentation classes, similar to [11,26]. We create the background, head, upper body, lower body, and shoes classes (evaluated using the mIoUscore, here referred to as $mIoU_5$). Since the automatic annotations are noisy, we evaluate our trained network's pose and segmentation performance on MPII and LIP instead.

4.2 Training Setup

We train our networks with Adam [13] using default parameters and a learning rate decay. For multi-task training, we sum the different losses[1]. In multi-dataset training, we interleave mini-batches from different datasets. We do not use mixed batches, since we require a specific batch composition for the batch hard triplet loss. Mixed batches can also lead to noisy gradients for the task-specific parameters [15,42]. We sample batches from the datasets with a frequency proportional to their sizes. For each training sample only losses with corresponding annotations are computed. Within a mini-batch it can thus occur that no gradients can be computed for some task head parameters, hence no updates or optimizer statistic updates are computed for these parameters in such iterations. In initial experiments, GroupNorm [40] performed significantly better for multi-task learning than BatchNorm [9], hence we apply it by default unless mentioned otherwise (see Table 7 and its discussion below). We initialize with ImageNet pretrained weights from [5]. We use PyTorch [24] and a Tesla V100 GPU with 16 GB memory. Especially training the multi-branch models require this amount of memory, whereas some of the single-task baselines can be trained with a fraction of the available GPU memory.

---

[1] Uncertainty weighting by Kendall *et al.* [12] gave no consistent improvements.

4.3 Experimental Results

Before discussing the multi-task and multi-datasets results, we first compare each single-task baseline to the state-of-the-art and confirm solid scores, on which we can base our multi-task experiments. Finally, we discuss some additional interesting insights and qualitative results.

Table 1 shows a selection of recent top-performing ReID methods. Even though the current top approach achieves 88.2% mAP on the Market dataset, we still outperform many recent methods by a large margin. Current top performing methods typically use a complex architecture [38,39,46] or tricks such as larger input images and more elaborate augmentations [20]. Our single-task baseline is essentially a simplified TriNet architecture [8], nevertheless, it still significantly improves the original mAP score of 69.14% by over 8%, yielding a solid baseline performance for person ReID.

Table 1. Baseline person ReID performance on Market-1501.

	Additional info	mAP	rank-1	rank-5	rank-10
PSE [31]	+Pose	69.0	87.7	94.5	96.8
TriNet [8]		69.1	84.9	94.2	–
PN-GAN [25]	+Pose	72.6	89.4	–	–
MANCS [38]	+Multi-loss	82.3	93.1	–	–
SPReID [11]	+Seg	83.4	93.7	97.6	98.4
Bag of Tricks [20]	+Multi-loss	85.9	94.5	–	–
MGN [39]	+Multi-loss	86.9	95.7	–	–
Pyramid [46]	+Multi-loss	88.2	95.7	98.4	99.0
Our baseline		77.4	91.1	96.9	98.1

For most attributes, our baseline obtains state-of-the-art accuracy as seen in Table 2. Due to an ambiguous evaluation protocol, some authors [19,34] evaluate multi-class color attributes as sets of binary attributes, resulting in incomparable scores. Excluding these two attributes for a consistent comparison shows that our baseline outperforms the current top method by 1.6%.

Table 3 compares our pose estimation baseline on the MPII and LIP validation sets. On the more commonly used MPII dataset, we achieve scores only 2% behind the state-of-the-art and almost match Sun et al.'s original soft-argmax approach [35], even though they use several task-specific network modifications. LIP seems to be a harder dataset and our baseline cannot directly compete with the state-of-the-art, which also uses part segmentation information.

Finally, Table 4 compares our part segmentation to state-of-the-art methods on the LIP validation set. Our baseline is 6.6% mIoU behind current top methods, however, all of those use the bigger ResNet-101 in combination with additional network modules or multi-scale information. Nevertheless, our baseline outperforms several previous approaches with bigger backbones, rendering it a good starting point for our experiments.

Multi-task Learning. Having verified our baseline results, we now turn to the multi-task evaluation. In a first round of experiments, we focus only on the Market-1501 dataset, employing our automatic annotations where necessary. Table 5 shows several task combinations, each one using the single-branch model ($\mathcal{M}^{SB}$) and the multi-branch model ($\mathcal{M}^{MB}$). For these comparisons, we present baseline results trained on the same automatic annotations, to see where performance is gained due to MTL. Some interesting observations can be made. ReID improves in all cases when using the single-branch model, as well as for most task combinations in the multi-branch case, especially when using more than one additional task. When considering only additional manual annotations

Table 2. Baseline attribute classification accuracy on Market-1501. *: Due to an unclear evaluation protocol the color attributes are not evaluated consistently.

	Gender	Age	Hair	L.slv	L.low	S.clth	B.pack	H.bag	Bag	Hat	Avg	C.up*	C.low*	Avg*
Sun et al. [34]	88.9	84.8	78.3	93.5	92.1	84.8	85.5	88.4	67.3	97.1	86.1	87.5	87.2	87.0
APR [18]	86.5	87.1	83.7	93.7	93.3	91.5	82.8	89.0	75.1	97.1	88.0	73.4	69.9	85.3
JCM [19]	89.7	87.4	82.5	93.7	93.3	89.2	85.2	86.2	86.9	97.2	89.1	92.4	93.1	89.7
Our baseline	92.9	87.0	89.7	93.6	94.8	94.6	88.0	89.4	79.7	98.0	90.8	79.4	71.9	88.2

Table 3. Pose results on the MPII and LIP validation sets (PCKh@0.5).

Dataset	Method	Head	Should	Elbow	Wrist	Hip	Knee	Ankle	Avg
MPII	Sun et al. [35]	–	–	–	–	–	–	–	87.3
	Tang et al. [36]	–	–	–	–	–	–	–	87.5
	Yang et al. [44]	–	–	–	–	–	–	–	88.5
	Our baseline	96.3	94.4	87.7	82.1	86.8	80.6	74.9	86.6
LIP	DeepLab [4,16]	91.2	84.3	78.0	74.9	62.3	69.5	71.1	76.5
	JPPNet [16] + Seg.	93.2	89.3	84.6	82.2	69.9	78.0	77.3	82.5
	Our baseline	90.4	84.3	76.7	74.0	62.6	67.4	70.0	73.9

Table 4. Body part segmentation performance on the LIP validation set.

	Backbone	Overall accuracy	Mean accuracy	Mean IoU
DeepLab (from [16])	ResNet-101	84.1	55.6	44.8
SS-JPPNet [16]	ResNet-101	84.5	54.8	44.6
JPPNet [16] (with pose)	ResNet-101	86.4	62.2	51.4
CE2P [29]	ResNet-101	87.4	63.2	53.1
CaseNet [10]	ResNet-101	–	–	54.4
Our baseline	ResNet-50	84.6	59.5	47.8

as well as when only using automatic annotations, the mAP score improves. Also when considering all tasks jointly, the mAP score still improves. For the other tasks a different set of tasks typically is able to achieve better scores.

Pose estimation suffers the most from the combination with other tasks, which becomes clear when considering the PCKh scores of the single and multi-branch models. When only trained with the ReID task, scores become the worst, which makes sense since pose and ReID are largely orthogonal tasks. Surprisingly though, the ReID score is not affected negatively by the pose task.

On the other hand, part segmentation benefits from being trained with ReID. When jointly trained with pose estimation, the segmentation scores even surpass the baselines in the single-branch model, but not in the multi-branch model.

Overall, the single-branch model seems to amplify the effects that different tasks have on each other, both positive and negative, while the multi-branch model performs more similarly to the independently trained baselines. Given that tasks share fewer parameters in the latter, this is not surprising.

Multi-dataset Training. The multi-task experiments have clearly shown that MTL can especially be beneficial for ReID performance, but pose estimation

Table 5. Multi-task learning on Market-1501 (manual and automatic annotations) using single- and multi-branch models, compared to the baseline of learning each task individually on market.

	Training: market						Evaluation			
	Manual			Auto			Market		MPII	LIP
	Tripl	Clas	Attr	Pose	Seg		ReID mAP	Attr acc	Pose PCKh	Pose PCKh	Seg mIoU$_5$
$\mathcal{M}^{SB}$	✓	✓					77.8	–	–	–	–
	✓		✓				78.0	87.9	–	–	–
	✓			✓			77.9	–	27.7	22.6	–
	✓				✓		77.6	–	–	–	48.5
	✓	✓	✓				77.8	87.7	–	–	–
	✓			✓	✓		78.6	–	30.8	22.4	49.6
	✓	✓	✓	✓	✓		79.2	88.0	28.8	21.3	47.9
$\mathcal{M}^{MB}$	✓	✓					76.9	–	–	–	–
	✓		✓				77.5	87.7	–	–	–
	✓			✓			77.4	–	34.4	27.0	–
	✓				✓		77.7	–	–	–	47.6
	✓	✓	✓				78.2	87.5	–	–	–
	✓			✓	✓		77.7	–	40.4	28.4	47.9
	✓	✓	✓	✓	✓		78.2	87.9	39.7	28.1	46.7
Baseline (individually trained)							77.4	88.2	46.9	29.9	48.7

and part segmentation results were not satisfactory, especially when compared to baselines trained on the respective datasets. Hence, we turn to multi-dataset training using interleaved mini-batches.

Table 6 shows the results for a series of multi-task trainings with a focus on different dataset combinations. Overall we observe similar effects to the single-dataset case discussed above. ReID typically benefits from additional tasks, apart for some multi-branch models. But with supervision from manual annotations, pose estimation and part segmentation now obtain scores that can match or improve the baseline scores.

Pose estimation still does not work well together with ReID or part segmentation. However, when using both MPII and LIP annotations, we also match the baseline pose results, which was not possible with automatic annotations.

For part segmentation trained only with ReID, the single-branch model consistently worked better than the multi-branch model when using automatic data, where now the multi-branch model works better at the cost of a lower ReID score. However, with additional pose estimation supervision, the single-branch model works better, as was the case before. We can now also evaluate all 20 LIP classes and the results correlate well with the reduced class set scores.

Table 6. Multi-task and multi-dataset learning on all considered datasets. Results from our single and multi-branch model, as well as the split output model are compared to the our baseline.

	Training							Evaluation				
	Market			MPII	LIP		Market		MPII	LIP		
	Tripl.	Clas.	Attr.	Pose	Pose	Seg.	ReID mAP	Attr. acc	Pose PCKh	Pose PCKh	Seg. mIoU	mIoU$_5$
$\mathcal{M}^{SB}$	✓			✓			77.5	–	82.2	40.5	–	–
	✓					✓	77.7	–	–	–	46.5	70.0
	✓		✓			✓	78.4	–	78.4	53.8	48.8	71.6
	✓		✓		✓	✓	78.0	–	86.8	74.3	49.9	71.8
	✓	✓	✓	✓	✓	✓	78.3	87.1	86.7	73.8	49.6	71.6
$\mathcal{M}^{MB}$	✓			✓			76.9	–	83.8	41.6	–	–
	✓					✓	76.8	–	–	–	47.2	70.8
	✓		✓			✓	77.8	–	83.9	52.9	47.5	71.0
	✓		✓		✓	✓	77.9	–	86.9	75.0	48.5	71.6
	✓	✓	✓	✓	✓	✓	— out of GPU memory —					
$\mathcal{M}^{SB/Split}$	✓			✓			77.9	–	86.7	44.5	–	–
	✓	✓	✓	✓	✓	✓	79.1	86.7	86.5	74.4	49.6	71.6
Baselines (individually trained)							77.4	88.2	86.6	73.9	47.8	71.0

The decrease in attribute classification accuracy is more noticeable than in the case of single-dataset training. The effect of multi-dataset training differs per attribute. Both the age and bag attribute accuracies improve, while the gender or hair accuracy significantly decrease. These effects will need further investigation.

When jointly training all tasks, the multi-branch model requires more than 16 GB GPU memory, highlighting a drawback of this backbone. The single-branch model only needs marginally more memory than the baseline, even when training all tasks jointly, but performance is slightly worse than variants trained on fewer tasks. Nevertheless, apart from the attribute classification task, this model can compete with all the baselines, often outperforming them. This indicates that synergies between the tasks exist and can be exploited in a single model with hard parameter sharing.

ReID and Pose Interference. The previous experiments suggest that the single-branch model is better overall, except that pose estimation degrades when trained jointly with ReID. As a possible solution, we make a slight modification to our single-branch model, where we split the backbone output into two separate tensors: one for pose heatmaps and one for the remaining tasks. This allows sharing all backbone weights, while still reducing interference between pose estimation and ReID gradients at the backbone output. Figure 3 shows this variant (with only ReID as an additional task). This modification only slightly changes most scores, but boosts the ReID performance by 0.8% as shown in Table 6.

Pretraining on MPII. As an alternative to joint training of tasks, we also evaluate pretraining the backbone on MPII and using these weights to initialize ReID training on Market. As Table 7 shows, the resulting mAP scores cannot match the baseline and the ReID training additionally has a very negative impact on pose estimation, while the joint training for both tasks gains the previously discussed results. Especially the single-branch model no longer produces a useful pose estimation after finetuning, probably because the largely pose-invariant ReID training erases pose-related information from the backbone output.

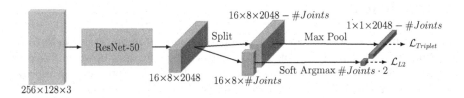

Fig. 3. Single-branch model with a split-pose head ($\mathcal{M}^{SB/Split}$). The backbone output is split channel-wise into two tensors, one for body joint heatmaps and one for other task heads. For simplicity only the triplet loss $\mathcal{L}_{Triplet}$ is shown.

Table 7. Comparison of multi-task training approaches and backbone normalizations. The three column-blocks show, respectively, the pose results trained only on MPII, ReID and pose after additional fine-tuning for ReID on Market, and finally, when jointly training both at once. LIP is only used for evaluation here.

		Train on MPII		→	Fine-tune on market			Train jointly		
		MPII	LIP		Market	MPII	LIP	Market	MPII	LIP
		PCKh	PCKh		mAP	PCKh	PCKh	mAP	PCKh	PCKh
$\mathcal{M}^{SB}$	BatchNorm	86.5	41.3		73.9	16.7	10.6	51.5	79.5	32.8
	GroupNorm	86.4	43.6		72.6	9.0	10.0	77.5	82.2	40.5
$\mathcal{M}^{MB}$	BatchNorm	86.2	39.5		77.7	57.4	15.6	73.9	80.1	32.8
	GroupNorm	86.6	43.3		75.6	70.1	33.9	76.9	83.8	41.6

GroupNorm vs BatchNorm. Initially we used a backbone with BatchNorm, which did not perform well during multi-dataset training. We hypothesize that different datasets result in different batch statistics, hence the overall collected statistics do not match the per-dataset train-time statistics, ultimately leading to worse results at test-time. While GroupNorm was initially developed to train with small mini-batches, a further benefit is that it does not accumulate batch statistics during training and thus should also improve joint training. Table 7 shows a comparison of the two different normalizations in the backbone, for the example of pose estimation and person ReID. The GroupNorm results for joint training are consistently better, outperforming the single-branch BatchNorm mAP score by over 25%. Furthermore, the generalization to different datasets (in this case LIP) is better for the GroupNorm models, which could again be explained by the fact that BatchNorm uses possibly unequal dataset statistics. Given these results, we use GroupNorm in all other experiments.

Qualitative Results. Figure 1 shows qualitative results for attribute classification, pose estimation and part segmentation on MOT16 sequences [22], showing that our network can also generalize to other datasets. Further qualitative results are found in the supplementary material.

5 Discussion

Our experiments show that several visual person understanding task can be tackled using a single unified model. We saw interesting synergies between different person-related tasks and datasets. Focusing on ReID, we were able to improve the mAP score by 1.7% by either utilizing additional tasks through automatic annotations, or multi-dataset training. Especially with the latter approach, our unified model can roughly match or even outperform the separately trained task- and dataset-specific baselines. More parameter sharing in the backbone proved beneficial for most tasks. For the particular case of ReID and pose estimation, the interference was overcome through a simple split of the network output.

Given our positive results, several directions open up for future work. Further person-related tasks and datasets can be added into the training. Better task heads from the specific domains or more complex multi-task training schemes will likely improve results. Ultimately, it will be interesting to integrate the tasks into a detector as an additional person understanding head. Combinations such as detection and ReID [43], or instance segmentation and pose estimation [6] have been evaluated, however there are no detectors jointly tackling all the tasks.

Most of the computation in our best-performing model is shared across tasks, adding almost no overhead to the single-task baseline. On a GTX 1080 Ti GPU it processes 50 person crops per second without batching and 122 with a batch size of 10. This could be further improved with a lighter backbone, rendering it well-suited for robotics applications, where resource constraints typically prohibit running several models in parallel.

6 Conclusion

We have shown that is possible to train a single model for four important person-centric tasks, offering a holistic person understanding without running separate models in parallel. We evaluated how different backbones and normalizations affect the resulting performance and found that GroupNorm is crucial for multi-dataset training. While person ReID and pose estimation interfere to a certain degree, a simple split of the backbone output can largely resolve this issue. Even though we make no complex modification to our ResNet backbone and use simple task heads, we can exploit task synergies using multi-task learning. Both automatic annotations and multiple datasets can be used to improve results and especially in the latter case we can roughly match or even outperform the single-task baseline scores. Based on these results, we see several interesting research directions to further advance visual person understanding. Nevertheless, even our current multi-task model is highly relevant for applications where people and machines interact, especially when computational resources are limited.

Acknowledgements. This project was funded, in parts, by ERC Consolidator Grant project "DeeViSe" (ERC-CoG-2017-773161) and the BMBF projects "FRAME" (16SV7830) and "PARIS" (16ES0602). Istvan Sarandi's research is funded by a grant from the Bosch Research Foundation. Most experiments were performed on the RWTH Aachen University CLAIX 2018 GPU Cluster.

References

1. Andriluka, M., Pishchulin, L., Gehler, P., Schiele, B.: 2D human pose estimation: new benchmark and state of the art analysis. In: CVPR (2014)
2. Bai, S., Bai, X., Tian, Q.: Scalable person re-identification on supervised smoothed manifold. In: CVPR (2017)
3. Caruana, R.: Multitask learning: a knowledge-based source of inductive bias. In: ICML (1993)

4. Chen, L.C., Papandreou, G., Kokkinos, I., Murphy, K., Yuille, A.L.: DeepLab: semantic image segmentation with deep convolutional nets, atrous convolution, and fully connected CRFs. PAMI **40**(4), 834–848 (2018)
5. Fu, C.Y.: Pytorch-groupnormalization. https://github.com/chengyangfu/pytorch-groupnormalization (2018). Accessed 08 Feb 2019
6. He, K., Gkioxari, G., Dollár, P., Girshick, R.: Mask R-CNN. In: CVPR (2017)
7. He, K., Zhang, X., Ren, S., Sun, J.: Deep residual learning for image recognition. In: CVPR (2016)
8. Hermans, A., Beyer, L., Leibe, B. In defense of the triplet loss for person re-identification. arXiv:1703.07737 (2017)
9. Ioffe, S., Szegedy, C.: Batch normalization: accelerating deep network training by reducing internal covariate shift. In: ICML (2015)
10. Jin, X., Lan, C., Zeng, W., Zhang, Z., Chen, Z.: CaseNet: content-adaptive scale interaction networks for scene parsing. arXiv:1904.08170 (2019)
11. Kalayeh, M.M., Basaran, E., Gökmen, M., Kamasak, M.E., Shah, M.: Human semantic parsing for person re-identification. In: CVPR (2018)
12. Kendall, A., Gal, Y., Cipolla, R.: Multi-task learning using uncertainty to weigh losses for scene geometry and semantics. In: CVPR (2018)
13. Kingma, D.P., Ba, J.: Adam: a method for stochastic optimization. In: ICLR (2015)
14. Kirillov,ˋA., Girshick, R., He, K., Dollár, P.: Panoptic feature pyramid networks. arXiv:1901.02446 (2019)
15. Kokkinos, I.: Ubernet: training a universal convolutional neural network for low-, mid-, and high-level vision using diverse datasets and limited memory. In: CVPR (2017)
16. Liang, X., Gong, K., Shen, X., Lin, L.: Look into person: joint body parsing & pose estimation network and a new benchmark. PAMI **41**(4), 871–885 (2018)
17. Lin, T.Y., Dollár, P., Girshick, R., He, K., Hariharan, B., Belongie, S.: Feature pyramid networks for object detection. In: CVPR (2017)
18. Lin, Y., Zheng, L., Zheng, Z., Wu, Y., Yang, Y.: Improving person re-identification by attribute and identity learning. arXiv:1703.07220 (2017)
19. Liu, H., Wu, J., Jiang, J., Qi, M., Bo, R.: Sequence-based person attribute recognition with joint CTC-attention model. W:1811.08115 (2018)
20. Luo, H., Gu, Y., Liao, X., Lai, S., Jiang, W.: Bag of tricks and a strong baseline for deep person re-identification. In: CVPR Workshops (2019)
21. Luvizon, D.C., Picard, D., Tabia, H.: 2D/3D pose estimation and action recognition using multitask deep learning. In: CVPR (2018)
22. Milan, A., Leal-Taixé, L., Reid, I., Roth, S., Schindler, K.: MOT16: a benchmark for multi-object tracking. arXiv:1603.00831 (2016)
23. Papandreou, G., Zhu, T., Chen, L.-C., Gidaris, S., Tompson, J., Murphy, K.: PersonLab: person pose estimation and instance segmentation with a bottom-up, part-based, geometric embedding model. In: Ferrari, V., Hebert, M., Sminchisescu, C., Weiss, Y. (eds.) Computer Vision – ECCV 2018. LNCS, vol. 11218, pp. 282–299. Springer, Cham (2018). https://doi.org/10.1007/978-3-030-01264-9_17
24. Paszke, A., et al.: Automatic differentiation in PyTorch. In: NIPS Autodiff Workshop (2017)
25. Qian, X., et al.: Pose-normalized image generation for person re-identification. In: Ferrari, V., Hebert, M., Sminchisescu, C., Weiss, Y. (eds.) ECCV 2018. LNCS, vol. 11213, pp. 661–678. Springer, Cham (2018). https://doi.org/10.1007/978-3-030-01240-3_40
26. Quispe, R., Pedrini, H.: Improved person re-identification based on saliency and semantic parsing with deep neural network models. arXiv:1807.05618 (2018)

27. Ranjan, R., Patel, V.M., Chellappa, R.: HyperFace: a deep multi-task learning framework for face detection, landmark localization, pose estimation, and gender recognition. PAMI **41**(1), 121–135 (2019)
28. Rebuffi, S.A., Bilen, H., Vedaldi, A.: Learning multiple visual domains with residual adapters. In: NIPS (2017)
29. Ruan, T., et al.: Devil in the details: towards accurate single and multiple human parsing. In: AAAI (2019)
30. Ruder, S.: An overview of multi-task learning in deep neural networks. arXiv:1706.05098 (2017)
31. Saquib Sarfraz, M., Schumann, A., Eberle, A., Stiefelhagen, R.: A pose-sensitive embedding for person re-identification with expanded cross neighborhood re-ranking. In: CVPR (2018)
32. Sárándi, I., Linder, T., Arras, K.O., Leibe, B.: Synthetic occlusion augmentation with volumetric heatmaps for the 2018 ECCV PoseTrack challenge on 3D human pose estimation. arXiv:1809.04987 (2018)
33. Suh, Y., Wang, J., Tang, S., Mei, T., Lee, K.M.: Part-aligned bilinear representations for person re-identification. In: Ferrari, V., Hebert, M., Sminchisescu, C., Weiss, Y. (eds.) Computer Vision – ECCV 2018. LNCS, vol. 11218, pp. 418–437. Springer, Cham (2018). https://doi.org/10.1007/978-3-030-01264-9_25
34. Sun, C., Jiang, N., Zhang, L., Wang, Y., Wu, W., Zhou, Z.: Unified framework for joint attribute classification and person re-identification. In: Kůrková, V., Manolopoulos, Y., Hammer, B., Iliadis, L., Maglogiannis, I. (eds.) ICANN 2018. LNCS, vol. 11139, pp. 637–647. Springer, Cham (2018). https://doi.org/10.1007/978-3-030-01418-6_63
35. Sun, X., Xiao, B., Wei, F., Liang, S., Wei, Y.: Integral human pose regression. In: Ferrari, V., Hebert, M., Sminchisescu, C., Weiss, Y. (eds.) ECCV 2018. LNCS, vol. 11210, pp. 536–553. Springer, Cham (2018). https://doi.org/10.1007/978-3-030-01231-1_33
36. Tang, W., Yu, P., Wu, Y.: Deeply learned compositional models for human pose estimation. In: Ferrari, V., Hebert, M., Sminchisescu, C., Weiss, Y. (eds.) ECCV 2018. LNCS, vol. 11207, pp. 197–214. Springer, Cham (2018). https://doi.org/10.1007/978-3-030-01219-9_12
37. Tompson, J., Goroshin, R., Jain, A., LeCun, Y., Bregler, C.: Efficient object localization using convolutional networks. In: CVPR (2015)
38. Wang, C., Zhang, Q., Huang, C., Liu, W., Wang, X.: Mancs: a multi-task attentional network with curriculum sampling for person re-identification. In: Ferrari, V., Hebert, M., Sminchisescu, C., Weiss, Y. (eds.) ECCV 2018. LNCS, vol. 11208, pp. 384–400. Springer, Cham (2018). https://doi.org/10.1007/978-3-030-01225-0_23
39. Wang, G., Yuan, Y., Chen, X., Li, J., Zhou, X.: learning discriminative features with multiple granularities for person re-identification. In: ACM MM (2018)
40. Wu, Y., He, K.: Group normalization. In: Ferrari, V., Hebert, M., Sminchisescu, C., Weiss, Y. (eds.) ECCV 2018. LNCS, vol. 11217, pp. 3–19. Springer, Cham (2018). https://doi.org/10.1007/978-3-030-01261-8_1
41. Wu, Z., Shen, C., v. d. Hengel, A.: Bridging category-level and instance-level semantic image segmentation. arXiv:1605.06885 (2016)
42. Xiao, T., Liu, Y., Zhou, B., Jiang, Y., Sun, J.: Unified perceptual parsing for scene understanding. In: Ferrari, V., Hebert, M., Sminchisescu, C., Weiss, Y. (eds.) ECCV 2018. LNCS, vol. 11209, pp. 432–448. Springer, Cham (2018). https://doi.org/10.1007/978-3-030-01228-1_26

43. Xiao, T., Li, S., Wang, B., Lin, L., Wang, X.: Joint detection and identification feature learning for person search. In: CVPR (2017)
44. Yang, W., Li, S., Ouyang, W., Li, H., Wang, X.: Learning feature pyramids for human pose estimation. In: ICCV (2017)
45. Zamir, A.R., Sax, A., Shen, W., Guibas, L.J., Malik, J., Savarese, S.: Taskonomy: disentangling task transfer learning. In: CVPR (2018)
46. Zheng, F., et al.: Pyramidal person re-identification via multi-loss dynamic training (2019)

Dynamic Classifier Chains for Multi-label Learning

Pawel Trajdos[(⊠)] and Marek Kurzynski

Department of Systems and Computer Networks, Wroclaw University of Science and Technology, Wybrzeze Wyspianskiego 27, 50-370 Wroclaw, Poland
pawel.trajdos@pwr.wroc.pl

Abstract. In this paper, we deal with the task of building a dynamic ensemble of chain classifiers for multi-label classification. To do so, we proposed two concepts of the classifier chain algorithms that are able to change the label order of the chain without rebuilding the entire model. Such models allow anticipating the instance-specific chain order without the significant increase in the computational burden. The proposed chain models are built using the Naive Bayes classifier and nearest neighbour approaches. To take the benefits of the proposed algorithms, we developed a simple heuristic that allows the system to find relatively good label order. The experimental results showed that the proposed models and the heuristic are efficient tools for building dynamic chain classifiers.

Keywords: Multi-label · Classifier chains · Naive Bayes · Dynamic chains · Nearest neighbour

1 Introduction

Under the well-known, single-label classification framework, an object is assigned to only one class. However, many real-world datasets contain objects assigned to different categories at the same time. Omitting one of those categories is considered as information loss. Classification process involving such a kind of data is called the multi-label classification [9]. Multi-label classification is a new and explored idea and it is employed in a wide range of practical applications [9].

Multi-label classification algorithms can be broadly partitioned into two main groups i.e. dataset transformation algorithms and algorithm adaptation approaches [9]. In this paper, only dataset transformation algorithms that decompose a multi-label problem into a set of single-label classification tasks are investigated. To reconstruct the multi-label response, during the inference phase, outputs of the underlying single-label classifiers are combined to create a multi-label prediction.

Electronic supplementary material The online version of this chapter (https://doi.org/10.1007/978-3-030-33676-9_40) contains supplementary material, which is available to authorized users.

G. A. Fink et al. (Eds.): DAGM GCPR 2019, LNCS 11824, pp. 567–580, 2019.
https://doi.org/10.1007/978-3-030-33676-9_40

Let's focus on one of the simplest decomposition methods: the *binary relevance* (BR) approach that decomposes a multi-label classification task into a set of *one-vs-rest* binary classification problems [1]. In this approach, it is assumed that labels are conditionally independent. Although the assumption does not hold in most of the real-life recognition problems, the BR framework is one of the most widespread multi-label classification methods. This is due to its excellent scalability and acceptable classification quality [16].

To preserve the scalability of BR systems, and provide a model of inter-label relations, Read et al. [22] developed the *Classifier Chain* model (CC) that establish a linked chain of modified one-vs-rest binary classifiers. The modification consists of an extension of the input space of single-label classifiers along the chain sequence. To be stricter, for a given label sequence, the feature space of each classifier along the chain is extended with a set of binary variables corresponding to the labels that precede the given one. The model implies that, during the training phase, input space of given classifier is extended using the ground-truth labels extracted from the training set. During the inference step, the binary labels predicted by preceding classifiers are employed. Thus, the described approach passes along the chain, information allowing the CC to take into account inter-label relations at the cost of allowing the label-prediction-errors to propagate along the chain [22]. As a consequence, the performance of a chain classifier strongly depends on chain configuration. To overcome these effects, the authors suggested generating an *ensemble of chain classifiers* (ECC). The ensemble consists of classifiers trained using different label sequences [22].

The originally proposed ECC ensemble uses the randomly generated label orders. Additionally, each chain classifier is built using a resampled dataset. This approach provides the additional diversity into the ensemble classifier. This simple, yet effective approach allows improving the classification quality significantly in comparison to single chain classifier.

Later research shows that the members of the ensemble may be chosen in such a way that provides further improvement of classification quality. Thus, Read et al. proposed a strategy that uses the Monte Carlo sampling to explore the label sequence space to find a classifier chain that offers the highest classification quality [20]. Another approach was proposed by Liu et al. [15]. They developed a method that establishes a model of inter-label relations that may be described using a *directed acyclic graph* (DAG). The ensemble is generated using topological sorting of the graph. Chen et al. [3] proposed a method that makes clusters of labels. Then, for each cluster of labels, an undirected graph describing inter-label relations is built. Then, a *minimum spanning tree* is created for the graph. After that, *breadth-first search* algorithm determines sequences for the cluster-specific ensemble of CC classifiers. A similar approach was proposed by Huang et al [14]. They proposed building the clusters using a meta-space that mixes input space and the label space. Then inter-label relations are modelled using correlation. The model is expressed using a DAG-like structure. Finally, the CC classifier is built for each cluster. The chain structure may also be induced using the Bayesian Network approach [30].

The chain sequence can also be found using the meta-heuristic approach. Goncalves et al. developed a strategy that utilises a *genetic algorithm* (GA) to find a good chain structure for the entire dataset [10]. To evaluate the label orders each corresponding classifier must be built and evaluated using the validation set. A similar approach was also used by Trajdos and Kurzynski who proposed to use the multi-objective genetic algorithm to optimize classification quality and chain diversity simultaneously [27].

Another way of dealing with the error propagation is to build a classifier that combines the CC algorithm with the BR-based approach [17,18].

The previously cited methods build the ensemble structure during the training procedure. Consequently, throughout this paper, this kind of methods will be called static methods. The dynamic chain classifiers, on the other hand, determines the best label order at the prediction phase [23]. The above-mentioned classifier produces a set of randomly generated label sequences and then validates the chain classifiers. During the validation phase, each point from the validation set is assigned with a label order that produces the most accurate output vector for this point. As the experimental research shows, the dynamic methods of building a label order may achieve better classification quality [23].

During the building of a dynamic chain classifier, multiple chain classifiers must be learned. These classifiers are built using the same training set and differ only in the chain order. As a consequence, the computational burden of the algorithm may be reduced if there exists a classifier that is trained once and changing the label sequence is done without rebuilding the model from scratch. To address this issue, two models based on the Naive Bayes approach and the nearest neighbour approach were proposed. Additionally, a dynamic method of determining the chain order based on the classification quality determined for each label separately is employed. This paper explores the idea previously presented in [26].

The rest of the paper is organised as follows. Next Sect. 2 provides a formal description of the multi-label classification problem and describes the developed algorithms. Section 3 contains a description of the conducted experiments. The results are presented and discussed in Sect. 4. Finally, Sect. 5 concludes the paper.

2   Proposed Methods

In this section, we introduce a formal notation of multi-label classification problem and provide a description of the proposed method.

2.1   Preliminaries

Under the *multi-label* (ML) formalism a d − dimensional object $x = [x_1, x_2, \ldots, x_d] \in \mathcal{X}$ is assigned to a set of labels indicated by the binary vector of length L: $y = [y_1, y_2, \ldots, y_L] \in \mathcal{Y} = \{0, 1\}^L$, where L denotes the number of labels.

In this paper, the statistical classification framework is followed. As a consequence, it is assumed that an object x and its set of labels y are realizations of the corresponding random vectors $\mathbf{X} = [\mathbf{X}_1, \mathbf{X}_2, \ldots, \mathbf{X}_d]$, $\mathbf{Y} = [\mathbf{Y}_1, \mathbf{Y}_2, \ldots, \mathbf{Y}_L]$ and the joint probability distribution $P(\mathbf{X}, \mathbf{Y})$ on $\mathcal{X} \times \mathcal{Y}$ is known. Because the above-mentioned assumption is never meet in real world, in this study, it is assumed that the multi-label classifier $h : \mathcal{X} \mapsto \mathcal{Y}$, that maps the feature space $\mathcal{X}$ to the set $\mathcal{Y}$, is built in a supervised learning procedure using the training set $\mathcal{T}$ containing N pairs of feature vectors x and corresponding class labels y.

2.2   Naive Bayes Classifier for Dynamic Classifier Chains

The CC classifier h is an ensemble of L single-label classifiers ψ_i that constitutes a linked chain that is built according to the permutation of label sequence π. Each single-label classifier $h_{\pi(i)}$ along with the chain makes its decision according to the maximum a posteriori rule:

$$h_{\pi(i)}(x) = \mathrm{argmax}_{y \in \{0,1\}} P(\mathbf{Y}_{\pi(i)} = y | B_{\pi(i)}(x)), \tag{1}$$

where $B_{\pi(i)}(x)$ is a random event defined below:

$$B_{\pi(i)}(x) = (\mathbf{X} = x, \mathbf{Y}_{\pi(i-1)} = h_{\pi(i-1)}(x), \mathbf{Y}_{\pi(i-2)} = h_{\pi(i-2)}(x), \cdots ,$$
$$\mathbf{Y}_{\pi(1)} = h_{\pi(1)}(x)), \forall i \in \{2, 3, \cdots, L\}, \tag{2}$$

and for $i = 1$ the terms related to labels disappear.

Conditioning on the random event $B_{\pi(i)}(x)$ instead of $\mathbf{X} = x$ allows the chain to take inter-label dependencies into account. The above-mentioned classification rule is a greedy rule that calculates the probability (1) using predictions of preceding classifiers.

The probability defined in (1) is then computed using the Bayes rule:

$$P(\mathbf{Y}_{\pi(i)} = y | B_{\pi(i)}(x)) = \frac{P(\mathbf{Y}_{\pi(i)} = y)}{P(B_{\pi(i)}(x))} P(B_{\pi(i)}(x) | \mathbf{Y}_{\pi(i)} = y). \tag{3}$$

The term $P(B_{\pi(i)}(x))$ does not depend on event $\mathbf{Y}_{\pi(i)} = y$. Consequently, the decision rule (1) is rewritten:

$$h_{\pi(i)}(x) = \mathrm{argmax}_{y \in \{0,1\}} P(\mathbf{Y}_{\pi(i)} = y) P(B_{\pi(i)}(x) | \mathbf{Y}_{\pi(i)} = y) \tag{4}$$

Now, to improve the readability we simplify the notation:

$$P(B_{\pi(i)}(x) | \mathbf{Y}_{\pi(i)} = y) = P(B_{\pi(i)}(x) | y). \tag{5}$$

Then, following the Naive Bayes rule, it is assumed that all random variables that constitute $B_{\pi(i)}(x)$ are conditionally independent given $\mathbf{Y}_{\pi(i)} = y$. Consequently, $P(B_{\pi(i)}(x)|y)$ is defined as follows:

$$P(B_{\pi(i)}(x)|y) = \prod_{m=1}^{d} P(\mathbf{X}_m = x_m | y) \prod_{l=1}^{l=i-1} P(\mathbf{Y}_{\pi(l)} = h_{\pi(l)}(x) | y). \tag{6}$$

Now, it is easy to see that the term $\prod_{l=1}^{l=i-1} P(\mathbf{Y}_{\pi(l)} = h_{\pi(l)}(\boldsymbol{x})|y)$, contrary to $\prod_{m=1}^{d} P(X_m = \boldsymbol{x}_m|y)$, depends on the chain structure. Furthermore, all probability distributions used in the above-mentioned terms can be estimated during the training phase when the chain structure is unknown.

The training and inference phases are described in detail using pseudocode shown in Algorithms 1 and 2.

Algorithm 2. Naive Bayes classifier – inference procedure.

```
Input data:
  x ∈ X -- input instance;
  V -- validation set;
BEGIN
  #Query the BR models
  FOR i ∈ {1, 2, · · · , L}:
    e_i^0 = ∏_{m=1}^{d} P(X_k = x_m|Y_i = 0);
    e_i^1 = ∏_{m=1}^{d} P(X_k = x_m|Y_i = 1);
  END FOR;
  Determine label permuatation π using V and x;
  SET i = 1;
  DO:
    h_{π(i)}(x) = argmax_{y∈{0,1}} e_{π(i)}^y P(Y_{π(i)} = y)
    FOR j ∈ {i + 1, i + 2, · · · , L}:
      d_{π(j)}^0 := e_{π(j)}^0 * P(Y_{π(i)} = h_{π(i)}(x)|Y_{π(j)} = 0)
      d_{π(j)}^1 := e_{π(j)}^1 * P(Y_{π(i)} = h_{π(i)}(x)|Y_{π(j)} = 1)
    END FOR;
    i := i + 1;
  WHILE(i < L);
  RETURN [h_1(x), h_2(x), · · · , h_L(x)];
END
```

Algorithm 1. Naive Bayes classifier – learning procedure.

```
Input data:
  T - training set;
BEGIN
  Split T into T_A and V so that:
  |T_A| = t|T| and |V| = (1 − t)|T|, t ∈ (0, 1)
  T_A ∩ V = ∅;
  Using T_A build estimators of
  the following distributions:
    P(Y_{π(i)} = y)∀i ∈ {1, 2, · · · , L}, y ∈ {0, 1}
    P(X_m|Y_{π(i)} = y)
    ∀i ∈ {1, 2, · · · , L}, y ∈ {0, 1}, m ∈ {1, 2, · · · , d}
    P(Y_{π(l)}|Y_{π(i)} = y)∀i, l ∈ {1, 2, · · · , L}; i ≠ l
END
```

2.3 KNN Classifier for Dynamic Classifier Chains

In this section, we define a dynamic classifier chain algorithm based on the nearest neighbours approach.

Let's begin with the definition of the distance function that depends on label permutation and the position along the chain:

$$\delta_{\pi,i}\left((\boldsymbol{x},\boldsymbol{y}),(\boldsymbol{x}',\boldsymbol{y}')\right) = \sqrt{\sum_{j=1}^{d}\left(\boldsymbol{x}_j - \boldsymbol{x}_j'\right)^2 + \sum_{l=1}^{i-1}(\boldsymbol{y}_{\pi(l)} - \boldsymbol{y}_{\pi(l)}')^2}. \quad (7)$$

For the first predicted label, the sum related to the label space is omitted. Such a defined distance function allows making the prediction using the chaining rule. The above-defined distance function is used to build the neighbourhood of a given point in the extended feature space: $M_{\pi,i}^R((\boldsymbol{x},\boldsymbol{y}))$. The neighbourhood contains the R closest instances selected from the training set according to the distance function $\delta_{\pi,i}$.

Given the neighbourhood, the probability $P(\mathbf{Y}_{\pi(i)} = y|B_{\pi(i)}(\boldsymbol{x}))$ is estimated as follows:

$$P(\mathbf{Y}_{\pi(i)} = y|B_{\pi(i)}(\boldsymbol{x})) \approx \frac{|\{(\boldsymbol{x}^n,\boldsymbol{y}^n)|(\boldsymbol{x}^n,\boldsymbol{y}^n) \in M_{\pi,i}^R((\boldsymbol{x},h(\boldsymbol{x}))), \boldsymbol{y}_i^n = y\}|}{R}. \quad (8)$$

Then, the label $\pi(i)$ is predicted using rule (1).

2.4   Dynamic Chain Order

In this subsection, the local measure of the classification quality is defined. To do so, we employed a modified version of the well-known F_1 measure.

First of all, the fuzzy neighbourhood in the input space is defined. The neighbourhood of an instance x is defined using the following fuzzy set:

$$\mathcal{N}(x) = \{(x^n, y^n, \mu(x, x^n)) : (x^n, y^n) \in \mathcal{V}\}, \tag{9}$$

where $\mathcal{V}$ is the validation set. The membership function $\mu(x, x^n)$ is defined using the gaussian function:

$$\mu(x, x^n) = \exp(-\beta\delta(x, x^n)^2). \tag{10}$$

The distance function $\delta(x, x^n)$ is simple euclidean distance and the β coefficient is tuned during the experiments.

Then, we define set of points $\mathcal{V}_l$ that belongs to given label:

$$\mathcal{V}_l = \{(x^n, y^n, 1) : (x^n, y^n) \in \mathcal{V}, y_l^n = 1\} \tag{11}$$

The set of points classified by the binary-relevance as label l is also defined:

$$\mathcal{D}_l = \{(x^n, y^n, 1) : (x^n, y^n) \in \mathcal{V}, h_l^{BR}(x^n) = 1\} \tag{12}$$

Using the above-mentioned sets we define the local True Positive rate, False Positive rate, False Negative rate respectively:

$$\mathrm{TP}_l(x) = |\mathcal{V}_l \cap \mathcal{D}_l \cap \mathcal{N}(x)|, \tag{13}$$

$$\mathrm{FP}_l(x) = |(\mathcal{D}_l \setminus \mathcal{V}_l) \cap \mathcal{N}(x)|, \tag{14}$$

$$\mathrm{FN}_l(x) = |(\mathcal{V}_l \setminus \mathcal{D}_l) \cap \mathcal{N}(x)|, \tag{15}$$

where $|\cdot|$ is the cardinality of the fuzzy set [7]. Then, we define the local measure of classification quality:

$$F_l(x) = \frac{2\mathrm{TP}_l(x)}{2\mathrm{TP}_l(x) + \mathrm{FP}_l(x) + \mathrm{FN}_l(x)} \tag{16}$$

Finally, the label order π is chosen so that the following inequalities are met:

$$F_{\pi(1)}(x) \geq F_{\pi(2)}(x) \geq \cdots \geq F_{\pi(L)}(x). \tag{17}$$

In other words, labels for whom the classification quality is higher precede other labels in the chain structure. This should reduce the propagation error.

2.5   The Ensemble Classifier

Now, let us define a ML $K-$element classifier ensemble: $eH = \{H_1, \ldots, H_K\}$. The ensemble is built using classifier chain algorithms defined in previous sections. Each ensemble classifier is built using a subset of the original dataset. The size of subset is 66% of the original training set.

The BR transformation may produce imbalanced single-label dataset. To prevent the classifier from learning from a highly imbalanced dataset, the random undersampling technique [8] is applied. The majority class is undersampled when imbalance ratio is higher than 20.

The research on the application of the Naive Bayes algorithm under the CC framework shows that when the number of features in the input space is significantly higher in comparison to the number of labels, the Naive Bayes classifier may not perform well [23]. To prevent the proposed system from being affected by this phenomenon, the feature selection procedure for each single-label separately is applied. The feature selection removes only attributes related to the original input space. We employed the selection procedure based on the correlation [12].

The final prediction vector of the ensemble is obtained via is a simple averaging of response vectors corresponding to base classifiers of the ensemble followed by the thresholding procedure.

3 Experimental Setup

The experimental study is divided into three main sections. The first one assesses the impact of employing the chaining approach. In this section, the binary relevance and classifier chains algorithms built using the following base classifiers are compared: J48 Classifier (C4.5 algorithm implemented in Weka) [19]; SVM algorithm with radial based kernel [4]; Naive Bayes Classifier [13]; Nearest Neighbour classifier [5].

In this section, the BR and CC ensembles built using a genetic algorithm tailored to optimise the macro-averaged F_1 loss are compared. For each ensemble, the size of the committee was set to $K = 20$. For the algorithm based on the genetic algorithm, the initial size of the committee was set to $3K$. Each numeric attribute used in the training and validation datasets was also standardised. After the standardisation, the mean value of the attribute is 0 and its standard deviation is 1. Each nominal attribute was converted into a set of binary attributes.

During the experimental study, the parameters of the SVM classifier ($C \in \{0.001, 1, 2, \cdots, 10\}$, $\gamma \in \{0.001, 1, 2, \cdots, 5\}$) were tuned using grid search and the 3-fold cross validation. The number of nearest neighbours was also tuned using 3-fold cross validation. The number of neighbours was chosen among the following values $R \in \{1, 3, 5, \cdots, 11\}$.

In two remaining sections, the conducted experimental study provides an empirical evaluation of the classification quality of the proposed methods and compares it to the reference methods. Namely, the experiments were conducted using the following algorithms for building the CC ensemble:

1. The proposed approach (Sect. 2.4).
2. Static ensemble generated using the genetic algorithm [27]. The ensemble is tuned to optimise the macro-averaged F_1 measure
3. ECC ensemble with randomly generated chain orders [22].

4. OOCC dynamic method proposed by da Silva et al. [23]. The ensemble is tuned to optimise the example based F_1 measure. Additionally, the reference method uses single split into training and validation sets.

The above-mentioned methods of building CC systems were evaluated using the Naive Bayes and the nearest neighbour algorithms as base classifiers. Systems built using different base classifiers were investigated in two separate sections. In the sections, the investigated algorithms are referred using the above-said numbers.

The reference algorithm also uses the Naive Bayes/nearest neighbour algorithm combined with the data preprocessing procedures described in Sect. 2.5.

The extraction of training and test datasets was performed using 10 fold cross-validation. For each ensemble, the proportion of the training set T_A was fixed at $t = 0.6$ of the original training set (see Algorithm 1).

The β coefficient was tuned during the training procedure using the 3 CV approach. The best value among $\{1, 2, \cdots, 10\}$ is chosen.

Single label classifiers were implemented using the WEKA software [11]. Multi-label classifier were implemented using the Mulan software [24].

The experiments were conducted using 30 multi-label benchmark datasets. The main characteristics of the datasets are summarized in Table 1. We used datasets from the sources abbreviated as follows: A [2], B [21] M–[24]; W–[28]; X–[29]; Z–[31]; T–[25]. Some of the employed sets needed some preprocessing. That is, we used multi-label multi-instance [31] sets (sources Z and W) which were transformed to single-instance multi-label datasets according to the suggestion made by Zhou et al. [31]. Multi-target regression sets (No 9, 30) were binarised using simple thresholding strategy. That is if the response is greater than 0 the resulting label is set '1'. To reduce the computational burden, we use only a subset of original Tmc2007 and IMDB datasets. Additionally, the number of labels in the Stackex datasets is reduced to 15.

The algorithms were compared in terms of 11 different quality criteria coming from two groups [16]: Instance-based Hamming, Zero-One, F_1, False Discovery Rate (FDR), False Negative Rate (FNR). Additionally, micro and macro averaged versions of F_1, FDR and FNR were used.

Statistical evaluation of the results was performed using the Wilcoxon signed-rank test [6] and the family-wise error rates were controlled using the Holm procedure [6]. For all statistical tests, the significance level was set to $\alpha = 0.1$. To check inner-group differences, we also applied the Friedman [6] test.

4   Results and Discussion

4.1   Assessing the Impact of Chaining Approach

In this section, the binary relevance ensembles with classifier chain ensembles built using the same base classifier are compared. The results are shown in Fig. 1a and Table 2. The compared algorithms are numbered as follows:

Table 1. Summarised properties of the datasets employed in the experimental study. Sr denotes the source of dataset, No. is the ordinal number of a set, N is the number of instances, d is the dimensionality of input space, L denotes the number of labels. LC, LD, avIR are label cardinality, label density and average imbalance ratio respectively [16].

No	Name	Sr	N	d	L	LC	LD	avIR	No	Name	Sr	N	d	L	LC	LD	avIR
1	Arts1	M	7484	1733	26	1.654	.064	94.74	16	LLOG	B	1460	1004	75	1.180	.016	39.27
2	Azotobacter	W	407	20	13	1.469	.113	2.225	17	Medical	M	978	1449	45	1.245	.028	89.50
3	Birds	M	645	260	19	1.014	.053	5.407	18	MimlImg	Z	2000	135	5	1.236	.247	1.193
4	Caenorhabditis	W	2512	20	21	2.419	.115	2.347	19	Ohsumed	B	13929	1002	23	1.663	.072	7.869
5	Drosophila	W	2605	20	22	2.656	.121	1.744	20	Plant	X	978	440	12	1.079	.090	6.690
6	Emotions	M	593	72	6	1.868	.311	1.478	21	Pyrococcus	W	425	20	18	2.136	.119	2.421
7	Enron	M	1702	1001	53	3.378	.064	73.95	22	Saccharomyces	W	3509	20	27	2.275	.084	2.077
8	Flags	X	194	43	7	3.392	.485	2.255	23	Scene	X	2407	294	6	1.074	.179	1.254
9	Flare2	M	1066	27	3	0.209	.070	14.15	24	SimpleHC	T	3000	30	10	1.900	.190	1.138
10	Genbase	M	662	1186	27	1.252	.046	37.32	25	SimpleHS	T	3000	30	10	2.307	.231	2.622
11	Geobacter	W	379	20	11	1.264	.115	2.750	26	SLASHDOT	B	3782	1079	22	1.181	.054	17.69
12	Haloarcula	W	304	20	13	1.602	.123	2.419	27	Stackex_chess	A	1675	585	15	1.137	.076	4.744
13	Human	X	3106	440	14	1.185	.085	15.29	28	Tmc2007-500	M	2857	500	22	2.222	.101	17.15
14	Image	M	2000	294	5	1.236	.247	1.193	29	water-quality	M	1060	16	14	5.073	.362	1.767
15	IMDB	M	3042	1001	28	1.987	.071	24.61	30	yeast	M	2417	103	14	4.237	.303	7.197

1. BR ensemble – J48.   4. CC ensemble – SVM.   7. BR ensemble – KNN.
2. CC ensemble – J48.   5. BR ensemble – NB.
3. BR ensemble – SVM.   6. CC ensemble – NB.   8. CC ensemble – KNN.

The analysis of the results clearly shows that there is a noticeable difference between the two groups of measures. It means, the differences between the BR-based and CC-based algorithms are greater in terms of example based criteria. On the other hand, the differences in mean ranks are lower for the example based measures.

For the example based measures, the average ranks achieved by the CC-based algorithms are lower than for the BR-based algorithms. However, only for algorithms based on the J48 classifier, the differences are significant for example-based FDR, FNR and F_1 measures. A similar trend is observed for the zero-one loss. In this case, only differences for the nearest neighbour classifier are insignificant.

On the other hand, for the label-based measures and the Hamming loss, almost no significant differences are observed. Nevertheless, the average ranks suggest that for this group of measures, the classification quality may deteriorate. The results clearly demonstrate that although label-specific quality measures do not change in a significant way, the prediction of the entire label-vector improves. This is an expected result since the CC-based approach incorporates the inter-label relations. This is a well-known fact that has been reported by authors that have previously compared both approaches [17].

The results also show that there are almost no significant differences between J48, NB and KNN based algorithms. Contrary, the SVM algorithm tends to outperform the remaining ones in terms of the example-based criteria, hamming loss and zero-one loss. It means that although J48 algorithm takes the biggest advantage of employing the chain rule, NB and KNN based classifiers are comparable to J48-based ensembles.

Table 2. Base classifier comparison. Result of the statistical evaluation. Rnk stands for average rank over all datasets, Frd is the p-value obtained using the Friedman test and Wp-i denotes the p-value associated with the Wilcoxon test that compares the i-th algorithm against the others.

Alg.	1	2	3	4	5	6	7	8	1	2	3	4	5	6	7	8	1	2	3	4	5	6	7	8
	Hamming								Zero-One								EX FDR							
Rnk	4.94	5.03	2.81	3.03	4.72	4.63	5.38	5.47	5.50	5.00	3.30	2.25	5.17	4.16	5.88	4.75	5.64	4.44	3.13	2.66	5.00	4.66	5.61	4.88
Frd	.000018								.000000								.000002							
Wp-1		1.00	.002	.148	1.00	1.00	1.00	.432		.032	.001	.000	1.00	.478	1.00	1.00		.070	.001	.001	1.00	.650	1.00	1.00
Wp-2			.000	.025	1.00	1.00	1.00	1.00			1.00	.001	1.00	1.00	.044	1.00			.845	.001	1.00	1.00	.056	1.00
Wp-3				1.00	.014	.022	.000	.000				.032	.005	.627	.001	.597				1.00	.002	.097	.001	.573
Wp-4					.552	.552	.017	.002					.000	.004	.000	.002					.002	.006	.000	.002
Wp-5						1.00	1.00	.591						.041	1.00	1.00						1.00	.964	1.00
Wp-6							1.00	1.00							.478	1.00							.666	1.00
Wp-7								1.00								.220								1.00
	EX F_1								Macro FDR								Macro FNR							
Rnk	5.72	4.47	4.06	2.53	4.53	4.25	5.63	4.81	4.25	5.50	3.00	4.91	3.97	5.25	4.00	5.13	4.63	4.45	5.20	4.97	4.03	4.78	3.41	4.53
Frd	0.000030								0.002491								0.312535							
Wp-1		.005	.041	.000	.200	.072	1.00	1.00		.019	.552	1.00	.390	1.00	1.00	.479		1.00	1.00	1.00	1.00	1.00	.022	1.00
Wp-2			1.00	.001	1.00	1.00	.189	1.00			.003	1.00	.697	1.00	1.00	.152			1.00	1.00	1.00	1.00	.441	1.00
Wp-3				.272	1.00	1.00	.089	1.00				.066	.552	.023	.349	.003				1.00	.077	1.00	.058	1.00
Wp-4					.014	.007	.000	.005					1.00	1.00	1.00	1.00					.419	1.00	.501	1.00
Wp-5						1.00	.200	1.00						.208	1.00	1.00						.998	1.00	1.00
Wp-6							.090	1.00							.101	1.00							1.00	1.00
Wp-7								1.00								.552								.143
	Micro FDR								Micro FNR								Micro F_1							
Rnk	4.81	4.84	2.72	3.13	4.81	4.78	5.19	5.72	4.66	4.44	5.31	4.66	4.31	4.66	3.78	4.19	4.56	4.69	4.41	3.75	4.69	5.03	4.25	4.63
Frd	0.000014								0.777721								0.777721							
Wp-1		1.00	.001	.141	1.00	1.00	1.00	.045		1.00	.706	1.00	1.00	1.00	.136	1.00		1.00	1.00	1.00	1.00	1.00	1.00	1.00
Wp-2			.000	.023	1.00	1.00	1.00	.564			1.00	1.00	1.00	1.00	1.00	1.00			1.00	1.00	1.00	1.00	1.00	1.00
Wp-3				1.00	.001	.001	.000	.001				1.00	.233	1.00	.215	.132				1.00	1.00	1.00	1.00	1.00
Wp-4					.091	.079	.015	.007					1.00	1.00	1.00	1.00					1.00	1.00	1.00	1.00
Wp-5						1.00	1.00	1.00						1.00	1.00	1.00						1.00	1.00	1.00
Wp-6							1.00	1.00							1.00	1.00							1.00	1.00
Wp-7								1.00								1.00								1.00
	EX FNR								Macro F_1															
Rnk	5.47	4.66	4.22	3.53	3.97	3.91	5.19	5.06	4.81	5.09	4.25	4.84	3.94	5.16	3.41	4.50								
Frd	.056423								0.224854															
Wp-1		.011	1.00	.009	.205	.054	1.00	1.00		1.00	1.00	1.00	1.00	1.00	.000	1.00								
Wp-2			1.00	.223	1.00	1.00	1.00	1.00			1.00	1.00	1.00	1.00	.031	1.00								
Wp-3				.937	1.00	1.00	1.00	1.00				1.00	1.00	1.00	1.00	1.00								
Wp-4					1.00	1.00	.169	.113					1.00	1.00	.824	1.00								
Wp-5						1.00	.221	1.00						.355	1.00	1.00								
Wp-6							.090	.266							.278	1.00								
Wp-7								1.00								.203								

4.2   Naive Bayes Classifier

The results of the experimental study are presented in Table 3 and Fig. 1b.

First, let's analyse differences between the proposed heuristic and the simple ECC ensemble. We begin with investigating the macro-averaged measures. It is easy to see that both methods are comparable in terms of the recall but the proposed one is significantly better in terms of precision. It means that the proposed method makes significantly less false positive predictions. Consequently, under the macro-averaged F_1 loss the proposed method outperforms the ECC ensemble. The same pattern is also present in results related to the micro-averaged measures. However, the difference for the micro-averaged F_1 measure is not significant. In contrast, under example based measures, except the Hamming loss, there are no significant differences between investigated methods.

The results show that the proposed heuristic provides an effective way of improving classification quality for the classifier chains ensemble. Moving the best performing, label-specific models at the beginning of the chain reduces the error that propagates along the chain.

Now, let's compare the proposed method to the other algorithm based on the dynamic chain approach. When we investigate the example-based criteria it is easy to see that the OOCC algorithm outperforms the proposed one in terms of FDR and Hamming loss. Those results combined with results achieved in terms

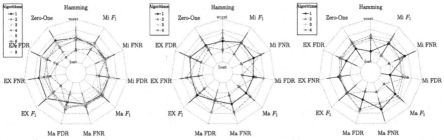

(a) Base classifier comparison (b) Naive Bayes classifier (c) Nearest Neighbour classi-
 – average ranks. fier.

Fig. 1. Visualisation of average ranks achieved by algorithms.

of macro and micro averaged measures shows that the OOCC method seems to be too much more conservative. In other words, it tends to make many false negative predictions in comparison to the other methods.

On the other hand, the average ranks clearly show that the method based on the genetic algorithm obtains the best results in comparison to the other investigated methods. The main reason is that the GA-based approach optimises the entire ensemble structure, whereas the investigated dynamic chain methods, choose the best label order for single classifier chain. Then the locally chosen chains are combined into the ensemble. It gives us a vital clue. Thus, when we consider an algorithm for dynamic chain order selection, we should think about a single chain and the global structure of the entire ensemble as well.

Table 3. Naive Bayes Based CC. Results of the statistical evaluation.

Alg.	1	2	3	4	1	2	3	4	1	2	3	4	1	2	3	4
		Hamming				Zero-One				EX FDR				EX FNR		
Rnk	2.45	2.67	3.03	**1.84**	2.52	**2.14**	2.97	2.38	2.84	**1.97**	2.91	2.28	2.56	**2.03**	2.53	2.88
Frd		.02113				.19410				.03824				.19410		
Wp-1		.702	.025	.063		.358	.199	.761		.019	.295	.134		.053	.700	.700
Wp-2			.319	.319			.006	.368			.005	.239			.136	.015
Wp-3				.001				.097				.040				.136
		EX F_1				Macro FDR				Macro FNR				Macro F_1		
Rnk	2.69	**2.03**	2.84	2.44	2.31	**2.22**	3.16	2.31	2.56	**1.94**	2.36	3.14	2.47	**1.81**	2.84	2.88
Frd		.19410				.04402				.02113				.02113		
Wp-1		.066	.821	.821		1.00	.012	1.00		.035	.919	.022		.156	.096	.248
Wp-2			.017	.112			.031	1.00			.174	.002			.003	.022
Wp-3				.590				.012				.105				.733
		Micro FDR				Micro FNR				Micro F_1						
Rnk	2.47	2.66	3.22	**1.66**	2.69	**1.72**	2.34	3.25	2.75	**1.78**	2.81	2.66				
Frd		.00027				.00029				.02242						
Wp-1		1.00	.028	.000		.005	.254	.239		.044	.610	1.00				
Wp-2			1.00	.008			.052	.000			.002	.044				
Wp-3				.000				.014				1.00				

4.3 Nearest Neighbour Classifier

The results of the experimental study are presented in Table 4 and Fig. 1c. The results show that for the group of example based measures and the zero-one loss, there are no significant differences in classification quality between all investigated algorithms.

For macro and micro averaged measures, the best performing algorithm is an ensemble optimised using the genetic algorithm. The proposed nearest-neighbour-based classifier does not differ significantly from ECC and OOCC algorithms. However, it tends to be more conservative because it achieves lower FDR and higher FDR. In other words, the classifier tends to decrease the false positive rate at the cost of decreasing the true positive rate. This phenomenon causes the highest classification quality in terms of the Hamming loss.

The results confirm the findings described in Sect. 4.1. The nearest-neighbour-based CC algorithm is unable to take all benefits of the chaining approach. On the other hand, the method is still comparable to chains built using different base classifiers.

Table 4. Nearest Neighbour based CC. Result of statistical evaluation.

Alg.	1	2	3	4	1	2	3	4	1	2	3	4	1	2	3	4
	Hamming				Zero-One				EX FDR				EX FNR			
Rnk	1.72	2.83	2.80	2.65	2.22	2.73	2.42	2.63	2.17	2.57	2.57	2.70	2.60	2.47	2.40	2.53
Frd	.008583				1.00000				1.00000				1.00000			
Wp-1		.004	.000	.006		1.00	1.00	1.00		1.00	1.00	.948		1.00	.985	1.00
Wp-2			.441	.173			1.00	1.00			1.00	1.00			1.00	1.00
Wp-3				.441				1.00				1.00				1.00
	EX F_1				Macro FDR				Macro FNR				Macro F_1			
Rnk	2.43	2.57	2.47	2.53	2.27	1.67	3.10	2.97	2.97	1.70	2.78	2.55	2.60	1.53	3.03	2.83
Frd	1.00000				.000265				.004979				.000259			
Wp-1		1.00	1.00	1.00		.017	.010	.012		.000	.617	.617		.000	.276	.579
Wp-2			1.00	1.00			.000	.003			.000	.004			.000	.000
Wp-3				1.00				.271				.561				.579
	Micro FDR				Micro FNR				Micro F_1							
Rnk	1.67	2.97	2.77	2.60	2.97	1.70	2.77	2.57	2.63	1.63	3.00	2.73				
Frd	.003725				.004979				.002113							
Wp-1		.009	.000	.028		.000	.926	.926		.002	.532	.657				
Wp-2			.382	.070			.002	.019			.001	.006				
Wp-3				.715				.926				.657				

5   Conclusions

The main goal of this research was to provide an effective chain classifier that allows changing label order at relatively low computational cost. We achieved it using a classifier based on the Naive Bayes and KNN approaches. To prove that the proposed method allows handling inter-label relations in an efficient way, we proposed a simple heuristic method that determines label order that should minimise label propagation error. Indeed, the experimental results showed that the proposed method is able to produce a good chain structure at a low computational cost. However, the proposed method of building a dynamic ensemble does not allow to outperform the static system that optimizes the entire ensemble structure. We believe that there is still a room for improvement. In our opinion, the performance of the system may be improved if we provide, a better heuristic that optimises the entire ensemble in a dynamic way.

Acknowledgments. This work is financed from Grant For Young Scientists and PhD Students Development, under agreement: 0402/0109/18.

References

1. Alvares Cherman, E., Metz, J., Monard, M.C.: A simple approach to incorporate label dependency in multi-label classification. In: Sidorov, G., Hernández Aguirre, A., Reyes García, C.A. (eds.) MICAI 2010. LNCS (LNAI), vol. 6438, pp. 33–43. Springer, Heidelberg (2010). https://doi.org/10.1007/978-3-642-16773-7_3

2. Charte, F., Rivera, A.J., del Jesus, M.J., Herrera, F.: Quinta: a question tagging assistant to improve the answering ratio in electronic forums. In: IEEE EURO-CON 2015 - International Conference on Computer as a Tool (EUROCON). IEEE, September 2015. https://doi.org/10.1109/eurocon.2015.7313677

3. Chen, B., Li, W., Zhang, Y., Hu, J.: Enhancing multi-label classification based on local label constraints and classifier chains. In: 2016 International Joint Conference on Neural Networks (IJCNN). IEEE, July 2016. https://doi.org/10.1109/ijcnn.2016.7727370

4. Cortes, C., Vapnik, V.: Support-vector networks. Mach. Learn. **20**(3), 273–297 (1995). https://doi.org/10.1007/bf00994018

5. Cover, T., Hart, P.: Nearest neighbor pattern classification. IEEE Trans. Inf. Theory **13**(1), 21–27 (1967). https://doi.org/10.1109/tit.1967.1053964

6. Demšar, J.: Statistical comparisons of classifiers over multiple data sets. J. Mach. Learn. Res. **7**, 1–30 (2006)

7. Dhar, M.: On cardinality of fuzzy sets. Int. J. Intell. Syst. Appl. **5**(6), 47–52 (2013). https://doi.org/10.5815/ijisa.2013.06.06

8. García, V., Sánchez, J., Mollineda, R.: On the effectiveness of preprocessing methods when dealing with different levels of class imbalance. Knowl.-Based Syst. **25**(1), 13–21 (2012). https://doi.org/10.1016/j.knosys.2011.06.013

9. Gibaja, E., Ventura, S.: Multi-label learning: a review of the state of the art and ongoing research. Wiley Interdisc. Rev. Data Min. Knowl. Discov. **4**(6), 411–444 (2014). https://doi.org/10.1002/widm.1139

10. Goncalves, E.C., Plastino, A., Freitas, A.A.: A genetic algorithm for optimizing the label ordering in multi-label classifier chains. In: 2013 IEEE 25th International Conference on Tools with Artificial Intelligence. IEEE, November 2013. https://doi.org/10.1109/ictai.2013.76

11. Hall, M., Frank, E., Holmes, G., Pfahringer, B., Reutemann, P., Witten, I.H.: The weka data mining software. ACM SIGKDD Explor. Newslett. **11**(1), 10 (2009). https://doi.org/10.1145/1656274.1656278

12. Hall, M.A.: Correlation-based feature selection for machine learning. Ph.D. thesis, The University of Waikato (1999)

13. Hand, D.J., Yu, K.: Idiot's Bayes: not so stupid after all? Int. Stat. Rev./Revue Internationale de Statistique **69**(3), 385 (2001). https://doi.org/10.2307/1403452

14. Huang, J., Li, G., Wang, S., Zhang, W., Huang, Q.: Group sensitive classifier chains for multi-label classification. In: 2015 IEEE International Conference on Multimedia and Expo (ICME). IEEE, June 2015. https://doi.org/10.1109/icme.2015.7177400

15. Liu, X., Shi, Z., Li, Z., Wang, X., Shi, Z.: Sorted label classifier chains for learning images with multi-label. In: Proceedings of the International Conference on Multimedia - MM 2010. ACM Press (2010). https://doi.org/10.1145/1873951.1874121

16. Luaces, O., Díez, J., Barranquero, J., del Coz, J.J., Bahamonde, A.: Binary relevance efficacy for multilabel classification. Progress in Artif. Intell. **1**(4), 303–313 (2012). https://doi.org/10.1007/s13748-012-0030-x

17. Madjarov, G., Kocev, D., Gjorgjevikj, D., Džeroski, S.: An extensive experimental comparison of methods for multi-label learning. Pattern Recogn. **45**(9), 3084–3104 (2012). https://doi.org/10.1016/j.patcog.2012.03.004
18. Montañes, E., et al.: Dependent binary relevance models for multi-label classification. Pattern Recogn. **47**(3), 1494–1508 (2014). https://doi.org/10.1016/j.patcog.2013.09.029
19. Quinlan, J.R.: C4.5: Programs for Machine Learning. Morgan Kaufmann Publishers Inc., San Francisco (1993)
20. Read, J., Martino, L., Luengo, D.: Efficient Monte Carlo methods for multidimensional learning with classifier chains. Pattern Recogn. **47**(3), 1535–1546 (2014). https://doi.org/10.1016/j.patcog.2013.10.006
21. Read, J., Peter, R.: (2017). http://meka.sourceforge.net/
22. Read, J., Pfahringer, B., Holmes, G., Frank, E.: Classifier chains for multi-label classification. Mach. Learn. **85**(3), 333–359 (2011). https://doi.org/10.1007/s10994-011-5256-5
23. da Silva, P.N., Gonçalves, E.C., Plastino, A., Freitas, A.A.: Distinct chains for different instances: an effective strategy for multi-label classifier chains. In: Calders, T., Esposito, F., Hüllermeier, E., Meo, R. (eds.) ECML PKDD 2014. LNCS (LNAI), vol. 8725, pp. 453–468. Springer, Heidelberg (2014). https://doi.org/10.1007/978-3-662-44851-9_29
24. Spyromitros-Xioufis, E., Tsoumakas, G., Groves, W., Vlahavas, I.: Multi-target regression via input space expansion: treating targets as inputs. Mach. Learn. **104**(1), 55–98 (2016). https://doi.org/10.1007/s10994-016-5546-z
25. Tomás, J.T., Spolaôr, N., Cherman, E.A., Monard, M.C.: A framework to generate synthetic multi-label datasets. Electron. Notes Theoret. Comput. Sci. **302**, 155–176 (2014). https://doi.org/10.1016/j.entcs.2014.01.025
26. Trajdos, P., Kurzynski, M.: Naive bayes classifier for dynamic chaining approach in multi-label learning. Int. J. Educ. Learn. Syst. **2**, 133–142 (2017)
27. Trajdos, P., Kurzynski, M.: Permutation-based diversity measure for classifier-chain approach. In: Kurzynski, M., Wozniak, M., Burduk, R. (eds.) CORES 2017. AISC, vol. 578, pp. 412–422. Springer, Cham (2018). https://doi.org/10.1007/978-3-319-59162-9_43
28. Wu, J.S., Huang, S.J., Zhou, Z.H.: Genome-wide protein function prediction through multi-instance multi-label learning. IEEE/ACM Trans. Comput. Biol. Bioinform. **11**(5), 891–902 (2014). https://doi.org/10.1109/tcbb.2014.2323058
29. Xu, J.: Fast multi-label core vector machine. Pattern Recogn. **46**(3), 885–898 (2013). https://doi.org/10.1016/j.patcog.2012.09.003
30. Zhang, P., Yang, Y., Zhu, X.: Approaching multi-dimensional classification by using Bayesian network chain classifiers. In: 2014 Sixth International Conference on Intelligent Human-Machine Systems and Cybernetics. IEEE, August 2014. https://doi.org/10.1109/ihmsc.2014.129
31. Zhou, Z.H., Zhang, M.L., Huang, S.J., Li, Y.F.: Multi-instance multi-label learning. Artif. Intell. **176**(1), 2291–2320 (2012). https://doi.org/10.1016/j.artint.2011.10.002

Learning 3D Semantic Reconstruction on Octrees

Xiaojuan Wang[1]([✉]), Martin R. Oswald[1], Ian Cherabier[1], and Marc Pollefeys[1,2]

[1] ETH Zurich, Zürich, Switzerland
xiaojwan@student.ethz.ch, xiaojuanwang.cs@gmail.com
[2] Microsoft, Redmond, USA

Abstract. We present a fully convolutional neural network that jointly predicts a semantic 3D reconstruction of a scene as well as a corresponding octree representation. This approach leverages the efficiency of an octree data structure to improve the capacities of volumetric semantic 3D reconstruction methods, especially in terms of scalability. At every octree level, the network predicts a semantic class for every voxel and decides which voxels should be further split in order to refine the reconstruction, thus working in a coarse-to-fine manner. The semantic prediction part of our method builds on recent work that combines traditional variational optimization and neural networks. In contrast to previous networks that work on dense voxel grids, our network is much more efficient in terms of memory consumption and inference efficiency, while achieving similar reconstruction performance. This allows for a high resolution reconstruction in case of limited memory. We perform experiments on the SUNCG and ScanNetv2 datasets on which our network shows comparable reconstruction results to the corresponding dense network while consuming less memory.

1 Introduction

Semantic 3D scene reconstruction from images aims at jointly reconstructing the geometry as well as the semantic meaning of a scene. It combines two important long-standing research topics: 3D reconstruction and semantic segmentation. In this paper, we are interested in dense approaches which focus on recovering realistic 3D models from real world data. Such methods can be especially useful to create content for graphics applications, or to model high-quality environments for mixed and virtual reality. Semantic segmentation is a well studied problem in 2D and has been extended to 3D in recent years. With the rise of deep learning, per-pixel semantic segmentation in 2D images has led to remarkable results [3,4,11,13]. A natural extension of these techniques to 3D consists in using a dense voxel grid representation, for which several recent methods have achieved compelling results [5–7,18]. However, in contrast to 2D scenarios, the memory usage and inference time for deep learning approaches increases cubically with the 3D volume size, which makes the training and especially the inference on large scenes difficult.

The scaling issue in dense voxel grid based 3D methods can be resolved by exploring structure in the grid data. To this end, we represent the data with an

© Springer Nature Switzerland AG 2019
G. A. Fink et al. (Eds.): DAGM GCPR 2019, LNCS 11824, pp. 581–594, 2019.
https://doi.org/10.1007/978-3-030-33676-9_41

Noisy, incomplete Input   *Cherabier et al. [5]* (11.8 GB)   *Ours* (4.3 GB)

Fig. 1. Semantic 3D reconstruction results. Our approach leverages an octree data structure to significantly reduce the memory usage during network inference while achieving similar performance compared to the dense voxel grid solution in [5].

octree which summarizes neighboring data cells with a single cell, if they contain the same value. This leads to significant memory savings. See Fig. 1 for an example input and output of our method. Recent work [16,17,20,21] have developed networks that perform convolution on octrees, but they assume that the octree structure of the data is known. Closer to us Tatarchenko *et al.* [19] proposed a network for generating high resolution 3D shapes in octree format, but it is not designed for semantic 3D reconstruction task from incomplete and noisy data. In this paper, we are interested in learning semantic 3D reconstruction on octrees, predicting both the semantics and the octree structure of the scene. The recent work by Cherabier *et al.* [5] presents a lightweight 3D semantic reconstruction method that combines traditional variational optimization and neural networks in order to learn the semantic 3D reconstruction from few training data. We adopt the same idea and our network embeds variational regularization and octree splitting together to predict the semantic label for each voxel in a coarse-to-fine manner. In each octree resolution level, the network predicts the semantic labeling by propagating information across voxels. Then it detects voxels that need to be split in order to refine the model, and propagate information to the next finer resolution level. In the end, the network outputs a semantic 3D reconstruction of the scene, with an octree representation provided by the splitting decisions. The network is optimized by two losses in each level, one is the sigmoid loss for predicting whether the octree cell should be split, and the other one is the cross entropy loss for per voxel semantic classification.

In summary, we make the following **contributions**:

- We present a novel framework for multi-view semantic 3D reconstruction that takes the octree of truncated signed distance functions (TSDFs) fused from different camera views as input, and generates an octree as semantic reconstruction output. Our network simultaneously learns the semantic segmentation labeling, as well as the octree structure, i.e., which cells should be subdivided.
- We propose a coarse-to-fine network architecture which is learned in an end-to-end manner. In each level, we apply variational optimization iterations to help propagate the semantic information across octree cells, and predict which set of octree cells contains fine details and thus propagate them to next

resolution level. In this way, large uniform areas such as floor, wall and ceiling are only processed in coarse levels and thus reduce the memory footprint.

- Our experiments on both synthetic and real 3D scene datasets demonstrate that our network operating on octrees can achieve comparable reconstruction and scene completion performance to the corresponding dense network in [5], while we use significantly less memory.

2   Related Work

Semantic 3D Reconstruction. Semantic 3D reconstruction has been an important research topic in computer vision for many years. Recent years deep learning based approaches have gained satisfactory performance in 3D vision tasks. Several deep learning based approaches have also been proposed targeting for 3D semantic reconstruction and scene completion. Dai et al. [6] introduced ScanComplete, an approach taking an incomplete 3D scan of a scene as input and predicting a complete 3D model along with per-voxel semantic labels. The presented fully convolutional network is in a coarse-to-fine inference strategy in order to produce high-resolution output. Later they also presented 3DMV [7], a novel method for 3D semantic scene segmentation of RGB-D scans in indoor environments using a joint 3D multi-view prediction network. They combined both data modalities (geometry and 2D RGB data) in a joint, end-to-end network architecture.

These networks usually require a very large number of parameters and enormous amounts of training data. Recently Cherabier et al. [5] proposed a lightweight neural network architecture which unifies the advantages of variational methods with those of deep neural networks, resulting in a simple, generic, and powerful model. It embeds variational regularization into the neural network, taking the TSDF-fused data cost as input and performing a fixed number of unrolled multi-scale primal dual optimization iterations with shared interaction weights to optimize the semantic probability likelihoods. Therefore it requires a moderate number of parameters, and can be trained from few scenes. In this work, we are interested in adapting the network in Cherabier et al. [5] to predict both the semantics and octree structures, aiming for much less memory usage and comparable reconstruction performance.

Deep Neural Network on Octrees. Different from 2D case, the cubic scaling of computational and memory requirements of 3D data makes convolutional neural networks training and inference infeasible for high-resolution inputs/outputs. This issue can be resolved by exploiting an octree structure to represent a scene.

Tatarchenko et al. [19] presented an octree generating network (OGN) for generating high resolution 3D shapes. Similar to a usual up-convolutional decoder for generating 3D output, the representation is gradually convolved with learned filters and up-sampled. The difference is that, starting from a certain layer in the network, dense regular grids are replaced by octrees, and only octree cells that need to be further refined will be propagated to later layers for subsequent processing such as convolution and deconvolution. However, it is designed for generating 3D geometry, i.e., predicting the occupancy of the voxel grid. There-fore it does not exploit the characteristics of 3D semantic reconstruction tasks and is hard to be applied to our task. Our proposed network adopts its *octree generating* idea, and predicts the voxel semantics by employing unrolled primal dual iterations and octree structure concurrently.

Wang *et al.* [20] proposed an octree-based convolutional neural network (O-CNN) for 3d shape analysis. Built upon the octree representation of 3D shapes, it takes the average normal vectors of a 3D model sampled in the finest leaf octants as input and performs 3D CNN operations on the octants occupied by the 3D shape surface. OctNet was proposed by Riegler *et al.* [17], and designed for deep learning with 3D sparse data. Following work is OctNetFusion [16] for depth map fusion. OctNet hierarchically partitions the 3D space into a set of unbalanced octrees. The convolutional network operations are directly defined on the structure of these trees. However, they are different from our octree network in the octree structure and application range. On the one hand, the octree in O-CNN only encode the surface information of 3D shape, whereas our work also accounts for the inner occupancy voxel grid. OctNet adopts a grid of shallow octrees to encode the voxel grid, the maximal depth of each shallow octree is 3, which becomes less efficient than the full-voxel-based solution when the volume resolution is lower than 64^3. On the other hand, both O-CNN and OctNet do not generate octree structure as output, but in 3D semantic reconstruction scenario, the structure of the octree is not known in advance and must be predicted.

3   Method

3.1   Octree Representation

An octree is a 3D grid structure with adaptive cell sizes. It can be generated by starting from a single cell representing the entire 3D space and recursively partitioning cells into eight octants. If every voxel within a cell has the same value, this cell is not subdivided and becomes a leaf of the tree. Therefore, it allows for memory reduction without losing any information compared with a dense voxel grid. Our network generates the octree semantic reconstruction output by starting from a coarse voxel grid, and learns to infer the semantic probabilities for the corresponding octree level in each level. Moreover, it predicts the octree structure supervised by the ground truth structure.

As done in [19], we use a hash table for an $O(1)$ access time. An octree cell (x, l) with spatial coordinates $x = (x, y, z)$ at level l is represented as a key-value pair (k, v) in the hash table. k is encoded from (x, l) by Z-order function [8], i.e., morton code $k = Z(x, l)$, and v can be a scalar or vector representing the value of an octree cell. The morton code can be efficiently computed using bit shifts. In sum, an octree O is represented as a set of all key-value pairs $O = \{(k, v)\}$.

3.2   Network Structure

We define the data cost as a volume computed from fused depth maps (e.g., from stereo or Kinect) and 2D semantic scene segmentations (e.g., obtained from a

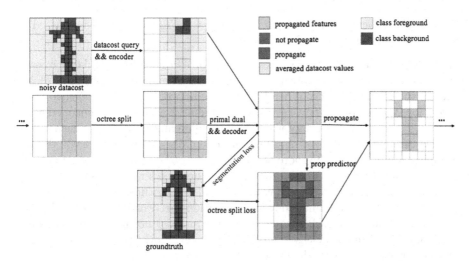

Fig. 2. Overview of our network architecture for one network block in one level. Noisy and incomplete depthmaps are aggregated into a datacost and represented as an octree. Our network predicts potential cell splittings and semantic label assignments.

semantic segmentation algorithm) and encoded by TSDFs [10]. Our proposed network takes the octree of the data cost as input, and generates an octree as semantic reconstruction output: both the structure, i.e., which cells are split, and the predicted semantic label. Instead of generating the data cost in a dense voxel grid as in Cherabier *et al.*'s work [5], we directly yield the data cost in octree representation by splitting the cells that are observed by the cameras and are set by the TSDF. The octree cells in the data cost can also be further merged if the values for the eight octants are the same.

We build the network level by level. Each level is responsible for optimizing the semantic label likelihoods, as well as predicting the octree splitting. The octree cells which need to be split indicate the existence of surfaces within the cell, and thus are split and propagated to the next level. Their semantic label likelihoods will be further refined. More specifically, each level is composed of five parts: *octree splitting, data cost encoder, unrolled primal dual, probability decoder*, and *propagation predictor*. We now describe these five components by taking a particular level l as an example (see Fig. 2).

Octree Splitting. We start the network from the coarsest level l_0, where we take a uniform distribution among semantic labels in regular grid of size $(2^{l_0}, 2^{l_0}, 2^{l_0}, C)$ as initial (C is the number of classes), and convert it to a set of octree cells, i.e., key-value pairs stored as a hash table (with values being semantic probabilities). The input to the subsequent level l is a set of octree cells of resolution $(2^{l-1}, 2^{l-1}, 2^{l-1}, C)$ propagated from the previous level $l-1$. Specifically, the value of each cell is the optimized semantic probability from the unrolled primal dual block in the previous level and is expected to be further optimized in this level. We thus split each cell into eight sub-cells by repeating its values, this will produce a new set of octree cells with resolution $(2^l, 2^l, 2^l, C)$.

We denote this octree level as $S_l = \{(x, l')|l' = l\}$. Then this will be passed to the unrolled primal dual block.

Data Cost Encoder. The data cost shows the evidence for each label in each voxel. We summarize the data cost to an octree (denoted by O^d) as a global input to the whole network. When training the network, we wish to generate an octree close to the ground truth semantic probability, which is also encoded as an octree O^u. These two octrees typically have a different structure. For each octree cell in S_l, we query the corresponding data cost from octree O^d. We will discuss this operation in Sect. 3.3 in more detail. Then we obtain the corresponding data cost O_l^d for level l, which will be the input of the encoder same as that of [5]: a residual unit that has two pairs of convolutional and rectified linear unit (ReLU) operations followed by a final convolution without activation. The convolutions are all with stride of one. According to [5], the encoder normalizes the influence of the different semantic classes with respect to each other and it also helps in reducing low-level noise in the data cost.

Unrolled Primal Dual. The block is composed of unrolled iterations of the primal-dual (PD) algorithm for minimizing the semantic reconstruction energy. Each PD update equation defines a layer in the network. Cherabier *et al.* [5] proposed to embed the variational optimization in a multi-scale network by unrolling the PD algorithm of Pock and Chambolle [15]. The energy minimization formulation is tailored to the multi-label semantic 3D reconstruction, and is parameterized by replacing the gradient operator with matrix convolutions which model the interaction of semantics and geometry for efficient label propagation. This already shows satisfactory performance in semantic 3D reconstruction. Therefore we adopt the same strategy. The difference is: every single PD step needs to be updated by propagating across different scales in [5], while for our method, each PD update propagates information within one scale and only the split octree cells will be optimized in the next finer level.

Probability Decoder. The outcome of the unrolled primal dual block, is passed to a residual decoder with the same structure as the data cost encoder to post process the optimized probability. Then a softmax activation layer is applied to normalize the semantic probability.

Propagation Predictor. After we obtain the probability from the decoder we need to decide which cells in S_l need to be propagated to the next level, and the rest stays in the current level. We make this prediction by applying a convolution layer over the decoder output with kernel size of 3 and stride of 1, followed by a sigmoid function to convert the convolution output into a propagation probability. We believe that looking at the semantic probability distributions of its neighboring cells can help decide whether there exist surfaces within the cell, i.e., whether the cell should be split. In the final level, the octree does not need to split and thus there is no *propagation predictor*.

The network was trained by two supervisions in each level: (1) The categorical cross-entropy loss for semantic segmentation for the cells in the octree level that is not propagated to next level (2) The sigmoid cross-entropy loss for binary classification of propagation for octree cells in S_l.

3.3   Customized Operations on Octrees

Data Cost Query. In each level l, we need to query the corresponding data cost value for each octree cell (x, l) in S_l from the global data cost input O^d. Then we obtain the data cost O_l^d for the corresponding octree level and this will be the input of the data cost encoder. Specifically, we search the key $k = Z(x, l)$ of the cell in the global data cost hash table. There exists two situations: (1) $Z(x, l)$ is stored at a level l or lower than l in O^d. Then, the queried data cost value can be uniquely determined. (2) $Z(x, l)$ does not exist in O^d, which means this cell is subdivided in O^d, and we denote this set of subdivided cells by $O^{(x,l)}$. $O^{(x,l)} \subset O^d$ and is a sub-octree rooted in cell (x, l). In this case, we take the weighted average of the data cost values in $O^{(x,l)}$. The corresponding weight is $\frac{1}{8^{l'-l}}$ where l' is the level of the cell in $O^{(x,l)}$. We formalize this data cost querying process from data cost octree O^d through function $q^d(k, O^d)$:

$$q^d(k, O^d) = \begin{cases} v & \text{if } \exists l' \leq l : (Z(x, l'), v) \in O^d \\ \displaystyle\sum_{(Z(x',l'),v') \in O^{(x,l)}} \frac{v'}{8^{l'-l}} & \text{otherwise} \end{cases} \tag{1}$$

Convolution. Each primal dual update step involves a convolution and a transposed convolution with a stride of one on the primal and dual variables. Besides, the residual encoder and decoder, as well as the propagation predictor are also based on one stride convolution on octree cells. We implement this convolution with stride one and arbitrary kernel size on octree cells in Caffe [12], which originally transforms convolution into matrix multiplication by laying out all patches in a feature tensor into a matrix. Then the convolution is achieved by multiplying the matrix with the kernel weight. The conversion between the feature tensor and the matrix with laid out patches is realized through the *im2col* function, and *col2im* reversely.

In our case, the convolution is not implemented on a regular feature tensor, but on hash table-based sparse features. We customize the *im2col* and *col2im* function, then the convolution is finalized also by matrix multiplication. The octree generating network in [19] also customizes this function on hash table based octrees, however, it realizes this on CPU by searching the neighbors within a patch in the hash table. Then the matrix multiplication is done in GPU. The frequent data transfer between CPU and GPU takes time and is thus not efficient. We improve this by maintaining the neighbor indices for each cell in every octree level, which is a minor storage overhead, but can avoid hash table search in CPU. In this way, the convolutions can all be done in GPU. Note that these convolutions could also be extended to any stride.

Currently, we maintain the hash table in CPU, so there are still some operations such as octree propagation, and some utility functions such as computing the neighbors for each octree cell, are done unavoidably in CPU. However, these operations are not frequent compared with the unrolled primal dual updates and they are therefore not a big overhead.

Primal Dual Update. For each octree level S_l in our network, we follow Cherabier *et al.*'s work [5] which embeds the following energy minimization into the unrolled primal dual block to optimize the semantic labeling likelihoods.

$$\underset{u}{\text{minimize}} \int_{S^l} (\|Wu\|_2 + fu)dx \quad \text{s.t. } \forall x \in S^l, \quad \sum_c u_c(x) = 1 \quad (2)$$

where u denotes the semantic probability for each level for octree cell x, and f indicates the corresponding data cost for each semantic label. This convex energy can be optimized by the PD algorithm [15], which transforms the problem into a saddle point energy minimization:

$$\underset{u}{\text{minimize}} \max_{\|\xi\|_\infty \leq 1} \langle Wu, \xi \rangle + \langle f, u \rangle + v(\sum_c u_c - 1) \quad (3)$$

where ξ denotes the dual variable, and v is the Lagrangian variable. For iteration $t + 1$, with step size σ and τ, the update is as follows:

$$v^{t+1} = v^t + \sigma(\sum_c \bar{u}_c^t - 1) \qquad\qquad \xi^{t+1} = \Pi_{\|\cdot\|\leq 1}[\xi^t + \sigma Wu^t]_* \quad (4)$$

$$u^{t+1} = \Pi_{[0,1]}[u^t - \tau(W^*\xi^{t+1} + f + v^{t+1})] \quad \bar{u}^{t+1} = 2u^{t+1} - u^t \quad (5)$$

where W^* denotes the adjoint of W.

3.4   Network Loss

Our proposed network is optimized by two losses in each resolution level, one is the sigmoid loss for predicting whether a octree cell should be split, and the other one is the cross entropy loss for predicting the semantic likelihoods.

Loss for Octree Propagation. For each set of octree cell S_l in level l, we compute the following sigmoid cross entropy binary classification loss:

$$L_s = \frac{-1}{|S_l|} \sum_{n=1}^{|S_l|} [p_n \log \hat{p}_n + (1 - p_n) \log(1 - \hat{p}_n)] \quad (6)$$

where $p_n \in \{0, 1\}$, and is determined by the groundtruth octree structure O^u, and $\hat{p}_n$ denotes the predicated propagation probability.

Cross Entropy Loss for Semantic Segmentation. For each set of octree cells S_l in level l, we only compute the cross entropy semantic classification loss for a subset of octree cells $S_l' = \{(x, l')|l' = l, x \in O^u\}$, where each cell must exist in the groundtruth octree O^u. In addition, to make the loss function agnostic to unobserved areas in the ground truth and to not penalize our solution in unlabeled regions, we use the same weighted loss with per voxel weighting function as in [5].

4   Experiments

4.1   Datasets and Settings

Datasets. We evaluate our network on two indoor datasets. The first one is the *synthetic* SUNCG dataset [18], and the other one is the recently released *real* ScanNetv2 dataset [6]. The SUNCG dataset contains over 45 K different scenes with manually created realistic room and furniture layouts. The dataset provides synthetic depth maps and volumetric ground truth annotation. All of the scenes are semantically annotated at the object level with 35 semantic classes. The ScanNetv2 dataset [6] comprises 1513 scene scans with fine-grained mesh semantic labeling. It also provides 2D segmentation labels for each frame view. We adopt the NYU [14] labeling with 40 semantic classes. For both datasets, we use a voxel size of 5 cm. In the SUNCG dataset, we randomly choose 400 scenes for training and 100 scenes for test. In the ScanNetv2, we train our network on the 1201 scenes among the provided 1513 scenes, and evaluate it in the remaining 312 scenes.

Data Cost Generation and Octree Encoding. For both datasets, we integrate the provided depth maps and 2D semantic segmentations using TSDF fusion with semantics similar to [5,9] based on the provided camera poses every 50th frame to establish voxelized data costs. Since the ScanNetv2 dataset only provides the ground truth semantic labeling in mesh format, we establish the voxelized ground truth by re-integrating the depth maps and 2D segmentations using all frames, which will provide strong evidence. Then we apply multi-label TV-L1 [1,2] optimization by minmizing Eq. (2) with $W = \nabla$ to obtain ground truth semantic probability distributions. The total variation (TV) norm effectively minimizes the surface area of a 3D shape.

We use 3 levels for octree encoding, but our network can be used with any number of resolution levels. For ground truth encoding in the SUNCG dataset, we recursively merge every eight voxels only if their semantic labels are the same until the depth 3 is reached. Since the ground truth for every scene in ScanNetv2 is our estimated probability distributions among the semantic labels, we merge the voxels if their most likely classes are the same, and the merged values take the average. For the data cost encoding in both datasets, we merge the voxels only if the voxel values for every class are the same.

Table 1. **Reconstruction performance on ScanNetv2** [6] **and SUNCG** [18]. "prop_known" means using the groundtruth octree split structure for cell propagation, while "prop_pred" uses the predicted octree split for propagation.

Method	ScanNetv2			SUNCG		
	Freespace	Semantic	Overall	Freespace	Semantic	Overall
Cherabier *et al.*	0.96	0.91	0.96	0.98	0.80	0.96
Ours, prop_known	0.96	0.86	0.94	0.95	0.79	0.93
Ours, prop_pred	0.95	0.84	0.93	0.94	0.76	0.92

Table 2. Reconstruction performance w.r.t. IOU on ScanNetv2 [6]. Our method yields comparable or slightly worse results than Cherabier *et al.* [5], but requires much less computing resources.

	wall	floor	cab	bed	chair	sofa	table	door	wind	bkshf	pic	cntr	desk	curt	fridg	show	toil	sink	bath	other	avg
Cherabier *et al.*	43.1	70.5	42.2	59.1	35.0	56.0	44.6	37.0	40.2	47.2	36.8	58.6	51.4	36.7	34.4	49.2	59.9	42.8	52.5	47.6	47.2
Ours, prop_known	44.2	73.1	45.3	56.7	37.9	57.5	50.7	40.3	43.7	44.9	35.8	61.1	54.2	38.9	39.2	42.6	59.4	42.9	26.0	47.1	47.1
Ours, prop_pred	43.2	70.7	42.7	55.4	34.6	51.9	46.6	37.1	34.7	35.0	36.4	55.8	50.1	38.8	38.9	44.0	52.2	39.9	56.0	39.5	45.2

Training and Inference Settings. For the ease of data transformation, such as random rotation and flip, we train on random crops of fixed size $32 \times 32 \times 32$, and perform data augmentation by randomly rotating and flipping around the gravity axis. Then we do octree encoding on the fly during training. For all the convolution layers, we use a kernel size of 3. We build the network in three levels, and for the first level, we unroll the primal dual for 50 iterations, and for the last two levels, we unroll 10 iterations. For the coarsest level, it is necessary to apply more primal dual iterations to do scene completion, and for the last two levels, we can use less iterations to refine the details. We use a batch size of 4, learning rate of 0.0001 and we use the ADAM optimizer for network training.

Since our network is fully convolutional, we can process arbitrary sized input. However, for the ease of octree encoding, we pad the rectangular scenes into square scenes. During inference, we adopt an octree input with a maximum of 7 levels, i.e., $128 \times 128 \times 128$, and output the reconstructed segmentation result in octree structure.

4.2   Reconstruction Performance Evaluation

We compare our network with the corresponding dense one in [5] in terms of semantic accuracy, separately for free space voxels and occupied voxels. On the ScanNetv2 dataset, we also measure the Intersection over Union (IoU) score among the 20 commonly used labels in ScanNet benchmark. The comparison results are shown in Table 1. The IoU comparison result on ScanNetv2 is shown in Table 2.

On both datasets, with ground truth octree split as propagation reference, the performance is comparable to the corresponding network working on regular voxel grids in Cherabier *et al.*'s work, and with the propagation predictor as reference, the accuracy drops within 4 points, which is in a reasonable range. On ScanNetv2, the mIOU is almost equivalent to Cherabier *et al.*'s work. We also show some reconstruction visualization examples on ScannNetv2 and SUNCG in Figs. 3 and 4. Both figures indicate that our network can produce visually similar reconstructions compared to the network working on voxel grids. In addition, on ScanNetv2, we can see that our network can also perform scene completion for the missing floor, walls, and so on.

Therefore we can draw the following conclusions given the experiment results on both datasets: (a) our network learning on octrees can achieve comparable reconstruction accuracy to the corresponding network learning on dense voxel grids, and almost equivalent visualization results. (b) our method can also produces results which are visually more pleasing than the ground truth used for training because of its scene completion function. (c) The propagation predictor still needs to be improved to predict the octree split in a better way.

4.3   Inference Efficiency Evaluation

We implement our network in Caffe, while Cherabier *et al.*'s network [5] is realized in Tensorflow and hardly to be transferred to Caffe. It is unfair to compare

Groundtruth	Cherabier et al.	Ours, prop_known	Ours, prop_pred

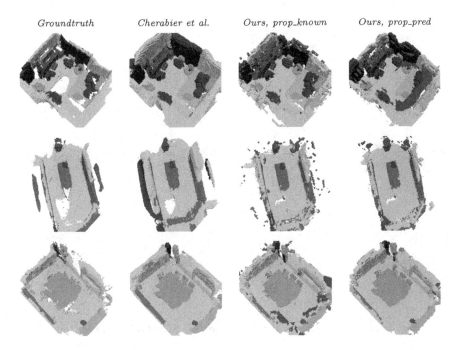

Fig. 3. Qualitative 3D reconstruction results on the ScanNet dataset for different scenes and methods. Our method often better fills holes to complete the geometry.

Table 3. Inference memory usage comparison on the ScanNetv2 (left) and SUNCG (right). N/A denotes not available, i.e., the memory usage exceeded the GPU memory limits (32 GB). The quantity of the number is GB. Our method uses significantly less memory than the corresponding dense grid approach.

Iterations	ScanNetv2				SUNCG			
	1	10	30	50	1	10	30	50
Cherabier *et al.*	11.8	N/A	N/A	N/A	10.67	N/A	N/A	N/A
Ours, prop_pred	4.3	14.7	20.2	22.1	3.2	9.3	15.7	21.1

the inference time between our method and theirs in different frameworks, so we skip the inference time comparison. To demonstrate the memory usage advantage of our octree primal dual network over the corresponding dense one, we list the peak memory consumption during inference with scene input size of 128^3. We vary the number of primal dual iterations in each network level to show the memory usage comparison. The inference is done in on a Nvidia Quadro GV100 GPU with 32 GB memory.

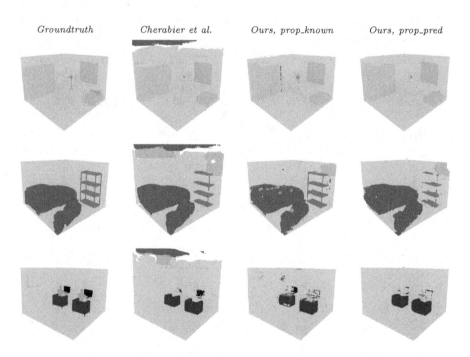

Groundtruth   *Cherabier et al.*   *Ours, prop_known*   *Ours, prop_pred*

Fig. 4. 3D reconstruction results on the SUNCG dataset [18].

As shown in Table 3, with primal dual iteration numbers larger than 1 in each level, the dense network cannot fit even one test scene in 32 GB GPU card, while ours use significantly less memory. However, Caffe itself is a naive framework and does not do memory optimization for neural network training and inference. Therefore, even our proposed network already reduces memory usage, the Caffe framework itself still takes a lot of memory.

5   Conclusion

We designed and implemented a deep network which estimates the learning of semantic 3D reconstruction and the corresponding octree representation of a scene. The octree data structure significantly reduces the methods memory footprint. Overall, our method solves a harder segmentation problem, since incorrect octree splitting estimates may reduce the segmentation performance too. Experiments on the SUNCG and ScanNetv2 datasets both show that our proposed network achieved comparable reconstruction performance to the corresponding network working on a dense voxel grid, while using much less memory.

Acknowledgements. This research was partially supported by the Intelligence Advanced Research Projects Activity (IARPA) via Department of Interior/Interior Business Center (DOI/IBC) contract number D17PC00280. The U.S. Government is authorized to reproduce and distribute reprints for Governmental purposes notwithstanding any copyright annotation thereon. Disclaimer: The views and conclusions contained herein are those of the authors and should not be interpreted as necessarily representing the official policies or endorsements, either expressed or implied, of IARPA, DOI/IBC, or the U.S. Government.

References

1. Bresson, X., Esedoḡlu, S., Vandergheynst, P., Thiran, J.P., Osher, S.: Fastglobal minimization of the active contour/snake model. J. Math. Imaging Vis. **28**(2), 151–167 (2007)
2. Chan, T., Esedoḡlu, S., Nikolova, M.: Algorithms for finding global minimizers of image segmentation and denoising models. SIAM J. Appl. Math. **66**(5), 1362–1648 (2006)
3. Chen, L.C., et al.: Searching for efficient multi-scale architectures for dense image prediction. In: Proceedings of Neural Information Processing Systems (NIPS) (2018)
4. Chen, L.-C., Zhu, Y., Papandreou, G., Schroff, F., Adam, H.: Encoder-decoder with atrous separable convolution for semantic image segmentation. In: Ferrari, V., Hebert, M., Sminchisescu, C., Weiss, Y. (eds.) ECCV 2018. LNCS, vol. 11211, pp. 833–851. Springer, Cham (2018). https://doi.org/10.1007/978-3-030-01234-2_49
5. Cherabier, I., Schönberger, J.L., Oswald, M.R., Pollefeys, M., Geiger, A.: Learning priors for semantic 3D reconstruction. In: Ferrari, V., Hebert, M., Sminchisescu, C., Weiss, Y. (eds.) ECCV 2018. LNCS, vol. 11216, pp. 325–341. Springer, Cham (2018). https://doi.org/10.1007/978-3-030-01258-8_20
6. Dai, A., Chang, A.X., Savva, M., Halber, M., Funkhouser, T., Nießner, M.: ScanNet: richly-annotated 3D reconstructions of indoor scenes. In: Proceedings of International Conference on Computer Vision and Pattern Recognition (CVPR) (2017)
7. Dai, A., Nießner, M.: 3DMV: joint 3D-multi-view prediction for 3D semantic scene segmentation. In: Ferrari, V., Hebert, M., Sminchisescu, C., Weiss, Y. (eds.) ECCV 2018. LNCS, vol. 11214, pp. 458–474. Springer, Cham (2018). https://doi.org/10.1007/978-3-030-01249-6_28
8. Gargantini, I.: Linear octree for fast processing of three-dimensional objects. Comput. Graph. Image Process. **20** (1982)
9. Häne, C., Zach, C., Cohen, A., Angst, R., Pollefeys, M.: Joint 3D scene reconstruction and class segmentation. In: Proceedings of International Conference on Computer Vision and Pattern Recognition (CVPR), pp. 97–104 (2013). https://doi.org/10.1109/CVPR.2013.20
10. Häne, C., Zach, C., Cohen, A., Pollefeys, M.: Dense semantic 3D reconstruction. IEEE Trans. Pattern Anal. Mach. Intell. **39**(9), 1730–1743 (2017). https://doi.org/10.1109/TPAMI.2016.2613051

11. He, K., Gkioxari, G., Dollar, P., Girshick, R.: Mask R-CNN. In: Proceedings of International Conference on Computer Vision (ICCV) (2017)
12. Jia, Y., et al.: Caffe: convolutional architecture for fast feature embedding. arXiv preprint arXiv:1408.5093 (2014)
13. Long, J., Shelhamer, E., Darrell, T.: Fully convolutional networks for semantic segmentation. In: Proceedings of International Conference on Computer Vision and Pattern Recognition (CVPR) (2015)
14. Silberman, N., Hoiem, D., Kohli, P., Fergus, R.: Indoor segmentation and support inference from RGBD images. In: Fitzgibbon, A., Lazebnik, S., Perona, P., Sato, Y., Schmid, C. (eds.) ECCV 2012. LNCS, vol. 7576, pp. 746–760. Springer, Heidelberg (2012). https://doi.org/10.1007/978-3-642-33715-4_54
15. Pock, T., Chambolle, A.: Diagonal preconditioning for first order primal-dual algorithms in convex optimization. In: International Conference on Computer Vision (ICCV) (2011)
16. Riegler, G., Ulusoy, A.O., Bischof, H., Geiger, A.: OctNetFusion: learning depth fusion from data. In: International Conference on 3D Vision (3DV) (2017)
17. Riegler, G., Ulusoy, A.O., Geiger, A.: OctNet: learning deep 3D representations at high resolutions. In: Proceedings of International Conference on Computer Vision and Pattern Recognition (CVPR) (2017)
18. Song, S., Yu, F., Zeng, A., Chang, A.X., Savva, M., Funkhouser, T.A.: Semantic scene completion from a single depth image. In: Proceedings of International Conference on Computer Vision and Pattern Recognition (CVPR) (2017)
19. Tatarchenko, M., Dosovitskiy, A., Brox, T.: Octree generating networks: Efficient convolutional architectures for high-resolution 3D outputs. In: Proceedings of International Conference on Computer Vision (ICCV) (2017). http://lmb.informatik. uni-freiburg.de/Publications/2017/TDB17b
20. Wang, P.S., Liu, Y., Guo, Y.X., Sun, C.Y., Tong, X.: O-CNN: octree-based Convolutional neural networks for 3D shape analysis. ACM Trans. Graph. (SIGGRAPH) **36**(4), 72 (2017)
21. Wang, P.S., Sun, C.Y., Liu, Y., Tong, X.: Adaptive O-CNN: a patch-based deep representation of 3D shapes. ACM Transactions on Graphics (SIGGRAPH Asia), vol. 37, no. 6 (2018)

Learning to Disentangle Latent Physical Factors for Video Prediction

Deyao Zhu[1,2(✉)], Marco Munderloh[2], Bodo Rosenhahn[2], and Jörg Stückler[1]

[1] Max Planck Institute for Intelligent Systems, Tübingen, Germany
tsu.tikgiau@gmail.com
[2] Leibniz Universität Hannover, Hanover, Germany

Abstract. Physical scene understanding is a fundamental human ability. Empowering artificial systems with such understanding is an important step towards flexible and adaptive behavior in the real world. As a step in this direction, we propose a novel approach to physical scene understanding in video. We train a deep neural network for video prediction which embeds the video sequence in a low-dimensional recurrent latent space representation. We optimize the total correlation of the latent dimensions within a variational recurrent auto-encoder framework. This encourages the representation to disentangle the latent physical factors of variation in the training data. To train and evaluate our approach, we use synthetic video sequences in three different physical scenarios with various degrees of difficulty. Our experiments demonstrate that our model can disentangle several appearance-related properties in the unsupervised case. If we add supervision signals for the latent code, our model can further improve the disentanglement of dynamics-related properties.

1 Introduction

A fundamental ability of humans for understanding dynamic scenes is to perceive physical properties of objects and predicting the physical evolution of a scene coarsely into the future. Providing cyber-physical systems with these abilities is a key ingredient to flexible and adaptive behavior in the real word. A large body of computer vision research has recently demonstrated the success of deep learning techniques for tasks such as object detection and recognition in images or video prediction. Learning to reason about the dynamic physical states of objects in video attracts increasing attention recently. A significant part of this research focuses on regressing the physical states of the system from images and using a physics-engine-like module to predict successive frames [2,25,28,30]. Although this is a straightforward approach, it requires hand-crafted tailoring of the state representation and simulator for the specific task. For example, one needs to

---

Electronic supplementary material The online version of this chapter (https:// doi.org/10.1007/978-3-030-33676-9_42) contains supplementary material, which is available to authorized users.

decide the physical laws to use or the number of represented objects. Some studies instead directly predict future frames end-to-end using deep learning based models [31]. Learning latent state representations that disentangle the physical factors of variation in the data such as object speed, position, mass, and friction, however, is still an open research problem. Such models would allow for introspection of the physical properties of a scene.

In this paper, we propose a variational approach to video prediction that learns a recurrent latent representation of the video and allows for predicting sequences into the future. Our network architecture is inspired by state-of-the-art approaches to video prediction [8,20,31]. To encourage the learning of a disentangled latent representation we minimize total correlation [4] of the latent dimensions and present videos of varying physical properties during training. We train and evaluate our model on synthetic videos of three physical scenarios with varying level of difficulty (sliding objects, collision scenarios). Our experiments demonstrate that our model can learn to disentangle several appearance-related properties such as shape or size of objects. For various dynamics-related physical properties such as speed and friction, we add supervision signals to the latent dimensions and demonstrate that training on total correlation can also improve disentanglement for these properties. To the best of our knowledge, our work is the first to apply total correlation minimization with the aim of discovering physical latent factors in the scene.

The main contributions in this paper are summarized as follows: (a) We propose a video prediction model inspired by [8,20,31] and train it using total correlation [4]. We also propose an approach to include supervision of dynamics-related properties for representation learning. Our model simultaneously predicts a sequence of future frames and generates latent representations which are physically interpretable for several appearance- and dynamics-related properties. (b) We analyze our approach on video datasets of three different physical scenarios with increasing difficulty[1]. We suggest evaluation metrics for reconstruction quality and disentanglement of latent physical properties for the datasets. (c) We provide detailed experiments and analysis which demonstrate that our method outperforms several variants in our datasets.

2   Related Work

Learning of Physical Scene Understanding: In recent years, the machine learning community has investigated several approaches to physical scene understanding [22,25,28,30–33]. Some approaches attempt to learn the dynamics of physical scenes from the explicit state representations (object positions, speed, etc.) which are provided by physics engines [25,30]. For instance, [25] represents the physical states as a graph and build a learnable and differentiable physics engines to update this graph. The approach in [30] introduces a pipeline to predict the next frame with a physics engine in their structure. Visual interaction networks [28] combine recurrent neural networks and interaction networks [2] to

---

[1] Dataset available from: https://github.com/TsuTikgiau/DisentPhys4VidPredict.

predict the next physical state. Our approach learns state representations and dynamics models directly from video sequences.

More closely related to our approach, instead of utilizing a physics engine to predict the future state, Ye et al. [31] learn to predict the next frame in an end-to-end way. The proposed architecture is an encoder-decoder network which takes four frames in sequence as input and predicts the next frame. For training, the paper proposes a special dataset that consists of multiple small batches where only a single physical property is varied while others are held fixed. Training then imposes a manual assignment of latent variables to physical properties and penalizes deviations of the fixed properties on each batch of sequences from the mean prediction. We instead combine supervision of dynamic properties on specific latent dimensions with a training objective that encourages disentanglement.

Physical Scene Understanding Datasets: A number of studies construct benchmarks with specific properties [21,23,24,29,31]. For example, Piloto et al. [23] and Riochet et al. [24] focus on the physical plausibility of videos. Lerer et al. introduce a benchmark [21] that includes sequences of wooden-block towers which might collapse for which models need to estimate the trajectories of blocks. [31] contains 5-frame videos of collisions between two objects with simple shapes in a simulator for which the last frame needs to be predicted from the first four frames. Wu et al. [29] record videos in various scenarios in the real world (sliding down a ramp, colliding objects, etc.). The evaluated models need to predict concrete physical properties like bounce height and acceleration. We propose a new video prediction dataset in physical scenes with three scenarios of varying difficulty (sliding objects, colliding objects). In each dataset we vary the physical properties of the objects for which adequate disentangled representations should be learned. Besides image reconstruction metrics, we also propose to use disentanglement metrics.

Video Prediction: Our proposed method is closely related to the field of video prediction. In this field, researchers focus on how to predict a sequence of future frames given a few initial frames [1,7,8,18,20,26,27,34]. For instance, [26] takes previous frames as input and predicts future frames at the pixel-level. Directly predicting images is prone to loosing details about the appearance of objects though. [27] instead predicts optical flow from the last to the next frame and warps the last frame with the optical flow to generate the prediction. [34] improve the optical flow method using a bilinear sampling layer to make the warping process differentiable. [8] introduces multiple convolutional flow kernels to warp the last frames and composites them into one final output as an alternative to the global optical flow. The optical flow generated images combined with a network stream that directly predicts on the pixel-level. The model also inputs the first frame in the sequence, mostly to maintain information about appearance of objects and background. Dynamics is modelled through LSTMs on the layers of the encoder. Based on [8,20] applies VAE-GAN [19] for better reconstruction quality. Our network architecture also predicts the future frame in a recurrent VAE structure. We only impose recurrency on the latent state and use total correlation to train for disentanglement.

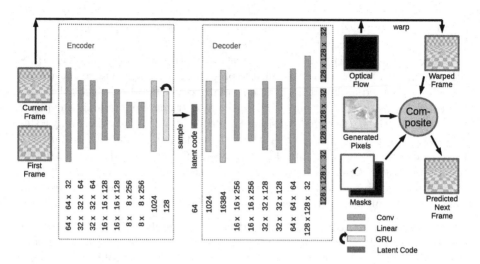

Fig. 1. An overview of our proposed recurrent encoder-decoder network for video prediction. All information about the scene dynamics needs to be maintained in the hidden state of the Gated Recurrent Unit at the last layer of the encoder.

Representation Learning: Representation learning is an important field to our work. A great deal of previous research has focused on unsupervised representation learning [3–5,12,15]. InfoGAN [5] trains to increase the mutual information between latent codes and generated frames in GANs [10]. Higgins et al. [12] analyze that increasing the weight of the KL-divergence loss in VAEs [17] helps to disentangle the latent code. Burgess et al. [3] explain this phenomenon using the information bottleneck theory and propose a method which smoothly decreases the weight for the KL-divergence loss. FactorVAE and β-TCVAE [4,15] decompose the KL-divergence term into three components and only increase the penalty to the part which is responsible for the disentanglement. Some works also investigate the learning of latent state representations and dynamics models in videos [9,11,14]. We apply total correlation minimization to learn a latent state representation to encourage discovering physical latent factors.

3 Method

Our deep learning approach to video prediction uses a recurrent stochastic encoder-decoder architecture which successively predicts the next frame from a sequence of input frames. We train the network using a variational approach which minimizes the total correlation between the encoded latent dimensions. This way, the network is encouraged to learn a representation that disentangles the latent factors of variation in the training videos.

Our model recursively predicts a low-dimensional latent code representation of video sequences. The latent code z_t causally explains the image observations o_t in the video with the observation model $p(o_t \mid z_t)$. For predicting the next latent code, we learn an encoder $q_\theta(z_t \mid o_{<t})$ that uses information from all previous observations. More specifically, we implement our encoder as a recurrent model. It takes in the previous hidden state s_{t-1} and the last observation o_{t-1} to compute the next hidden state $s_t = f_\theta(s_{t-1}, o_{t-1})$. The hidden state s_t defines a distribution $\tilde{z}_t \sim q_\theta(z_t \mid s_t)$ from which the latent code at this step is sampled. The recurrent autoencoder also requires to learn the observation model $p_\psi(o_t \mid z_t)$ with parameters ψ (the decoder).

3.1   Learning Objective

For training this model, we derive a variational lower bound similar to the variational autoencoder [17] and PlaNet [11]. We maximize the data likelihood of the image observations in the video,

$$\ln p(o_{1:T}) = \ln \prod_t \int p(o_t \mid z_t) p(z_t \mid o_{t-1}, s_{t-1}) dz_t$$

$$\geq \sum_t \underbrace{E_{q_\theta(z_t \mid o_{t-1}, s_{t-1})}\left[\ln p(o_t \mid z_t)\right]}_{-L_{rec,t}} - \underbrace{KL(q_\theta(z_t \mid o_{t-1}, s_{t-1}) \parallel p(z_t \mid o_{t-1}, s_{t-1}))}_{L_{KL,t}},$$

$$(1)$$

where we assume an uninformed Gaussian prior with zero mean and unit diagonal covariance for the state-transition model $p(z_t \mid o_{t-1}, s_{t-1})$. By this approximation, we can use techniques such as β-VAE and β-TCVAE to encourage the latent code to disentangle the latent factors of variation in the training data. The derivation of Eq. 1 can be found in the supplementary material.

The ELBO decomposes in a reconstruction $L_{rec,t}$ and a complexity term $L_{KL,t}$ per time step. We use the Laplace distribution $\frac{1}{2b} \exp(-\frac{|x-\hat{x}|}{b})$ with fixed scale parameter b as the output distribution of decoder. By this, the reconstruction loss can be written as $L_{rec,t} = \frac{1}{b} \sum |x_t - \hat{x}_t|$, where x_t denotes the ground truth frame and $\hat{x}_t$ is the predicted frame. The KL-divergence term can be determined in closed form, since our encoder predicts a normal distribution with diagonal covariance.

The final training objective for our VAE model is

$$L_{VAE} = L_{rec} + L_{KL}, \tag{2}$$

where $L_{rec} = \sum_t L_{rec,t}$ and $L_{KL} = \sum_t L_{KL,t}$.

Recent representation learning approaches have demonstrated that augmentations to this loss function can improve the disentanglement of the representation into the latent factors of variation in the training data. β-VAE increases the penalty to the KL-divergence term,

$$L_{\beta-VAE} = L_{rec} + \beta L_{KL}. \tag{3}$$

Here, $\beta > 1$. β-TCVAE instead decomposes the KL-divergence term into three components

$$L_{KL,t} = \text{KL}(q(o_{t-1}, z_t \mid s_{t-1}) \parallel p(o_{t-1} \mid s_{t-1}) q(z_t \mid s_{t-1}))$$
$$+ \text{KL}(q(z_t \mid s_{t-1}) \parallel \prod_i q(z_{t,i} \mid s_{t-1})) + \sum_i \text{KL}(q(z_{t,i} \mid s_{t-1}) \parallel p(z_{t,i}))$$

$$(4)$$

and only increases the penalty to the total correlation $\text{KL}(q(z_t \mid s_{t-1}) \parallel \prod_i q(z_{t,i} \mid s_{t-1}))$ which is mainly responsible for disentanglement as explained in [4].

Supervision of Latent Dimensions: We also explore training specific dimensions of our latent representation in a supervised way. For selected properties, we normalize their values to the range $[-10, 10]$ and impose an L1 loss between them and specific dimensions of the latent code as an additional loss term. The final training objective in this case is,

$$L_{sup} = L_{unsup} + \lambda \sum_t \sum_i |f_{t,i} - \widetilde{z}_{t,i}|. \tag{5}$$

Here, L_{unsup} is either L_{VAE} or $L_{\beta-VAE}$, $f_{t,i}$ is the value of the i-th property to be supervised at time step t, and $\widetilde{z}_{t,i}$ is the corresponding dimension of the latent code sample.

3.2   Network Structure

Our encoder is a recurrent neural network which receives the last hidden state s_{t-1}, the latest image o_{t-1} and the first image o_1 in the sequence. It outputs a prediction for the state s_t of the next frame which we interpret and split into the mean and diagonal log variances of a normal distribution $q_\theta(z_t \mid s_t) = q_\theta(z_t \mid s_{t-1}, o_{t-1})$. The decoder deconvolves samples from the encoder distribution into a Laplace distribution over the pixels in the predicted image. In Fig. 1 we give an overview and details of our network structure.

Besides the last frame, the encoder also takes in the first frame as input for a better conditioning of the reconstruction of background and object shapes. To remember information from previous steps, a GRU [6] layer is used for the last layer of the encoder. Note that the current output of the GRU layer is also its hidden state for the next step (unlike in an LSTM [13]). By this, the model needs to store all information about dynamics in the latent code distribution.

The decoder takes the latent code sample from the encoder and assembles it into the predicted next frame. It first generates a shared feature map via an upsampling network. Then, three small nets convert the shared feature map into optical flow, generated pixels and masks, respectively. The optical flow is used to warp the last frame towards the next frame. Warped frame and generated pixels are composed together via the masks to yield the predicted next frame.

For better image quality, adding skip connections between encoder and decoder or adding recurrency into the decoder are effective approaches [7,8,20]. However, these approaches circumvent the representational bottleneck in the

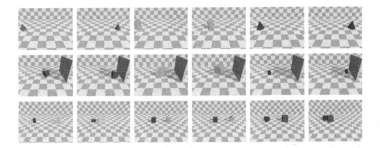

Fig. 2. Samples from our datasets. Row 1, 2, 3 are from the sliding set, the wall set and the collision set, respectively.

latent code and can store dynamics information in other layers. Since we aim at a latent code that represents the appearance and dynamics information required to predict the next frame, we don't adopt these approaches.

Our model takes the first and current frame as input to predict the next frame in each step. The current frame can be either the ground truth data or the predicted one from the last step. At the beginning of the sequence, we feed our model four consecutive ground truth frames to initialize the hidden state of the recurrent encoder. Then, the system recursively uses the predicted image from the last step to perform multi-step prediction.

4   Physical Scene Datasets

We evaluate our approach in videos of physical scenarios of increasing difficulty. We employ the physics engine *PyBullet* to create three datasets. In the sliding set, objects of various shapes and friction coefficients slide with various initial speeds on a plane. The wall set shows collisions of a sliding object with a wall. The collision set contains collision scenarios of two objects that slide into each others. In the latter two, we also vary the density and the restitution coefficients of objects. Example sequences for the datasets are shown in Fig. 2.

For each sequence, we record 10 frames with a rate of 10 Hz. Besides, segmentation masks and depth maps are saved, too. The objects in our dataset have 5 different shapes: cylinder, prism, cube, cone and pyramid. The ratios among edges are fixed, but the scales of objects are changeable for the diversity of data.

Sliding Dataset: The sliding dataset describes a physics scene where an object with various appearances and physical properties slides from left to the right. We do not include sequences in which the object would fall over. Objects in this dataset have 5 properties: shape, scale, friction coefficient, initial speed, and initial position. Different sequences have different combination of these properties which we choose from a finite set of discrete values per property. The set totally has 26000 sequences including a training set with 20000 sequences, a validation set with 3000 sequences, and a test set with 3000 sequences.

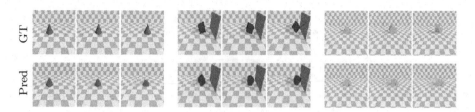

Fig. 3. Prediction examples of β-TCVAE in different datasets. First row demonstrates the ground truth frames. Second row shows the 1st ($t = 5$), 3rd, and 5th predicted frames in three datasets.

Wall Dataset: Similar to the sliding dataset, the objects in the wall dataset also slide from left to the right. However, the object slides into a fixed wall in the right of the scene. If the object is fast enough, it will hit the wall and bounce back. In this dataset, objects may also fall over. We have 5 properties in this set: shape, scale, material, initial speed, and initial position. Each material has its own setting of density, restitution, friction, and color. Again we choose a discrete set of possible values for each property. We have totally 10125 sequences in this set including 7425 sequences in the training set, 1350 in the validation set and 1350 in the test set.

Collision Dataset: In the collision dataset, 2 objects slide into each other from left and right. Both objects have their own settings of shapes, scales, materials, initial speeds and positions from a discrete set of values. This set has 25000 sequences in the training set, 2500 sequences in the validation set and 2500 sequences in the test set.

5   Experiments

We evaluate our video representation learning approach on our proposed datasets. To measure the level of the latent code's disentanglement we use the mutual information gap (MIG) proposed in [4]. We also measure the disentanglement of a property separately by computing the mutual information gap for the single property. Additionally, we assess the quality of the video prediction using the peak signal-to-noise ratio (PSNR).

Experiments for Unsupervised Learning: We first assess unsupervised learning with our approach and compare VAE, β-VAE [12] and β-TCVAE [4] objectives for various β values. The models are trained to predict the remaining six frames in each sequence given the first four ground truth frames as inputs.

To explore the relationship between the coefficient β and the level of disentanglement, we evaluate a set of β values. In the sliding set, we set β to 1, 5, 9, 13, 17, 21, 25; in the wall and the collision set, β are set to 1, 6, 11, 16, 21, 26 and 1, 11, 21, 31, respectively. Each setting is trained 22 times in the sliding set and 12 times in the other sets. Each model is trained for 12000 iterations. We use the Adam optimizer [16] with parameters $\beta_1 = 0.5$, $\beta_2 = 0.999$ and learning rate

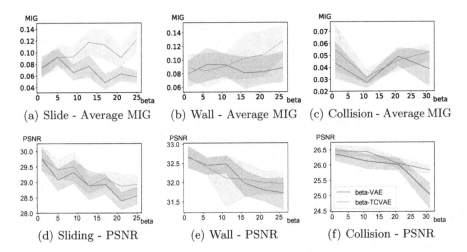

(a) Slide - Average MIG   (b) Wall - Average MIG   (c) Collision - Average MIG

(d) Sliding - PSNR   (e) Wall - PSNR   (f) Collision - PSNR

Fig. 4. MIG and performance reduction (average and 90% confidence intervals) for unsupervised learning. In the sliding set and the wall set, β-TCVAE outperforms β-VAE and successfully increase the average MIG. Besides, larger β leads to bigger performance reduction in both approaches.

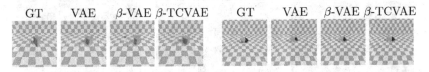

Fig. 5. Predicted last frame of two sequences for different approaches.

$6e-9$. Batch size is set to 8. For the scale parameter of the decoder's Laplace distribution we empirically choose $b = 0.0147$. Schedule sampling [8] is applied for training: The model is first trained to predict only one future step at the beginning of training. Then we smoothly transition to full sequence prediction from iteration 1000 to iteration 9000.

Some prediction examples of β-TCVAE are given in Fig. 3. The average MIG curves are shown in Fig. 4(a)–(c). We show means and 90% confidence intervals of evaluated MIG values. For the sliding set and wall set, a higher β helps to increase the average MIG in β-TCVAE. In contrast, β-VAE struggles to improve it. For the most difficult collision set, β-TCVAE slightly improves over β-VAE, while there is no obvious improvement over VAE ($\beta = 1$). Larger β values limit the capacity of the model by forcing it to stay closer to the prior which negatively influences the video prediction quality. This can be seen in Fig. 4(d)–(f) in the reduction in PSNR. We observe that the reduction for β-TCVAE is smaller than for β-VAE in most cases. Figure 5 shows the last predicted frame in a video sequence by the different approaches.

To figure out which kinds of properties benefit from a larger β, we present the MIGs for individual properties in Fig. 6. Both β-TCVAE and β-VAE can

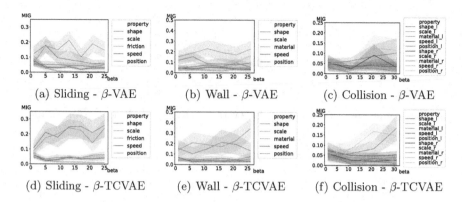

(a) Sliding - β-VAE   (b) Wall - β-VAE   (c) Collision - β-VAE

(d) Sliding - β-TCVAE   (e) Wall - β-TCVAE   (f) Collision - β-TCVAE

Fig. 6. Individual MIG of properties for unsupervised learning. Both β-TCVAE and β-VAE work better for properties which have high influence on the reconstruction loss like shape in the sliding sets and position in the collision set. β-TCVAE outperforms β-VAE in such properties. For other properties they are comparable to VAE ($\beta = 1$).

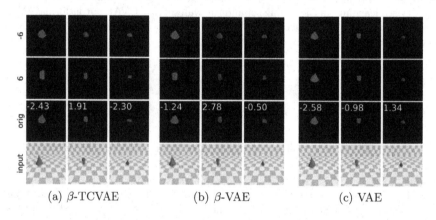

(a) β-TCVAE   (b) β-VAE   (c) VAE

Fig. 7. Latent traversals for the shape property in the sliding set. We manually modify the value (given in row headers) of the dimension corresponding to the specific property and show the predicted optical flows in the first 2 rows. The orig row shows the prediction for the estimated value of the dimension. In the first 2 examples, the contour changes from a triangle-like shape to a rectangular-like shape as we increase the value in β-TCVAE and β-VAE models while this is not the case for standard VAE.

disentangle some properties better like shapes in the sliding set or position in the collision set. β-TCVAE achieves better results than β-VAE. However, the approaches struggle to disentangle dynamic-related properties like speed or friction. To visualize the results of β-TCVAE and β-VAE, we select our best β-TCVAE, β-VAE and VAE ($\beta = 1$) models and show latent traversals for shapes in the sliding set in Fig. 7. For the traversals, we select the dimension of the latent code that has the highest mutual information with the shape.

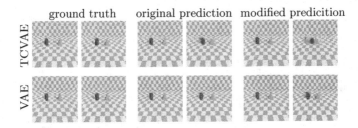

Fig. 8. Effect of latent code modification. We show predicted 1st and last frames from β-TCVAE and VAE. In the last column, we modified the latent code dimension corresponding to the speed at $t = 4$ and show subsequent predictions. While β-TCVAE generates a collision event, there is only little change for VAE.

Experiments for Supervised Learning: Although unsupervised learning in our model using the β-TCVAE objective can improve the disentanglement of properties like shape, scale and position in our datasets, dynamics-related properties like speed and friction are not well disentangled. In this section, we analyze if supervision of some properties can be included into representation learning and if the disentanglement of these properties can be improved.

We train our model in two ways: using the VAE ($\beta = 1$) objective and the β-TCVAE objective with $\beta = 31$. We select dynamics-related properties for supervision in each dataset, and add a supervised loss term for them as detailed in Sect. 3.1. We set $\lambda = \frac{1}{3} \times 10^4$ in our experiments and cap the log variance of the latent code's distribution from below at $\log \sigma^2 = -10$. We train each approach 12 times for 12000 iterations for all datasets. In the sliding set, we supervise friction, speed and position. In the wall and the collision set, speed and position are supervised. The settings of schedule sampling and the Adam optimizer are the same as in the previous experiments.

We show the MIG graphs in Fig. 9. In (a) we observe that β-TCVAE successfully increases the average MIG in all datasets. Subfigures (b) and (d) demonstrate that unlike in the unsupervised learning case, with supervision the model can disentangle dynamic-related properties better in the sliding and collision sets. However, the approach cannot improve the MIG for these properties in the wall set as shown in (c). In addition, the supervised approach also achieves higher MIG for some properties without supervision compared to the unsupervised approach like the shape and the scale in (b). This may be due to the reduction of the supervised properties information in the representation of unsupervised properties. We also show latent traversals in Fig. 10 which compare the results of β-TCVAE and VAE. Figure 8 demonstrates predictions when dynamics-related properties are changed by their corresponding latent codes in our model. The model trained with the β-TCVAE objective demonstrates a noticable speed change of the objects in this example, making the objects collide. We provide further examples in the supplementary material and video.

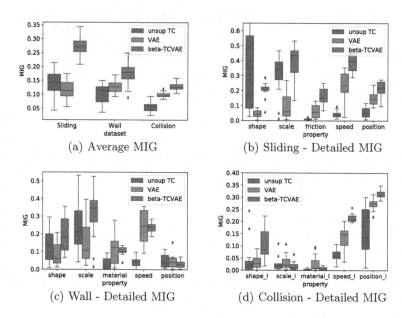

(a) Average MIG

(b) Sliding - Detailed MIG

(c) Wall - Detailed MIG

(d) Collision - Detailed MIG

Fig. 9. MIG for supervised learning (mean and 90% confidence intervals) and unsupervised learning for comparison (β-TCVAE). β-TCVAE achieves higher average MIG compared to VAE. There is no significant MIG increase for the wall set for the supervised properties (speed and position). In the sliding and collision sets, β-TCVAE further increases the MIG of the supervised properties (friction, speed and position in sliding set and speed and position in collision set).

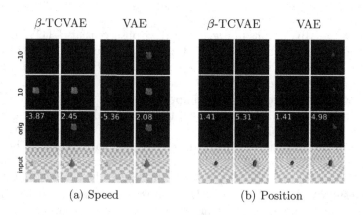

(a) Speed

(b) Position

Fig. 10. Latent traversals for supervised learning. The brighter red, the faster. β-TCVAE shows more obvious changes of brightness when we modify the corresponding latent code dimension compared to the VAE case. For the property position, the changes for β-TCVAE are also more significant than for VAE. (Color figure online)

6   Conclusion

In this paper, we propose a recurrent variational autoencoder model that learns a latent dynamics representation for video prediction. We use total correlation to improve the disentanglement of the learned representation into the latent factors of variation in the training data. In this way, the model can discover several properties related to the physics of the scenarios such as shape or positions of objects. We also demonstrate that partial supervision of dynamics-related properties can be added which further improves the disentanglement of the representation. We evaluate our approach on a new dataset of three physical scenarios with increasing levels of difficulty. In future work we plan to extend our dataset to more complex scenarios and investigate other network architectures to further improve the level of scene understanding.

Acknowledgements. This work has been supported through Cyber Valley.

References

1. Babaeizadeh, M., Finn, C., Erhan, D., Campbell, R., Levine, S.: Stochastic variational video prediction. In: ICLR (2018)
2. Battaglia, P., Pascanu, R., Lai, M., Rezende, D., Kavukcuoglu, K.: Interaction networks for learning about objects, relations and physics. In: NIPS (2016)
3. Burgess, C., Higgins, I., Pal, A., Matthey, L., Watters, N., Desjardins, G., Lerchner, A.: Understanding disentangling in beta -VAE. In: Learning Disentangle Representations: From Perception to Control workshop (2017)
4. Chen, T., Li, X., Grosse, R., Duvenaud, D.: Isolating sources of disentanglement in VAEs. In: NIPS (2018)
5. Chen, X., Duan, Y., Houthooft, R., Schulman, J., Sutskever, I., Abbeel, P.: InfoGAN: interpretable representation learning by information maximizing generative adversarial nets. In: NIPS (2016)
6. Chung, J., Gulcehre, C., Cho, K., Bengio, Y.: Empirical evaluation of gated recurrent neural networks on sequence modeling. In: NIPS Workshop (2014)
7. Ebert, F., Finn, C., Lee, X., Levine, S.: Self-supervised visual planning with temporal skip connections. In: CoRL (2017)
8. Finn, C., Goodfellow, I., Levine, S.: Unsupervised learning for physical interaction through video prediction. In: NIPS (2016)
9. Fraccaro, M., Kamronn, S., Paquet, U., Winther, O.: A disentangled recognition and nonlinear dynamics model for unsupervised learning (2017)
10. Goodfellow, I., et al.: Generative adversarial nets. In: NIPS (2014)
11. Hafner, D., et al.: Learning latent dynamics for planning from pixels. In: Chaudhuri, K., Salakhutdinov, R. (eds.) Proceedings of the 36th International Conference on Machine Learning. Proceedings of Machine Learning Research, vol. 97, pp. 2555–2565. PMLR (2019)
12. Higgins, I., et al.: beta-VAE: learning basic visual concepts with a constrained variational framework. In: ICLR (2017)
13. Hochreiter, S., Schmidhuber, J.: Convolutional LSTM network: a machine learning approach for precipitation nowcasting. In: Neural Computation (1997)
14. Johnson, M., Duvenaud, D.K., Wiltschko, A., Adams, R.P., Datta, S.R.: Composing graphical models with neural networks for structured representations and fast inference. In: Advances in Neural Information Processing Systems 29 (NIPS), pp. 2946–2954 (2016)

15. Kim, H., Mnih, A.: Disentangling by factorising. In: CoRR (2018)
16. Kingma, D., Ba, J.: Adam: a method for stochastic optimization. In: ICLR (2015)
17. Kingma, D., Welling, M.: Auto-encoding variational Bayes. In: CoRR (2013)
18. Kitani, K.M., Ziebart, B.D., Bagnell, J.A., Hebert, M.: Activity forecasting. In: Fitzgibbon, A., Lazebnik, S., Perona, P., Sato, Y., Schmid, C. (eds.) ECCV 2012. LNCS, vol. 7575, pp. 201–214. Springer, Heidelberg (2012). https://doi.org/10.1007/978-3-642-33765-9_15
19. Larsen, A., Sønderby, S., Larochelle, H., Winther, O.: Autoencoding beyond pixels using a learned similarity metric. In: ICML (2016)
20. Lee, X., Zhang, R., Ebert, F., Abbeel, P., Finn, C., Levine, S.: Stochastic adversarial video prediction. In: arXiv preprint (2018)
21. Lerer, A., Gross, S., Fergus, R.: Learning physical intuition of block towers by example. In: ICML (2016)
22. Mottaghi, R., Bagherinezhad, H., Rastegari, M., Farhadi, A.: Newtonian scene understanding: Unfolding the dynamics of objects in static images. In: CVPR (2016)
23. Piloto, L., et al.: Probing physics knowledge using tools from developmental psychology. In: CoRR (2018)
24. Riochet, R., et al.: IntPhys: a framework and benchmark for visual intuitive physics reasoning. In: arXiv preprint (2018)
25. Sanchez-Gonzalez, A., et al.: Graph networks as learnable physics engines for inference and control. In: ICML (2018)
26. Srivastava, N., Mansimov, E., Salakhutdinov, R.: Unsupervised learning of video representations using LSTMs. In: ICML (2015)
27. Walker, J., Doersch, C., Gupta, A., Hebert, M.: An uncertain future: forecasting from static images using variational autoencoders. In: Leibe, B., Matas, J., Sebe, N., Welling, M. (eds.) ECCV 2016. LNCS, vol. 9911, pp. 835–851. Springer, Cham (2016). https://doi.org/10.1007/978-3-319-46478-7_51
28. Watters, N., Tacchetti, A., Weber, T., Pascanu, R., Battaglia, P., Zoran, D.: Visual interaction networks. In: NIPS (2017)
29. Wu, J., Lim, J.J., Zhang, H., Tenenbaum, J.B., Freeman, W.T.: Physics 101: learning physical object properties from unlabeled videos. In: BMVC (2016)
30. Wu, J., Lu, E., Kohli, P., Freeman, W., Tenenbaum, J.: Learning to see physics via visual de-animation. In: NIPS (2017)
31. Ye, T., Wang, X., Davidson, J., Gupta, A.: Interpretable intuitive physics model. In: Ferrari, V., Hebert, M., Sminchisescu, C., Weiss, Y. (eds.) ECCV 2018. LNCS, vol. 11216, pp. 89–105. Springer, Cham (2018). https://doi.org/10.1007/978-3-030-01258-8_6
32. Zhang, R., Wu, J., Zhang, C., Freeman, W., Tenenbaum, J.: A comparative evaluation of approximate probabilistic simulation and deep neural networks as accounts of human physical scene understanding. In: Annual Conference of the Cognitive Science Society (2016)
33. Zheng, B., Zhao, Y., Yu, J., Ikeuchi, K., Zhu, S.: Scene understanding by reasoning stability and safety. In: IJCV (2015)
34. Zhou, T., Tulsiani, S., Sun, W., Malik, J., Efros, A.A.: View synthesis by appearance flow. In: Leibe, B., Matas, J., Sebe, N., Welling, M. (eds.) ECCV 2016. LNCS, vol. 9908, pp. 286–301. Springer, Cham (2016). https://doi.org/10.1007/978-3-319-46493-0_18

Learning to Train with Synthetic Humans

David T. Hoffmann[1(✉)], Dimitrios Tzionas[1], Michael J. Black[1],
and Siyu Tang[1,2,3]

[1] Max Planck Institute for Intelligent Systems, Tübingen, Germany
{dhoffmann,dtzionas,black,stang}@tuebingen.mpg.de
[2] University of Tübingen, Tübingen, Germany
[3] ETH Zürich, Zürich, Switzerland

Abstract. Neural networks need big annotated datasets for training. However, manual annotation can be too expensive or even unfeasible for certain tasks, like multi-person 2D pose estimation with severe occlusions. A remedy for this is synthetic data with perfect ground truth. Here we explore two variations of synthetic data for this challenging problem; a dataset with purely synthetic humans and a real dataset augmented with synthetic humans. We then study which approach better generalizes to real data, as well as the influence of virtual humans in the training loss. Using the augmented dataset, without considering synthetic humans in the loss, leads to the best results. We observe that not all synthetic samples are equally informative for training, while the informative samples are different for each training stage. To exploit this observation, we employ an adversarial student-teacher framework; the teacher improves the student by providing the hardest samples for its current state as a challenge. Experiments show that the student-teacher framework outperforms normal training on the purely synthetic dataset.

1 Introduction

The broad success of deep neural networks comes at a price: the ever growing need for huge amounts of labeled training data. For many tasks, the lack of data seems to be one of the major limiting factors of progress. It is particularly problematic for the tasks where manual labeling requires significant human effort, or is even unfeasible. For example, in multi-person 2D pose estimation, a major challenge is that people are often partially visible. Manual annotation of body joints that are severely occluded is error prone and the resulting labels are noisy. Computer graphics can help to resolve these issues. 3D rendering engines offer the opportunity to generate a large amount of data with perfect labels: e.g., the location of occluded body parts and the precise pose of the camera.

Nowadays, large scale synthetic datasets with reasonable realism can be generated relatively easy and the idea of synthesizing training data has been widely

Electronic supplementary material The online version of this chapter (https:// doi.org/10.1007/978-3-030-33676-9_43) contains supplementary material, which is available to authorized users.

G. A. Fink et al. (Eds.): DAGM GCPR 2019, LNCS 11824, pp. 609–623, 2019.
https://doi.org/10.1007/978-3-030-33676-9_43

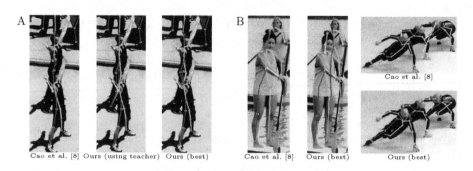

Fig. 1. Qualitative comparisons between our models and Cao et al. [8].

explored. In general, there are two common strategies for generating a synthetic dataset: rendering a purely synthetic dataset, and augmenting real training images with synthetic instances. The advantage of the former is the full control over the virtual 3D world and ability to generate high variance datasets [4,5,12,29,35,36,38,44]. The advantage of the second approach is that some of the instances in the dataset are real, resulting in overall higher realism [2,11,40].

We generate both types of synthetic datasets. One purely synthetic dataset and a mixed dataset, which is generated by augmenting the MPII pose estimation dataset [3] with synthetic humans. In particular, we design these datasets to improve on frequent failure cases that we observe with state-of-the-art models (see Fig. 1), namely uncommon camera angles and strong occlusion. By comparing generalization performance using these two datasets we obtain insights into which way of generating data is preferable. We further investigate how strongly the lack of photorealism of the synthetic humans limits generalization. To make the synthetic data more realistic, we propose a simple synthetic-to-real human style transfer algorithm, based on the work of Dundar et al. [10].

These experiments show that naive training with synthetic data leads only to limited improvements. One explanation is that training on large synthetic datasets leads to overfitting of the model to the features of synthetic data. We observe that some synthetic images convey more information than others. Overfitting to features of synthetic data could be limited by generating only useful, i.e. difficult synthetic data, and thus limiting the training on synthetic data.

As a step in this direction, we propose a method to use synthetic datasets more effectively. Specifically, we introduce an adversarial student-teacher framework. The teacher learns online which training data is still difficult. This information is then used to increase the sampling probability of similar examples. By taking into account feedback from the student, the teacher keeps on updating the sampling probabilities throughout training and adapts them to the specific needs of the student. Training with the teacher on the purely synthetic data outperforms normal training.

Our contributions can be summarized as follows: (1) We propose a large-scale synthetic multi-person dataset, a mixed dataset, and a domain-adapted version of the latter. (2) We explore which way of generating synthetic data is superior for our task. (3) We propose a student-teacher framework to train on the most difficult images and show that this method outperforms random sampling of training data on the synthetic dataset. We provide datasets and code[1].

2   Related Work

Synthetic Datasets with Humans. The need for labelled training data has fueled development of datasets with synthetic humans. Many methods use 3D models of the human body to generate data [4,5,16,35]. Other approaches augment 3D training data by utilizing 2D pose datasets [9,37], while [40,43] augment datasets with cut-outs of objects or animals. Closely related to our approach, [36,44] render the SMPL model [27] on top of random indoor images. These methods generate datasets with a single synthetic human. Multi-person datasets were created by employing video games for pedestrian detection [29] and pose tracking [12]. Similarly, [30] develop a simulation environment in a game engine, including virtual humans. Related to our approach, [38] augment real training images similar to the ones in [44] but with multiple synthetic humans occluding each other.

Domain Adaptation. The quality of synthetic data is often insufficient to generalize well to real data. Several domain adaptation methods have been developed to overcome this problem. Shrivastava et al. [42] train a Generative Adversarial Network (GAN) to refine synthetic images, while keeping the label information intact. Recently, Cycle-GAN has been used to map images from one domain to another [4,31]. However, GAN-based methods are prone to unstable training and require tedious hyper-parameter tuning. As a practical alternative, recently [10] proposed domain stylization to stylize synthetic images to real ones, using the fast photorealistic image stylization method of [25].

Human Pose Estimation. Multi-person pose estimation has attracted substantial attention over the last years [8,14,15,19,23,28,32,33]. One of the most popular datasets is the MPII multi-person pose estimation dataset [3]. Among the best performing methods on MPII are: [33], which uses a pose partition network, [28], which uses context information, [15], which refines pose predictions, and [32], which predicts "tag maps" to solve the grouping problem. The most widely used method is OpenPose [8], a bottom-up approach that first predicts keypoints and then estimates Part Affinity Fields (PAFs) to group them.

Learning to Train. Bengio et al. [6] introduce curriculum learning for learning systems, exploiting the idea that different data samples are informative at different training stages. As a proof of concept they manually define the samples for each stage with gradually increasing difficulty. Multiple methods have focused on automating curriculum learning [7,13,20,24]. These approaches try

---

[1] https://ltsh.is.tue.mpg.de.

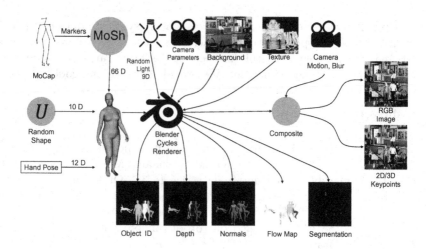

Fig. 2. Schematic of the data generation pipeline.

to maximize information gain during training by carefully monitoring the learning success of the model. Alternatively, adversarial methods [21,22,41] try to pick the hardest samples at each training stage; [21] favors samples resulting in higher loss, [22] learns weights for the loss of each training sample as a soft curriculum, while [41] uses online hard example mining for object detection. Peng et al. [34] propose an adversarial training scheme to optimize data augmentation online. They train two teacher networks to learn a probability distribution over the hyper-parameters for data augmentation; one predicts the most difficult image rotations, while the other predicts parameters for deep feature occlusion.

3   Multi-person Synthetic Data

In the following we describe the generation of the datasets (Sects. 3.1, 3.2, 3.3) and the domain adaptation used to increase visual appearance of the mixed dataset (Sect. 3.4).

3.1   Data Generation Pipeline

To generate realistic synthetic training data we build on top of [36,44]. We use multiple different sources of data to build a realistic synthetic scene. Images and ground truth annotations are rendered using Cycles, the rendering engine of Blender[2]. An overview can be seen in Fig. 2.

Body Model and MoCap Data. We use the parametric body model SMPL+H [39] to generate realistic synthetic humans. SMPL+H is parameterized by pose $\theta \in \mathbb{R}^{78}$ and shape $\beta \in \mathbb{R}^{10}$. We collect realistic pose and shape parameters by fitting SMPL+H to standard MoCap data by using MoSh [26].

---

[2] https://www.blender.org.

Details. We draw inspiration from [36,44] who generate small video sequences, each having different but fixed parameters for the position, pose, shape and texture of a synthetic human, the background image, camera position, lighting, etc. In contrast, we generate single images and render multiple synthetic humans, while randomizing the number of them. As a result, we generate a dataset with much higher variance. Images with inter-penetrating meshes of virtual humans are rejected to avoid artifacts in the generated ground truth.

Further details regarding the description of the data generation pipeline, posing of hands and a quantitative comparison of our datasets to other datasets can be found in **Supp. Mat.**

Fig. 3. Example images from the purely synthetic dataset. It contains high occlusion, extreme poses, various camera angles and various challenging backgrounds.

3.2 Synthetic Dataset

Background Images. To generalize well to in-the-wild pose estimation datasets the background images should come from many different scenes. To this end we use images from SUN397 [45] and reject all images with a resolution smaller than 512×512 pixels to ensure high quality backgrounds. Additionally, we reject all images containing humans, as we do not have ground truth annotations for them. We use mask-RCNN [1,17] as our human detector.

Generative Factors. We sample the number of synthetic humans per image from a Poisson distribution with $\lambda = 9$, to encourage many humans per image, while avoiding too extreme values. The datasets of [36,44] have only very small variance in camera position. However, preliminary experiments show that the camera position significantly influences the difficulty of multi-person pose estimation. Therefore we increase the range of possible camera positions, by sampling the camera pitch uniformly from $[0,45]°$. The resolution of the final rendered images is set to 640×640 pixels. We refer to this dataset as $\mathcal{D}_S$.

3.3 Mixed Dataset

We build upon the finding of [40] that realistic occluding objects lead to larger improvements than abstract objects. We choose our occluders to be from the same class as our target objects; i.e. humans, to simulate crowded scenes with multiple humans. To generate the dataset we use the pipeline described above with a few differences. Instead of SUN397 [45] we use the training images of the MPII human pose dataset [3] as background images. To keep the MPII ground truth intact, we render the images with the same resolution as the background MPII image, and keep the camera pose fixed. We then augment the MPII human pose dataset by superimposing synthetic humans. Their number is drawn from a Poisson distribution with $\lambda = 4$ to introduce interesting and intense occlusions as shown in Fig. 4(A), without extreme occlusions by too many synthetic humans. We render each of the 15,956 images in our training set 5 times with different parameters for increased variance. We refer to this dataset as $\mathcal{D}_M$.

Fig. 4. (A) Example images from $\mathcal{D}_M$. (B) Corresponding images of $\mathcal{D}_{Style}$. For the last image, the segmentation network included non-human parts in the segmentation masks. Resulting artifacts can be seen for rightmost synthetic human.

3.4 Domain Stylization

The appearance of real and synthetic humans differs strongly. Factors contributing to these differences are the low quality of textures and differences in lighting conditions for synthetic humans and background images. Additionally, the small number of human textures limits the variability. These differences in appearance might limit the generalization. We draw inspiration from Dundar et al. [10] to reduce these differences by using the fast photorealistic style transfer method of [25]. Style transfer methods require a pair of images as input, a content image I_C and a style image I_S. While the style of these images can be largely different, their content should have similarities. Finding such pairs is a non-trivial problem. However, for the $\mathcal{D}_M$, we have a canonical choice of image pairs: the image from $\mathcal{D}_M$ and its background as I_C and I_S, respectively.

Naive application of style transfer methods on the whole image, leads to severe artifacts. Therefore, only the style of semantically similar classes should be transferred. To obtain a good semantic segmentation network Dundar et al. [10] iterate between stylizing a dataset and training a network for semantic segmentation on the stylized dataset. Here, we are only interested in transferring the style of real to synthetic humans. Fine-grained human detection is important to avoid parts of the background bleeding into the foreground after style transfer (see Fig. 4(B) right panel). We therefore employ Mask-RCNN [1,17] to predict pixel-wise masks for humans. Ground truth masks for the synthetic humans are generated during data generation. Since the style-transfer algorithm can not handle images of arbitrary size, we rescale the larger images to 600 pixels before applying the style transfer. We refer to the resulting dataset as $\mathcal{D}_{Style}$. Examples can be seen in Fig. 4(B).

4   Learning to Train with Multi-person Synthetic Data

We now turn to the task of training a pose estimation network with synthetic data. We first provide general information about our model. This is followed by a brief description of the training procedure. Finally, we detail the student-teacher framework and explain how the teacher is trained.

Pose Estimation Network. For all experiments we use our Tensorflow implementation of the network proposed in [8], which we will refer to as *OpenPose* network. Our training differs only slightly from [8]; details are provided in **Supp. Mat.** Because of these differences, we use a self-trained model on real data as the baseline throughout the paper.

Training with Synthetic Data. Following the advice of [18], we freeze the weights of our feature extractor whenever training on synthetic data. In particular, we freeze the first 4 layers of the OpenPose network. Additionally, we make sure that each batch is composed of 50% real and 50% synthetic images. More details on our training procedure with synthetic data are provided in **Supp. Mat.**

Grouping. Sampling the most difficult samples with higher probability comes with the risk of oversampling a small amount of data. To avoid such behavior, and ease the task for the teacher, we group the synthetic data into meaningful groups. We found empirically that the position of the camera and the distance of people in an image contribute to the difficulty of multi-person pose estimation. Thus, we use these two image characteristics to group our data. We assume 10 *groups* to yield a good trade-off between precision and difficulty for the teacher. For minimal distance grouping[3], denoted as mD, we decide for linearly spaced values between $[0, 640)$ px. For the camera pitch grouping, denoted as C we space the group boundaries linearly in the interval $[\min(X) + \text{Var}(X), \ \max(X) - \text{Var}(X))$, where X contains all values for the camera pitch in the dataset.

---

[3] We sample persons not images. The image is cropped around this person. The minimal distance is defined as smallest distance of this person to any other person.

4.1   Adversarial Teacher

The teacher network is trained simultaneously with the student network to adapt the sampling strategy dynamically to the current training state of the student. A schematic of the forward pass can be seen in Fig. 5. The input to the teacher should represent the training state of the student. We choose the real image resulting in highest mean loss per joint within the previous N training steps. This provides some information about the type of images that are still difficult for the student. The output of the teacher network is a probability distribution $\tilde{P}$ over a set of groups $\{g_1, \ldots, g_i\}$. This probability distribution is used to sample one of them. For the next N training steps, synthetic training samples are drawn from this group only.

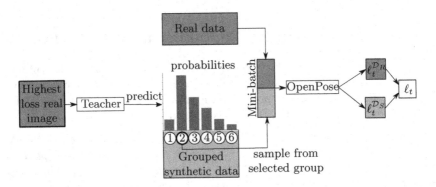

Fig. 5. Diagram of the forward pass. The total loss is denoted as ℓ_t, the loss on real images as $\ell_t^{\mathcal{D}_R}$ and on synthetic images as $\ell_t^{\mathcal{D}_S}$. The reward signal and backward pass are explained in the main text. For clarity only 6 instead of 10 groups are displayed.

Table 1. Results on the held out validation set. $\mathcal{M}_{\mathcal{D}_R}$ is trained only with real data. $\mathcal{M}_{\mathcal{D}_S}$ was trained solely on synthetic data. $\mathcal{M}_{\mathcal{D}_R + \mathcal{D}_S}$ is trained on real and synthetic data. $\mathcal{M}_{\mathcal{D}_R + \mathcal{D}_M}$ was trained on real and the mixed dataset.

Model	Head	Shoulder	Elbow	Wrist	Hip	Knee	Ankle	mAP
$\mathcal{M}_{\mathcal{D}_R}$	**91.3**	89.1	79.2	70.4	**75.9**	71.5	66.7	77.7
$\mathcal{M}_{\mathcal{D}_S}$	37.9	23.5	12.7	7.3	5.6	3.4	3.2	13.4
$\mathcal{M}_{\mathcal{D}_R + \mathcal{D}_S}$	91.1	89.2	80.5	71.0	75.2	**73.6**	**68.1**	**78.4**
$\mathcal{M}_{\mathcal{D}_R + \mathcal{D}_M}$	**91.3**	**89.5**	**80.7**	**71.7**	75.4	72.5	67.7	**78.4**

Training the Teacher. The objective of the adversarial teacher should be to maximize the loss, $\ell_t^{\mathcal{D}_S}$. Unfortunately, sampling and data augmentation are non-differentiable operations, prohibiting end-to-end training of the teacher network.

An alternative method to provide a supervision signal is needed. We draw inspiration from [34] and employ a reward/penalty training scheme. To determine whether the teacher is rewarded or penalized we monitor $\ell_t^{\mathcal{D}_S}$. If $\ell_t^{\mathcal{D}_S} \geq \ell_{t-1}^{\mathcal{D}_S}$ the teacher succeeded in finding more difficult examples than before and is rewarded. Unfortunately, $\ell_t^{\mathcal{D}_S}$ has a high variance. To reduce the variance of the teaching signal we reward if

$$\ell_t^{\mathcal{D}_S} \geq \frac{1}{H} \sum_{h=0}^{H} \ell_{t-1-h}^{\mathcal{D}_S}, \tag{1}$$

where H denotes the number of past loss values to be considered. To avoid favoring images with many people, we use the mean loss per joint on the image. Equation 1 provides the direction of the gradient descent step but no ground truth is given to compute the gradients. To efficiently get a reward signal we follow [34] and increase the probability of a group being chosen, if the teacher gets rewarded. Probabilities for other groups are decreased accordingly. Formally, we update P_i and P_j, where i denotes the selected group and $j \neq i$ denotes all other groups, by

$$P_i = \tilde{P}_i + \delta \alpha \tilde{P}_i, \text{ and } P_j = \tilde{P}_j - \delta \frac{\alpha \tilde{P}_i}{|g| - 1}. \tag{2}$$

Here $\tilde{P}_i$ denotes the prediction of the teacher, P_i is the updated pseudo ground truth probability, $0 \leq \alpha \leq 1$ controls the size of the update, $|g|$ denotes the number of groups and δ is a sign indicator $\delta = \{+1, \text{ if Eq. 1 holds}; -1, \text{ otherwise}\}$. Finally, we obtain gradients to update the teacher network by computing the KL-divergence loss between P and $\tilde{P}$. Information on optimization related hyperparameters and the architecture are provided in **Supp. Mat.**

During training we face a exploration/exploitation trade-off. The group with highest probability, might not be optimal. To overcome this problem, we sample a group from a uniform distribution instead of the predicted probabilities with probability $\epsilon = 0.1$.

5   Experiments

We test our models on the MPII multi-person pose dataset [3]. For that purpose we use the toolkit provided by [3]. Following the standard validation procedure, the test metric is only computed for people within close proximity. We split the real training data, denoted as $\mathcal{D}_R$, into a training and a validation set. Our validation set consist of 343 randomly selected groups of people in close proximity. The respective images are not used for training. We report mAP (mean Average Precision), the main metric of the benchmark [3] for each model.

5.1   Which Dataset Generalizes Best?

We hypothesize that multi-person pose estimation methods are limited by a lack of training data. To test this hypothesis we train our model on $\mathcal{D}_S$ and $\mathcal{D}_R + \mathcal{D}_S$.

Table 2. Results for the models $\mathcal{M}_{\mathcal{D}_R+\mathcal{D}_M}$, $\mathcal{M}_{\mathcal{D}_R+\mathcal{D}_{Style}}$, $\mathcal{M}_{\mathcal{D}_R+\mathcal{D}_M+\text{masks}}$ and $\mathcal{M}_{\mathcal{D}_R+\mathcal{D}_{Style}+\text{masks}}$ datasets, where "+ masks" denotes masking out loss generated by synthetic humans. All reported results are on the held out validation set.

Model	Head	Shoulder	Elbow	Wrist	Hip	Knee	Ankle	mAP
$\mathcal{M}_{\mathcal{D}_R+\mathcal{D}_M}$	91.3	89.5	80.7	71.7	75.4	**72.5**	67.7	78.4
$\mathcal{M}_{\mathcal{D}_R+\mathcal{D}_M+\text{masks}}$	**92.3**	**90.9**	80.5	**72.2**	76.0	71.7	68.3	78.9
$\mathcal{M}_{\mathcal{D}_R+\mathcal{D}_{Style}}$	91.8	89.8	80.4	70.9	75.5	71.6	67.9	78.3
$\mathcal{M}_{\mathcal{D}_R+\mathcal{D}_{Style}+\text{masks}}$	91.6	90.6	**80.8**	71.8	**77.7**	72.2	**68.8**	**79.1**

Interestingly, for $\mathcal{M}_{\mathcal{D}_S}$, the model resulting from training only on $\mathcal{D}_S$, mAP is very low, suggesting that the model overfits to the synthetic data. However, when training on $\mathcal{D}_R + \mathcal{D}_S$ the mAP improves over the mAP of $\mathcal{M}_{\mathcal{D}_R}$ (Table 1).

While synthetic data can improve the accuracy of multi-person pose estimation, the improvements are relatively small given the extensive amount of additional training data. Multiple factors might limit the generalization. It could well be that the dataset bias between the synthetic and real dataset is just too strong. Generating the $\mathcal{D}_M$ is a straightforward way of generating a dataset with similar dataset bias as the original dataset. By training on $\mathcal{D}_M$ we can quantify the influence of it on the generalization. When training with $\mathcal{D}_M$ we consider only real humans as samples. The rationale behind that decision is that we primarily want to increase the frequency of occlusion of real humans. However, the network is also trained on all synthetic humans that are within the cropped training image. As can be seen in Table 1, training on $\mathcal{D}_R + \mathcal{D}_M$ results in similar accuracy as $\mathcal{M}_{\mathcal{D}_R+\mathcal{D}_S}$. Therefore, the two methods of generating data are equivalently good. The dataset bias seems not to be the main limiting factor.

5.2   Does Stylization Improve Generalization?

The generalization might be limited by the appearance of synthetic humans. To overcome the limited generalization and measure how the difference in appearance influences performance we train on $\mathcal{D}_R + \mathcal{D}_{Style}$. This improves accuracy over $\mathcal{M}_{\mathcal{D}_R}$, but leads to a decrease of mAP compared to $\mathcal{M}_{\mathcal{D}_R+\mathcal{D}_M}$ (see Table 2). This result is surprising, as many factors believed to limit generalization are improved and the data is visually more realistic. A possible explanation is that the network learns to detect artifacts of the style transfer. Alternatively, the failure cases of the style transfer method might lead to "confusion" of the network.

In an ablation study, we test whether training on synthetic humans actually improves the mAP or if the improvement when training with $\mathcal{D}_M$ or $\mathcal{D}_{Style}$ is mostly caused by additional occlusion. For that purpose, we mask out all the loss that is generated by synthetic humans. Comparing $\mathcal{M}_{\mathcal{D}_R+\mathcal{D}_M+\text{masks}}$ with $\mathcal{M}_{\mathcal{D}_R+\mathcal{D}_M}$, it can be seen that masking out the loss generated by synthetic humans increases the accuracy. Therefore, the domain gap between synthetic and real humans limits the generalization, and the improvement of $\mathcal{M}_{\mathcal{D}_R+\mathcal{D}_M}$

over $\mathcal{M}_{\mathcal{D}_R}$ is due to more occlusion. Stylization in combination with masks leads to the best model (see Fig. 1 and **Supp. Mat.** for qualitative results), suggesting that a smaller gap between synthetic occluder and real parts of the image improves generalization.

5.3   Does Informed Sampling Improve Results?

Finally, we test whether the teacher network can help to use the synthetic data more effectively. For that purpose we use the adversarial teacher with $\mathcal{D}_R + \mathcal{D}_S$. The results can be seen in Table 3. Grouping according to the camera pitch leads to an additional improvement of 0.5 mAP in comparison to $\mathcal{M}_{\mathcal{D}_R+\mathcal{D}_S}$. See Fig. 1 and **Supp. Mat.** for qualitative results. For usage of the teacher in combination with the mixed and stylized datasets we do not observe further improvements. Since we only consider real humans as samples some groups are very small. We assume that oversampling of these groups inhibits improvements.

Table 3. Comparison of the $\mathcal{M}_{\mathcal{D}_R}$ and $\mathcal{M}_{\mathcal{D}_R+\mathcal{D}_S}$ baselines (copied from Table 1) to the student-teacher model using different groupings. Results on the validation set.

Model	Grouping	Head	Shoulder	Elbow	Wrist	Hip	Knee	Ankle	mAP
$\mathcal{M}_{\mathcal{D}_R}$		91.3	89.1	79.2	70.4	75.9	71.5	66.7	77.7
$\mathcal{M}_{\mathcal{D}_R+\mathcal{D}_S}$		91.1	89.2	80.5	71.0	75.2	73.6	**68.1**	78.4
"adversarial Teacher"	C	**91.7**	90.0	**80.9**	71.2	**77.1**	**73.6**	67.7	**78.9**
"adversarial Teacher"	mD	91.5	**90.4**	80.5	**72.2**	75.8	73.1	67.6	78.7

As can be seen in Fig. 6, improvements for highly occluded people are strongest for models trained with the teacher. Clear differences to $\mathcal{M}_{\mathcal{D}_R+\mathcal{D}_M}+$masks and $\mathcal{M}_{\mathcal{D}_R+\mathcal{D}_{Style}}+$masks can only be seen for the highest occlusion level. For all but the lowest occlusion levels $\mathcal{M}_{\mathcal{D}_R}$ is outperformed by all other models. Thus, our methods of training improve accuracy for difficult high occlusion cases.

Sampling Probabilities. The teacher often assigns high probability to few groups early in training. In most cases the teacher converges to a uniform sampling strategy over the groups, as training progresses. This is not equivalent to random sampling, as samples are not uniformly distributed across groups. As a result the training data follows a uniform distribution for the respective image characteristic. A uniform distribution over an image characteristic like camera pitch is more extreme than the distribution in the real training data. Training on more extreme samples seems to improve the generalization. We find that improvements are largest for the camera pitch grouping. This might be due to the bias to small camera pitch in the real training data.

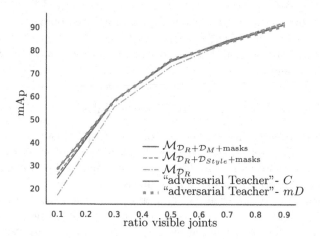

Fig. 6. Detection performance for varying ratio of visible joints (mAP). The validation data is grouped into 5 linearly spaced groups in range $[0,1]$. The groups contain 14, 111, 289, 286, 180 persons respectively. The teacher methods are hard to distinguish because of similar values.

6   Conclusion

In summary, we created multiple synthetic datasets and analyze their effectiveness. We show that training with synthetic data improves multi-person pose estimation methods. We find that both our methods of generating synthetic datasets perform on par. Surprisingly, our approach for improving visual appearance of synthetic humans decreased the accuracy. More elaborate domain adaptation methods might provide better results. For example, GAN-based approaches ensure that no obvious artifacts can be used to distinguish real from synthetic. We find that improvements of the $\mathcal{M}_{\mathcal{D}_R+\mathcal{D}_M}$ and $\mathcal{M}_{\mathcal{D}_R+\mathcal{D}_{Style}}$ can be explained by more occlusion, as mAP increases when masking out the loss of synthetic humans. Here the stylization leads to further improvements, suggesting that visual quality of occluding objects is important. Finally, we find that training on the most difficult synthetic samples at each point of training improves the results. This suggest that, for large synthetic datasets, random sampling is not optimal and better strategies exist. More research in this direction is necessary to draw final conclusions. $\mathcal{M}_{\mathcal{D}_R+\mathcal{D}_{Style}+masks}$ outperforms the "adversarial Teacher" C model. We assume that the potential of the teacher is limited by the small amount and the quality of human textures. Given better textures we expect this approach to outperform $\mathcal{M}_{\mathcal{D}_R+\mathcal{D}_{Style}+masks}$.

Limitations. The teacher network is limited in multiple ways. First, the current implementation requires grouping of data. The size and spacing of groups might have a large influence on the training success and applicability of teacher networks. Furthermore, the grouping is based on one feature only. This is suboptimal, since difficulty of an image is determined by multiple factors. We plan to extend the teachers to handle multiple characteristics at once. A more elaborate formulation that does not require grouping might be superior. Last, the teacher can be applied to other tasks and networks, here we evaluate it only for multi-person pose estimation with the OpenPose network.

The style transfer occasionally produces artifacts in the stylized image. Especially the skin color of the synthetic humans might be unnatural. In rare cases, large parts of the background are included in the human mask. These failures in segmentation can lead to ghost-like synthetic humans (see **Supp. Mat.**).

Acknowledgement. S. Tang acknowledges funding by Deutsche Forschungsgemeinschaft (DFG, German Research Foundation) Projektnummer 276693517 SFB 1233.

Disclosure. MJB has received research gift funds from Intel, Nvidia, Adobe, Facebook, and Amazon. While MJB is a part-time employee of Amazon, his research was performed solely at, and funded solely by, MPI. MJB has financial interests in Amazon and Meshcapade GmbH.

References

1. Abdulla, W.: Mask R-CNN for object detection and instance segmentation on Keras and TensorFlow (2017). https://github.com/matterport/Mask_RCNN
2. Alhaija, H.A., Mustikovela, S.K., Mescheder, L., Geiger, A., Rother, C.: Augmented reality meets computer vision: Efficient data generation for urban driving scenes. IJCV **126**(9), 961–972 (2018)
3. Andriluka, M., Pishchulin, L., Gehler, P., Schiele, B.: 2D human pose estimation: new benchmark and state of the art analysis. In: CVPR, June 2014
4. Bąk, S., Carr, P., Lalonde, J.-F.: Domain adaptation through synthesis for unsupervised person re-identification. In: Ferrari, V., Hebert, M., Sminchisescu, C., Weiss, Y. (eds.) ECCV 2018. LNCS, vol. 11217, pp. 193–209. Springer, Cham (2018). https://doi.org/10.1007/978-3-030-01261-8_12
5. Barbosa, I.B., Cristani, M., Caputo, B., Rognhaugen, A., Theoharis, T.: Looking beyond appearances: synthetic training data for deep CNNs in re-identification. CVIU **167**, 50–62 (2018)
6. Bengio, Y., Louradour, J., Collobert, R., Weston, J.: Curriculum learning. In: ICML (2009)
7. Büchler, U., Brattoli, B., Ommer, B.: Improving spatiotemporal self-supervision by deep reinforcement learning. In: Ferrari, V., Hebert, M., Sminchisescu, C., Weiss, Y. (eds.) ECCV 2018. LNCS, vol. 11219, pp. 797–814. Springer, Cham (2018). https://doi.org/10.1007/978-3-030-01267-0_47
8. Cao, Z., Simon, T., Wei, S.E., Sheikh, Y.: Realtime multi-person 2D pose estimation using part affinity fields. In: CVPR (2017)
9. Chen, W., et al.: Synthesizing training images for boosting human 3D pose estimation. In: 3DV. IEEE (2016)
10. Dundar, A., Liu, M.Y., Wang, T.C., Zedlewski, J., Kautz, J.: Domain stylization: a strong, simple baseline for synthetic to real image domain adaptation. arXiv preprint arXiv:1807.09384 (2018)
11. Dvornik, N., Mairal, J., Schmid, C.: On the importance of visual context for data augmentation in scene understanding. arXiv preprint arXiv:1809.02492 (2018)

12. Fabbri, M., Lanzi, F., Calderara, S., Palazzi, A., Vezzani, R., Cucchiara, R.: Learning to detect and track visible and occluded body joints in a virtual world. In: Ferrari, V., Hebert, M., Sminchisescu, C., Weiss, Y. (eds.) ECCV 2018. LNCS, vol. 11208, pp. 450–466. Springer, Cham (2018). https://doi.org/10.1007/978-3-030-01225-0_27

13. Fan, Y., Tian, F., Qin, T., Bian, J., Liu, T.Y.: Learning what data to learn. arXiv preprint arXiv:1702.08635 (2017)

14. Fang, H., Xie, S., Tai, Y.W., Lu, C.: RMPE: regional multi-person pose estimation. In: ICCV (2017)

15. Fieraru, M., Khoreva, A., Pishchulin, L., Schiele, B.: Learning to refine human pose estimation. In: CVPR Workshops (2018)

16. Ghezelghieh, M.F., Kasturi, R., Sarkar, S.: Learning camera viewpoint using CNN to improve 3D body pose estimation. In: 3DV (2016)

17. He, K., Gkioxari, G., Dollár, P., Girshick, R.: Mask R-CNN. In: ICCV (2017)

18. Hinterstoisser, S., Lepetit, V., Wohlhart, P., Konolige, K.: On pre-trained image features and synthetic images for deep learning. In: Leal-Taixé, L., Roth, S. (eds.) ECCV 2018. LNCS, vol. 11129, pp. 682–697. Springer, Cham (2019). https://doi.org/10.1007/978-3-030-11009-3_42

19. Insafutdinov, E., Pishchulin, L., Andres, B., Andriluka, M., Schiele, B.: DeeperCut: a deeper, stronger, and faster multi-person pose estimation model. In: Leibe, B., Matas, J., Sebe, N., Welling, M. (eds.) ECCV 2016. LNCS, vol. 9910, pp. 34–50. Springer, Cham (2016). https://doi.org/10.1007/978-3-319-46466-4_3

20. Jiang, L., Zhou, Z., Leung, T., Li, L.J., Fei-Fei, L.: MentorNet: learning data-driven curriculum for very deep neural networks on corrupted labels. arXiv preprint arXiv:1712.05055 (2017)

21. Katharopoulos, A., Fleuret, F.: Biased importance sampling for deep neural network training. arXiv preprint arXiv:1706.00043 (2017)

22. Kim, T.H., Choi, J.: ScreenerNet: learning self-paced curriculum for deep neural networks. arXiv preprint arXiv:1801.00904 (2018)

23. Kocabas, M., Karagoz, S., Akbas, E.: MultiPoseNet: fast multi-person pose estimation using pose residual network. In: ECCV (2018)

24. Kumar, M.P., Packer, B., Koller, D.: Self-paced learning for latent variable models. In: NIPS (2010)

25. Li, Y., Liu, M.Y., Li, X., Yang, M.H., Kautz, J.: A closed-form solution to photo-realistic image stylization. In: ECCV (2018)

26. Loper, M., Mahmood, N., Black, M.J.: MoSh: motion and shape capture from sparse markers. TOG **33**(6), 220 (2014)

27. Loper, M., Mahmood, N., Romero, J., Pons-Moll, G., Black, M.J.: SMPL: a skinned multi-person linear model. TOG **34**(6), 248 (2015)

28. Luo, Y., Xu, Z., Liu, P., Du, Y., Guo, J.M.: Multi-person pose estimation via multi-layer fractal network and joints kinship pattern. TIP **28**(1), 142–155 (2019)

29. Marin, J., Vázquez, D., Gerónimo, D., López, A.M.: Learning appearance in virtual scenarios for pedestrian detection. In: CVPR (2010)

30. Müller, M., Casser, V., Lahoud, J., Smith, N., Ghanem, B.: Sim4CV: a photo-realistic simulator for computer vision applications. IJCV 1–18 (2018)

31. Murez, Z., Kolouri, S., Kriegman, D., Ramamoorthi, R., Kim, K.: Image to image translation for domain adaptation. In: CVPR (2018)

32. Newell, A., Huang, Z., Deng, J.: Associative embedding: End-to-end learning for joint detection and grouping. In: NIPS (2017)

33. Nie, X., Feng, J., Xing, J., Yan, S.: Pose Partition networks for multi-person pose estimation. In: Ferrari, V., Hebert, M., Sminchisescu, C., Weiss, Y. (eds.) ECCV 2018. LNCS, vol. 11209, pp. 705–720. Springer, Cham (2018). https://doi.org/10.1007/978-3-030-01228-1_42

34. Peng, X., Tang, Z., Yang, F., Feris, R.S., Metaxas, D.: Jointly optimize data augmentation and network training: adversarial data augmentation in human pose estimation. In: CVPR (2018)

35. Pishchulin, L., Jain, A., Wojek, C., Andriluka, M., Thormählen, T., Schiele, B.: Learning people detection models from few training samples. In: CVPR (2011)

36. Ranjan, A., Romero, J., Black, M.J.: Learning human optical flow. In: BMVC (2018)

37. Rogez, G., Schmid, C.: Image-based synthesis for deep 3D human pose estimation. IJCV 126(9), 993–1008 (2018)

38. Rogez, G., Weinzaepfel, P., Schmid, C.: LCR-Net++: multi-person 2D and 3D pose detection in natural images. In: TPAMI (2019)

39. Romero, J., Tzionas, D., Black, M.J.: Embodied hands: modeling and capturing hands and bodies together. ACM TOG 36(6), 245 (2017). (Proceedings of SIGGRAPH Asia)

40. Sárándi, I., Linder, T., Arras, K.O., Leibe, B.: How robust is 3D human pose estimation to occlusion? arXiv preprint arXiv:1808.09316 (2018)

41. Shrivastava, A., Gupta, A., Girshick, R.: Training region-based object detectors with online hard example mining. In: CVPR (2016)

42. Shrivastava, A., Pfister, T., Tuzel, O., Susskind, J., Wang, W., Webb, R.: Learning from simulated and unsupervised images through adversarial training. In: CVPR (2017)

43. Tripathi, S., Chandra, S., Agrawal, A., Tyagi, A., Rehg, J.M., Chari, V.: Learning to generate synthetic data via compositing. arXiv preprint arXiv:1904.05475 (2019)

44. Varol, G., et al.: Learning from synthetic humans. In: CVPR (2017)

45. Xiao, J., Hays, J., Ehinger, K.A., Oliva, A., Torralba, A.: Sun database: large-scale scene recognition from abbey to zoo. In: CVPR (2010)

Author Index

Akgul, Yusuf Sinan 513
Al-Halah, Ziad 428
Antunović, Tonći 189
Ardizzone, Lynton 442
Aslan, Enes 513

Babakhin, Yauhen 218
Banerjee, Biplab 485
Bevandić, Petra 33
Black, Michael J. 609
Bodesheim, Paul 62
Brox, Thomas 139
Brust, Clemens-Alexander 414
Buhmann, Joachim M. 232, 247

Chaudhuri, Subhasis 485
Cherabier, Ian 581

Denzler, Joachim 62, 203, 261, 414, 499
Durall, Ricard 303

Elich, Cathrin 48
Engelmann, Francis 48
Erdler, Oliver 18
Eyring, Veronika 261

Fischer, Kai 387
Fischer, Volker 139

Gall, Juergen 107, 537
García, Yanira Guanche 499
Gehler, Peter V. 345
Geisen, Ulf 374
Genewein, Tim 139
Giuliari, Giacomo 232
Glüer, Claus-C. 374
Gross, Horst-Michael 387
Gupta, Puneet 401

Haring-Bolívar, Peter 93
Haurilet, Monica 428
Hermans, Alexander 551
Hoffmann, David T. 609

Hörold, Maurice 247
Hu, Tongxin 331

Kahl, Matthias 93
Keller, Sebastian Mathias 171
Keuper, Janis 303
Kiefel, Martin 345
Kissner, Michael 471
Kitamura, Hirotoshi 218
Knöbelreiter, Patrick 3
Koch, Reinhard 374
Kolb, Andreas 93
Kontogianni, Theodora 48
Korsch, Dimitri 62
Köser, Kevin 79
Kotera, Jan 122
Köthe, Ullrich 303, 442
Kraft, Basil 203
Krešo, Ivan 33
Kretz, Adrian 288
Kuhn, Andreas 18
Kurzynski, Marek 567

Laermann, Jan 360
Leibe, Bastian 48, 551
Liao, Wentong 331
Lin, Shan 18
Lui, Kam To 456

Mahecha, Miguel 203, 499
Majumder, Soumajit 522
Matas, Jiří 122, 317
Mayer, Helmut 471
Mester, Rudolf 288
Milz, Stefan 387
Mohrmann, Jochen 79
Möller, Michael 93
Mummadi, Chaithanya Kumar 139
Munderloh, Marco 595

Nguyen, The-Gia Leo 442

Ochs, Matthias 288
Ommer, Björn 456

Oršić, Marin   33, 189
Oswald, Martin R.   581

Panareda Busto, Pau   107
Pfeiffer, Kilian   551
Pfreundt, Franz-Josef   303
Pinetz, Thomas   156
Pock, Thomas   3, 156
Pollefeys, Marc   581
Pöpperl, Maximillian   387

Rahtu, Esa   401
Rakshit, Sayan   485
Razumenić, Ivan   274
Reichstein, Markus   203, 261
Requena-Mesa, Christian   203
Roig, Gemma   485
Rosenhahn, Bodo   331, 595
Roth, Stefan   345
Roth, Volker   171
Rozumnyi, Denys   122
Runge, Jakob   261

Samarin, Maxim   171
Samek, Wojciech   360
Sanakoyeu, Artsiom   218
Sárándi, István   551
Šarić, Josip   189
Schmarje, Lars   374
Schwarz, Katja   456
Šegvić, Siniša   33, 189
Šerých, Jonáš   317
Shadaydeh, Maha   261, 499
She, Mengkun   79

Simon, Martin   387
Song, Yifan   79
Soukup, Daniel   156
Špetlík, Radim   274
Šroubek, Filip   122
Stiefelhagen, Rainer   428
Strodthoff, Nils   360
Stückler, Jörg   595

Tang, Siyu   609
Tanke, Julian   537
Trajdos, Pawel   567
Trifunov, Violeta Teodora   261
Tzionas, Dimitrios   609

Ufer, Nikolai   456

Vražić, Sacha   189

Wang, Xiaojuan   581
Wannenwetsch, Anne S.   345
Warkentin, Paul   456
Weber, Mark   551
Wegmayr, Viktor   232, 247
Wieser, Mario   171
Wong, Tak Ming   93

Yang, Michael Ying   331
Yao, Angela   522

Zelenka, Claudius   374
Zhang, Dan   139
Zhu, Deyao   595

Printed in the United States
By Bookmasters